PASTORS AND VISIONARIES

Religion and Secular Life in Late Medieval Yorkshire

PASTORS AND VISIONARIES

Religion and Secular Life in Late Medieval Yorkshire

JONATHAN HUGHES

THE BOYDELL PRESS

First published 1988 by The Boydell Press
an imprint of Boydell & Brewer Ltd
PO Box 9, Woodbridge, Suffolk IP12 3DF
and of Boydell & Brewer Inc.
Wolfeboro, New Hampshire 03894-2069, USA

ISBN 0 85115 496 4

British Library Cataloguing in Publication Data

Hughes, Jonathan, *1952-*
Pastors and visionaries.
1. Church of England, Diocese of York. Clergy.
Clerical life, 1350-1450
I. Title
253'.2
ISBN 0-85115-496-4

Library of Congress Cataloging-in-Publication Data

Hughes, Jonathan, 1952-
Pastors and visionaries : religion and secular life
in late medieval Yorkshire / Jonathan Hughes.
p. cm.
Bibliography: p.
Includes index.
ISBN 0-85115-496-4 (alk. paper)
1. Yorkshire — Church history. 2. Catholic
Church. Diocese of York (England) — History.
3. Yorkshire — History. I. Title.
BR763.Y6H84 1988
282'.4281 — dc 19 88-10210
CIP

∞ Printed on long life paper
made to the full American Standard

Printed and bound in Great Britain at
The Camelot Press plc, Southampton

Contents

Acknowledgements

It is a pleasure to acknowledge my gratitude to Dr Jeremy Catto who supervised the D.Phil thesis on which this study has been based. He has shown a careful interest in all stages of this work and has always provided friendly support and generous help. I am also grateful to Dr V. Flint for supervising my early research into late medieval piety. In addition I wish to thank those who have read this manuscript in its various stages and offered helpful criticisms and comments: they include Mr James Campbell, Professor Barrie Dobson and Dr Roger Highfield (who examined the doctoral thesis) Dr Barbara Harvey and Dr Henry Mayr-Harting. I am grateful for the assistance and cooperation of the staff of the Bodleian Library, Oxford; Cambridge University Library; York Minster Library; St Edwards; and David Smith of the Borthwick Institute of Historical Research.

I am also indebted to the support of my parents and my parents-in-law; but above all I wish to express my gratitude to my wife, Nikki, who helped to correct the proofs and to compile the index. Her patience and understanding made all this possible.

Abbreviations

Bodl. Lib.	Bodleian Library
B.I.H.R.	Borthwick Institute of Historical Research
B.R.U.C.	Biographical Register of the University of Cambridge
B.R.U.O.	Biographical Register of the University of Oxford
B.R.P.	Biographical Register of Peterhouse
B.J.R.L.	Bulletin of the John Rylands Library
B.L.	British Library
CPL	Calendar of Papal Letters
CPR	Calendar of Patent Rolls
C.U.L.	Cambridge University Library
C.W.A.S.	Cumberland and Westmorland Antiquarian Society
E.D.R.	Ely Diocesan Register
E.H.R.	English Historical Review
E.E.T.S.	Early English Text Society
J.B.A.A.	Journal of British Archaeological Association
J.E.H.	Journal of Ecclesiastical History
J.W.C.I.	Journal of Warburg and Courtauld Institute
P.L.	Patrologia Migne
M.L.A.	Modern Languages Association
M.L.R.	Modern Language Review
Mod. Phil.	Modern Philology
N.C.W.	North Country Wills
P.M.L.A.	Publications of Modern Languages Association
Prob. Reg.	Probate Register
Reg. Thores.	Register of Thoresby
R.E.S.	Review of English Studies
R.S.	Rolls Series
S.S.	Surtees Society
TE	Testamenta Eboracensia
TRHS	Transactions of the Royal Historical Society
W.S.	Wyclif Society
Y.A.S.	Yorkshire Archeological Society Record Series
Y.A.J.	Yorkshire Archeological Journal
T.V.	Testamenta Vetusta
W.I.	Wills and Inventories
Y.M.L.	York Minster Library

For Nikki and Venetia

Introduction

The period between the Black Death and the Wars of the Roses, when the French wars helped to create a sense of national pride and identity, was a social and cultural watershed in English history. A larger more complex ruling class, composed of prosperous tenant farmers, merchants, lawyers, administrators and other occupations, was evolving as the narrow pastoral base of the economy broadened, and educated men were required to serve in an expanding bureaucracy which was keeping paper records for the first time. Opportunities for education were expanding in the newly founded grammar and cathedral schools and the university colleges. English was becoming the national spoken and written language used in the administration of magnate households and the civil service. The representatives of this dynamic new society made the Commons into a formidable critic of administrative and financial inefficiency, and at times, government policy.

These social changes were matched by cultural developments. The first great vernacular literary movement of the country occurred in the late fourteenth and early fifteenth century. Narrative poems were written that offered a broader and more realistic perspective on human nature than that conveyed in the earlier aristocratic courtly romances. Chaucer's *Canterbury Tales* celebrated the new diversity in English society, and his contemporaries and followers included Langland, Gower, Hoccleve and Lydgate. These authors and others offered members of the expanding literate class of England a mirror image of their own society. In this period more people than ever before were reading books for instruction and entertainment.

One aspect of these social and intellectual changes was the composition and copying of spiritual literature in England. Most of the devotional works which were copied and circulated throughout England in the fifteenth century were originally composed or translated by men who lived and worked in the area administered by the archbishop of York. The first of these writers was Richard Rolle, who died prematurely of the plague in 1349. Other religious authors in the period between 1350 and 1430 included William Nassyngton of the consistory court of York, the anonymous author of *The Prick of Conscience*, John Waldeby of the

Austin friars of York, William Rymyngton of the Cistercian abbey of Sawley, Walter Hilton, a canon of Thurgarton priory in Nottinghamshire, the author of *The Cloud of Unknowing* and its related treatises, who lived and wrote in the north-east midlands, Nicholas Love, the prior of Mount Grace, the authors of *'The Holy Boke Gratia Dei'* and the treatise *Of Angel's Song*, who wrote in a north-east dialect, and the authors of the York and Wakefield Corpus Christi plays, which were expanded and elaborated in this period.

All of these writers were saying something socially significant. Even a cursory reading of the works of Rolle, Hilton, and Nicholas Love, reveals that their teaching was not hermetic mysticism confined to monasteries and circles of elites. They may have described the relationship between the individual and God; but they were also concerned with the relationship between the pious man and his society. These works were written in English for large numbers of readers; and they offered practical advice to secular clergy and laymen on how to integrate their personal meditations with social responsibilities, conformity to the sacraments of the church, especially to compulsory annual confession, and the performance of penitential satisfaction. The broad social concerns of these authors suggest that the spiritual literature of the diocese represents another aspect of the social and intellectual changes of the period. Hilton and his contemporaries were influenced by lay piety, and in their turn they encouraged and exerted some control over its development.

There were profound social consequences. As laymen showed more initiative and independence in religious practice and belief, their expectations for the church and their hunger for moral and spiritual teaching became such that by the end of the fourteenth century some priests and laymen felt that the church was not doing enough; and the Lollard movement arose from this dissatisfaction. The English church responded to the threat of heresy, the schism, and the protracted conflict with France with a remarkable show of assertion and independence; and in the course of the fifteenth century its authorities established a firm control over all aspects of religious life.

However, there has been no general survey of religion in this period which might relate it to these social and intellectual changes. There has been considerable work on episcopal administration and some political matters, including Wyclif; and on some religious orders, the Lollards, and religious practices in certain regions.[1] There is still need for a general survey that places the spiritual literature of the period within its

[1] M. Aston, *Thomas Arundel* (Oxford, 1967); K. B. McFarlane, *John Wycliffe and the Beginnings of English Nonconformity* (London, 1952), and *Lancastrian Kings and Lollard Knights* (Oxford, 1972), J. I. Catto, 'Religious Change under Henvy V' in G. L. Harriss

historical context. Some contributions have been made the the editors of *The Cloud of Unknowing* and its related texts, *The Revelations of Divine Love* by Julian of Norwich, *The Book of Margery Kempe,* and in the biographical studies of Richard Rolle.[2] This thesis adds to such work by asking the question: why was so much of this spiritual literature written in the diocese of York? It traces a particular impulse — late fourteenth century northern spiritual literature — to its originators, and explores its readership. Social developments in the diocese suggest that the writing of contemplative literature in this region was no accident, and that historical explanations for the phenomenon lay in the study of religious practices and beliefs. In this period the diocese of York was the centre of an eremitic movement that rivalled the earlier movements of the eleventh and twelfth centuries. The increase in the numbers of recluses and the foundation of Carthusian monasteries in the region suggests that the religious literature of the diocese reflected social conditions and had social implications. The popularity of the cults of some of the leaders of the contemplative movement: Richard Rolle, St John of Bridlington and Richard Scrope, the archbishop of York, also implies that this eremitic movement may have impinged itself on the beliefs of even the less sophisticated and educated inhabitants of the diocese, and that there was a relationship between contemplation and popular religion.

This study is confined to the administrative unit of the diocese of York, which included the North, East and West Ridings, and the counties of Nottinghamshire and Lancashire, and excludes the other two bishoprics of the northern province, Durham and Carlisle. No attempt is made to study the administration of the important religious institutions of the diocese, which included the cathedrals of York and Beverley, the semi-autonomous archdeaconry of Richmond, and the 10 Cistercian, 7 Benedictine, 18 Augustinian and 3 Premonstratensian houses of the region. The appropriate starting point for the thesis was taken to be 1350 to allow for consideration of the impact of Rolle's life and teaching within the diocese. The study continues into at least the mid-fifteenth century to consider the impact of the religious literature of the diocese, both in York and, briefly, in the rest of the kingdom. This is

(ed.) *Henry V: The Practice of Kingship* (Oxford, 1985); R. B. Dobson, *Durham Priory, 1400 – 1450* (Cambridge, 1973); J. A. Thompson, 'Clergy and Laity in London, 1376 – 1453' (Oxford Univ. D. Phil. thesis 1960); N. P. Tanner 'Popular Religion in Norwich with special Reference to the Evidence of Wills, 1370 – 1532' (Oxford Univ. D. Phil. thesis 1973), and *The Church in Late Medieval Norwich* (Toronto, 1984).

2 *The Cloud of Unknowing and the Book of Privy Counselling,* ed. P. Hodgson (London, EETS, 1944); *A Book of the Shewings to the Anchoress Julian of Norwich,* ed. E. Colledge and J. Walsh (Toronto, 1978); *The Book of Margery Kempe,* ed. S. B. Meech and H. E. Allen (London, EETS, 1940); H. E. Allen, *Writings Ascribed to Richard Rolle* (New York, 1927).

not a regional history in the strictest sense of the work, and the clergy and magnates, who are studied in an attempt to find out who may have been responsible for initiating the religious changes within the diocese, were not provincials, but important figures in the universities, the court and the government administration.

The study of religion in the diocese of York between 1350 and 1450 is divided into six sections. The first chapter is concerned with the religious conventions of the Yorkshire nobility, which were neither peculiar to this period nor this region. Chapter Two looks at the patronage of the eremitic movement of the diocese and the social functions of the recluse. The third chapter reviews the pastoral contributions of the church of York to the movement between 1350 and 1372, and the fourth chapter deals with the church's response to the increasing popularity of recluses and their teaching between 1370 and 1450. In the fifth chapter the content of the religious literature of the diocese is placed in its social context; and the final chapter is concerned with saints' cults and the relationship between popular religion and the eremitic movement. The conclusion briefly examines the relationship between the religious changes of the diocese of York and those of the continent, and evaluates the contribution of later-medieval Yorkshire towards the development of a national religion.

CHAPTER ONE

The Religious Character of the Nobility of the Diocese

The main emphasis in this investigation into religious practices and beliefs in the diocese of York will be placed on those developments that were unique to the period between 1350 and 1450 and to the region. The nobility of Yorkshire played a crucial role in encouraging these religious changes: magnates' patronage of recluses and reading of devotional literature will be studied in chapter two; and the contribution of circles of high ecclesiastics towards the eremitic movement and their response to it, which consisted of a conscious formulation and articulation of changes in religious sensibility, will be studied in chapters three and four. However, considering the importance of magnates and high ecclesiastics in facilitating these changes, it is necessary to define precisely the Yorkshire nobility; and furthermore, before looking at the popularity of recluses and their teachings, which obviously entailed a re-evaluation of the relationship between the pious patron and his community, it is necessary to examine the traditional relationship between the nobility and religious communities of the diocese, including the family, and religious institutions, especially the parish church. This entails establishing the character of the religious conventions in the diocese that were not unique to either the region or the period. Such a survey is dependent on the surviving evidence of religious attitudes left behind by a social elite defined in terms of wealth, education and administrative and social responsibilities. These attitudes had not been determined by either superior literacy or the broader horizons formed by travel because they had never been consciously formulated, although they were consciously held and cultivated. Despite their cosmopolitan life-style, the nobility shared their aspirations and fears with the poorer, less educated and peripatetic Yorkshiremen as well as with their fellow aristocrats in other regions. This was because all noblemen traditionally depended on the spiritual comforts offered in the diocese by their families and their parish neighbours. Even the bondsmen and cottars of a nobleman's estate and the beggars of his parish played an important role in the rituals and intercessions provided by these two communities.

The Nobility

The diocese of York cannot be considered as a distinctive social or geographical entity: the rich plains along the Rivers Ouse and Derwent, and in Holderness and South Yorkshire, which supported grain and light industry, were more economically and socially significant than the sparsely settled uplands of West Yorkshire and the border regions; this is testified by the range of parish churches, monasteries and castles that dotted the landscape. These prosperous areas were really an extension of the plains in the south-east of the kingdom; and the nobility that they supported had too many southern interests to be considered provincials. They were a dynamic and expanding class, distinguished by their inherited landed estates and their new wealth which came from many sources; they also held positions of authority at a local and national level which required considerable literacy and practical ability.

The wealth of the upper baronage, of families such as Percy, Mowbray and Neville, was based on landed estates and a military power that served as a buffer against the Scots, but it was possible to join the lower ranks of the aristocracy by acquiring wealth through war, land, trade, or by the practice of law or service in the church. The Hundred Years war provided fortunes in prizes and ransom money for captains such as Thomas Lord Roos and Sir Brian Stapleton, who rose to prominence through the territorial connections in the north-east of John of Gaunt. Military service itself could bring noble status: when commissioners set about finding witnesses for the Grosvenor family in an armorial dispute who were *generosi*, they assigned this status after noting the length of each man's military service.[1] The availability of cheap land for leasing and purchase after the Black Death offered opportunities for the country gentry to expand into the fertile areas of the diocese. It was in this period that the East Riding families such as Roos and Dependen rose to prominence. The export of Yorkshire wool from the expanding port of Hull provided opportunities for enterprising merchants such as the De la Pole brothers, William and Michael, who rose from yeoman status in 1330 to become money lenders to Edward III.[2] Careers in common law provided wealth and social advancement for families who were to play an important part in the evolution of religious practices in the diocese. The two sons of William Scrope of Castle Bolton in Wensleydale, Henry and Geoffrey, made a fortune as pleaders in the court of common pleas which was frequently held in York. Henry was chief baron of the

1 N. H. Nicolas, *The Controversy between Sir Richard Scrope and Sir Robert Grosvenor in the Court of Chivalry* (London, 1832), i, 248 – 51.

2 K. B. McFarlane, *The English Nobility* (Oxford, 1973), pp. 165 – 7.

exchequer from 1330 to 1336, and Geoffrey was chief justice of the king's bench from 1324 to 1349. By obtaining estates through private negotiation they became the leading landowners in the North Riding and founders of the respective dynasties of Bolton and Masham.[3] The church, in what was the largest diocese in the kingdom, provided lucrative careers for loyal civil servants in the fourteenth century and canon lawyers at the turn of the fifteenth century as episcopal and archidiaconal officials, titular heads of landed prebends, hospitals and parish churches, and in the valuable prebends of York Minster. Vows of clerical celibacy did not prevent clergy forming clerical dynasties of relatives and friends: John Thoresby, the archbishop of York (1353 – 1373), secured preferment for his relatives from the Waltham and Ravenser families in the church of York and in chancery in Westminster.

Despite their varied origins, noblemen had distinctive literary and administrative skills which they used in crown service. Yorkshire magnates were prominent as councillors and administrators in the household of the king and in his council. The Scropes of Bolton and Masham were civil servants of the royal household for fifty years, and Henry Lord Scrope of Masham was highly valued by Henry V, who employed him as a diplomat, and after the Cambridge plot of 1415 his place as a prominent royal advisor was taken by his kinsman and neighbour Henry Lord FitzHugh of Tanfield, the chamberlain of the king's household and constable of England. The gentry of the diocese also served the crown by attending parliament as knights of the shire and many, through John of Gaunt's influence, were engaged in administering and commanding the English troops in France, Gascony and Spain. York clergy dominated the expanding civil service during Edward III's reign: chancery was controlled by members of the Ravenser and Waltham families, who were responsible for the administrative techniques of parliament from expence writs to the sifting of petitions;[4] Richard Ravenser was frequently summoned from Yorkshire to see the accounts of the Queen. These clerks upheld the sound business traditions of an efficient bureaucracy.

The nobility, above all, applied their skills to conscientious administrative service in the local communities of the diocese. The York Minster chapter, the most distinguished in England, supervised the affairs of a complex and centralized administration responsible for ninety parishes.[5] Under their guidance minor officials, chosen from the ranks of vicars

3 E. L. G. Stones, 'Sir Geoffrey le Scrope, Chief Justice of the King's Bench', *E.H.R.*, lxix (1954), 1 – 17. J. L. Grassi, 'Clerical Dynasties in the Royal Administration 1230 – 1340' (Oxford Univ. D. Phil. thesis 1960).

4 ibid, p. 186.

5 R. B. Dobson, 'The Residentiary Canons of York in the Fifteenth Century', *J.E.H.*, 30 (1979).

choral and chantry priests, kept written records and accounts in Latin of the daily administration of the cathedral.[6] The organization of the magnate household required equal bureaucratic skills. The voluminous records of Lancaster testify to the mass of documentation needed to administer a household such as John of Gaunt's which employed a staff of minor clergy and lesser noblemen; and even the humblest baron in the diocese had his knights, clerks, squires, seals and wardrobe and presided over an incipient system of financial control and registry.[7] Magnates, landed gentry and city merchants were part-time civil servants in their local communities, supplementing the work of the secular clergy by encouraging social order and discipline through their administrative duties. The contribution of local regions to the war effort, and their defensive precautions, depended on the organizing ability of this class.[8] Knights such as Sir Ralph Hastings, and Sir William Neville, in cooperation with local sheriffs, were frequently required to serve on commissions of array and to organize the recruitment and equipping of troops from the East Riding for serving in France and Scotland. Local commissions, which fell heavily on a small minority with no legal training, played an important role in the administration of local justice and law and order: between 1381 and 1391 Sir Ralph Hastings, Sir Robert Hilton, Sir Brian Stapleton and Sir John Dependen were involved in ten commissions investigating such local incidents as breaches of the peace, vandalism of churches, property disputes and coastal defences. In the boroughs of York, Beverley, and Hull, prominent merchants in the town councils were responsible for maintaining law and order and preserving the liberties and customs of their communities.[9]

The nobility were also distinguished by wealth. From the surviving poll tax returns for the West Riding in 1379 it has been established that there was one member of the gentry — assessed at 20s per head — to every five hundred males.[10] They were aware of their distinction and emphasized it. The manor house of every nobleman contained a display of gold, gilt and silver plate engraved with the family arms. With gold

6 F. Harrison, *Life in a Medieval College* (London, 1952).

7 R. Somerville, *History of the Duchy of Lancster*, I, 1265 – 1603 (London, 1953), 90 – 133; Robert Avesbury, *De Gestis Mirabilis Edwardi Tertii*, ed. E. Maunde Thompson (London, R.S., 1889), 372 – 4, 416 – 17, 434 – 7; H.J. Hewitt, *The Organization of War under Edward III* (Manchester, 1966); McFarlane, *Nobility*, 33, 44 – 5.

8 A. Gooder, 'The Parliamentary Representation of County York, 1258 – 1832' *Y.A.S.*, I (1935), 16.

9 CPR (1367 – 70) pp. 24, 57; CPR (1370 – 74) pp. 204, 494; CPR (1374 – 77) pp. 321; CPR (1381 – 85) pp. 506, 585, 592; CPR (1385 – 89) pp. 471, 214, 263, 475; CPR (1388 – 92) pp. 137, 208, 212, 219, 343.

10 M. G. Vale, 'Piety, Charity and Literacy Among the Yorkshire Gentry, 1370 – 1480', *Borthwick Institute of Historical Research*, 50 (1976), 4.

fetching 40s the ounce troy, and silver 2s 10d, they could represent a considerable fortune.[11] The plate in Henry Lord Scrope's London home alone was worth £480 9s 2d, and Richard Ravenser, the archdeacon of Lincoln, had over thirty-six silver dishes engraved with his arms in his Lindsey manor.[12] Jewellery was a distinctive ostentation. Richard Roos bequeathed gold rings to twenty-four people in 1406, and Richard Ravenser had twenty-seven gold rings.[13] They shared a cosmopolitan life-style. Many knights had seen active service abroad, where they could observe customs and obtain spoil. In 1384, Sir Thomas Ughtred bequeathed a linen bed-cover, decorated with images of the king of France and his arms, which were bordered by images of the French people.[14] High officials, such as Henry Lord Scrope of Masham and John Newton, the treasurer of York Minster, travelled in their own barges and the magnate families of Scrope of Masham and Neville of Raby possessed town houses in London. Fashions were extravagant and opulent. Richard Ravenser had a collection of furred cloaks, surcoats, mantles and capes worth £23 in his London manor.[15] Isabella Wyleby, in 1414, bequeathed a colourful collection of furred coats of red, grey and mottled violet, and tunics of blue and violet with silver belts.[16] Bed hangings, curtains and tapestries were ostentatious displays of state. The inventory of Henry Lord Scrope's confiscated goods records sixty bed curtains, twenty coverlets, twenty nine curtains and nineteen tapestries, all sumptuously decorated in the fashion of the time with exotic beasts and colours.[17]

Wealth provided the nobility with the means to express their religious impulses freely. The regular incomes of landed estates allowed noblemen to make foundations and endowments. The urban society of York on the other hand did not have such freedom: fluctuations in the cloth trade and industrial production had an adverse effect on religious benefaction in this period.[18] The noble families of the diocese also had cash and moveable goods which they could dispose of in their last wills and testaments according to their religious inclinations. All members of

11 McFarlane, *Nobility*, p. 98.

12 C. L. Kingsford, 'Two forfeitures in the Year of Agincourt', *Archeologia*, 70 (1919), 79; the inventory of Richard Ravenser is in *Memoirs of the History and County of Lincoln* (Lincoln, 1848), pp. 317 – 26.

13 ibid, p. 319.

14 The printed wills from the York Probate Registers of the Exchequer Court occur in *Testamenta Eboracensia*, ed. J. Raine and J. Raine, S.S. vols. 4, (1300 – 1429); 30, (1429 – 67); 45 (1467 – 85). Subsequently referred to as TE. I, II, III. Ughtred's will is in TE. 1, p. 243.

15 *Memoirs Lincoln*, pp. 317 – 18.

16 TE. I, p. 382.

17 Kingsford, 80.

18 R. B. Dobson, 'The Foundation of perpetual chantries by the citizens of medieval York', *Studies in Church History*, iv (1967).

this class had valuables such as chapel furniture, vestments, secular plate, and garments, and at least £10 in cash, to give to their favourite churches and charities. Most had over £50 in cash to bequeath, and great magnates such as William Lord Roos could give away as much as £748.[19]

The nobility of the diocese did not, therefore, have a distinctive regional identity. Military ethics, as befitting a border country, and nepotism, among the Thoresby affinity, were important in the region; but the social experiences of the nobility were not unique. Career opportunities in administration, diplomacy, war and international trade took them to the universities, to London and to Europe.[20] Any analysis of their religious attitudes must, therefore, begin with those beliefs which were shared among the ruling class of England. These were not related to social mobility, literacy or a cosmopolitan lifestyle, which were all recent developments, but to traditional, fundamental values of the aristocracy that newcomers to the class were anxious to endorse. Their religion reinforced the close bonds existing between the nobleman and his community, which consisted of the extended family and the local society that was served so ably by lay and ecclesiastical ministers in the fourteenth century. These communities exerted ties more powerful than the blandishments of new-found education, wealth and travel.

FAMILIAL RELIGION

Families, like cathedral chapters or fraternities, functioned as religious communities conducting religious services, providing patronage for religious artists, and asserting their importance. For centuries the centre for the rituals of familial religion had been the domestic chapel, run by a resident chaplain. The Percies had a chapel at Seamer, where Lady Eleanor heard daily mass, and the FitzHughs had a chapel in their castle at Ravensworth. By the end of the thirteenth century as the acquisition of a domestic chapel began to be regarded as a mark of gentry, lesser gentry began to include private chapels in their manor houses, and licences were obtained by Sir Miles Stapleton in 1388 and Sir John Ingleby in 1397 permitting them to celebrate mass in their oratories. These chapels were becoming more elaborate because the heads of families, instead of founding new chantries, diverted their money into the family chapel where services were regularly held for members of

19 TE. I, pp. 57 – 60; *The Register of Henry Chichele*, ed. E. G. Jacob (Oxford) ii, (1938), pp. 23 – 24.

20 R. B. Cooke, 'Some Early Civic Wills of York', *Assoc. Archit. Soc.*, 28 (1406) 841 – 69. York merchants were involved in the wool trade. Thomas Holme (d. 1406) owned tenements in Calais.

their family. In 1412 William Lord Roos left £400 for ten chaplains to celebrate in his chapel in Belvoir manor.[1] Architectural changes in the domestic chapels allowed the family to attend mass apart from the rest of the household in a first floor pew, which was connected by a gallery with private apartments and offered a secluded view of the altar.[2]

These chapels could become a formidable expression of the financial and social status of the family. Their furnishings comprised a considerable part of a nobleman's fortune. Ralph Newton, onetime dean of the Scrope chapel, claimed in 1415 that Henry Lord Scrope possessed one hundred and twenty copes, ninety-two of which were recorded in Knighteley's inventory.[3] The average value of each of these vestments could have been as much as £60, for they were made of satin, velvet and silk and decorated with gold. The combination on these garments of religious symbols, like the holy names, and symbols of family rank, such as the coat of arms, shows that religious ceremonies in the family chapel were used to reinforce a sense of social position.[4] The furnishings of these chapels were considered family heirlooms: Sir Stephen Scrope of Masham, Thomas Percy and Isabella Wyleby are among those who left candelabras, silver and gold ewers and cruets, and jewelled crucifixes to their heirs.[5] Service books were also considered part of the chapel treasure: Knighteley listed over fifty antiphonars and other service books among the goods in Lord Scrope's chapel; many were illuminated and covered heirlooms from his mother; Robert Roos left psalters to his children in 1392 and Elizabeth Lady FitzHugh left primers to all of her grandchildren.[6] The wealthy were art collectors, patrons of silversmiths and goldsmiths, manuscript illuminists and sculptors; but they created an atmosphere that could arouse religious sensibility.

The family maintained its own staff of clergy: the Percies had three chaplains supervising the services of their Alnwick chapel, and the chantry of Richard Lord Scrope at Bolton was served by a staff of six. The family chaplain was an intimate of the household frequently the recipient of legacies such as the bequests of ten marks made by Sir Ralph Hastings in 1367 and Beatrice Roos in 1414,[7] and sometimes responsible

1 *Reg. Chichele*, ii, pp. 22 – 6.

2 W. A. Pantin, 'Instructions for a devout and literate layman', in J. J. G. Alexander and M. T. Gibson (eds), *Medieval Learning and Literature, Essays presented to Richard William Hunt* (Oxford, 1976), 405.

3 Kingsford, 76; *Foedera*, ed. T. Rymer (London, 1704 – 35), IX, 272 – 80.

4 J. I. Catto, 'Religion and the English Nobility in the later fourteenth century', in H. Lloyd-Jones, V. Pearl and B. Worden (eds.) *History and Imagination, Essays in honour of H. R. Trevor-Roper* (London, 1981), 46.

5 TE. I, p. 57; Scrope and Grosvenor, ii, 55; *Wills and Inventories* . . . (chiefly from the Registry at Durham), vol. i, ed. J. Raine, SS, vol. 38, p. 38; TE, I, p. 382.

6 *Testamenta Vetusta*, ed. N. H. Nicolas (London, 1826), p. 212.

7 TE. I, p. 217.

for the education of children: the chantry established by William Lord Roos at Belvoir in 1414 also served as a school. Another important member of the household was the family confessor. The friars stimulated the development of private confession in the thirteenth century and by 1300, certainly by 1350, it was customary for noble families to have their own confessors, usually friars who were sometimes leading members of their order. Thomas Wyntton, the provincial of the Augustinian Friars, was confessor and executor to Sir William Marmion of Keesby in 1390. The frequency with which confessors served as executors indicates their important position in the family: Ralph Hastings of Slingsby made his confessor his executor in 1446 because he considered him to be one of the people who had helped him the most.[8] Confessors were sometimes left life pensions: in 1398 Sir William Chaworth left his confessor an annual income of nine marks for the rest of his life.[9]

The noble families of the diocese provided in their chapels a religious environment that was ancillary to the parish church; the family, like a monastic community, represented an ideal of permanence that was upheld by those individual members who fought for its institutional survival by protecting family lands and estates. Laws of property and especially the fourteenth century laws of entail, were introduced to ensure that estates were not lost to the male family line because a member of the family failed to produce issue; after the death of the head of a family younger male children could, through entail, receive land with the proviso that they could never alienate it, and that in the event of their male line perishing it would revert back to the head of the family or his rightful heir.[10] The motive for preserving the continuity of a family community and its assets was as religious as it was for religious orders and secular communities of canons: the family would provide intercession for its members in the same way as a monastic brotherhood or guild. For this reason there was little emphasis in wills on displays of familial affection. Children were regarded as an insurance that the family would continue to provide prayers for the souls of their ancestors. Thomas Lord Roos left all his personal possessions to his eldest son Richard, ignoring the other children, and added the proviso that if his heir died this property would be distributed to his younger sons. In the event of all his children dying the goods were to be sold and the money used for prayers of his soul.[11] Surviving children fulfilled their obligation to provide for the souls of their parents and ancestors,

8 ibid., p. 20; *The Academy*, V (Lincoln, 1879), pp. 220 – 22, 280 – 85.
9 ibid, p. 247.
10 McFarlane, *Nobility*, pp. 63 – 72
11 TE. I, pp. 251 – 2.

and some of the provisions were generous. Mary Lady Roos provided for six priests to celebrate at Rievaulx for her parents, and Lady Beatrice Roos left 100 marks for the celebration of masses for her ancestors and parents.[12] The increase in chantry foundations in the diocese between 1350 and 1400 demonstrates the importance of the spiritual funcations of the family. Most of these new foundations of families like Roos, Constable and Stapleton were intended to provide masses for parents and ancestors. However, families did not merely constitute another branch of the institutional church, and there evolved among them independent religious attitudes and rituals that clergy nevertheless approved of and participated in. These aspects of familial religion will now be studied.

The Lineage

Families, as we have seen, could provide an important setting for Christian ritual, but there would appear to be little place for a direct influence of family sentiments on Christian belief, and little connection between heraldic and Christian symbols. However, the family coat of arms was a potent symbol that gave to the lineage a spiritual significance that could be termed religious. A sense of well-being and religious affiliation accompanied membership of an armigerous family: it provided the security of a permanent institution like a religious fraternity, and just as the church was a vehicle for the collective salvation of its members through the sacraments and the collective merits of prayer and penance, so too the family offered redemption through chivalric rituals and collective merits attained through deeds of honour. In analysing familial religion it is necessary to demonstrate that when families in the diocese showed an interest in heraldry, chivalry and war they were expressing sentiments as fundamentally religious as those they expressed within the more obviously Christian framework of parish society.

Before discussing the religious attitudes associated with heraldry it is necessary to establish the importance of heraldry in the environment. The prevalence of heraldic evidence on domestic architecture, in the windows of cathedrals and private chapels, on the gatehouses of monasteries and in the larger parish churches shows that its potential as a source of evidence of religious beliefs cannot be ignored. The importance of heraldry within the domestic household can be seen in the inscription of the arms of Richard Lord Scrope of Bolton on his halls,

12 TE. 1, pp. 375, 359.

beds, windows and plate, and in the bequests of bed-hangings and tapestries to the heirs of Ralph Lord Neville and Sir Ralph Hastings.[1] The furnishings of the family chapels, including such liturgical books as the surviving books of hours of the Neville and Pullein families and the only extant service book among the fifty mentioned in the will of Henry Lord Scrope of Masham also contained family coats of arms.[2] So did Chapel vestments: the wills of Ralph Lord Neville and Sir Ralph Hastings mention collections of different vestments inscribed with the family lineage, and Henry Lord Scrope bequeathed sixty-five copies bearing his arms to Yorkshire parish churches.[3] The same symbols occurred on churches and religious houses throughout the diocese. The most dominant were the saltire of the Neville's of Raby and the bend azure of the Scropes of Bolton which survived in twenty churches in the north until the nineteenth century. In the fourteenth century the Scrope crest was found in all of the major religious houses of Yorkshire and one of the deponents in the Scrope-Grosvenor lawsuit, William Troy, a canon of Aske, testified that the Scrope arms were in glass windows and wall paintings in over forty Yorkshire churches.[4] Ecclesiastics as well as soldiers displayed their arms: Walter Skirlaw, the bishop of Durham, placed his coat on his new building projects in York Minster and Howden.[5]

The churches of the diocese recorded the history of noble families. Magnates, knights and esquires could consult, in York Minster, one of the largest displays of chivalric heraldry and insignia in the north. It was in the chapter house that the greatest lords of the north were required to give evidence in the Scrope-Grosvenor lawsuit of their knowledge of the history of the Scrope family arms. The cathedral was the family burial place for the Scropes of Masham: Stephen Lord Scrope was buried in St Stephen's chapel and his son Lord Henry Scrope asked to be buried there and left money for an image of himself in armour with his shield bearing a coat of arms.[6] The minster windows also contained the arms of Scrope of Masham, Stapleton, Hastings, Neville and Percy. Gentry families demonstrated their pedigrees in parish churches. A fifteenth century monument in Cowthorpe church shows Sir Thomas Heslarton and his wife recumbent under a sheet covered by the family tree: on the branches of the tree are the heads of their thirteen children, and the roots of the tree have shields bearing the family coat of arms.[7] Gentry in

1 Scrope and Grosvenor, ii, 350 (the deposition of Sir William Acton); *W.I.*, 71, 38; TE. 1, pp. 57, 197.
2 Kingsford, p. 91; Y.M.L., MS. Add. 54; Y.M.L. MS. xvi, k.6.
3 *Foedera*, ix, pp. 271 – 8.
4 *Scrope and Grosvenor*, ii, 331.
5 Gough, *Sepulchral Monuments*, 19.
6 *Foedera*, ix. p. 274.
7 N. Pevsner, *The Buildings of England, Yorkshire: York and the East Riding* (London, 1972), p. 309.

other regions had the same interest in genealogy: John Pympe of Kent had a tomb built which showed an account if his lineage going back five generations; he also arranged for the arms of leading families of the country with whom he believed he was related to be inserted into the windows of the nave of his burial church.[8]

Under the patronage of noble families churches resembled private mausolea as more space was appropriated for monuments and heraldic signs were perpetuated on effigies in brass and stone. Within the choir of the church of St Agatha's in Easby Abbey the history of the Scropes of Bolton was carved in freestone and alabaster:[9] their heraldry displayed around family tombs in glass windows, before altars, on panels, abbey vestments, in the refectory, and on the pavements of the church. Above the choir stood effigies of the founders, Henry Scrope and William Scrope, with their arms painted on their shields. Others of their lineage were interred under flat stones where their effigies and arms were sculptured. Statues of the nobility displaying the family arms must have constituted an important part of the religious surroundings of parishioners. These monuments showed the lord in full armour, usually in a recumbent pose, with his lady by his side. The family arms were displayed on his shield and jupon and the monument was frequently surrounded by carvings of knights or angels bearing the family arms. Such sculptures were to be found in parish churches throughout the diocese including those of Bedale, Howden, Pickering, and Tanfield.[10] Patrons of these churches ensured that they and their ancestors were remembered by displaying their effigies and arms on brasses, frequently in the family chapel within the church: in 1362, in the parish church of Aldborough, a six-foot two-inch brass figure of William Aldborough was set on the floor of the family chapel and his arms were emblazoned on his shield and jupon.[11] Brasses were often placed on marble slabs in chancels to secure a position near the high altar: Sir John St Quintin had a brass figure of himself in full armour set on a nine foot marble slab alongside an effigy of his first wife Lora in the parish church of Brandesburton in 1397.[12]

Heraldry then, was an important visual aspect of the social and religious environment. The coat of arms represented status especially to newcomers to noble rank, and until the heraldic visitations of the Tudors, the assumption of badges on coats of arms was relatively

8 P. W. Fleming, 'Charity, faith and the gentry of Kent', in A. J. Pollard (ed.) *Property and Politics*, (Gloucester, 1984), p. 51.

9 H. C. Colvin, *The White Canons in England* (Oxford, 1977), p. 108.

10 *Sepulchral Monuments*, i, pp. 171 – 81.

11 M. Stephenson, 'Monumental brasses in the North Riding', *Y.A.J.*, (1903), 203.

12 M. Stephenson, 'Monumental brasses in the West Riding', *Y.A.J.*, (1900), 3. M. Stephenson, 'Monumental brasses in the East Riding', *Y.A.J.*, (1893), 211.

uncontrolled, leading to armigerous disputes over the right to bear a particular emblem. The most notable of these was the Scrope Grosvenor lawsuit. However, these disputes and the evidence from wills, funerals, architecture and chapel furnishings also provided evidence of religious attitudes that went beyond family pride and social status. The coat of arms was a symbol of continuity that could be upheld against the ravages of death and infertility; childless men attempted to ensure that their family coat did not perish with them. The last heir of the Hastings, the Earl of Pembroke, bypassed his legal heir, a distant cousin, by enfeoffing his lands to Sir William Beauchamp, his cousin on his mother's side, on condition that he take the entire arms of the Hastings family.[13] The different images adopted by families acted as powerful totems for onlookers and owners: the badge of the white hart was a focal point of loyalty to Richard II in the 1390's, especially in the diocese of York where he was popular: a chained hart was placed on a capital above the entry to the south choir of York Minster, which the king visited in 1394.[14] Although there is an episode in a poetic romance, *Floreant et Florete*, (probably compiled in its final form for the household of Ralph Lord Neville of Raby between 1390 and 1399) featuring the white hart entering a court as a pledge of redemption,[15] it must be said that the precise psychological significance of such family coats as the Percy crescent, the crab of the Scropes of Masham, and the plumed feathers of the Scropes of Bolton has been lost. Nevertheless it is possible to appreciate their religious significance through an understanding of the attitudes that underlay the emphasis that families placed on the antiquity of their coats of arms and the honour that they accumulated.

Most noble families of this period were willing to defend the antiquity of their coats of arms. In the mid-fourteenth century a Latin book of hours was commissioned for Joan Mountenay, an heiress in Ecclesfield near Sheffield, which was emblazoned with sixteen shields containing the arms of her ancestors and showing the evolution of her family through marriage the consequent changes in her arms.[16] Families were eager to defend the continuity of their lineage against any challenges. In 1373, during an expedition to France, Sir Richard Scrope was involved

13 McFarlane, *Nobility*, p. 74.

14 J. H. Harvey, Richard II and York, in F. R. H. Du Boulay and Caroline M. Barron (eds.), *The Reign of Richard II, Essays in Honour of May McKisack* (London, 1971), 207.

15 Gervase Mathew, *The Court of Richard II* (London, 1968), pp. 47 – 9; M. V. Clarke, *Fourteenth Century Studies* (Oxford, 1937), p. 286; See also J. Huizinga, *The Waning of the Middle Ages* (1924), who said 'With the emblem and motto we enter the sphere of heraldic thought, of which the psychology is yet to be written'. pp. 222 – 23.

16 Y.M.L. MS. add. 54. For description see J. Hunter, *Hallamshire: the History of Topography of the Parish of Sheffield in County York*, (London, 1869), p. 391; and *Archeol. Journal*, III, 46.

in a controversy with Carmilow of Cornwall over the right to bear the arms *azure a bend or.*[17] The jealousy with which members of the Scrope family guarded their arms is revealed in an attack on the garrison of Geneville by an English contingent that included Sir William Scrope, the eldest son of Sir Richard Scrope. A French hostage was found wearing the arms of Scrope of Bolton and ordered to remove them immediately before Sir William found out and had him killed.[18] The importance of the lineage in religious conventions is best illustrated from the Scrope Grosvenor lawsuit, a dispute that arose in 1385 during a military expedition to Scotland when Sir Richard Scrope of Bolton found Sir Robert Grosvenor of Cheshire wearing his coat of armour. All members of the nobility who were able to give any information relevant to the dispute were required to give their depositions in various parts of the country.

There was more to this case, which was finally resolved in favour of Sir Richard Scrope in 1390, than an attempt to prove by the ancestry of the Scrope arms that they were gentlemen as well as lawyers. Witnesses such as Sir Robert Laton and Sir John Mauleverer who claimed they had never heard of the Scrope arms becoming extinct through a lack of male heirs or a successful challenge to their arms, were upholding an ideal of permanence that was threatened when a coat of arms was usurped by another family.[19] The Yorkshire knights and the abbots and monks of religious houses of the diocese who made depositions in favour of the Scropes were concerned to demonstrate the antiquity and continuity of the lineage by using the physical presence of the Scrope arms in the diocese, their own oral and armorial traditions and armorial and historical evidence. Sir Thomas Merkingfield and Sir John Wade deposed that it was common knowledge that the Scrope arms could be traced back to the conquest, and Sir Brian Mountbacher in claiming an antiquity of over three hundred years for these arms, pointed to their presence in the churches and abbeys of Sir Richard Scrope's birth-place.[20] Historical evidence was provided by the religious houses of the diocese which displayed the arms of their founders and benefactors. The prior of the Augustinian abbey of Bridlington sent two canons with property grants and a book of chronicles to York Minster chapter house to show that the Scropes had continually used the *azure a bend or* without default of male heir since the conquest. This chronicle traced the history of the Scrope family to a Henry Scrope living in the time of King Stephen, whose son Richard granted property to the priory. The

17 *Scrope and Grosvenor,* ii, 165.
18 *Scrope and Grosvenor,* ii, 108.
19 ibid, 300.
20 ibid, 318; 313; 381; 324; 387.

chronicle also referred to a Scrope in the retinue of John Gant, who arrived in England with William the Conqueror, and an illustration of the Scrope arms at this time was provided.[21] The chronicle was known in other Yorkshire houses: the abbot of the Premonstratensian abbey of St Agatha's referred to it in his deposition and described it as the Bridlington chronicle.[22] Bridlington priory also provided as evidence property grants made to the house by John Gant and witnessed by the Scrope family.[23] Other houses to give evidence on the antiquity of the Scropes' lineage were the Gilbertine priory of Watton, which produced a chronicle written at the time of the conquest that contained a list of the lords who came over from Normandy, including the Scropes; and the Cistercian abbey of Fountains which provided many old vestments embroidered with the Scrope arms.[24] The religious houses, by defending the Scrope lineage, were upholding an ideal of permanence. The prior of the Augustinian house of Gisburn testified to the presence of the Scrope arms in his priory, which was nearly one hundred years old, and said the same arms had been on Skelton since time immemorial.[25]

Behind the emphasis placed on the antiquity of these family coats there lay ideas concerning the collective merit of honour which had accumulated in the family through the contributions of individual members, like the accumulation of collective merits of prayer and penance. Such honour was aquired through a martial code of behaviour, and especially by the bearing of the family coat of arms in battle. Honour was perhaps as important a motive as the acquisition of booty and ransom money among the nobility fighting in France during the Hundred Years War. Witnesses for the Scropes therefore testified to the honour brought to the Bend Azure in Scotland, Normandy, Brittany and Gascony. John Ryther, the esquire to the younger Geoffrey Scrope of Masham, witnessed the presence of the arms of Sir Richard Scrope of Bolton at Paris, Sir Henry Scrope of Masham in France and Ireland, and the arms of his son Sir Geoffrey in Brittany; he also mentioned the famous battlefields such as Crecy and Berwick where members of the family had served.[26] Bravery in battle brought special honour. Sir William Chauncy testified that in thirty years of bearing arms he had never seen a family do so much honour to their arms as Sir Richard and his blood lineage, and Sir Geoffrey St Quintin deposed that he had heard that the Scrope family had frequently acquired much honour in

21 ibid, 279.
22 ibid, 274.
23 ibid, 279.
24 ibid, 28; 278.
25 ibid, 278; 274.
26 *Scrope and Grosvenor*, ii, 339.

their arms in great expeditions, journeys and battles.[27] Some deponents provided specific details: Sir William Moigne, who was at the siege of Calais, testified that the plaintiff's son Sir William, who was to be Earl of Wiltshire, conducted himself so gallantly one night in capturing French supplies that every Englishman spoke of him with honour.[28] The death of one of the family in battle was seen as a sacrifice which rebounded to the honour of the lineage, and Sir William Hesilrigg pointed out that Sir Richard Scrope's eldest brother, Sir William, had been mortally wounded at the siege of Morlieux.[29] These deponents were as concerned as the Scropes to contribute towards the collective honour of their lineage and they proudly recounted the fields of battle where they had carried their banners: John Ryther esq. had been at Crécy, Sluys and Najera.[30] Many could testify to a lifetime's service with the sword: Nicholas Sabraham, before settling down as a husband of a Northumberland heiress, spent thirty years as a professional soldier.[31] The martial ideal was not restricted to the diocese of York. Many of the most notable warriors who participated in this dispute were from other regions: Sir Richard Waldegrave was a Suffolk knight, and Thomas FitzHenry was from Lincolnshire.

Honour could also be acquired through other martial pursuits, including jousting, which provided an opportunity for schooling in the knowledge of heraldry and for symbolic displays of family lineages. Sir Thomas, Lord Roos of Kendal, a notable tourneyer, testified that the Grosvenor arms had never appeared in tournaments and that it was through service and jousting that a knowledge was acquired of these matters.[32] He had taken his banner to tournaments at Dunstable and Newmarket, and he had seen Sir Geoffrey Scrope, the founder of the Masham line, acquire much honour for the lineage by serving as an esquire to those who appeared in tournaments, and by becoming, after his knighthood, one of the most famous jousters in England. He also saw Geoffrey's son Sir Henry, the first lord of Masham, tourney very ably in the Scrope arms and receive acknowledgement from Edward III. Other prominent Yorkshire jousters included Sir Thomas Roos and Henry Lord Roos of Igmanthorpe.[33] The importance of martial pursuits for family honour was such that armour itself was invested with some of the symbolic significance associated with the coat of arms and regarded

27 ibid, ii, 304.
28 ibid, ii, 377.
29 ibid., ii, 324.
30 ibid., ii, 338.
31 ibid, i. 124 – 24; ii, 323 – 5; Maurice Keen, 'Chaucer's Knight', in V. J. Scattergood and J. W. Sherbourne (eds.), *English Court Culture in the Later Middle Ages* (London, 1983), 53.
32 *Scrope and Grosvenor*, ii, 300, 335.
33 ibid., ii, 300, 335.

as a repository of honour to be preserved in the male line. Henry Lord Scrope of Masham left his eldest brother and heir, Geoffrey, in 1415 all the armour bequeathed him by his father and a considerable collection of jousting equipment, including a great tent with a hall and six turrets, many bastard saddles and his jousting pole, with the stipulation that they were to remain in the hands of his heirs and were never to be sold.[34] Sir John Constable, Sir Ralph Hastings and Sir Thomas Roos bequeathed their armour in a similar manner.[35]

The essentially religious attitude towards the martial life was manifested in the continuing importance of the crusading ideal in the second half of the fourteenth century. Englishmen still fought in the eastern Mediterranean against the heathen Turks, where their efforts culminated in the Alexandrian campaign of 1365; and in Prussia against the pagan Lithuanians, where they helped the Teutonic knights to conquer and settle the lands beyond the River Memel. There is no evidence that the Grosvenor family participated in these crusades but the Scropes were a great crusading family and their case was considerably strengthened by those who gave witness to the honour such pious and gentlemanly activity bestowed on their lineage. The plaintiff's son, William Scrope of Bolton, served in Prussia,[36] but most attention was paid to the Scropes of Masham. Sir William Waldegrave testified to the presence of Sir William Scrope, a younger son of the chief justice, in the retinue of the earl of Hereford in the siege of the town of Satalia in Asia Minor in 1362.[37] Nicholas Sabraham had also seen him in Spain, where he would have entertained hopes of encountering the Moors, and Sir John Godard had seen him in the Holy Land beyond Venice bearing the Scrope arms in the retinue of the Duke of Duras.[38] Henry's eldest son Geoffrey served in Prussia at the siege of Wellan, and according to the testimony of his faithful squire John Ryther, he died in the Scrope arms at the siege of Piskre. Ryther buried his master's body and stayed in Königsberg at the end of the *Reise* to see to the placing of a glass panel with the Scrope arms in the Marienkirche of Königsberg.[39] Geoffrey's brother Stephen, who eventually succeeded as lord of Masham, followed his crusading example, and Sir Nicholas Sabraham testified to his presence in the army of Peter of Cyprus and at the taking of Alexandria in 1362, where he was knighted by the king. Henry, a younger brother of these two, died in the Holy Land, and

34 *Foedera*, ix, p. 275; Kingsford, 82.
35 TE 1, pp. 350, 197, 251, 254, 358.
36 *Scrope and Grosvenor*, i, 172; Keen, 'Chaucer's Knight', 51.
37 *Scrope and Grosvenor*, i, 166.
38 ibid, ii, 324.
39 ibid, i, 146; ii, 351 – 2; Henry Ferrers deposed that he had seen Sir Geoffrey's arms on a table before the high altar in this cathedral, i, 146; ii, 351.

Sabraham noted his arms on a tomb in Messembria.[40] Crusading was pursued by other families in the diocese. Sir Thomas Malbysse mortgaged his estate at Acastre to William Fairfax of Scalton in 1366 in order to raise money for a crusade.[41] The Stapleton family of Bedale had a long history of sympathy for crusading ideals: their patron saint was St Nicholas, the protector of crusaders. Between 1360 and 1365 Sir Miles Stapleton of Bedale and Ingham established a college of Trinitarians or Maturins, an order dedicated to the redemption of captives taken by the Turks, at Ingham in Norfolk.[42] Some of the Roos family of Helmsley were also crusaders. Thomas, the fourth Lord Roos (1337-1384), died while preparing to go on a crusade, and his eldest son John, the fifth Lord Roos (1367-93), died in Paphos in Cyprus on return from a pilgrimage to the Holy Land.

Northern courtiers helped to contribute to the considerable enthusiasm for the crusading ideal that existed among court circles during the reign of Richard II. Chaucer may have used the collective experience of the Scropes of Masham for his description of the crusading knights in the prologue to the Canterbury Tales; he appeared as a witness for the family in the Scrope-Grosvenor dispute and testified to the presence of their arms in a London inn.[43] His friends included, Sir William Neville, brother of John Lord Neville of Raby, and Sir John Clanvowe, who were both deponents in this dispute, and who were in the Duke of Bourbon's expedition to the Barbary coast in 1390.[44] In the 1390s crusades involving northerners were organized against the Prussians and Turks: Sir Thomas Percy, Hotspur, and Peter Buckton, another friend of Chaucer, accompanied Bolingbroke to Prussia in 1390.[45] Courtiers, including the Earl of Northumberland's son Sir Ralph Percy, who died in the Holy Land in 1399, were members of a lay order dedicated to the recapture of Jerusalem, the Order of the Passion. One of its founders, Philippe de Mézières, tried to achieve this objective by proposing an Anglo French crusade in a letter to Richard II in 1395.[46] The small but expensive Wilton diptych, not improbably painted for Richard II's private altar in 1395, demonstrates the importance of the crusade as a means of acquiring honour and heavenly approval for a coat of arms: the king, whose arms, the royal leopard impaling the arms of Edward the Confessor, are shown on a reverse panel, is depicted receiving the banner of St George from Christ, the Virgin and eleven angels who are

40 ibid, i, 124 – 5; Keen, 'Chaucer's Knight', 52.
41 *Sepulchral Monuments*, i, pp. 17 and 122.
42 Chetwynd-Stapleton, 95 – 6; 232; 237.
43 *Scrope and Grosvenor*, ii, 411.
44 ibid, ii, 437 – 38.
45 Gooder, p. 169.
46 Philippe de Mézières, *Letter to King Richard II*, ed. G. W. Coopland (Liverpool, 1975).

wearing the badge of the white hart.[47] Similar symbolism was used at a tournament in Smithfield in 1394 when twenty-four Garter knights, including Sir Brian Stapleton, wore the white hart livery and heard a mass of St George.[48] The crusading ideals of courtiers even survived the defeat at Nicopolis in 1396 of a crusading host. Henry Lord FitzHugh of Tanfield, a neighbour and relative of the Scropes of Masham, indicated an interest in the order of the Passion, and in 1408 he went to Prussia with gifts of armour for which he paid no customs. Little is known of his activities in Prussia, but in October 1409 he obtained permission to take a supply of bows, arrows and bowstrings to St Peter Castle on the island of Rhodes, which was in the process of being built by the knights of Jerusalem as a defence against the Saracens. The details of FitzHugh's expedition in the Mediterranean and Asia Minor have been lost; but according to the family chronicles he penetrated as far as Cairo, and on his return he fought against the Turks and Saracens and helped the knights to complete their castle; seventeen shields of the knights of the garter, including FitzHugh's, were placed on the south side of this castle.[49] FitzHugh's younger relatives continued the connection with Rhodes: in 1434 John, the fifth Lord Scrope of Masham, took with him on an embassy to the grand master of the Order of St John of Jerusalem at Rhodes the sixteen-year old Henry Lord Scrope of Bolton.[50] FitzHugh's castle even attracted the patronage of a Yorkshire squire: Sir John Pigott left 40s to its fabric for its defence against the Turks and a further 10 marks for a crusade against the Hussites in Bohemia.[51]

The Code of Honour of the Nobility: its Social and Religious Significance

The evidence associated with heraldry indicates that some religious significance was attached to the pursuit of honour through aggression. It is now necessary to establish what other virtues were associated with honour apart from physical prowess, and to explain how the rest of society, including the church, could approve of, and indeed identify with, the interests and rights of noble families through symbol and ritual

47 Mathew, *Richard II*, pp. 47 – 8; Clarke, *Fourteenth Century Studies*, p. 286; J. N. Palmer, *England, France and Christendom* (London, 1972); J. Harvey, The Wilton Diptych, a re-examination', *Archeologia*, xcviii (1961), 1 – 28; F. Wormald, 'The Wilton Diptych', *JWCI* xvii (1954), 191 – 203.

48 H. E. Chetwynd-Stapleton, 'The Stapletons of Yorkshire', *YAJ*, viii (1883 – 84).

49 A. C. Reeves, *Lancastrian Englishmen* (Washington, 1981), p. 81; T. D. Whitaker, *A History of the County of York*, vol. 1, Richmondshire (London, 1821), p. 126.

50 Whitaker, i, 126.

51 Prob. Reg. 2, f.544v; M. G. A. Vale, 31.

to the extent that these symbols and rituals consisted an important aspect of the religious conventions of the diocese.

The code of honour among noblemen of the diocese was narrowly orientated towards the family because it had been taught within magnate and gentry households. Grievances were expressed in terms of family honour rather than in generalized philosophical, political or constitutional concepts. Such abstract notions were known at the universities; but they would not have been taught within the family.[1] The households of magnates, higher ecclesiastics and important knights functioned as educational institutions in the same way as the schools and monasteries. However, whereas the latter provided training for clergy and lawyers, the former offered instruction from the age of seven to members of the family, relatives and wards, preparing them for military careers which usually began at the age of eighteen, or for careers in a household. Domestic chaplains instructed their charges in the elements of religious faith, including the Creed and daily prayers and observances, and clergy or professional schoolmasters prepared their charges for the responsibility of administering their estates by conducting reading and writing lessons in the vernacular. The lord of the household, or experienced knights, offered instruction in genealogy, good manners, dress and the rituals of serving at table and hunting.[2] The most important educational function of the household, however, was to teach the young how to defend their family honour through jousting and fighting. Physical fitness and dexterity with weapons were encouraged at an early age, and around fourteen formal military training through sword fighting, riding, tilting, archery and staged competitions commenced.[3]

Such training did not encourage self analysis: the nobility received no university education; therefore they did not see honour in generalized philosophical, political or constitutional concepts, but as part of very specific notions of family dignity which allowed a considerable degree of moral latitude. Questions of honour could therefore be settled by violence: Sir William Neville and Henry Bolingbroke the earl of Derby were prepared to engage in personal combats;[4] Sir Ralph Hastings was charged with manslaughter in 1394; and Sir Thomas Percy, while accompanying Bolingbroke in Lithuania, caused a bloody fracas between English and German troops in his desire for honour by

[1] For a discussion of the bounded horizons formed by the grievances and aspirations of lineage societies in seventeenth century Durham see Mervyn James, *Family, Lineage, and Civil Society* (Oxford, 1974), p. 184ff.

[2] A. R. Myers, *The Household of Edward IV* (Manchester, 1959), pp. 2 – 3.

[3] N. Orme, *From Childhood to Chivalry* (London, 1984), pp. 55 – 60, 180 – 205.

[4] Whittaker, ii, 125.

usurping the Germans' privilege of bearing the banner of St George.[5] The violence which loyalty to a family inspired extended to a family's retainers and officials who frequently disturbed the peace in this period. In 1393 Sir William Beckwith, one of Lancaster's retainers, was engaged in a private war that necessitated the return of John of Gaunt from France in 1393.[6] Observers of aristocratic behaviour seldom considered the motives behind such violence because they were more interested in the consistency of a nobleman's chosen course of action than his morality.[7] Contemporaries approved of the loyalty of Sir Stephen Scrope of Bolton who accompanied Richard II to Conway in 1399: the monk of Evesham described him as a valiant knight, right valiant in arms; and a French nobleman eulogized the loyalty of Scrope and William Ferriby, claiming that none could help pitying them.[8] The tolerance of individual weakness and respect for the collective honour of the lineage helps to explain the leniency which was shown to the heirs of convicted traitors. By the late fourteenth century the honour and estates of families were protected by law and entailed estates were free from the over-lordship of the king and could not be forfeit for treason because the tenant was in law only a life tenant.[9] Henry V was reported to have experienced death-bed remorse for having inflicted injury on the innocent heirs of Henry Lord Scrope of Masham, by presenting to Scrope's cousin, Henry Lord FitzHugh, the confiscated Richmondshire estates that contained entailed land. His dying wish was that the estates be returned to the rightful heir.[10] Scrope's younger brother and heir, Henry Scrope, took forcible possession of the estates after FitzHugh's death, and in 1442 a petition of John Lord Scrope to parliament that he be given permanent possession of the estates was accepted.[11] The treason of one individual rarely did permanent damage to the honour of a family. John Scrope became a prominent servant of the Lancastrians; the Percies came back to power within a decade of their quarrel with Henry IV, and in two generations they had reclaimed all their estates.[12] Any remorse that a condemned traitor might feel was concerned with the fate of his lineage: Sir Richard Scrope, because of his advanced age, received no conviction for possible involvement in the cause of Richard II, although his sons William Scrope the Earl of Wiltshire and Sir

5 Gooder, p. 165.
6 M. McKisack, *The Fourteenth Century* (Oxford, 1959), p. 463.
7 Mervyn James, 'English Politics and the Concept of Honour, 1485 – 1642; *Past and Present* Suppl. 3, (1978), 54; and 'The Concept of Order and the Northern Rising of 1569', *Past and Present* (1973), 53ff.
8 *Scrope and Grosvenor*, ii, 46.
9 McFarlane, *Nobility*, p. 76.
10 Ross, 'Baronage', pp. 206 – 11.
11 Reeves, pp. 91 – 2.
12 Ross, pp. 211 – 19.

Stephen Scrope were deeply implicated, and when sentence of death was pronounced against his eldest son Sir Richard consented to the decision, begging Parliament not to disinherit himself and his children.[13] Richard II's unprecedented confiscation of Bolingbroke's Lancastrian inheritance helped to arouse the opposition of the leading northern families of Percy and Neville.

Constancy, self assertion and violence were the natural expressions of men of honour and reached their most idealized form when the family arms were borne in war. Richard Lord Scrope's grandson was, appropriately, one of the spokesmen for the war ethic. Lord Scrope's son, Sir Stephen of Bentley, the deputy lieutenant in Ireland, died in 1409 leaving his son Stephen a minor of twelve years of age. His widow immediately remarried his lieutenant in Ireland, the prominent captain Sir John Fastolf. Stephen, who inherited the sword which had been given to Richard Lord Scrope by Edward II, and family heirlooms bearing the *azure a bend or*, grew up in a household that was closely attached to chivalric ideals; and he attended his stepfather on the French campaign between 1415 and 1425.[14] As an invalid he was excluded from military service, but he learned French and became an observer of the military exploits of such men as his stepfather and the Duke of Berry.[15] In 1450, in collaboration with William Worcester, Fastolf's secretary, he translated material from Christine de Pisan's *Livre de fais d'armes et de Chevalerie* and produced the *Boke of Noblesse*. The theme of the original and the translation is that war is a virtuous activity for the man of honour. The possibility of some participants in the war being morally in the wrong was considered to be irrelevant as long as they believed themselves to be right. The conviction that if the disputants held their cause sincerely they would all be saved is summed up when Scrope asks: "Where is a holier, juster, or more perfect thing than to make war in your rightful title."[16] Such conviction of the justice of an honourable cause could explain the moral autonomy of the captains who perpetrated such massacres as the sack of Limoges in 1369; Henry Duke of Lancaster confessed to acts of butchery and it is probable that others, such as FitzHugh, could have made similar confessions. The code of honour could also explain why so many campaigns were rashly undertaken. Although crusades frequently ended in disaster, or in

13 *Scrope and Grosvenor*, ii, 37.

14 For the will of Sir Stephen Scrope of Bentley, the third son of Richard Lord Scrope of Bolton, see *Scrope and Grosvenor*, ii, 50.

15 For details of Stephen Scrope's life and his relationship with Sir John Fastolf see *The Boke of Knyghthode*, ed. E. Warner (London, EETS, 1904), xlv ff.; and G. Poulett Scrope, *A History of Castle Combe*.

16 *Boke of Knyghthode*, p. 3. M. H. Keen, 'Chivalry nobility and the man at arms', in C. T. Allmand (ed.), *War, Literature and Politics in the the Late Middle Ages* (Liverpool, 1976), 35.

looting and pillaging, the ideal remained untarnished and the outcome was of less importance than its symbolic significance.

The general social acceptance of martial values is demonstrated by the church's interest in and approval of the attitudes of familial religion. Secular knights had believed in the piety of the martial assertion of the lineage since pre-Christian times, and such ideals were celebrated in the heroic Anglo-Saxon epics.[17] The church first recognized the concept of a just war and knighthood as a Christian vocation during the crusades of the eleventh century. By the fourteenth century the English church had come to accept that even the secular pursuit of warfare had a religious virtue. A considerable section of the civil service accompanied Edward III to France, including many clerical administrators. They were responsible for organizing the war and keeping the king in touch with the home government. Clerks of the privy seal served the interests and honour of a feudal king by taking an active part in defensive operations and suffering the hardships of campaigning alongside the knights.[18] It was not only the archbishops from magnate families such as Richard Scrope of Masham and Alexander Neville who held aristocratic values. John Thoresby, a civil servant from a humble background, went to France in 1344 to press Edward III's claim to the French throne, and in 1352 he called for prayers in the diocese of York for Henry Duke of Lancaster who was about to engage in personal combat with Otto of Brunswick over a slight to his honour.[19] Even members of the mendicant orders participated: a York Augustinian friar, John Erghome, who belonged to the East Riding family of Erghome near Bridlington priory, wrote a commentary on the prophetic poem of Robert of Bridlington for his patron Humphrey Bohun Earl of Hereford, satirizing the excesses of court life and calling for greater moral purpose among the knights in furthering Edward III's cause in France.[20] The churches and monasteries of the diocese were repositories of knights' armour and the trophies of battle: the prior of Marton preserved in his treasury the coat of arms that Sir Alexander Neville wore at the battle of Homildon Hill.[21]

It has been claimed that the motives of these Yorkshire clergymen who lived near to the Scottish borders were patriotic, and that they mistakenly ascribed the same motives to the knights because they had

17 M. H. Keen, *Chivalry* (London, 1984), pp. 1 ff.

18 J. R. L. Highfield, 'The relations between the Church and the English crown from the death of Archbishop Stratford to the opening of the great schism 1349 – 78' (Oxford D. Phil thesis, 1951), pp. 197 – 99.

19 W. H. Dixon and J. Raine, *Fasti Eboracenses, Lives of the Archbishops of York*, vol. I (York, 1863), p. 458.

20 *Political Poems and Songs*, ed. T. Wright (London, Rolls Ser. 14a, 1856), vol. I, p. 206; H. M. Peck, 'The Prophecy of John of Bridlington', (Chicago Univ. Ph.D. thesis 1930), pp. 25 and 61.

21 *Scrope and Grosvenor*, ii, 344.

little understanding of their code of honour.[22] Such a distinction fails to take into account the prevalence of "lineage values" throughout society. They were expressed in history, tragedy and romance, and they constituted an important part of the education of the nobility, which often occurred under clerical direction in the noble household. The process is described in a fourteenth century metrical romance called *Ipomydon*, where a clerk teaches the younger sons of the king to read, sing, hunt and ride.[23] Noblemen were schooled at an early age in the history of the lineage of the great families of the north, either by their parents or older knights. Many deponents in the Scrope Grosvenor lawsuit, including Sir Ralph Hastings, Sir Nicholas Sabraham and John Ryther, esquire, testified that they had been instructed in the history of family lineage from their fathers and ancestors.[24] Such an education included the memorizing of the different family arms: Sir Robert Laton related how his father, an old man of seventy with a long record of service in wars and tournaments, commanded him to write a schedule of all the arms that he had learned from his ancestors which had belonged to princes, lords, barons, knights and esquires who had flourished since the conquest.[25] It was upbringings such as these that enabled deponents such as Sir John Boswell and Sir Thomas Merkingfield to testify that the history of the Scrope arms was common knowledge throughout the county of York and the whole kingdom.[26] The knights who recognized these arms in churchyards, monasteries and manor houses were exercising carefully trained memories.

The clergy were equally well schooled in these traditions and those born in an armigerous family retained pride in their lineage. Sir John Gildesburgh as a twelve year old at Oxford saw the commencement of a clerk by the name of Scrope, one of the younger sons of Sir Geoffrey Scrope of Masham, accompanied by trumpeters carrying on their instruments peonids bearing the Scrope arms.[27] The monks who gave evidence in the Scrope Grosvenor controversy appear to have received the same grounding in the lineages of the nobility as the knights. The abbots of Selby, Jervaulx and Rievaulx deposed that in their youth they had been told about the Scrope arms from old lords and knights.[28] Novice monks, who were brought up within monasteries, were instructed in the history of lineages to enable them to identify the arms

22 J. Barnie, *War in Medieval Society* (London, 1974), pp. 106 – 12.
23 M. James, 'Concept of Order', 51; *Early English Meals and Manners*, ed. F. J. Furnivall, (EETS, London, 1868), Hue de Rotelande, *Ipomydon*, ed. Kolbing and Koschwitz, lines 194 – 212.
24 *Scrope and Grosvenor*, ii, 168; 323 – 5; 351 – 2; 124 – 5; 146.
25 ibid, ii, 300.
26 ibid, ii, 279; 320.
27 ibid, ii, 111.
28 ibid, ii, 270 – 73.

on their walls and windows and the coats of arms borne by distinguished visitors to their house. The priors of Lanercost and Gisburn identified the Scrope arms in their windows because it was a tradition of the monks and canons to learn the ancestry of family coats, and the abbot of the Cistercian house of Byland saw Sir Richard Scrope arrive at his house when he was a youth, and he knew his arms because he had been told about them by the older monks.[29] The Benedictine abbey of Selby even possessed an old book illuminated with columns of the escutcheons of the arms of earls, barons, knights and esquires with the names of their families above them.[30]

Such concern with the history of the family arms represented a deep need to identify with the permanence they represented. The canons of Bridlington, who were witnesses in the Scrope-Grosvenor dispute, appreciated the length of time spanned in the history of a great family and the ability of the lineage to survive its ravages. They produced charters witnessed by the Scropes, and pointed to the seals which bore effigies of knights holding swords of the type used at the time of the conquest.[31] The sense of awe that was felt about the age of a lineage can be seen in the deposition of Sir Simon Wensley, the parish priest of Wensley church and a member of the family who were once lords of Wensley. The church was in the shadow of Bolton castle, under the patronage of Richard Lord Scrope, and it contained windows showing the arms of Scrope and Neville. Within the churchyard there were many tombs of the Scrope family, and Sir Simon described the oldest, which belonged to a period when ancient burial customs were followed. It was one of a number of stone chests submerged under large square stones that were so massive that they had sunk into the earth and only their summits remained. Many of the Scrope lineage were buried under these stones, the last being William Scrope, the father of Sir Henry, who was buried in the Premonstratensian house of St Agatha's. The priest described with wonder the defacement worked on the inscriptions and dates of these monuments by time and weather, and the persistent survival of the family arms.[32] The same admiration of permanence can be seen in the testimony of William Irby, the master of St Nicholas' Hospital in Richmond, who described the custom of the old men of his hospital of learning about the history and antiquity of the coats of arms of such families as the Scropes.[33]

The lineage, and the code of honour associated with it, was so respected in society and by the church because chivalry was seen as a

29 ibid, ii, 279; 275.
30 ibid, ii, 270.
31 ibid, ii, 279.
32 ibid, ii, 329.
33 ibid, ii, 321.

religion. The dispute over the *azure a bend or* was a national controversy, probably one of the most significant events in the lives of this generation of aristocrats. Uppermost in the minds of the participants was their sense of blood as the vehicle for collective family genius and virtue which was transmitted from the past to the future along an unbroken male line.[34] Birth in an honourable lineage and the immortality that honourable deeds conferred on their arms were important elements of their religious convictions, and this was expressed in funerals in the diocese.

Funerals were an occasion to mourn the passing of the body; but they were also a celebration of the immortality of the family and its honour. The deeds of honour of the veterans of the French wars were symbolically commemorated. John Lord Neville asked for two men at his funeral, fitted out in his armour with escutcheons of his arms, who were to carry between them a banner bearing the Neville arms.[35] The distinguished soldier, Ralph Lord Neville of Raby, arranged for his body to be borne by a chariot drawn by seven horses; and before burial he was to be carried to the nave on the shoulders of eight soldiers, four of whom were to display his peacetime arms — the device and badge worn at tournaments — and four of whom were to display his arms of war.[36] The survival of the deeds of honour achieved during the exercise of noble office was also celebrated in the stone effigies depicting the deceased in full armour at an ideal age of thirty; these can still be seen in the parish churches of Bedale, Pickering and Tanfield where members of the Marmion family are commemorated.[37]

The triumphant concentration on the dignity of the family lineage allowed a shift in emphasis away from the mortal remains of the deceased. Since the funeral of Edward II it was customary to have a second symbolic burial of an effigy of the deceased, of wood or leather, displaying his armour and the family arms.[38] There was therefore a less exclusive attention to the lying in state of the mortal body. The smell of putrefaction could lead to gossip and scandal, as in the funeral of John of Gaunt; and William Lord Roos in 1415 and Elizabeth Lady FitzHugh in 1427 preferred a quick despatch of their bodies.[39] Others chose a simple interment: Thomas Lord Boynton consigned his body to burial in the same linen cloth in which he happened to die.[40] The use of effigies

34 James, 'The Concept of Order', 47 – 54; English politics, 14.
35 *W.I.*, p. 39.
36 ibid, p. 27.
37 *Sepulchral Monuments*, i, 171 – 81.
38 E. Kantorowicz, *The King's Two Bodies*, (Princeton, 1957), pp. 419 – 36; M. Vale, *War and Chivalry*, (London, 1981), p. 90.
39 *The Register of Henry Chichele*, ii, pp. 22 – 6; T.V., i, p. 212; T. Gascoigne, *Loci e libro Veritatum*, (ed. Rogers, p. 138).
40 *W.I.*, p. 32.

bearing the immortal arms in funerals allowed mourners to face and give expression to the mortality and corruptibility of the body, and attention was even drawn to the contrast between the mutability of the earthly body, and the eternity of the family honour and dignity commemorated on these effigies. In 1394 Sir Brian Stapleton made a will similar to the Black Prince's, in which he denigrated his body as a 'caitiff' and requested the presence at his funeral of a good-looking and well-mounted man of any state who was to wear his armour and display the Stapleton arms.[41] High ecclesiastics such as Thomas Haxey, a residentiary canon of York, and Richard Fleming, the bishop of Lincoln, were each commemorated by two effigies, one showing them in the dignity of their noble office dressed in their ecclesiastical vestments and surrounded by their family arms, and another which depicted their bodies in a state of putrification.[42]

These ceremonies show that the code of honour and the ideals of familial religion were not confined to the nuclear family. A nobleman commanded a loyality from relatives and members of his household. The solemn and pious procession of mourners, paupers and parish church and cathedral singers who accompanied the hearse was followed by a brilliant display of heraldic banners and escutcheons of the dead man's family depicting his alliances and descent.[43] A collection of such funeral banners, embroidered with the arms of great lords, was produced by the prior of Lanercost in the Scrope-Grosvenor dispute.[44] Knights and esquires at funerals wore the arms of the deceased, and his badge was worn by his household. These arms, which were painted on the tomb chest, symbolized the greatness and continuity of the nobleman's family, and its representative was the male heir to whom the whole family owed allegiance. This loyalty penetrated deeply into the religious convictions of the humblest, and it was demonstrated by the liveried poor who would follow and pray around the hearse of a great householder. This loyalty could take political and military forms. The Richmondshire tenants of the duke of Lancaster joined Henry Bolingbroke when he landed at Ravenspur in 1399, and the Percy rebellion of 1405 inspired the allegiance of some members of the families of Scrope of Masham and the Plumptons.

The wide acceptance and the Christian application of chivalry was expressed in symbol and ritual which demonstrated its redemptive significance. Christ was portrayed as a knight who quested for men's

41 Prob, Reg. 1, f.69v; Vale, 'The Yorkshire Gentry', 12; Kantorowicz, p. 420ff.

42 *North Country Wills*, (SS., 116, 1908), pp. 32–4; York Minister lib. Reg. Test i, fol. 239v. and f.281.

43 M. E. James, 'Two Tudor Funerals', C.W.A.S., lxvi (1966), 169.

44 *Scrope and Grosvenor*, ii, 274.

souls.[45] His arms could be seen on the walls of cathedrals, in the stained-glass windows of parish churches, and they frequently occur in the primers that were used in domestic chapels. Stitched onto one of the folios of a *Liber Precum*, written in 1420 for the Pullein family of Pontefract and Ulleskelf, is a fifteenth century woodcut illustration of the instruments of the Passion arranged heraldically for use as an indulgence.[46] The shield is divided by the cross, which has a crown of thorns and a bleeding heart, and within each of the four sections formed by the cross the instruments of the Passion, the pinchers, nails, scourges and the sheaves of wheat, are displayed heraldically in the manner of a knight-at-arms. The implication of such heraldry was that Christ was born to the most honourable of lineages, and as a man of the highest honour he secured for mortal man a heritage in this immortal lineage through His Passion. This belief was endorsed by an inscription in a North Lincolnshire dialect under the arms of Christ which says that whoever beholds these arms has the pardon of the kingdom of men.[47] Some illustrations of Christ's face in books of hours imply that in His Passion he exhibited the same constant and heroic behaviour valued in the family code of honour. In the Pullein prayer book there is a representation of a victorious and smiling Christ facing Pilate.[48] In a book of hours written in the diocese between 1405 and 1413, possibly for the Scrope family or their supporters, there is a portrait showing Christ in an aristocratic posture, seated on an opulent gold and red chair with a golden ball at his feet and a pair of crossed swords behind him.[49] In such a context the wound that is shown on his side is reminiscent of a battle wound. The theme of such illustrations was the precept for aristocratic behaviour provided by Christ's constancy to the honour of his lineage. In the Pullein hours Our Lord's noble bearded face is set against the chivalric background of a purple castle, lush garden and decorative tiles, and around his head a motto says: 'Constancy in our Lord and redeemer'.[50] Family arms were closely identified with the Passion. Underneath a picture in the *Mountenay Hours* showing the Descent from the Cross there is a shield bearing the Mountenay arms.[51] In a manuscript of Michael de Massa's gospel harmony, which was copied at

45 J. A. W. Bennett, *Poetry of the Passion* (Oxford, 1982), p. 138.

46 Y.M.L. MS. xvi, k6. This prayer book consists of 120 folios of vellum, bound in calf, of which 112 are illuminated Latin text. A calendar occupies six folios with entries of a later date, including those relating to the Pullein family. The folios are 8½ by 6½ inches; there are 19 lines to the page and the capitals are illuminated.

47 ibid, fo. 44.

48 ibid. fo. 45a.

49 Oxford, Bodl. MS. Latin Liturg. f2, fo. 59v; for description see O. Pacht and J. Alexander, *Illuminated Manuscripts in the Bodleian Library* (Oxford, 1973), iii, 67.

50 Y.M.L. MS. xvi, k6, fo. 94a.

51 Y.M.L. MS. 54 add. fo. 64.

the request of Sir Miles Stapleton of Ingham and Bedale in 1405, there is a depiction of the Crucifixion above the Stapleton arms, a lion rampant on a black and white border.[52]

Armour and weapons were even absorbed into the liturgy, and this was facilitated by the popular concept of the sacrifice of Christ, manifested in the high mass, as an honourable death in the battle for men's souls. The northern homily cycle allegorized each item of a knight's armour as instruments of the Passion, and *Piers Ploughman* contains a vision of the resurrected Christ as a jouster displaying his banner and coat of arms, which were his cross and blood.[53] The monasteries of the diocese would have been familiar with the image of Christ the soldier, and it was at Bridlington, that repository of chivalric memorabilia, that Peter Langtoft depicted Christ in his chronicle as a knight-errant.[54] The armour and weapons of knights, therefore, could have considerable religious significance and play an important part in the liturgical commemoration of the Passion. The *Ancrene Wisse* used the knight's shield, hanging high on the rood screen after his death, as a meditative image of the Passion. The Norman triangular shape, narrowing at the bottom, recalled the cross, and the materials of wood, leather, and paint evoked the cross, body and blood.[55] In the funeral processions of the Yorkshire knights, Sir Brian Stapleton, Sir Robert Swillington and Sir Ralph Bulmer, their best armour was paraded and deposited as mortuary offerings in their burial churches in the manner of their fathers.[56] The swords, helmets and shields borne by the chief mourners formed the centre of the funeral procession; they were presented at the altar at the same time as the priest's offering, thereby fitting naturally into the requiem mass: the armour of these knights was associated symbolically with the offering of the mass and secured intercession for their souls.[57]

These and other chivalric rituals, as Chaucer showed, circumscribed the harsh realities of human nature and the code of honour.[58] They originated among secular knights, remained under their control, and justified knighthood as an order like the monastic and clerical orders, which was dedicated to God within a secular sphere.[59] The ceremony of dubbing to knighthood, with its sacramental undertones, was in the

52 Oxford, Bodl. MS. 758, fo. i; for description see Pacht and Alexander, iii, 170.
53 Bennett, *Passion*, p. 66.
54 ibid, p. 67; *Chronicle of Peter Langtoft* (Rolls Series, 47), 126.
55 Bennett, *Passion*, pp. 64 – 5.
56 Prob. Reg. i, fo.69v; TE, I, p. 107; p. 344; see also TE, I, pp. 147 and 287.
57 James, 'Two Tudor Funerals', 270.
58 See 'The Knight's Tale in *The Works of Geoffrey Chaucer*, ed. F. N. Robinson (London, 1957) lines 975 – 1010, 2484 – 2560.
59 Keen, Chivalry, pp. 65 – 82; Vale, *War and Chivalry*, pp. 33 – 62; Huizinga, *Waning of the Middle Ages*, trans. F. Hopman, pp. 83ff.

hands of secular lords.[60] The independence of chivalry from clerical initiative was shown in the self-confidence of the deponents in the Scrope Grosvenor dispute who projected the importance and piety of their chivalric ethics. Thomas, Lord Roos claimed that his chivalry had been learned on the battlefield and in the tourney.[61] Many witnesses described the battles they fought in as chivalric undertakings, and all took serious oaths on their knighthood or chivalry. The proud and quarrelsome English captains saw one another as fellow members of a chivalric order, and different families would emblazon their arms alongside one another. The prior of the Gilbertine priory of Old Malton deposed that Alexander Neville, uncle of the then Lord Neville of Raby, had a coat of arms in the priory embroidered with the Neville arms and quarters filled with small escutcheons of the arms of his friends, including Sir Ralph Hastings, Sir William Marmion, the Scropes and others.[62]

The monastic vocation provided the model for many of the secular rituals of chivalric fellowships. The Order of the Passion required four vows and two of them were monastic.[63] The Order of the Garter, formed by Edward III in 1348, was a fellowship of twenty-four of the leading soldiers of their day. Yorkshire members included Sir Miles Stapleton, Sir Brian Stapleton, Richard Lord Scrope of Bolton, Henry Lord Scrope of Masham, and Henry Lord FitzHugh of Tanfield. This society of knights conducted themselves like a monastic order, formulating their own rules and statutes which required religious orthodoxy, courage in battle, loyalty, and making provision for commemoratory masses for members.[64] A roll of honour was maintained recording the virtues of members such as their deeds in battle and the details of their military service. The order had its offices and chapters which met in stalls like a cathedral, at St George's Chapel, Windsor. Above each stall the armorial achievements of the knights were recorded as a reminder that the man born to arms could save his soul in the honourable discharge of his office. The Garter was founded on an Arthurian model; and the pentecostal vow of the Knights of the Round Table to dedicate themselves to the quest of the Holy Grail imparted a sense of mystical vocation to the order. *Sir Gawain and the Green Knight*, which appears to have been written by a north-west countryman in the patronage of the

60 Keen, *Chivalry*, p. 76.
61 *Scrope and Grosvenor*, ii, 355.
62 ibid, ii, 344.
63 Huizinga, *The Waning of the Middle Ages*, p. 75.
64 See E. Ashmole, *The Institution, Laws and Governances of the Order of the Garter* (London, 1672). Sir John Fastolf was expelled from the order for allegedly craven conduct in June 1428. Monstrelet, *Chronicles*, ed. T. Johnes (London, 1840), p. 555; cit. Vale, *War and Chivalry*, p. 43.

Lancastrians, contains many details of court life and ends with the motto of the Order of the Garter.[65] It is possible that the religious symbolism of this work was employed at Garter ceremonies at Windsor. John of Gaunt, possibly the patron of the author, may have considered when making his will the coat on Gawain's shield, which was a magic pentangle symbolizing the knight's perfection through the deeds of arms that he performed through his five wits and with his five fingers. Gaunt displayed his own family coat at his funeral, but like Gawain he recognized his own frailty and used the same fivefold symbolism to refer to *mes cynk sens les quelx juy multz negligentment despendie.*[66] It is also possible that Sir Brian Stapleton and the other garter knights who participated in a ceremony at Smithfield in 1391 — when they were led in chains by twenty-four ladies — were symbolically reenacting the poem and identifying their garters with Gawain's girdle, a symbol of the knight's penitence.[67]

The rituals of the Garter may also have penetrated the distinctively penitential wills made by the so-called 'Lollard knights' of Richard II's chamber, three of whom, Sir John Montagu, Sir Lewis Clifford and Sir John Cheyne, were members of the order. In the wills of Clifford and Cheyne, written in 1404 and 1413, the testator describes himself as an unworthy knight and traitor to God and consigns his stinking carrion to the corner of a churchyard with only a russet burial cloth and a candle for the head and feet.[68] Their austerity, befitting to soldiers, is reminiscent of the plainness of Henry Duke of Lancaster, also a garter knight, and is echoed in the wills of other members of the order. Sir Brian Stapleton, whose stepdaughter Elizabeth Waleys was married to Sir William Neville, a "Lollard knight", made a will in 1391 containing some of the features of these wills. He asked that his wretched body be buried in Helaugh church and provided a penny dole for paupers who prayed for his wretched soul. All his household, servants and paupers were clothed in blue and russet, the livery of the Garter.[69] Other members of the Garter retained in their funerals elements of monastic austerity and Garter symbolism. The coffin of John Lord Neville of Raby, in 1389, was covered with russet and the cross of St George, and all his mourners wore the same livery.[70] In 1415 Henry Lord Scrope of Masham requested that there be no hearse for his body, which was to be draped in a white woollen cloth bearing the arms of St George with two candles for the

65 C. J. Peterson, 'The Pearl Poet and John Massey of Cotton, Cheshire', *R.E.S.* 25 (1974), p. 257ff.
66 *Sir Gawain and the Green Knight*, (ed. Tolkien and Gordon); TE. 1, p. 186.
67 Chetwynd-Stapylton, 242.
68 K. B. McFarlane, *Lancastrian Kings and Lollard Knights* (Oxford, 1972), pp. 207 – 26.
69 Prob. Reg. 1, fo.69v.
70 *W.I.* p. 39.

head and feet.[71]

The observers of aristocratic rituals all accepted the piety of chivalric values. Stephen Scrope in 1440 presented his *Boke of Knyghthode,* a translation of Christine de Pisan's *Epistle of Othea to Hector,* to his hard-bitten stepfather, addressing him as: *Moult sage et vaillant chevalier.*[72] In the dedicatory preface he says that Sir John and his fellow knights have been received into the order of chivalry because they have kept and defended the Christian faith, the rights of the church and the land.[73] Chroniclers described the activities of the nobility in similar terms. A northern cleric celebrated the victory of Neville's Cross in a poem praising the conduct of Henry Percy, who defended his people armed with the "breastplate of faith".[74] The Lanercost chronicler interpreted the actions of Henry Percy in the same way and described Sir Thomas de Rokeby as a model on how to fight with valour for a pious cause.[75] Two Yorkshire knights who were famous for their piety were Henry Lord Scrope of Masham and Henry Lord FitzHugh of Tanfield. A contemporary described Scrope as a knight of the "excellent Order of the Garter" who fought for his faith and his king; and the family chronicler of the FitzHughs described Henry Lord FitzHugh as a great gentleman and a noble and courageous knight who delighted in games of love and war, and who, with God's help, waged honourable wars for his sovereign and made honourable journeys to the Holy Land.[76] Both men, as we shall see, were more than conventionally pious, but like Henry Duke of Lancaster before them, they and their contemporaries would have regarded their chivalric ideals as an integral part of their religion.

SOCIAL RELIGION

The evidence of heraldry, besides helping to define the nobility of the diocese as a group, provides evidence that the family could be a focus for religious ideals that were upheld by its members, the household, and all others who participated in and identified with its chivalric rituals. However, the nobility was also distinguished as a group by its wealth; and the way families confidently invested their money in chantry foundations, testamentary bequests, obits, masses and funeral arrange-

71 *Foedera,* ix, p. 276.
72 *Boke of Knygthode.*
73 ibid, 3.
74 *Political Poems and Songs,* i, p. 45; cit. Barnie, p. 106.
75 *Chronicon de Lanercost,* ed. Stevenson (Edinburgh, 1839), p. 350ff. cit. Barnie, p. 106.
76 *Rotuli Parliamentorum,* ed. J. Strachey, 6 vols (London, 1767 – 77) iv, p. 66; Whittaker, *Richmondshire,* i, 125.

ments provides an equally important body of evidence for religious conventions. A spiritual aridity has been detected in such conventions, a drought not to be broken until the arrival of protestantism in the north.[1] However, there is a need to understand institutional, communal religion in late medieval terms, and to see it as a sincere, articulate and sometimes compassionate expression of the spiritual relationship existing between the individual and his local community. Any moral, intellectual or spiritual limitations in such a relationship were more than compensated for by the religious changes in the diocese, which will be discussed in subsequent chapters.

Magnates, despite their peripatetic lives, their domestic chapels, and their family confessors and chaplains, depended on the good will and intercession of parishioners because of a common and deeply felt concern with the afterlife and the fate of the soul of the deceased. The concept of a voyage of the soul to the otherworld through Purgatory had pagan origins, and the dead in the fourteenth century were frequently buried with provisions and money for their journey. However, after the clarification of the doctrine of Purgatory at the second council of Lyons in 1274 it was widely believed that this journey could be hastened with the intercession of Christian prayers and rites which were regarded as necessary to bring the soul to rest and prevent hauntings.[2] Dreams of Purgatory were reported which contained urgent requests from the dead for specific prayers and masses which would speed their release. A Hampole nun dreamed of her brother, a squire, shortly after his death in the battle of Shrewsbury, and he showed her a great letter on which was written specific prayers which she was to recite fifty times and psalms which she was to sing twenty times if she was to secure his release. The lineage, for all its powers, could not guarantee such intercession.[3] Families were never free from the threat of extinction through the failure of the male line. Noblemen, whose affairs were conducted in the environment of international affairs, trade and national politics, needed the prayers and masses of the local communities of the lowlands of the diocese including the poorer nunneries of the countryside, the friaries and hospitals of the towns, and the parish churches, which were in the villages that clustered around the manor houses of the nobility. These they secured in their foundations and endowments and in their bequests to the church and their local community. Ideals of unity, continuity and a belief in a collective salvation involving the entire

1 Peter Heath, 'Urban Piety in the Later Middle Ages: the Evidence of Hull Wills', in R. B. Dobson, (ed.) *The Church, Politics and Patronage in the Fifteenth Century* (Gloucester), 1984), p. 229.

2 cf, James, *Family Lineage and Civil Society*, pp. 52 – 4.

3 C.U.L., MS. Li, vi, 43, fo. 80 – 81v.

community both complemented and balanced the more abrasively assertive attitudes of familial religion.

Foundations and Endowments

Until 1250 the most important testimony to the influence of the Yorkshire nobility as founders had been the religious houses, especially those of the Benedictine, Cisterican and Augustinian orders. In the fourteenth century the only new houses established were those of the Carthusian order, which will be included in the discussion of the eremitic movement in chapter two. However, brief consideration of these older communities is merited because the abbeys and priories to some extent upheld the same religious sentiments and performed the same spiritual functions as families and local communities in the diocese. Monasteries, which produced and traded in wool, were an important part of aristocratic society. Monks have been described as celibate landlords: they had considerable contact with the lay nobility who acted as their stewards and legal advisers; and in turn, monks, like those of Durham priory, the largest house in the north with fifty or so resident members,[1] would have settled disputes among lay noblemen, and provided hospitality and banking facilities. Most regulars were probably from the lesser gentry of the diocese, and they were just as concerned with the history, continuity and honour of their house as they were with that of their lineages. This explains why the monks of Durham were so concerned with the defence of property rights, ancient privileges, rights of institution and advowson; and why so much of Prior Wessington's later literary works were devoted to the monasteries rights and liberties.[2] It is likely that the monks of other religious houses of the north, who were such authorities on heraldry, were as zealous in defence of the rights of their houses as the disputants in the Scrope Grosvenor dispute. Membership of such a community, either as a monk or lay benefactor, could offer the same sort of spiritual security as that provided by the family: behind the preservation of the rights of founders and their descendents in canon law were sentiments that saw in the deathless community and the founder's descendents a body of persons with an undying relationship to one another. If the key to the family's redemption was honour, for the religious community and its patrons it was prayer and the liturgy.

In the twelfth and thirteenth centuries the names of the greatest

1 The largest house in the diocese was Fountains which had thirty-five members.
2 R. B. Dobson, *Durham Priory, 1400 – 1450* (Cambridge, 1973).

families of the diocese were recorded in the obit rolls of the monks, and established families in the fourteenth century maintained their historical links with the religious houses of the diocese while rising families established close connections with local houses; in both cases they used their patronage to secure intercession. The Percies were an honoured name at the Augustinian abbey of Whitby and continued to patronize other houses connected with the family such as the Cistercian abbey of Sawley, which received from Henry Lord Percy in 1392 all the rents from his manor of Gisburn.[3] The Scropes of Bolton demonstrated their more recent social arrival by creating a close family connection which the Premonstratensian house of St Agatha's at Easby near Richmond in the reign of Edward II, and in 1393 Richard Lord Scrope obtained a licence to grant the convent a yearly rent of £150 to support ten chaplains celebrating for his good estate.[4] Patronage of the regular orders in the form of endowments of lands and rents in the fourteenth century seems, with the exception of the Carthusian order, to have been primarily motivated by these family traditions, and there is little evidence of an informed interest in a particular order. It is significant that among gentry families who had no historical connections with any monasteries there is little evidence of an informed interest in the older religious orders, although there were knights like Sir James Pickering, who in giving 160 acres in Spaldingmore to the Gilbertine priory of Ellerton on the Derwent, were seeking the intercession of religious houses near their estates.[5] Some civil service clerks, such as the brothers Richard and Robert Ravenser who gave £10 yearly rent from lands in Kingston to the canons of Guisborough, showed some interest in religious houses; but even they were much more generous patrons of secular institutions.[6] In general the record of patronage of the older religious houses among the lesser nobility is not impressive, and in the county of Kent, where there were few magnates of any significance, there was a similar neglect of the older religious orders except among the more established gentry families.[7] The fact that the nobility of the diocese were neither founding religious houses nor endowing existing ones to any great extent in the late fourteenth century perhaps provides a background to the hostility shown towards the possessioned orders among such courtiers as John of Gaunt; but many noblemen had simply come to prefer the perpetual chantry, which only required a comparatively small endowment sufficient to ensure its perpetual survival, and offered an opportunity

3 CPR, 1391 – 6, p. 150.
4 ibid, p. 244.
5 CPR, 1385 – 89, p. 7.
6 CPR, 1374 – 77, p. 176; 1377 – 81, p. 482.
7 Fleming, 'The gentry of Kent', pp. 36 – 53.

for those from less substantial families to become founders. The eleventh and twelfth centuries had witnessed the growth of the monastic movement and the fourteen and fifteenth centuries were the age of the perpetual chantry.

A perpetual chantry was established by an endowment of land and property; this would bring in an income sufficient to create and sustain a living for at least one priest and his successors, whose daily duty was to celebrate a requiem mass for the repose of the founder's soul and the souls of other specified individuals. These chantries were founded either by the purchase from the crown of a licence to alienate property to the church or through the rents of lands held in trust.[8] In Kent, where perpetual chantries were just as popular among testators of armigerous rank, the latter method was preferred as a means of by-passing the sometimes slow progress of purchasing a licence which had to be assessed and paid into the hanaper.[9] Licences to alienate were more common in the diocese of York, especially among civil servants and former hanaper officials who were perhaps able to hasten the process through their London contacts. The Black Death of 1349 and the subsequent epidemics of 1361 and 1367 created a demand for offices, masses and anniversaries for the dead. The perpetual chantry, which was exclusively devoted to intercession, was better suited than the religious houses to meet this demand. Chantry chapels crowded York Minster and the parish churches of the diocese and took many forms. The grandest were the "stone-cage" chapels containing an alter and the founder's tomb, which were built between the pillars of the nave or aisle of greater churches. There were also parclose wooden chapels found in the aisles of parish churches, and the chantry tombs, which consisted of portable altars used as table-tops. Chantries could be fully instituted benefices where appointments were conducted by the archbishop; or services where endowments and appointments were entrusted to trustees who could supervise the conduct of the priest.[10] All founders were free to dictate what rules they pleased in their foundation charters, and therefore they enjoyed a greater control over the perpetual chantry than would have been possible if they had founded a monastery. Few of these foundation deeds survive, but after the statute of mortmain in 1279 endowments to chantries required a royal licence and were enrolled on the patent rolls.[11]

Although noblemen lived cosmopolitan lives worshipping in many churches and having access to many potential sources of intercession,

[8] K. L. Wood-Legh, *Perpetual Chantries in Britain* (Cambridge, 1965), pp. 32 – 65.
[9] ibid, p. 48; Fleming, 'The Gentry of Kent', 39.
[10] Wood-Legh, pp. 65 – 92.
[11] Wood-Legh, p. 46 – 7; W. Page, *Chantry certificates in county York*, 2 vols. (55, 91, 92, Durham, 1894 – 5), p. 37.

they placed special emphasis on the intercessions provided by chantries within the diocese. The Percys had perpetual chantries in York and Beverley, and the Scropes of Masham and the Vavasours in York Minster.[12] Most cathedral chantries however were founded by cathedral clergy, such as Henry Bowet's stone chapel, built in York Minster in 1415; or the chantries established by the royal clerks who held offices in the cathedrals: members of the Ferriby family founded chantries in York Minster in 1352, 1374 and 1393; and chantries were founded in Beverley Minster in 1380 by Richard and John Ravenser and Walter Skirlaw.[13] However, despite the prestige of these two cathedrals, the nobility considered the family parish church to be the most fitting place to establish a pertetual chantry.

The Percys, who were the patrons of the parish church of Tadcaster, established a chantry there in 1384, and Ralph Lord Neville founded a chantry in the church of Sheriff Hutton, which was endowed by John Neville in 1370.[14] The residentiary canons and king's clerks, besides establishing chantries among their colleagues in York and Beverley cathedrals, founded chantries in the parish churches of their ancestral villages. In 1396 Robert Beverley founded a chantry in the parish church of North Barton, and John Ravenser endowed a chantry in the village of Waltham.[15] Leading East Riding knights Sir Marmaduke Constable and Sir Robert Flamborough founded chantries in their parish church of Helmesly in 1359 and 1360.[16] Some of the endowments made by the gentry were impressive: in 1396 Sir John Saville endowed a single chaplain chantry in the parish church of Halifax with the income from 200 acres.[17] Merchants also preferred to establish perpetual chantries in their parish churches: the Greys in St Mary's York and the Acastres in All Saint's North Street,[18] and Robert Holme left £400 to ensure the survival of his chantry.[19] These perpetual chantries had become such a dominant feature of parish churches that it was not possible even to provide an altar in the church for many foundations; and churches were also confronted with the problem of disciplining a large body of chantry priests who were all supported by separate endowments. One solution

12 R. B. Dobson, 'A History of York Minster in the later Middle Ages, 1215 – 1500' in G. E. Aymler and R. Cant (eds.), *A History of York Minster* (Oxford, 1977), 96; Ross, 'Yorks. Baronage' p. 100.

13 CPR, 1350 – 54, p. 318; CPR, 1374 – 77, p. 18; CPR, 1391 – 96, p. 278; CPR, 1396 – 99, p. 404; CPR, 1370 – 74, p. 5; CPR, 1377 – 81, pp. 260, 553.

14 Ross, 'Baronage', p. 100; CPR, 1370 – 74, p. 366; Ross, Baronage, p. 200.

15 CPR, 1391 – 96, p. 581; CPR, 1370 – 74, p. 410; CPR, 1374 – 77, p. 18.

16 CPR, 1358 – 61, pp. 214, 436.

17 CPR, 1396 – 99, p. 9.

18 CPR, 1377 – 81, p. 21; CPR, 1381 – 85, p. 318.

19 Prob. Reg., i, fo. 102; J. I. Kermode, 'The merchants of three northern English towns', in C. H. Clough (ed.), *Profession Vocation and Culture in Later Medieval England* (Liverpool, 1982), p. 25.

to these problems was to convert a parish church into a collegiate body of chantry priests who shared a common fund under the presidency of one of their number.[20] Some of the leading magnates of the diocese attempted to do this in the parish churches where they possessed the advowson. Richard Lord Scrope of Bolton failed in his attempt in 1398 to convert his parish church of Wensley, in the shadow of his recently crenellated manor of Bolton, into a college;[21] but Ralph Lord Neville was more successful: in 1410 he obtained a licence to convert his parish church of Staindrop into a college of a master, warden, six clerks, six paupers and six poor priests, and he successfully converted the north side of the choir of this church into a chamber for members of this college.[22] Another indication of the importance of perpetual chantries between 1350 and 1400 is that over two-thirds of the 135 licences for the alienation of property and rents in the diocese recorded by the crown were for the foundation of perpetual chantries. The motives behind these foundations, the rules of the chantry and the lists of the beneficiaries of the chaplain's intercessions, which were under the founder's control, are therefore an important source of evidence of social and religious attitudes.

Patronage in the fourteenth century was as powerful a social force as chivalry and the inheritance of wealth and economic success, and it was based on the church livings at the disposal of the crown, the bishops, the religious houses and the lay nobility. The presentation of church livings by the archbishops of York enabled many from relatively humble origins, such as members of the Waltham, Ravenser, and Ferriby families, to enter the ranks of the nobility as civil servants, ecclesiastical lawyers, and cathedral canons. Those who were born into titles and wealth used the patronage at their disposal to further careers in the church for their officials and those relatives who were younger children and would therefore inherit relatively little. In Richmondshire the patronage of church livings was shared among families ranging from the barons Scrope of Bolton and Masham, the lords FitzHugh of Tanfield, and knights like Sir Miles Stapleton of Bedale, to lesser gentry such as Sir John Wyclif. It is not therefore surprising that the chantry foundations of such families reflect the founder's preoccupations with patronage. Cantarists were instructed to celebrate for the welfare of the founder's living patrons and the souls of his deceased patrons; and in this way the chantry was used to express gratitude, and to reciprocate patronage by exercising through prayer and masses a form of patronage

20 A. H. Thompson, *The English Clergy and their Organization in the Later Middle Ages* (Oxford, 1947), p. 146.

21 CPR, 1396 – 99, p. 489.

22 W. Dugdale, *Monasticon Anglicanum*, ed. J. Caley, H. Ellis, and B. Bandinel (1817 – 30, reprint 1846), vi, I, 401.

in the courts of heaven. The inter-related families of Thoresby, Waltham, Ravenser and Ferriby, who were helped in their careers in the civil service and in the church of York by the patronage of archbishops Melton and Thoresby, made over thirty alienations to chantries between 1350 and 1400, usually with the request that their patrons and colleagues be remembered in the services. William Ferriby, the archdeacon of Cleveland, and Archbishop John Thoresby founded chantries in York Minster to celebrate for the soul of William Melton in 1350 and 1359; and John Ravenser endowed a chantry in Waltham for the purpose of providing intercession for the souls of all his benefactors.[23]

These clerical families, especially the Ravensers, were mindful in their chantry foundations of their chief patron the crown, and their inclusion of the king and queen in the benefits of the mass constituted part of the price paid for an overlord's licence for the necessary endowments. In 1370 Richard Ravenser, a canon of Beverley Cathedral and former attorney and receiver of Queen Isabella's household, founded a chantry in Beverley for two chaplains who were to celebrate for the souls of Isabella and Philippa, the late queens of England, and the welfare of Edward III; he also organized the two queens' anniversaries.[24] In 1378 Richard Ravenser obtained a licence to establish a *maisondieu* of twelve poor men and one chaplain who were to pray and celebrate for the good estate of the king, his mother Joan, and Henry Earl of Northumberland.[25] Some gentry were equally concerned to secure the welfare and gratitude of royal patrons: in 1371 Sir John Rouclif secured a chaplain in the York hospital that he founded to pray for the good estate of the king and the soul of the late queen Philippa, and in 1394 Sir Robert Persay endowed a chaplain to celebrate for Richard II's welfare.[26] Even the most powerful families were mindful of the crown. In 1378 Henry Percy, who had been created earl of Northumberland in the previous year, acknowledged his gratitude by establishing a chantry with three chaplains in Hextildesham in Yorkshire to celebrate for the good estate of the king.[27] By 1393 Sir Wiliam Scrope of Bolton was a chamber knight of Richard II and an established royal favourite, and in this year his father, Richard Lord Scrope of Bolton, established a chantry in his castle at Bolton with six chaplains celebrating for the good estate of Richard II and his heirs,[28] perhaps in acknowledgement of the fact that his son, Sir William, had become a chamber knight and established royal favourite.

23 Riley, p. 156; *Historians of the Church of York and its Archbishops*, ed. J. Raine (R.S., 111, 1879–94), p. 275.
24 CPR, 1370–74, p. 5.
25 CPR, 1377–81, p. 31; p. 260.
26 CPR, 1370–74, p. 47.
27 CPR, 1377–81, p. 218.
28 CPr, 1391–96, p. 244.

The founders of perpetual chantries, by using the currency of prayer and the language of patronage, were revealing the social and material bias of their religion; and this was expressed in their attempts to use the chantry to harmonize the pursuit of wealth and heaven. Soldiers, landlords, civil servants and merchants could pursue prosperous careers and use their profits to finance a chaplain who would celebrate for the success of their careers and the prosperity of friends, colleagues and patrons. Any contradictions between their pursuit of wealth and their preoccupation with their fate in the next world could be reconciled if they contributed some of the profits of their enterprises into chantries. In this way chancery clerk Henry of Edenstowe hoped to secure a profitable career and ensure that he still inherited the richer and more permanent profits of heaven. In 1342 he established a double perpetual chantry in his native town of Edwinstowe in Nottinghamshire, requesting masses for himself, his family and benefactors. In the preamble to the foundation charter, which reads like a business transaction, he declares that among all the means of restoring fallen humanity the solemn celebration of masses for the well being of the living and the repose of the departed was the most worthy to draw down the mercy of God. He therefore stated his intention to use his wealth to purchase masses with the earnest desire of acquiring the permanent wealth of heavenly treasure in place of the earthly wealth that perishes.[29] The landed nobility could use their wealth in the same way by alienating the yearly rent from their estates to support cantarists. Sometimes other profitable businesses were contributed, such as the nineteen shops provided by Isolda Acastre, the widow of a wealthy York merchant, for the upkeep of a chantry in All Saints' parish church.[30]

Through intercession a nobleman could integrate his worldly success with his spiritual aspirations; and furthermore, if a chantry had a charitable function the founder could secure intercession from the grateful recipients, while at the same time facilitating the performance of the charitable works which were prescribed as the duties of the active life. Founders sometimes prescribed charitable works as part of the priest's duties, and some chantries, such as the one founded by William Lord Roos in 1412, were intended to function as schools. The hospital, a home for the aged and infirm, and the *maisondieu*, a combination of alms house and hospital, were types of chantry, and many were founded by the nobility in this period. Ralph Lord Neville founded a hospital at Welle in 1343, which was further endowed by John Neville in 1365, and

29 K. L. Wood-Legh, 'Some aspects of the history of chantries in the later Middle Ages', *T.R.H.S.* (1946), 48; see *Trans. Thoroton. Soc.* 1904, p. 80.
30 Riley, p. 277.

king's clerk Richard Ravenser founded St Nicholas' Hospital in Beverley in 1384 and later extended it into a *maisondieu*.[31] Merchants were especially prominent as founders: the wool merchant and money lender, Michael de-la-Pole, founded a *maisondieu* at Kingston-on-Hull in 1377 for twenty-six poor men and women who were granted a daily allowance of 8d.[32] Two brothers who were merchants, Robert Holme who died in 1396 and Thomas Holme who died in 1406, each established a *maisondieu* in the city of York, and a Beverley merchant, John Aske, founded the Trinity hospital in Beverley for twenty-four inmates.[33] Founders were motivated by charity. Foundation charters stipulated that the master of the hospital was required to prepare the souls of inmates for the life to come and to provide for their bodily welfare; Michael de-la-Pole granted the inmates of his *maisondieu* 8d a day for this purpose.[34] The main motive behind the foundation of hospitals was to make provision for the celebration of offices and the performance of prayers for the founder's soul. The founder laid down the rules of religious observance for the bedesfolk and clergy; and the priest in charge of the hospital was responsible for ensuring that the inmates prayed for his soul: Robert Holme stated in his foundation charter that his hospital was founded for the benefit of his soul.[35] Founders also determined the offices to be celebrated by the clergy, and the inmates were requested to be present and to remember the soul of the founder. Robert Knowles prescribed an elaborate routine of masses and offices for the chantry chaplains of the hospital he founded in 1384, many of which were to be attended by the alms folk in a livery of his own choosing, a white gown with a red rose in his memory.[36] Michael de-la-Pole prescribed for a priest to celebrate daily mass with the twenty-six bedesfolk of his hospital, and a chaplain in Richard Ravenser's hospital was instructed to celebrate for the souls of Richard Ravenser and all the benefactors of the hospital.[37] Because these hospitals were private chantries they were almost ignored by the rest of the nobility, although Robert Roos gave 12d in 1406 to the poor of Richard Ravenser's hospital and 2s to the poor of St Giles' Hospital in Beverley.[38]

The above concerns of founders implies an aristocratic, elitist attitude towards salvation and a willingness to use wealth to achieve it, which

31 CPR, 1364 – 67, p. 60; M. Riley, 'The foundation of chantries in the counties of Nottingham and York', *Y.A.J.*, 33 (1936 – 38), 281.

32 Riley, 278.

33 Kermode, p. 31, Cooke, 'Early Civil Wills' 839 – 71. These two brothers left individual bequests to ten alms houses and hospitals in the city.

34 Riley, 278.

35 Prob. Reg., i, fo. 102.

36 Riley, 274.

37 ibid., 278.

38 ibid, 281.

suggests that some of the ideals of social religion were not far removed from some of the more assertive aspects of the codes of honour held by the family; but the perpetual chantry also reveals a more humble awareness of the mutually dependent relationship existing between noblemen and their local communities. The family was a unified community that provided intercession for its members; but its survival could never be guaranteed and the chantry therefore demonstrates the important intercessory function of the local communities of the diocese where nearly all the chantries of the Yorkshire nobility were founded. Such intercession depended on the unity and stability that such communities could offer. The Mass could only aid the living and the dead if the community in which it was being celebrated, whether a small village or cathedral chapter, was in a state of peace. No-one who was in a state of hostility towards his neighbours could benefit from the celebration of the Mass.[39] The masses conducted by a chantry priest and purchased by a grandee could therefore evoke the close relationship between the noblemen and his local community, including his household, and would take place presumably after the lord had settled his accounts and paid his tenants' wages. They were organized so that the local community could participate in them and were often conducted at daybreak and sunrise so that the workers and servants could attend; those present were enjoined to pray for the souls of the founder of the chantry.[40] No matter how much a Yorkshire nobleman was involved in other parts of the country, his name remained an integral part of the religion of his local community. Secular canons were especially dependent on the intercessions of a unified community of colleagues and friends in the cathedral (among whom there were occasional quarrels) because they could not rely on direct descendants to perpetuate their memory. In the chantries of residentiary canons the cantarist was instructed to pray for the souls of fellow canons, and because it was believed that the power of the mass was diluted as it was spread among people — the normal order of precedence was the founder, spouse, parents and children — this naming of another person in a foundation charter was an important testimony of friendship.[41] The artisans and humbler citizens of York formed societies for mutual help and protection, known as guilds, which could finance a chantry to secure intercession for all its members. In 1426 the Guild of St Christopher established a chantry in York Minster.

The chantry was not just intended to help the individual or

[39] A claim made in all confession manuals of the period. See J. Bossy, 'Social history of confession', *T.R.H.S.* (1974).
[40] Wood-Legh, 'Some aspects of the History of chantries', 49.
[41] Wood-Legh, *Perpetual Chantries*, p. 307.

corporative founders and those named in the foundation charters; the communities of the diocese also benefited. Founders of chantries believed they were not only contributing towards the physical splendour of the church but helping in the spiritual elevation of their communities. The rise in the number of chantry foundations in the second half of the fourteenth century increased the number of daily masses being celebrated because chantry priests were not allowed to celebrate at the same time as the parish priest. In some churches a mass was celebrated every hour, and Doncaster parish church celebrated every hour from 5 a.m. to 10 p.m.[42] A multitude of masses was believed to bring intercession to the entire community. This idea was expressed by Archbishop Richard Scrope in the ordination of a chantry at Elland near Halifax. It was claimed that some founders of chantries possessed a deep piety and a reverence for things beautiful and believed that they were not only ensuring their own particular welfare, but that they were engaged in a work of charity outshining all others because it brought about the collective salvation of the faithful. The endowment of chantries, so the writer claimed, provided the necessary support for worthy ministers to offer a service to God in memory of the Passion and to celebrate this sacrament for the salvation of many.[43] Some founders made more specific provision for the spiritual welfare of their communities: Sir Thomas Cumberworth's concern for the souls of the parishioners on his estates was praised by Thomas Gascoigne who testified that Cumberworth improved the endowments of certain poor vicarages in Argon, county York and Somerby in Lincoln county. According to Gascoigne, Cumberworth lamented the appropriation of parishes to monasteries because of the consequent loss of good rectors and neglect of the pastoral office; and he made up the loss suffered by incumbents by giving lands and tenaments to the parish church. When Cumberworth also established a chantry of St Mary in the church of Somerby adjoining his manor in 1439 he was helping to provide intercession for the souls of his tenants.[44] John Pigot, esquire, provided for the celebration of mass for the souls of the poor in 1429 by leaving a missal and ornaments to an altar at Ripon where paupers' funerals were conducted.[45]

This emphasis on the dependence of the departed on the suffrages of those still in this world was not necessarily a pessimistic and fearful view of God and Purgatory. It was a way of confronting death, which was made all the more poignant in an age of frequent epidemics, with an expression of solidarity in the local community that encompassed the

42 Wood-Legh, *Perpetual Chantries*, p. 307.
43 Riley, p. 255; Reg. Scrope, fo.17 – 18.
44 *Loci e libro veritatum*, p. 62.
45 Prob. Reg. 2, fol.544v.

living and the dead. The crisis of separation was met with an ideal of unity and permanence, represented by the perpetual chantry, which was akin to the ideals propagated in familial religion.

Testamentary Bequests

The land and property that a nobleman wished to endow for chantry foundations was either alienated during his lifetime or enfeoffed to uses, which enabled him to leave instructions on his deathbed in his will to his feofees to use the enfeoffed property to found a perpetual chantry.[1] A testament, usually made and revised up to within two years of a nobleman's death, disposed of the testator's body and moveable property, including money, for the aid of his own soul, and although it could be used to purchase the masses of a chantry priest, it did not deal with land, and therefore it could not guarantee an income for a perpetual chantry; chantries established in testaments, such as those of Robert Roos in 1392 and Mary Lady Vavasour in 1414, were only secure for as long as the money lasted.[2] However, although the circumstances surrounding the making of a will were different from those involved in establishing a perpetual chantry, the religious attitudes expressed were essentially the same. Moveable property was disposed of for the benefit of the testator's soul in the purchase of intercessory prayers from the secular religious institutions of the diocese and the testator's local community. Wills, like chantries, were used to perform charitable works in exchange for grateful prayers; and like chantry foundations they expressed a commitment to the concept of the active life, and an understanding of salvation that was not individualistic or familial but dependent on a nobleman's conviction that he belonged to a united local community. The importance of religious sentiments that were directed towards the entire community, and not just a family affinity, became especially apparent when testators near death were giving thought to the mutability of family lineages and estates, and recognizing the importance of taking the precaution of using cash to purchase prayers for the soul: in 1399 Sir William Mowbray left all the moveable property of his household to his wife and children with the stipulation that if these children died the property was to be used for prayers for his soul.[3] Some moveable property, especially the armour handed down from father to son, was a potent symbol of family honour, but it was

1 McFarlane, *Nobility*, p. 69.
2 Prob. Reg. i, fo.51; TE, I, pp. 179–80; TE, I, p. 368.
3 TE, I, p. 159.

recognized that if a lineage died out it would be of most help to the testator if such heirlooms were reduced to cash and used for the purchase of prayers. In 1399 Thomas Roos of Ingmanthorpe bequeathed his arras, bed curtains, sword and armour, and hunting horn, all important symbols of family status, to his son and heir Robert, stipulating that if all his heirs died they were to be sold and the money was to be used for prayers for the whole family.[4] These prayers would be obtained from the local community, including religious institutions, the household and the poor, all of whom a nobleman needed as much as his family for spiritual intercession. Despite the national interests of the nobility they made few bequests to religious institutions or charities outside the sees of York and Lincoln — the donations of William Latimer to the Austin Friars of London were exceptions to this rule — and the bequests of Richard Lord Scrope of Bolton in 1400 to twenty monasteries, hospitals and churches in the diocese, and of Ralph Lord Neville, who left money to each friary, religious house and chantry in the diocese, are more representative of the active interest taken by the nobility in the religious life of their local society.[5]

Such interest did not embrace the wealthy houses of the regular orders, and this conforms to the patterns of endowment. Testamentary bequests to these monasteries were rare, and as with endowments of land and rents, they were motivated by family traditions rather than an interest in a particular order. In 1351 Henry Percy left 100 marks to one of the family's favourite abbeys, the Cistercian house of Sawley in West Yorkshire.[6] Rievaulx, a house with traditional connections with the Roos family, received £24 from Lady Mary Roos in return for prayers in 1394, and a mark for every monk from William Lord Roos in 1414.[7] Donations to Cistercian and Benedictine monks also seem to have fallen off by the fourteenth century in other regions, such as Sussex.[8] The richest houses only attracted the patronage of the wealthy, and even they seemed to have been afraid that their generosity would not be appreciated enough to inspire grateful and conscientious prayers from the monks. The nobility were therefore attracted to the smaller and poorer houses of Premonstratensian canons: in 1400 Richard Lord Scrope left 20 marks and 100s respectively to the impoverished houses of Eggleston and Coverham, and a mark to each canon;[9] and in 1415 Henry Lord Scrope of Masham donated furniture, vestments and 25 marks to Coverham,

4 Prob. Reg. 3, ff.23v – 24.
5 *W.I.* p. 74.
6 TE, I, p. 57.
7 *Register Chichele*, p. 23.
8 N. Saul, *Scenes from Provincial Life. Knightly families in Sussex 1280 – 1400* (Oxford, 1986), p. 152.
9 *Scrope and Grosvenor*, ii, 31.

stipulating that in return the canons were to celebrate mass devoutly for his soul and to remember him in their calendars.[10]

The interest shown by the nobility in the many small nunneries in Yorkshire and Lincolnshire was also inspired by the poverty of most of these houses and the likelihood that generosity would be rewarded with grateful prayers. Comprehensive interest was shown by Sir Brian Stapleton who left £10 in 1394 specifically for the poor nunneries of Yorkshire, and Sir John Dependen left 20s to each of twelve Yorkshire nunneries. Despite their poverty, many of these nunneries were almost exclusively composed of unmarried women of aristocratic birth,[11] and as such they constituted an important part of the social world of the nobility. Many individual bequests to nuns were dowries: Elizabeth Sewerby left a legacy £10 7s 6d to her niece and namesake to enable her to become a nun of Nunmonkton; two of the four daughters of York merchant, Roger Moreton, were nuns of Clementhorpe, who received doweries of four marks from their father for the purchase of black flannels.[12] Many, through their relatives, had close contacts with these religious communities: John St Quintin in 1396 left 40s to Stixwold nunnery where his sister was a nun, and Stainfield where another of his sisters was a prioress.[13] The close social interaction between the lay nobility and these convents was shown in the funeral of Sir Thomas Cumberworth, which was attended by nuns, and prioresses of the diocese; and by the bequests of great ladies to their friends in convents, such as the best linen given by Agnes St Quintin to the prioress of Swine, Joan Skirlaw, the sister of Walter Skirlaw Bishop of Durham, and the furred mantle given by Margaret Stapleton to Isabella Vavasour in 1465.[14]

The most popular of the regular orders were the four orders of Franciscan, Dominican, Carmelite and Augustinian friars, whose traditional activities of preaching and administering confession gave them an important pastoral role in society. Many were private confessors of the nobility: John Kenningham, provincial of the Carmelites, was the confessor of John of Gaunt; and friar Henry Newton was the confessor of Sir William Chaworth, who died in 1394.[15] There is no evidence until the late fifteenth century of friars preaching sermons at

10 *Foedera*, ix, pp. 272 – 80.

11 E. Power, *English Medieval Nunneries* (Cambridge, 1922), p. 329ff. Among the high born nuns there was a continual need for admonition concernng their secular fashions and habits; the prioress of Nunmonkton, Margaret Fairfax, was regarded as a great lady of the neighbourhood. See the visitations of Yorks nunneries in Reg. Thoresby, fo.16; and Reg. Bowet, fos.101 – 2.

12 TE, II, p. 196.

13 TE, I, p.

14 Prob. Reg. 3, fo.231v; TE, I, p. 382; Prob. Reg. 4, fo.110.

15 TE, I, p. 247.

funerals, but their importance as preachers in the fourteenth century is suggested by the popularity of the sermons of the Austin friar John Waldeby, which were delivered outside the church of the Austin friars in York between 1354 and 1370.[16] The houses of the friars were located in the larger settlements of the diocese of York, in Hull, Scarborough, Beverley, Pontefract and Hartlepool, which all had two or more orders, and Kildale, Yarm, Tickhill, Northallerton and Richmond. They were therefore naturally supported by the merchants and burghers who all left bequests to the friaries of their towns. The friars had no rural estates and would have had few economic connections with the great landowners of the diocese, who were prevented by the friars' vows of poverty from alienating any property to them; the only property grants made were infrequent and modest endowments of adjacent plots of land necessary for the enlargement of a manse such as that made by Richard Lord Scrope to the Friars Minor of Richmond.[17] However, magnates and gentry were able to leave substantial legacies in their testaments, and these bequests indicate a widespread interest in the order and what it represented rather than the traditional family support shown for individual monasteries. Many bequests were made to all the orders: Sir Brian Stapleton and Richard Lord Scrope left bequests of one mark and 20s to each of the friars' houses in the diocese.[18] Many bequests were made to all the orders of the major towns: Sir Marmaduke Constable left a mark to all the friars' houses in York, Hull and Beverley in 1377 and Henry Lord Scrope left 40s to the four orders of York, and 20s to the friars of Beverley and Hull.[19] The nobility saw the friars, who were dependent on alms, as begging orders whose prayers and services would be especially valuable for their souls. Margery, widow of Sir William Aldeburgh, left the residue of all her goods to the Dominicans of York to finance anniversaries for herself, her husband, and for the maintenance of 'the poor brothers of the York convent'.[20] Sir Thomas Ughtred laid special value on the intercession of the friars: in 1398 he bequeathed 90s to all the orders of York and Scarborough in return for trentals and annual obits for his soul and the souls of his wife and brother.[21]

The nobility also gave enthusiastic support to the secular clergy and their institutions. They were proud of the imposing cathedral in York,

16 Prob. Reg. 4, fo.110, Margaret Stapleton left 6s 8d to a friar called Rotham who was to ensure that a sermon was preached on the day of her funeral. cit. Vale, 'Piety, Yorks. gentry', 16.

17 *Scrope and Grosvenor*, ii, 32; TE, I, p. 57.

18 Prob. Reg. I, fo. 69v.

19 Archb. Reg. 12, fo.59, TE, I, p. 97; TE, I, p. 101; Rymer, p. 275.

20 *W.I.* p. 69.

21 TE, I, p. 243.

and bequests ranging from a mark to £40 were made to the fabric fund of the Minster by leading magnates and gentry including, Henry Lord Scrope, Sir Robert Swillington, Sir Henry Vavasour, and Sir Marmaduke Constable. But the universally respected institution was the parish church, which received bequests from all testators, lay and ecclesiastic. Some of the wealthiest were actively interested in the spiritual welfare of the parish communities where their interests lay. Henry Lord Scrope of Masham left copes to ten parish churches in the diocese and vestments to a further three, instructing his executors to give two marks to those churches whose needs were greater and to give missals to any parish church that did not have the missals to allow the daily celebration of mass.[22] Sir Marmaduke Constable left 40s to the East Riding churches of Flamborough, Holme and Nafferton for their upkeep.[23] All members of the nobility left bequests, usually between a mark and 20s, to their own parish churches to help in their upkeep. Some were knowledgeable about the affairs of their churches and left bequests for specific repairs: Sir Marmaduke left two marks for a pavement over the chancel of his parish church of Flamborough and 20s for the repair of the altar of St Katherine in the same church.[24] The gentry of the county of Kent, whose horizons were narrower than those of the York nobility, were even more actively involved in parish affairs, and in a recent survey of charity among the Kent gentry in the fifteenth century over half of the testators left money for specific repairs.[25] The growth of interest in the local parish church occurred throughout England in the fourteenth century, and it has been suggested that this was a consequence of the flourishing of the local and central courts at the expense of the old feudal honour: gentry began to identify more with their own locality, and the parish church reflected their standing in local society.[26]

The intercessions of the secular clergy were as highly valued as those of the friars, perhaps because both were equally active in pastoral work, and the local parish priest nearly always received a monetary bequests in return for which the donor would be remembered in parish services. Henry Lord Scrope requested that all rectors and chaplains of the churches which had received bequests from him were to organize prayers for his soul every Sunday and to preserve his memory in their masses. Sir John Constable, Margaret Plays, and William Heghfield were among those who left generous gifts to their priests for this purpose.[27] Some testators made general bequests to secular clergy to

22 Rymer, p. 273.
23 TE, I, pp. 97, 99.
24 Prob. Reg. 2, fo.242v; TE, I, p. 98.
25 Fleming, 'The Gentry of Kent', pp. 36 – 53.
26 Saul, *Provincial Life*, p. 153.
27 TE, I, pp. 99, 164, 53, 258, 325.

encourage as many parish priests as possible to celebrate for their souls. Richard Lord Scrope left 2s to all the parish priests and chantry chaplains coming to his funeral, and Isabella Persay left each priest at her funeral 12d.[28] The value placed on the prayers of the local parish priest and his community is illustrated by Joan Ogle's bequest of half a mark to her parish priest to enable him to pray with his parishioners for her soul.[29] These bequests indicate that the Yorkshire nobility, despite their family chapels, perpetual chantries and their links with religious houses, had a special and highly valued relationship with their local parish church.

This was a mutually dependent spiritual relationship and not a case of high-handed patronage, because all testators in securing the spiritual intercession of these parishes needed to ensure that their departure from this world was peaceful, and that they did not leave behind any ill feeling. Confession manuals written for parish priests in the fourteenth century defined all sins as transgressions against the unity and stability of parish society; forgiveness, ratified by reception of the sacraments, including extreme unction, could not take place until penitents, including testators, had made tangible restitution for any wrongs that they had perpetrated on their communities.[30] These handbooks may have defined different sins for different social classes,[31] but no nobleman could afford to ignore these basic principles of parish unity and sacramental grace when making a will, which to some extent served as a penitential document.

Most testators set aside the residue of their moveable property for the purpose of repayment of debts and other forms of restitution: between 1392 and 1412 Robert Lord Roos, Sir John Constable and William Lord Roos arranged for inventories of their goods to be made, and whatever was needed for the payment of debts and the payment of compensation to those claiming unjust treatment at their hands was to be sold for this purpose.[32] Some, like Richard and Stephen Scrope, made provision to sell a manor if their goods were not sufficient.[33] Such provisions were as necessary for the welfare of the soul as expenditure on prayers and masses. In 1391 Sir William Mowbray concluded his will, in which he arranged for the payment of his brother's debts, by declaring that all his lands, profits and goods had been accounted for in expenditure for the

28 *Scrope and Grosvenor*, ii, 32; TE, I, p. 271.
29 TE, I, p. 139; *W.I.* p. 33.
30 Myrk, *Instructions for Parish Priests*, ed. E. Peacock (London, E.E.T.S., 1905), pp. 52, 72. Bishops made the same point in their sermons; see the sermons of FitzRalph in Dundalk, K. Walsh, *A Fourteenth Century Scholar and Primate: Richard FitzRalph in Oxford, Avignon and Armagh* (Oxford, 1981), p. 373.
31 *Speculum Sacerdotale*, ed. E. H. Weatherley (E.E.T.S., London, 1936).
32 TE, I, pp. 7, 179, 210, 350; *Reg. Chichele*, p. 23.
33 *Scrope and Grosvenor*, ii, p. 55; TE, III, p. 39.

good of his soul and any left over had been set aside for restitution: his wife, one of his executors, had given him an assurance that she would not allow his soul to go to Hell because of a failure to make restitution.[34] Restitution was not only believed to be necessary for the salvation of the testator's soul, but also his executors, who were frequently reminded of it. Sir Marmaduke Constable in 1376, Sir William Mowbray and Sir Brian Stapleton in 1394, all impressed on their executors that they would be answerable to God on the day of judgement if they failed to make proper disposition of the testator's goods.[35]

The nobility used the last testament in a belated attempt to rectify the wrongs and abuses on the estates from which they drew their incomes, which had perhaps been caused by long absences on various forms of government service. Villeinage had survived in the north and some noblemen were troubled that they had abused their positiions of authority over bondsmen. Some of the villeins of Sir John Constable at Holderness had entrusted into his safekeeping after their deaths goods and chattels for the convenience of their sons. Sir John, in his testament in 1449, confessed that he had failed to return this property and instructed his executors to pay it back to these sons without decrease, furthermore adding that if he had swindled anyone in either immoveable or moveable goods, harmed their bodies, or kept back the wages of any servant unjustly, then his executors were to satisfy them immediately.[36] Sir Thomas Ughtred of Kexby emancipated two of his villeins from all bondage in 1398 and gave them a mark each,[37] and Richard Lord Scrope, a prominent royal servant and soldier who was absent from his estates for long periods, expressed concern about his moral negligence as a landlord and willed that all those tenants in Richmondshire who had infertile or enclosed fields or no houses to live in were to receive a mark each.[38] The return for such belated paternalism was prayers: in 1386 John Lord Neville set aside all the rents due from his husbandmen, cottars, bondsmen and free tenants in an effort to secure their prayers, and Sir Marmaduke Constable left 10 marks to the poor tenants of his native Flamborough and Holme.[39]

The thirty-six prebend holders of York Minster who were responsible for the administration of ninety parishes were equally concerned to ensure that the parishioners and tenants of their prebendal estates harboured no ill feeling towards them. The sense of responsibility canons felt towards parishioners with whom they may have had little contact

34 TE, I, p. 159.
35 TE, I, pp. 99, 159, 198; *N.C.W.* p. 1.
36 Prob. Reg. 2, fo. 242v.
37 Prob. Reg. 3, fo. 68; TE, I, pp. 242 – 3.
38 *Scrope and Grosvenor*, ii, 32.
39 *W.I.* p. 40; TE, I, pp. 99, 375.

during their lives reflects the dependence that the York clergy felt, near death at least, on the prayers of laymen. In 1386 Richard Ravenser left £22 to his needy parishioners of Knaresborough and Empyngham; and Thomas Haxey, treasurer of York, left bequests of 40s to the needy parishioners of twelve churches in the East Riding and Howdenshire.[40] There is no evidence that the York Minster clergy felt such kinship with the benefices from other regions that they had acquired or exchanged early in their careers. Such benefices are ignored in their wills, in which they show no retrospective concern with their careers apart from the affectionate memories of their first benefices, usually in their family neighbourhoods, and their university college.[41] Thomas Greenwood, canon of York, left a gift to the fabric of Thirsk, his first church, and Robert Wycliffe left 40s to the church of Kirkby Ravensworth, where he was rector from 1377 – 82, and the ancestral parish of Wycliffe.[42] Near death these clergy, who were anything but provincial, showed a strong sense of their identity as Yorkshiremen.

The nobility also turned to their households for spiritual intercession. These communities of servants, clerks, squires, administrators and dependents were responsible for maintaining schools and religious services within the domestic chapel; they were probably more important in the upbringing of noblemen than the nuclear family, for which few testators expressed any intimate feelings. The imminence of a lord's death created concern among retainers about the future of the household and their own material security. But the lord, when confronted with death, was equally anxious about the fate of his household and its influence on the welfare of his soul. He therefore left generous legacies to maintain the continuity and harmony of his household and to secure the prayers of his retainers and servants. Sir William Latimer asked his executors to ensure that all his servants would be kept in future, according to their state and service, for as long a time as they had served him before his death in such a manner that they would account themselves happy.[43] The largest legacies were to the intimates of the household: Henry Lord Scrope of Masham left goods to the value of 100s to Halneth Mauleverer, Geoffrey Savage, Robert Wyvill and Robert Lane, as long as they were in his service at the time of his death. These men were all from prosperous families and were presumably squires and chamberlains of the household. Scrope left sums of 40s to a further ten named persons including valets and clerks,

40 *Memoirs Lincoln*, p. 315; TE, III, p. 56; York Minster Library, Wills in Dean and Chapter's peculiar (Reg. Test.) I, fo. 219.

41 J. T. Rosenthal, 'The Fifteenth century Episcopate, Careers and Bequests', in D. Baker (ed.), *The Church and the World*, 10, 117 – 26.

42 Reg. Test. I, fo.203; *W.L.* p. 67.

43 TE, I, p. 114.

and 40s to each man in his service at the time of his death in the expectation that they would pray for him, and two marks to those servants who would pray for him at his funeral.[44] The humblest household servants, those who laboured on the lord's demesne and did not possess their own holdings, unlike the tenants and bondsmen of the estates, were remembered in their master's testaments. Sir Brian Stapleton left 40s to his ploughmen and carters and 20s to each cook and groom not mentioned in his will, and John Lord Neville left 200s to be distributed among his ploughmen, wagoners, cattlemen and shepherds.[45]

The nobility also had a spiritual relationship with a more anonymous body of people, who constituted an underworld in the diocese, of beggars, lepers, and outlaws, many of whom drifted into the larger towns such as York. There is no way of knowing their exact numbers, but it is possible that they outnumbered the recorded populace of the tax returns of 1379. On Good Friday in 1396 Richard II was reported to have distributed 4d with his own hands to each of the 12,040 people outside York Minster. A separate record in the official court book ratifies this figure by giving the total amount spent at £200 13s 4d.[46] Although they lacked a definite status these outcasts were an important source of intercession for the community. Charitable bequests were not attempts at social control or reform, but they were made in anticipation of grateful prayers.[47] Thomas Scargill of Leeds had the inmates of St Leonard's Hospital praying at his funeral in 1432, and Richard Lord Scrope left 2s to each prisoner in the castles of York, Durham, Carlisle, Richmond, and Appleby in return for prayers for his soul.[48] Sir Ralph Hastings and Sir John Constable were among those who left generous legacies to the lepers of York in return for their prayers.[49] The most popular form of charitable bequest was the funeral dole, often a penny, which, as in the case of the funerals of Sir Brian Stapleton and Sir Stephen Scrope of Masham, was distributed to all the poor attending the funeral in return for their carrying tapers and candles and praying around the body of the testator.[50] Funeral alms ensured that there would be an impressive gathering of mourners and some testators left substantial legacies to the poor: in 1352 Henry Percy left £20 to be distributed as alms along the funeral procession and £200 to be distributed at the funeral itself; Richard Lord Scrope left £100 in funeral alms and Ralph Lord Neville

44 Rymer, p. 275.
45 Prob. Reg. I, fo.69v; *W.I.* p. 40.
46 Harvey, *Richard II and York*, p. 210.
47 J. T. Rosenthal, *The Purchase of Paradise* (London, 1972), p. 105ff.
48 *Scrope and Grosvenor*, ii, 32.
49 TE, I, pp. 218, 350, 372. Reg. Test. I, fo.138.
50 Prob. Reg. I, fo.69v; TE, III, p. 39.

and Agnes St Quintin left £40.[51] Such charity was inevitably impersonal: noblemen rarely put money into the hands of paupers personally, except on ceremonial occasions such as Maundy Thursday, and their executors used clerical intermediaries and almoners to distribute alms on the funeral procession and at interment to paupers who would pray for a man they may never have seen. Charity was rarely motivated by an emotional concern with the misfortunes of particular individuals and was often a mechanical act generated by the donor's concern for the welfare of his soul. For this reason it frequently took a symbolic form. The inmates of St Leonard's Hospital were clothed in uniforms of symbolic colours and emblems; and testators, whose confessors stressed the moral value of the numbers three, five, seven and ten, arranged their charities in symbolic patterns. Sir Stephen Scrope of Masham left ten pennies to ten paupers and seven pennies to seven paupers in 1406.[52]

However, some of the wealthy did have a social conscience. The burghers of Hull took an oath promising to act and work for the common weal, and some charitable bequests indicate a first-hand acquaintance with social problems.[53] Sir John Dependen left 100s to the needy and bedridden of his native town of Helaugh, and Richard Lord Scrope of Bolton left £40 for the repair of a bridge in Wensley, the residue of his estate to the poor of this town, and a mark to each blind beggar in Richmondshire.[54] Much interest was shown in St Leonard's Hospital, which was not a private chantry but a genuine alms house with an important social function. It was the largest hospital of its kind in England with 224 sick and poor in its infirmary in 1370, and 23 children in the orphanage, all under the supervision of a matron.[55] The master of St Leonard's was usually a chancery official, and this explains the generous legacies to the matron, the brothers and sisters, and the poor of the hospital, left by William Waltham and Walter Skirlaw.[56] Others to leave bequests to the poor of St Leonard's included Sir Marmaduke Constable and William Gascoigne.[57]

No matter how impersonal charity may have been at times it was usually accompanied with genuine religious sentiment. Sermons frequently taught that it was the duty of Christians who remained in the world to live an active life by following the way of Martha and caring for

51 TE, I, p. 57; *Scrope and Grosvenor*, ii, 32; *W.I.*, p. 73; Prob. Reg. 3, fo. 231v; TE, 1, p. 322 and p. 375.
52 TE, III, p. 39.
53 Kermode, 'Merchants', 8.
54 Prob. Reg. 3, fo.88v; *Scrope and Grosvenor*, ii, 33.
55 M.R. Clay, *The Medieval Hospitals of England* (London, 1908), p. 156.
56 Reg. Test. I, fo.179; TE, III, p. 55; TE, I, 306.
57 TE, I, 98; *N.C.W.*, p. 2.

Christ's limbs, or the needy. Nicholas Blackburn senior, who was responsible for many acts of charity in York, commissioned a window in All Saints' church in North Street depicting the corporeal acts of mercy.[58] Acts of compassion towards the unfortunate were believed to speed the passage of the soul towards purgatory. In 1409 William Stauton, who was from an armigerous Durham family, slept in the cave of St Patrick's Purgatory in Lough Dergh and dreamed that he was assisted out of purgatory by a woman who guided him up a ladder and cord. Staunton had been influenced by the parable of the good samaritan, for the woman explained to him that the cord was one that he had given to a merchant who had been robbed by thieves and had approached him for alms. In his dreams he entered Paradise and was told by a company of monks and canons that whenever he did a good deed they thanked him.[59] Norfolk's leading knight, Sir John Fastolf, had similar views on charity, and in 1459 he asked his executors to distribute his property in alms and deeds of piety 'for the more hasty delyveraunce of my soule from the peynefull flawmes of the fyre of Purgatory'.[60] Some testators arranged for a final gesture of compassionate charity at their funerals in an attempt to safeguard their passage through purgatory. Sir William Mennevil in 1372 requested that his russet burial cloth be distributed to the poor around his grave; but few matched the gesture of Sir Thomas Cumberworth who requested that the coffin made for him be given at his funeral to the digger of his grave.[61] The last will and testament then, like the foundation charters of perpetual chantries, was used by the nobility to express, in the face of death, strong feelings of social concord. However, these sentiments received a more dramatic depiction in the rituals associated with the funerals of the great families of Yorkshire.

The Funeral

Since the thirteenth century the funerals of an increasingly prosperous nobility were becoming more elaborate as alms giving became more conspicuous; additional prayers were used in the ceremonial procession, and private masses and prayers for the dead proliferated; and new altars were also incorporated in parish churches to facilitate these services. Such funerals were a time of heightened religious activity for

58 Prob. Reg. 2, fo.605.
59 S. Leslie, *St. Patrick's Purgatory* (London, 1932), pp. 28 – 33.
60 *The Paston Letters*, ed. J. Gairdner, (2nd ed. Gloucester, 1983), vol. 3, p. 159.
61 The Academy, 5, pp. 230 – 2 and pp. 280 – 85.

the whole community. Some historians have criticized such activity from a social perspective: the apparently disinterested distribution of funeral arms in return for prayers has been seen as a failure on the part of the nobility to control and dictate social developments and to advance social status; and alms have been described as a form of class distinction used to transmit only the rich man's soul to heaven.[1] Social religion was concerned with neither of these things. The crisis of death inspired in noblemen the desire for an expression of communal unity within the parish and the household which was provided by the funeral. Salvation was not seen in isolated or elitist terms because death was regarded as a social crisis that threatened to divide the dead from the living; funeral and burial rites not only provided consolation for the bereaved, but ritually enacted the ultimate inseparability of the living and the dead, expressing a nobleman's desire for a salvation that included his family and local community, and which was achieved by securing the intercession of all the dead in purgatory, including the poor. In 1400, Roger Wandesford asked for many rites at his funeral because the rites of the living, he claimed, could bring comfort in securing intercession for the dead. In 1414 John Newton, the treasurer of York Minster, left instructions to his executors to provide a sumptuous funeral with as much pomp as possible for the honour of God, the refreshment of the poor, the benefit of his soul and the souls of all the faithful dead.[2] He further added that his wealth was to be spent by his executors to ensure that all the faithful were delivered from punishment. Testators naturally requested prayers at their funeral for their families, but they also made separate bequests for prayers for their own souls and the souls of all the faithful dead; and these outnumber bequests made for prayers for the soul of the testator alone. Sir Ralph Hastings left £10 to the poor for prayers for his soul and the souls of all the faithful, and Isabella Wyleby left 10 marks for prayers for her soul and the souls of all the faithful.[3]

The death of a great lord affected all the members of his local society because it emphasized the salutory message of transience. His funeral was a rite of passage that made it easier for mourners in the community to come to terms with the transition of death through rituals that projected an ideal image of the human condition, and made it available for human participation.[4] One such image for a nobleman was the family and its lineage, but another was his local society, focussed on the parish church or the household. Despite parish feuds and the social

1 Rosenthal, *Purchase of Paradise*, pp. 124 – 32; F. R. DuBoulay, *An Age of Ambition* (London, 1970); Rosentham, *Purchase*, p. 23 also asserts that funeral pomp shows a selfish preoccupation with the fate of the individual soul.
2 T.E., I, p. 256; Reg. Test, I, fo.168.
3 TE, I, p, 217, p, 382,
4 James, 'Two Tudor Funerals', 164.

divisions complained of in the pastoral manuals, the funeral expressed a sense of Christian solidarity in these communities. Parish churches and household chapels were reserves of spiritual power which was dispensed in sacraments that were needed by even the mightiest in times of crisis. The successful operation of these sacraments depended on the unity of the communities conducting them. The deceased's confession, and the arrangements made for restitution in the last will and testament, reconciled the testator with his community and allowed intercessions provided in the funeral to be effective. The funeral procession, a triumphant voyage of the dead man's soul that onlookers participated in, symbolized this unity that triumphed over death. Stephen Scrope, the second lord of Masham, gave instructions for his coffin to be clothed in a black cloth with a white cross on which were to be placed two three-pound candles at either end. After prayers his body was to be conveyed along the River Ouse at night to Selby near the manor of his son Henry, where mass was to be celebrated. The following night the coffin was to continue its journey to York, where a mass would be celebrated on its arrival.[5] John Lord Neville's triumphant and solemn procession cost two hundred pounds, and twenty-four russet-clad paupers bore his coffin in a hearse bearing twenty-four candles and five ten-pound tapers.[6] The same ceremonies were conducted for noble families in other regions, notably East Anglia: in 1466, during the funeral procession of Sir John Paston from London to Bromholme, the body was laid out overnight in the Paston family church at St Peter Hungate in Norwich surrounded by thirty-nine choir boys, twenty-six clerks and four torchbearers.[7] The souls of the wealthy were launched to a chorus of song: Sir Ralph Hastings and Sir John Clifford had two-thousand masses sung immediately after their deaths, and Elizabeth Lady FitzHugh had a thousand masses and ten trentals performed immediately after her death.[8] The blaze of lights accompanying the procession created a sense of triumph and union. During Ralph Lord Neville's funeral procession in 1367 sixty torches burned around the body, and Elizabeth Lady FitzHugh's body was taken to Jervaulx Abbey by the light of twenty-four torches and fifteen tapers, each weighing one pound.[9] This sense of triumph and unity was shared by the whole community including the poor. At a time when the continuity of the household appeared to be under threat, the funeral gave

5 TE, III, p. 33.
6 *W.I.*, p. 39.
7 *Paston Letters*, ed. Gairdner, IV, p. 255 – 9. See also C. Richmond, 'Religion and the fifteenth-century gentleman', in R. B. Dobson (ed.), *The Church Politics and Patronage in the Fifteenth Century* (Gloucester, 1984), 196.
8 TE, I, p. 197; p. 167; Test. Vetusta, p. 212.
9 *W.I.*, p. 27; TV, p. 212.

prominence to the funeral livery of the departed and provided for a symbolic union between a great lord and the anonymous poor by clothing their representatives in a livery of the testator's choosing. The most common livery given to the poor torch bearers in the funeral procession was russet: Isabella Fauconbergh and Joan Hesilrig had thirteen russet clad paupers following their processions, and Sir Marmaduke Constable and Richard Ravenser had twelve.[10] A black livery was chosen by Sir John Dependen; Agnes Burton left thirteen black hoods and tunics for poor men who were to carry torches on her burial day;[11] and Elizabeth Wortelay had twelve paupers clad in white tunics and capes standing around her body on the day of her funeral.[12]

After the funeral candles continued to burn in the parish churches of the diocese to affirm the deceased person's triumph over death, and the survival of a spiritual bond between him and the communities that continued to intercede for his soul and the souls of all the dead. Twelve candles from Henry Lord Scrope's funeral procession were distributed to the most needy parish churches in Richmondshire, and thirteen torches from the procession of Sir Brian Stapleton's body were distributed to the nearby churches of Wighill, Helaugh and Tadcaster.[13] The liveried poor continued to watch and pray over the body until interment. Nicholas Strelley requested that twenty-pounds of wax and four tapers be burnt around his coffin in the parish church of Strelley for seven days and that five paupers, clad in a livery of black cloaks and hoods, were to be paid 2d a day to watch over his body.[14]

The interment of the body was also an opportunity for the expression of communal religious values. The careers of the York nobility took them far beyond the diocese, and they cannot be dismissed as provincial in taste or behaviour. But despite their cosmopolitan lives they showed, in their choice of a final resting place, a desire for the human comforts provided in the more immediate horizons of their local community. The decision of the privy seal clerk, Richard Ferriby, in 1346 to be buried in the house of the Austin Friars of Rouen was an exception.[15] Nearly all testators wished to be buried in the diocese of York, and over half of them chose to be buried in their local parish church. Magnates who chose interment in the parish church included Robert Roos of Igmanthorpe, who was buried in Igmanthorpe church; and high ecclesiastics who

10 TE, I, pp. 282; 269; 101; *Memoirs Linc.*, p. 313; TE, I, p. 107.
11 Prob. Reg. 3, fo.88v; TE, I, p.36.
12 *Foedera*, ix, p. 276; TE, I, p. 125.
13 *Foedera*, ix, p. 276; Prob. Reg. I, fo.69v.
14 TE, II, p. 3.
15 Prob. Reg. 3, fo.490.

were buried in parish churches included John Ravenser and John Prophete.[16] Among the gentry the proportion of those choosing burial in parish churches was higher at 60%.[17] In the large churches of Richmondshire, built between 1250 and 1350, families were laid out in large aisleless choirs to outnumber the worshipping congregation, and in the East Riding church of Flamborough the monuments of the Constable family dominated. Personal possessions were presented to the church as mortuary gifts; knights would give their best horse and ladies their best cloth, and these would sometimes be accompanied by valuables from private chapels. In Kent, where there were few magnates of the same status as the northern families, an even higher proportion of 90% of the gentry were buried in their parish churches within a few miles of their residences.[18] Most of those who were not buried in parish churches still chose a local community that they knew well for their final resting place. Most of the Benedictine, Cistercian, Cluniac and Augustinian houses were ignored as burial places by the nobility, but some local abbeys did serve as a traditional place of interment for the leading families. The Roos family of Helmesley used the nearby Cisterican abbey of Rievaulx, and the FitzHugh of Ravensworth the nearby Cistercian abbey of Jervaulx. The cathedral at York served as a natural resting place for the residentiary canons who spent most of their later years in the cathedral close, including John Newton and Thomas Dalby. The only exceptions to this pattern of burial among family and friends in the local community were the 10% of testators who chose to be buried among the friars minor, especially in the churches of the four orders of York and the friars preachers of Beverley.

These ritually expressive burial ceremonies were not new to this period, and they expressed cultural traditions in the face of the irruptions of individual mortality. However, despite the lack of testamentary evidence before 1375, it can be assumed that these customs themselves would have been drastically curtailed during the outbreaks of the Black Death in 1349, 1362 and 1369 along with the dispensing of the sacraments of Confession and Extreme Unction.[19] It is therefore possible that these elaborate ceremonies of social harmony in the years between 1375 and 1450 represent, like the realistic, non-allegorical illuminations of funerals and burials accompanying the office of the dead in books of hours in northern Europe in the same period, a reassertion of tradition, faith and social optimism after a traumatic

16 TE, I, p. 179; Reg. Test., I, fo.202; TE, III, p. 56; *W.I.*, p. 46.
17 Vale, 'Piety', 8.
18 Fleming, 'Charity and Gentry', 50.
19 *Concilia Magnae Britanniae*, ed. D. Wilkins (Oxford, 1798), Vol. iii, p. 12.

epidemic and the consequent suspension of the consolations of communal religion.[20]

CONCLUSION

The religious convictions of the families and communities of the diocese can be labelled conventional for two reasons. Firstly, they were not unique to the diocese. The clannish parish and county gentry of Kent, who comprised 2% of the population of the county, supplied the senior personnel of county administration and held important positions in central government. They were equally dependent in their religious beliefs and practices on the family and parish society.[1] Secondly, these religious attitudes had not been determined by anything peculiar to the diocese of York in terms of geography, social conditions or individual personalities: the particular experiences, formulative reading, and friendships between individuals or among circles of intellectuals had no real influence on the evolution of a religion that, through such concepts as the materially assisted voyage to the other world, had things in common with all religions and parallels with folk conventions. The conventions of familial and social religion can be considered in this light because, although they were fostered by the church, they had not been consciously formulated by its leaders. They were shared by all classes of society who relied in times of crisis on the support of the family and the social environment. For all their administrative responsibilities, their cosmopolitan experiences and their elite social status, the nobility of the diocese upheld spiritual attitudes that could have been determined by horizons as narrow as those in the lives of the tanners, yeomen, potters and tilemakers of the parish of All Saints' church in North Street in York. The small world of these urban craftsmen was dominated by the parish church and its clergy and the high altar. They were able to share the benefits of perpetual chantries by joining the guilds of St Christopher, St Francis and St Anthony; in the forty testaments that these artisans made between 1390 and 1450 they left the humble tools of their trade to their children, in the same way that noblemen bequeathed their armour; and they left small bequests to the fabric of the parish church, and made restitution to their community by paying forgotten tithes.[2] This explains why the religious ideals of the noble family were

[20] G. K. Fiero, 'Death Ritual in Fifteenth Century Manuscript Illuminations', *Journal Medieval Hist.*, 10 (1984) 270ff.

[1] Fleming, 'Charity', p. 37.

[2] P. J. Shaw, 'Wills relating to All Saints North Street', in P.J. Shaw, *An Old York Church* (York, 1908), pp. 83 – 98.

shared by other sections of the community; why tenants and paupers could wear the arms of a deceased nobleman and identify with the lineage commemorated in his funeral; and why so much of Yorkshire society participated in and benefited from the spiritual intercessions paid for by the investments of the ruling class.

There was nothing in the religious conventions of the ruling class of the diocese that suggested they self-consciously distinguished themselves spiritually or intellectually from parish societies within the diocese or elsewhere. These conventions expressed no broad interest in, or understanding of, abstract ideas on the universal church and its laws; rather they reveal an unreflective dependence on the local community. Chivalry, as we have seen, was not concerned with self-examination or the formulation of a moral code based on human experiences; and it was not a distinctively aristocratic code: bravery and aggression were widely admired in a vendetta society where physical violence and intimidation were important means of self expression. However, there is evidence that some intellectuals within the church were consciously modifying the character of religious practice and belief in Yorkshire society. The third chapter will survey the fundamental work undertaken by a group of York clergy to increase the moral awareness of parishioners and reduce the incidence of violence in the diocese. There were spiritual as well as moral limitations to religious conventions based so exclusively on familial and social models. The nobility defined salvation in terms of the dynamic social forces formulating their personalities, such as warfare and patronage. A religion formulated and expressed in such self-assertive social and material terms clearly lacks a sense of the transcendent, and while an emphasis on membership of a family could overcome a sense of isolation and vulnerability in the face of death, it also left little room for individuality; and the emphases on ritual and clerical intercession gave little recognition to the possibility of a direct relationship with God. However, there is evidence that some intellectuals within the church were addressing themselves to these limitations and consciously modifying religious practice and belief within Yorkshire society. The following chapter is concerned with the growing interest in the eremitic movement as a private form of religious vocation in which the practitioners aspired to a detachment from the pressures and consolations of communal religion. The changes surveyed in the following chapters were not conventional in the sense that they can be linked to the innovations of strong personalities within the diocese of York.

CHAPTER TWO

The Eremitic Movement in the Diocese of York

Patronage

The most important indication that those upholding the religious conventions of the diocese were also witnessing and participating in important changes in religious sensibility was that the same families who were investing the lives of their members in the pursuit of honour, and their capital in communal religious rites, were also producing and supporting solitaries: men and women who, in an attempt to get closer to God, strove to achieve a physical and emotional detachment from human society. Anchorites and anchoresses in particular, shunned companionship and communication. They were enclosed in cells, or narrow small houses, usually in a parish churchyard or adjacent to the church, in a ceremony that emphasized their death to the world: the doors to their cells were symbolically barred and the office of the dead celebrated for them; unlike the rituals of excommunication, confession and penance, there followed no symbolic re-integration into society. Any close involvement or interest in such a life suggests an important departure from the conventions of family and social religion. Before discussing the nature of the nobility's participation in the eremitic life through consulting recluses and reading literature on the contemplative life, it is necessary to establish that recluses in Yorkshire enjoyed a special relationship with their patrons in this period.

Recluses, whether they were anchoresses and anchorites confined to a single cell for their lives, Carthusian monks who lived in a community comprised of single cells, or hermits, males licenced to the solitary life in a ceremony of dedication but free to roam at will[1], were neither a new

[1] Because of their unstructured lives recluses were required to carry letters testimonial, and episcopal registers began to record the taking of professions of individual hermits. The two best known eremitical rules in the fifteenth century were the *regula heremitarum*, erroneously attributed to Richard Rolle, and the rule of St Paul the first hermit, which counselled hard physical work and simple prayers in the ascetic tradition of the desert fathers. See Virginia Davis, 'The Rule of Saint Paul, the First hermit, in late Medieval England', in W. J. Sheils, (ed.) *Monks, Hermits and the Ascetic Tradition*, (Eccl. Hist. Soc., 22, Oxford, 1985), pp. 203 – 14.

phenomenon nor restricted to the diocese of York. In the twelfth century they were found mainly in rural regions, patronized in remote places by the Anglo-Saxon gentry. By the thirteenth century increasing numbers of laywomen, usually maidens, were enclosed throughout the eastern counties of the kingdom under royal patronage, especially that of Henry II who supported forty-eight solitaries.[2] By the fourteenth century however, more men were becoming recluses, and royal patronage was not as significant as the support of local magnates and gentry; and recluses therefore became more common in those areas where there was local interest: in London and in the counties of Lincolnshire, Norfolk, Kent and especially Yorkshire. There are over 185 surviving references to the cells of recluses in the north-east; 128 of these are in the diocese of York and 100 are concentrated in Yorkshire, especially in the East Riding and Richmondshire. Over sixty of these cells were established in the fourteenth and fifteenth centuries, compared to thirty in the twelfth and thirteenth centuries.[3] This represents the greatest concentration of recluses in the kingdom: only Norfolk, with thirty-six cells founded in the fourteenth and fifteenth centuries, comes close to this; and in some regions, such as the less populated diocese of Bath and Wells, there are very few references to recluses.[4] Some indication of the importance of noble patronage is provided by the distribution of cells. Some were in isolated areas, such as caves overlooking the Humber at Saltfleet, or in woods near Doncaster, and others were attached to religious communities like the Augustinian canons of Guisborough and Bridlington. However, by this period recluses were no longer a purely rural phenomenon. Most lived among lay communities in cells or narrow houses that were in churchyards, such as the chapel of St Simon and Jude at Coverham, or attached to the chapel of the high altar of the parish church. Many recluses occupied cells in busy centres of thoroughfare at such town gates as Frenchgate in Richmond and Hungate in York, and in the market towns of Wakefield and Wath.[5] By the fourteenth century as many as a third of the recluses in the kingdom were living in towns and cities. In the diocese of York it was the patronage of the nobility that enabled large numbers of recluses to live independently from monastic institutions for the first time. In the city of Norwich, where the first references to recluses occur by 1400, the patronage of the nobility was not such an important factor.[6] Some recluses of the city were supported by a circle of citizens, but most were attached to religious houses, especially of the Benedictine order.

2 A. K. Warren, *Anchorites and their Patrons* (Berkeley, 1986) p. 26ff.
3 R. M. Clay, *Hermits and Anchorites of England* (London, 1914) Appendix.
4 *Somerset Medieval Wills*, ed. F. W. Weaver (Somerset Rec. Soc., 1901), pp. 24 – 88.
5 Clay, *Hermits*, pp. 203 – 63.
6 N. P. Tanner, *The Church in Late Medieval Norwich* (Toronto, 1984), pp. 57 – 66.

However, the statistical evidence itself is not as important as evidence of the exact nature of the patronage of solitaries: the special relationship that existed between individual recluses in the diocese and circles of clergy and magnates, gentry and merchant families was unique. In London, a larger, more anonymous city than York, where the population was expanding by 1380 with the arrival of rural migrants and the dispossessed, the patronage of recluses was more general and indiscriminate. Among the wills of the burghers and tradesmen of the city made between 1350 and 1400 there were thirty-one bequests to solitaries, twenty-seven of which were to unspecified anchorites of the city or individual parishes.[7] Among such patronage there is little evidence of particular support for influential recluses, and these London bequests were nearly always made in conjunction with grants to friars, lepers, prisoners and the poor, thereby assigning to the recluse a status that was somewhere between that of an outcast and a poor friar: a grateful recipient of alms who would pray for the donor's soul. A typical bequest was that of William Bury, fishmonger, who left money to the various orders of the friars, to the inmates of hospitals, and to the lepers and anchorites of the city.[8] After 1400 this charity towards recluses tailed off noticeably. The impressive financial patronage of recluses in general, and individual solitaries in the diocese of York, was of a different order, and implies that the local nobility established special relationships with recluses and that they had a profound admiration for the eremitic life.

The most influential patrons of recluses in this period were the dukes of Lancaster whose hereditary lordship, which included large areas of Richmondshire, Nottinghamshire and Cumberland, entailed many commitments to solitaries. The Pontefract reclusarium in the chapel of St Helen near the castle had been established before 1240 and passed to the Lancasters in 1311. Henry, the first duke of Lancaster, took a personal interest in the two anchoresses living in the reclusarium, and in 1359 he received a licence to assign to them a livery (a conventual loaf of bread, a gallon of wine and a general allowance for food) which would support a chaplain to celebrate divine service for the anchoresses daily in the chapel.[9] Not long after, Henry founded his own reclusarium in the churchyard of the parish church of Whalley in Lancashire, which consisted of one anchoress and two female servants. Extensive lands were granted to Whalley abbey in return for which the monks would feed the anchoress and her servants, maintain their buildings and provide a chaplain; the duke of Lancaster retained the right of admission

7 *Calendar of Wills Enrolled in the Court of Husting*, ed. R. Sharpe (London, 1890) 11, p. 161.

8 ibid, p. 161.

9 M. Wade Labarge, 'Henry of Lancaster and Livre de Seyntz Medicines', *Florilegium* 2 (1980) 183 – 91; Warren, *Anchorites*, p. 274.

to any vacancies for himself and his heirs.[10] His involvement with these recluses was probably intense for he was himself the author of an ascetic, penitential work of confession, *Livre de Seyntz Medicines*. Similarly his successor as Duke of Lancaster, John of Gaunt, who showed an interest in the religious issues of the time, was a patron and protector of a number of anchorites and hermits. Besides leaving three nobles (one and a half marks) to each hermit or recluse living in London or within five leagues of the city centre, he honoured regular commitments to recluses within the duchy at Beverley, Pontefract, Whalley, Snaith near Pontefract, Richmond, Bishop's Lynn, Leicester and Chatterburn in Lancashire.[11] He took a personal interest in some of these recluses: describing John the hermit of Singleton in West Lancashire as 'our good friend', arranging for the repair and refurbishing of houses at the site of the execution of Thomas earl of Lancaster for the habitation of William, a hermit of Bingham near Nottingham,[12] and granting the wardenship of the hermitage of the chapel of St Martin at Chatterburn to Richard Goldburn 'as long as he behaves himself decently'.[13] Most revealing is Gaunt's involvement with the itinerant Lollard preacher, William Swinderby, a hermit who came from Swinderby on the borders of Nottinghamshire and Lincolnshire and arrived in Leicester. Gaunt, as patron of Leicester abbey, befriended the hermit, who would accept food from the duke while refusing it from local people. When William was accused of holding heretical views by the mayor and burgers of Lincoln in 1382, Swinderby attested that Gaunts's presence at the hearing strengthened him.[14] When the crown passed to the house of Lancaster in 1399, royal patronage of hermits which had previously been confined to London passed to Yorkshire, Lancashire, and Northumberland in grants ranging from 1d to 3d a day.[15] Both Henry IV and Henry V had close relationships with the recluses inhabiting the Westminster reclusory, John Murymouth, John London and William Alnwick. Anchorites played an especially important part in the life of Henry V who endowed a permanent reclusory at Sheen with twenty marks.[16] Henry VI, who tried at times to live like a recluse, continued all previous royal commitments and accepted the anchorite foundation at Richmond as his own when he assumed control over the lordship that

10 Warren, *Anchorites*, p. 274; CRP 1358 – 61, p. 246.
11 Warren, *Anchorites*, p. 174ff.
12 *John of Gaunt's Register 1372 – 76*, ed. J. Armitage-Smith (Camden 3rd Series, xx – xxi), 1911, vol. ii, p. 949.
13 ibid, vol. i, p. 437.
14 J. Compton, 'Leicestershire Lollards', *Leicestershire Archeological and Historical Society*, 44 (1968 – 9) 11dd.
15 Warren, *Anchorites*, p. 170.
16 CPR, 1413 – 19, p. 114.

endowed it, and in 1439 he granted 20s to the anchoress who had been immured in St Edmund's chapel, Richmond, for forty years.[17]

The same close interest in the eremitic life and individual recluses was shared by the leading magnate families in the diocese. John of Gaunt's lordship of Richmond (1272 – 99) and the patronage of St Edmund's chapel, Richmond, passed to Ralph Lord Neville of Raby, who married Gaunt's fifth daughter Joan Beaufort; and both Lord Neville and his wife, besides honouring their responsibilities to the Richmond anchoress, left substantial legacies to anchorites within the diocese and the bishopric of Durham. Significantly, it was among a Yorkshire family who were staunch upholders of the conventions of familial religion, the Scropes of Masham, that such interests were most prominent. Testamentary evidence for this and other Yorkshire families is scarce before 1350, and it is possible that Geoffrey Scrope of Masham, a canon of York and Lincoln who left 20s in 1383 to the anchorite of Holy Trinity church in Lincoln and bequests to three recluses in the diocese of York,[18] was not the first member of this family to patronize solitaries. In 1405 Stephen, the second Lord Scrope of Masham, left a gilt image of the patron saint of hermits, John the Baptist, to his son and heir, Henry Lord Scrope of Masham in 1405,[19] and they both supported Robert, a recluse of Beverley. However, it was Henry, who became the third Lord Scrope in 1405, who demonstrated in his will in 1415 the sense of responsibility that he felt towards practitioners of the eremitic life throughout the kingdom. Lord Scrope, besides leaving half a mark to each anchorite and anchoress living in the city and suburbs of York and London, made bequests ranging from 100s to one mark to seventeen anchorites throughout the diocese of York and one hermit (including recluses at the family manor of Upsall and at Leek) and in London, Shrewsbury, Wighton in Norfolk and Newcastle.[20] His younger brother and heir John, the fourth Lord Scrope, continued the family's long-term commitment to recluses within the diocese and left 3s 4d to specified anchorites in the city of York.[21]

Among magnate families outside the diocese only the Beauchamps of Warwick[22] exerted the same comprehensive and consistent patronage of solitaries as the Lancasters and Scropes. However, in Yorkshire throughout this period many of the leading families who were friends or

17 Warren, *Anchorites*, p. 189.

18 *Memoirs Lincoln*, p. 315; *Lincoln Wills*, ed. C. W. Foster (Lincoln, 1914) vol. ii, pp. 11 – 19.

19 TE, II, pp. 31 – 7.

20 *Foedera*, ix, pp. 272 – 8.

21 TE, II, pp. 31 – 7.

22 C. Ross, 'The Estates and Finances of Richard Beauchamp', *Dugdale Soc. Occasional Papers*, 12 (1956) 3 – 22.

relatives of the Scropes, or witnesses in their favour in the Scrope Grosvenor dispute, supported anchorites within their lordships. Among the most important patrons were the Roos family, lords of Helmesley in the East Riding and connected through marriage with the Scropes of Masham. John, the son of Lord and Lady Thomas and Beatrice Roos and an important crusader, desired to be buried opposite the sepulchre of St Aelred of Rievaulx, author of the *Rule for Recluses,* and left 20s to each anchorite living within the area of his lordship in Helmesley, Byland, Beverley and Harpham. His brother William, who succeeded to the patrimony as 7th Lord Roos of Helmesley in 1393, left £100 to be distributed among those hermits and recluses who had been ordained and whose honesty in serving God assiduously and devotedly was known, and who would pray specially for their patron.[23] Their mother, lady Beatrice, also supported recluses within the lordship and left 40s in 1414 to anchoresses in Leek near Helmesley and Nun Appleton.[24]

Convincing evidence of the close relationship maintained between recluses and patrons also exists in the interest shown among gentry circles in certain anchorages and solitaries. Doncaster, where there was a reclusarium for two anchoresses at Doncaster bridge, was an especially important centre for the eremitic life. The Doncaster bridge anchorage, which received bequests in 1360 and 1382 from the vicar of Doncaster, William Nelson, and Geoffrey Scrope, canon of Lincoln, had been founded by the FitzWilliam family in 1270 and endowed with lands supervised by the master of St Edmund's Hospital and his assistant.[25] This family continued to supervise closely the reclusarium: in 1348 Lady Isabel FitzWilliam, widow of William lord of Elmley and Spotborough, bequeathed a robe to the incumbent Lady Joan, and in the mid-fifteenth century John FitzWilliam, the lord of Spotborough restructured the duties of the master of St Edmund's and his assistant, giving the master charge of the recluses and the property endowed to them; Lord John also exhorted the master on his priestly duties and provision for the anchoresses. The family retained the right of nomination to the reclusarium; an important privilege considering that recluses like Margaret Tattersall had family connections.[26] Around the time that John FitzWilliam was rearranging responsibilities at the Doncaster reclusarium, his sister, Lady Joan Wombwell, made a bequest to the anchoress

23 *Early Lincoln Wills*, ed. A. Gibbons (Lincoln, 1888), pp. 70 – 71.
24 TE, I, p. 376.
25 *Early Lincoln Wills*, p. 103; *Lincoln Wills*, p. 17; Warren, *Anchorites*, pp. 208ff.
26 Warren, *Anchorites*, p. 208ff; *Testamenta Karleolensia*, C.W.A.S., Ex. Ser. 9, (1839), 30; TE, I, p. 51; N. Smedley, 'An Incised Stone from the Free Chapel of Ancres near Doncaster', *Y.A.J.*, 37 (1948 – 9), 505 – 7.

of Beeston in Yorkshire. Equally close contact with recluses was maintained by the FitzWilliam's relatives, the Stapletons of Bedale, Carlton and Wighill. Sir Brian Stapleton, the famous garter knight, remembered solitaries in his will in 1394, and his executor, Sir John Dependen left 3s 4d to all anchorites in the diocese.[27] Sir Brian's nephew and executor, Sir Miles Stapleton of Ingham, twenty miles from Norwich, had a daughter Emma who was enclosed at the Carmelite friary in Norwich from 1421 to 1442. The will of Sir Brian Stapleton's son does not survive, but his son's daughter-in-law, Agnes, took an interest in the eremitic life, as did her son John and daughter-in-law, Margaret Stapleton: in 1455 John Stapleton left one mark to each anchorite in the city of York, and in 1466 Margaret Stapleton remembered in her will the anchoress of Clementhorpe, where she was herself secluded, and two York anchoresses in Walmgate and Fishergate.[28]

The city of York itself was, with the patronage of local priests and merchants, an important focus for this new interest in the eremitic life. There were two active anchorite sites around 1360, and seven between 1380 and 1415, three of which, St Cuthbert's, St John's Hungate, and St Martin's chapel, were near the parish church of St Saviour's.[29] This increase in the number of cells can be attributed to the support of leading aldermen and mayors of York: between 1370 and 1440 over half the mayors of the city left bequests to anchorites, and parishioners of St Saviour's church figure prominently in this patronage, which implies a more personal involvement than the rather anonymous charity shown towards recluses in the city of London in the same period. The rector of St Saviour's from 1390 to 1433 was Adam Wigan, a scholar of Balliol, who left three legacies to anchoresses within the walls of York at All Saint's church North Street, Fishergate, and Walmgate, and three to anchoresses in the diocese at Thorganby south east of the city, Pontefract and Beeston.[30] Wigan appears to have influenced leading York merchants who were connected with his parish. In 1434 Thomas Bracebrigg, a parishioner of St Saviour's, made bequests to the same three York anchoresses who were patronized by Wigan and to the Thorganby recluse, who inhabited a cell supported by Henry Lord Scrope of Masham.[31] In 1458 Richard Wartere, who bequeathed £20 for the rebuilding of St Saviour's church tower and roof, left money to three York anchoresses, including two patronized by Wigan and Bracebrigg, and to the Thurganby anchoress.[32] Richard Russel, a parishioner of the

27 Prob. Reg. 3, fo. 88.
28 Prob. Reg. 4, fo. 116; TE, II, p. 270.
29 Warren, *Anchorites*, p. 242.
30 B.I.H.R. Prob. Reg. 3, fo. 363; TE, II, pp. 25 – 6.
31 Prob. Reg. 3, fo. 487.
32 Prob. Reg. 4, fo. 115; CRP, 1408 – 13, p. 187.

nearby church of St John's Hungate, who left 100s to St Saviour's churchwardens and gifts to the poor of that parish, left large grants to anchoresses at Walmgate, All Saints North Street, and St Helen's Fishergate;[33] and John Bolton, besides making general bequests to anchorites in the city, asked to be buried at St Saviour's.[34]

Another indication of an increasingly informed and personal interest in solitaries among the nobility is the presence in the diocese of recluses who were establishing considerable reputations and attracting a number of important patrons. These included Robert of Beverley, who was supported by Stephen and Henry Lord Scrope of Masham, and Robert Manfield a canon of Beverley;[35] John, the hermit who inhabited the hermitage founded by John of Gaunt at the site of Thomas of Lancaster's execution and who was also supported by Henry Lord Scrope;[36] Elizabeth Hotham, an anchoress whose benefactors included Richard Plumpton and Matilda Mauley, daughter of Ralph Neville Earl of Westmoreland; and Joan de Ayleston, the anchoress who was established at Nottingham by Anne of Bohemia with Richard II's knowledge and consent.[37] The personal contact between recluses and their benefactors that such patronage brought can be seen in the interest shown by the Scropes of Masham, especially Henry Lord Scrope, in individual solitaries throughout the diocese. There was no equivalent development in any other region until the influence of the Scropes and FitzHugh was felt in court circles. Although there were considerable numbers of recluses in the city of Norwich and in the country of Norfolk after 1400 there is no evidence that the nobility of Norfolk showed any particular interest in them. Sir John Fastolf, who patronized alms houses, parish churches and friaries in Norwich, left no bequests to recluses.[38] The Pastons, whose estates were situated 20 miles north of the city of Norwich, were by origin a legal family like the Scropes; they held a similar status in the country to such families as Stapleton and Dependen in the East Riding. But the Pastons showed no interest in solitaries, apart from Margaret Paston who left 3s 4d to recluses at the friars' preachers and the White Friars of Norwich in 1482.[39]

An equally distinctive feature of the nobility's interest in recluses was their activity as founders and supporters of the new Carthusian monasteries. The Carthusians were committed to an institutional

33 Prob. Reg. 3, fo. 439; TE, II, pp. 52 – 7.
34 Prob. Reg. 2, fo. 107.
35 *Foedera*, ix, 275; TE, II, pp. 31 – 7.
36 Clay, *Anchorites*, p. 70; *Foedera*, ix, 275.
37 *The Plumpton Correspondence*, ed. T. Stapleton (Camden Soc. 1834), pp. xxiii – xxxiv.
38 For Fastolf's will see *Paston Letters*, ed. J. Gardner, (1904, Repr. Gloucester, 1983), iii, pp. 160 – 64.
39 *Paston Letters*, v, p. 322; for recent account of the Pastons and their religion see Richmond, 'Religion and the fifteenth century gentleman', pp. 193 – 207.

following of the cenobitic life and the monks lived as anchorites in separate cells, maintaining vows of silence. The original charterhouses of Witham and Hinton had been established in 1178 and 1225 in remote West Country districts; but the seven houses founded by courtiers, including north-countrymen, between 1343 and 1415, were built in the more populous east; and four of them were in the north. These communities of recluses represented another aspect of the increase in the incidence of the solitary life in the late fourteenth and early fifteenth centuries.

In 1343 Nicholas Cantilupe, one of Edward III's captains, built a charterhouse in a private park at Beauvale near Thurgarton. The king granted the house an annual tun of wine, and his daughter, Isabella, granted her ''beloved very dear in Christ'' an annual pension of 100s.[40] In 1370 John of Gaunt gave his manor of Etwell, worth £12 yearly, to help maintain the monastery.[41] The monks of Beauvale also had the continued support of a local gentry family. In 1362 William Aldeburgh of Nottinghamshire declared his special affection for the piety of the prior and his monks and made over to them land near Sherwood forest, which adjoined the grounds of the priory, to supplement what he considered to be a modest endowment.[42] In 1393 Aldeburgh's daughter, Elizabeth Stapleton, wife of Sir Brian the younger, became the benefactress of the abbey. With her sister, Sybil Ryther, and brother-in-law, Sir William Ryther, she alienated two manors for the house.[43] The Hull merchant family of de-la-Pole were responsible for establishing an urban charterhouse immediately outside the north gate of Kingston-on-Hull. William de-la-Pole gave seventy acres of land and £20 in yearly rent for the establishment of a hospital; and in 1377 Michael de-la-Pole, who was to become Earl of Suffolk and Chancellor, converted his brother's proposed hospital and nunnery into a joint foundation, a charterhouse and hospital, which were to be separately administered.[44] In the foundation charter he declared his spiritual affection for the very devout religion of the Carthusian order and his belief that the Carthusian monks would serve God more diligently than nuns. The north-countrymen connected with the foundation charter were the founder's brother-in-law Richard Scrope of Bolton, Walter Fauconbergh, Richard Ferriby and Robert Selby.[45] Although Michael de-la-Pole

40 E. M. Thompson, *The Carthusian Order in England* (London, 1930), p. 158.
41 ibid, pp. 161 – 2.
42 ibid, pp. 159 – 60.
43 CPR, 1391 – 96, 308.
44 Sir William Dugdale, *Monasticon Anglicanum*, ed. J. Caley, H. Ellis and B. Bandinel (1817 – 30, vi), p. 26; White, *Peerage*, p. 458; M. R. Clay, *Medieval Hospitals*, p. 80. William de la Pole purchased the advowson for the hospital from Richard Lord Scrope.
45 *Monasticon*, vi, 182; Thompson, *Carthusian Order*, pp. 200 – 1.

was buried in the church of Hull Charterhouse his impeachment for treason in 1386 meant that the monastery was not able to benefit in full from his endowment. His son Michael, restored to his father's honours in 1397, alienated lands and goods to the yearly value of 38s 4d to the monastery.[46] John Waltham and three local parish priests alienated a parish church to the charterhouse with the support of Richard II; and in 1402 Richard Lord Scrope of Bolton and Edmund de-la-Pole alienated land worth £20 a year to St Michael's charterhouse.[47] Throughout the fifteenth century members of the de-la-Pole family continued to support the monastery and chose to be buried there.[48] St Michael's also enjoyed the support of the Yorkshire nobility in the first half of the fifteenth century. In 1404 Marmaduke Constable, the lord of Flamborough in the East Riding, left £20 to the brothers of Hull.[49] In 1437 John Dautre left a silver plate bearing the name 'Jesu' to the brothers; and Sir Thomas Cumberworth left his best gilt chalice and 100s to the monks in 1450.[50]

The most influential of all these charterhouses of the north-east was founded in 1398 on the manor of the Ingilby family in the Cleveland hills. The founder of Mount Grace priory, Thomas Holland, Duke of Surrey, possessed considerable estates in Yorkshire in Kirkby Moorside and Cottingham; and he was a father-in-law of Henry Lord Scrope of Masham. In his foundation charter Holland stated that although from a very early age he believed that all orders of the holy church were good and devout, yet by God's inspiration he bore a special devotion and most peculiar affection for the holy order of Carthusians; he furthermore entertained a great admiration for their holy observances and for persons living in that order, whose number by God's grace he hoped to increase.[51] In 1400 the Duke of Surrey was beheaded for his part in an uprising against Henry IV, and in 1412 his body was conveyed from the manor of Bordelby to its final resting place in Mount Grace. Another opponent of Bolingbroke, Archbishop Richard Scrope, probably financed the building of one of the cells because his arms are still to be found over the doorway of the first cell. The arms of Sir William Gascoigne, the chief justice, are above the doorway of the second cell. In 1417 Thomas Duke of Exeter, brother of Joan Beaufort, built five new cells at Mount Grace.[52] The Ingilby family, on whose manor the priory

46 Thompson, *Carthusian Order*, p. 203.
47 CPR, 1401 – 5, p. 111. John Lord Neville endowed prayers at Hull; see *Wills and Inv.* p. 40.
48 TE, I, p. 372; TE, VI, pp. 76, 179.
49 TE, I, p. 98.
50 TE, II, p. 233; *The Academy*, v, p. 230 – 2.
51 ibid, p. 229; *Monasticon*, vi, 23.
52 H. V. Le Bas, 'The Founding of the Carthusian Order', in W. A. Brown, 'A History of Mount Grace', *Y.A.J.*, xviii (1904 – 5), 257; W. H. St John Hope, 'The Architectural History of Mount Grace', in Brown, 'A History of Mount Grace', 308.

was built, were probably joint founders; the names of John and Thomas Ingilby and their wives occur in the foundation charter, and in 1438 Sir William Ingilby died in possession of the advowson of Mount Grace priory where his widow Joan, daughter of Sir Brian Stapleton, was buried.[53] The monks of Mount Grace also had the support of the local nobility of the North Riding. Sir John Dependen left £6 13s 4d to the house, 10 marks for the repair of a cell, and a tablet and crucifix to the prior. In 1414 Sir Henry Vavascour left 20 marks to the prior and convent, and his widow in the same year left 10 marks to Nicholas Love.[54]

The last of the new charterhouses was the royal foundation of Sheen, which was established by Henry V in 1415 on the south bank of the Thames. It is reasonable to assume that those who advised the king on this new foundation were those north-countrymen who were so actively interested in the eremitic life, especially Henry Lord Scrope and Henry Lord Fitzhugh of Tanfield, who were Henry V's closest advisors at the time. Henry Lord Scrope was probably associated with Mount Grace in some way through his wife Joan, Duchess of York, the daughter of Thomas Holland. Scrope's enthusiasm for the Carthusian order is shown by his bequest in 1415 of £5 to each of seven charterhouses in England.[55] This Carthusian revival occurred in a period between 1343 and 1415 when numbers in the old Cistercian and Benedictine monasteries, founded in the twelfth century, were declining, and when there were no new foundations of canons or friars' houses. The piety of the foundation documents of the new charterhouses and the generosity of patronage suggests that the Carthusians represented for some a revival of the old contemplative ideals of the monastic orders. The large Benedictine and Cistercian monasteries, relatively neglected by testators in this period, had become in their prosperity and adminstrative complexity what Reginald Pecock termed microcosms of society.[56] But the Carthusian monks were regarded as contemplatives and solitaries. The York merchant Richard Russel, a benefactor of solitaries, left bequests in 1431 to the 'monk recluses' of St Michael's at Kingston-on-Hull and Mount Grace.[57] This view of the Carthusians was summed up by the prior of Mount Grace, Richard Methley, towards the end of the fifteenth century when, in an annotation to *The Cloud of Unknowing*, he described the Carthusian monks as the modern hermits.[58]

53 Thompson, p. 231.
54 Prob. Reg. 3, fo. 88 – 9v; TE, I, p. 361.
55 *Foedera*, ix, pp. 272 – 8.
56 Pecock, *Reule of Crysten Religioun*, ed. W. G. Skeat (London, EETS. 1927), p. 416.
57 Prob. Reg. 3, for 439.
58 Ms. Pembroke Coll. Camb. 221, fo. 4v; *The Chastizing of God's Children*, ed. J. Bazire and F. Colledge (Oxford, 1957), p. 56.

A new religious order that had affinities with the Carthusians was the Brigittine Order, established by St Bridget in Sweden in 1371 to enable men and women to pursue a contemplative and eremitical life. Many of the first novices were anchoresses who were granted dispensation to leave their cells to join the order. The only Brigittine house in England was Syon, which was founded through the efforts made between 1406 and 1415 of a circle of north-countrymen who had influence over the king. They included Henry Lord Fitzhugh of Tanfield, the king's chamberlain, who visited Vadstena in 1406 with Sir Halneth Mauleverer and enfeoffed lands in Cambridgeshire for the establishment of a Brigittine house that was originally intended to occupy the site of the ruined hospital of St Nicholas in York.[59] Other enfeoffees included FitzHugh's neighbour and brother-in-law, the treasurer, Henry Lord Scrope of Masham, who was also a friend and neighbour of Sir Halneth Mauleverer; Thomas Fishbourne, a chaplain of Henry V, who was described by Thomas Gascoigne as a devout Yorkshire squire and was probably a member of the Fishbourne family of Richmondshire — one of whom, Matilda, was the recipient of a bequest for prayers in Lord Scrope's will — and Thomas Langley, the bishop of Durham and keeper of the privy seal, who was also benefactor in Scrope's will.[60] FitzHugh supported some Swedish monks of the Brigittine order and continued to correspond with Vadstena until Henry V founded Syon in March 1415 on the northern banks of the Thames opposite its twin foundation of Sheen.[61]

This patronage establishes that recluses were becoming an important part of rural and urban communities within the diocese of York. Legislation in the thirteenth century restricting the size of the anchorites window and forbidding them to hear confessions or to use their cells to store vestments and valuables indicates that despite strict rules of enclosure, anchorites had considerable contact with local communities. This was certainly the case by the late fourteenth century. Emma Sherman, an anchoress enclosed for many years in a cell in Doncaster, enjoyed the use of a little garden and was allowed to transfer from this place in 1404 on account of the clamouring of the people there, and to move to another cell with a garden which she was allowed to leave annually, without episcopal licence, in order to visit churches or other pious places for the purpose of obtaining indulgences.[62] Such social

59 J. H. Wylie, *The Reign of Henry the Fifth* (Cambridge, 1914), i, 221.

60 For a summary of the foundation of Syon see: *The Incendium Amoris of Richard Rolle*, ed. and Introduced by M. Deanesly (Manchester, 1915), pp. 91 – 141; D. Knowles, *The Religious Orders in England* (Cambridge, 4th edn; 1979), ii, pp. 180 – 84; CRP, 1416 – 22, pp. 34 – 5.

61 For an account of this correspondence see M. B. Tait, 'The Brigittine Monastery of Syon', (Oxford D.Phil. thesis 1975).

62 Clay, *Anchorites*, p. 140; CPL, 1396 – 1404, p. 477.

contact allowed recluses to continue to perform the same practical duties that have been attributed to twelfth century solitaries.[63] John of Gaunt gave twenty-six oak trees to John, the hermit of Singleton in West Lancashire to enable him to construct a bridge as quickly as possible near the town of Lancaster;[64] and he also sent oak trees to the recluse of Snayth near Doncaster for work in his park at Crydelyng.[65] Hermits at Skipwith and Stainforth collected money for the repairing of roads, and many served as turnpike men and bridge wardens.[66] Those whose cells were attached to the chancel of the parish church or who acted as chantry priests, like Thomas Coke, priest and anchorite in the chantry chapel of Kexby, would have looked after the parish church at night. Some may have continued to perform pastoral duties in the parish church, but these were being eroded in the fourteenth century as the educational standards of the parish priest rose.[67]

Such involvement in parish life meant that recluses, like chantry priests, nuns and friars, the other main beneficiaries of noble patronage in this period, were expected to involve themselves in the conventions of familial religion by providing intercession for their benefactors. The Lancastrians especially relied on the prayers of hermits and anchorites: Henry Grosmont, the first duke of Lancaster, requested prayers and masses for his soul from the recluses of St Helen's Pontefract and Whalley;[68] and John of Gaunt required prayers for his soul and the souls of his ancestors from Richard Goldburn, the recluse of St Martin's chapel in Chatterburn.[69] Henry V used the intercessions of recluses to strengthen his disputable claim to the throne: the houses of Syon and Sheen served as great prayer houses for the Lancastrian dynasty, and the monks of Sheen and London Charterhouse and the recluse of Westminster were asked to pray for the king's success in battle. Two Lancastrian servants, William Lord Roos, privy councillor of Henry IV and Henry V, and Henry Lord Scrope of Masham, chamberlain of Henry V, both left substantial legacies for the prayers of anchoresses and anchorites (Lord Scrope left 6s 8d to each anchoress and anchorite, apart from those mentioned in his will, who would pray for his soul within six weeks of his death).[70] The high values placed on the intercessions of Carthusian monks did much to break down the strict isolation of the order. The foundation charters of all these monasteries

63 H. Mayr-Harting, 'Functions of a Twelfth Century Recluse', *History* (1975).
64 *John of Gaunt's Register 1372 – 76*, ii, p. 949.
65 ibid, ii, p. 512.
66 Clay, *Anchorites*, p. 60.
67 See Chapter Three.
68 CPR, 1558 – 61, p. 246.
69 *John of Gaunt's Register*, i, p. 437.
70 *Foedera*, ix, 272 – 80.

recorded the monk's obligation to commemorate their founders and patrons in their services: the Carthusians of Mount Grace were obliged to perform masses for the prosperity of leading courtiers including the de-la-Pole family, Alexander Neville, the archbishop of York, Richard Lord Scrope of Bolton, John Lord Neville of Raby, and the mayor of Kingston, Richard Ferriby.[71] Benefactors of the Carthusians also stipulated that they wished to be remembered in the monks' services, although this was against the custom of the order. When William Aldeburgh alienated land to Beauvale in 1362 he asked that he and his wife and family share a part in all masses, canonical hours, prayers, vigils, fasts, abstinences, alms and other spiritual exercises performed in the priory.[72] The Carthusians, who did not have the estates of the older orders, had to oblige. When Aldeburgh's daughter, Elizabeth Stapleton, alienated land to Beauvale she stated that all the services requested by the founders were to be continued along with anniversary masses commemorating the deaths of her parents. The prior agreed, in consideration of the great sums which Sir William Aldeburgh, Sybil Ryther and Elizabeth Stapleton had provided to relieve the difficulties of the house.[73]

Such demand for the intercessions of recluses does not mean that they were regarded in the same light as parish and chantry priests; rather it indicates that there was a widespread admiration for their holiness. This can be observed in the foundation charters of the Carthusian monasteries, and even in the writings of John Wyclif: Wyclif compared recluses to the ten just men of Sodom who by their superior virtue assuaged the wrath of God, and he explained that this was the reason that their prayers and offices were sought after.[74] However, the close personal interest shown in solitaries by such pious men as Henry Duke of Lancaster and Henry Lord Scrope suggests that there was more to the patronage of recluses than passive admiration of holiness. The prestige of some individual recluses, the significance of particular anchorages at Doncaster, Richmond, and St Saviour's, and the interest in particular recluses shared by circles of friends and relatives such as the Scropes of Masham, the Stapletons, Willoughbys and the parishioners of St Saviour's, indicates that solitaries were beginning to occupy an intimate and important place in people's lives. It is therefore necessary to look more closely at the social and spiritual functions that recluses performed for their patrons. The career of Richard Rolle of Hampole was of fundamental inportance in elevating the status of the recluse as

71 Le Bas, 'The Founding of Mount Grace', 256 – 8.
72 Thompson, *The Carthusian Order*, pp. 160 – 61.
73 CPR, 1391 – 96, p. 308.
74 Wyclif, *De Civili Domino*, ed. J. Loserth (W.S.), i, pp. 170 – 77.

someone who was consulted on spiritual matters by laymen, and who therefore initiated changes in religious sensibility by influencing the development of lay participation in the contemplative life.

The Spiritual and Social Significance of the Eremitic Movement

In order to understand the influence that Rolle and recluses following him had on the development of religious sensibility in the period between 1350 and 1450, it is necessary to trace eremiticism to the late eleventh century, when significant numbers of men dedicated themselves to the desert ideal of controlling their physical and social needs in an attempt to free their spirits and encounter God. In so doing they developed the concept of a contemplative life of detachment from social ties, and made innovations in traditional communal forms of worship. The eremitic movement of the fourteenth century was in some ways a culmination of this movement, although it differed from it in the important respect that recluses in the fourteenth and fifteenth centuries were influential members of lay society who communicated to their patrons their experiences of the contemplative life, and who suggested ways that laymen could aspire towards these same experiences.

In the late eleventh and early twelfth century a new and assertive body of hermits established themselves in Italy, France and north-east England. Increasing numbers of laymen, secular clergy and monks adopted an eremitic life very different from the one practised by earlier hermits, who had believed that a holy life could only be lived outside human society. These new hermits aspired to a simple life of prayer, the personal contemplation of God, charity and manual work; in their zeal they showed an interest in the spiritual and moral welfare of society; they were active as preachers and stressed private sins and their expiation rather than monastic prayer for the corporate sins of the world. Such men strove for spiritual detachment rather than withdrawal into a desert.[1] Most of these hermits eventually formed their own religious communities, comprised of ordained hermits, who become monks, and lay hermits, who became *conversi*. It has been shown that Cistercian, Carthusian and Augustinian houses were founded in this period through the direct or indirect inspiration of hermits who were opposed to simony, and over-elaborate liturgy, possessions, and property, and who were interested in reforming the monastic orders and returning them to the simplicity of the rule of Benedict or that attributed to Augustine.[2] In the north-east of

1 Henrietta Leyser, *Hermits and the New Monasticism* (London, 1984), pp. 18 – 28.
2 ibid, pp. 38 – 68.

England in this period hermits, inspired by Bede's account of the lives of the Northumbrian monks, established eremitical communities at the great Anglo-Saxon shrines, including Durham. Hermits formed the community of canons regular at Nostell in Yorkshire in 1120, and monks who left St Mary's abbey in York because it was too lax established the Cistercian community of Fountains.[3]

These hermit communities initiated important changes in religious sensibility: the Cistercians encouraged the development of a more personal religion based on a respect for the humanity of Christ. One of their most influential spokesmen was Aelred of Rievaulx, the son of a hereditary priest of Hexham. His decision to leave this position as steward of the Scottish court to become a monk of Rievalux was described by St Bernard as a passage from the kitchen to the hermitage.[4] Aelred wrote a number of religious works expressing the Cistercians' belief that it was necessary to renounce one's place in a competitive society to discover the basic human values of friendship and self-understanding, and to attain the realization that God could be found in human relationships.[5] This was achieved by a compassionate participation in Christ's suffering; Cistercian authors in the north-east continued to write on these themes: Stephen Easton, a monk of Sawley abbey in the West Riding, wrote before his death in 1252 the *Mirror For Novices*, which provided instructions for daily meditations on the physical details of Our Lord's Nativity and life and their spiritual significance.[6] Although Cistercians were no longer such active leaders of religious movements by the fourteenth century, they continued to maintain the traditions of Cistercian spirituality. The monks of Rievaulx treasured Aelred's *Oratio Pastoralis*, an autobiographical reflection written near his death, and there were some Cistercian spiritual writers in this period.[7] The most important of them was William Rymyngton, who was born in the village of Rymyngton in Yorkshire, and who spent nearly all his life in the small Cistercian abbey of Sawley in Craven, West Yorkshire, where he was prior in 1380. Rymyngton, chancellor of Oxford in 1372, wrote a dialogue against the followers of Wyclif and a series of meditations on divine love known as the *Stimulus Peccatoris*.[8] The *Stimulus*, which was originally written for an anchorite monk and made up *ex sentenciis beati*

3 ibid, p. 37.
4 *The Life of Ailred of Rievaulx by Walter Daniel*, ed. F. M. Powicke, London (1950), p. 7.
5 See C. Morris, *The Discovery of the Individual* (London, 1972), pp. 64 – 120. For a discussion of Aelred's *Oratio Pastoralis* see Dom. Wilmart, *Auteurs Spirituels et Texts devots du moyen age Latin* (Paris, 1932), p. 287.
6 *John Hoveden, Poems*, ed. F. Raby (SS. 1939), p. xxiii; D. H. Farmer, 'Stephen of Sawley', *The Month* (1963), 332 – 42.
7 Wilmart, p. 287; Raby, p. xxiii.
8 A. B. Emden, *A Biographical Register of the University of Oxford* (Oxford, 1953), 111, p. 1617.

Augustini beati et venerabilis Anselmi, achieved some popularity: there are fourteen extant manuscripts; one text was taken back to France in 1440 by Charles of Orléans, who may have first read the work at Pontefract where he was imprisoned; and the *Stimulus* was included in the Syon library catalogue.[9] Rymyngton reached a wider audience through preaching: a chancellor of Oxford, he preached two sermons to the synod of York clergy in 1372, which included emotive provocations of the sufferings of Christ; the manuscript of these sermons was copied in the neighbouring abbey of Whalley, along with the works of Bernard and Aelred of Rievaulx.[10] Another Cistercian to attempt to teach the laity about the sufferings of Christ was a monk of Sawley abbey, who translated Grosseteste's *Chasteau d'Amor* 'only for lewed men's sake' and called it *The Myrour of lewed Men:* the translator added to this work his own affective meditations of the Passion of Christ and Mary.[11]

Towards the end of the thirteenth century there was initial eremitic enthusiasm among the Franciscans. By the beginning of the fourteenth century two Franciscan works, the *Stimulus Amoris* of James of Milan and the *Meditationes de Vitae Christi* — mistakenly attributed to Bonaventura and probably written by John de Caulibus in Tuscany — arrived in the north of England, and their circulation was widespread. The *Stimulus Amoris* survives in complete form in 222 manuscripts and the *Meditations* in an even greater number. The rhapsodical prose of these works was patterned to move the reader's feelings of compassion towards Christ's suffering. They had considerable influence on the affective sermons delivered by the fairs of all orders: in the library catalogue of the Augustinian friars compiled in 1372, there were four copies of the *Meditations.*[12] Although the Cistercians and Franciscans were most exclusively associated with the eremitic life in the twelfth and thirteenth centuries, there were recluses and contemplative writers who resisted the pull of religious communities. Robert Flower, a York merchant's son, lived in a cell near Knaresborough until his death in 1218, where he was visited by King Henry III; and in the thirteenth century Peter the hermit of Wakefield achieved a national reputation as a holy man and prophet.[13] One religious writer of the thirteenth century who absorbed Franciscan and Cistercian influences without joining a monastic community was John Hoveden. Hoveden was born in Howden in the East Riding, and after a period at Oxford he secured a

9 J. McNulty, 'William of Rymyngton, prior of Sawley', *Y.A.J.*, xxx (1931), 231ff.

10 G. R. Owst, *Literature and Pulpit in Medieval England* (Cambridge, 1933), pp. 272 – 77.

11 M. Deanesly, *The Lollard Bible* (Cambridge, 1920), p. 637. For edition see *Myror of Lewed Men*, ed. C. Horstmann (London, EETS, 1892), p. 407ff.

12 A. I. Doyle, 'A Survey of the Origins and Circulation of Theological Writings in English', (Cambridge Univ. Ph.D. thesis, 1956), I, pp. 207 – 11; M. Deanesly, 'The Gospel Harmony of John de Calibus', *Collect. Francisc.*, B.S.F.S. ii, 10 – 79.

13 Clay, *Anchorites*, p. 46.

post as clerk in the household of Queen Eleanor, the wife of Henry III.[14] He was the author of a Latin poem, *Philomena*, and a series of ecstatic meditations on the Passions of Christ and Mary.[15] His influence continued into the fourteenth century: the canons of Howden venerated him as a saint and John Wyclif described him as *Sanctus et devotus*.[16] The *Philomena* was translated into English at the end of the fourteenth century and a Franciscan, Walter Wilburn, referred to him as his hymn to the Virgin.[17] A north-countryman who followed the traditions of the Northumberland hermits was the monk solitary of Farne, a Benedictine monk of Durham who left Durham college, Oxford, at the beginning of the first decade of the fourteenth century to retire to the island of Farne off the Northumberland coast, the home of such notable hermits as St Cuthbert and Bartholemew of Farne. During the Black Death of 1349 he wrote a series of meditations on Christ's Passion containing autobiographical descriptions of his own religious experiences.[18]

The diocese of York, therefore, had long been a centre of eremitic movements, the most important of which were those of the late eleventh and early twelfth centuries. Many of these eremitic traditions were maintained until the fourteenth century among Cistercian monks, and individual solitaries. But although the Carthusians and solitaries of the fourteenth and fifteenth centuries depended on some of these traditions, they departed from them in important respects. Neither the Cistercians and canons of the twelfth century nor the friars of the thirteenth century were able to sustain all their eremitic ideals: as religious houses founded in the twelfth century grew in size and administrative complexity they came closer to the traditional forms of monasticism that the hermit monks had been trying to avoid; and as the friars, who enjoyed a wider popularity than the Cistercians in the fouteenth century, were acquiring more possessions, they were losing their status as an eremitic order.[19] The recluses of the fourteenth and fifteenth centuries never compromised their eremitic ideals in this way: some joined the Carthusians, who remained commited to an austere ascetic life until the dissolution of the monasteries; others chose to remain attached to their religious communities and attempted to reform them to the supposed original purity existing at the time of their foundation in the eleventh century;

14 Emden, *B.R.U.O.*, ii, pp. 974 – 5; *Hoveden Poems*, ed. Raby, p. xxiii ff.

15 *Philomena*, ed. C. Blume (Hymnologische Beiträge, Leipzig, iv, 1930).

16 J. Wyclif, *De Ecclesia* (Wyclif Soc.), p. 101; Emden, *B.R.U.O.*, ii, pp. 974.

17 F.J.E. Raby, 'A Middle English Paraphrase of John Hoveden's *Philomena*', *M.L.R.*; 30 (1935), 339 – 42; For text see *Meditations on the life and Passion of Christ*, ed. L. D. Evelyn (London, E.E.T.S. 1921).

18 W. A. Pantin, 'The monk solitary of Farne', *E.H.R.*, LIX, (1944), 162 – 86.

19 Leyser, *Hermits*, pp. 97 – 105.

and others, thanks to the patronage of the local nobility, were able to live apart from monastic orders. Neither the Cistercians nor the Franciscans provided practical help and guidance on the contemplative life for those ordinary men and women who may have wished to pursue meditative exercises in their spare time. Rymyngton and Waldeby were notable fourteenth century preachers, but none of their sermons and meditations were translated into the vernacular; and the friars remained aloof from the contemplative movement in the fourteenth century: in the huge library of the Austin friars of York there were no works of those recluses and religious writers of the north-east whose main priority was to teach the principles of the contemplative life to their patrons.[20] The man who initiated these important developments was Richard Rolle of Hampole.

Rolle was born around 1300 in the village of Thornton-le-Dale near Pickering, and sometime in his childhood his parents moved to Richmondshire, probably to Aiskew near Bedale. He attended Oxford, possibly as a contemporary of the Monk of Farne, and like the monk solitary he left to become a hermit. Rolle fled to his old childhood home of Thornton where he stayed in various cells before moving to Richmondshire where his parents were living. He finally settled down in a cell in the cemetery of the Cistercian nunnery of Hampole where he died in 1349, probably from the plague.[21] Rolle was influenced by the eremitic traditions of the north-east. He may have had contact as a child with the Cistercian abbey of Rievaulx in the East Riding, and he later translated Aelred of Rievaulx's *Rule for Recluses,* probably for the various Cistercian nuns for whom he was acting as a councellor at Yedingham and Hampole.[22] Like the twelfth century hermits of the diocese and the monk solitary of Farne he was influenced by Bede's accounts of the life of Cuthbert: he once described the eremitical life as one that followed the traditions of John the Baptist and Cuthbert.[23] He also referred to and was influenced by John of Hoveden's *Philomena*.[24] But Rolle was also very unconventional, and by projecting his own personality he inspired a circle of followers and lay patrons who were responsible for creating a widespread interest in Rolle's life and teachings.

20 Hackett, pp. 421 – 92; Morrin, *John Waldeby*, p. 14ff.

21 For full account of Rolle's life see H. E. Allen, *Writings Ascribed to Richard Rolle* (New York, 1927). See also C. Whiting, 'Richard Rolle of Hampole' *Y.A.J.* (1948 – 51), 3ff; Emden, *B.R.U.O.* iii, pp. 1586 – 7. See also the office of Richard Rolle compiled at Hampole c. 1380 – 83 in *The York Breviary, (Brev Ebor)*, (SS, 75, 1882), II, Appendix.

22 Allen, *Writings*, pp. 324 – 35.

23 *Brev. Ebor.*

24 Allen, *Writings*, p. 420.

The key to this hermit's individuality and popularity was probably the unique emphasis he placed on his own experiences, especially in the Latin autobiographies, *Contra Amatores Mundi* (surviving in seven complete copies), *Incendium Amoris* (which survives in forty-two complete manuscripts and six fragments, and in three copies of an English translation) and *Melos Amoris* (of which there are ten complete and three fragmentary manuscripts).[25] Rolle's last and most popular Latin treatise was *Emendatio Vitae,* which survives in ninety-five manuscripts and sixteen English texts, representing seven separate translations.[26] Rolle applied Hoveden's terms *calor, canor* and *dulcedo* to his own ecstatic descriptions of the warmth, songs and sweetness of God's love. These simple accounts of a supernatural and physical understanding of divine love would have been easily comprehended by Rolle's humble neighbours in Yorkshire, and he used them to exalt himself as a holy man in their eyes by repeatedly claiming that such experiences were a foretaste of heavenly bliss. He found his disciplines in the Yorkshire nunneries among the younger daughters of gentry families; for them he wrote English letters of spiritual advice on beginning the contemplative life. About 1343, he wrote *Ego Dormio* for a lady of Yedingham in which he advised her to become a nun, and the *Commandment* for a nun of Hampole. Rolle's closest disciple was Margaret Kirkby, a Richmondshire recluse who was probably originally from Kirkby Ravensworth.[27] In 1340 Rolle, who lived twelve miles from her cell in East Layton or Ainderby, translated the psalms into English for her, providing commentaries that contained his mystical responses to them.[28] When he moved to Hampole he continued to visit her, and near the end of his life he wrote for her the most advanced of his English works of spiritual counsel, the *Form of Living.*[29] In these works Rolle was pioneering a change in the conception of the anchoress's vocation. The guides for recluses of the twelfth and thirteenth century, including Aelred's *Rule for Recluses* and the *Ancren Riwle,* emphasized the penitential process of reliving Christ's agony by chastizing the body, and they provided strict rules to free the recluse from an emotional dependence on human society.[30] Such ascetic disciplines were intended to start recluses on the process of self-perfection; but the ascetic

25 M. Sargent, 'Contemporary Criticism of Richard Rolle', *Analecta Cartusiana,* 55, (1981), 197.

26 M. G. Amossian, 'The Rolle Material in Bradfer-Lawrence MS 10 and its Relationship to other Rolle Manuscripts' *Manuscripta,* 23 (1979), 67 – 78.

27 ibid, pp. 246 – 56.

28 ibid, p. 174; Oxford Bodl. lib. MS. Laud. Misc. 286.

29 ibid, pp. 256 – 68.

30 Warren, *Anchorites;* C. H. Talbot, Godric of Finchdale and Christina of Markyate', *The Month* (1963), 26 – 31.

emphasis was such that the achievement of mystic communion with God was only mentioned in passing. In the epistles of Rolle and his followers, the recluse is seen as a contemplative as well as an ascetic, for whom the purgative process was only a beginning, and for whom a union with God is envisaged and expressed in explicit, joyful terms. This contemplative conception of the eremitic life was beginning to be shared by the archbishop of York and his officials who were responsible for enclosing recluses; and it was also the aspiration of the anchoresses who were advised by Rolle. This can be established from the changes in the language of the episcopal registers of the diocese where the enclosure of recluses is recorded. In the registers of the archbishops of York in the late thirteenth century the emphasis is on the seclusion of the anchorite and their serving God with a penitential, humble and chaste life.[31] In 1320 the conception of enclosure was still ascetic: a nun petitioned Archbishop Melton to be enclosed so that she could serve God more strictly by leading a solitary life.[32] It can be no coincidence that contemplative language was beginning to be used in 1357, within a few years of Rolle's death, and in connection with the enclosure of his disciple Margaret Kirkby. Margaret secured from Archbishop John Thoresby the unusual concession of being allowed to leave her cell in East Layton to move to another cell in Ainderby so that she could observe the celebration of mass in the parish church. The archbishop's register notes the confirmation of her petition saying she greatly desired the anchorite life in order that she might fashion herself as a servant of God more freely and more quietly with pious prayers and vigils.[33] This is a gentler more celebratory tone with the emphasis on quiet seclusion and prayer; and by the end of the fourteenth century the phrase 'contemplation' was being widely used in registers, such as Bishop Repingdon's of Lincoln, to record the enclosure of recluses.[34]

Rolle's influence after his death in 1349 extended further than the anchoresses he had advised. He was held in affectionate regard by the nuns of Hampole and their neighbours, thanks to the efforts of Margaret Kirkby, who moved to the priory, probably between 1381 and 1383, to be near the body of her master who was buried in Hampole cemetery. Margaret spent the last ten years of her life here, and between 1381 and

31 Warren, *Anchorites*, p. 117; see *Register of Wickwane, 1279 – 80*; ed. W. N. Brown (SS, 114, 1907), p. 74; *Register of John le Romeyn and Henry of Newark 1286 – 99* (SS, 123, 128, 1913 – 17), i, pp. 126, 196.

32 *V.C.H. Yorkshire*, 3, 113.

33 B.I.H.R., Reg. Thoresby, fo. 287; Allen, *Writings*, p. 502.

34 J. Nichols, *History and Antiquities of County Leicestershire*, (London, 1795 – 1815), vol. 1, part 2, p. 65.

1383 a biographical office of the hermit was written with the help of reminiscences of Margaret and some of the older nuns.[35] Pilgrims to Rolle's shrine recorded a series of miracles which the nuns included in their office. The affectionate regard with which the hermit was held among the Hampole nuns and their neighbours is a testimony to the influence of this charismatic personality in elevating the status of the solitary to that of a holy man.

Rolle's most significant contribution to the growth of the eremitic movement in this period was the patronage that he inspired among the Yorkshire nobility. When he ran away from Oxford and his parents to become a hermit he turned to his childhood home of Thornton le Dale, where there was a certain wildness that he loved, probably in the expectation of receiving help from his father's old friend, squire John Dalton, the constable of Pickering Castle and agent of Thomas, Earl of Lancaster. He appeared in his hermit's garb in Pickering church about 1318, praying in Lady Dalton's side-chapel, where he was recognized by her sons who had been the hermit's fellow students at Oxford. The Daltons maintained Rolle in their house, providing him with a cell in their manor, where he stayed, probably from 1318 to 1322, giving guidance to Lady Dalton and her friends,[36] and perhaps serving as the Daltons' family confessor; soon after 1327 he composed a manual of confession, *Judica Me Deus*, and in this work he alluded to his stay with the Daltons and his being continually disturbed during the summer harvest; the biographical office of the Hampole nuns claims that his patron and her friends interrupted his contemplation by seeking his holy counsel.[37] Rolle probably left the Daltons in the confusion surrounding the fall of Thomas

35 There are some problems in reconciling the facts in the register with the vague statements about Margaret Kirkby made in the office by the nuns of Hampole; but there is no need for such a complicated resolution as that proposed by Allen in *Writings*, pp. 502 – 11. She identifies a Margaret le Boteler, a nun of Hampole who was enclosed at E. Layton in Dec. 1348, with Margaret Kirkby. In doing so she telescopes the events described in the office involving Rolle's visits to Margaret Kirkby to the ten months between Dec. 1348 and Rolle's death in Oct. 1349. But the office states clearly that several years elapsed between Margaret's first two seizures. Allen's theory also forces her to juggle with the chronology of Rolle's writings. *The Form* was dedicated to Margaret Kirkby, recluse, and if she is to be identified with Margaret le Boteler then Rolle must have written *The Form* shortly before his death, very quickly. The vagueness of the office encourages the impression that Margaret moved to Hampole shortly after the hermit's death; but it is unlikely that the nuns could have got the facts wrong when they had Margaret's own testimony, unless they were lying to encourage the cult. It is perhaps safest to assume that Margaret Kirkby had originally been a recluse at Ainderby; and when she was enclosed there in 1357 she was simply returning to her old cell.

36 *Brev. Ebor.* Allen is incorrect when she assigns a date of 1322 for *Judica Me Deus*: *Judica B2* is Rolle's summary of Pagula's *Pars Oculi*, which was written between 1326 and 1328, probably in 1327. See J. P. Daly, 'An Edition of the Judica Me Deus of Richard Rolle' (Univ. North Carolina Phd. thesis, 1960) p. lxiii.

37 ibid; Allen, p. 463.

Earl of Lancaster and the arrest of John Dalton in 1322.[38] In a later work written in 1343 he referred to a series of four aristocratic ladies who were his patrons; and in another work he described himself as being at home with the rich and conversing with magnates and great ladies.[39] The first of these patrons was probably Lady Eleanor Percy, who intervened to have Dalton released from prison after the execution of Lancaster.[40] Another was the lady described in *Contra Amatores Mundi*, whose aspect in death so greatly disturbed him: she and her husband had supported him at Oxford, and they sustained him in a solitary cell on their estate a considerable distance from their home until the death of the husband.[41] This couple were probably Ralph Lord Neville, the second baron of Raby, and his wife Margery Thweng, because Ralph Neville's fifth son Thomas, who held preferment in York, including canonries of York and Beverley from 1332 and the archdeaconry of Durham from 1334, was Rolle's only known patron at Oxford, and Thomas was only fifteen at that time.[42] The deaths of Eleanor Percy in 1328, Ralph Neville in 1331 and Margery Thweng in 1332, probably occasioned the period of hardship described in Rolle's later writings and the local difficulties alluded to in the office. His move to Richmondshire, which he described as being for urgent and practical reasons, may have been an attempt to find secure patronage in the neighbourhood where his family was living.

The area was a centre of piety and patronage in this period: the parish churches of Masham, Well, and Kirkby Wiske were all rebuilt between 1330 and 1350.[43] Although Rolle may have maintained some contact with John Dalton, who was squire of Kirkby by 1343, his main source of

38 The Lancastrians may have been among Rolle's early patrons. Dalton was retained by Thomas Earl of Lancaster, the lord of Pickering, and Henry, the first Duke of Lancaster, a patron of hermits and author of a devotional work, was a descendant of this house.

39 Allen, *Writings*, pp. 121 – 22, 227, 246.

40 ibid, p. 459.

41 ibid, p. 465. See also E. J. Arnould, 'Richard Rolle's patrons: a new reading', *Medium Aevum*, 6 (1937), 122 – 24. Rolle, while he was dwelling in a solitary cell, was so upset after witnessing the death of a great lady who was his acquaintance that for a long time he was plagued by fear and despondency. This was not Lady Percy. In two manuscripts of the *Contra Amatores Mundi* the sentence ends: *quod quendam matrona suo, per annos nonullos sustentaverat ad scolos*. The lady and her husband were therefore Rolle's patrons at Oxford. Arnould thinks they were John Dalton and his wife; but if so why would Rolle — who was running away from Oxford and his parents — go to his Oxford patrons, who in fact failed to recognize him. Rolle's cell was also in the Dalton's house and the cell described in *Contra Amatores* was distant.

42 One of Ralph Neville's sons was imprisoned in 1332 as a supporter of Thomas Earl of Lancaster. For Thomas Neville's career see Emden, *B.R.U.O.* ii, p. 1351. For the Thweng family see G. H. White, *The Complete Peerage* (London, 1953), XII, part I, 641. For further details of Margery Neville, whose dower house was the manor of Faceby in Cleveland, see W. M. L'Anson, 'Kilton Castle', *YAJ*, xxii, (1912 – 13), 75 – 96; and Whittaker, *Hist. Yorks*, ii, 82. Margery Neville died in 1331, the same year as her husband, and she was buried at Well.

43 Allen, *Writings*, p. 508.

patronage would have been fron such leading Richmondshire families as the Scropes of Masham, the FitzHughs of Tanfield, and the Stapletons of Bedale, who all lived within a twelve mile radius of Layton where Rolle lived and wandered.[44] His patrons may have included Sir Geoffrey Scrope, who purchased the manor of Masham early in the reign of Edward III and who died in 1340; his son and heir Henry, the first Lord Scrope of Masham, who lived until 1391; and Sir Geoffrey's son, Geoffrey, a canon of Lincoln in 1334, rector of Bolton Percy near York in 1340, and rector of Great Bowden. This family were patrons of the Richmondshire anchoresses who dedicated themselves to following Rolle's counsels on the contemplative life. Their castle was a visible landmark from Margaret Kirkby's cell in East Layton, where the Stapletons were lords of the manor, and the cell in Ainderby churchyard, a Scrope family living, where she moved in 1357, was in the Scrope's manor. Richard Scrope, who was born the third son of Henry the first baron of Masham in 1346, was presented to the rectory of Ainderby in 1368 at a time when Margaret Kirkby would have still been a recluse at Ainderby church.[45] In 1376 Scrope resigned as rector of Ainderby to succeed his uncle Geoffrey Scrope as rector of Great Bowden. Geoffrey in 1382 bequeathed twenty shillings to an anchoress of Hampole.[46] The anchoress of Hampole was probably Margaret Kirkby, and the bequest confirms that she was at Hampole to help in the compiling of the miracles for the office between 1381 and 1383. An unreliable account of Rolle's life, written before 1405, says that Margaret Kirkby lived at Hampole for ten years until her death.[47] If the biographical office and the miracles were, as seems likely, both compiled between 1381 and 1383 as a result of Margaret's arrival at Hampole, then she may have lived until 1391. Her death by 1394 is implied by the interest shown in her by the Stapletons, who until 1373 were the lords of Bedale and the manor of East Layton where Margaret Kirkby had her cell. In 1394 Sir Brian Stapleton left his niece Ainste de Medilton 'a round silver ewer with an image of Our Lady that once belonged to a anchorite of Hampole'; this may refer to Rolle but more probably it

44 ibid, p. 508.

45 Emden, *B.R.U.O.* iii, 1659. In the part of East Layton which lay in the parish of Stanwick the FitzHughs, Scropes and Nevilles had territorial connections.

46 *Market Harborough Records*, ed. J. E. Stokes and W. B. Bragg (London, 1890) p. 50. Geoffrey, the fifth son of Sir Geoffrey of Masham was an M.A. Oxon in 1338, C.C.L. in 1348 and a canon of York and Lincoln. See Emden, *B.R.U.O.* III. The Scropes had other links with Ainderby church: Stephen Lord Scrope of Masham made a bequest to William Blase, rector of Ainderby and executor of Henry Lord Scrope of Masham who bequeathed the church a cape.

47 Allen, *Writings*, p. 40; Whiting, 'Richard Rolle' 12; Osterreichische National-bibliothek, Vienna, MS 4483.

refers to Margaret Kirkby.[48] Her patrons may also have included the FitzHughs, who owned estates around Ravensworth and East Layton since 1357 and who were lords of Tanfield two miles from Masham. The above families also showed an interest in Margaret Kirkby's servant, Elizabeth, and the anchoress of Kirkby Wiske, who seems to have been closely associated with both Margaret and Elizabeth. Geoffrey Scrope, the rector of Great Bowden, left one mark to the anchoress of Kirkby Wiske five miles south of Ainderby; and in 1405 his nephew Stephen, the second Lord Scrope of Masham, left 20s to Elizabeth Hampole and 13s to the anchoresses of Kirkby Wiske.[49] Stephen's son and heir Henry the third Lord Scrope, left a legacy in 1415 to Elizabeth, whom he described as *quondam servienti Anachoritate de Hampole,* and 13s to the anchoress of Kirkby Wiske.[50] Both of these ladies were also remembered in 1401 by Peter Dalton, a canon and treasurer of Lincoln and possibly a relative of Rolle's original patrons, who left 16s to the anchoress of Kirkby Wiske and Hampole.[51] In 1393 a York chandler, John Croxton, who was involved in progagating the cult of Rolle, left bequests to the anchoress of Kirkby Wiske, and a number of anchoresses who appear to have followed the example of these disciples of Rolle including; two anchoresses of Westheton, an anchoress of Thurgansby, who was also supported by Henry Lord Scrope, and her servant Allison.[52] An interest in Rolle and his followers is also implied in the interest shown by nobility in Hampole: Sir John Dependen and Henry Lord Scrope were among those to leave large bequests to the priory. Joan Beaufort was probably one of a group of aristocratic ladies who were patrons of Hampole: Isabella Wyleby, who lived in the manor house at Raby, had many connections with Hampole and she, along with Matilda, Countess of Cambridge, was a patron of the house.[53]

This support that Rolle generated for himself and his followers was unique: no such interest was aroused by individual recluses in other regions. Julian of Norwich, an anchoress of St Julian's church who was attached to the Benedictine nunnery of Carrow from 1393, was the author of a distinguished series of autobiographical revelations and visions of God's love. But no cult was established in her honour, and

48 Prob. Reg: 6, fo. 133; TE, I, p. 199. Sir Brian Stapleton was connected with the FitzWilliams and Methams, the lords of Melsonby. Sir Brian held land in 1376 in Skelbroke near Hampole. He therefore had connections with all the places important in Margaret Kirkby's life.

49 *Market Harborough Records,* p. 50; TE, II, p. 32.

50 *Foedera* ix, 275.

51 *Early Lincoln Wills,* p. 97. There was a Peter Dalton who studied at Oxford in 1360 – 62 and who knew Wycliffe. He was a vicar general of Alexander Neville.

52 TE, I, p. 180.

53 TE, I, p. 383; TE, II, p. 121. Matilda kept royal state for many years at Conisborough near Hampole. Allen, *Writings,* p. 522.

there is little evidence that recluses were patronized by the citizens of Norwich or the Norfolk nobility. The absence of any recluse in the city of Norwich between the 1320s and 1390s suggests that there was little in the way of inspiration or support in her local invironment to encourage her to become an anchoress.[54] It is likely that she was influenced by eremitical developments in the diocese of York: she was dedicated to St John of Beverley, who was little known in the fourteenth century outside the diocese of York; and the northern forms in the earliest surviving manuscripts of her work suggests that she or her scribe were northerners. One such manuscript, containing a short version of Julian's vision along with a copy of Rolle's *Amending of Life*, was copied in 1435 and owned by a north-countryman, William Constable; according to the *incipit*, it was faithfully transcribed from an exemplar in 1413, the year that Julian made her short version available for copying.[55] Julian was certainly influenced by northern writers, including Rolle; and even if she was not from the north it is likely that she was influenced in her choice of an eremitical vocation by the writings of Rolle, which were written for anchoresses, and by the example of Margaret Kirkby. She may have learned about the Hampole hermit and his disciple from their patrons the Stapletons, because a branch of this family settled in Norfolk. Sir Miles Stapleton, brother of Sir Brian Stapleton, the lord of Bedale and owner of a ewer once belonging to Margaret Kirkby or Rolle, moved from Bedale to Norfolk in 1360.[56] When he died his son Miles, who was to become Sir Miles of Ingham, was still a minor, and throughout his life he remained closely attached to his uncle Sir Brian, the lord of Bedale: his uncle remembered him with affection in his will in 1394 and appointed him as one of his executors.[57] Sir Miles of Ingham was a prominent patron of the arts in Norfolk and owner of Michael of Massa's *Life of Christ*.[58] He would almost certainly have known about Rolle and Margaret Kirkby from his uncle, and he had dealings with Julian of Norwich while acting as executor of Isabel Gifford, the Countess of Suffolk and a sister of Thomas Beauchamp earl of Warwick. In 1416 Sir Miles was appointed by her to give 20s to Julian the recluse of Norwich.[59] It is therefore possible that the Stapleton family, and especially Sir Miles, had earlier contact with Julian. Sir Miles'

54 Tanner, *The Church in Late Medieval Norwich*, p. 63.

55 *A Book of the Shewings to the Anchoress Julian of Norwich*, ed. E. Colledge and J. Walsh (Toronto, 1978); *Julian of Norwich's Revelations of Divine Love, the Shorter Version*, ed. (from MS, B.L. Add. 37790) by F. Beer (Heidelberg, 1978), pp. 12 and 18.

56 Chetwynd-Stapleton, 'The Stapleton's, 231 – 32.

57 Prob. Reg, 6, fo. 133.

58 Bodl. Lib. MS. 758 (Sum. Cat. 2676), written in 1405 in Latin and English by Ralph Medilton on the order of Miles Stapleton. For description see O. Pacht and J. Alexander, *Illuminated Manuscripts in the Bodleian Library* (Oxford, 1973), III.70.

59 *Reg. Chichele*, ii, p. 95.

daughter, Emma Stapleton, seems to have followed Julian's example after the death of her father in 1419: between 1421 and 1442 she was enclosed as an anchoress at the Carmelite priory of Norwich.[60] Between 1420 and 1470 Norwich had more recluses than any other city, but considering Julian's relative obscurity and the absence of recluses in fourteenth century Norwich it is possible to see this increase in solitaries as a reflection of the spread of Rolle's influence to East Anglia by the beginning of the fifteenth century: in 1405 a Norwich hermit, Thomas Basset, wrote a defence against the detractors of the hermit of Hampole.[61]

An important aspect of Rolle's influence in the diocese and elsewhere was the interest he aroused in the contemplative teachings of the recluse; this is implied by the large number of surviving manuscripts of his Latin and English writings. Many of Rolle's works were written for nuns and recluses who were from the gentry families of Yorkshire; and according to the compilers of his office Rolle converted many to God through his holy exhortations and his sweet writings, which were in the form of treatises and little books that he composed for the edification of his neighbours.[62] Evidence of the circulation of Rolle's English works in the fourteenth century is exiguous: few wills survive before 1370 and the earliest surviving manuscripts are from the last quarter of the fourteenth century. The most widely circulated of these English works was his translations of and commentary on the psalms. These glosses contained subjective accounts of the author's solitary life, his dedication to the Holy Name, and the physical sensations that it inspired, which he regarded as an apprehension of Christ's love. An early reference to the presence of the psalter in a gentry household is suggested in the will of Joan Walkyngham, a friend of Sir Geoffrey Scrope and his wife, made on her manor of Ravensthorpe in 1346 in the presence of Thomas Thweng, a relative of one of Rolle's patrons. Joan bequeathed *meum psalterium cum littera grossa et quendam librum scriptum littera anglicana*.[63] One third of the thirty-six surviving manuscripts of the English psalter are plain with little decoration; and this implies that the earliest circulation of this work was mainly in the monasteries and nunneries of Yorkshire.[64] However, the rapidity with which manuscripts were copied and worn out suggests a wider popularity for this work by the end of the fourteenth century. Those surviving early fifteenth century manuscripts

60 Clay, *Hermits*, p. 70, Emma was enclosed in a chamber under Holy Cross chapel Warren, *Anchorites*, p. 203. Sir Miles Stapleton made a will in 1414. His grandson Sir Brian died without issue and the properties of this family reverted to the elder branch of the descendents of Sir Brian Stapleton of Bedale.

61 Allen, *Writings*, pp. 403 – 4, and App. pp. 529 – 37 for text.

62 *Brev. Ebor.*

63 TE, 1, p. 17. Joan left silver to Joan, the daughter of Geoffrey Scrope

64 Doyle, '*A Survey*', i, p. 103ff.

which are expensive volumes in large, handsome script, decorated borders and elaborate capitals were clearly designed for such aristocratic households as those in which Rolle and Margaret Kirkby found patronage.[65]

The aristocracy, who were among Rolle's first patrons and who supported Margaret Kirkby, were earlier readers of his works and followers of his teachings. The Nevilles were early devotees to the cult of the Holy Name, and it is possible that the 'Lollard knight', Sir William Neville, may have introduced Rolle's works to his two friends at court, Sir John Clanvowe, the author of a devotional tract, and Sir William Beauchamp, who owned the works of Rolle and Clanvowe. Joan Beaufort, wife of Ralph Neville of Westmorland and daughter of John Gaunt, owned a copy of Rolle's *Meditations on the Passion*: a page of one copy of this work bears the inscription *Johanna unfortunata Westmerlandiae Cowntes*.[66] The Scropes of Masham, the FitzHughs of Tanfield and the Stapletons of Bedale were all owners of Rolle's works. The will of Henry Lord Scrope of Masham provides evidence that there were important manuscripts of Rolle's works in this family. He bequeathed to his younger brother and heir, John Scrope, a large, glossed psalter, and he also left a glossed psalter to his chaplain, John Foxholes; these volumes may have been Rolle's English or Latin psalters. Lord Scrope was also the owner of a compilation of Rolle's works written in the author's own hand, which had presumably been in the family since the time when they were patrons of the hermit. In 1415 Lord Scrope bequeathed this volume to his brother-in-law, Henry Lord FitzHugh, describing it as: *unum librum incipit cum libro vocato Sintillar et in continetur incendium amoris, quem Ricardus Heremita composuit, et unum Quaternum parvum, in quo continetur expositio super Judica me Deus quod Ricardus Heremita composuit et scripsit, pro Rembrancia*.[67] If, as this description implies, the *Incendium* in the same volume as the *Judica* was also an autograph, then this compilation could have been made available by the Scropes for their protégée Margaret Kirkby, and used for the inclusion in the office of the autobiographical passages from the fifteenth chapter of the *Incendium*. The Stapletons of Bedale may have owned Rolle's works from an early date, and in 1448 Agnes Stapleton, widow of Sir Brian Stapleton, a grandson of Sir Brian, the patron of Margaret Kirkby, bequeathed a great psalter to the Plumpton family in 1448.[68]

65 See Oxford Bodl. MS. 953, MS Tanner, I, Hutton 12 and MS Laud. Misc. 448. These can be compared with MS Bodl. Lib. 877 and MS. Laud Misc. 286, which are smaller and less legible script. MS Laud is abbreviated and was probably intended for a clerical audience.

66 CUL., MS Add. 3042; Allen, *Writings*, p. 279.

67 *Foedera*, ix, p. 276.

68 *N.C.W.*, p. 116, Doyle, 'Survey', i, p. 316.

These northerners were responsible for extending Rolle's influence at the court. The Nevilles were early devotees to the cult of the Holy Name, and it is possible that Sir William Neville, the 'Lollard knight', may have introduced Rolle's works to his friends and fellow chamber knights at Richard II's court, including Sir John Clanvowe, author of a devotional tract, and Sir William Beauchamp, executor of the princess of Wales and owner of the works of Rolle and Clanvowe. The brothers-in-law Henry Lord Scrope and Henry Lord FitzHugh were responsible for influencing religious sensibility in the court of Henry V. Both were king's chamberlains, and Scrope, according to Walsingham, was valued by the king for his piety.[69] Together with Thomas Fishbourne, a Yorkshire squire and owner of a tract on the Holy Name who became an anchorite confessor to Henry V and leading ladies of the court, they helped to make the royal Brigittine foundation of Syon a centre for the study of Rolle's writings. They were among the first to appreciate the close affinity between his works and the ecstatic and supernatural revelations of St Bridget. Lord Scrope left a copy of Bridget's *Revelations*, which he obtained in Beverley, to his nephew Stephen Scrope, the archdeacon of Richmond; FitzHugh would probably have read the *Revelations* about the time of his visit to Vadstena in 1406; and in Fishbourne's large library there were two copies of the *Revelations*.[70] It was probably through their encouragement, and perhaps donations, that the monastery began to acquire a large collection of Rolle's works: Lord Scrope left £20 and a collection of books to Syon; and the brother's library contained 13 volumes of the *Emendatio Vitae*, four of *de Contra amatores mundi*, six of the commentary on the Book of Job, five of the *Incendium amoris* and single copies of *The commentary on the Canticles* and *The Mending of Life*.[71] This monastery in turn inspired the study of Rolle in another royal foundation of 1415, the Carthusian monastery of Sheen directly across the Thames: two Latin manuscripts of the *Incendium* and a compilation of Rolle's writing *De Excellentia Contemplacionis* are related to Brigittine manuscripts.[72] It is also possible that the atmosphere of piety that these northern courtiers encouraged helped to shape the excessive religious sensibilities of Henry VI, a devotee of Rolle's mystical doctrine, in his formative years.

69 *The St Albans Chronicle*, ed. V. H. Galbraith (Oxford, 1937), p. 78.

70 *Foedera*, ix, p. 275. The Revelations may have been copied at Beverley Cathedral. For information concerning the scribal activities of Thomas Dautre, who served in the household of the Archbishop of York at Bishop Burton and was employed as a scribe in his capacity as chapter clerk in 1400, see *Register of Thomas Langley*, ed. R. L. Storey (SS; 164, 166, 169, 1956), p. 19.

71 Sargent, 'Contemporary Critics of Rolle', 171. An important annotator of Rolle manuscripts in the latter half of the fifteenth century, James Greenhalgh, was a monk of Sheen.

72 *Catalogue of Syon Monastery*, ed. M. Bateson (Cambridge, 1898), p. 226.

By the fifteenth century evidence survives of the presence of Rolle's works among the East Riding gentry whose ancestors may have befriended the hermit and listened to his sermons. Robert Thornton was a member of a minor gentry family who had been lords of the manor of East Newton near Pickering, where Rolle had his first cell, since the reign of Edward III. Thornton copied into the collection of religious and secular works that he compiled for his family a body of fragmentary exampla and lyrics ascribed to Rolle, which combined pastoral teaching with his distinctive devotional edification; these are perhaps survivals of the 'little books and holy exhortations' that Rolle was supposed to have composed for, and delivered to, his neighbours: they include an English comentary on the Decalogue, and exempla on the contemplative life and the administration of confession.[73] Thornton's sources may have included the libraries of Lord Scrope, who asked for prayers for a Robert Thornton, and Lord FitzHugh, who was constable of Pickering castle. In the inventory of the East Riding widow Elizabeth Sewerby, the daughter of Sir Henry Vavasour, there was a copy of Bridget's *Revelations*, valued at 66s 8d and a copy of Rolle's *Meditations on the Passion* valued at 4d.[74] This unique reference indicates the circulation of cheap paper copies of Rolle's works, which were worn out quickly and too cheap to warrant mentioning in wills. There is also evidence that copies of Rolle's English psalter were being used in gentry households in the fifteenth century: one copy was owned in the first quarter of the fifteenth century by a gentleman of northern connections; the manuscript records the death of Katherine Hampton, *ma femme*, in 1414 and the birth of Richard Hampton in 1422.[75] In 1450 Sir Thomas Cumberworth, who was related to many East Riding families such as Gascoigne and Constable, left to the parson of Somerby 'my grete boke of david sauter as was at the Frerys'; this was probably an expensive copy of the psalter previously the property of the friars.[76] A common lawyer and baron of the exchequer, Sir Peter Ardene, also left his 'sawter glossed' to his brother Thomas, a priest.[77] The popularity of Rolle's writings in York was an aspect of the growth of devotion in this town from the late fourteenth century. The Benedictine abbey of St Mary's in York would have been an early centre for studying his works: a former monk of the house, Christopher Braystones, who died in 1374 or 1375, owned a manuscript containing the *Incendium Amoris* and *Emendatio Vitae*.[78] In 1407 Isabel

73 *Brev. Ebor*; Allen, *Writings*, pp. 268 – 75.
74 TE, II, p. 196.
75 Doyle, 'A Survey', p. 108.
76 The Academy, pp. 230 – 32 and 280 – 85.
77 TE, II, p. 232.
78 Sargent, 'Contemporary Criticism of Rolle', 162.

Percy left a 'psalter anglice' to a York curate,[79] and in 1427 John Maltster, a chaplain of St Giles' church, York, and supporter of York recluses, left a copy of Rolle's commentary on Job to Robert Semer of St Leonard's hospital, and to the library of this hospital a book written on paper containing the office of Richard Rolle.[80] Another York chaplain, Robert Wasselyn, transcribed and annotated a manuscript containing extracts from the *Incendium Amoris*.[81]

Rolle's importance in the eremitical movement of the late fourteenth and early fifteenth century can be measured not only in the interest he inspired among the nobility in anchorites and their teaching, but also in the influence that he had on other recluses and religious writers in the diocese. Some of these people acquired reputations as holy men and wrote spiritual treatises for recluses and those in secular life. Although all these imitators of Rolle attempted at some stage in their lives to live the solitary life, they differed from the Hampole hermit in their affiliation to religious orders. They were therefore less idiosyncratic and generally showed a greater pastoral awareness of their potentially wide audience. Some responded in a directly critical way to aspects of Rolle's teachings. Walter Hilton and the author of the *Cloud of Unknowing* were aware of the unsophisticated and potentially influential elements in Rolle's works, such as his emphasis on physical and supernatural experiences. They were in a position to observe, through the success of Rolle's cult, that these accounts of his experiences had aroused the interest of the less educated in the diocese, for the nuns of Hampole emphasized the ecstatic aspects of Rolle's doctrine in their biographical office of the hermit. In their writings, the recluses of the late fourteenth century expressed their concern about the possibility that some of Rolle's enthusiastic imitators would take his descriptions of the 'fire of Love' and heavenly song out of context and react to them in too literal a way. The author of *The Cloud of Unknowing* observed that many inexperienced followers had been misled into a spurious spirituality; Hilton warned that the experiences described by Rolle were physical and therefore possibly deceptive. Hilton, especially, was concerned with providing an intellectual tightness to Rolle's teachings and adapting them with an eye to their pastoral dissemination. This aspect of the work of Hilton and his contemporaries will be discussed in chapter four, when the reaction of York clergy to the growing popularity of recluses and their teachings, and the contribution of the church to the development of religious sensibility in the diocese is considered. However, Hilton, and other writers of the north-east, many of whom

79 TE, I, p. 271.
80 B.I.H.R. Prob. Reg. 2, fo. 533.
81 C.U.L. MS., Ff 7 14.

are anonymous, had specialist as well as pastoral objectives, both of which are revealed in the same works. These writers belonged to the same eremitic tradition as Rolle, and they were probably inspired by him. In their meditative works they provided instructions of a highly sophisticated nature on the principles and practices of the contemplative life for recluses, Carthusians, nuns, and those secular clergy and laymen who were interested.

Rolle's influences were predominantly Cistercian and Franciscan, but the most influential spiritual tradition in the late fourteenth century for Hilton and his contemporaries was Augustinian. By the middle of the century some Augustinian friars and canons were attempting to recapture the eremitic ideals of the Augustinian rule, and they involved the two orders in a rivalry in which both claimed to be the true followers of St Augustine.[82] Both orders appear to have been more notable in this period than the Cistercians, and even the Franciscans, as teachers on the solitary life. Augustinian friars and canons emphasized in their discussions on the rules for the eremitic life, for individuals and communities, the need for charity, cooperation, discipline and obedience; and when giving guidance on meditation they drew on the works of Augustine to provide sensible psychological advice for solitaries and their followers, which suggests that they envisaged a wider audience than Rolle.

Perhaps the most influential Austin friar of the fourteenth century was John Waldeby of the York convent, the provincial of the order until 1357. Waldeby was influenced by Franciscan teaching at the York friary where he studied from 1339 to 1346 (there were four copies of the pseudo Bonaventuran *Meditationes de Vitae Christi* in the convent library) and he was exposed to further Franciscan influences at Oxford where he studied from 1346 to 1356. Like most of the religious writers of the north-east, Waldeby was influenced by an ecclesiastical household. He was connected to the circle of doctors, clerks and friars attached to Thomas de la Mare, a relative of Grandisson and correspondent of John Thoresby, who was prior of the Benedictine cell of Tynemouth near Newcastle from 1340 to 1349; Waldeby was probably one of the Augustinian friars who, according to Walsingham, was accustomed to visit Tynemouth before 1349.[83] He continued to have contact with de la Mare after the latter became abbot of St Albans, and around 1354, while the abbot was spending a year in his cell in Tynemouth, Waldeby visited him and told him about the sermons he was delivering in York on the Creed. The abbot urged him to arrange them in permanent form, and at his request

[82] A. Gwynn, *The English Austin Friars in the Time of Wyclif* (Oxford, 1940), p. 94.
[83] ibid, pp. 120 – 121; *Gesta Abbatum Monasterii Sancti Albani*, ed. H. T. Riley, 2 vols. (R.S., 28/4 a – c, 1867 – 69), 11, 380.

Waldeby went back to York to compose them in Latin.[84] The completed twelve homilies were sent to de la Mare with a dedicatory preface which describes the difficult circumstances of their composition: the author's need to escape to Tickhill hermitage from the noise and bustle of York and the continuous demands on his time and energy; this preface therefore gives some indication of the eremitic ideals of this circle.

Another Austin friar who was dedicated to the pursuit of an eremitic life, and who also taught others, was William Flete of the Cambridge convent. Flete was more of an East Anglian than a northerner by origin (he was probably born in South-East Lincolnshire); but his career at Cambridge[85] (where he lectured on the sentences from 1354 to 1355, and where he obtained his baccalaureate in Theology by 1358) and his pastoral work in Ely diocese (where he was licenced to hear confessions in 1352) has affinities with the careers of members of the circle of Walter Hilton, a writer whom Flete influenced. Before 1359 Flete declined to proceed to the degree of Master of Theology, and in July 1359 he left England and built himself a cell in a wood near the Augustinian convent of Lecceto. For the next twenty years Flete corresponded with some of the Italian mystics, advised leading citizens of Siena and involved himself in papal politics.[86] His most important contribution to the eremitic movement in England was made between 1352 and 1358 at Cambridge with the composition of *De Remediis Contra Temptacionem*, which deals with temptations against faith afflicting those attempting to live a contemplative life. The work was influential: there are twenty-two surviving Latin manuscripts comprising four recensions, and an English translation surviving in sixteen manuscripts,[87] made by Walter Hilton, whose early Cambridge career may have coincided with Flete's. Among the readers of *De Remediis* were Charles duke of Orléans, who had a manuscript copied during his captivity in England, and two Yorkshiremen who copied their own versions: Robert Wasselyn, a York priest, and John Morton, a York layman. Another copy, possibly transcribed at Mount Grace, was given by Dame Wade, before she resigned as prioress of Swine in 1487, to Joan Hitoft of Nuncotham nunnery.[88] Although he probably never returned to England between 1359 and his death in 1390, Flete followed eremitical developments in this country, especially the dispute between the Austin friars and the Augustinian canons as to which order could rightfully call St Augustine their founder. The Austin prior provincial, Geoffrey Hardeby, who was connected with York

[84] Gwynn, *Austin Friars*, pp. 120 – 121.
[85] Emden, *B.R.U.C.*, p. 234.
[86] Gwynn, *Austin Friars*, pp. 139 – 92; *Dictionnaire de Spiritualité*, pp. 1204 – 1208.
[87] F. Roth, *English Austin Friars* (New York), p. 405.
[88] M. B. Hackett, 'William Flete and the *De remediis contra temptaciones*', in *Medieval Studies Presented to Aubrey Gwynn* (Dublin, 1961).

convent, stated the friars' claim in 1356 in his *De Vita Evangelica*, and Flete made his own contribution by addressing three letters to the English province of Austin friars in 1380 calling for a stricter observance of the rule and the eremitic traditions of the order.[89] The first was addressed to all the brethren of the province; the second to all masters and doctors; and the third to the prior provincial. These letters, probably copied at Cambridge, constituted a programme of eremitical reform for the order: Flete urged his brothers to observe perfectly the rule of St Augustine by preaching, performing deeds of charity, observing scrupulously the choral offices, and above all by spending as much time as possible in study and contemplation in their cells.[90]

Flete's letters suggest that despite the activities of such friars as Waldeby and William of Nottingham, the Austin friars were not comparing favourably with the Augustinian canons in their attempts to recapture the eremitical purity of the Augustinian rule. The type of worldly friar Flete may have had in mind in his letters was John Erghome of the Austin convent of York.[91] Erghome was a man of intellectual versatility whose personal library consisted of over two hundred volumes; but although he was interested in medicine, astrology, magic, history and the classics, there is little evidence in his library of interest in the contemplative life, and he was more drawn to the affairs and scandals of Edward III's court, which he alluded to in his Bridlington prophecies and commentary.[92] Erghome was probably not atypical, for in the late fourteenth century catalogue of the large library of the York convent there is no mention of any of the recluses and religious writers of the north-east whose main priority was to teach the principles of the contemplative life to their patrons.[93] Even the two known religious writers of the order, Waldeby and Flete, did not choose to write in the vernacular for wider circulation. Despite the efforts of the Austin friars to reform their order along eremitic lines and to extend their activities as religious teachers they were probably not as successful as their rivals the Augustinian canons in accepting the challenge posed by Rolle, who was the first to open up the possibility of a more widespread involvement in the contemplative life.

Some indication that the canons were more in touch with the religious enthusiasms aroused by Rolle can be seen in the popularity of John

89 Gwynn, *Austin Friars*, p. 94.

90 M. B. Hackett, *The Spiritual Life of the English Austin Friars of the Fourteenth Century* (Studia Augustinas: Vitae Spiritualis Magister, 11, Rome, 1959), ii, 471 – 92; and 'William Flete', *The Month*, xxvi (1961), 69 – 80.

91 Gwynn, *Austin Friars*, p. 138.

92 P. Meyvaert, 'John Erghome and the *Vaticinium Roberti Bridlington*', *Speculum* (1966), 656ff.

93 Hackett, *Spiritual Life of English Austin Friars*, pp. 421 – 92; M. J. Morrin, *John Waldeby O.S.A.* c. 1315 to 75 (Studia Augustinia Historica Roma, 1975), p. 14 ff.

Thweng, a canon and prior of the Augustinian house of Bridlington, who was directly influenced by Rolle, and who achieved a reputation as a holy man widespread enough by 1362, when he was still a canon, to inspire John Erghome's envious attempt to mock the priory and its saintly canon by foisting his pseudo prophetic satire on Edward's court onto 'St John of Bridlington'. John Thweng was born about 1320 in the village of Thweng on the Wolds, nine miles west of Bridlington; Rolle spent part of his life in the same area. According to Thweng's biographers he was of some social standing: they described his parents as worthy and his descent as *generosus*.[94] It is therefore likely that he was a member of the branch of the Thwengs who had been established at Kilton since 1257; this family were leading landowners in the Wolds, with estates throughout the East Riding at Northcave, Foxholes and Thweng. The family was pious: at least one of its members was a patron of Rolle; two were churchmen, and John Thweng's parents were credited with giving their son a devout upbringing.[95] The possibility that the Thwengs knew Rolle is suggested in the patronage of the hermit by Thomas Neville, and presumably his stepmother Margery Thweng, the youngest daughter of Marmaduke Lord Thweng. There are aspects of Thweng's career and piety which strongly suggest the direct influence of the Hampole hermit. Thweng began his education at the age of five in the village school, run by a priest; he acquired a reputation as a devout child, and at the age of twelve he took a vow of chastity before being professed at the age of fourteen as a novice canon. By 1336 he had proceeded to Oxford; like Rolle he left after three years, and he returned to his native region in 1339, occupying a post as tutor to the children of a wealthy and influential personage, possibly a member of the Neville family. At the age of twenty he entered the Augustinian priory of Bridlington, where he remained from 1340 until his death in 1379, holding from 1361 the offices of cellarer and prior.[96]

Although he did not remain a recluse like Rolle, Thweng was an important figure in the eremitic movement. A canon called Hugh, probably of Bridlington, wrote a biography of the prior depecting him as an innovative monk who tried to introduce an ascetic zeal into the monastic life.[97] This was perhaps a conscious attempt on Thweng's part to recapture the eremitic ideals of some of the Augustinian canons of the

94 *Vita S. Joannis de Bridlingtona*. (Acta Sanctorum Oct.; Collecta, Digesta, V, Brussels, 1786), p. 137; *Capgrave, Nova Leganda Angliae*, II (ed. Horstmann, p. 67).

95 White, *Peerage*, XII, part I, p. 741; L'Anson, 'Kilton Castle', (8). The Thweng family of Kilton were an extinct barony: the last baron, Thomas Thweng, died in 1474, and John Thweng could have been a member of this family. Thweng, the manor house of the last baron was only 9 miles from Bridlington.

96 *Vita S. Joannis*, p. 137; *Nova Legenda Angliae*, II, p. 67.

97 *Vita S. Joannis*, pp. 137 – 42.

twelfth century. He brought a new asceticism and charity to his duties as cellarer, and despite the opposition of other monks he gave alms to the poor. As prior he replaced administrative power with charismatic leadership, based on a personal holiness that elicited loyalty and affection. He introduced into the priory a rule of simplicity, equality, abstinence and prayer; and although he did not write a new rule he acquired a reputation as a monastic reformer.[98] Another of his biographers, John Capgrave, claimed that Thweng had a reputation for learning that encouraged scholars from all over England to visit him. Capgrave also described Thweng's dedication to the Gospel of St John, a favourite text among mystics which the prior of Bridlington had recommended as a rule for monastic discipline exceeding all others. Thweng achieved some fame through his experiences of the fires of love; Capgrave gave a detailed account of the physical manifestations of the ecstasies experienced by the prior during the daily celebration of the mass, which closely correspond to descriptions in Rolle's *Incendium*.[99] The bull of his canonization in 1401 described John Bridlington as a man surpassingly proficient in holy scriptures which he read burning with fire of love; and this was how Rolle recommended that the psalter should be read.[100] It is possible that Thweng wrote mystical works that have not survived: Bale credited him with a volume of commentaries on the psalter along with a volume of homilies and a work on the Lord's prayer, but none of these works has been identified.[101]

Thweng had acquired a national reputation for holiness: after his death miracles were reported at his tomb at the same time as Rolle's cult was being established, probably with the help of the Scrope family. Thweng's cult too was established with the help of a leading Northern family, the Nevilles, relatives of Thweng by marriage. Ralph Neville, before his death in 1367, gave stone for the fabric of the priory church when Thweng was prior.[102] Alexander Neville, the archbishop of York, and his vicar general, Peter Dalton, examined the miracles in 1386, and in 1401 Thweng was canonized as St John of Bridlington; supporters of the cult included Richard Scrope, the archbishop of York, Henry Lord Scrope, and Joan Beaufort.[103] Like Rolle, Thweng was survived by disciples, and they too were supported by the Nevilles. William Sleightholme, his closest disciple, was a canon of Bridlington whose reputation before his death in 1420 rivalled that of his master.

98 ibid. pp. 137 – 42.
99 *Nova Legenda Angliae*, II, p. 67ff.
100 Archiv; Vaticii Regesta Lateran, Bonifacii ix an 12, Vol. 97, fos. 241 – 4. cit. J. S. Purvis, 'St John of Bridlington', *Journal of Bridlington and Augustinian Society*, II (1924), 31 – 7.
101 Purvis, St John of Bridlington, 38.
102 Ross, 'Yorkshire Baronage', p. 295.
103 See chapter on saint's cults for further details.

Sleightholme was confessor to John Neville, the lord of Raby from whom he received ten marks in 1382, and possibly to Lord Neville's son Ralph, Earl of Westmorland, and his wife Joan Beaufort: in 1413 Joan Beaufort was host to Margery Kempe at Raby during Mrs Kempe's visit to her confessor, Sleightholme, and to the shrine of John Bridlington.[104]

The Augustinian canon who did most to extend the scope and significance of eremitic teaching in the late fourteenth century was Walter Hilton of Thurgarton priory in the diocese of York. Hilton used the vernacular to teach clerks, priests, lawyers, nuns and laymen about the contemplative life. His early career in Cambridge and Ely has some affiliations with William Flete's. At his inception to study law at Cambridge in 1371 he was described as a clerk of Lincoln, but the dialect of the surviving manuscripts of his works suggests that he was from the north of the diocese, the same area as Thoresby and his affinity. Like Waldeby, Hilton was associated with a household, the circle of northern clerks closely associated with Thomas Arundel the bishop of Ely and archbishop of York. However, Hilton is different from the religious writers of the diocese preceding him in that he probably started writing on the eremitic life while he was still committed to secular life as a Cambridge canonist and Ely consistory court lawyer between 1371 and 1384.[105] It was possibly during his Cambridge period, under the influence of the works of the Franciscans and William Flete, that he started to write for recluses and nuns. He freely translated and adapted James of Milan's *Stimulus Amoris*, a series of Franciscan meditations on the life of Christ; this is attributed in two early northern manuscripts to Walter Hilton, and according to one manuscript the translation was made for non-Latin-speaking nuns, possibly of the Franciscan abbey of Denny.[106] It is also probable that Hilton translated during this period Flete's *De Remediis contra temptacionem* to provide a guide on the problems of the contemplative life: the earliest manuscript, which is northern, describes the translation as 'a devout matier of the drawing of Mr Waltere Hylton'.[107] Hilton left Cambridge around 1384 and, fired no doubt by the example of Rolle and others, he became a hermit. During his short period as a recluse, from 1384 to 1385, he wrote letters on counsel on the solitary life to administrators and secular clergy of Cambridge who were contemplating becoming recluses. Hilton himself compromised, like Thweng, and joined the Augustinian canons. He became an official in the small Nottinghamshire priory of Thurgarton in

104 *W.I.*, p. 39; *The Book of Margery Kemp*, ed. S. B. Meech (London, EETS, 1940), p. 133.
105 B.M. Add. MS, 11748. cit. J. M. Russel-Smith, 'Walter Hilton and a Tract in defence of the Veneration of Images', *Dominican Studies*, vii, (1954) 181 – 214; Emden, *B.R.U.C.*, pp. 305 – 306. See Chapter four for further details.
106 Doyle, 'A Survey', i, p. 208.
107 ibid, i, p. 187.

the diocese of York where he remained until his death in 1396. It was during this last period of his life when he was a hermit and a canon that he wrote extensively on the solitary life in the vernacular.[108] *The Scale of Perfection* was composed in two books: book one was addressed to an anchoress, but the author had in mind the diverse requirements of the religious, both regular and solitary, and the seculars, who included the clergy and laity; book two was written after an interval of time; addressed to a 'ghostly friend', possibly a person of similar background to the author, it appealed to anyone of sufficient education and piety who wished to live a life that combined reading, contemplation and activity.[109] Because of the size of the audience that Hilton envisaged, he expressed concern about the dangers of an uncritical following of Rolle's teaching on ecstatic experiences and offered spiritual instructions of a much moderate and practical nature. Hilton's most original contribution towards increased participation in the contemplative life was his composition of a letter to a layman, generally titled *Epistle on Mixed Life,* in which he defined the life that combined action and contemplation as the mixed life in an attempt to give it greater dignity.

During the course of the fifteenth century the letter on the mixed life was read by Northern gentry such as Robert Thornton and Sir Thomas Cumberworth, and moreover *The Scale of Perfection* attained a popularity rivalling that of Rolle's *Psalter*: forty-five manuscripts of *The Scale of Perfection* have been discovered, and the complication and variation of these manuscripts testifies to widespread and indiscriminate copying.[110] Initial circulation was probably among anchoresses and anchorites. The earliest manuscript of the expanded version, containing the end of book two and passages on the Holy Name, which were omitted from the original manuscript, was owned by Margery Pensax, an anchoress of Hawton in Nottinghamshire.[111] However, Margery Pensax, and another recluse from the diocese of York, Thomas Fishbourne, introduced Hilton's English works to the courts of Henry IV and Henry V at a time when northerners were also encouraging an interest in the teachings of Rolle and St Bridget. In 1399 Margery left Hawton and was granted by Henry IV an exceptionally large annual royal pension of 40s, enabling her to live at a cell in Bishop's Gate, London until 1415.[112] Her manuscript of *The Scale of Perfection* was bequeathed to Syon monastery

108 Knowles, *Mystical Tradition*, pp. 101 – 2.

109 There is still no critical edition of the Scale of Perfection: see Knowles, *Religious Orders*, ii, p. 124.

110 Doyle, 'A Survey', i, p. 256.

111 Doyle, 'A Survey', i, pp. 256 – 58; *Calendar of the Register of*

112 *Calendar of the Register of Richard Scrope*, ed. R. N. Swanson, 2 vols. (B.I.H.R., York, 1981, 1983), p. 73.

one year before its foundation. The royal confessor, Thomas Fishbourne, who was also confessor to the nuns of Syon, owned two copies of *The Scale* which are described in the Syon Catalogue. The influence of these northern recluses among courtiers was undoubtedly an important factor in generating an interest in Walter Hilton's teachings among the most powerful dowagers of the fifteenth century including Joan Beaufort and her daughter Cecily Neville. The enthusiasm of such patronage may have influenced the printing of *The Scale of Perfection* and the *Mixed Life* at the end of the fifteenth century.[113] *The Scale of Perfection* was also read in the fifteenth century by those East Riding gentry who supported solitaries and read the works of Rolle. Lady Eleanor Roos, daughter of Sir Thomas Roos of Igmanthorpe, received *unum librum vocatum primum Mr Walteri Hilton,* from William Authorpe, a rector of Kirk Deighton in Yorkshire who was buried in Mount Grace.[114] In 1438 she left this copy of *The Scale* to the wife of her nephew Robert Roos of Igmanthorpe. Sir Thomas Cumberworth also owned a copy of an English work of Walter Hilton.[115] Lay readers in the diocese may have helped in the dissemination of Hilton's works among the burghers of London: the Killum family of Thurgarton were responsible for passing a manuscript of *The Scale* into the hands of John Killum, a London grocer, and Richard Colop, a London parchener.[116]

Most of the religious authors of the north-east drew mainly on a native mediative heritage represented by the *Ancren Riwle,* Cistercian traditions (strong in Yorkshire) and on the Franciscan sermons and meditations of Italy. All of these traditions emphasized the emotional aspect of devotion, and an English writer who found an alternative source of inspiration was the author of *The Cloud of Unknowing* and its attendent treatises, who shows a heavy reliance on the Dominican writers of the Rhineland, Eckart and Tauler, and on more speculative and abstract mysticism.[117] This suggests that although he lived as a solitary he was at sometime a member of the Dominican order. There are similarities between his writings and Hilton's, and there is evidence that he was connected with Hilton's Cambridge circle: in the English treatise *Of Angel's Song,* which is probably by Hilton, there is a reference to the author of *The Cloud of Unknowing,* and the author of *The Cloud* probably referred to Hilton when he spoke of 'redyng, thinkyng and preiing . . . wretyn in another book of another man's werk moche betyr then I can tell thee': these were topics dealt with more fully in the *Scale of*

113 W. A. Pantin, *The English Church in the Fourteenth Century* (Cambridge, 1955), p. 254.
114 B.I.H.R., Prob. Reg. 3, fo. 529.
115 *The Academy,* 5, p. 220ff.
116 Jones, *Minor Works of Hilton,* p. 1ff.
117 D. Knowles, *The English Mystical Tradition* (London, 1961), p. 70.

Perfection.[118] It is, therefore, possible that he was a member of the Cambridge convent which had many contacts with the Cologne convent in the 1390s. What can be stated with reasonable certainty is that he was writing sometime between 1350 and 1400.[119] These dates have been determined by references to Rolle's doctrine and the teachings of the author of *The Cloud of Unknowing* in a manuscript of *Of Angel's Song* which was copied about 1400.[120] The earliest of the seventeen manuscripts of *The Cloud of Unknowing* are from the first decades of the fifteenth century; and all are written in an East Midlands dialect. The fact that the original was written in the north of this region is suggested by the presence of northern forms in the rarer words of *The Cloud* and in the earliest and most consistent of the manuscripts. On this basis the editor of *The Cloud* had concluded that the original works were written by someone from the north-east Midlands, in the region of Nottinghamshire, which accords well with the provenance of the surviving manuscripts.[121]

The writer's audience in the first instance was probably a circle of spiritual élites and professional contemplatives. His earliest work, *The Cloud,* was addressed to a young man of twenty-four in a 'singular' or 'solitary form of living'.[122] The subsequent treatises: the *Book of Privy Counselling,* the *Epistle of Prayer,* the *Pistle of Discrecioun,* the translations of *Denis Hid Divinity* and *Benjamin Minor,* the paraphrase of two sermons of Bernard, and *The Discerning of Spirits,* were English works of spiritual direction, like Rolle's later works, written for a circle of disciples. *The Pistle of Discrecioun* was conceived as an answer to questions put to the author by his pupils. These works were of a more refined nature than Rolle's *Form of Living,* substituting for his idiosyncratic and personal experiences a clear programme of contemplation based on the works of Pseudo Dyonisius and the *via negativa.* Subsequent circulation undoubtly occurred among recluses and the monks of the expanding Carthusian order who were professional contemplatives: one volume containing all these works was copied at Mount Grace from an older manuscript.[123] It has been suggested that the circulation of these treaties was restricted to these circles: the relationship between the seventeen manuscripts of *The Cloud* and the ten of the *Book of Privy Counselling* is so close that copying and circulation could not have been as extensive as it was for the works of Rolle; the volumes are small humble affairs of the

118 *The Cloud of Unknowing and the Book of Privy Counselling,* ed. P. Hodgson (London, EETS, 1944), pp. 71; P. Hodgson, 'Walter Hilton and the *Cloud of Unknowing, M.L.A.,* 50 (1955), 404.

119 Knowles, *Mystical Tradition,* p. 70.

120 W. Hilton, *Angel's Song,* ed. T. Takamiya (Tokyo, 1977), p. 7.

121 Knowles, *Mystical Tradition,* p. 70; *The Cloud of Unknowing,* pp. ix – li. The earliest surviving manuscript MS Harl, 674 was written in the early fifteenth century.

122 Doyle, 'A Survey', pp. 274 – 77.

123 ibid, pp. 274 – 77. MS Harl 2372.

sort that would have been owned by recluses.[124] But it is equally possible that these volumes were owned by ordinary people: one was made 'for the common profit' by arrangement of a London layman; and a colophon to another containing a *Treatise of Discerning of Spirits* bears the name of a London sheerman called Robert Holland.[125] The printing of *The Book of Privy Counselling, Denis Hid Divinity*, and *The Epistle of Prayer* in the fifteenth century suggests interest in this author outside the regular orders. It is also significant that for the first time treatises of psychological subtlety were written in English prose. The works of Rolle and the author of *The Cloud* are a testimony to the importance of the initiative of solitaries and others outside the regular orders in private religion.

The order most dedicated to the practice of the eremitic life, and whose members did most to elaborate and disseminate Rolle's teachings was the Carthusian order. The monks of Mount Grace in particular closely studied the intensely emotional mystical doctrine of Rolle and elaborated it in their works as authors and translators. Richard Methley, who was born in the West Riding in 1451, was at Mount Grace in 1476; he wrote at least five mystical treatises, including a spiritual epistle to Hugh the hermit, who was probably a recluse living in the hermitage above the priory. Methley's descriptions of the mystical ecstasy and fire of love, experienced after the celebration of mass, are closely derived from the *Incendium Amoris*.[126] A contemporary of Methley, John Morton, who entered Mount Grace in 1482, wrote three mystical treatises that contain sensational accounts of his visions.[127] The Carthusians were quick to perceive the affinities between Rolle's writings and the *Horologium Sapientiae*, an emotive, romantic and even fervid autobiography by the Dominican Henry Suso.[128] Their new communities on the east coast were allied to their mother houses in Europe and were an important link with Rhineland spirituality: in 1415 Henry V made provision for seven monks from Germany in his monastery of Sheen.[129] Mount Grace was an especially important centre for the early study of the *Horologium* and probably for the transmission of the earliest English versions of this work.[130] Nicholas Love, prior of Mount Grace in 1410,

124 ibid, pp. 200 – 207.

125 *The Minor Works of Walter Hilton*, ed. D. Jones (London, 1929), pp. xiii – xvi; MS Harl. 993.

126 Knowles, *Religious Orders*, ii, p. 225; Allen, *Writings*, p. 416. Methley's autobiographical and mystical writings occur in Trin. College, Camb. MS 1160; see M. R. James, *Catalogue of MSS of Trinity College Cambridge*, III, no. 1160, pp. 176 – 8.

127 A. G. Dickens, *The English Reformation*, (London, 1922), pp. 33 – 7.

128 Henry Suso, *Horologium Sapientiae*, ed. J. Strange (Cologne, 1861).

129 R. Lovatt, 'The Influence of Religious Literature of Germany and the Low Countries on English Spirituality' (Oxford Univ. D. Phil. thesis 1965), p. 64.

130 ibid, p. 169. E. Zeeman, *Archiv für das Studium der Neueren Sprachen* 194, (1954), pp. 117 – 8.

paraphrased into English Suso's treatise on the sacrament, which was taken from the *Horologium*. In Fishbourne's library there was a tract on the eucharist which may have been this work. The first translation of the entire *Horologium* probably originated from this house: *The Tretys of the Seven Poyntes of Trewe loue and euerlastynge wisdame drowen out of the boke that is writen in latyn and called Orologium Sapiencie* was a free translation in a north-east dialect. Two manuscripts of this work conclude with the identical colophon: *scriptum finaliter in monte gracio ultimo die mensis mayi 1419.*[131] The translator, like many readers of Suso, was an enthusiastic follower of Rolle and he gives an account of his feeling 'the hete of the fyre of love of oure lord jhesu'. To make the *Horologium* accessible to the lay person he omitted material of a clerical nature, reducing the repetitive and fluctuating emotional states of the original into seven points, each devoted to an aspect of the love of Jesus, while retaining the fervour and overall purpose of the original, which was to strengthen the recipients' love of Jesus.[132] The author was aware of the richness of the literary tradition preceding him: 'considering the multitude of bokes and treaties drawen in englisse that now be generally comyid my wille hath be withdrawen dredyng that werk somwhat was in wast'. He described himself as a 'sympele true chapeleyne unworthi the name of fader' and dedicated the work to a 'most worshipful lady'.[133] This suggests that he was not a regular of the monastery, but perhaps a private chaplain of a lady associated with the priory, such as Joan Holland Countess of Kent, widow of the founder, and sister-in-law of the wife of Henry Lord Scrope of Masham. There are eight surviving manuscripts of the Tretys; one, and probably two, were copied at Mount Grace; and another belonged to Beauvale and was in all likelihood transcribed there,[134] perhaps at the instigation of benefactors of Beauvale such as Sibella Rither and Elizabeth Stapleton. The monastery was probably the source of the copy of the *Tretys* owned by Sir Thomas Chaworth, a member of a family in Uverton, Nottinghamshire with many links with Beauvale. In 1458 Chaworth bequeathed an English book called the *Orologium Sapiencis* to Richard Byngham, Justice of the King's bench.[135] Also in this family was a copy of the *Speculum Devotorum*, a Carthusian compilation of translated quotations from devotional works from the Continent including: the *Horologium, The revelations of St Bridget,* and *The revelations of Catherine of Siena, Elizabeth of Hungary and Mechthild*. This manuscript

131 ed. Horstmann, *Anglia*, X (1888); Wichgraaf, *Anglia* XLI 1/2, 352; Lovatt, p. 197; Doyle 'A Survey', i, p. 213 – 15.
132 Wichgraaf, p. 352.
133 Doyle 'A Survey', i. pp. 213. – 19.
134 ibid. i, p. 215, Douce MS 114.
135 TE, pp. 220 – 28.

was transcribed at Sheen and contains the arms of Scrope and Chaworth; it was probably a presentation copy for Elizabeth, daughter of Sir Thomas Chaworth, and her husband, John Lord Scrope. Through the efforts of these Carthusian monks the *Horologium* became a popular work in England closely associated with the writings of Rolle: over half of the surviving English manuscripts of the *Horologium* contain his works.[136]

The Carthusians also shared the same awareness as the author of *The Cloud* and Hilton about the unsuitability of such mystical teachings for many ordinary people. Between 1408 and 1411 Nicholas Love translated and adapted the Franciscan *Meditatione de Vitae Christi* into *The Mirror of the Blessed Lyfe of Jesu Christ*.[137] This work contained Love's reflections on the contemplative life, including criticisms of untutored enthusiasm and the preoccupation with supernatural experiences. He countered this by providing meditations that were less subjective and abstract than those of Rolle and the author of *The Cloud* and more suitable for those with no special contemplative gifts. The first copies of Love's *Mirror* were probably used for communal reading and private meditation in the Carthusian community of Mount Grace; the earliest lay owners of the work were aristocratic patrons of the monastery. At the turn of this century there was still a manuscript of Love's translation at Ripley Castle, the seat of the Ingilbys, who owned the manor house where Mount Grace was founded; and Henry Lord Scrope of Masham, whose father-in-law Thomas Holland, Duke of Surrey, was the founder, left a book of meditations beginning *Bonaventura cum Passione* to the Countess of Dorset in 1415.[138] Eleanor Roos, the spinster daughter of Sir Thomas Roos of Igmanthorpe who was buried at Mount Grace where she probably lived a life of seclusion, left a copy of *The Passion of Our Lord* in English to her nephew, Robert Roos, in 1438.[139] Elaborate versions of *The Mirror* would have been made for magnate households: one containing fine borders and initials, bears the arms of Neville and Beaufort, and was probably intended for Joan Beaufort, an important literary patron, and her husband, Ralph Neville, Earl of Westmorland.[140] Twenty years after its publication *The Mirror* was being circulated among the gentry of the diocese. A copy was made on paper and parchment

136 Doyle, 'A Survey' ii, p. 267; MS Beebeigh Abbey.

137 N. Love, *The Mirror of the Blessed Lyfe of Jesu Crist*, ed. L. F. Powell (Oxford, 1911); C. Zeeman, 'Nicholas Love, a fifteenth century translator'. *R.E.S.*, (1915), 118. See Doyle I, pp. 37 – 44 for discussion of the north-east dialect of the early manuscripts of *The Mirror*.

138 These Ripley Castle manuscripts are now in the collection of Mr H. L. Bradford-Lawrence; Le Bas, 'The Founding of Mount Grace', 259; *Foedera*, ix, pp. 272 – 8.

139 Prob. Reg. 3, fo.529.

140 Oxford Bodl. MS e. Mus. 35 (sum. cat. 3615) has the initials M.N. and the arms of Neville and Beaufort on p. xvi. See Pacht and Alexander, *Illum. Manuscripts*, iii, 939.

with illuminated capitals in the first half of the fifteenth century by a York layman, John Morton, who was probably the brother of an important book collector of the city.[141] The manuscript contains *The Mirror of the Blessed Lyfe of Jesu Crist* and other meditations on the Passion and two letters of fraternity, one of 1396 from the Carmelities of Scarborough for members of the Wyndhill family who had given books to the convent, and the other of 1438 from the York convent for John Morton and his wife Juliana; it is therefore possible that this manuscript was one of the benefactions of Morton connected with the letter of fraternity.[142] In 1448 Agnes Stapleton left *Librum meum vocatum Bonaventura* to the nuns of Sinningthwaite, and in 1450 Sir Thomas Cumberworth left 'my boke de Vita Christi' to William Gaunstede, who was possibly a secular priest of Yorkshire or Nottinghamshire.[143] The inventory of Elizabeth Sewerby, in 1468, records *unum librum de Vita Christi in lingua materna* valued at 10s, which fell into the hands of Thomas Hornby, a secular priest of York and one of Elizabeth's legatees.[144] Hornby left the work to her niece of the same name who was a nun of Nunmonkton. *The Mirror* was also read by secular lawyers: in 1437 Thomas Dautre left *unum librum meum vocatum Bonaventura* to his son John Dautre, who in turn left it to his son William; and in 1468 Arthur Ormsby, a Lincolnshire lawyer, left 'my boke called bonaventure de Christi' to George Neville, the archbishop of York.[145]

Another Carthusian monk, who knew of the existence of Love's work, also paraphrased the *Meditations* in thirty chapters; he addressed the work to a nun and included quotations from Suso's *Horologium*, the *Revelations* of Bridget and other mystical works.[146] This work was also read by the Yorkshire gentry: a second manuscript of the *Life of Our Lord* was made in the mid-fifteenth century for John Lord Scrope and Elizabeth Chaworth, and in the Thornton manuscript this work has been divided into the liturgical hours of the day.[147]

Recluses not only significantly contributed to the religious life of the diocese as authors; they also made eremitical literature available to a wider audience through their activities as scribes. The scribe of the

141 Doyle, 'A Survey', ii, p. 68. For the will of the scribe's brother, John Morton see TE, II, p. 13.
142 Doyle, 'A Survey', ii, p. 68 – 9; Oxford Bodl. MS, 131 (sum. cat. 999), a mid-fifteenth century manuscript on parchment and paper. For text of *Mirror* see fos. 1 – 122.
143 *N.C.W.*, p. 116; *The Academy*, p. 220ff.
144 TE, p. 196.
145 TE, p. 59; Prob. Reg. 2, fo. 413.
146 Doyle, Survey i, p. 159.
147 ibid, p. 160, see Deanesly, 'The Gospel harmony of Jon de Caulibus' for the translation known as *The Privity of the Passion* written in northern dialect. This prose translation predates Love's. See Thornton Manuscript Lincoln Cathedral, fos. 178 – 89; *Yorkshire Writers*, ed. C. Horstmann (London, 1896) I, pp. 198 – 219.

largest surviving compilation of Rolle's Latin works was probably a north-country hermit; showing a scholarly interest in the care of texts and in the details of Rolle's life, he attempted to complete his compilation from many sources and included biographical details of a scholarly rather than a hagiographical nature. He wandered throughout the country of Richmondshire and the regions east of Hampole in search of a new manuscript that would provide a missing verse to Rolle's Latin commentary on the psalter; his success testifies to the rapid and indiscriminate copying of Rolle's works.[148] Between 1409 and 1411 the scribe passed through Tanfield; and in compiling a text for the first book of the *Judica Me Deus* he used a manuscript that had been copied by the hermit of Tanfield, who resided in an abandoned manor house on the manor of Henry Lord FitzHugh of Tanfield.[149] The Tanfield hermit's manuscript was also probably the source for a copy of the *Judica* found in another important compilation of Rolle's works: in both of these compilations there are autobiographical passages missing. It has been suggested that the first scribe to omit these autobiographical passages was the Tanfield hermit, who was primarily interested in the works from an instructive point of view.[150] The Tanfield hermit's manuscript was so authoritative because his source was probably the autographed compilation owned by his patron Lord FitzHugh and Lord Scrope. The crucial Tanfield manuscript, which has unfortunately been lost, was possibly commissioned by these two brothers-in-law. Another recluse scribe was John Lacy, the anchorite of the Black Friars of Newcastle, who was possibly supported by Lord Scrope. Between 1420 and 1430, Lacy transcribed and illuminated a manuscript of 151 folios which contained some of the works of Rolle and Hilton and some of his own devotions, including a commentary on the Ten Commandments, the Seven Deadly Sins and instructions on the administration of Confession. Lacy wrote for his lay neighbours, using their speech and idiom. He left his manuscript to Roger Stonysdale, the chaplain of St Nicholas' Church, with the condition that it was to be handed down from parish priest to parish priest. This recluse also left St John's church, which was near his cell, a copy of the Wycliffite bible.[151]

Carthusian scribes played an important role in making devotional literature available to those in active life, and they probably saw it as their duty to do so; when London Charterhouse was founded Michael Northburgh, the bishop of London, wrote to the priors of Witham and Hinton arguing that it was the duty of the Carthusians to teach and edify

148 Allen, *Writings*, pp. 22 – 34. Oxford, Bodl. MS 861.
149 ibid, pp. 28 – 30.
150 ibid, pp. 28 – 30, Trin. Coll. MS. 153.
151 TE, II, p. 356; M. R. Clay, 'Further studies on medieval recluses' *J.B.A.A.* (1953), 73

others.[152] Mount Grace and Beauvale were especially important centres for studying and transcribing religious literature. Mount Grace owned collections of the works of Rolle, Hilton, the author of *The Cloud*, Bridget, Suso and Margery Kempe, and copies of the works of the author of *The Cloud*, Rolle and Suso were made here.[153] A collection of the major works of Rolle was copied at Beauvale in the mid-fifteenth century; Sir Thomas Chaworth's copy of the *Treatise of Seven Points of True Love* was copied at the monastery; and a volume containing the *Speculum Devotorum*, a compendium of the spiritual life, was transcribed by the Carthusians for John Lord Scrope and his wife Elizabeth Chaworth.[154] Such activity would suggest that the influence of the Carthusians was not confined, as has been claimed, to a close-knit spiritual aristocracy in London.[155]

Recluses were also able to communicate the principles of the contemplative life to the nobility and provide them with spiritual advice in their capacity as private confessors; this was a function which had previously been mainly performed by the friars. The most common reason for consulting a solitary would have been for his or her acknowledged expertise in contemplative matters. Recluses were at the forefront of the devotion to Christ's Passion: their cells were sparsely furnished with an oratory and crucifix to encourage meditation, and some, such as Emma Rawghton's two-storied cell in All Saints' church in North Street, overlooked the high altar of the parish church to allow continual contemplation of Christ's sacrifice.[156] It is possible that recluses were responsible for carving the alabaster tablets depicting scenes from the Passion that were so common in York. The leading devotional writers and holy men of the diocese either served as private confessors to leading families or as public penitentiaries. Rolle was probably the first hermit to establish himself as a leading confessor among the gentry of the East Riding and the baronage of East Riding and Richmondshire. In 1354 Friar John Waldeby was licenced by Archbishop Thoresby to act as public penitentiary in the diocese for two years. The most famous confessor of the second half of the fourteenth century was probably William Sleightholme, who was appointed public penitentiary in 1398 and served as confessor to John Lord Neville, Margery Kempe and possibly Joan Beaufort. Walter Hilton and the author of *The Cloud* both served as confessors and advisors to recluses and

152 Thompson, *Carthusian Order*, p. 119.
153 Doyle, 'A Survey', i, pp. 200–6 and 216, Harl MS 2372 (The works of the Cloud author) MS. Add 37049 (The works of Rolle and Suso).
154 ibid, i, pp. 200–6, 221; ii, p. 267. Douce MS 114.
155 R. Lovatt, '*The Imitation of Christ in Late Medieval England*'. *TRHS*, series xviii (1968), 100; Jeremy Catto, 'Religious Change under Henry V', in G. L. Harris, ed. *Henry V The Practice of Kingship* (Oxford, 1985), p. 111.
156 Clay, *Anchorites*, p. 83.

religious communities, and to men in public life. Hilton advised a lawyer, John Thorpe, and Adam Horsley, clerk of the exchequer. As an advisor of pious laywomen he was famous enough to be consulted by a confessor who wished to know how to direct a woman who was attempting to live a quasi-monastic life in the world. Hilton's reply was conveyed by letter from the confessor to the woman concerned.[157] John Lacy, the scribe and author who occupied a two-storied annexe in the priory of the friars preachers of Newcastle, was probably the anchorite remembered in the will of Lord Scrope. Lacy also received bequests from Cecilia Homildon and the Newcastle merchant Roger Thornton.[158] Richard Misyn, a Carmelite friar and one-time hermit, translated Rolle's *Incendium Amoris* in 1433 for Margaret Heslington, a recluse of Heslington near York and a member of the York Corpus Christi guild since 1428.[159] Misyn also served as the private chaplain of Henry Percy, Earl of Northumberland, in 1441.[160] In the light of the bequests that the Carthusians of Mount Grace and Beauvale attracted and their activity as devotional writers, translators and scribes, it is likely that the monks of these houses acted as confessors or guides to the local nobility.

It is, furthermore, probable that many other recluses not noted as authors still established reputations in the diocese as authorities on spiritual matters, and that they were consulted as such by their lay patrons. Rolle's disciples Margaret Kirkby, her servant Elizabeth, and the anchoress of Kirkby Wiske may have given spiritual guidance to members of the Scrope and Stapleton families. The anchorites supported by the parishioners of St Saviour's York were possibly spiritually and intellectually distinguished. Their popularity coincides with Mr Adam Wigan's rectorship. Wigan was educated at Balliol, and he bequeathed a copy of St Gregory on Ezechiel to his friend Richard Stapleton, master of the college.[161] His long residence in one parish, St Saviour's from 1399 until his death in 1433 was, considering his intellectual stature, exceptional, and it is likely that he provided spiritual guidance as well as material help to the anchoresses of All Saints', Fishergate, Walmgate and Thurganby. He also probably helped to foster a close relationship between recluses and their patrons, the York merchants Richard Russel, Thomas Bracebrige and John Bolton, perhaps creating a similar religious atmosphere to the one inspired by Richard Rolle in the areas around Ainderby and Hampole. Another scholar with

157 C. Riehle, *The Middle English Mystics* (London, 1981), p. 19. The letter does not survive but is referred to in B.L. MS. Harl. 2406 fos. 50 – 60v.

158 W.I., pp. 44 and 78 – 80.

159 *The Fire of Love and the Mending of Life*, ed. R. Harvey, (London, EETS, 1896); *Register of the Guild of Corpus Christi in the city of York*, ed. R. H. Skaife (SS; 1872).

160 Emden, *B.R.U.O.* II, 1286; C.P.L. ix, p. 210 – 11.

161 Emden, *B.R.U.O.*, iii, p.

a close involvement in the solitary life who was connected to this St Saviour's circle was John Raventhorpe, who resided with his servant in St Martin's chapel within the parish of St Saviour's (quarters formerly occupied by a priest anchorite). Raventhorpe left a large library to various York citizens, a psalter and an alabaster image of the Pietà to the parishioners of St Saviour's church where he was buried, and a large portifor to Richard Russel.[162] Emma Rawghton, the anchoress of All Saints' church, North Street, who had a national reputation, may also have been connected with this circle: she received forty shillings from the will of Richard Russel. In Richmond towards the end of the fourteenth century there was an anchoress sufficiently well known to be visited by John Thweng.[163] She was probably Joan Samson who was supported by John Fairfax and the Nevilles, the lords of Richmond. Alice Derby, an anchoress of Clementhorpe whose cell was probably attached to the small fashionable nunnery of the same name, had a distinguished and learned clientèle and received legacies from Thomas Howren, the rector of All Saints'; Lady Margaret Stapleton, who made her will in 1465 while residing in the nunnery; Elizabeth Sewerby; and the York chantry priest Robert Est: all these patrons had libraries of the devotional writings of the north-east.[164]

These recluses, in their work as confessors and spiritual counsellors, exchanged contemplative literature with their clients. An anchorite of Lichfield, possibly the author of an English version of the *Ancren Riwle* known as the *Treatise on Five Wits*, attributed in one manuscript to a person with the name of Lichfield, left a book of devotion, perhaps this same work, to Robert Wolveden, the treasurer of York Minster; Wolveden in turn bequeathed the book to John Appilton, a subtreasurer, in 1432.[165] Sir Thomas Ughtred received a breviary and a missal from Thomas Coke, an anchorite who served as his chantry priest in a chapel on his manor of Kexby; and Matilda, an anchoress who inhabited an old cell at the foot of the town steps of Lincoln at the foot of Holy Trinity, received alms and a scroll of prayers and devotions from Sir Thomas Cumberworth, the owner of a substantial collection of devotional literature.[166] It is probable that the Carthusians of Mount Grace loaned books: in 1458 William Banks, a gentleman of York, left 20s to the monastery to satisfy any claims concerning a book called '*Florarium Bartholomei*'.[167]

162 TE, II, p. 28.
163 TE, I, pp. 50 – 52, 180, *Nova Legenda* ii, p. 67.
164 Y.M.L. Dean and Chapter Wills, Reg. Test. I, fo. 317; *N.C.W.*, p. 48; TE, II, p. 64; and p. 159.
165 Prob. Reg. I, fo. 235; Doyle, *A Survey*, ii, p. 135; Bod. Lib. Rawl. MS. 8c.
166 TE, I, p. 244; *The Academy*, pp. 280 – 5.
167 Lovatt, 'Rhineland Spirituality' p. 375, TE, II, p. 217.

The role of recluses as confessors and intimate counsellors for the nobility is further demonstrated by their importance in the court; most of the prominent anchorites at Westminster were northerners and associated with Syon (a monastery with strong northern affiliations). There were two reclusaria near the palace itself at Westminster Abbey. One near the infirmary housed Dan John Murymouth (d.1393) who heard the confession of Richard II on the night before he rode out to meet the peasants, and his successor John London, a former treasurer of Queen Eleanor's manor who occupied this cell soon after 1390 until his death in 1429. London was consulted by Thomas Earl of Warwick, Thomas Beaufort Duke of Exeter, and Henry Lord Scrope of Masham who left the recluse 100s and a rosary.[168] London was also probably a confessor to the nuns of Syon because his name occurs on the obit roll of the monastery.[169] The other Westminster cell was built in the fourteenth century between the south transept of St Benedict's chapel and was inhabited in the early fifteenth century by a northerner, William Alnwick, a Benedictine monk of St Albans who was probably the Westminster recluse to whom Henry V made a full confession on the evening following his father's funeral.[170] The King's trust in him was shown in his appointment as the first confessor general of Syon. Another recluse influential in the court and at Syon was Thomas Fishbourne, once a landed gentleman of Yorkshire who had acted as steward to abbot William Heyworth of St Albans before being ordained and enclosed in a cell at St Germain's near the abbey in 1409.[171] During his enclosure from 1409 to 1413 Fishbourne acted as confessor to a number of ladies of the court who were members of the lay fraternity of this abbey, including Lady Eleanor Hull, a servant of Joan of Navarre (the wife of Henry IV) and Elizabeth Beauchamp, wife of Richard Beauchamp, Earl of Warwick,[172] Through these ladies Fishbourne came to the notice of Henry IV; he served as his chaplain in 1413 before his appointment in 1421 as Alnwick's successor as confessor to the nuns of Syon. Many of these nuns were of aristocratic background and Fishbourne's library was appropriate to the needs of a court confessor and included: tracts on the active and contemplative lives; aids to meditation in the form of St Edmund's *Speculum Ecclesie*; and confession manuals such as the *Summa Summarum* and the *Pupilla oculi*.[173] The Beauchamp family were especially influenced by solitaries

168 Clay, *Anchorites*, p. 154; Knowles, *Religious Orders*, ii, pp. 220 – 22, 367 – 8; C. Peers, and L. E. Tanner, 'On Some Recent Discoveries in Westminster Abbey', *Archaeologia*, 93, (1949), 151 – 64.

169 T. Gascoigne, *Loci e Libro Veritatum*, ed. J. Rodgers (Oxford, 1881), p. 170.

170 *Festa Henrici Quinto*, ed. F. Taylor and J. S. Roskell (Oxford, 1975), pp. 15, 147.

171 Wylie, *Henry V*, I, 224.

172 CPR, 1413 – 16, pp. 26, 71; CPR, 1420 – 24, p. 304.

173 Bateson, *Syon Catalogue*, pp. 102, 108, 110.

from the north: while Elizabeth was consulting Fishbourne, her husband Richard Beauchamp (a nephew of Isabella Gifford, the patron of Julian of Norwich) was obeying the specific prophecies of Emma Rawghton, anchoress of All Saints' North Street in York. In the first year of Henry IV's reign Emma prophesied that if Richard founded a chantry in the chapel of the hermitage of Guy's Cliff, a mile from Warwick, he would have a male heir. In 1428, one year before the rise of prominence of Joan of Arc, she made it known that it had been shown to her by Our Lady that the infant king Henry VI ought to be crowned in France as well as England, and that no person was better fitted to be his guardian than Richard Beauchamp.[174] Perhaps Emma influenced royal policy, for shortly afterwards Beauchamp became a member of the council that ruled for the king, who was crowned in France, and from 1428 to 1436 he was king's tutor. These prophecies were at least widely regarded as truthful and at the end of the fifteenth century a life of Richard Beauchamp was commissioned consisting of fifty-three pencil drawings and epistles, including two legends showing the success of Emma's two predictions, the crowning of the king and the birth of Richard's heir in 1425.[175]

Recluses, therefore, were significant in the upper levels of society within the diocese of York, at the university of Cambridge, to a lesser extent Oxford, and at Westminster. They provided personal spiritual guidance to the leaders of the diocese and the kingdom, and it was therefore inevitable that by the late fourteenth century their teachings would have considerable social significance.

The Teachings of the Recluse and their Social Application

Hermits and anchorites of late fourteenth century Yorkshire still performed the same functions as their predecessors in the eleventh and twelfth centuries: Carthusian monks, anchorites and hermits continued to write for their fellow professionals who were attempting to master the contemplative art. However, their teachings were different in that they were adapted to fit the needs of their lay patrons who depended on recluses as spiritual guides and confessors. Their writing therefore had social significance and influenced the development of religious sensibilities throughout society. The solitaries of the late fourteenth century may have provided guidance on the principles of the contemplative life but they were not isolated professionals, for even Rolle's teachings had

174 Clay, *Anchorites*, pp. 157; John Rous, *Rous Rol*, (London, 1845), no. 50; Warren, *Anchorites*, p. 204.

175 Warren, *Anchorites*, p. 204.

affinities with the sensibilities of his less educated neighbours; and more importantly, his followers in the late fourteenth century showed an awareness of the social implications of all teachings on the eremitic life. This they analysed in their discussions on the conflicts between the active and contemplative lives.

The ideal of the cenobitic life was to reach a state of detachment from the community; and the writers of devotional literature in this period concerned themselves with the place occupied in society by the individual who had dedicated himself to God. The clearest resolution of this question lay in theoretical definitions of two separate modes of living: the active and contemplative lives. These terms originated in the works of Augustine, which were available in most fourteenth century libraries. Augustine was the first to allegorize Luke X.38 – 42 as a description of the two lives: Martha, busy around Christ, symbolized a life of worthwhile but transitory activity, and Mary, resting at Christ's feet, represented the detached contemplation of eternity. Genesis XXIV.30 provided further material for exposition on the two lives: Jacob's fertile wife Leah, who is merely endured by Jacob, symbolized a life of activity, undertaken from a sense of duty rather than joy for the sake of the fruits of such good works as preaching; and Rachel, Jacob's sterile wife who is loved for her own sake, betokened a life of joy in a contemplation that was free from all responsibility.[1] Gregory elaborated Augustine's expositions to give, as Wyclif was to acknowledge, the first formal definition of the active and contemplative lives. Gregory defined more precisely the duties of the blind and fertile Leah, which included (for laymen) feeding the poor, helping and correcting neighbours, caring for dependents, and (for clergy) teaching and preaching by word and example. The duties of Rachel included resting in silence and cultivating the beauties of a mind that is unable to communicate what it has seen.[2]

The connection between these two scriptural passages and the theory of the active and contemplative lives became standard by the fourteenth century: instructions on the duties of the two lives were absorbed into the liturgical calendar, the gospel reading for the Feast of the Assumption in all uses was Luke X.38 – 42; and expositions were provided by contemplative writers of the diocese.[3] Shortly after becoming a hermit Rolle preached his first public sermon at Pickering church on the Feast of the Assumption, probably justifying his newly

1 F. J. Steele, 'Definitions of the Active Life in Middle English Literature of the thirteenth, fourteenth and fifteenth Centuries' (Oxf. D. Phil. thesis 1979), pp. 12 – 25. C. Butler, *Western Mysticism* (London, 1927), p. 171.

2 Butler, pp. 172 and 182. *Moralia in Iob*, PL 75 – 6 vl. 61. *Moralia* P.L. 75, 727. *Hom. in Ezech.* P.L. 76

3 Steele, p. 79.

closen contemplative vocation.[4] His treatment of the mutual exclusiveness to the two lives was extreme: discussing the active duties of the clergy, he claimed that those of the most mystical dispositions do not desire a cure of souls, and even if they did feel the call from contemplation to action they would find it impossible to obey it.[5] The individuality of Rolle's treatment of the two lives lies in his defence of a contemplative vocation, the eremitical or enclosed life. For him the one controlling motive for such a life was love of God. For this the hermit will disown human contact, wordly approval and power. Rolle claimed that he found it necessary to flee to the wilderness because he found it impossible to live harmoniously with other men who were an obstacle to his inner joy. Away from the tumult of the town, the noise and distractions of communal life, and the cares of the world, he experienced with a clear conscience the gifts of *calor, dulcedo* and *canor*. Because of this knowledge of things hidden and insights into spiritual matters he proclaimed the eremitical or enclosed life, which followed the traditions of John the Baptist, the prince of hermits, and Cuthbert, to be the highest state in the church.[6]

The later contemplative writers of the diocese all recognized the inevitability of the conflicting claims of the two ways of life, and in elaborating on the differences between them they did not draw a distinction between clergy and laity, but between those clergy and laymen who lived a secular life, and those who laid aside all the privileges and duties of the active life for the love of God. They all interpreted the *pars Marthae* as the willingness of clerics to answer the call to pastoral duty, and the readiness of laymen to live up to the dictates of the pastoral manuals. The Yorkshireman, John Wyclif, shared this interest in the eremitic life and wrote a number of Assumption sermons on the text of Luke X.38 – 42. He saw the active life as the bulwark of the authority of the church and its pastoral ideals: the superiority of the active life was maintained in canon law by the pope and other doctors in the interests of church government, secular dominion and the obligations inherent in the offices within the church: he saw this as a rationalization affording clergy with an excuse to engage in purely secular pursuits; and he described the commitments of the active life as spiritually harmful: 'It is impossible for a man to lead an active life without falling into sin.[7] Walter Hilton also maintained that the preoccupation of the followers of Martha with their duties prevented

4 *Brev. Ebor.* Appendix.
5 *The Incendium Amoris of Richard Rolle*, ed. M. Deanesly (Manchester, 1915), pp. 204 – 7.
6 ibid, pp. 182 – 6.
7 *Wyclif Super Evangelia de Sanctis xx and Sermones Miscellanei* xlviii in Johnannis Wyclif *Sermones*, ed. J. Loserth (Wyclif Soc. 1887 – 90) Vol. II p. 147 1 – 5 Vol. VI 387/ 33 – 5.

them, to their peril, from profiting from the spiritual works which were more rewarding and pleasing to God. In the letter of legal and spiritual direction written for John Thorpe, Hilton revealed his own dissatisfaction with the competitive and emotionally charged atmosphere of society, and his own profession in particular. He warned Thorpe that no matter now much he was able to profit from his education in legal consultations and law suits, there lurked within such worldly intercourse a pride, avarice, falsehood and servility that could poison the affections. Advising his friend to despise the world by abandoning the study and practice of the law and relinquishing his benefices, he told him to resist the pressure of those who condemned any attempt to follow Christ in purity and simplicity as foolish madness; such people, Hilton claimed, tried to implicate converts in their own dependence on human society under the pretence of offering them employment in a legal capacity.[8] The author of *The Cloud* also commented on the incompatibility of the two lives; and the conflict was expressed from the layman's viewpoint by Stephen Scrope, who included Gregory's commentary on Ezechiel in his translation of *The Epistle to Othea*. Scrope discussed the tensions felt by one who feels the call of the contemplative life and is faced with the duties of knighthood; the knight with contemplative aspirations is advised to abandon his active life: 'þe good knyt goosli tending oonly to þe knyghthood of heven, shulde be whooly drawen fro þe worlde and chese contemplatiif liif'.[9] The conviction of these writers in the superiority of the contemplative life and the need for those feeling its call to abandon their active lives is the theoretical background to the growth of the eremitic movement in the fourteenth century.

The prestige of recluses in society was derived from their status as solitary figures who appeared, symbolically at least, to have detached themselves from human society and the corporate rituals of communities centred on the parish church and the guilds. This social detachment gave solitaries more prestige than they would have had before taking their vows, and it is possible that in some cases an original decision to live an eremitic life was inspired by dissatisfaction with uncertain social status. Rolle's father was a prosperous but landless yeoman, and Richard Bradley, the preaching hermit, was probably the illegitimate son of Richard Lord Scrope of Bolton.[10] Many anchoresses were probably from small gentry families who had been unable to

8 Cit. J. M. Russel-Smith, 'Walter Hilton and a Tract in Defence of the Veneration of Images' *Dominican Studies* VII (1954), 185; MS. Royal E III fol. 115 r b.

9 Scrope, *Epistle to Othea*, ed. C. F. Butler (London, EETS, 1970), p. 97/15; *The Cloud of Unknowing*, ed. P. Hodgson (London, EETS, 1944), p. 30/21 – 3 31/16 47/3 55/6.

10 Tanner, 'Popular Religion in Norwich', p. 119. For the books allegedly written by Bradley see Bale, *Scriptorum Catalogus*, pp. 629 – 30.

provide them with sufficient dowers to enable them to join fashionable nunneries, or to enter into marriages that could eventually give them the status as pious widows enjoyed by Agnes and Margaret Stapleton. Recluses frequently continued to betray their social origins in their new vocation. Many of the miracles of St Robert of Knaresborough are concerned with the ferocious defence of his rights on his small plots of land against the encroachments of the local landlord.[11] Many solitaries cultivated small gardens attached to their cells, and Margaret Kirkby, whose family were small landowning gentry, continued to keep a servant. But for most people recluses escaped social definition: they could not be categorized as bond or freeman, landlords or retainers, or ordained priests or laymen. Their new respect came from social detachment. The Richmondshire nobility who visited Rolle in his cell admired his ability to remain apart while engaging in the social ritual of conversation. Thomas Samson, a paralytic who demonstrated his conquest of his body and his social environment by abstaining from eating for seven years, attracted the attention of Archbishop John Thoresby in 1355.[12]

Recluses interested in influencing the spiritual development of clients and lay society in general were confronted with the problem that theories about the two lives and superiority of the hermit's social detachment could do little to help the spiritual development of those in active life. Such theories could merely encourage a passive admiration, or even worship, of such detachment; this can be seen in bequests to solitaries and the prolification of saints' cults; they could, on the other hand, arouse dissatisfaction and cause people to discard impulsively their responsibilities and become hermits. These difficulties had been foreseen, and recluses made their detachment into a source of objective social authority, like the hermits of Egypt and Syria in the fifth century; fourteenth century recluses, in their work as confessors, performed tasks of social arbitration, reconciling penitents to their communities by encouraging outward social conformity and inner detachment.[13]

The traditional social mediator had been the parish priest: the handbook for confessors written by William Pagula of Humberside between 1320 and 1322 outlined the role of the parish priest as a guarantor of social harmony. The *Pars oculi* and subsequent adaptations such as John Myrk's *Instructions for Parish Priests* were not concerned with introspection for its own sake and instructed confessors to enquire

11 *The Life of St Robert of Knaresborough*, ed. H. J. T. Drury (Roxburgh Club, 1824); see chapter six for further details.

12 *The Kirkstall Chronicle*, ed. M. V. Clarke and N. Denholme (J.R.L. 1931), p. 121; Oxf. Bodl. MS Dods. 140.

13 P. Brown, *The Making of Late Antiquity*, (Harvard, 1978), pp. 80 – 82; and 'The Holy Man in Late Antiquity', in P. Brown, *Society and the Holy in Late Antiquity* (London, 1982), pp. 127 – 38.

into the thoughts and actions that threatened to disrupt a penitent's relationship with his community. Confessors were therefore required to examine the social behaviour of their parishioners, to define sins as impulses and activities that indicated hostility towards others in the parish: gluttony was not regarded as a compulsive habit but an anti-social act depriving others in the community of food;[14] even barely conscious impulses were defined in this way: a penitent who felt pleasure at a neighbour's misfortunes and disappointment at his success would be expected to confess to the sin of envy. In assigning penance the priest determined the gravity of confessed sins by the degree of hostility shown and the amount of disruption caused to the community; and he required penitents to make restitution to those they had wronged in thought, word or deed: gluttons were to give alms to the poor,[15] the envious man had to reconcile himself with his neighbours and provide him with tangible help. The penitential handbooks therefore depicted religion as a buttress for the continuity and stability of society[16], and penance was seen as an act of social atonement sealed by the celebration of mass. There was little sympathy for individuality: the most severe penances were reserved for the sins of self-assertion, pride and anger. However, there were penitents, namely the very devout, who would have seen their thoughts and sinful impulses in a much more private context, and who felt the need to reconcile themselves primarily to God. Recluses such as Rolle, Hilton and the author of *The Cloud of Unknowing*, who acted as confessors, catered for such people by helping them to reconcile themselves to God as well as their communities.

An individualist such as Rolle must have found Pagula's lack of sympathy for individuality hard to accept, and he wrote his own confession manual, *Judica Me Deus*, which he adapted from Pagula's *Pars oculi* for a friend who was a parish priest. Rolle altered the social dimension of this standard confession manual to provide a subjective interpretation of sin and confession. He began his manual with a devotional sermon, *Judica A*, in which he urged his friend to become a hermit, claiming that noone but God could know a man's heart. Among his instructions on the administration of confession, which comprised *Judica B2*, he included advice to the parish priest on preaching to his parishioners from texts urging them to love God and to live in solitutde from other men. Throughout the work the author stressed that virtue was to be found only in the heart, and that only through loving Christ

14 John Myrk, *Instructions for Parish Priests*, ed. E. Peacock (E.E.T.S., London, 1905), 11 1315 – 16.

15 ibid, 11. 1705 – 10.

16 cf. J. Bossy, 'Social History of Confession', *TRHS*, (1974); for discussion of Pagula see L. E. Boyle, 'A Study of the Works attributed to William of Pagula' (Oxford Univ. D Phil. thesis, 1956).

could forgiveness be obtained. Descriptions of mystical ecstacy, Rolle's only criteria for salvation, were included to undermine further the social ideals of the author's source.[17] *The Judica Me Deus* may have been used as a confession manual by Rolle in the Scrope household, because Henry Lord Scrope of Masham bequeathed the autographed *Judica* to Henry Lord FitzHugh in 1415. Another anchorite to introduce a more personal devotional element to a confession manual was John Lacy, the anchorite of the Black Friars' in Newcastle; between 1420 and 1434 Lacy combined Thoresby's *Lay Folk's Catechism* with his own private devotions.[18]

Walter Hilton wrote at length on confession, especially in the *Scale of Perfection*, where he described the administration of confession as the means whereby the church extended its pastoral authority by encouraging people to conform to the social standards taught by parish priests and providing them with the opportunity to do so; this entailed avoiding the Seven Deadly Sins, living in peace with one's neighbours and performing good deeds, all of which was supervised by the confessor.[19] He defined the conscience nurtured in such confessions as purely social, motivated by fear or disobeying the precepts of the church rather than from personal sense of dissatisfaction. Such confessions, he claimed, no matter how frequent, brought no change of feeling in the penitent and did not distinguish him from an irregular attender at confession; such penitents are described as: 'Simple souls, the which feel not the gift of special devotion, nor ghostly knowing of God . . . but trow generally as holy kirk troweth, and not fully wit that is'.[20] Compulsory annual confession was, he claimed, instituted for the minority of people who would neither feel contrition nor leave their sins without a social system to measure themselves against. It linked such people with a devout minority by a reformation in faith rather than feeling: 'But for all men are not so perfect, and peradventure mickle of the more part of Christian men is unperfect, therefore Holy Kirk ordained confession by way of general bond to all Christian men'.[21] The author of *The Cloud of Unknowing* drew the same distinction between a spiritual minority and the uninitiated who needed compulsory confession to show them the stains on their consciences.[22] He showed no interest in the social context of confession, and discussed the Seven Deadly Sins as inner rather than social failings. John Wyclif also showed no interest in the routine of parish work and the problems of the parish confessor and

17 Allen, *Writings*, pp. 93 – 101.
18 J. F. Royster, 'A Treatise on the Ten Commandments', 21.
19 W. Hilton, *The Scale of Perfection*, ed. E. Underhill (London, 1923).
20 ibid, p. 257.
21 ibid, p. 248.
22 *The Cloud of Unknowing*, p. 71.

ignored in his writings the social sins discussed in the confession manuals.

Such contrasting views on confession were not socially divisive because all devotional writers recognized that it was the duty of a sympathetic confessor to reconcile devout penitents to their society through outward conformity and inner detachment. Hilton described the attendance of a devout minority at compulsory annual confession as a necessary concession to the community; absolution was necessary to ensure an isolated and pious man's acceptance in society and his safety from his enemies, like the charter or pardon obtained by an outlaw from the king. It ratified his acceptance. For such a man society could be inherently repressive because it was the duty of the clergy to seek and correct faults, and laymen were required to correct the faults of their neighbours, although both clergy and laity were ideally motivated by charity and not a love of chastisement.[23] Hilton advised the devout man to remain detached from such activity, and other devotional writers recommended that the piously individualistic, who were required to perform the penances of the parish confessor, showed the same detachment. Nicholas Love, in *The Myrour,* instructed penitents to follow the footsteps of Christ by feeling compassion for men's sins and the misery of this transitory life; Christ's life was a penitential existence, and he was the first to communicate the allienation of the devout man when he spoke to his disciples: 'He confortede her hope agenst tribulacions and hate of the worlde, seyenge thus, if the world hate yow, wieth wele that it hated me firste byfare yowe'.[24] Therefore lovers of Christ can perform with detachment any penance assigned to them, because they 'knawen oure self here as pilgrims and strangers'.[25] The same message was given by Julian of Norwich to Margery Kempe who visited her cell: 'the more despyte, schame, and repref that ye haue in the world the more is your meryte in the syghth of God'.[26]

But although devotional writers advised attendance at compulsory annual parish confession, there was a recognition that there was also a need for an alternative form of shriving. Hilton said the parish priest's sign of absolution could mean little for the devout because no matter how frequently they were shriven they would still feel the biting and fretting of conscience. Sinful impulses which caused one to doubt one's love of God and his forgiveness could not be combatted by a conventional confession.[27] Both the monk solitary of Farne and Julian the anchoress of Norwich discussed at length the devout person's

23 *Scale,* p. 246.
24 *The Mirror,* p. 213.
25 ibid, p. 86.
26 *The Book of Margery Kemp,* p. 43.
27 *The Scale,* p. 77.

struggle to reconcile their love and fear of God. For Julian this took the form of a conflict between intimations of God's love and forgiveness and the institutional discipline of the church.[28] Her greatest moment of spiritual crisis occurred when she had doubts about the sincerity of her experiences of God's love after speaking flippantly with a parish priest; and she could find no one to absolve her.[29] According to Hilton social forgiveness and reconciliation was of little use to such people; what was required was a reformation in thought and feeling that brought a genuine inner richness and a belief in one's own worthiness.[30] This could only be obtained through introspective meditation and confession to someone who did not repress inner potential but encouraged it. For penitents who felt a sense of conflict between their respect for the social discipline of the church, administered through the sacrament of penance, and their faith in and doubt about their own private intimations of God's love and forgiveness, the only valid shrift was that made to one who had left society to dedicate himself to the love of God: such penitents would turn to the solitary. It was a recluse that Hilton had in mind when he advised the devout man to keep experiences of the visitation of the Lord to himself and to show it only to his confessor.[31] Margery Kempe revealed her experiences to an anchorite of Lynn, but once during his absence she was forced to take her confession to the parish priest, and she did not find him so tolerant; she complained to her regular confessor that her feelings were repudiated as 'mere japes'.[32] Anchorite confessors such as John London and Thomas Fishbourne had a clientèle that was more exclusive and wide ranging than that of the parish priest, and there was less chance that they would arouse the resentment of secular priests as the friars had done. Henry Scrope of Masham, the owner of a large library of devotional books, knew recluses all over the country; and he is an example of a devout layman who would have confessed to solitaries. Recluses were responsible for encouraging introspection in their clients, and they taught him to regard confession as an intimate disclosure to an understanding spiritual guide. Parish confessions were made in front of the congregation to a parish priest who covered his eyes with his hood; they were public affairs, but confessions were made to anchorites through barred windows in what was the first step towards the development of the private confessional.[33]

[28] Julian of Norwich, *Revelations of Divine Love*, ed. R. Hudleston (London, 1927), pp. 80 – 83.
[29] ibid, p. 137.
[30] *The Scale*, p. 256.
[31] ibid, p. 11.
[32] *The Book of Margery Kempe*, p. 44.
[33] J. Myrc, *Instructions for Parish Priests*, ed. E. Pecock (London, EETS, 1868), ll 845 and ll 851 – 2.

The recluses' concern with the spiritual problems of those in active life was an important new development. The eremitic movement of the twelfth century had expanded into an attempt to reform the monastic communities and increase their spirituality; but by the fourteenth century eremitic zeal was being directed towards the much larger community that constituted society in general. Many hermits and anchorites were not ordained, and their lives could therefore be seen as an extreme manifestation of lay piety. Many laymen and secular clergy attempted to emulate such piety by incorporating eremitic teaching and practices into their active lives. One way of achieving this was through membership of the lay fraternities of contemplative communities. Charterhouses could provide temporary retreats for those unable to retire from the world; Thomas Arundel, Archbishop of Canterbury, and Robert Est, the York chantry chaplain with connections with Clementhorpe, were members of the lay fraternity of Mount Grace; and Sir Hugh Willoughby, a former friend of Philip Repyndon — the bishop of Lincoln who retired to a charterhouse — was a member of the Beauvale fraternity. These men anticipated Sir Thomas More who made periodic retreats to London charterhouse.[34] In the city of York the Corpus Christi Guild, founded in 1408, was a popular fraternity that also attracted men and women of intellectual and social distinction. Most of the leading book owners of the diocese were members including: Margery Scrope, mother of Henry Lord Scrope, her son Stephen, Archdeacon of Richmond, John, the fourth lord of Masham, Sir John Stapleton, Elizabeth Sewerby, Richard Misyn and Margaret Heslington, Thomas and John Dautre, John Newton and Robert Wolvedon.[35] The popular lay fraternity in court circles that was influenced by eremitic teaching was the fraternity of the Benedictine abbey of St Alban's, situated on the great road to the north about a day's ride from the court. John London and Thomas Fishbourne were closely associated with the abbey, and Fishbourne encouraged some of his clients at the court to enter its lay fraternity. In 1416 he and Eleanor Hull, a former prioress of Sopwell, were admitted to the honorary fraternity, and later in the same year Eleanor's husband and son were admitted, to be followed in 1417 by another of Fishbourne's patrons, Elizabeth Beauchanp.[36] Eleanor resided periodically at St Alban's Sopwell until 1427; her mistress, Queen Joan of Navarre was also connected with the abbey, and the

34 *Sede Vacante Wills*, ed. C. E. Woodruff (Kent Arch. Soc; III, 1914), pp. 81 – 2; Reg. Test; I fo. 331, TE, II, p. 131, Willougby owned a collection of plate once belonging to Repyndon.

35 *Register of the Guild of Corpus Christi.*

36 CPR, 1408 – 12, p. 397; CPR, 1413 – 16, pp. 27, 71; 1420 – 24, p. 304; C. E. Hodge, 'The Abbey of St Albans under John Whethampstede', (Manchester Univ. Ph.D. thesis, 1933), p. 143.

Queen's treasurer and receiver, John Foxholes, a former chaplain of Henry Lord Scrope, made frequent visits there. Other members of the fraternity included: Joan Beaufort, who joined in 1424; the infant king Henry VI and his nurses, who joined in 1424; Margaret Duchess of Clarence; Humphrey Duke of Gloucester and his wife Eleanor Cobham, Oldcastle's widow, who owned a copy of the *Ancren Riwle*.[37]

The temporary retreats offered by lay fraternities were not always sufficient: some wives regarded their widowhood as a release from active responsibilities, and they took vows of chastity to become 'vowesses'. In a ceremony conducted by the archbishop or his suffragan, either before or during the celebration of mass, the 'vowess' was given a mantle, veil and ring, and she took a vow of chastity and made a sign of the cross, promising to God and Our Lady to live stably in chastity all her life. The investiture closely resembled the profession of an anchoress, but the vowess was entitled to live in the world, to make a will and to dispose of property. Between 1370 and 1470, widows in the diocese of York were regularly professed as vowesses, and some were attached to Yorkshire nunneries, especially Clementhorpe, where they lived lives of contemplation and seclusion. Widows taking the veil at Clementhorpe included: Joan Scargill, whose husband was buried in the convent in 1400, Margaret Norton, the widow of John Stapleton, Elizabeth de-la-River and Isabella Bruce. Elizabeth Chaworth, the widow of John Lord Scrope, took the veil as a vowess in 1455, but her place of retirement is unknown.[38] The vow of chastity, especially if it was made by couples such as Mr and Mrs Kempe, symbolized the rejection of the claims of the flesh and a formal attachment to an eremitic life. Richard Andrew and his wife Anne both vowed in 1479 'to be chaste from this time on and to live in fasting, prayer and works of piety'; and Andrew described himself as a hermit, promising to live stably in this vow after the order of hermits.[39]

Another appropriate time to express eremitic sentiments was during the drawing up of the last will and testament. Testamentary language provides ambiguous evidence of religious sentiment because it can merely reflect the conventions of testators and their notaries. Nevertheless, during the period between 1370 and 1420 when recluses were playing an increasingly important role in the religious life of the diocese, there was a significant change in the convention; self-denigratory language towards the soul and body and expressions of contempt for

37 *Chronicum Rerum Gestarum in Monasterio S. Albani*, AD 1422–31, in Johanne Amundesham, *Annales Monasterii S. Albani*, ed. H. T. Riley (Rolls ser; London, 1870), I. pp. 12, 16, 27, 33, 40, 65. The author, an unknown monk, was a court chronicler as much as a monastic chronicler.

38 TE, III, Appendix, p. 312ff.

39 ibid.

the world were being used for the first time. The contemplation of human bones as a penance for the sin of pride had been recommended in confession manuals, but in its extreme form it was normally reserved for the recluse, as can be seen in illustrations of St Jerome holding a skull. When Yorkshire gentry and magnates chose to contemplate the corruptibility of their mortal remains and express hatred for the world in their wills, then at least part of the explanation must lie with the growing importance of recluses in the diocese and the increased reading of devotional literature. One of the earliest of these wills was that of Sir William Mowbray, a friend of Sir Brian Stapleton and son-in-law of Sir John Dependen; in 1391 Mowbray, writing in his own hand in French, asked to be buried in the house of the friars minor of York with one dimly lit candle, no dignitaries or crowds and no vain glory around his vile body.[40] Sir Brian Stapleton referred to his miserable soul, and in 1397 Sir Ralph Hastings asked for burial at Selby Abbey without any distinctions, apart from a candle at his head and feet, and asked to be drawn in a simple cart on the day of his departure from this miserable world.[41] By the first half of the fifteenth century such self-denigratory language was becoming common among those Yorkshire men and women who were reading devotional texts and patronizing solitaries. In 1424 Henry Lord FitzHugh requested that his wretched body be carried openly as quickly as possible and interred at night if necessary.[42] His widow Elizabeth referred in her will in 1427 to 'her bones', and Margaret Stapleton in 1465 made a reference to *post humacionem completam*.[43] Thomas and John Dautre, who both had large collections of devotional works, referred to their putrid cadavers and described themselves as miserable sinners.[44] Such language was rare, especially before 1420, and outside the diocese it was confined to the wills of courtiers and ecclesiastical dignitaries. The wills of the gentry of a diocese like Bath and Wells, where there is little evidence of the ownership of devotional texts, reveal no such penitential language.

More common, but equally perhaps a reflection of the popularity of eremitic teaching in this period and the changes it brought about in religious conventions in the diocese were the innovations in Yorkshire funerals between 1370 and 1410. In a significant number of funerals the traditional assertion of familial and communal ties was replaced by a more austere and even private service. East Riding landowners Sir Marmaduke Constable and Sir William Heghfield requested, in 1373 and

40 TE, I, pp. 158 – 60.
41 ibid, I, p. 217.
42 For an abstract of this will, which no longer survives, see *Register of the Archdeaconry of Richmond* 1361 – 1442, ed. A. H. Thompson (YAJ xcv.) pp. 206 – 7.
43 *Test. Vet*; p. 212.
44 TE, p. 97; Prob. Reg. 2, fo 413.

1403, that expenditure on their funerals did not exceed alms payments; and in 1402 Sir John Dependen wanted no gathering of feasting neighbours at his funeral, and requested that all his mourners wear black.[45] Displays of chivalry, of escutcheons and arms, were giving way to interments that were more appropriate for a Carthusian monk or recluse. Burial cloths of gold or silk, displaying the family arms, were replaced by coarse woollen cloth in the funeral of Sir William Mennevill in 1372 and Sir John Dependen in 1402.[46] In 1373 and 1420, Sir Marmaduke Constable and Robert Germyn, esquire, presented the mortuary gift of horses without customary armour and family banners.[47] Some requested no memorials: Michael de la Pole, whose family founded Hull Charterhouse, and John Lord Neville of Latimer asked for blank burial stones.[48] Such wills, when seen in conjunction with the increased lay participation in the contemplative life of the north-east, can be seen as genuine expressions of piety. The expressions of self-negatory and world-hating sentiments near death, and the desire for simple and humble burials was perhaps the nearest that those living lives of conflicting ties and responsibilities could come to the unambigious rejection of the world that was achieved by Rolle and his followers.

The Lollard heresy can also be seen as an aspect of the eremitic movement as it spread beyond the diocese. Although all devotional writers were of impeccable orthodoxy, there was in their writings a tension between their recognition of the importance of a direct personal relationship between the individual and God and the role of the church as the social and institutional guarantor of men's souls. Lollard literature expressed this conflict in more extreme form: criticisms of institutional religion and authority; the advocation of disendowment in the interests of biblical simplicity and the emphasis on personal faith and penance were all concepts based on eremitic traditions. Devotional literature such as Rolle's psalter was interpolated with Lollard doctrine; a biography of the hermit, which was written in 1405, probably reached Vienna through Hussite channels; and the *Ancren Riwle* was adapted for laymen. Sir John Clanvowe, a close friend of Sir William Neville, wrote a lay sermon in which he declared his hatred of the world and welcomed the abuse of those who labelled him and his fellow courtiers as 'Lollards'.[49] He and his fellow chamber knights were merely using in their wills the same ascetic vocabulary as Rolle and Hilton. Wyclif himself expressed his admiration for recluses; he was reputed to have

45 TE, p. 98; p. 321.
46 W.I. p. 321.
47 TE, I, p. 98; TE, p. 98; TE, I, p. 300.
48 *Reg. Chichele*; T.V., I, pp. 212.
49 McFarlane, *Lancastrian Kings*, pp. 204 – 5.

dressed in the russet tunic and sandals of the hermit; he answered criticisms in the decretals of the uselessness and irrevelance of hermits in civil life by applying such criticisms to pastoral education and government; and he claimed that many could help a community by good works, but only a minority who were separated from other men could bring grace into the church. One such hermit, according to him, was John the Baptist, who baptized the people of Jerusalem while the Pharisees and clerks followed their traditions and governed the city.[50] The leading preachers William Smith and William Swinderby were hermits who had probably been inspired by Rolle. Advocates of the disendowment of the religious houses had considerably sympathy for the Carthusian order. Nicholas Hereford eventually retired to a Carthusian monastery, after recanting, and John of Gaunt left £20 to each charterhouse in England.[51] Schemes for the disendowment of the religious orders exempted the Carthusians: John Trevisa added notes advocating the disendowment of the older religious orders only to his translation of the *Polychronicon*; and although Sir Thomas Chaworth, who owned both the Latin *Polychronicon* and Trevisa's translation, made no bequests to Benedictine or Cistercian houses, he maintained his family's links with Beauvale.[52]

Historical reasons can only provide a partial answer to the phenomenon of Richard Rolle; in some ways he represented a culmination of eremitic traditions in the diocese; but he was also a unique personality.[53] What is more significant, especially in relation to the church of York, was the subsequent popularity of his teachings; the widespread patronage of recluses among the nobility of the diocese; and the increasing lay participation in the contemplative life, especially through the reading of the contemplative literature provided by recluses. These important developments, which were of historical significance throughout England by the mid-fifteenth century, must have satisfied the most ambitious pastoral objectives of York clergy. Before studying their response to the growing popularity of Rolle's teachings and recluses in general, which was becoming evident by the mid 1370s and which would have been crucial to the subsequent history of the eremitic movement, it is necessary to examine a less obvious contribution of the church to this movement. This involved the provision of fundamental religious instruction and guidance in the diocese, without which there have been no place for less educated people in the contemplative life The archiepiscopate of John Thoresby from 1352 to 1373 was of central importance in this respect.

50 *De Civili Domino*, I, p. 173.
51 TE, I, p. 186.
52 D. Fowler, *The Bible in Early English Literature* (London, 1977).
653 TE, II, pp. 220 – 28.

CHAPTER THREE

Pastoral Care in the Diocese of York, 1352 – 1373

We have so far seen, in chapter one, the religious character of the Yorkshire nobility which could, especially in familial religion, have been formed with little control on the part of ecclesiastical authorities; and the illusion of uncontrolled religious practices might be confirmed by the distinctive features of northern religion in the fourteenth century: the proliferation of recluses and the wide readership of northern contemplative literature. But this is a misleading impression. We have seen hints of close ecclesiastical supervision of religious life in the doubts expressed by some recluses, who were in fact also churchmen, about the implications of some of Rolle's teachings when taken out of context and applied too literally by the less educated. In order to understand the misgivings felt by ecclesiastical authorities of the diocese and their theological counsellors, and their reaction, which constituted a gloss and a refinement on the teachings of the recluse, we now have to consider more closely the leadership of the church of York: especially the way the art of contemplation was related to pastoral care and distinguished in the 1380s and 1390s from Lollardy; which, in its turn, as we shall see, may have first emerged from within ecclesiastical circles in the diocese. The work of the clergy of York who adapted the teachings of Rolle for the growing numbers of recluses and lay followers is the most significant religious development of this period and central to this study. However, before examining this it is necessary to see the work of the York clergy in the context of more elementary pastoral policies. The increased significance of solitaries and their teaching in secular life depended on there being a healthy state of self-criticism and reform within the church of York (for after all many recluses were ordained clergy); and on a strong sense of pastoral initiative within the church: for lay support of solitaries and wider appreciation of eremitic teaching depended on the clergy of York raising the standards of literacy and religious knowledge throughout the diocese. John Thoresby, archbishop of York from 1353 to 1373, did not have to formulate a response to the growing popularity of the recluse because this did not become apparent until after his death; but he helped prepare the way for the widespread interest and participation in the eremitic life by creating a more educated priesthood and laity, and by establishing the guidelines of pastoral care that ensured that churchmen would direct their pastoral skills to adapting eremitic teaching for those in secular life. During his archiepiscopate we can see something very different from the impression of ecclesiastical slackness that the material in chapters one and two created. Individual clergy trained in Westminster, Oxford, York Cathedral, and the archiepiscopal household, were formed into a circle by Thoresby; and they used their legal and theological expertise to establish a firm control over all aspects of diocesan life. Thoresby, their patron and leader, was an effective administrator and reformer who supervised closely clerical conduct and who attempted to control some of the more abrasive aspects of the religious conventions of the diocese by providing legislation and elementary moral and doctrinal teaching to encourage self-control, moral sensibility and social cooperation. This was an attempt to reduce the violence and vendettas habitual among York parishioners that owed something to the prevalence of chivalric codes of honour in the diocese. In the years that precede the rise in popularity of the recluse in the 1380s, the clergy of York closely supervised all aspects of the religious life of the diocese. The fundamental religious instruction that they provided during confession, in sermons and in the cycle plays, made the responsible reception of contemplative teachings possible; and established the precedent for the church of York's more exclusive concern with the pastoral application of eremitic teachings after 1370, when the challenge posed by Rolle's popularity had become apparent: Thoresby and his clergy were the first in a series of tough-minded men who imposed order and structure on the piety of the north. Any evaluation of the contribution of the church of York to the subsequent increase in the interest in recluses and spiritual literature must therefore begin with an analysis of the development of the pastoral office during Thoresby's archiepiscopate.

Hints about the significance of Thoresby's twenty-one year archiepiscopate, which began three years after Rolle's death in 1352, are provided in a near contemporary account of the archbishop written by a Dominican friar Thomas Stubbs.[1] Stubbs, a doctor of divinity of Oxford and a Yorkshireman from the forest of Knaresborough, was closely acquainted with two men who were members of the York Minster chapter, bishops Bury and Thomas Hatfield of Durham. He acted as Hatfield's executor in 1381 and probably wrote his continuation of the lives of the archbishops of York in the 1380s.[2] He originally only

1 *Continuatio Chronicae de vitis archiepiscoporum Eboracensium per Thomas Stubbs* in *Historians of the Church of York and its Archbishops*, ed. J. Raine, (R.S., 3 vols., 1879 – 94), ii, pp. 388 – 41.

2 L. H. Butler, 'Archbishop Melton, his neighbours and kinsmen', *J.E.H.*, ii, (1951), 54; TE, 1, p. 122.

intended to take his work up to 1353, later adding his account of Thoresby's life, probably at the suggestion of the archbishop's nephew, John Thoresby, Hatfield's chancellor in 1373.[3] Stubbs described the archbishop as a peacemaker and a settler of disputes, emphasized the diligent and regular way he discharged his episcopal duties, the strict piety of his private life, and claimed that Thoresby wore out his clerical household by his diligent celebration of the canonical house and matins in chapel.[4] Such an account, drawn from the testimony of Thoresby's colleagues and members of his household, warrants serious consideration; fortunately Stubbs' assertions can be tested in Thoresby's well-kept register and in some of the elegant letters and pronouncements bearing his name which are to be found in the register of his successor Alexander Neville.[5] However, before examining the development of the pastoral office under Thoresby, it is necessary to consider the training and experience that made him such an efficient diocesan.

Thoresby the King's Archbishop

A brief consideration of the major themes of Thoresby's career — his pluralism, his nepotistic patronage of friends and relatives to positions in the church of York; his application of his legal and diplomatic skills in the service of the crown and in the defence and maintenance of the liberties and unity of the church; and his struggle to reconcile the conflicting ties of church and state — may not appear to be of obvious relevance to a study of recluses and contemplative teaching in the late fourteenth century. However, Thoresby and his circle provides an example of how practical, public administrators could be closely in touch with the religious, moral and social needs of others. They were at the forefront of religious change and with their pastoral commitment they gave a spiritual dimension to the active life. They also provided their successors in the church of York including John Wyclif and Walter Hilton, whose early careers are similar and who were equally torn between the commitments of the active life, whether they included practising law, claiming benefices, or working for the crown, with an exacting pastoral ideal that they felt they had to live up to; this was to be the basis of many of the conflicts appearing in the autobiographical and instructional religious writings that appeared in the diocese in the late

3 Emden, *B.R.U.O.*, iii, pp. 2103 – 4.

4 *Historians of the Church of York, ii, p. 419.*

5 For descriptions of the register see D. M. Smith, *Guide to the Bishop's Registers of England and Wales* (London, 1981), p. 239; and A. H. Thompson, 'The Registers of the archbishops of York', *Y.A.T.* 32 (1936) 245 – 63.

fourteenth century. The only difference was that while Thoresby and his clerks were committed to elementary religious and moral instruction of clergy and layfolk in the diocese, their successors, thanks to the work of their predecessors, were faced with a pastoral challenge and responsibilities that had a greater spiritual dimension.

The efficiency of the administrative centres of government, the Privy Seal, Exchequer and Chancery, depended on the legal expertise and administrative skills of the clergy, especially those from the north-east, which had been acquired at university and in archiepiscopal households. Thoresby's early career was typical of the northerners of his generation; and such experience offered little practical or theoretical training on such aspects of the pastoral office as the administration of confession or the preaching of sermons. The friars, who were a missionary order, were more trained for these duties. However, years of crown service helped to make Thoresby an efficient and dedicated archbishop. His attempts to challenge the friars' superiority in pastoral affairs by providing elementary religious instruction for all those under his care shows that administrative, diplomatic and political experience could be an adequate preparation for the successful performance of the pastoral office.

John Thoresby was from a modest family in the village of North Thoresby in Lindesey, a few miles south of Grimsby in Lincolnshire. His neighbour and possible kinsman was Archbishop William Melton and therefore, like many of the aspiring clergy from the East Lindesey and Howdenshire families of Melton, de-la-Mare, Hugate and Ferriby, he was favourably positioned for ecclesiastical preferment.[1] Like Rolle, he attended Oxford during Melton's archiepiscopate and he was supported by the living of Brunwith in Yorkshire, which had been presented to him in 1320 by Thomas Earl of Lancaster, a possible patron of Rolle, and by 1326 he had reached graduate status.[2] It is possible that he studied theology in these years: according to Bale, Thoresby had such a great reputation as a theologian that Baconthorpe dedicated his commentary on Aristotle's *Ethics* to him.[3] In 1341 Thoresby qualified for the degree of Bachelor of Canon Law; this training in canon law, and presumably civil law, would have given him a knowledge of the laws of the church, international Roman law and the laws of diplomacy, which

1 For biographical material on Archbishop Thoresby see J. L. Grassi, 'The Clerical Dynasties from Howdenshire, Nottinghamshire and Lindsey in the Royal Administration, 1280 – 1340' (Oxford Univ. D. Phil, thesis 1960), pp. 473 – 78; Emden, *B.R.U.O.*, iii, p. 1863; Highfield, 'Relations between the Church and the English Crown 1349 – 78' pp. 575 – 80; T. F. Tout, *Chapters in the Administrative History of Medieval England* (Manchester, 1920 – 32), iii, p. 86ff.

2 Emden, *B.R.U.O.*, iii, p. 1863.

3 *Fasti Ebor.*, p. 157; J. Bale, *Scriptorum Illustrium maioris Brytannie quam* 1557, centuria sexta, p. 493.

he first applied in the service of Melton, an extremely conscientious archbishop of York. In 1323 he served as Melton's chaplain, and by 1328 he was a public notary of the diocese.[4] His knowledge of Roman Law probably secured his employment at the Papal Curia in 1323 and 1324, and by the 1340s Thoresby had become a regular and friendly correspondent with Pope Clement VI.[5]

However, Thoresby's early career was not dominated either by university study or service to the English or Roman church, but by governmental responsibilities. Melton was Edward II's most important civil servant: he dominated the wardrobe from 1307 to 1315, and introduced into the royal administration the Ferribys, Hugates, and Thoresby, beginning a nepotistic tradition of advancement of Lindsey and Howdenshire men in crown service that was to last eighty years.[6] Melton became treasurer in 1325, and again in 1330, when he introduced Thoresby into the exchequer as the treasurer's clerk.[7] His protégé soon entered the office of chancery as a notary on an annual salary of forty marks a year, and he became one of the leading officials of the government.[8] Thoresby's knowledge of international law and diplomacy, and his notarial skills, were employed during Edward III's tortuous foreign policy between 1338 and 1344 when the king was trying to formulate alliances between the imperial princes and the English crown against Philip VI of France: he became a member of the king's council in Flanders in 1338 and was involved in diplomatic negotiations with the French in 1340, 1344 and 1346.[9] In these years of dual government he and Simon Islip were the king's first ministers: Islip held the post of keeper of the regent's seal in 1346; Thoresby accompanied Edward III abroad as keeper of the Privy Seal and held the most important administrative position in England including the keeper of the Rolls of chancery from 1341 – 45, keeper of the Privy Seal in 1345, and chancellor in 1349.[10]

The post of keeper of the Privy Seal was an advancement that opened the way for episcopal promotion. From 1345 – 55 each keeper of the privy seal had become a bishop of a prestigious see or an archbishop. Thoresby's experiences prior to his episcopal appointments to the bishopric of St David's in 1347, the bishopric of Worcester in 1349 and the archbishopric of York in 1352, primarily consisted of administrative and diplomatic service for the crown. His income as a prominent civil

4 Grassi, 'Clerical Dynasties', p. 473; Reg. Melton, fo. 189.
5 *Foedera*, iii, p. 64.
6 Butler, 'Archbishop Melton', 54ff.
7 Grassi, p. 473.
8 CPR, 1334 – 38, p. 329.
9 Grassi, p. 473; Emden, *B.R.U.O.*, iii, p. 1863.
10 Grassi, p. 474.

servant had been supplemented by the revenues from a total of twenty-one benefices that he held between 1326 and 1346; but there is no evidence that he performed any pastoral functions during these years.[11] Many of these offices, such as the archdeaconry of London and the deanery of Lincoln, were important pastoral and administrative positions, but Thoresby's commitments as a university student and an important official of state would have prevented him from regarding them as anything more than profitable sinecures that supplemented his civil service income. The office for which he retained most affection was probably the canonry and prebend of the Chapel of St Mary and the Holy Angels in York Cathedral, which, under his influence, was to become an early preferment for some of the most influential York clergy of the fourteenth century.[12]

Thoresby's first two episcopal appointments had no special pastoral significance. He only held St David's from September 1347 to September 1349 and Worcester from September 1349 to September 1351, and he had little time to make an impact on either diocese. His appointment to York in 1352 was more significant. It was normal practice for the crown to relinquish its most outstanding administrators at the height of their careers to the most important positions in the church. Islip resigned as keeper of the privy seal in 1349 to become archbishop of Canterbury. Edward needed the skills and qualities that both Islip and Thoresby had shown as royal servants in the two most important ecclesiastical positions, because he was anxious to have men of proven loyalty as leaders of the church. The previous archbishop of Canterbury and chancellor, John Stratford, had opposed him over the issue of war taxation and, perhaps modelling himself on Becket, had defended the privileges and independence of the clergy. In Thoresby and Islip, the king had two churchmen on whom he could rely for support in the war and for the provision of taxes to pay for it. Both men had spent a great part of their professional careers working for a government that was dedicated to war against France and Scotland: they had both accompanied Edward at the siege of Calais in 1347.[13] Their loyalty was also assured in that they were not of aristocratic birth and would be unencumbered by the magnate affiliations that played an important part in the careers of their successors Richard Scrope and Thomas Arundel in the second half of the fourteenth century. Thoresby, as archbishop of York, endorsed Edward III's war policies and secured for them the spiritual and material support of his diocese; in 1352 he issued an order to solicit the prayers of the faithful on behalf of Henry

11 Emden, *B.R.U.O.*, iii, p. 1863.
12 *The Chapel of St. Mary's York*, ed. A. H. Thompson (Y.A.J., xxvi, 1944 – 47), p. 266ff.
13 Highfield, 'The Church and the English Crown', p. 203.

Duke of Lancaster who was about to engage in mortal combat with the Duke of Brunswick; in 1356, the year following his appointment as guardian of the kingdom, he ordered prayers of thanksgiving throughout the diocese for the victory at Poitiers; and on 17 November 1366 he ordered prayers for the Black Prince who was going to the aid of King Pedro of Castile against the French mercenaries.[14] Edward's wars depended on taxation, including the clerical tenths, and Thoresby was cooperative in this respect: in July 1359 his tenants were exempted from the payment of tenths because of his enthusiastic work as a commissioner of array in 1355.[15] In 1367 he issued provincial legislation to enforce the collection of tenths in the diocese, probably in part at least in an effort to help the war effort; in these constitutions Thoresby referred to parishioners who impeded churchmen in the free gathering of tithes and who went to such lengths to avoid the paying of tithes that they allowed their sheaves to be wasted or destroyed; instructions were issued forbidding any such avoidance or the attempted impeding of rectors who were collecting the tenth.[16] In many of his pronouncements as an archbishop Thoresby showed that he conceived the church to be both an English and a state institution.

Edward also needed a diplomat of proven worth to administer the difficult see of York. The peculiar privileges of the archdeaconry of Richmond and the chapters of the mother churches of York, Beverley, Ripon and Southwell all enjoyed the right of institution and required the supervision of a diplomat; and to the north there was a troublesome suffragan, the bishop of Durham, whose see enjoyed palatine rights. Thoresby's diplomatic skills had been noticed by the bishop of Porto, who praised his part in the Anglo-French negotiations to Innocent VI. On 25 November 1345 Clement VI besought him to assist two cardinals who were coming to England in an attempt to preserve peace between France and England, and in 1346 Clement wrote him a letter full of gratitude for his services.[17] Thoresby gave notice of his ability to settle disputes in the church as bishop of Worcester in March 1350 when a conflict involving the opposition of the larger monasteries, especially Cirencester, to primatial visitation was solved by the drawing up of a compromise agreement defining the limits of the prior's visitation rights.[18] One of his first acts as archbishop of York was to effect a reconciliation between the mayor and citizens of York and the abbots

14 *Fasti Ebor.*, p. 458; Oxford, Bodl. MS.C. iv, 2080.

15 *Foedera*, iii, p. 436; Reg. Neville, ii, fo.20.

16 *Concilia Magnae Britanniae*, ed. D. Wilkins (Oxford, 1738), iii, pp. 69 – 70.

17 *Foedera*, iii, p. 64; J. Le Neve, *Fasti Ecclesiae Anglicanae*, ed. T. D. Hardy (Oxford, 1854), i, p. 294.

18 R. M. Haines, *The Administration of the Diocese of Worcester in the First Half of the Fourteenth Century* (London, 1965), p. 308.

and monks of St Mary's abbey who were on the verge of going to the king's court over a boundary dispute.[19] Pope Urban V's high opinion of him as a diplomat can be gauged from the fact that in the dispute between Alexander Neville, archdeacon of Cornwall, and John Grandisson, bishop of Exeter, Urban entrusted the case to Thoresby, who issued instructions to the Bishop of Exeter summoning him to York.[20] The most long standing conflict in the church in this period was the dispute between Canterbury and York regarding the right of the archbishop of York to bear his cross erect in both provinces and other questions of prerogative. This was finally ended in 1353 through the friendship of Thoresby, Islip and Edward III; it was resolved that each archbishop could bear his cross in the other's province; and as a concession each new archbishop of York was required to send to the shrine of St Thomas Becket, within two months of his election, a golden image of an archbishop bearing a cross or jewels to the value of £40. At parliament and councils the southern primate was to have precedence by sitting to the right of the sovereign; if the two prelates were to encounter one another in a narrow street the archbishop of York would have to give way. These decisions were confirmed by Pope Clememt VI in 1353 who made a further distinction between the two sees: the archbishop of York bore the title of Primate of England and the archbishop that of Primate of All England.[21]

Thoresby also applied the legal, administrative and notarial skills that he acquired at university and the civil service to the administration of his archbishopric. His register was the last of a great series, including those of Melton and Greenfield, kept while the see was controlled by civil servants. After his death in 1373 the standard of the archbishop's registers in York declined, giving the impression that the efficiency of diocesan administration, at least as far as keeping records went, had deteriorated.[22] The constitutions that Thoresby issued at Cawood in 1367 confronted such legal problems as the fraudulent alienation of small amounts of property to the church that did not belong to the donor, but to wives or creditors; he ordained that no one was to assist in such cunning frauds, and that only property that was free could be alienated to the church.[23]

By serving his king, nation and church loyally and efficiently, Thoresby would have been considered by his contemporaries a successful bishop. But such devoted service alone provides no evidence

19 *Fasti Ebor.*, p. 457; *Historians of York*, ii, p. 419; Francis Drake, *Eboracum* (York and London, 1736), p. 581.
20 CPR, 1364 – 67, p. 153.
21 *Fasti Ebor*, p. 452.
22 Grassi, 'Clerical Dynasties', p. 184.
23 *Concilia*, iii, p. 70.

of the church's role in the profound religious changes that were occurring in the north-east. It has been maintained that there was a weakness in the metropolitan's leadership of the church after the end of Stratford's tenure of the see of Canterbury; and this has been attributed to the subsequent appointment of permanent government civil servants who acted less like independent churchmen than royal servants unable to defend the freedom of the church from royal exactions.[24] A special diocesan importance has also been claimed for a group of English bishops, including John Grandisson, who were not in royal service or ecclesiastic households and who were appointed to the less important sees like Exeter.[25] Thoresby may have proved himself a loyal servant of the king as an archbishop by endorsing many of his policies, but he and Islip were first and foremost loyal churchmen who were capable of standing up to Edward III. They did so in 1355 when the king intervened in parliament and ordered the confiscation of the temporalities of Thomas Lisle, the bishop of Ely, because some of the followers of the bishop had allegedly attacked members of the household of Lady Blanche Lancaster. Chancellor Thoresby and his treasurer, Edington, with the support of Islip, passively resisted the order, which engendered a furious reply from the king.[26] The temporalities of Ely were not seized until October 1356, and Thoresby resigned as chancellor one month later. Thoresby's subsequent energetic work in the diocese suggests that Edward's acceptance of his resignation was welcome; and his period of government service should not obscure the fact that his first priority was pastoral service to the church. He and Islip attended to these duties as conscientiously as they had performed their governmental responsibilities, continuing to work together as they had done in the civil service. Both men came to their sees at a critical time, when the plague had decimated the numbers of the clergy. Near the start of Thoresby's archiepiscopate Islip wrote a letter to his fellow primate complaining about the wretched state of the church of England which had received no support from the high and mighty and which had consequently lost all its power and influence. Thoresby, in his reply, attempted to comfort his friend by signifying his intention to confront the problem.[27] This he did by implementing a coherent programme of reform in the church of York and making provisions for the education of clergy and laity. Without such policies there would have been little

24 J. R. L. Highfield, 'The English Church Hierarchy in the Reign of Edward III', *T.R.Hist.S.*, 5th ser. vi, (1956), 115 – 38.
25 ibid, 115 – 118.
26 B. Wilkinson, 'A Letter of Edward III to his Chancellor and Treasurer', *EHR*, xlii, (1927), 248 – 50.
27 *Fasti Ebor.*, p. 467.

chance of the eremitic movement of the diocese reaching the numbers it did.

Reform of the Church of York

Thoresby's reforms can be seen as a concerted effort to combat the disastrous effects of three epidemics of the Plague in his diocese. In 1349 nearly half the clergy and laity of the diocese perished from the Black Death. The mortality figures can only be estimated by the numbers of benefices vacated by death; it is probable that between 42% and 45% of the beneficed clergy died between July and August.[1] A further outbreak occurred in June 1361 when Thoresby issued an order for the people to pray for the removal of wars, pestilence and other troubles in the kingdom.[2] The severity of this visitation is only partially indicated by the institution figures for March 1361 to March 1362; in this period there were thirty-three institutions to benefices void by death, compared to fifteen in the year after the Black Death of 1349; some idea of the mortality can be gained from the figures for the deanery of Pontefract where one third of the beneficed clergy died between 1361 and 1362. Another epidemic occurred in the summer of 1369 when 72 benefices were vacated by death, 61 between June and November; and Thoresby was forced to order prayers for the removal of the pestilence in October 1368 and 8 May 1369.[3] Such mortality and social upheaval had profound effects on the church and its administration of the pastoral office. The deaths of so many priests necessitated emergency measures including lay administration of sacraments such as confession, and hasty, temporary consecration of churches and cemeteries, many of which were undertaken in 1349 by the suffragan archbishop of York, Hugh archbishop of Damascus.[4] This disaster threatened the reputation and sanctity of the church, the authority of parish priests and their relationship with the laity.

There were more tangible and long-term effects within the church itself, especially in the lower levels of the church where the daily pastoral work was performed and the impact of the epidemics was greatest. The bulk of the clergy of the diocese comprised unbeneficed chaplains who, until 1349, provided a surplus of labour for the church.

1 A. H. Thompson, 'The Pestilence of the fourteenth Century in the Diocese of York', *Y.A.J.*, lxxi, (1914), 99 – 113.
2 *Fasti Ebor.*, p. 461.
3 Thompson, 'Pestilences', 115.
4 Thompson, 'Pestilences', 109. He had been excommunicated for impersonating an archbishop and consecrating a chapel.

Most of them made a living from the celebration of masses, for which most people made provision before their deaths. Distinct from the holders of perpetual chantries, they were a property-less labour force aware of the fluctuations of their market. A smaller proportion of these unbeneficed chaplains found employment as parish or stipendiary chaplains (*capellani curati*) who assisted or took the place of incumbents in the administration of a cure of souls for notoriously low wages. The mortality of the Black Death, which was relatively slight among the great pluralists, was highest among the parish and stipendary chaplains who performed the often fatal pastoral tasks of hearing confessions and administering extreme unction to the dying. The shortage of parish priests was further exacerbated by the heavy demand for masses for the dying, which reduced the normal labour surplus among the chantry chaplains. In 1349 Archbishop Zouche issued licences allowing minor clergy to celebrate masses, and his suffragan, the archbishop of Damascus, hurriedly ordained new priests, persuading them to take up pastoral work by offering all stipendary chaplains a temporary stipend of six marks.[5] Inevitably parish priests exploited this situation and left their parishes to become chantry priests performing the safer and now more lucrative work of celebrating masses; landless tenants were to show opportunism when they deserted their landlords' estates in search of higher wages. In 1350 Islip complained about the priests who survived the plague and neglected the cure of souls by celebrating masses for which they demanded extortionate salaries.[6] In 1361 the rector of Horsham in the diocese of York complained that the current pestilence was so severe that it had carried off all the chantry chaplains who celebrated mass; he asked a chantry chaplain, Adam de Brantyngham, to assume the office of parochial chaplain, but Adam flatly refused.[7] In the poorer parishes of the diocese there was even difficulty in finding clergy to accept benefices. After the 1349 pestilence the religious of poorer houses, especially the Premonstratensian canons, were allowed to hold incumbencies in vacant benefices. In 1369 Thoresby was forced to admit a canon of Marton to the vicarage of Colston (Notts) because the vicarages were so poor that no secular priest would take them.[8] Such incumbents either employed a curate or stretched their depleted resources to administer the parish themselves.

The plague also caused abuses within clerical communities. The communal life of the religious orders made them very vulnerable during epidemics. In 1349 the heads of eighteen religious houses died and a

5 Wood-Legh, 'Perpetual Chantries', 191 – 92; Thompson, 'Pestilences', 118.
6 Wood-Legh, 'Perpetual Chantries', 192.
7 Thompson, 'Pestilences', 115; Reg. Thoresby, fo.204v.
8 Thompson, 119.

decline of discipline followed.[9] In 1353 there were reports that the few survivors of the alien priory of Blyth were living dissolutely and neglecting to observe their rule or celebrate mass. Indiscreet governance was reported to be threatening the extinction of Shelford priory, and there were reports of strife and scandal in Keldholme and Newburgh priories.[10] Morale was so low that in 1354 the prior of Drax, feeling himself unable to cope with the great and intolerable burdens of his office, resigned his dignity.[11] Discipline also declined among the communities of chantry priests who survived and profited from epidemics. Thoresby received complaints that the chantry priests of St Mary's hurried over morning masses and directed the mass offerings of parishioners to themselves by finishing their services before the parish priest at the high altar. It was also reported that they neglected their choir offices and spent the day in idle visiting or walking in the fields during which, if they said their office at all, it was hurried and abridged.[12]

The Black Death undermined complacency, especially where the dignity of clergy and their institutions were concerned; this would have forced a conscientious, strong diocesan or metropolitan into a reappraisal of pastoral work and the value of those who were performing it. Thoresby regarded the plague as a challenge, a call to reform; and this can be seen in a preamble to a mandate that he issued in July 1361 ordering the singing of the litany in procession every Wednesday and Friday throughout the diocese, with the special saying of daily collects at Mass for the cessation of the pestilence.[13] He did not question the necessity of the plague or its purging function and in this preamble he described it as the scourge of the Almighty that filled the faces of his people with shame and made them repent.[14] The author of this preamble gave no indication that God should or would be merciful and advised all the faithful that all they could do was pray for his clemency. This was a contrast to the more fatalistic preamble to the same mandate written by Thoresby's predecessor: Archbishop Zouche described the plague as a just punishment by God for men's sins, but suggested that men should appeal to Christ who will hear their knocking and protect those whom he has redeemed with his blood.[15] Zouche's resignation seems to have been the reaction of a man who panicked: in the summer of 1349, when the pestilence was at its height, he stayed at his rural

9 ibid, 123.
10 ibid, 123; Reg. Thoresby, fo.13.
11 Thompson, 124; Reg. Thoresby, fo.29d.
12 Thompson, *The English Clergy*, p. 145.
13 *Fasti Ebor.*, p. 461.
14 Thompson 'Pestilences', 102, 114.
15 ibid, 102.

manor near Ripon and he did no visitation work that year.[16] Thoresby, whose response seems to have been more pragmatic, wasted little time in applying practical measures to the problems raised by the epidemics. He conducted a series of visitations of religious houses as soon as he became archbishop, and in 1353 and 1354 he issued a number of commissions of enquiry into religious houses including the Augustinian houses of Kirkham, Shelford and Newburgh, the alien priory of Blyth, the Clunic priory of Monkbretton — where Thoresby even had to warn the convent to treat his official properly — and the Cistercian nunnery of Hampole.[17] Thoresby addressed himself to the problem of laxity among chantry priests and sent a mandate to the dean of Nottingham telling him to warn priests, under pain of suspension, against neglecting to take part in the daily choirs or beginning their daily masses before the parish priest had completed his.[18] This mandate was probably preserved in the register to serve as a model for further issues to other churches.

Thoresby confronted the disastrously high mortality among parish priests by increasing the numbers of priests ordained in the diocese. Four or five ordinations were conducted each year, and after the third epidemic in 1369 there were three special and four general ordinations creating 306 acolytes, 187 sub-deacons, 163 deacons and 161 priests to supervise in Yorkshire, Lancashire, Nottinghamshire and Westmorland.[19] The initiative behind this extraordinary recruiting drive in the priesthood was Thoresby's. Even in normal circumstances it was customary for the archbishop to devolve the responsibility for officiating at ordination services to his suffragan as Zouche had done in 1349. Thoresby, however, chose whenever possible to supervise this arduous task himself. Between 1356, when he was finally free from state service, and 1362, he officiated at all ceremonies himself; from 1361 to 1370 he only delegated the ordination ceremonies to his officials nine times; in all he assisted in seventy out of eighty-one ordinations between 1356 and 1370 and only relinquished this task in his old age; from 1370 until his death the labour of ordinations fell on Richard Sermen.[20] This increased recruitment to the priesthood did have its critics, and William Rymyngton expressed concern, in a sermon delivered at York Minster in 1373, that it would lead to a fall in standards.

Thoresby and Islip were more concerned about the erosion of respect for the sacraments, the institutions and rituals of the church, and its priesthood. In 1351 the archbishop of Canterbury sent a mandate to the

16 ibid, 123.
17 Reg. Thoresby, fos. 13 – 15; Thompson, 'Pestilences', 123.
18 Reg. Thoresby, fo. 204v; Thompson, 'Pestilences', 115.
19 *Fasti Ebor.*, pp. 475 – 76; J. A. Hoeppner Moran, 'Clerical Recruitment in the Diocese of York', *J.E.H.*, 34, (1983), 33.
20 *Fasti Ebor.*, pp. 475 – 6; Hoeppner-Moran, 33ff.

bishop of Bath and Wells, claiming that his appointment of lay confessors during the 1349 pestilence had done irreparable damage to the prestige and authority of the clergy.[21] Thoresby rebuked the citizens of Fulford for continuing to use their temporary cemetery at St Oswald's long after the Black Death had passed.[22] Concern was also shown in these years for the problem of those ordained priests who deserted their parishes and the pastoral office because of the plague and other reasons. A mandate was issued from Cawood between January 1361 and January 1362 to the rural dean of Harthill in the East Riding on the question of chaplains, such as one Adam Brantyngham, who deserted their parishes to celebrate masses; Thoresby stated that anyone ordained to a cure of souls could not desert his living without doing damage to the church; and he exhorted the rural dean to help him to combat this problem by finding those priests who hid to avoid taking their posts, and by maintaining vigilance concerning the presentation of priests in the parish.[23] In a series of letters found in Neville's register Thoresby complained about the problem of non-residence in the chapter of York and in the archdeaconries of the diocese, which was compounded by the high proportion of aliens promoted by the pope; such people, he writes, are deaf, mute and unaware of the bleating of the flock; they do not watch out for wolves, but leave behind servants while they concentrate merely on milking wealth.[24] Thoresby conducted a visitation of the chapter of York in May 1362 and reprehended the non-residence of English canons which Melton had complained of to him. He observed the non-residence of the dean, the decay of his home in the close, the absence of the treasurer Banktre since his appointment, and his failure even to pay the wages of the sacristans and the clerks of the vestry; he also criticized the dean for neglecting to fulfil a promise to supply forty poor people with food and expressed a wish to have the poor stalls augmented with the rich in the church.[25] It is significant that after his death there were fewer problems of non-residence in the chapter and the cathedral had a series of outstanding treasurers including John Clifford and John Newton.

Thoresby's most concerted effort to correct specific abuses within the church of York was his issuing of the constitutions from Bishopthorpe on September 30 1367. He took the unusual step of having these constitutions approved before convocation because, in his own words, he wished to resist with all his strength certain errors and abuses which were increasing seriously in the church; and he wanted to have these

21 *Concilia*, iii, p. 745.
22 Reg. Thoresby, fo. 11v.
23 Reg. Thoresby, fo. 204; Thompson, 'Pestilences', 115.
24 Reg. Neville, Vol. 4, fo.6b.
25 *Fasti Ebor.*, p. 468.

statutes modified in provincial council to lessen the chances of excommunication for careless priests.[26] The archbishop ordered the publication of the constitutions throughout the deaneries; plentiful copies were to be given to all rectors and vicars, and parish priests were to expound them every Sunday. With the excuse of ignorance removed any clergy guilty of lack of vigour in this matter would be canonically punished.[27]

The precedent for Thoresby's legislation fixing the wages of stipendiary chaplains was the government's statute of labourers, issued when Thoresby was chancellor in 1351. The archbishop was undoubtedly just as concerned to maintain the status quo within the church, but he also attempted to give formal recognition to the important pastoral work done by stipendiary chaplains in order to prevent them deserting their pastoral office to celebrate chantry masses. This particular constitution opens with the statement that the clergy are bound to exercise the pastoral office and to watch diligently and vigilantly over their subjects. After considering the recent considerable hardships of the stipendary chaplains, caused by the depletion of their numbers in the pestilence, the archbishop decided to alleviate their suffering and bring them closer together by fixing the annual stipend of all such priests ordained in the past, present and future at six marks; priests paid in this way for parochial administration were to be content with their stipends and they were forbidden, under pain of suspension, from earning additional money by the celebration of masses. The same constitution, in an effort to make the office of chantry priest less of a lucrative temptation for those in pastoral office, legislated against chantry priests taking mass offerings from parishioners it was decreed that chantry priests with permission to celebrate mass could not conduct their celebration before the parish official. An enquiry into the observance of this law was to be conducted throughout the churches of York during the synods of Easter Sunday, St Michael's day and any other convenient time.[28]

These constitutions were also concerned with the correct administration of the sacraments, which had suffered some damage in the plague years. It was decreed that all clergy with cognizance over marriage settlements and divorce should not, on pain of excommunication, deputize this power. According to Thoresby, the selling of jurisdiction to inexperienced or incompetent persons could lead to unjust sentences, scandal to the church, and endanger the souls of all those involved. Another decree enforced the sentence of excommunication on any clergy who drew up secret and illegal marriage contracts without the

26 *Records of the Northern Convocation*, ed. J. Raine (S.S., 113, 1906) p. xlvii.
27 *Concilia*, iii, p. 70.
28 ibid., iii, p. 69.

due formality of publishing banns.[29] These constitutions, like much of the provincial legislation of Canterbury, closed with penitential legislation concerning the jurisdiction of absolution. Thoresby observed that parish priests had been admitting to confession penitents guilty of sins which could only be absolved by the archbishop's penitentiaries.[30] The catalogue of sins reserved for his jurisdiction numbered thirty-seven, and many, such as homicide and simony, had long been the preserve of episcopal judgement.[31]

Despite these epidemics, Thoresby restored confidence and a sense of purpose in the church of York. This is demonstrated by the amount of rebuilding in York Minster that occurred during his tenure of the see which can be attributed to his initiative and support.[32] When the minster architect, Thomas Pacenham, died of the plague in 1349 the nave, which had been begun about 1290, was still far from finished. During the next eleven years the whole of the timber vaulting was built by the carpenter, Philip of Lincoln, and by 1360 the nave was substantially complete.[33] This could not have been achieved without the personal contributions of Thoresby. In January 1356 the chapter, overburdened with debts, wrote to him asking him to give them timber; and in April 1359 he gave John de Godyngham, master of the fabric of the church of York, £20 towards the fabric fund, a donation he repeated in November 1360.[34] The completion of the nave allowed for the commencement of work on the eastern arm of the church. The project for the rebuilding of the choir existed before 1349 when one of the canons, Thomas Samson, bequeathed £20 to the fabric of a new choir, provided that it was begun within a year of his death.[35] The project was underway in 1350 with the commencement of the Zouche chapel, which probably took thirty years to complete.[36] The aisles and the eastern front of the choir were begun in 1361, aided by Thoresby's donations to the fabric fund of £20 in January 1361 and £30 in April 1361. The archbishop also ordered the demolition of his manor house at Sherborne so that stone could be used for the building work in the minster; ten days later, in July 1361, Thoresby laid the foundation stone of his lady chapel, which was to comprise the four eastern bays of the choir, accompanying the act with a gift of 100 marks.[37] In April 1362 he gave £20 to Robert Rithre, the lord of Rithre,

29 ibid, iii, pp. 69 – 70.
30 ibid, iii, p. 72.
31 ibid, iii, p. 73.
32 *Historians of York*, ii, p. 420.
33 J. H. Harvey, 'An Architectural History of York Minister from 1291 to 1558, in Aymler and Cant, eds. *A History of York Minster*, p. 158.
34 *The Fabric Rolls of York Minster*, ed. J. Raine, (SS, xxxv, 1859), pp. 51 – 6.
35 TE, I, p. 54.
36 *Fasti Ebor.*, pp. 447 – 48; Harvey, 'York Minster', p. 160.
37 Fabric Rolls, pp. 51 – 6; *Fasti Ebor.*, p. 483; *Hists. York* ii, 420.

for twenty-four oaks for building work at the cathedral; and for the rest of his life, from 1361 to 1373, Thoresby gave twice yearly payments of £100 to the fabric fund, making a total sum of £2,376.[38] By his death, on 6 November 1373, the lady chapel had been substantially completed by William Haton junior and Robert Patryngton, who also designed the clerestory after 1368.[39] The value of Thoresby's personal donations can be seen in the virtual cessation of active work on the cathedral for ten or twelve years after his death because of a shortage of funds. The east end of the minster was finally completed by 1405 when the west bays and the east window were finished.

Religious Instruction

The most urgent pastoral need in the diocese in these years was the provision of a system of religious education for clergy and laymen. Thoresby realistically met this by initiating a pastoral policy that had the practical objective of providing guidance on how to live a Christian life. This was to be provided during annual confession, and the clergy responsible for its administration were provided with guidelines in handbooks such as the *Pars oculi*, written during Melton's archiepiscopate by a theologian and penitentiary from the region where Thoresby was born and where the archbishop recruited heavily for the church, and in a simple more accessible handbook written by Thoresby himself for less educated priests and laymen. In these manuals, and in Thoresby's other reforms, an attempt was made to create more peaceful, supportive Christian communities, and the administration of compulsory annual confession was of fundamental importance in administering the necessary social discipline. By increasing standards of religious knowledge and moral awareness, Thoresby made a positive contribution towards the growing importance of recluses and their teachings in the diocese; but he also inadvertently made a more negative contribution towards the context of devotional literature in the late fourteenth century because, as we have seen, the most religious and individualistic personalities reacted in their writings against the communal pressure of the corporate social definition of personality and sin contained in the confession manuals. Both the communal pressures and the devotional reactions were paradoxically creations of the church of York.

Thoresby's most urgent priority was to get clergy to occupy a pacificatory, civilizing role in local parishes: to bring a measure of social

[38] *Fasti Ebor.*, p. 484.
[39] Harvey, 'York Minster', p. 163.

unity where the preservation of law and order was threatened by the revenge mentality of the community. Some indication of the problems facing a pastoral archbishop can be gained from the record of violence in Thoresby's register, which shows the power of vendetta among clergy and laity. Attacks on clergy by laymen were frequent: on February 26, 1362 a commission was issued to absolve Sir Adam de Everingham, a knight who had been excommunicated for laying violent hands on Richard de Halghton, the rector of Derfield; absolution was given on April 27 1365 to John de Gayford and Gervase de Pecco for cutting off the head of a chaplain called John de Wynteworth until they could go to Rome for absolution; and a sentence of excommunication was given on April 20 1366 against those who laid violent hands on the dean of Pontefract and killed his servants.[1] The looting of churches was not uncommon. On May 11 1348 an event occurred during the Whitsuntide processions which was described as a yearly occurrence: laymen, armed with swords and clubs, attacked the priests who stood at the high altar receiving the offerings of their parishioners and filled a dragon's head with the offerings of wax and coin which they carried away on a pole.[2] On 26 July 1365 excommunication was delivered on those who broke into the monastery at Pontefract and carried away plate and jewels.[3] The clergy in their turn were often heavily armed and quick to resort to violence. On August 8 1356 a commission of enquiry was given to John de Crakall, a canon of Ripon, to investigate a claim of Hugh Knight, a priest who described how he was attacked at Wath by certain armed laymen and how he killed one of them in self-defence.[4] Two laymen, William Roston and his son, were absolved on 21 February 1358 from wounding a chaplain, John Pie, with a sword and arrow after they had been pursued by Pie and his dog and attacked with a gisarme.[5] Thoresby's concern with the problem of violence and disorder in his diocese is shown in the catalogue of crimes drawn up in 1367 for the absolution of the archbishop and his penitentiaries. Five of them involved hostility towards clerics, and the archbishop also reserved for his own absolution all public offences disturbing the peace of city, town or countryside.[6] He also confronted these problems with patient attempts to provide elementary moral guidelines for clergy and laity to follow.

Many of Thoresby's provincial laws and instructions provided such advice to laymen. In one of his 1367 constitutions he gave instructions

1 *Fasti Ebor.*, p. 465, ibid, p. 363.
2 Thompson, 'Pestilences', 116.
3 *Fasti Ebor.*, p. 362.
4 ibid, p. 459.
5 ibid, p. 460.
6 ibid, p. 73.

on the rearing of infants, a matter that had been discussed in Pagula's *Pars oculi*; observing that mothers and nurses through negligence suckle infants in their own beds and subsequently fall asleep, suffocating the child, he instructed parents, nurses and any who have custody of infants, to feed infants in their cradles without falling asleep.[7] He also concerned himself with such rudimentary matters as profanity in churchyards and conduct in church. On 9 September 1365 he ordered that parishioners of Workshop to desist from conducting wrestling and archery contests, performing indecent dances, and singing in their churchyard; and on December 6 1367 he issued an order preventing the holding of markets and eating and drinking in the porch and churchyard of Whitgift.[8] In September of this year the archbishop gave a general order forbidding buying, selling, archery, wrestling and games in any church or churchyard and on Sundays and festival days; he gave a small paternal homily pointing out that Christ would not allow business to be conducted in the temple. In this same decree Thoresby declared that only catholics who agreed to go to church to pray reverently and humbly beg forgiveness of sins would gain admittance.[9]

Ordained clergy needed such elementary guidance just as badly. Few bore the title of *magister*, which signified graduation from Oxford or Cambridge, and the shortage of clergy in these plague years meant that the admission test for the lower clerical offices was very slight. Most clergy on Thoresby's extensive ordination lists bore a patronymic derived from their place of origin, which suggests that they were humble villagers whose identity had previously been determined by their father's Christian names; such men would have regarded the clerical profession as a chance to acquire social status and a surname.[10] The archbishop's sense of responsibility towards their education can be seen in his personal involvement in their ordination, and in his concern over their dress, bearing and decency. It was especially important that clergy distinguished themselves in such matters in the fourteenth century because they had no special dress, and there were many complaints that they were indistinguishable from laymen. In one of the 1367 constitutions Thoresby observed that some clergy, even priests, in defiance of decorum and canon law, which forbade short cassocks, continued to seek glory in ostentatious shoes and garments of a deformed shortness — these were probably short jackets worn in the manner of the gentry to display red hose above the knee; he ordered such behaviour to be censured and penalized. In addition Thoresby

7 *Concilia*, iii, p. 69.
8 ibid, iii, p. 68.
9 ibid, iii, p. 68.
10 Reg. Thoresby, fos. 329 – 496.

tried to exhort his clergy to greater self-esteem and dignity: he pointed out that sober dress and actions pleased God and slovenly bodies betrayed diseased minds; furthermore by dressing in an undignified manner they were not only harming their own souls, but failing their flocks to whom they were an example.[11]

Such legislation, however paternal, was not enough, and some system of instruction for clergy and laity was needed. Before discussing the measures introduced by Thoresby it is necessary to consider the inadequate provisions that existed in the church at the time. In the provincial council of Lambeth in 1281 Archbishop Pecham denounced clerical ignorance and issued a code dealing especially with the administration of confession. A section of his legislation, entitled *De informatione simplicium* and beginning *Ignorantia sacerdotum*, outlined a programme of religious instruction on the six articles which was to be expounded to the people in the vernacular four times a year. The six articles comprised the fourteen articles of faith, the ten commandments, the seven works of mercy, the seven vices and the seven sacraments.[12] But Pecham did not provide secular priests with instructions on these matters, or any practical help in delivering these sermons, and the only education available to them was that provided in some secular cathedrals and metropolitan churches. Because of this situation much of the pastoral work was done by Pecham's fellow friars who, by the end of the thirteenth century, were localized conventual bodies devoted to theological teaching, popular preaching and the administration of the sacraments. An attempt was made to advance the education of beneficed secular clergy in the decree of Boniface, *Cum ex eo*, in May 1298: this allowed bishops the freedom to grant licences for study to rectors whom they had instituted to a cure of souls, provided that they proceeded to the priesthood within a year of the termination of their studies and that suitable substitutes took over the running of the parishes while they were away at university.[13] However, in its operation it was used to facilitate extended university study for magisters and did nothing to help the parish chaplains who knew no Latin, who were hired to administer the benefices with cure of souls.[14]

In the first half of the fourteenth century canonists attempted to rectify this situation by writing manuals on the administration of confession and basic Christian dogma for their fellow secular clergy. The best and most influential was the *Oculus sacerdotis*, composed between 1320 and

11 *Records of the Northern Convocation*, p. 95.

12 Pantin, *The English Church*, p. 193.

13 L. E. Boyle, 'A Study of the Works attributed to William of Pagula (Oxford Univ. D.Phil. thesis 1954), p. 98.

14 R. M. Haines, 'The Education of the English Clergy During the later Middle Ages', *Canadian Journal of History*, 4 (1969).

1328. The author, William of Pagula, came from Paull, or Pagula, three miles south-east of Hull, in an area from which Melton, and later Thoresby, drew heavily for recruitment to the church.[15] Pagula, like Thoresby in his diocean legislation, was concerned with parochial evils such as ignorance, pluralism, and non-residence; but the ignorance that he tried to eliminate was that of his fellow graduates who administered the cure of souls as penitentiaries, rural deans and parish priests, but who had not been prepared for such work in their studies of the seven liberal arts. Pagula denounced the ignorance of his colleagues concerning the sacraments, but as a canonist he was primarily concerned with the administration of penance which he considered to be a judicial matter founded on canon law.[16] The first part of the *Oculus Sacerdotis* is a detachable confession manual, a work of psychological subtlety that explains the social ideology that lies behind the administration of confession and the development of conscience. Pagula saw the penitential as more important than preaching as a teaching medium, and he showed those with cure of souls what things they were bound to teach during the administration of confession. Although the *Oculus Sacerdotis* became popular throughout the diocese and influenced subsequent manuals for the next sixty years, its length and prolix Latin prose would have rendered it inaccessible for the humblest parish chaplains.

By the 1340s there was a growing confidence and sense of pastoral initiative among secular clergy, thanks to the efforts of bishops like John Grandisson who, while he was bishop of Exeter from 1327 to 1369, was a model for his contemporaries as a preacher, churchbuilder, and in his regular and meticulous attention to the everyday details of diocesan life.[17] An important aspect of this increased pastoral zeal among seculars was their opposition to the friars over the question of pastoral jurisdiction. Grandisson was active in issuing mandates concerning the hearing of confessions and the appointment of penitentiaries to hear confessions on the bishop's behalf. In 1342 and 1354 he complained that friars were acting as bishop's penitentiaries without authority; and he revoked the faculties granted to friars in 1354.[18] His policies probably influenced the views of his protégé, the theologian Ralph FitzRalph, who depicted the friar's privileges in his sermons and in the *Defensorium curatorum* as a threat to the central place of the parish church in popular religion. While FitzRalph was at the papal Curia in 1344 an English doctor of canon law wrote the *Memoriale presbiterorum*, a handbook for parish priests which confronted the friar's mastery of the theology of

15 Boyle, 'William of Pagula', p. 98.

16 R. M. Ball, 'The Education of English Parish Clergy in the Later Middle Ages', (Cambridge Univ. Ph.D. thesis, 1977), pp. 49 – 51.

17 K. Walsh, *Richard FitzRalph in Oxford, Avignon and Armagh* (Oxford, 1981), p. 67.

18 Pantin, *The English Church*, pp. 158 – 59.

penance by demonstrating that the administration of confession was an enquiry into the legal transgression of the different social classes, and that the assignation of penance was a means of enforcing the canon law of the Church.[19] Such an assertion of the legalistic basis of confession was an effective retort to any mendicant assumptions about the friar's superior learning and eligibility for the pastoral office; but it offered no real practical aid to the semi-literate priests who were the butt of the friar's criticisms. However, Thoresby and his clergy, notably William Nassyngton and John Gaytrik, did attempt to provide ordinary incumbents and laymen with elementary religious knowledge, and in so doing they became the first in an impressive series of York clergy to write in the vernacular.

William Nassyngton was a member of Grandisson's circle before he secured a career in York diocese. He was auditor of causes in Exeter in 1322 and served as Grandisson's chancellor from 1331 to 1334. Shortly before his death in 1359, Nassington requested prayers for the soul of his patron; but his later career was spent in the north-east: he served as advocate in the court of York from 1346 to 1350, and was vicar general in Durham in 1443. Nassington was the author of the most ambitious of all teaching aids for parish priests, the *Speculum Vitae,* an exposition of the Lord's Prayer and an analysis of the division of the seven deadly sins and seven virtues that enabled confessors to find out from a penitent 'qwat synne he is most gilty/ And remedy it there agayne'/. Nassington showed the same legal and social interests as the author of the *Memoriale* and analysed the different sins appropriate to different classes.[20] Despite the address to 'lewed' men, the *Speculum Vitae* is a virtual *summa* that would have served as a penitential reference work to clergy of the diocese. The strong northern affiliations of the text, the use of northern works such as the *Desert of Religion,* and the large numbers of surviving manuscripts of northern provenance, several of which were used in northern religious houses, suggests that it was composed while Nassington was advocate at York.[21] Forty manuscripts of the *Speculum Vitae* survive, a number exceeded only by another northern work of moral instruction, the *Prick of Conscience.*[22] Its circulation in the fifteenth century suggests that it was read, perhaps out loud, among the same

19 M. Haren, 'A Study of the Memoriale Presbiterorum, a fourteenth Century Confession Manual for Parish Priests' (Oxford Univ. D.Phil. thesis 1975), p. 397.

20 Emden, *B.R.U.O.*, ii, p. 1337; Doyle, 'A Survey', i, pp. 79 – 83; Wells, *Manual*, 348 (vi, 8); Allen, *Writings*, pp. 371 – 2; MS Bodl. Lib. 446, fo.224; Haren, *Memoriale Presbiterorum*', p. 173.

21 See V. A. Gillespie, 'The Literary Form of the Middle English Pastoral Manual with Particular Reference to the *Speculum Christiani*' (Oxford Univ. D.Phil. thesis, 1981), pp. 132 – 3; and V. A. Nelson, 'Problems of Transcription in the *Speculum Vitae* Manuscripts', *Scriptorium*, 31 (1977), 254 – 59.

22 Pantin, *The English Church*, p. 228.

middle ranks of clergy and gentry who owned copies of the *Prick of Conscience.*[23] In 1446 a York chantry priest, William Revetour, left Alice Bolton, the wife of a prosperous York merchant, a *librum de oratione Dominica et Stimulus Conscientia in Anglia;* and John Lord Scrope left an English book of the Pater Noster to his daughter in 1455.[24] Such works were important aids to the minute analysis of conscience, but their length and complexity would have put them beyond the reach of many poorer priests and their parishioners.

It is likely that Thoresby, before becoming archbishop of York, was influenced by the attempts made by the secular clergy and canon lawyers of Grandisson's circle (such as Nassington) to wrest the pastoral initiative from the friars. He was a Bachelor of Canon Law in 1341 and was one of eighteen canon lawyers who were at the papal Curia in Avignon in 1344 at the same time as FitzRalph and the author of the *Memoriale.*[25] When he became archbishop of York he would have worked with Nassington, and he had dealings with Grandisson. It is possible that he also opposed the friars; according to Bale he attacked the mendicants when they preached that mortuaries ought not to be rendered to the parish priest, and he wrote against them a work which commenced with the words *Pridem sanctissimus in Christo pater.*[26] None of the activity of these clergy provided an effective answer to the friars' justification for their pastoral activity, which was that many secular clergy were too uneducated to perform the pastoral office themselves. Even in Grandisson's Exeter it was only the friars who were able to preach in Cornish, and in York during the early years of Thoresby's archiepiscopate the most notable public preacher was friar John Waldeby, a public penitentiary in the diocese in 1354, whose collection of Sunday sermons, *Novum opus Dominicale,* were originally delivered to the laity in the vernacular at the church of the Austin friars in York every Sunday, with the aim of arousing people to conversation and penance.[27]

Thoresby's most realistic attempt to combat clerical ignorance was his composition of a Latin catechism, which summarized the six articles that were the subject of Pecham's decree *Ignorantia sacerdotum.* He instructed a Benedictine monk of St Mary's York, John Gaytrick, to make an expanded version of his catechism in English verse. This was probably arranged in the Christmas of 1356 when a monk of the abbey, called John de G., visited Thoresby's household. Thoresby wrote to the

23 See Doyle, 'A Survey', i, p. 84 for description of surviving manuscripts; Bodl. MS. Eng. poet. d.5. was copied by John Kylyngyke (a Yorkshire name).
24 TE, III, p. 268.
25 Haren, 'Memoriale Presbiterorum', Appendix.
26 Bale, *Scriptorum,* cent. sexta, p. 493.
27 Walsh, *Richard FitzRalph,* p. 359; Hackett, 'English Austin Friars', 456; Owst, *Preaching,* pp. 64 – 5.

abbot about the monk telling him that he had made himself so popular at his household that his fellow monks must be fearing that he was laying charges of monastic corruption and arranging a visitation.[28] The archbishop asked the abbot if he could have him back at the beginning of Lent, and on 25 November 1357 the Latin catechism was issued from Cawood and enrolled in the archbishop's register, along with Gaytrick's translation, and approved by the convocation of York.[29] In a preamble to the Latin original Thoresby gave his reasons for composing the work, emphasizing the culpable ignorance of priests and his intention to prevent them from avoiding their collective duty: he ascribed the troubles of his diocese to the neglect and ignorance of the clergy and complained that none of those whom he is unworthily permitted to preside over — a burden he dolefully bears — follows Christ; he complains that the laity are in need of instruction in the observation of the basic and necessary Christian laws, which are derived from himself, rectors, vicars and parish priests — who are in just as much need of instruction themselves — lest ignorance and negligence come to pass, facilitating grave errors and endangering souls.[30] The first section of the work attempted to forestall errors in belief by giving a simple outline of the fourteen articles of belief concerning the knowledge of God. Seven articles dealt with the operation of the Godhead, including the mysteries of the Trinity, the penitential functions of the holy church and the reuniting of the body and soul at the Day of Judgement. The other seven were dedicated to Christ's manhood, his Incarnation, Passion, the Harrowing of Hell, the Resurrection, Ascension and the Judgement.[31] In Gaytrick's vernacular version the principle behind the work is restated and directed primarily at the laity as the translator informs his readers that the archbishop, to prevent people from excusing themselves from knowing these things, has ordained that they be taught them in English. Gaytrick also expanded the original, using other manuals, perhaps at St Mary's, and while Thoresby was concerned with the implementation of a teaching programme, his adaptor attempted to give the laity a rationale for this programme by giving the teaching function of the church a wider spiritual and historical context. An account is therefore provided of the origin of creation, and man's loss of God given reason and knowledge through the fall of Adam and Eve, rendering mankind dependent on the teaching and laws of the church for this knowledge, which is the only way to salvation.[32]

28 ibid, p. 55.

29 Reg. Thoresby, fos.295a – 298. For circulation of surviving MSS. see Doyle, Survey 11.

30 ibid, fo.298b; *The Lay Folk's Catechism*, ed. T. P. Simmons and H. E. Nolloth (London, EETS, 1901), pp. 2 – 4.

31 Reg. Thoresby fo. 296a; *Catechism*, 11. 566 ff.

32 ibid, fo.295b; 11.1-29; Gillespie, 'The Middle English Pastoral Manual', pp. 21 – 34

Most of the *Lay Folk's Catechism*, as it became known, was concerned with the teaching of the laws of the church, which comprised the ten commandments, the seven sacraments, the seven works of mercy, the seven virtues and the seven sins. Conduct according to these precepts was monitored during confession, for this work was essentially a penitential manual. Its originality lay not in its content, but in its simplicity and conciseness,which may have been a reaction against the obfuscation of the moral teaching of the *Speculum Vitae* and *The Prick of Conscience* behind formidable length and elaborate allegory.[33] Thoresby and Gaytrick made little attempt to give a social and legal rationale to moral precepts like the authors of the *Pars oculi* and the *Memoriale presbiterorum*; they merely gave simple instructions showing people how to live their lives.

Thoresby realistically applied his knowledge of theology and canon law to this task and did not concern himself unduly with the impulses of penitents. He was one of the few canonists to observe the Thomist distinction between cardinal and capital sins, which were in themselves punishable by damnation, and the seven deadly sins, which were specific manifestations of those general impulses.[34] This must have lessened the severity of the penitential examination and encouraged a more regular attendance at confession because Thoresby's manual showed that impulses could not be punished by damnation. Instead the author concentrated on social conduct; the catalogue of the seven deadly sins was used to castigate social hostility: envy, backbiting, slander, adultery, violence, anger and all types of theft, were censured. As was usual in such cases of social hostility, absolution was to be refused until restitution had been made to the injured party.[35] One of the complaints about friars was that they granted absolution without restitution: in their concern with the spiritual dimensions of confession they neglected its role as an agent of communal reconciliation and harmony.[36] But Thoresby, like Pagula, had a clear sense of the church's pacificatory role; obedience to the ten commandments could encourage social harmony and stability: theft, manslaughter, adultery, swearing and sacrilege were forbidden, holy days were to be observed and parishioners were to be content with their lives, to look up to their betters and respect the clergy. The positive virtues of social responsibility were also encouraged: parents should be respected and looked after, and the seven

33 E. J. Arnould, *Le manuel des peches* (Paris, 1940), p. 37.

34 M. W. Bloomfield, *The Seven Deadly Sins* (Michigan, 1952), pp. 43 – 4.

35 Reg. Thoresby, fo.296b; *Catechism*, ll 245 – 7. For a more detailed discussion of the relationship between the administration of confession and restitution see Myrk, *Instructions for Parish Priests*, pp. 52, 71.

36 This criticism of friars as confessors was expressed on 16 May 1356 in a bill of complaints, drawn up by the clergy of the province of Canterbury and submitted to a provincial council in London. Walsh, *Richard FitzRalph*, p. 408.

deeds of mercy were used to exhort parishioners to an active involvement in society by performing their duties providing spiritual and material help to the less fortunate.[37] The rhymed couplets, provided in Gaytrick's translation as an inducement to follow these instructions, show that he was under no illusions about the nature of his audience:

> 'These til our neghlebors er ful needful
> And to tham that dos tham wondir medefull,
> For he sal find merci that mercifull is,
> And man withouten merci of merci sal misse.'[38]

Thoresby envisaged the parish priest performing a disciplinary role in society by administering the sacrament of penance, but this did not preclude confessors from arousing a degree of psychological and spiritual awareness in their penitents. Self-discipline was encouraged because it could make parishioners into more useful, happier people. Those guilty of the deadly sin of sloth, claimed the author, lacked such discipline, and in their repugnance to do good deeds they suffered a heaviness of heart that prevented them from deriving pleasure from loving and serving God; they showed an unnatural hostility towards fellow parishioners, because all men were born to work for others.[39] Thoresby recorded in his register the violent and intemperate crimes of clergy and laymen, and he tried in this work to encourage a greater degree of rationality in the behaviour and attitudes of people. The seventh virtue of temperance or moderation was described as the measure of all that people do to enable them to live rationally without excess and greed. The author did not encourage asceticism, but a rational and moderate attitude to life which would bring strength of mind and body, defined as the ability to confront sorrow and happiness without undue elation or depression.[40] Within the examination envisaged by Thoresby there was scope for the encouragement of greater sensitivity of conscience that is also found in the *Pars oculi*. The fifth virtue of prudence was described as the ability to discern good from evil, and in the discussion of the deadly sin of covetousness it was pointed out that in crimes such as usury, simony and fraud, there was often a degree of cleverness and craft obscuring the moral wrong of obtaining something in this way.[41] The discussion of the sin of envy involved such subconscious motivations as the rejoicing at the misfortune of others

37 Reg. Thoresby, fo.296b; *Catechism*, ll 200 – 6.
38 Reg. Thoresby, fo.297a; *Catechism*, ll 376 – 79.
39 Reg. Thoresby, fo.297b; *Catechism*, ll 562 – 38.
40 Reg. Thoresby, fo.297b; *Catechism*, ll 430 – 45.
41 Reg. Thoresby, fo.297b; *Catechism*, ll 425 – 26; 510 – 15.

regretting hearing the praises of those one envies, and misinterpreting and misrepresenting their actions by turning their good deeds into sins.[42] Considerable self-examination was also required for the sin of backbiting, for it was pointed out that the listener was also guilty, 'For war ther no herer ther were no bacbiter.'[43]

In the prelude to the Latin version of the work Thoresby envisaged a considerable extension of the importance of compulsory confession in the lives of parishioners by requiring everyone in his diocese to learn his catechism and to be examined on it during confession. He declared that knowledge of the laws of the church was essential for salvation, and to prevent the excuse of ignorance being offered he composed this work, offering forty days indulgence and ratifying inducements given by other clergy to all those who would remember, or try their hardest to remember, these laws.[44] The simple rhyming verse of this work was also probably intended as an aid to memory. Knowledge of Thoresby's instructions was to be tested in the forty days preceding Easter by the parish clergy who were to enjoin a health giving penance on those who failed the examination.[45] The exhortation to parishioners to remember this catechism shows that self examination was encouraged outside confession. Thoresby also saw the possibility of annual confession becoming a spiritual dialogue between priest and penitent in which penitents were instructed and examined on their religious knowledge. This was a rudimentary but basic step towards a wider understanding of self-analysis and a personal sense of sin that was envisaged by Rolle and other recluses. Robert Thornton probably saw the *Catechism* performing this function for members of his family and household when he included it in his manuscript alongside the devotional works of northern England. An attempt was also made in the English version of the instructions to increase the significance of the sacrament of communion in parishioners lives, and Gaytrick, in an addition on the Eucharist attempted to foster devotion to the sacrament by exhorting annual communion.

Thoresby, besides affirming the traditional importance of the sacrament of penance as an instrument of pastoral care, was also responsible for giving a new impetus to the role of preaching in the pastoral office. The religious instruction provided in annual confession and the four parish sermons delivered annually, in accordance with Pecham's statute of 1281, would not have been sufficient to enable parishioners to memorize the *Catechism*, despite its simplicity. In an important advance on Pecham's legislation Thoresby commanded rectors, vicars, parish

42 Reg. Thoresby, fo.297b; *Catechism*, ll 470 – 77.
43 Reg. Thoresby, fo.297b; *Catechism*, ll 480 – 83.
44 Reg. Thoresby, fo.298a; *Catechism*, p. 4.
45 Reg. Thoresby, fo.298a; *Catechism*, p. 4.

priest and other curates to expound to the people, carefully and exactly in the vernacular, at least on every Sunday, the outline of the six articles he had provided for them. The laity were enjoined to pay close attention to these sermons so that they could learn these six points, and they were to make provision for their children to learn them.[46] Gaytrick, in his adaptation, also emphasized the importance of preaching in the pastoral office and in doing so he, like Thoresby in the original, took the unusual step of openly castigating the clergy for failing in the performance of the pastoral office.[47] Previous and subsequent manuals such as the *Pars oculi* and the *Speculum sacerdotale,* and much penitential legislation, was concerned with protecting the prestige of the priesthood, and ways were even devised for preventing laymen from working out the nature of priests' sins from their public penances by keeping clerical penances secret.[48] Gaytrick declared that there were many people in this world who were not educated enough to know and serve God and whose deeds proclaimed this; the responsibility for this, he claimed, lay with those who had charge of their souls and who were duty bound to teach them.[49] The catechism was designed to help priests to meet this pastoral responsibility, and Gaytrick conveyed to his readers an image of their archbishop as a caring pastor who was intent on providing his flock with the religious knowledge that would secure their salvation: 'so mikel couaites he the hele of yhour soules'.[50]

This pastoral initiative was emulated in the province of Canterbury by Simon Islip, who administered the church with Thoresby in the same spirit of friendship and cooperation that they shared as civil servants. On 21 February 1361 Islip sent to all the parish priests of his diocese a *brevis libellus,* which does not survive, on the seven sins and their species and the ten commandments, which they were to copy, learn and teach to their parishioners before his next visitation after Easter. He also followed Thoresby's example in using confession to check on the laity's knowledge of these things, and at the synod of Ely in 1364 he ordered every priest to examine adults frequently on their religious knowledge when they attended confession, and to make sure that they were teaching their children their prayers. He too emphasized the importance of regular preaching, and at the same synod he ordered priests to devote themselves to studying the scriptures, and to preach frequently in English on the ten commandments, the creed and the seven deadly sins.[51]

46 Reg. Thoresby, fo.298b.
47 *Catechism,* pp. 2 – 4.
48 *Speculum Sacerdotale,* ed. E. H. Weatherly (London, EETS, 1922), pp.87 – 8.
49 *Catechism,* ll 34 – 41; Reg. Thoresby, fo.295b.
50 Reg. Thoresby, fo.298a; *Catechism,* 11566 – 70.
51 Pantin, *The English Church,* p. 212; Lambeth, Reg. Islip, fo.182.

The Oculus Sacerdotis, Speculum Vitae and the *Lay Folk's Catechism* were popular and influential in the diocese in the second half of the fourteenth century, and this can be attributed to some extent to the pastoral initiative of Thoresby. The official status of the Latin and English versions of Thoresby's instructions would have guaranteed the wider influence of the pastoral manual. The *Catechism* would have been distributed down the ecclesiastical administration from archdeacons to clergy, and exemplars may have been distributed at chapters for circulation among parish priests. The archdeacons were responsible for ensuring that all parish clergy possessed copies, and it is probable that they were expected to transcribe them themselves.[52] It is possible that Islip, in ordering priests of his diocese to transcribe their own copies of his *brevis libellus*, was following the example set by Thoresby in York.[53] The *Speculum Vitae* was popular despite its length and survives in forty manuscripts, and the *Oculus Sacerdotis*, although not an official work like the *Catechism*, reached and assisted the penitentiary class to which Pagula belonged in the second half of the fourteenth century and circulated among the rural parish clergy of the diocese. The earliest known owner of the *Oculus* in Yorkshire is Richard Rickhale, chaplain of Topcliffe in North Riding who owned a copy in 1359. Another North Riding rector, Thomas Halton of Abel, bequeathed a copy to Kirkstall in 1391, and John Sandall rector of Wheldrake in East Riding left a copy in 1397. A fourteenth century manuscript of *Oculus Sacerdotis* with penitential annotations was owned by the vicar of Skipworth, and a York canon, Walter Bruge left his copy to a parish priest.[54] The transmission of these texts, judging by the humble nature of surviving manuscripts and their lack of uniformity, was unorganized and diffuse, suggesting that they were copied by the priests themselves. The popularity of the *Oculus* throughout the parish clergy of rural Yorkshire in the later fourteenth century is testimony to the success of Thoresby's pastoral drive to extend religious education through the administration of confession.

Behind Thoresby's *Catechism* there lay a belief in the church's pastoral mission to create a more compassionate and civilized society. This achievement depended on the activities of conscientious priests who were prepared to make the sacrament of penance a source of comfort and strength as well as instruction and correction. There is evidence that by the end of Thoresby's archiepiscopate parish

[52] Ball, 'Education of Parish Priests', p. 83.
[53] Pantin, *The English Church*, p. 312.
[54] Ball, 'Parish Priests', . 87; Prob. Reg. 2, fo.11; TE, I, p. 156.

societies and their priests were accepting their pacificatory and comforting role. In St Mary's church in Beverley in 1372 a priest called Peter Aldgate heard the confession of a madman, William Watton, who had been cared for with understanding by his master Thomas Waghen, his mother and his neighbours, despite his frequent violent outbursts. Watton threatened suicide and expressed paranoiac delusions that some of his neighbours were trying to kill him. Aldgate humoured the man, telling him to trust in God and pray, and went to inform his kinsmen and master. On his return Watton stabbed the priest, and he was seized by the bailiffs. The dying man, however, abjured them by Christ's body to do Watton no harm because he did not know what he was doing, and he forgave him before God.[55]

Further evidence for the successful dissemination of pastoral teaching can be seen in the activities of the religious guilds that performed cycles of religious plays dramatizing the moral teachings found in the *Catechism*. In a Lollard vernacular adaptation of Richard Ullerston's *Defensorium dotacionis ecclesie,* written shortly after 1401, it was claimed that Thoresby sent Gaytrick's English translation of the *Catechism* in small 'pagynes' to the common people to help them to learn and know it.[56] If the writer meant pageants he could have been referring to the inspiration that Thoresby and Gaytrick provided for the composition and performance in York of two cycles on the seven deadly sins and the creed. In 1378 Wyclif, in *De officio pastorali*, referred to an English version of the *Pater Noster* being taught in English in the play of York.[57] The seven petitions of the lord's prayer were traditionally regarded as a means of salvation for each of the seven sins, and it is possible that the miracle plays of the *pater noster* cycle dramatized the resistance of seven saints to each of the seven sins with the aid of the divinely efficient clauses of the lord's prayer.[58] Possible references to such plays were made in 1446 when a play of St Jacob in six pageants was bequeathed to the guild of Corpus Christi, and in 1455 when Robert Lasingby left the church of St Dionysius a play of St Dionysius.[59] In 1389 a guild of Our Lord's Prayer was

55 *Fasti Ebor*., p. 465 – 46.

56 M. Aston, 'Lollardy and Literacy', in M. Aston, *Lollards and Reformers* (London, 1984), p. 209. For Ullerston see A. Hudson, 'The Debate on Bible translation, Oxford 1401', *E.H.R.*, xc (1975), 1 – 18.

57 H. Craig, *English Religious Drama*, (Oxford, 1955), p. 338; Wyclif, *De Officio Pastorali*, ed. G. Lechler (Leipzig, 1869).

58 Craig, *Religious Drama*, pp. 338 – 41.

59 ibid, p. 340.

founded in York, which maintained seven lights in token of the seven supplications of the Lord's prayer. This guild owned no property, apart from the properties of the *Pater Noster* play, and its members were bound to accompany the players through the city and ensure good order during their performances.[60] They were also dedicated to uphold the values propagated in Thoresby's *Catechism*: members were bound to make and remember a table showing the whole meaning and use of the Lord's Prayer, which was to hang against a pillar in York Minster, and all potential members were questioned by the warden to determine whether or not they intended to live rightly, possibly according to the archbishop's precepts.[61] It was perhaps also in the period of Thoresby's archiepiscopate that the creed, which is also outlined in the *Catechism,* was first dramatized. In 1446 William Revetour, a warden of the guild of Corpus Christi, bequeathed to the guild a book of the *Creed Play* and appertaining books and banners, with the stipulation that this play was to be performed every ten years.[62] The length of this play — according to a 1465 inventory it consisted of twenty two quires — suggests that it dramatized the composition of the Apostle's Creed, with the help of the *Northern Legendary,* in twelve pageants dedicated to the lives of the twelve apostles.[63]

The most impressive aspect of the wider dissemination of religious teaching was the use of drama to extend biblical, theological knowledge and devotional awareness. The first English Corpus Christi cycles were developed in the diocese of York, probably during Thoresby's archiepiscopate, and they can be tentatively connected with the influence of the archbishop and his clergy at York and Beverley. This cycle was an important foundation for the growth of lay piety towards the end of the fourteenth century. From the tenth to the thirteenth century Latin liturgical plays commemorating the Nativity and Passion and complementing the mass had been performed in churches. Although they were in Latin they fulfilled, through the use of mime, an educational function and as early as 1200 they were being performed outdoors to lay audiences: in this year on the north side of the cemetery of a Beverley church a resurrection play

60 For foundation charter see *Records of Early English Drama,* York, ed. A. T. Johnson and A. Rogerson, (Toronto, 1979), pp. 6 – 7; *Early English Guilds,* ed. L. Toulmin-Smith (London, 1870), pp. 137 – 9.

61 ibid, p. 139. In 1466 the guild merged with the guild of St Anthony's.

62 *Register of the Guild of Corpus Christi,* p. 294; TE, II, pp. 116 – 18.

63 Craig, *Religious Drama,* pp. 334 – 38.

was staged.[64] In the thirteenth century in Werburgh Abbey in Chester and in York Minster (1255) there were liturgical cycles concerning the Fall, Nativity, Resurrection and Last Judgement, which by the end of the thirteenth century were probably being performed outdoors at Whitsun as important civic occasions: the mayor of Chester, John Arnway, was responsible for giving the Chester cycle civic status by 1278,[65] and at Cividale near Friuli in Italy in 1304 a Whitsunday cycle was performed by the clergy and chapter of the diocese in the presence of the patriarch of Aquilea and notables of the region.[66] The passing of the performance of the York Latin cycle from secular clergy of the minster, and perhaps monks of St Mary's Abbey, to the craft guilds is connected with the institution of the Civic Riding and the Feast of Corpus Christi. The Civic Riding was instituted in 1298 as a civic procession of craft guilds using visual symbols to demonstrate the nature of their craft; a eucharistic equivalent was the Feast of Corpus Christi, instituted throughout England in 1318: in York, as in other cities, an annual procession of clergy and laymen carried the host in a prescribed circular route from the central church. The implementation of this feast in the diocese in the first half of the fourteenth century was an important aspect of a pastoral campaign to make Christ's life and sacrifice relevant to secular life; and this encouraged the integration of the procession and the mid-summer liturgical plays with the civic riding procession, in which guilds were depicting the performance of their crafts with increasingly sophisticated mimed pageants. The guilds therefore began to stage versions of these plays, often with the appropriateness of the craft in mind.[67] The translation and adaptation of these Latin Cycles into a vernacular cycle depicting history from creation to doomsday first occurred in the diocese of York sometime between the institution of Corpus Christi in 1318 and 1376, the date of the first documentary evidence for the existence of a vernacular Corpus Christi cycle in the diocese. In 1376 2s yearly rent was paid for the use of one tenement to house three pageant wagons; and in the same year a York priest, William Thorpe, left his book of plays to a layman, Sir Richard Yedingham, which suggests that these plays performed on pageant wagons were in English.[68] In 1378 a fine paid by the shearers for their pageant establishes that these plays were being performed by craft guilds in

64 G. Wickham, *Early English Stages* (London, 1966), i, p.123ff.
65 F. Salter, *Medieval Drama in Chester* (Toronto, 1955).
66 Wickham, *English Stages*, 1, p. 123ff.
67 ibid.
68 *Records of English Drama*, p. 3.

the city.[69] Another vernacular Corpus Christi cycle was probably established in the diocese about the same time in the town of Beverley, for in 1377 there occurs a reference to expenses for the pageant of the Corpus Christi play. The Beverley cycle was spoken of in 1390 as *antiqua consuetudo*, and in 1394 it was agreed to play the York Corpus Christi plays in places appointed from ancient times.[70] The term anciently implies a generation or so and suggests that both cycles were first performed around 1360 shortly after the publication of Gaytrick's English version of Thoresby's *Lay Folk's Catechism*, and in the wake of the production of the English works of Rolle, Nassington and other vernacular religious writers of the diocese. Further evidence that the Corpus Christi cycle was a conscious pastoral initiative comes from a description occurring in an application to the mayor and council of the play of Corpus Christi day as being instituted from ancient time for the sake of great devotion, extirpation of vices and reformation of morality.[71] It is also possible that the Cornish *Ordinalia*, composed between 1350 and 1375, during the time when Grandisson was bishop of Exeter, was the result of pastoral initiative. There is no direct evidence of Thoresby's personal initiative behind the York Corpus Christi plays, unless he was related in some way to Richard Thoresby, a bailiff since 1361 and a friend of the mayor of York, John Sancton.[72] The mayor and town council, elected from representatives of the guilds, was responsible for the supervision of these plays, and Richard Thoresby was also a master of the Guild of Jesus Christ and the Blessed Virgin, which was dedicated to the honour of Christ's body and was a possible forerunner of the Corpus Christi guild, founded in 1408 to supervise the Corpus Christi procession.[73] It is also probable that the authorship and supervision of these plays was in the hands of the clergy of the most important city church. The Chester cycle was translated and adapted from the Werburgh Abbey liturgical cycle by a senior monk of the abbey, Sir Henry Francis, between 1377 and 1389.[74] The York cycle was therefore probably composed and supervised by the minster clergy who performed the liturgical cycle, perhaps with the assistance of monks of St Mary's Abbey including Gaytrick. The Corpus Christi cycle at Beverley, where there was no monastery, would also have been in the control of the cathedral clergy, where Thoresby's nephew, Dr John Thoresby, was provost.

69 ibid.
70 W. Tydeman, *The Theatre in the Middle Ages* (Cambridge, 1978), p. 114.
71 Tydeman, *Theatre in Middle Ages*, p. 100.
72 York City Library MS., 'Civic Officials and Parliamentary Officials of York, by R.H. Skaife, fo.650.
73 ibid, fo.750.
74 Salter, *Drama in Chester*, p. 8ff.

Both the Beverley and York cycles provided a comprehensive survey of biblical history: in 1396 an order to the thirty-nine craft guilds of Beverley to have their plays ready every Corpus Christi day suggests that there were thirty-nine plays in the cycle. The York cycle contained forty-eight plays which were described in a list compiled by the town clerk in 1415.[75] The craft assembled to perform at 4.30am on Corpus Christi day at nine stations rented by leading citizens, including the mayor and aldermen (in 1416 it was to the highest bidder), and on the tenth unrented site at the pavement, a public space allowing the cycle to be performed for the largest possible audience.[76] The evidence that these cycles were somehow performed in their entirety at the ten stations includes: the maintenance of lights by the guilds for evening performances; fines imposed by the council on guilds failing to perform pageants; the application from two guilds in 1421 for permission from the council to abbreviate and amalgamate their crucifixion play; and the fines imposed by guilds on members whose acting was substandard.[77] Some of the York plays, such as the Cain and Abel drama, which exhorts people to pay tithes in the manner of 1367 constitutions, directly endorse pastoral policies. However, in a more profound way these forty-eight biblical plays staged with the cooperation of the town council and the craft guilds represent the church of York's finest pastoral achievement, and it is possible to see a close relationship between the *Lay Folk's Catechism* and the concept of the Corpus Christi cycle. Gaytrick, in presenting Thoresby's instructions as a scheme for salvation in which the archbishop willed that 'al men be saufe' was giving the work a comprehensive rationale for the collective salvation of members of the church of York similar to that expounded in the York Corpus Christi cycle, which through sophisticated use of typology and symbolism depicted man's defections from divine grace and his responses to God's saving initiatives. The role of the church as the medium of God's grace was repeatedly stressed through the symbols of the Ark and the Cross to give a different but equally important emphasis on the pastoral role of the church as a vehicle of salvation. The importance of the local church in this typological demonstration of the operation of God's grace would have been stressed in the cults of local saints such as William, and in the table that the vicars choral of York Minster were obliged to memorize, which related the history of the church of York to world and biblical history.[78] The cycle was intended to

75 Craig, *English Drama*, pp. 200 – 203; *York Plays*, ed. L. Toulmin-Smith (Oxford, 1885), pp. xi – xii.

76 M. Twycross, 'Places to Hear the Play: Pageant Stations at York', *Records Early English Drama*, Newsletter (1978).

77 Tydeman, *English Theatre*, p. 100ff.

78 J.S. Purvis, 'The Tables of the York Vicars Choral', *Y.A.J.*, 41, (1966).

be a more complete fulfilment of the instructions commenced in the *Catechism*, and in adapting the liturgical plays the authors used the religious and pastoral literature of the diocese, including the *Northern Passion*, a simple English poem on Christ's ministry and Passion which had been translated from the original French in the early fourteenth century in the north of England, to infuse greater spirituality into the cycle.[79] The Passion plays in the York cycle were especially affected by the use made of the *Northern Passion* and, like the Franciscan meditations and gospel harmonies, they were expanded to show Christ's life in greater detail, with the purpose of arousing affective responses from the audience. The York crucifixion play also shows the influence of the realistic descriptions of the crucifixion found in Nassyngton's poem *The Band of Loving* and in Thoresby's *Catechism*.[80] Some seventeen plays were also amplified far beyond their liturgical bounds by the introduction of apocryphal stories from the gospel of Nicodemus, which had been translated into a northern English poem. Apocryphal stories were selected with a strong sense of dramatic propriety to provide a spiritual dimension to the pastoral policies of the period.

The Influence of Thoresby's Pastoral Policies

Thoresby, as a patron who continued the nepotistic practices of Greenfield and Melton, was in an especially strong position to create around him a circle of like-minded men to implement his policies. Through his patronage northerners, many of whom were relatives from Howdenshire and Lindsey, were able to receive the same sort of training that he had received in the civil service, the university of Oxford, and in the archbishop's household. Nearly all these clerks eventually applied their learning, skills and experience in the administration of York diocese.

As a leading government official, Thoresby gave a new impetus to the recruiting and promotion of clerks from Lindsey and Howdenshire. While he was keeper of the chancery rolls his brother Richard Thoresby became keeper of the hanaper in 1343, and in 1357 and 1379 he was succeeded by two of the archbishop's nephews, Richard and John Ravenser.[1] The Ravensers were established in Lindsey, North Thoresby, and were related to the Thoresbys through the marriage of John Thoresby's sister to a member of the Waltham family in nearby South

79 Craig, *Religious Drama*, pp. 155 – 57.

80 For Nassyngton's poem, also known as *De Trinitate et Unitate* see Religious Pieces, ed. G. G. Perry, (London, EETS, 1914), pp. 63 – 7.

1 Tout, *Chapters*, iii, pp. 215 – 16; Grassi, 'Clerical Dynasties', p. 478; CPR, 1350 – 54, p. 185.

Grimsby. Their son John Waltham married Margaret Ravenser, a sister of Richard and John Ravenser. The children of John Waltham and Margaret Ravenser also found employment in the civil service: John Waltham, the eldest and the archbishop's great nephew, was brought into chancery by his uncle, and he became keeper of the Privy Seal from 1386 to 1389; his younger brother William was probably introduced into the royal administration by the two Ravenspur brothers, and William Waltham succeeded John Ravenspur as keeper of the hanaper in 1389.[2] The Ferribys were related to the Meltons, who in turn could have been related to the Walthams, and they were introduced into the great wardrobe by Archbishop Melton at the same time as Thoresby was introduced into the chancery; by 1361 the wardrobe was still in the hands of William Ferriby.[3] A number of Thoresby's household chaplains were also employed by the crown: Thomas Buckton and Henry Barton were described as king's clerks in 1362 and 1363, and Walter Skirlaw, a Howdenshire man who was a king's clerk in 1372, was probably first introduced into administration by Thoresby.[4] Another Howdenshire clerk, Thomas Brantingham, a kinsman of the Ferribys, was a clerk of the controller in 1355 and a keeper of the wardrobe in 1368; and a canon of York, Henry Ingleby, was one of Thoresby's leading privy seal clerks from 1340 to 1354.[5]

Thoresby also used his influence as an archbishop and a respected Oxford graduate — he wrote to the chancellor in 1352 thanking his for his enrolment in the list of the university's benefactors — to help his protégé through university. His interest in the training of his clergy at Oxford was shown in 1367 when he passed legislation forbidding clergy of the diocese from attending lectures on Physic. He took special interest in the career of his nephew, John Thoresby, and in 1352 he wrote to the chancellor on his behalf.[6] This nephew had a distinguished career at Oxford: he received his Baccalaureate of Canon Law in 1353 and incepted as Doctor in 1356; before 1364 he lectured at the university on Civil and Canon Law.[7] His studies were aided by the influence of his uncle, who wrote to the bishop of Lincoln in 1353 asking him to grant his nephew a licence of non-residence for two years from the rectory of Lifford so that he could study, and in 1364 the archbishop provided him with the rectory of Brantingham in Yorkshire.[8] Members of the Thoresby

2 Tout, *Chapters*, iii, pp. 215 – 16; Grassi, 'Clerical Dynasties', p. 184.
3 Grassi, 'Clerical Dynasties', p. 543.
4 CPR, 1361 – 64, p. 199.
5 Grassi, 'Clerical Dynasties', p. 188; Tout, *Chapters*.
6 Emden, *B.R.U.O.*, iii, p. 1863.
7 ibid, iii, p. 1864; For Dr John Thoresby's career see *Beverley Chapter Act Book*, ed. A. F Leach (S.S., 1903), ii, pp. lxxii – iv; Grassi, 'Clerical Dynasties', p. 478.
8 *Fasti Ebor.*, p. 449.

dynasty and other northern clergy and civil servants were a force in Balliol College. John Waltham, son of Thoresby's sister Margaret, was a fellow of Balliol before 1349; he received his B. A. and baccalaureate of canon law before 1358 and his doctorate of canon law by 1379.[9] He too received help from his uncle: in 1352 Waltham was mentioned solicitiously in a letter from Archbishop Thoresby to the chancellor of the university; and while Thoresby was bishop of St David's he provided his nephew with a canonry and prebend of Abergwili in Carmarthenshire. Waltham's academic career was as distinguished as his cousins: in his will in 1375 he left a collection of books to Balliol, and in 1379 he obtained his doctorate in canon law.[10] Two others who may have received encouragement and help from Thoresby during their studies at Balliol were John Hugate and William Ferriby: Hugate, whose family had been introduced into royal administration by Melton, was a fellow of Balliol College in 1361, and in 1370 he was granted a licence by Thoresby to study at Oxford; Ferriby, the keeper of the wardrobe from 1360 – 1361, was a fellow of Balliol from 1364 to 1375 and a distinguished scholar; he deposited the works of Burley and Ockham in the college library in 1368.[11]

Dr John Wyclif and other members of the clerical family of Wyclif, the lords of Wycliffe near Richmond, studied at Balliol, perhaps with the support of Thoresby.[12] The proof establishing John Wyclif's connection with this family is his relationship with Robert Wyclif, possibly a nephew, and a subdeacon of York Minster by 1368: in May 1371 the king granted Mr John Wyclif, the rector of Ludgershall, a portion of the tithes belonging to the prior of Bermondsey in Ludgershall which had come into the crown's hands as a result of the seizure of alien priories; Wyclif found as mainpernors Robert Wyclif, clerk, and the mayor of York, John Sancton.[13] The lords of Wyclif from 1349 to 1362 were Roger Wyclif, who was dead by 1362, and William Wyclif, who was probably his eldest son; in 1363 the lord of Wyclif was John Wyclif, who was probably a younger son of William.[14] By controlling the advowson of Wyclif church this family maintained a clerical dynasty in this rectory which included: Roger Wyclif, rector until 1363; William Wyclif, rector from 1363 to 1369

9 Emden, *B.R.U.O.*, iii, p. 1913.
10 ibid, iii, pp. 1913 – 4.
11 ibid, ii, pp. 979; Grassi, 'Clerical Dynasties', pp. 115, 129.
12 Richard Fleming, Bishop of Lincoln said in 1422 that Wyclif was from the diocese of York and was born of respectable parents. See Vaclav Mudroch, 'John Wyclif and Richard Fleming: gleanings from German sources', *BIHR*, xxxvii (1964), 239.
13 G. A. Holmes, *The Good Parliament* (Oxford, 1975), p. 168 n. 3; McFarlane had been sceptical about the tradition that John Wyclif had Richmondshire origins: K. B. McFarlane, *John Wyclif and the Beginnings of English Nonconformity* (London, 1952), p. 3.
14 H. B. Workman, *John Wyclif* (Oxford, 1926), ii, 45 – 46.

on the presentation of John Wyclif, who was probably his elder brother; and Robert Wyclif, whose connection with Dr John Wyclif has been established and who succeeded William as rector of Wyclif; another clerical member of the family was Nicholas Wyclif, the son of John Wyclif, who was ordained as a priest in York in 1363.[15] The reformer Dr John Wyclif was probably one of two John Wyclifs who were ordained deacons in St Mary's Abbey York and priests in York Minster in 1351.[16] The family, like other northerners, had connections with Balliol: Dr John Wyclif was master of the college from May 1360 to 1362, and his mastership coincided with the fellowship of William Wyclif, the rector of Wyclif, who attended Balliol from April 1361 to 1363; in 1362 John Wyclif, the master, and ten fellows, including William Wyclif, were witnesses to a deed in which the church of Abbotsley was appropriated to the college.[17]

This clerical Richmondshire family, to which Wyclif belonged, can be considered part of Thoresby's affinity. The archbishop's patronage of the family is implied in the licence he granted to William Wyclif to study at Balliol on 5 August 1365.[18] Robert Wyclif, Dr John Wyclif's mainpernor, was closely connected with two of Thoresby's private chaplains, Walter Skirlaw and John Clone. The Wyclifs also had links with the Hugate family, many of whose members served Melton and Thoresby: the Wyclif's hold on the rectory of Wyclif was finally relinquished in 1367 when the lord of Wyclif, John Wyclif, presented the church to Henry Hugate, and Henry Hugate was a contemporary of John and William Wyclif at Balliol.[19] The family of Wyclif's other mainpernor, John Sancton, was also connected with the Hugates. John Sancton's relative Richard appeared with John Hugate, fellow of Balliol as executor to Marshalsea clerk Nicholas Hugate.[20] Dr John Wyclif's membership of the Wyclif family of Richmondshire, and his links with Robert Wyclif and the mayor of York, John Sancton, suggests that he was, at least in the early stages of his career, a member of the circle of York clergy patronized by Thoresby. There is also circumstantial evidence that Wyclif directly benefitted from Thoresby's patronage. In 1356, the year that Dr John Thoresby, the archbishop's nephew, contributed to a feast in Merton College, John Wyclif was a probationary fellow; his name occurs as a steward of the week paying bills to the fellows' commons.[21] Another of Archbishop Thoresby's nephews, John Waltham, was a contemporary of Wyclif's at Balliol. It is likely that

15 ibid, ii, 45 – 46, 38 – 40.

16 *Fasti Ebor.*, p. 465.

17 J. A. Robson, *Wyclif and the Oxford Schools* (Cambridge, 1961), p. 13.

18 Emden, *B.R.U.O.*, iii, p. 2106; Reg. Thoresby, fo.291v.

19 *Early Lincoln Wills*, p. 25; Workman, *John Wyclif*, p. 45; McFarlane, *John Wyclif*, p. 4

20 *Beverley Chapter Act Book*, ii, pp. 122 – 25.2

21 Emden, *B.R.U.O.*, ii, p. 976; Robson, *Wyclif*, pp. 10 – 13.

Thoresby's influence secured for Wyclif the patronage of the archbishop's old friend Simon Islip. In 1357 Islip visited Merton, perhaps meeting Wyclif and Dr John Thorseby, and in 1366 he made John Wyclif the head of his new foundation of Canterbury Hall, a secular society based on the rule of Merton, with which the college was to have close associations; but Islip died in 1366 before the statutes of Canterbury Hall were formalized, and without his protection Wyclif lost his position because of the opposition of the monks.[22]

Wyclif's career disappointments and abnormally bad luck may have influenced the bitter attacks he was later to make on the church, but his pluralism, his application through the university for a York canonry and prebend in 1362, and prospects of a bishopric (perhaps at Thoresby's old see of Worcester[23]) suggests that Wyclif showed in his early career the ambitions and attitudes of his fellow northern clerks. In the 1370s his academic and ecclesiastic career did diverge from the pattern established among Thoresby and his servants: Wyclif did not return to York diocese, and he remained at Oxford where instead of specializing in canon law he took a doctorate in theology in 1372. However, like many of Thoresby's affinity, he did serve the government. By 1374 John of Gaunt had found a use for Wyclif's theological skills as a government propogandist. It is possible that this involvement of a university academic in politics can be attributed to the intervention of Edward III's eldest and most trusted civil servants John Thoresby and Simon Islip. There is evidence of Wyclif's connections with northerners in the civil service: in 1371 he acted as executor to William Askeby, an exchequer clerk and archdeacon of Nottingham.[24] Wyclif's connections with exchequer clerks in this year raises the further possibility that the lay patron who brought him to the attention of John of Gaunt, the feudal overlord of Richmond, was Thoresby's executor Richard Lord Scrope of Bolton, the treasurer of the Exchequer from 1371 to 1371. Scrope had served in Gaunt's retinue in Aquitaine in 1369, and apart from his government service his interests were primarily in Richmondshire in the region where Wyclif was born. The crown grant to Wyclif of the portion of the tithes of Ludgershall belonging to the prior of Bermondsey was paid and announced by Lord Scrope from the treasury; and in July 1373 Wyclif was advanced £60 by the Exchequer, again probably by the keeper Richard Scrope, for his wages and expenses as one of the English envoys meeting the papal envoys at Bruges to press the English

22 H. S. Cronin, 'John Wyclif, the Reformer, the Canterbury Hall, Oxford', *T.R.H.S.*, 3rd ser. (1914), 73; B. W. Henderson, *History of Merton College* (London, 1889), p. 46.

23 Workman, *Wyclif*, i, p. 153; R. W. Maitland, 'Wyclif's Preferments', *E.H.R.*, xv (1900), 529; Pop. Pet. 1, 390.

24 *Early Lincoln Wills*, p. 25.

government claims.[25] Wyclif's service for John of Gaunt perhaps ensured that he did not lose contact entirely with his family and Robert Wyclif in particular. Robert, a leading executor in the diocese, entered the king's service in 1377, perhaps with John Wyclif's assistance, when he was appointed on a commission to ascertain the value of the yearly revenues of the alien priories of Northumberland, Westmorland and Cumberland.[26]

Some of Thoresby's administrative and pastoral experience was gained in the service of the personal retinue of Archbishop Melton, and he in turn offered similar opportunities in his own household. One of his first household clerks was Thomas Buckton D.C.L., his vicar general from October 1354 to 1356 and an official at the court of York. He was preferred by Thoresby to the rectory of Rudby in Cleveland in 1355, and he was made a canon of York in 1363.[27] One clerk who received most of his training in Thoresby's household was John Clone, the archbishop's chaplain from April 1353; he was possibly the same John Clone who was described as a king's clerk in 1340, and he was rector of the important parish church of All Saints' in North Street, York from 1356 to 1359.[28] Clone was closely associated with Robert Wyclif and exchanged the rectory of Kirkby Ravensworth, which he had held since 1371, for Wyclif's rectory of St Cross in York in February 1379.[29] In the same month Clone was inducted into Robert Wyclif's stall at Auckland as part of the exchange. Wyclif was ordained sub-dean of York Minster in 1368, and as he did not attend university it is possible that he received his early training like Clone, in Thoresby's household. Robert Wyclif later became the most important household clerk of the bishop of Durham, Walter Skirlaw, serving as his chancellor and receiver from 1390 to 1405; Skirlaw was another member of the Thoresby household: he served as Thoresby's domestic chaplain in 1354 and 1356, his secretary in 1359, and he became the archbishop's proctor in the chapter of York at the 1361 parliament; he was given expenses to attend the papal curia in Rome in this year and was described by the archbishop as 'our beloved clerk'.[30] Another who received his early training in this household was Henry Barton, Thoresby's attorney in 1358, his domestic chaplain in

25 Holmes, *Good Parliament*, p. 168 n. 3.
26 Workman, *John Wyclif*, p. 45; McFarlane, *John Wyclif*, p. 4.
27 Emden, *B.R.U.O.*, i, p. 300; Reg. Thoresby fo.82v; See also Thoresby's will in TE, 1, p. 90. Buckton's will, made in 1366 is in TE, 1, p. 77.
28 For biography see Thompson, 'Registry of the Archdeaconry of Richmond', 238 – 39; for activities in diocese see C.P.R., 1354 – 58, p. 209, C.P.R., 1358 – 61, p. 129.
29 Reg. Hatfield, fo.169b.
30 Workman, *John Wyclif*, p. 41. For biography of Skirlaw see R. G. Davies, 'The Episcopate in England and Wales, 1375 – 1433' (Manchester Univ. Ph.D. thesis 1974) Vol. 1, p. 90 and Vol. III, p. cixlvii; Reg. Thoresby, fo.317. Cal.Pap.Pet., pp. 342, 345 and 349.

1360 and holder of the prebend of Osbaldwick.[31] Other members of the archbishop's household included Henry Ingleby, treasurer of York Minster in 1369; Robert Hackthorpe, a notary; John Gaytrick; the archbishop's nephew John Waltham, who was ordained by Thoresby in 1356 and who received expenses from him to attend parliament in 1361; and Dr John Thoresby, who was appointed the archbishop's chancellor in 1370.[32] The archbishop's great-nephew John Waltham, the future archbishop of Salisbury, may also have been trained in this household because there is no record of his having attended university.[33] Another relative, Elias Thoresby, served as the receiver of the archbishop's chamber and obtained £1,000 for expenses in October 1361; and a nephew, Robert Thoresby, was an esquire in the household in 1364.[34] The archbishop's testament, which was witnessed and executed by Henry Barton, John Clone, Elias Thoresby and Robert Thakthorpe, suggests that Thoresby's household was not as extravagant as those of contemporaries like William Wykeham, and probably more intimate. He left large sums of money to John, Robert and Elias Thoresby, and silver and plate to John Clone and all the clerks of his household who had no benefices.[35] Members of the household remembered their patron with affection: Thomas Buckton left 'my lord the archbishop' silver dishes in 1366; Mr John Waltham left £20 for two chaplains to pray for his uncle's soul, and John Ravenser left 400 marks in 1390 for twenty-one chaplains to celebrate for the soul of 'my dear master and uncle'.[36]

These household clerks, government servants, and college fellows constituted a close-knit circle of relatives and friends who appeared together in property transactions and who acted as one another's executors: Richard Ravenser, John Ravenser and Henry Barton were feofees together in 1371; Dr John Thoresby and Henry Ingleby were executors of Mr John Waltham; and Walter Skirlaw was a legatee of Richard Ravenser.[37] They also left one another personal possessions and books: John Waltham made bequests to Dr John Thoresby, William Waltham, Robert Thoresby and Thomas Gaytrick, perhaps a relative of John Gaytrick, and Richard Ravenser left a book of chronicles to Walter Skirlaw and a *portiforium* to John Waltham.[38] Thomas Buckton's legacy

31 TE, 1, p. 90; C.P.R. 1361 – 64, pp. 199, 531; C.P.R. 1358 – 61, p. 199; C.P.R. 1367 – 70, p. 463; C.P.R., 1370 – 74, p. 147. See also J. Le Neve, *Fasti Ecclesiae Anglicanae*, compiled B. Jones (London, 1963) 6, pp. 11, 13 and 73, for biography.

32 Thompson, 'Registry of Richmond', 247, 257 – 60; TE, 1, p. 90; Emden, *B.R.U.O.*, iii, pp. 1913 – 14, 1863 – 64.

33 For biography see Davies, 'The Episcopate', 111, p. ccciv.

34 Grassi, 'Clerical Dynasties', p. 477; Reg. Thoresby, fo.315; fo.316.

35 TE, 1, p. 90.

36 TE, 1, p. 77 (Buckton); York Dean and Chapter Wills, fo.80v (J. Waltham); TE, 111, p. 56 (Ravenser).

37 C.P.R., 1370 – 74, p. 147; Dean and Chapter Wills, fo.81; TE, 111, p. 56.

38 Dean and Chapter Wills, fo.80v – 81; TE, 111, p. 56.

of books to St Mary's Abbey may have been inspired by a friendship with John Gaytrick of St Mary's.[39] It was perhaps inevitable that these clerks would share and express pastoral values acquired in the service of the archbishop of York.

Pastoral ideals were expressed in Stubbs' life of Melton, written with the help of Bishop Bury, which celebrates the virtues of a bishop who was a kind and accessible patron, a lover of the poor, and a good pastor; this life, together with the life of Archbishop Thoresby, to which Dr John Thoresby probably contributed, gives some indication of the values of Thoresby's clergy.[40] The most explicit expression of the problems of living up to high pastoral ideals was made by the negligent pluralist Dr John Wyclif, whose writings perhaps reflected the attitudes of the Thoresby affinity for whom patronage was a way of life. His *De officio pastorali*, written in 1378 while he was still a king's clerk and an absentee benefice holder, is perhaps to be regarded as the confession of a careerist from the diocese of York, who acknowledged the benefits that he enjoyed from the patronage of Thoresby and Islip while admitting his failure to justify these privileges by not living up to the high pastoral ideals of his patrons and their households. All too often, Wyclif says, the love of parents, friends and neighbours is stronger than the love of the flock: men aspire to become curates to rise above their humble station and enter the ranks of the nobility. Wyclif confesses his own guilt by associating himself with those government servants who neglected the pastoral office by hanging around the court, flattering royal patrons and accepting the bribes and payments of office. He also castigated the cathedral clergy and college fellows, whom he described as fawners of princes, for neglecting the pastoral office by hiring paid incumbents to look after the flocks they fleeced.[41] In his writings the sacrifice of ideals to self-interest was transformed into a comprehensive attack on the system that offered the privileges of patronage. In *De civili dominio* he discussed the church's failure to live up to Gregory's notion of the pastoral office, which consisted of preaching and performing works of mercy. Wyclif claimed that many who tried to perform this office merely wove webs for themselves which could become spiders' webs formed by human traditions and the sin of hypocrisy; Wyclif could only have been thinking of the web of connections and patrons formed by himself and other northern clergy.[42] He confessed to the sins of hypocrisy and ambition in *De veritate sacrae scripturae*, and in *De officio* he described negligent pluralism as a greater sin than lechery and urged members of

[39] TE, 1, p. 77.
[40] *Historians of the Church of York*, ii, p. 417.
[41] *De Officio Pastorali*, pp. 43ff.
[42] J. Wyclif, *De civili dominio*, ed. J. Loserth, (Wycl. Soc. 1902), ii, pp. 180 – 83.

his class, who like him had lapsed in their neglect of pastoral responsibility, to confess and repent.[43]

The clergy of York were equally conscious of their pastoral responsibilities, and they all made provisions for the poor parishioners of their prebends and parish churches in their wills: Thomas Buckton left money to his poor parishioners, and Richard Ravenser left £22 to be distributed among the poor parishioners of his prebend of Knaresborough, which he had held since 1371.[44] They also expressed concern about their failure to live up to the high pastoral ideals of their patron, especially in their wills. In 1375 the chancellor of York, Thomas Farnlawe, declared himself to be an unworthy and negligent minister of the church, and in 1402 Walter Skirlaw, who treasured a missal once belonging to Thomas Grandisson, described himself as a wretched sinner and a useless and unworthy minister.[45] John Ravenser, who was keeper of the hanaper and a canon of York, gave expression to the conflict that he felt between his pastoral vocation, which was satisfied in the service of the archbishop of York, and his duties as a crown servant frequently required at Westminster; Ravenser financed twenty-one chaplains in 1391 to celebrate for the souls of his royal patrons and the parochial incumbents of four of his parish churches; in addition he left £40 in his will to Richard II to compensate for his negligent service as keeper of the hanaper; and he left his coarse russet burial cloth to be distributed as clothes for his poor parishioners.[46]

Thoresby's patronage secured government, university and cathedral posts for many northern clerks; but this did not always have the negative effect on the performance of the pastoral office claimed by Wyclif. The archbishop's clergy did not just pay lip service to their sense of pastoral responsibility: they were well trained administrators, and their patron's determination to employ the legal and administrative skills of these civil servants, university graduates and household clerks in the effective administration of his diocese can be seen in his opposition to the papal provision of aliens in York Minster.[47] He no doubt envisaged a harmonious working relationship with his kinsmen, friends and neighbours — similar to the one he enjoyed with Islip when he served the government — which would ensure that his pastoral policies were implemented.

43 *De Officio Pastorali*, p. 58; see also *De officio regis*, ed. A. W. Pollard, and C. Sayle (Wycl. Soc. 1887) ii, p. 54; B. Smalley, 'The Bible and Eternity, John Wyclif's Dilemma', *J.W.C.I.*, (1964), 77.

44 TE, 1, p. 77; *Memoirs of Lincoln*, pp. 312 – 14.

45 TE, 1, pp. and 94.

46 TE, 111, p. 56.

47 Reg. Neville, fo.6b.

The important administrative positions in the diocese were virtually reserved for civil servants of the Thoresby affinity: prebends in the collegiate chapel of St Mary and the Holy Angels in York provided early preferment for Archbishop Thoresby and his nephew Dr John Thoresby: the treasury of the cathedral was held by Henry Ingleby and Henry Barton; and the mastership of St Leonard's Hospital in York was held by Richard Ravenser in 1365 and by members of the Ferriby family.[48] Dr John Thoresby was collated to the provostship of Beverley Minster just before his uncle's death in 1373, and he was an active provost until his own death in 1380.[49] The Thoresby affinity also held many of the most important pastoral positions in the diocese. The cooperation of archdeacons would have been essential if the instructions outlined in Thoresby's Catechism were to be enforced, for they were responsible for examining parish priests during visitations and ensuring that the archbishop's instructions were expounded and observed in chapters, and that each church possessed a copy. Two of Thoresby's protégés were archdeacons: Walter Skirlaw was archdeacon of Cleveland.[50] Officials of the court of York were responsible for hearing causes and pronouncing sentence; but it is possible that they also wielded the power of correction and punishment, and they may therefore have supplemented the work of archdeacons and rural deans; William Nassyngton, Thomas Buckton and Mr John Waltham were all officials of this court.[51] Few records of the activities of these clerks survive: Dr John Thoresby and Mr John Waltham were public notaries, and they served on commissions, including a visitation of Gisburn Priory; and Henry Ingleby and Henry Barton conducted a visitation of St Leonard's in 1364.[52] It is possible that members of the Thoresby household were responsible for supervising the activities of the Corpus Christi day celebrations, including the performance of the York cycle plays: in 1366 Thomas Buckton left 100s to the solemnity of Corpus Christi in York to maintain the bearing of four torches in the procession around the body of Christ on the feast of Corpus Christi.[53] This bequest may have been entrusted to Richard Thoresby, the master of the Guild of Jesus Christ, and the mayor John Sancton, who had connections with the Hugate family and John Wyclif.[54]

48 *The Chapel of St Mary's York*, pp. 266ff; Tout, *Chapters*, v, pp. 30, 77.

49 *Beverley Chapter Act Book*, ii, pp. lxxii – iv.

50 For biography of Ferriby see Tout, *Chapters*, iii, pp. 215 – 17, iv, pp. 146 – 53 and pp. 168 – 72; for appointment as archdeacon of Cleveland see C.P.R., 1354 – 58, p. 183.

51 Thompson, *The English Clergy*, p. 43; Emden, *B.R.U.O.*, ii, pp. 1337 – 8; i, p. 300; iii, p. 1913 – 4.

52 ibid, iii, p. 1863 – 4; C.P.R., 1361 – 4, p. 531.

53 TE, 1, p. 77.

54 In 1388 this bequest was in the hands of the mayor of York William Selby.

Thoresby's influence can also be detected among those clerks who found careers outside York diocese. Richard Ravenser was archdeacon of Lincoln from 1368 – 86, and he took his duties seriously enough to compose a tract on the jurisdiction and duties of the archdeacon of Richmond. Thoresby's great-nephew John Waltham, bishop of Salisbury, administered his diocese effectively, despite his civil service commitments, and conducted a thorough visitation of religious houses in his diocese.[55] William Wykeham had been associated with Thoresby in the Privy Seal until 1357; he received a York prebend from the archbishop and a letter of congratulations on his appointment as a bishop. Wykeham was an exemplary diocesan; he was a noted church-builder in Winchester, and he founded a school in Winchester and a college in Oxford which were intended to provide relief for poor scholars and training for secular clergy, who were to fill the gaps in the priesthood caused by the plague.[56] Walter Skirlaw was appointed bishop of Durham in 1389, and despite his governmental responsibilities he resided in his diocese whenever possible after 1394. His register does not survive, but his commitment to the education of the clergy is shown in his endowment of three fellowships for northerners at Michael Hall; and like Thoresby he was a great builder in his diocese, donating large sums to the building of the Lantern tower of York Minster.[57]

John Wyclif's connections with the northern clerks seem effectively to have ended by 1371 when he was lecturing at Queen's, although he would probably have been friendly with the 'Lollard knight' Sir William Neville, who was a brother of the future archbishop of York and a professional administrator in the royal household. Nevertheless, the influence that Wyclif exerted at Oxford through his teaching and writings on the lollard preachers may have owed something to the pastoral inspiration of Thoresby and his circle. *The Lay Folk's Catechism*, which he may have heard about from Dr John Thoresby at Merton, or John Waltham at Balliol, may have encouraged him to advocate regular preaching in the vernacular on the Lord's prayer, the seven deadly sins, and the ten commandments, and the translation of the scriptures. Lollards certainly capitalized on the popularity of the *Catechism* and interpolated various manuscripts with Lollard doctrine, although not all these manuscripts were single and coherent revisions.[58] They clearly appreciated its potential for improving the pastoral qualifications of

55 Davies, 'The Episcopate in England', iii, p. ccciv.
56 Reg. Neville, fo.26a; Tout, *Chapters*, iii, p. 235.
57 Davies, 'The Episcopate in England', iii, p. ccxlvii; Tout, *Chapters*, iii, p. 436.
58 Lambeth MS. 408. I am indebted to Anne Hudson who advised me on the relationship between these texts. See also A. L. Kellog and E. W. Talbot, 'The Wycliffite Pater Noster and Ten Commandments', *B.J.R.L.*, Vol. 42 (1959 – 60), 356 – 58.

parish priests: one reviser, in an attempt to provide a comprehensive reference book for like-minded clergy, added to Gaytryge's framework Wyclifite doctrine and material from other handbooks that covered all aspects of the teaching syllabus.[59] Wyclif himself may have learned about the York *Pater Noster* cycle, which he cited in *De officio pastorali* as a precedent for a vernacular bible, from the mayor of York, John Sancton.

The strong sense of pastoral mission shared by Thoresby and his household facilitated the subsequent development of the contemplative movement in the diocese by raising moral and educational standards, which were an essential step in the impingement of eremitic values on the consciousness of the ordinary man. By the 1370s this increased religious awareness and independence could be seen in the activities of the craft guilds of Beverley and York which staged the cycle plays. The Guild of Our Lord's Prayer, which supervised the performance of the *Pater Noster* cycle, demanded high moral standards among its members; the inspiration may have come from the penitential enquiries recommended in Thoresby's *Catechism*: members, who met every six weeks, were bound to maintain seven lights in York Cathedral every Sunday and feast day in token of the seven supplications of the Lord's prayer and to make and remember a table, which was to hang in the minster, showing the meaning and use of the lord's prayer; new members were to be examined on the rightness of their lives.[60] An indication of the moral fervour of some tenant farmers can be seen in the will of John Kyneton written in 1374: recalling the words of consolation of Our Lord, who counselled those wishing to be perfect to renounce their goods and follow him in poverty, Kyneton left all his wheat and livestock to his brothers who were told to distribute it among the poor after his death.[61]

The widespread influence that Thoresby had on clergy who were working in many parts of the kingdom should, however, warn us against using his pastoral policies as a complete explanation for the subsequent development of the contemplative movement in the diocese. Even in its earliest stages the pastoral programme of Thoresby cannot be considered as a phenomenon that was unique to the diocese of York: Thoresby worked in unison with Islip; and John Grandisson was a pastoral bishop who influenced a group of clergy, including FitzRalph, Roger Northburgh, bishop of Lichfield, and probably John Trevisa, who were all just as influential as members of Thoresby's circle.[62] The *Oculus sacerdotis*, although written by a northerner in the archbishop of York's own recruiting ground, was not officially distributed by

59 Lambeth Palace Library MS 408; Gillespie, 'Speculum Christiani', p. 31ff.

60 *English Guilds*, pp. 137 – 39.

61 TE, I, p. 93.

62 Walsh, *Richard FitzRalph*; Pantin, *The English Church*, pp. 151 – 52.

Thoresby or any other churchman, and yet through random distribution it became popular throughout the kingdom: a late fourteenth century inventory records the goods of thirty-five Norfolk churches, eleven of which owned the *Oculus*.[63] Nor is there much evidence that Thoresby had any particular interest in the teachings of Rolle or recluses, apart from commending the humility and devotion of an anchoress called Lucy Newmarch when he was bishop of Worcester, conducting a visitation of Hampole in 1353, and giving 100s to a nun of the house in 1373.[64] His clergy showed no special interest in Rolle's writings or recluses until towards the end of the fourteenth century.[65] They were primarily practical men, and in administering the pastoral office they were concerned with administration, church reform, and moral teaching, much of which, considering its social dimension, had little in common with some of Rolle's eremitic teachings. To explain why recluses became so popular in York society, and why their writings and teachings became socially acceptable as a means of pastoral and religious instruction in the diocese, it is necessary to look at the next generation of York clergy who enjoyed the patronage of Thomas Arundel.

63 Ball, 'Education Parish Priests', p. 175ff.
64 Clay, *Anchorites of England*, p. 91; Reg. Thoresby, fo.398r; TE, 1, p. 90.
65 See the will of Richard Ravenser, *Memoirs of Lincoln*, p. 312.,

CHAPTER FOUR

Pastoral Care and its Adaptation to Eremitic Teachings in the Diocese of York, 1370 – 1450

During the twenty years that he administered the diocese of York Thoresby, as we have seen, exerted firm control over the appointments of his clergy, their conduct and education; he thereby ensured that his diocese was harmoniously and efficiently administered by tried and trusted friends, neighbours and relatives. This embraced all aspects of parish life; under his guidance the church of York supervised the moral and social conduct of its parishioners. Subsequent leaders of the church of York, however, would have to face more complex pastoral problems that had an internal spiritual dimension: they would need to formulate a response to the growing popularity of recluses and their teachings among parishioners who, thanks to Thoresby's policies, were more educated and independent; and they would need to show diligence and subtlety in distinguishing between the genuine piety of recluses and their followers, and either irresponsible emotional enthusiasm, or the heretical beliefs of the lollards, which may have originated from within Thoresby's own circle. Nevertheless, the legacy that Thoresby and his clergy left of a tough-minded and energetic approach to diocesan problems would have encouraged their successors to adapt themselves to the changing dimensions of pastoral care and to exercise the same control over all aspects of the religious life of the diocese. Before discussing the response of Thoresby's successors to these spiritual problems, it is necessary to establish that there was some continuity in the diocese after Thoresby's death in terms of the composition of close-knit clerical affinities with a conscientious approach to pastoral duty.

Between 1388 and 1424 the see was held, with the exception of Waldeby's short tenure in 1397, by three men, Thomas Arundel, Richard Scrope, and Henry Bowet, who were at the centre of a circle, the origins of which can be traced to Arundel's tenure of the see of Ely between 1376 and 1388. These three archbishops were able to exert considerable control over patronage within the church of York, and were able to ensure that their friends and servants all secured employment in the diocese. A similar pattern of preferment was therefore established to that operated by Thoresby; but whereas Thoresby's affinity had a relatively narrow base of relatives and neighbours in north Lincolnshire and Yorkshire, the circle of Thomas Arundel, while still made up of predominantly north Lincolnshire men and Yorkshiremen, was far more broadly based on the friendships established during diocesan service, especially at Ely, and at the university of Cambridge. Obviously careful attention will have to be paid to the intellectual and spiritual interests of these clergy, and their commitment to the contemplative life. However, first it is necessary to look at the careers of the northerners who served Arundel, Scrope and Bowet, to appreciate how their secular experiences helped to formulate their religious outlook from a personal, pastoral perspective. In the course of their careers these clerks acquired a number of skills, legal, pastoral and literary, which they used in the service of the diocese; and their secular experiences were crucial in determining the way they performed their pastoral duties. Some worked for the government, although not as many as had done under Thoresby's tenure of the see; most studied at Cambridge; and for all of them patronage, especially that of Arundel, Scrope and Bowet, was a fundamental factor in their careers. Such apparently unpromising material: the world of university colleges, the consistory law courts and the bishop's household, where friends competed for and exchanged benefices, was the inspiration behind the contemplative movement of the late fourteenth century. The role of the Carthusians in transmitting contemplative teachings has perhaps been over-emphasized at the expense of the secular clergy. The religious literature of northern England was primarily written in the late fourteenth century before Mount Grace and Sheen, the two most important charterhouses (from a literary point of view) had even been founded. It was the secular clergy of North Lincolnshire and Yorkshire who graduated in canon law who were the real innovators. When members of this circle, including Hilton, began to write, they did not do so from a purely theological and monastic perspective, but from a personal experience of the secular world: they expressed their dissatisfaction with ambition and success and their yearnings for a less complicated and more studious and introspective basis for their lives. When these clerks approached the contemplative life, they experienced and expressed the tension they felt over their inability or refusal to turn their backs on their social environment; and they strove to reconcile these conflicting pastoral, administrative and spiritual claims. These personal conflicts also gave them insight into the spiritual problems of laymen with whom they had much more in common, and determined the way they would adapt eremitic teachings in the course of their pastoral work.

Clerical Households and Affinities in the Diocese of York, 1373 – 1430

When Thoresby's successor, Alexander Neville, was elected by the York chapter, it may have seemed possible to some contemporaries that he would be the sort of man to give a pastoral structure to the activities of recluses and their followers: his uncle Thomas Neville, the archdeacon of Durham, had been a patron of Rolle, and his elder brother John Neville, the lord of Raby, was a patron of William Sleightholme and possibly, John Thweng.[1] Neville's election, perhaps at the expense of the former treasurer of the exchequer, Thomas Brantingham, occurred at a time when the crown was exerting less influence over appointments to the episcopate than the papacy and the magnates.[2] Neville was an acceptable candidate to Pope Gregory XI and the Neville family, but unlike Thoresby, who was a crown candidate, he lacked experience in government and diocesan administration; this was to have serious consequences for the diocese of York, undermining the achievements of Thoresby and his clergy.[3] In 1381 he alienated his suffragan, the bishop of Durham, over visitation rights, and in 1382 precipitated a five year strike at Beverley Minster by insisting on his right to preside over the chapter as a canon of the cathedral; he then proceeded to interfere with the harmony and efficiency of York Minster by moving some of the vicars choral to Beverley and, by his insistence in 1384, on moving the consistory court of York and all synods and convocations to Beverley.[4] Neville, therefore, managed within fifteen years to destroy the harmonious and efficient working relationship between the archbishop of York and his friends, fellow government officials and relatives that had been established by Melton and Thoresby: he alienated the York and Beverley chapters and surviving members of the Thoresby affinity, especially Richard Ravenser, the leader of the Beverley strike, John Ravenser and possibly their nephew John Waltham.[5] According to contemporaries, Neville was equally reviled by his subjects in the diocese as a poor pastor. After his primary visitation in the autumn of 1375, he seems to have spent an inordinate time behind the walls of his Cawood palace until he virtually deserted the diocese in 1386 to become

1. *W.I.*, p. 39.
2. Davies, 'The Episcopate in England', II, p. 93.
3. R. G. Davies, 'Alexander Neville, archbishop of York, 1373 – 1388', *Y.A.J.*, 47 (1975), 87 – 101.
4. ibid, 87 – 101, A. F. Leach, 'A Clerical Strike at Beverley Minster', *Archeologia*, lv (1896), pp. 1 – 20; A. F. Leach, *Memorials of Beverley Minster*, ii (S.S. cviii, 1903), pp. lxxix – lxxi; *Hist. Church of York*, iii, pp. 284 – 86, ii, p. 423; M. Aston, *Thomas Arundel* (Oxford, 1967), pp. 289 – 93.
5. A. H. Thompson, 'The Registers of the Archdeaconry of Richmond', pp. 251 – 3; le Neve, *Fasti Ecclesiae Anglicanae*, i, pp. 4, 6, 49, 63, 123.

the intemperate counsellor of Richard II.[6] By 1388, when Alexander Neville was translated in disgrace to the Avignon see of St Andrews, there had been, not only a deterioration in the fabric of some of the archbishop's buildings, but a breakdown in the exercise of the patronage and diplomatic tact that was necessary for the effective administration of the diocese.[7] Such matters were an added embarrassment when seen against the larger issues of the Papal Schism and lollard criticisms of the church.

Neville's successor, Thomas Arundel, the brother of Richard FitzAlan Earl of Arundel, was a political opponent; but his translation from Ely to York in 1388 was a sound pastoral appointment. Like Thoresby, Arundel, who was chancellor from 1386 – 89, had experience in government administration, diplomacy and diocesan work; he was also the ideal person to heal the divisions between the archbishop and his clergy caused by Neville and to restore the harmonious working efficiency of the clergy of the diocese. His credentials for the task had been established while he was bishop of Ely from 1373 to 1388: during the troubled years of Neville's archiepiscopate he maintained Thoresby's methods of patronage, employing a number of northern clerks in diocesan administration and offering them the opportunity of study at Cambridge, and especially Peterhouse, which was to replace Oxford and Balliol as the intellectual centre of the life of the Yorkshire clergy.[8] These clerks accompanied Arundel to York in 1388, serving their archbishop with the same loyality and efficiency as their predecessors had served Thoresby; and they continued to hold together and extend this close-knit circle of friends and professional administrators after Arundel's departure to Canterbury. It was the clergy led by Arundel, and his successors at York, Scrope and Bowet, who were to impose order and structure on the piety of the north between 1373 and 1430.

Arundel's appointment as bishop Ely in 1373 at the age of twenty was another example of the initiative taken by magnate families in the matter of episcopal appointments during Edward III's dotage. His aristocratic origins allowed him to offer preferment to outsiders because he did not have to cater to ambitious relatives like Thoresby. Clergy from the diocese of York would have been attracted to Arundel's service because

6 *Historians of York*, ii, p. 423; Davies, 'Alexander Neville', 87 – 101; *Gesta Abbatum Monasterii Sancti Albani*, ed. H. T. Riley (R.S., 1867 – 9), iii, p. 278; W. Illingworth, 'Copy of a Libel against Archbishop Neville, temp. Rich. II', *Archeologia*, xvi (1812), 82 – 3.

7 Aston, *Thomas Arundel*, pp. 278 – 79.

8 Although Yorkshire contained only 13% of the national population, the proportion of Yorkshiremen in the colleges of Cambridge rose in the fourteenth and fifteenth centuries from 2% to 27%. The recruitment of fellows from Yorkshire was especially high in the smaller colleges like Peterhouse and Michaelhouse. See T. H. Aston, 'Medieval Alumni of Cambridge', *Past and Present*, 86 (1980), 30.

the bishop of Ely was an influential figure in Cambridge, retaining the right of admission to Peterhouse, a graduate society of fourteen fellows and one master, founded by Hugh Balsham, the bishop of Ely in 1257.[9] Arundel, who was probably educated at Cambridge, was favourably disposed to the Peterhouse society, and at his request Richard II in 1388 revived the licence granted by his grandfather to Simon Langham, which allowed the fellows custody of the manor of Hinton.[10] The college specialized in the study of canon law and provided the theoretical training for clerks working in the consistory court of Ely and the archdeaconry of the diocese.[11] While he was still young, Arundel would have relied on his family for guidance in matters of ecclesiastical patronage. His father's friend, Richard Lord Scrope of Bolton, who attended the enthronement of the bishop of Ely in 1376, probably introduced into Arundel's administration Scrope's younger cousin and godson, Richard Scrope, the fifth son of Henry Scrope the first lord of Masham.[12] Richard Scrope was an important link between the clerical circles of Thoresby and the circle that was formed around Arundel. He was a rector of Ainderby in 1367, and his godfather Richard Lord Scrope was one of Thoresby's executors.[13] Scrope served as an advocate in the consistory court of Ely which was held in St Michael's parish church in Cambridge; and he presided over the consistory court from November 1375 to 1379. He combined this activity with the study of canon law at Cambridge: he was a licentiate in civil law in 1375, and he was awarded his doctorate in both civil and canon law in 1379.[14]

The most important diocesan servant and scholar that Scrope introduced into Arundel's administration was John Newton of York, who became an advocate in the consistory court of Ely in 1376. He acted as a commissary in this court in September 1376, and presided over it from May 1379 to March 1382 at St Mary's church in Cambridge. In September 1379 he succeeded Scrope as Arundel's official, a post he held until 1388.[15] One of his rewards for this service to Arundel was a long and distinguished career at Peterhouse. His college fellowship probably dates from the 1370s; during this period he became a bachelor of civil law (by 1375) and doctor of civil law (by 1378). In 1382 he succeeded Thomas Worminghall, another official of the consistory court, as master of

9 Aston, *Thomas Arundel*, p. 27.

10 Deanesly, *The Incendium Amoris*, pp. 97 – 9; T. A. Walter, *A Biographical Register of Peterhouse Men* (Cambridge, 1927, 1930).

11 The rising importance of canon law in Cambridge in the fourteenth century reflected the importance of law as a vocational training for positions in the ecclesiastical bureaucracy. For the dominance of Cambridge graduates in the Ely administration see Aston, 'Medieval Alumni', 77.

12 Aston, *Thomas Arundel*, p. 305.

13 TE, I, p. 90.

14 Aston, pp. 54 – 7; Emden, *B.R.U.C.*, pp. 513 – 14.

15 Aston, pp. 54 – 59.

Peterhouse, a post he was to hold until 1397.[16] Scrope, or Newton, may have been responsible for introducing a number of other northerners with Peterhouse connections into the Ely administration. Thomas of Barnard Castle, a fellow of the college and master in 1400, served as Arundel's registrar from 1374 to 1378; and William Noion, who was also a member of the college, was Arundel's wardrobe clerk from 1375 to 1376 and from 1382 to 1383.[17] He was promoted from Arundel's own household to the rich living of Haddenham in 1382 in an exchange with Thomas of Barnard Castle. Noion served as Arundel's receiver from 1381 – 1388 and he was a benefactor of Peterhouse.[18] Another northerner who was a fellow of the college was William Irby of Humberside, the college bursar from 1374 – 1375 and a fellow in 1401; Irby was a penitentiary of Ely in 1376.[19] Two other members of this circle who were Cambridge graduates and who may have had associations with Peterhouse, were Mr Richard Pittes and Mr Thomas Dalby. Pittes, shortly after 1373, was appointed proctor in the bishop's consistory court.[20] Dalby was a magister by 1375 and a leading Cambridge figure by 1384 when he witnessed with John Newton the confirmation to the chancellorship of John de Burgo. Dalby, like Newton, was a member of Arundel's domestic household; he was presented to a living in the gift of Ely in 1375 and was present at episcopal functions in Ely in March 1376; by May 1377 he was receiving commissions to hold synods with other deputies of Arundel, and in 1387 and in 1388 he served as archdeacon of Ely.[21] Dalby may have come to the notice of Arundel and Richard Scrope through the patronage of a friend of the Earl of Arundel and Richard Lord Scrope of Bolton, Sir Roger Beauchamp, a veteran royal servant and chamberlain in 1376. Dalby owned a dish, a gift from Thomas Arundel, with the arms of Roger Beauchamp, and he founded a chantry in York Minster for the souls of Thomas Arundel and Roger Beauchamp's son Philip, archdeacon of Exeter, warden of Tickhill, and an executor of Grandisson. Another Cambridge scholar in this circle was John Gilby, a protégé of Scrope's, who was studying in Cambridge in 1381 when he was ordained in Ely.[22]

Walter Hilton was also a member of Arundel's circle, and he probably enjoyed a more tangible working relationship with his fellow northern

16 Walker, *B.R.P.*, i, pp. 19 – 20; Deanesly, *The Incendium Amoris*, pp. 63 – 79; Emden, *B.R.U.C.*, pp. 421 – 2.

17 Walker, i, pp. 29 – 30; Aston, pp. 312 – 313.

18 Walker, i, pp. 33; Aston, pp. 313 – 314; C.P.R. 1385 – 89, p. 512; Cal. Pap. Reg. Letters, iv, 1362 – 1404, pp. 209 – 10; Cal. Pap. Reg., Letters, iv, p. 317.

19 Walker, *B.R.P.*, i, pp. 17 – 18; Emden, *B.R.U.C.*, PP. 327 ÷ 8.

20 Aston, pp. 307 – 9; H. E. D. Blakiston, 'Two More Medieval Ghost Stories', *E.H.R.*, xxxviii (1923), 85 – 6.

21 Aston, pp. 76 – 7, pp. 309 – 10.

22 Emden, *B.R.U.C.*, p. 258.

clerks than had Wyclif. Hilton was described as clerk of Lincoln in 1371 and may have been related to Thomas Hilton, a canon of Lincoln who later became a member of Richard Scrope's household at York.[23] No record of his ordination at Ely survives, but by 1375 he was serving as an advocate in the Ely consistory court in Cambridge in a case involving tithes with another advocate, Mr Thomas Gloucester.[24] Hilton, therefore, as an Ely diocesan administrator in the 1370's, was a working colleague of Thomas Dalby, Arundel's leading commissioner, and the consistory court officials, Richard Scrope, John Newton and Richard Pittes. He was also an academic colleague of these administrators, studying canon and civil law with them at the adjacent university of Cambridge. He was described as a Bachelor of Civil Law and a clerk of Lincoln diocese in a papal mandate to the official of Ely, which granted him the reservation of the canonry and prebend of Abergwili, Carmarthen on the 28th of January 1371 in succession to William Appliton of Pembroke Hall.[25] In 1375 Hilton was referred to in the Ely Consistory court register as a Bachelor of Civil Law, and, like Thomas Dalby, with whom he perhaps had closest associations, he was described as a magister. The chronology of the careers of these two men, who died in 1396 and 1400, depends on whether or not these titles were genuine because, if they were, both men would have been older than Arundel and the other Ely officials. If Hilton took an M.A. he could only have completed it before commencing his study for the baccalaureate of Civil Law which, if he was a B.C.L. in 1371, would have been in 1364. He would therefore have come up to Cambridge by 1357 at the age of fourteen, and this places his birth at no later than 1343. However, it was common for bachelors of Civil Law to usurp the title of magister, and this would imply that Hilton studied for the baccalaureate of Civil Law between 1364 and 1370 as an undergraduate.[26] This would mean that he, and perhaps Dalby, would be exact contemporaries of Arundel and his

23 ibid., pp. 305 – 6; Reg. vin. 179, f.532v. Mandate to the official of Ely for Walte Hilton, bach. of laws, Linc. dioc. for can. and preb. of Abergwili 28 Jan. 1370 – 71. Cit J. P. H. Clarke, 'Walter Hilton in Defence of the Religious Life and of the Veneratio of Images', *Downside Review*, (1985), n. 8. For T. Hilton, see *Register Richard Scrope*, ed R. N. Swanson, (B.I.H.R., 1981), I, p. 3.

24 Emden, *B.R.U.C.*, pp. 305 – 6; see Clarke, 'Walter Hilton', for the reference in th Consistory Register, checked by Mrs D. M. Owen of Camb. Univ. liv., where th judgement of the official of the consistory in a cause concerning tithes of Willinghan ends: *Presentibus magistris Thomas Gloucestr et Waltero Hilton bacular' in legibus Linc dioc. testibus vocatis*. See Emden, *B.R.U.C.*, p. 260 for Gloucester's career, and Walker *B.R.P.*, i, p. 18.

25 See Clarke, 'Walter Hilton', n. 8 for reference in Reg. Avenion. 179, f.532, checked b Father Benedict Hackett, O.S.A., which reads: *Dilecto filio Offic. Elien. Salutem Volentes itaque dilectum filium Walterum de Hilton, clericum Lincoln. diocesis, Baccalariu in legibus apud vos, de litterarum scientia, vite ac morum honeste.*

26 For discussion of this chronology see Clarke, I, n. 10.

diocesan servants. Nevertheless, Hilton would have been brought into academic contact with Scrope, Newton and the other clerks in Arundel's circle when he decided to specialize in the study of canon law: there is evidence that Hilton qualified as an inceptor in canon law, although he did not go on to the magisterium.[27] He presumably started the study of canon law between 1371 and 1375 when he was still a B.C.L. serving in the Ely consistory court; and he may have been a bachelor of canon law by 1376 and ready to incept as doctor of canon law in 1381 – 1382.[28] Until his decision to renounce the academic life while he was a *baccalarius formatus*, sometime between 1383 and 1386, Hilton was following an academic career in the footsteps of Scrope and Newton who both qualified as doctors of canon and civil law by 1379.[29] Hilton may have studied canon law at Peterhouse where the bishop of Ely retained the right of admission. The possibility that he was a member of the Peterhouse society is strengthened through his association with fellow canonist Thomas Gloucester, who graduated B.C.L. in 1371, and whose appointment as Arundel's deputy official in Ely on 6 January 1374 was recorded in the Peterhouse register and the compotus rolls. Gloucester was a member of Arundel's circle: he was the bishop's commissary general in 1378 and was associated with Richard Scrope and John Newton, who was to be master of the college: in 1377 Gloucester and Scrope obtained a licence from the bishop of Ely to choose their own confessor; and in 1378 he was engaged with John Newton in the election of a prioress of St Radegund. Another less likely possibility, if Hilton was already a graduate before obtaining the baccalaureate of civil law by 1370, is that he studied at Pembroke with William Appilton, and on Appilton's death, or removal elsewhere, he applied to succeed him in the canonry of Abergwili in 1371. There were of course connections between the two colleges: Arundel's chaplain John Bottisham, who succeeded Newton as master of Peterhouse in 1397, left books to Pembroke library.[30] What can be stated with reasonable certainty is that Hilton belonged to this society of northern clerks from North Lincolnshire and Yorkshire who enjoyed the patronage of Thoresby at Oxford and Arundel at Cambridge.

27 ibid, I.
28 ibid, I, n. 10.
29 Russel Smith, 'Walter Hilton in Defence of the Veneration of Images', 110ff.
30 Pembroke College was dominated by northerners, and it had a tradition of studying contemplative literature and providing spritual guidance for nuns: the foundress Mary de St Pol left injunctions to the fellows of the college to visit the sisters of Denny and give them spiritual counsel, and according to an early manuscript of the *Stimulus Amoris*, North Cosin vii, Hilton translated this work for minors who knew no Latin, a description that could apply to the Franciscan prior of Denny. See A. Attwater, *Pembroke College* (Cambridge, 1936), p. 10ff.; Doyle, 'A Survey', i, p. 208.

Arundel, as bishop of Ely, was primarily the patron of canon law students who applied their skills to his diocesan administration. But, like Thoresby, he was also a government servant and chancellor from 1386 – 1389, and as such he was a patron of civil servants, mainly through King's Hall, a college endowed by Edward III, whose function it was to equip King's clerks with the skill in international law and diplomacy needed in the period of the conciliar movement and the French wars.[31] Two northerners who attended this college were Henry Bowet from Cumberland and William Waltham, the nephew of John Ravenser, the keeper of the hanaper. Bowet, who was a king's clerk by 1372 and a leading diplomat by 1388, was the presiding official in the Bishop of Ely's court on 11 May 1374 at All Saints' church in Cambridge, and he served as an advocate in this court in 1376 when he was ordained by Arundel; he would therefore have had contact with Scrope, Newton and Hilton, who were all Ely consistory court officials in this year. In the following year Bowet was made archdeacon of Ely.[32] William Waltham, who succeeded his uncle as keeper of the hanaper in 1393, was a King's Hall fellow from 1377 – 1388 and he was ordained by Arundel in 1378.[33] Two King's Hall clerks served Arundel as officials of the archdeacon of Ely: Robert Ragnell, official in 1380, was a fellow of the college before 1388; Ralph Selby D.C.L., archdeacon's official in the preceding year, was the eleventh warden of King's Hall from 1391 to 1398, and he was a member of Richard II's council and a leading royal diplomat.[34]

The development of King's Hall in the fourteenth century into one of the two largest colleges in England, and its use as an educational supplement to the royal household and the court, providing educated personnel for service in government departments, illustrates the decline in importance of the episcopal household as a training centre for government officials, even from Thoresby's time. Arundel probably provided training for two northerners who became civil servants and whose careers closely resemble those of many of the clerks of Thoresby's circle who did not attend university. John Waltham was a guest of Arundel's on Christmas Day in 1383, and he probably received training in Arundel's household as well as in the household of his great uncle Thoresby; Waltham's career, like Scrope's represents the most tangible of the links that existed between the two circles of Thoresby and Arundel.[35] Thomas Haxey, who also did not attend a university, received his first preferments from Arundel in 1384 and was probably

[31] A. B. Cobban, *The King's Hall* (Cambridge, 1969), pp. 9 – 28.

[32] Aston, *Thomas Arundel*, pp. 306 – 7; Emden, *B.R.U.C.*, pp. 83 – 4.

[33] Emden, *B.R.U.C.*, p. 614; Cobban, p. 250.

[34] Aston, *Thomas Arundel*, p. 308; Emden, *B.R.U.C.*, p. 470.

[35] Aston, *Thomas Arundel*, p. 204; Davies, 'The Episcopate in England', I, p. 128, III, p ccciv.

trained in his household.[36] During his years as chancellor, from 1386 – 1389 and 1391 – 1398, Arundel used these King's Hall and household clerks, like Thoresby before him, to assist him in government administration: Henry Bowet was a leading diplomat and counsellor in the 1380s; John Ravenser was keeper of the hanaper in 1393; John Waltham was keeper of the Rolls in 1388 and treasurer in 1390 when Arundel was chancellor; and Thomas Haxey was chief clerk and keeper of the writs and rolls of the common bench in the 1390's.[37] It is perhaps significant, in the light of the presence of these northerners in the royal administration, that in 1392 the chancery and departments of the exchequer and common bench were removed to York and Waltham and Arundel were blamed by contemporary southern chroniclers for the move.[38]

This circle was not exclusively confined to canonists, and some Cambridge friars would have worked with Arundel's Ely clerks and been valued for their theological knowledge and pastoral skills. Thomas Fishlake, from Fishlake in Yorkshire, was originally a member of the Carmelite convent of Doncaster and was ordained by Thoresby in 1358. He joined the Cambridge convent in 1371, obtained his Bachelor of Theology at the university and preached at the Ely diocesan synod in 1377.[39] John Pole, also a Carmelite of the Cambridge convent (by 1377) incepted for a doctorate in Theology in 1381, and was licensed to hear confessions in the Ely diocese in 1377.[40] As Cambridge had the only Dominican convent in the diocese of Ely, and this in close contact with the bishop of Ely who ordained all Cambridge Dominicans, it is likely that members of this order came into contact with Arundel and his clerks. One Dominican who can be considered a member of this circle was Dr John Paris, confessor of Sir Roger Beauchamp, vicar general of the English province in 1378, and preacher at the Ely diocesan synod in 1376. If, as seems likely, the author of the *Cloud of Unknowing* was a Dominican, his northern origins and knowledge of Rolle's works, the similarity between some of the ideas and pastoral objectives in the writings of the author of *The Cloud* and Walter Hilton, and Hilton's knowledge of this author, would suggest that he belonged in some way to the circle of northern clerks and writers at Cambridge and Ely, and that he was a member of the Cambridge convent. The possibility that he studied at Cambridge is

[36] Aston, *Thomas Arundel*, pp. 310 – 11.
[37] Davies, 'The Episcopate in England', I, pp. 128, 213, 250; III, p. xl.
[38] C. M. Barron, 'The Quarrel of Richard II with London, 1392 – 7', in Du Boulay and Barron, *The Reign of Richard II*, p. 181.
[39] H. Gardner, 'The Scale of Perfection', *Medium Aevum*, 5 (1936) 22. Emden, *B.R.U.C.*, p. 231.
[40] Emden, *B.R.U.C.*, p. 441.

strengthened when his dependence on the Dominican writers of the Rhineland is considered. Cambridge convent had a large number of Germans and considerable contact with Cologne: in 1397 three friars of the convent had leave to study there.

Ely, unlike York, was a diocese offering little scope for advancement, apart from preferment to Cambridge colleges such as Peterhouse, and it was inevitable that some members of this circle that formed around Arundel in Cambridge and Ely were dispersed when they found ecclesiastical preferment in other dioceses, but they used their new positions to boost the careers of their friends and colleagues in Ely and so maintained the continuity of this community. In 1385 Richard Scrope was made bishop of Coventry and Lichfield, and during his thirteen years of tenure of the see he provided Mr John Gylby to the rectory of Chesterfield in his diocese.[41] In 1388 John Waltham was made bishop of Salisbury, and by 1399 he was being assisted by Robert Ragnall who was made archdeacon of Dorset in 1388; Waltham also made Richard Pittes a canon of Salisbury.[42] Henry Bowet first found preferment in the service of Henry Despencer the bishop of Norwich; in 1400 he was appointed by the Crown to the bishopric of Bath and Wells, and in 1408 he appointed his old associate Richard Pittes as his vicar general.

The tightness and coherence of this circle, however, is best demonstrated by the fact that nearly all these clerks eventually ended their careers serving the church of York. Some preceded Arundel's arrival in the diocese. The first of the Ely clergy to find preferment here were: Ralph Selby, who was appointed auditor of causes in the court of York in 1386; John Gylby, who obtained the rectory of Knesall in Yorkshire in 1387; and William Waltham, who was archdeacon of the East Riding from 1386 until his death in 1416.[43] Walter Hilton indirectly served the church of York when, after a brief attempt to live as a hermit, he became a canon at Thurgarton priory in Nottinghamshire in the diocese of York. The Augustinian canons were the most practical and pastorally active of the religious orders, and it was at Thurgarton that Hilton's religious writings became more pastorally oriented. He also probably continued to maintain contact with his Cambridge friends and this is implied in his obtaining from Cambridge, sometime after his departure, a copy of the book of Louis de Fontibus, which he translated into English under the title *The Eight Chapters on Perfection*.[44] Another of the circle who was a

41 Emden, *B.R.U.C.*, pp. 513 – 14.

42 Aston, *Thomas Arundel*, pp. 308 – 09; Emden, *B.R.U.C.*, p. 470.

43 Emden, *B.R.U.C.*, p. 614.

44 Clark, 'Walter Hilton in Defence of the Religious Life', 2. This book was presumably found after Louis had left the university and passed to Hilton at Thurgarton by a Cambridge friend.

member of an enclosed order in the diocese was the Dominican Dr John Paris who was in the York convocation from 1391 – 96.

Many of the Ely clergy, however, profited from the victory of the appellants and Arundel's promotion to York in 1388, and secured positions in the administration of the diocese, although many of them continued to maintain their contacts with Cambridge, especially Peterhouse. John Newton, who obtained a York prebend in 1385, was Arundel's vicar general in York by 1390 and obtained the post of treasurer of York Minster in 1391. He remained master of Peterhouse until 1393 and retained connections with the college at least until 1403.[45] John Bottisham, a native of Ely, became Arundel's vicar general at York and his chancellor in 1399. He also succeeded John Newton as master of Peterhouse from 1397 to 1400.[46] From 1400 to 1421 the mastership of Peterhouse was held by Thomas of Barnard Castle, who obtained preferment in his native diocese when his canonry and prebend of St Mary and the Holy Angels, a favourite preferment for household clerks of the archbishop of York, was ratified.[47] William Noion followed Arundel to York and obtained the prebend of South Cave in 1388 when he was Arundel's treasurer; by 1399 he had obtained the prebend of Dennington in York in an exchange with William Waltham. He too continued with his studies at Peterhouse, and in 1401 he obtained a papal indult allowing him to enjoy the fruits of his benefice for the rest of his life while absent for university study.[48] Dalby's fortunes were also closely tied up with Arundel's: he obtained a canonry in York in 1390, and he was granted by the crown the archdeaconry of Richmond, which he held until his death in 1400.[49] Thomas Haxey's first appointment in York was in 1393, and in 1395 and 1405 he obtained prebends in Southwell and York, which he resigned when he became treasurer in 1418.[50] During his years at York Arundel continued to extend his patronage to clerks recommended by his clergy, resident clergy of the minster and Cambridge graduates including: Mr John Scarborough, a Cambridge graduate from the diocese of Coventry and Lichfield who was probably introduced into Arundel's administration by Richard Scrope; Mr William Cawood, a north countryman who was Arundel's vicar general in 1393; John Clifford, the treasurer of York; Mr Thomas Walworth, vicar general in 1389; and William Helperby, a Peterhouse

45 Walker, *B.R.P.*, pp. 19 – 20. In 1403 – 04 Newton gave £6 13s 4d to Peterhouse.
46 Emden, *B.R.U.C.*, p. 76; Walker, *B.R.P.*, pp. 28 – 9; Aston, *Thomas Arundel*, p. 316.
47 Walker, *B.R.P.*, pp. 29 – 30; Emden, *B.R.U.C.*, p. 39.
48 Walker, p. 33; *Fasti Ecclesiae Anglicanae*, vii, pp. 16, 21; C.P.R., 1385 – 89, p. 449; C.P.R., 1396 – 99, pp. 477, 478, 480.
49 Aston, *Thomas Arundel*, pp. 309 – 10; Thompson, 'The Registers of the Archdeaconry of Richmond', pp. 239 – 40; Emden, *B.R.U.C.*, p. 174.
50 Aston, *Thomas Arundel*, p. 311; Fabric Rolls of York Minster, pp. 203 – 6.

fellow from 1388 – 93, who was a petitioner for the prebend of St Mary's of the Holy Angels, York.[51] The association that existed between Arundel and Nicholas Love between 1408 and 1411 may have originated during Arundel's years at York.

Arundel was translated in 1396 to Canterbury, a diocese that offered less scope for advancement for his York officials; they continued to prosper at York from where there was no obvious promotion except to a bishopric. The decision these clerks made to end their careers at York was also probably encouraged by the successive appointment of their old friends and colleagues Richard Scrope and Henry Bowet to the archbishopric of York. Their arrival in the diocese brought further reunions between old Ely and Cambridge associates. When Richard Scrope replaced Waldby in 1398 he was accompanied by Mr John Gylby, one of his household clerks at Lichfield who served in Scrope's household in 1401 and 1403.[52] Other Cambridge scholars to secure positions in Scrope's administration were Mr John Bottisham, who presided over convocation on 20 July 1398 with Dalby, Newton, Walworth and Robert Ragnall, who was a minster priest by 1400 and an advocate of the court of York by 9 March 1402.[53] Scrope also brought with him from Lichfield a number of household clerks including: Thomas Hilton, who was described as a clerk of the archbishop's household in 1403, and his precentor at Lichfield Cathedral, Robert Wolveden, who was described as a clerk in Scrope's household in September 1399 when he was acting as the archbishop's vicar general with full powers.[54] The names of Hilton, Gylby, Wolveden and another of Scrope's servants, Geoffrey Scrope, occur on many documents of this period.[55] Wolveden may have received help from Thomas Dalby, whose prebends of Thockrington in York Minster he received in 1400, and he served as the proctor of Stephen Scrope, who succeeded Dalby as the archdeacon of Richmond.[56] Stephen Scrope, like his uncle the archbishop, had a distinguished career at Cambridge: he was a graduate by 1399 and chancellor in 1414.[57]

By the beginning of the fifteenth century nearly all of Arundel's leading Ely clerks, their kinsmen and servants, had been reunited in the

51 Emden, *B.R.U.C.*, p. 510 (Scarborough); Aston, *Thomas Arundel*, p. 310; *Miscellanea II*, ed. A. H. Thompson (S.S. cxxvii, 1916), *Memorials of Ripon*, ii, pp. 212 – 13, (Cawood); TE, I, p. 166 (Clifford); Aston, *Thomas Arundel*, p. 297 – 8, 316n. (Walworth); Walker, *B.R.P.*, i, p. 22; *B.R.U.C.*, p. 297 (Helperby).

52 Gylby and Robert Wovenden and other clerks of the archbishop's household witnessed the profession of obedience of William Beverley master of the order of Sempringham, *Register of Scrope*, ed. Swanson, p. 91.

53 *Calendar of Register of Scrope*, p. 25, 37; Reg. Scrope, fos. 25, 37 – 38v.

54 *Calendar of the Register of Scrope*, pp. 1 – 3; Reg. Scrope, fo.1.

55 *Calendar of Register of Scrope*, pp. 3 – 5, 91, 100; Reg. Scrope, fo.56v – 57, 100.

56 *Calendar Reg. Scrope*, pp. 4 – 5; Reg. Scrope, fo.7.

57 Emden, *B.R.U.C.*, p. 515.

service of the church of York. Arundel had helped to heal the divisions created by Neville, and he established an administration as formidable and loyal as Thoresby's. During the first three decades of the fifteenth century Arundel's former servants and their households dominated the church of York. William Waltham decided to take up residentiary status in York Minster in 1401, possibly because of the arrival of Richard Scrope and the presence of Newton among the residentiary canons. In 1407 Scrope was succeeded as archbishop of York by Henry Bowet, who brought with him his old friend Richard Pittes and made him his vicar general in the same year.[58] Bowet held the see of York until 1423, and during the first three decades of the fifteenth century the treasurers of York were John Newton, who was succeeded by Pittes in 1414, Thomas Haxey, who was appointed in 1418, and Robert Wolveden who was treasurer from 1426 to 1432.

These clerks in turn offered patronage to the York Minster priests who were ordained in the opening years of the fifteenth century. Some of these priests followed the example of their patrons and combined diocesan administration with study at Peterhouse. Robert Alne, who was ordained in York in 1401, was made a fellow of Peterhouse in 1400 on the same day as his friend John Oteringham of Holderness.[59] Alne's academic career from the time of his appointment as a fellow until 1421, when he stopped studying arts and began a course in canon law, would probably have been assisted by Thomas of Barnard Castle, who was master of the college from 1400 until his death in 1421. Like his predecessors, Alne applied his training in canon law in the church courts: he was examiner of the court of York from 1421 until his death in 1440, besides serving as a chantry priest at the altar of St Nicholas in York Minster.[60] Most of these younger clerks, however, devoted themselves exclusively to diocesan administration. John Langtofte, who witnessed Dalby's will in 1400, secured an important prebend in the college of St Mary and the Holy Angels in York.[61] Robert Semer, who was remembered in Dalby's will, was ordained by Scrope in 1402. John Kendale, who was a friend of John Newton, was ordained in the same year and he served as a vicar choral in York Minster. Thomas Beelby, a friend of William Waltham, was ordained in 1403 and William Gate, Waltham's chaplain, served as a priest in the cathedral.[62]

Most members of the clerical affinities of the diocese in the period between 1380 and 1430 were not so closely bound by kinship ties as the clerks of Thoresby's circle; but they had the same sense of gratitude

58 Thompson, *The English Secular Clergy*, p. 189.
59 Walker, *B.R.P.*, p. 30; *Calendar Reg. Scrope*, p. 48; Reg. Scrope, fo.175.
60 TE, II, p. 78.
61 Y.M.L. Reg. Test. I, fo.124.
62 *Calendar Reg. Scrope*, pp. 48 – 9; Reg. Scrope, fo.175.

towards their patrons, especially Arundel who outlived many of them. John Clifford left Arundel a silver dish requesting him to be as good a lord to him after his death as he was during his life; Thomas Dalby in 1400 made provisions for a chantry priest at York to celebrate for the soul, after his death, of the one-time archbishop of York whom he had served; William Noion, in 1405, declaring his trust in Arundel's lordship, made him his executor, 'humbly requesting his paternity to be a good lord to me after my death, as he was during my life'.[63] Similar language was used by John Bottisham, who addressed 'my most special lord, the lord Thomas archbishop of Canterbury', requesting him 'in whose lordship I have special trust' to be an executor.[64] Henry Bowet founded a chantry in 1413 in which the body of 'our beloved son Richard Pittes, our archdeacon of Cleveland' was to be buried.[65] Pittes died before Bowet, in 1415, and requested burial in York Minster 'next the newly built tomb of the reverend father in Christ, my lord Henry the archbishop of York'.[66] In 1418 Stephen Scrope similarly desired burial 'near by lord the archbishop [Richard Scrope] who laid his helping hands on me when he was alive and whose prayers I beseech now that he is in heaven'.[67] The servants of Arundel, Scrope and Bowet were evidently close friends and acted as one another's executors: Newton's executors and witnesses were William Waltham, Thomas Haxey and John Gylby; and Robert Semer and Robert Ragnall were executors to Stephen Scrope.[68] Many of them chose to be buried in adjoining graves: the residentiary canons Thomas Haxey, William Cawood, Stephen Scrope, Richard Pittes and Robert Wolveden were all buried within the cathedral close where they had dedicated the latter part of their lives. The prebendal houses of the canons of York were centres of wealth and patronage, and most of these clerks left portions of their valuable plate and cash to one another. Thomas Dalby remembered Arundel, John Newton and Robert Ragnall; Robert Wolveden made bequests to Robert Semer and John Langtofte.[69]

Despite the difficult years under Alexander Neville, Arundel and his successors in the diocese of York were able to maintain the traditions of patronage established by Melton and Thoresby, in which the services of close-knit and cooperating groups of ecclesiastical administrators and scholars were secured for the church of York. This helped to ensure that

63 TE, I, p. 166; Y.M.L. Reg. Test. I, fo. 124 (Dalby); Y.M.L. Reg. Test., I, fos. 139 – 40; TE, III, pp. 28 – 9 (Noion).
64 Aston, *Thomas Arundel*, pp. 316 – 17.
65 Reg. Test. I, fo.216.
66 Y.M.L. Reg. Test., I, fo.172.
67 TE, I, pp. 385 – 89.
68 Reg. Test. I, fo.168; TE, I, p.364ff.
69 Reg. Test. I, fo.124; Reg. Test. I, fo.235.

the high pastoral standards of the Thoresby circle were also maintained. Faced with illiteracy and disorder, Thoresby and Islip tried to make the parish church a civilized centre of moral discipline and social order. Arundel and his clerks were concerned with defending these achievements, and this can be seen in their legal and disciplinary work in the diocese of Ely. Much of the original impetus for the pastoral activity of the Ely clergy must have come from those York clergy who had started their ecclesiastical careers during Thoresby's archiepiscopate, such as Richard Scrope, William and John Waltham, and Robert Ragnall, a clerk of Richard Ravenser. They would have instilled into the young bishop of Ely the exalted notions of pastoral duty that he was later to show as archbishop of Canterbury.

Pastoral discipline in Ely was exercised through the consistory court, which met fifteen times a year and dealt with cases involving ordinary parishioners ranging from the non-payment of tithes to adultery. The court was also an important instrument for supervising the conduct of parochial clergy by dealing with suits brought by parishioners against their priests for such derelictions of duty as non-residence.[70] The responsibility for the active role played by the consistory court in discovering and dealing with abuse lay, not with Arundel who was rarely there, but with the northern clerks who dominated it and applied the methods of pastoral discipline established by Thoresby. The officials of the court with the most extensive powers were Richard Scrope and John Newton, who operated the court in two Cambridge churches, and were therefore able to use the services of such canon lawyers as Walter Hilton. Other important officials included Henry Bowet and Richard Pittes. These clerks were concerned to improve the efficiency of this court; in 1382 John Newton attempted to reform procedures in this court concerning cases in which officials were the subject of litigation.[71] Under them the consistory court expanded as the most important instrument of diocesan administration: officials of the court had the power to summon diocesan synods where provincial statutes could be published; these were supervised by Scrope, Thomas Dalby, and in his absence, John Newton.[72] The judiciary proceedings of the consistory court and the sanctioning publicity of diocesan synods provided Arundel's clerks with the means of dealing with abuses and keeping a watchful eye on the moral state of the diocese. The diocesan meetings were also an occasion for the preaching of sermons of ceremony and importance: among the speakers were the Dominican John Paris in 1376 and the Carmelite

70 Aston, *Thomas Arundel*, p. 67, p. 98ff.
71 ibid, p. 62.
72 ibid, p. 80.

Thomas Fishlake, the future translator of the *Scale of Perfection*, who was appointed by Arundel himself in 1377.[73]

These clerks also dominated the administration of York after Arundel's translation. Arundel resided in the diocese of York from May 1389 to September 1391 when he was reappointed chancellor. From that time on he only managed to visit his diocese yearly, and he ordained in person only once in 1395.[74] This activity reflects both his genuine interest in his pastoral duty and his heavy commitment to government.[75] Fortunately he could rely on the proven services of his Ely administrators who helped to create the favourable impression he left as archbishop of York. His first vicar general, Thomas Walworth, was succeeded in 1390 by John Newton who held the vicarship for the next five and a half years, the last two in conjunction with William Cawood. In 1396 John Bottisham was appointed vicar general.[76] The most influential of these officials was John Newton who, while he was vicar general, had extensive powers including collation to benefices and canonical correction with the full power to convoke the clergy; from 1393 – 1395 he presided over convocation.[77] Another official with extensive powers was Thomas Dalby, the archdeacon of Richmond from 1389: in 1397 both Newton and Dalby were involved in the collection of tithes. Evidence that Arundel and Thomas Dalby attempted to enforce Thoresby's pastoral policies in the outer reaches of the diocese is provided in a mandate that the archbishop of York sent to his archdeacon in 1396 offering indulgences in return for contributions towards the building of a church in a remote area of Richmondshire; Arundel explained that this was part of a move to build up the church in such areas of the diocese, and he sent a collector, John Denygham, with the power to compel people to purchase these indulgences: he defined the faithful as those who helped to finance church building and who attended confession regularly.[78] Little can be said of the administrative work of the vicars choral: the record of their personal activity, and that of their archbishop, may have been in Arundel's lost register.[79] However, the high standards of efficiency shown in the administration of church justice in Ely were maintained. Newton was described as an official of the court of York in 1391, and one of the advocates of this court was Robert Ragnall.[80] The records of the court of the dean and chapter's

73 ibid, pp. 74 – 5.
74 ibid, p. 285 – 304.
75 R. G. Davies, 'Thomas Arundel as Archbishop of Canterbury', *J.E.H.* (1973), p. 10ff
76 ibid, pp. 390 – 400.
77 ibid, pp. 287, 288n., 294 – 98, 394 – 95.
78 Wilkins, *Concilia*, iii, p. 226.
79 Aston, *Thomas Arundel*, pp. 287 – 98.
80 *Calendar of Reg. Scrope*, p. 87; Reg. Scrope, fo.37v – 38.

peculiar in York are less informative than those of the bishop's consistory court at Ely, but Newton and his fellow residentiary canons Thomas Walworth, Thomas Dalby and Nicholas Ferriby showed some pastoral zeal: the court dealt with a high proportion of marital cases.[81]

After Arundel's translation to Canterbury in September 1396 the control of the diocese of York passed officially into the hands of Arundel's servants. Richard Scrope, who had administered Lichfield conscientiously for twelve years, left a good impression during his short tenure of the see of York. He was probably conscious of the pastoral heritage of Thoresby and Grandisson for he owned a copy of FitzRalph's sermons.[82] Despite being a member of the royal council in 1397, he was seldom absent from his diocese; he maintained good relations with the bishop of Durham, who was his friend Walter Skirlaw, and he contributed towards the building of the minster. His popularity as a leader of the church is suggested by the thriving cult that was established at his tomb.[83] Henry Bowet, his successor, had been high in the confidence of Henry Bolingbroke as his attorney general, but after his translation to York in 1407 he gave the diocese energetic service until he was incapacitated by ill health.[84] His primary visitation of the diocese from May 1409 until the summer of 1410 was the longest in living memory, and he issued a large number of mandates for carrying out extensive repairs in the run-down parishes.[85] During his tenure of the see building work at the minster was accelerated, and £500 a year was expended.[86] Bowet's interest in preaching and instruction is shown in his ownership of Bromyard's *Distinctiones* and an alphabetical compendium for preachers.[87] These three leaders of the church, Arundel, Scrope and Bowet, were all in their different ways trying to protect the achievements of Thoresby and Islip, who had created a more efficient pastoral church and established harmony between lay and ecclesiastical governments. Arundel and Scrope showed courage in protecting the liberties of the church in the face of calls for increased church taxation and disendowment in the parliaments of 1401 and 1404; Arundel, as chancellor, showed a keen interest in establishing sound principles of government during the period of political unrest surrounding Bolingbroke's usurpation of the crown. In Henry V's reign internal stability and a strong relationship between crown, commons and the church was

81 Aston, *Thomas Arundel*, p. 298.
82 Emden, *B.R.U.C.*, p. 514.
83 See Ch. 6.
84 Davies, 'The Episcopate in England', p. 213.
85 Reg. Bowet, fos. 87v, 88 – 88v, 91 – 91v, 155v, 169v – 170, 173; J. Palmer, 'The Career of Henry Bowet, Archbishop of York' (Oxford Univ. M.Litt. thesis, 1964), p. 73.
86 *York Fabric Rolls*, pp. 41, 45, 46, 202; Palmer, 'Henry Bowet', p. 77.
87 Reg. Test. I, fo.216.

achieved; and in this same period Bowet's long residence in the diocese of York, his building activities and generous hospitality, were all important factors in the local economy that helped to ensure a period of peace in the diocese.[88]

The most impressive consolidation of the work of Thoresby achieved by Arundel's clerks, especially during the archiepiscopates of Scrope and Bowet, was in their creation of a purely resident and professional ecclesiastical administration. Thoresby's decision to devote the latter part of his life to diocesan administration illustrates the reluctance with which many good pastoral bishops took on government duties. By the 1370's, when King's Hall was rising to prominence, the northern clerks were no longer such a dominant force in the civil service as they had been when Thoresby was archbishop. Although Arundel was never able to relinquish the responsibilities of state service for long, most of his clerks at Ely, with the exception of the King's Hall scholars, were purely engaged in university study and diocesan work. When Newton, Scrope and Bowet took over the administration of the diocese of York, along with the archdeacons of Cleveland, the East Riding and Richmond, who were Richard Pittes, William Waltham, Thomas Dalby and Stephen Scrope, they were, with the exception of Stephen Scrope, the chancellor of Cambridge, a resident clergy. They were assisted by the residentiary canons of the minster such as Robert Wolveden, who also served as vicar general, and Robert Semer, and the minster priests and vicars choral including William Gate, John Langtofte, Thomas Beelby, John Kendale and Robert Alne. Most of these clergy had no training in either the civil service or in the university; the cathedral of York was replacing both institutions as a source of training and experience for clergy of the diocese in law, administration, liturgical organization and municipal affairs. The canons, vicars choral and minster priests were required to care for the fabric of the church and its estates and to supervise the daily liturgy and the activities of the Corpus Christi Guild, of which Wolveden, Stephen Scrope and Newton were all members.[89] In the years between Scrope's execution and Bowet's enthronement they extended the cathedral's educational function by contracting John Thornton of Coventry to provide narrative panels in the Great East Window of the cathedral illustrating the words *Ego sum alpha et omega* with twenty-seven scenes from the Old Testament and eighty-one from the Revelation of St John.[90] The archiepiscopates of Scrope and Bowet and the emergence of York Minster as a centre of ecclesiastical training

88 Palmer, 'Henry Bowet', p. 78.
89 See B. Dobson, 'The Residentiary Canons of York', *J.E.H.*, 30, (1979), pp. 145 – 73.
90 D. E. O'Connor and J. Haselock, 'The Stained and Painted Glass of York Minster', in G. E. Aylmer and R. Cant (eds.) *A History of York Minster* (Oxford, 1977), pp. 364 – 67.

and employment provided proof that the ideal of a purely resident and professional clergy, upheld by the Salisbury chapter and Richard Ullerston at the council of Pisa in 1408, was achievable.[91]

These developments represent a culmination of Thoresby's methods of patronage and his conscientious approach to pastoral duty, and it is therefore not surprising that this circle also produced the most popular pastoral manual of the late fourteenth and fifteenth century, the *Pupilla oculi*. The author, John de Burgo from Lincoln diocese, was a proctor of Cambridge in 1370 and a doctor of divinity by 1384. In his early career there is no evidence of Arundel's patronage, although as chancellor of Cambridge he would have had some contact with the bishop of Ely. However, he did know Thomas Dalby, who was a witness to his confirmation as chancellor in 1384 along with Simon Romeyn, a household clerk of Arundel's who was rewarded with a York prebend before his death in 1394.[92] Burgo too obtained preferment in York during Arundel's tenure of the see, and like Dalby, Newton and others of the circle, he ended a distinguished academic career to settle down to administrative parochial work in the diocese of York: between 1388 and 1398 he was rector of South Collingham in Nottinghamshire, and he was licenced to hear confessions in the diocese in 1398.[93] If he is identified with the John Burgh who was a member of the collegiate church of Auckland in the diocese of Durham then he also served as executor to Walter Skirlaw in 1405.[94] Between 1380 and 1385, at the instance of his fellows, he adapted Pagula's *Oculus sacerdotis* to meet the special requirements of an elite group of Cambridge graduates and benefice holders, providing information on such technicalities of priestly life as the correct office to follow in cases where a priest holds several benefices, and adding civil law citations useful for consistory court officials such as an extra chapter on the conduct of matrimonial cases and questions of consanguinity, and information on tithes, vows, mortuaries and funerals.[95] The special appeal of the *Pupilla oculi* to graduates working in the Ely diocesan court on matrimonial cases suggests that the fellows who urged Burgo to write the work were those northern adminstrators at the Ely consistory court who were influential at Cambridge, such as Richard Scrope, chancellor in 1378, Thomas Dalby, and John Newton, the master of Peterhouse, who probably acquired his

91 See M. Harvey, 'English Views on the Reforms to be Undertaken in the General Councils 1400 – 18, with special reference to the Proposals made by Richard Ullerston', (Oxford Univ. D.Phil. thesis, 1964), pp. 1 – 20.

92 *E.D.R.*, (Reg. Arundel, 1896), p. 30.

93 Emden, *BRUC*, p. 107.

94 TE, I, p. 311.

95 Ball, 'Education of Secular Clergy', pp. 70 – 74; John de Burgo, *Pupilla oculi* (Paris, 1510).

copy of *Pupilla oculi* while he was working in Ely as Arundel's official. Another member of this circle, John Gylby, who bequeathed a copy of *Pupilla oculi* to his parish church, probably obtained it when he was in Cambridge in the 1380s. The university with its stationers was an important distribution centre for the *Pupilla*: among early owners were Richard Dunmow, fellow of Pembroke in 1380, and Thomas Markaunt, fellow of Corpus Christi in 1413; and in the fifteenth century twelve owners of the work were Cambridge men and five colleges owned copies.[96] The other important distribution centre was York Minster, and this too can be attributed to the northern clergy in Arundel's circle, including Burgh himself and John Newton, who introduced the work to ecclesiastical administrators in the diocese of York and Durham. Newton, who left his copy to his steward Nicholas Ackeld, acted as executor to two owners of the *Pupilla*, Walter Skirlaw, bishop of Durham, whose other executor was John Burgh, and Thomas Langley Dean of York and later bishop of Durham. Langley left two copies to two members of his administration, and two other members of his administration, Nicholas Holme and Thomas Fishbourne owned copies.[97] Throughout the fifteenth century the *Pupilla* was used by such York Minster administrators as William Duffield and fellows of Cambridge with Yorkshire connections like Robert Fitzhugh D.D., a canon of York in 1418 and master of St Leonard's in 1415, and Robert Wodelarke of King's Hall who was licenced to preach in York diocese in 1446.[98] This pattern of circulation among Cambridge graduates and ecclesiastical officials of York, differing as it does from the earlier diffuse circulation of the *Oculus Sacerdotis* among parish clergy throughout the country, confirms that Burgo adapted Pagula's work to meet the administrative needs of Cambridge scholars and northern clergy.

The arrival of these clergy at York in the 1390's coincides with the production of two other influential pastoral manuals associated with York Minster: *Cibus Anime*, a book of pastoral reference on the teachings of the church related to the cure of souls; and a vernacular adaptation of the *Speculum Christiani*. The compiler of *Cibus Anime* perhaps took his title from a phrase in Gaytrick's *Catechism* describing the church's teaching as the food of the food of the soul, and he is heavily dependent on the religious literature of the north, including the works of Rolle and the *Pupilla oculi* to which he refers his readers.[99] The York Minster origins of the work are further corroborated by a request in a colophon to one of the manuscripts for prayers for the souls of Thomas and Robert

96 ibid, pp. 86 – 7, 165 – 70.

97 *Catalogi Veteres Librorum Cathedralis Dunelmensis*, (SS, 7, 1838), p. 119 – 21.

98 TE, III, p. 132; *Reg. Chichele*, II, p. 540.

99 Gillespie, '*Speculum Christiani*', p. 202 – 39.

Garton, which may indicate ownership, scribal activity, or even authorship.[100] Both men probably belonged to the East Riding clerical family: Robert was parson of Kirklington in 1396, a prebendary of Newton in Durham and a king's clerk in 1399[101]; but Thomas is a more likely candidate as compiler of *Cibus Anime*. Possibly a Cambridge graduate (he is referred to in the will of a York mason in 1411 as *domine*)[102] he was rector of the church of St John the Baptist, and like Burgo he was licenced to act as Richard Scrope's penitentiary in 1398 and 1399.[103] He was also a long-serving administrator in York cathedral and had close associations with John Newton: from 1388 to 1405 he was chamberlain and in 1406 he was appointed Newton's sub-treasurer, a post he held until a year before his death in 1418. His closest friends were probably Newton, from whom he received bequests in 1414, Robert Semer, a beneficiary of his will, and with whom he was involved in a chantry foundation, and Robert Wolveden, who was granted probate of the will.[104] Thomas Garton's experience as penitentiary and administrator was similar to Burgo's; this and his scholarship (he was appointed one of the keepers of Newton's library in 1414) make him a plausible candidate as the compiler of *Cibus Anime*. The fact that the earliest manuscripts of this work are from the first quarter of the fifteenth century and the reference to *Pupilla oculi* suggests a date of composition between 1390 and 1400. Early circulation was restricted to the diocese of York, probably York Minster and Mount Grace: one early manuscript was copied by a York chantry chaplain, Robert Wasselyn, and another was owned by the monks of Mount Grace.[105] Shortly after the compilation of this work some of its Latin authorities were illustrated with vernacular verse to provide a comprehensive vernacular reference book on pastoral care more comprehensive than Gaytrick's English adaptation of Thoresby's Latin Catechism. The *Speculum Christiani*, as it was known, survives in sixty manuscripts, the earliest of which are in a North Lincolnshire dialect. A York Minster provenance is suggested by the compilers dependence, for vernacular sources, on the religious literature of the north.[106] Initial circulation of the *Speculum*, like that of *Cibus Anime*, occurred in the diocese; one of the earliest manuscripts was owned by the abbot of Rievaulx, William Spenser, and another early owner was a married clerk, John Crove, who left a copy in Wenlock church for the instruction of souls. Among owners in the

[100] ibid, p. 230.
[101] CPR, 1396 – 99, p. 1.
[102] TE, III, p. 47.
[103] *Calendar Reg. Scrope*, i, p. 17.
[104] TE, III, p. 15.
[105] Gillespie, '*Speculum Christiani*' p. 217.
[106] ibid, p. 239ff.

second half of the fifteenth century were York Minster priests, Robert Est and Thomas Symson.[107] The possibility that the compiler belonged to the circle of administrators associated with John Newton is strengthened by consideration of the close relationship between *Cibus Anime, Speculum Christiani,* and another closely related text that also employs Latin authorities and vernacular verse and discusses a table of Our Lady in York Minster. In fact the *Cibus Anime* and *Speculum Christiani* may have been compiled by the same person, for in the concluding colophon to one manuscript there occurs the name of Garton.[108]

The composition and circulation of two Latin pastoral works of reference on ecclesiastical administration and the cure of souls, the *Pupilla oculi* and *Cibus Anime,* and a vernacular work of reference on the cure of souls, *Speculum Christiani,* towards the end of the fourteenth century among a largely resident and highly qualified body of ecclesiastical administrators, penitentiaries and residentiary canons at York Minster, represents a culmination of Thoresby's methods of patronage and his conscientious approach to pastoral duty. However, in some fundamental respects the conception of the pastoral office held by these York clergy who served Arundel, Richard Scrope and Henry Bowet, was changing; and this can be seen in some of the alterations that Burgo made to the *Oculus sacerdotis*. Pagula, Thoresby and Gaytryge understood pastoral care as primarily the administration of confession, and they emphasized the public, social functions of this sacrament and the role of parish priests as moral instructors and agents of social harmony. The first religious writer of the diocese to alter the concept of the pastoral office was Richard Rolle, who adapted the first section of *Oculus sacerdotis,* the *Pars oculi,* to give a more private, interior dimension to the sacrament of penance in 1324. Sixty years later Hilton was cautiously doing the same thing, and his contemporary at Cambridge, John de Burgo, may have had a similar objective when he gave the sacrament of penance a less dominant position in the *Pupilla oculi*: owners of the work in the early fifteenth century annotated the penitential section of the work with observations on the need for frequent confession and contrition in the manner espoused by Rolle and Hilton. Similar additions on the need for prayer with utmost devotion to Jesus occur in Robert Wasselyn's copy of *Cibus anime.*[109] Furthermore, the fifth tabula of the *Speculum Christiani* is a reworking of the sixth chapter of Rolle's *Form of Living* and deals with sin, penitential cleansing, despair, the pains of Hell and the joys of Heaven; and this implies that it was designed for confessional use as a vehicle for private

[107] TE, III, pp. 159, 199, 160.
[108] Gillespie, '*Speculum Christiani*', p. 230ff.
[109] Ball, 'Education of Parish Priests', p. 257ff.

devotion and self-examination,[110] which in turn suggests that the pastoral office was broadening to include inner devotion. Burgo and his readers were consequently less concerned than Pagula and his readers with the use of the sacrament of penance as a means of social and dogmatic instruction. Burgo furthermore reduced preaching, which occupies one third of the *Oculus sacerdotis*, to one tenth of the content of his pastoral manual,[111] and this too indicates that there was a reduction in emphasis on fundamental instruction in the exercise of the pastoral office occurring among a devout circle of ecclesiastical administrators; this would have been occasioned by the growth of literacy and spirituality among clergy and laymen. Thoresby and Islip merely faced illiteracy and social discord, and the contents of *Oculus sacerdotis* and the *Lay Folk's Catechism* reflect this. Arundel and his clergy, in attempting to defend the social stability and harmony created by these pastoral bishops, were confronted by the growing internal dimension to pastoral problems, such as the threats to the individual and his community posed by the popularity of contemplative teachings and the spread of heresy. They were therefore less concerned with the dissemination of religious knowledge, whether in the administration of confession or through preaching, than they were with formulating a pastoral policy that created a doctrinal and social orthodoxy out of the growing religious enthusiasm and independence of the period. Before considering this pastoral policy in the pastoral and religious writings of this circle and their administrative work, it is necessary to establish that they were not specialized lawyers, administrators and academics, but that they had the necessary versatility and intellectual and spiritual qualities to make York minster into a centre of learning and contemplation which was relevant to social problems and could confront the challenge posed by the religious literature of the north.

York Clergy and the Contemplative Life

At the beginning of this period of growing lay piety and literacy, many professions such as the craft guilds (or mysteries), the theology schools, and the circles of common lawyers near St Paul's still maintained the secrecy of their skills and their elite status through ritual, specialized techniques and technical language. The monks of the Benedictine and Cistercian orders similarly showed little interest in making their ascetic

[110] V. Gillespie, 'The *Cibus Anime* book three, A guide to Contemplatives?', *Spiritualität Heute und Gestern*, (Aug. 1982), 90ff.

[111] Ball, 'Education of Parish Priests', p. 281.

and liturgical disciplines accessible to outsiders, and abbeys such as Durham priory remained intellectually inward looking, to the extent that even their concept of history was closely connected with the rights and privileges of their house. Two notable exceptions however were the recluses and Carthusian monks who adapted devotional routines and skills for interested amateurs. Rolle and the author of *The Cloud of Unknowing* made some efforts in this direction, but they still evoked some of the language and skills of a closed profession and described the contemplative experience as the special reward for elite practitioners of the contemplative art which was essentially incommunicable to outsiders, and therefore of little social relevance. Arundel and his clerks were responsible for demystifying and opening up this profession by adapting and applying the teachings of the recluse to amateurs who did not live the solitary life. They prescribed and defined for such people a 'mixed life' of activity and contemplation and reduced the recluses' emphasis on skills and elusive experiences, to make contemplative doctrine applicable and relevant to all members of society. By doing this they were of course concerned with reducing the likelihood of people being lead astray through ignorance; but before discussing the specific pastoral work of these clerks in this field, it is necessary to see their efforts in the context of these general trends occurring in English culture at the turn of the fourteenth century, in which academic disciplines and professions were becoming more accessible and relevant to the non-specialist.

Henry Lord Scrope of Masham and Humphrey Duke of Gloucester were soldiers whose interests ranged far beyond warfare to include law, diplomacy, administration, and the collecting of books of such diverse subjects as history, romance, theology, and the contemplative life. Apart from the growing numbers of literate laymen wanting a knowledge of these subjects, the impetus for the popularization of academic, monastic and courtly disciplines came from the work of professionals such as Wyclif and Pecock in theology, Fortesque in common law, Chaucer in court culture and conventions, Thomas Hoccleve in the civil service, and Stephen Scrope in chivalry and the art of warfare. None of these men allowed their interests to be confined by their professions, and in their writings they all showed an ability to command a knowledge and understanding of the different disciplines, while revealing the intellectual versatility to see beyond the confines of these professions. By showing an interest in, and understanding of, human nature at an individual and social level they were able to make the arcane mysteries of specialist teachings, convention and language, relevant and comprehensible to most individuals, whether it be courtly love etiquette, heraldry and chivalry, or the rhetorical conventions of letter writing. Two theologians, Wyclif, who was occasionally employed by the government, and later Pecock, a bishop, helped to transform abstract scholastic theology into a subject of lively debate and importance in contemporary English society, through their interest in Augustinian psychology, textual scholarship, and biblical and ecclesiastical history. The subject of canon law was similarly given a broader human perspective, and Arundel and his clerks, through their work in this field, can be considered, along with Wyclif and Chaucer, among the forerunners of the dissemination of culture and learning. As trained canonists they shared a broad and humane understanding of their profession which extended beyond such narrow aspects of ecclesiastical law as jurisdiction, property disputes or questions of consanguinity. Hilton, in his discussions on the personal dimensions of sin and penance and their social implications for the administration of confession, showed an interest in the spiritual, psychological and social dimensions of ecclesiastical law. The rest of the circle, as we shall see, also applied their legal training in this area, and they were able to do so because, as scholars and practical men, they had the versatility to treat learning as a key both to understanding and improving contemporary society; by doing so they contributed to the integration of the university in the national life.

Arundel and his clerks specialized in canon law, but this subject also aroused in them an interest in book collecting and such diverse subjects as ecclesiastical, secular and biblical history, theology and classical society. The three archbishops of York were all bibliophiles and scholars. Arundel's library was valued at £500. He was in contact with intellectual developments in Italy; he had travelled to Florence during his exile from 1397 to 1399 and had discussed his library with the humanist Coluccio Salutati, who had promised to send him his own treatise *De Nobilitate legum et Medicine*.[1] Richard Scrope, according to Walsingham, had an incomparable knowledge of scholarship, and the inventory of Henry Bowet's collection of theological and legal texts may have only represented a portion of his library.[2] The focal point of the intellectual life of their circle was Cambridge. Both Richard and Stephen Scrope were chancellors of the university; William Waltham left a collection of theological and legal works to King's Hall; and Robert Alne left the works of Aristotle, Boethius and Aquinas to the university library.[3]

However, it was to Peterhouse that most of these clerks would gravitate, especially before 1414, and many of them donated books,

1 *Epistolario di Coluccio Salutati*, ed. F. Novati (Rome, 1891 – 1911), iii, pp. 360 – 63, 497 – 501, 618 – 21; Jacob, *The Fifteenth Century*, p. 666.
2 TE, III, pp. 69 – 85.
3 Reg. Test. I, fo. 91; TE, II, p. 78.

including new humanist works from Italy, to the library. Thomas Arundel bequeathed to the college a collection of the works of Aristotle including the *Physica Parva,* and John Bottisham left Peterhouse all his books on canon and civil law and some of the works of Gregory and Aquinas to Pembroke Hall.[4] Thomas of Barnard Castle, the master of Peterhouse from 1400 – 1421 and his friend William Noion, who was studying there in 1401, were also benefactors and probably donated books.[5] The leading intellectual figure in the college was John Newton, the master from 1382 to 1397. Newton, like Arundel, may have been in touch with Italian scholars because he left seventeen volumes to the Peterhouse fellows in 1414, three of which were written in Italy.[6] Among the collection there was an Italian manuscript of Bartolus of Sassoferrato on the *Digestum Novum,* an example of the work of the Italian humanist jurists of the fourteenth century.[7] Newton's interest in ancient Rome, which is demonstrated in the substantial collection of classical texts that he left to Peterhouse, may have originated from his training in Roman law. Included in this collection were Seneca's *Declamations,* with Trivet's commentary, which was given to the college in 1411; the *Variae* of Cassiodorus, a collection of 468 official letters and documents serving as rhetorical models and contained in an Italian manuscript along with Giles of Rome's *History of the Destruction of Troy;* Macrobius' *Saturnalia;* Valerius Maximus' book for rhetoricians; the *Historia Tripartita* of Cassiodorus; the Roman military treatise of Flavius Vegetius Renatus, and Pierre Bersuire's secular glosses on Ovid's *Metamorphoses* with Trivet's allegorical commentary.[8] Newton's interest in secular history was shown in his bequest of an eleventh century history of the Franks, *De abbreviacione historiarum* by Aimonius of Fleury, and a history of the arrival of William the Conqueror in England.[9] The theological collection contained Jerome's *Contra Jovinianum,* Augustine's *Contra Pelagianos,* Boethius' *De Trinitare* and the works of St Bernard and the Victorine school. Also in the legacy were Boethius' *De Consolatione Philosophiae* and Alan of Lille's *De Planctu Naturae,* both of which discuss the workings of fortune in the natural world; and there was even a short scientific tract on the laws of motion.[10] Robert Alne, who was a fellow from 1400 and probably a protégé of Newton and Richard Scrope, donated to the college library in 1418 a manuscript of Augustine's *De*

4 *Sede Vacante Wills,* ed. C. E. Woodruff (Kent Arch. Soc., iii, 1914), pp. 81 – 2; Walker, *B.R.P.*, i, pp. 28 – 29, Emden, *B.R.U.C.*, p. 76.

5 Walker, i, pp. 29 – 39.

6 M. R. James, *A Catalogue of Manuscripts in the Library of Peterhouse* (Cambridge, 1880), nos. 167, 173, 233.

7 ibid, n. 233.

8 ibid, n. 162.

9 Reg. Test. I, fo. 168; TE, I, p. 364ff.

10 ibid; *Catalogue Peterhouse Manuscripts,* n. 275.

Trinitate and *De Civitate Dei*. Alne also bequeathed a collection of books to a fellow Yorkshireman and Peterhouse fellow, John Oteringham, including Seneca's letters and Petrarch's *De Remediis*, with the stipulation that they were to go to the college after his death.[11] The Peterhouse scholars shared common interests in human personality which is revealed in their following contemporary theological debates on free will, and in different societies, which is indicated by their interest in classical culture; they would have been conscious of the need to find an immediate social utility for their studies. The earliest statutes of the college, framed by Simon Montacute, the bishop of Ely in 1344, were designed to fulfil the intention of the founder, which was to encourage self-preparation for the service of the common weal by advanced study; this policy had been pursued by Arundel who had found ecclesiastical preferment for many of its fellows.[12]

Newton and his circle helped to bring these scholarly interests to York, and the first indication of the emergence of York Minster as a centre of scholarship coincides with Newton's arrival at the cathedral in the early 1390s. In 1391 Mr John Percy of Swynton in Appliton, Yorkshire, who may have been another Cambridge member of this circle, left a book of saints' lives, a work of Trevisa, a letter collection associated with Peter of Blois containing expositions on the episcopal office to John Newton, and a French Brut to Mr John Scarborough, a canon of York who had been one of Richard Scrope's clerks at Lichfield.[13] Scarborough in 1395 left Pagula's *Summa summarum* and a Clement with two glosses to Thomas Arundel.[14] In 1406 an advocate at York, John Harwood, left John Newton 'my special lord', the choice of all his books.[15] In 1414 Newton laid the foundations for the cathedral library in a bequest to the canons of seventy volumes. Although there was not such an emphasis on the classics in this bequest, it would still have helped to make York a centre of scholarship in a variety of subjects. The responsibility for setting up this library rested with Newton's executors, his Ely and Cambridge colleagues William Waltham and John Gylby. Forty volumes were books on civil law and canon law including the works of the Italian jurists Bartolus of Sassoferrato and Cino of Pistoia. Most of these were to be deposited in a chest standing in the vestry of the cathedral, with the reservation that they were to be given to any nephew of Newton's who wished to specialize in law. In the rest of the collection there were works of biblical exegesis and such aids to biblical scholarship as Jerome's interpretations of Hebrew names and a

11 TE, II, p. 78.
12 Walker, *B.R.P.*, i, pp. 1 – 4.
13 BI, Reg. 14 (Arundel), f.27, TE, I, p. 164.
14 TE, III, p. 6.
15 Reg. Test. I, fo.142.

gloss on the letters of St Paul. There was a theological collection, dominated by the works of Augustine, Gregory and Bernard. The scholastic theologians of the thirteenth century, with the exception of Aquinas, were poorly represented, suggesting that Newton and his circle were more interested in the psychological and practical application of theology, and there was a comparative rarity in the collection, namely Holcot's Sunday sermons. Newton's interest in the secular society of Rome was to some extent represented in the bequest of John of Salisbury's *Policraticus* and his historical interests were demonstrated in such works of ecclesiastical and secular history as a history of England from the British period until 1129, written by Alfred the treasurer of Beverley, William of Malmesbury's Gesta *Pontificum Anglorum* and Bede's *Ecclesiastical History*.[16] In 1430 another member of Arundel's circle, Robert Ragnall, an advocate in the court of York, supplemented this bequest by leaving to the canons of York the pick of any of the books from his library not found in the cathedral; the treasurer of York, Robert Wolveden, was to have the choice of any of the remaining books.[17]

By this date York Minster had emerged as a centre where canon lawyers could, during their studies, consider the individual and his relationship to society along Peterhouse lines; it no longer only provided basic pastoral administration, training and education as it had done in Thoresby's time. The servants of Arundel, Scrope and Bowet had a greater breadth of scholarship than Thoresby's clerks, and they were well equiped to meet the challenges posed by Rolle and other recluses because they brought a humane and practical perspective on their own and other professions; they could apply these criteria to the contemplative profession. The Italian civilians who were read at Peterhouse and York defined the active life as the expression of the social will of the people through secular laws. The canonists of Peterhouse and York did something similar with religious experience and ecclesiastical laws by placing them in the social context of the common weal or the mixed life.

These clerks were in an ideal position to recognize at a very early stage the pastoral difficulties and potential represented by the growing popularity of Rolle's teachings and the activities of his followers in the 1370s and 1380s. Most of them were Yorkshiremen, and Richard Scrope of Masham, one of the clerks closest to Arundel during the early days of his Ely administration, was a member of the family which had probably been among the hermit's patrons. Richard Scrope's own acquaintance with Margaret Kirkby and Rolle's writings may have

16 Reg. Test. I, fo. 168; TE, I, p. 364ff; For Alfred of Beverley see Antonia Gransden, *Historical Writings in England* (London, 1976), p. 212. For text of this history see *Aluredi Beverlacensis Annales*, ed. T. Hearne (Oxford, 1716).

17 Reg. Test. I, fo. 202.

occurred during the time he held the rectory of Ainderby from 1367 to 1376 when Margaret was a recluse there. He may have received further encouragement from his uncle Geoffrey Scrope, a canon of Lincoln in 1381, from whom he received the rectory of Great Bowden in 1376; in 1383 Geoffrey Scrope left a book of devotion to John Bautre, a vicar choral of York Minster, a copy of *Hostienses* to his nephew Richard Scrope, and some chessmen to Henry Lord FitzHugh, a kinsman and neighbour of the Scropes who collected Scrope's works.[18] Richard Scrope's interest in Rolle may explain the compilation at Lichfield during his episcopate of one of the finest collections of Rolle's writings; between 1386 and 1398 *Ego Dormio, The Commandment, The Form of Living* and the *Incendium Amoris,* all in northern dialect, and other northern works such as the *Prick of Conscience* and Hovenden's *Philomena,* were copied into a single volume. The quality of the English texts bespeaks good sources, and the attribution of the unified text of *The Form* and *Ego Dormio* to *quodam notabile Ricardi Rolle hermite* suggests an informed ancestry within the region that Rolle lived.[19] Richard Scrope, as rector of Ainderby and a member of a family who were such important patrons of recluses, was in a very good position to acquire the English texts, which were written for the nuns and anchoresses of Yorkshire, from Margaret Kirkby and her fellow recluses; he probably had access to autographed manuscripts because his nephew Henry Lord Scrope of Masham owned an autographed volume of Rolle's works.[20] It is also likely that Richard Scrope was the first to introduce Rolle's works to the clerks of Arundel's circle, including Scrope's colleague at the Ely consistory court in 1376, Walter Hilton. There is no evidence that Rolle was being read at Cambridge prior to the arrival of these northern clerks at the university, and in Flete's *De Remediis Temptationem,* composed at Cambridge between 1352 and 1358, there is no trace of Rolle's influence.

Evidence of the interest shown by Arundel and his household in Rolle's works comes from the will of Sir William Thorpe, who was a member of Arundel's household in 1380; in 1396 Thorpe, who asked to be buried in Ely Cathedral, bequeathed a protifor which he had received from Arundel and left his chaplain a book composed by 'Richard the Hermit', which may also have been a gift from Arundel.[21] The interest shown by the fellows of Peterhouse in Rolle's works, which is testified by the presence of Rolle's *Commentary on Job,* the *Form of Living* and *Judica*

18 Thompson, 'Register of the Archdeaconry of Richmond', 253 – 54. Richard Scrope was also warden of the free chapel of Tickhill, a contemplative retreat of John Waldeby; *Market Harborough Records,* p. 50.

19 Oxford, Bodl. MS. Rawl. A., 389; see Doyle, 'A Survey', II, pp. 143 – 5; Allen, *Rolle, Writings,* p. 45.

20 *Foedera,* ix, p. 276.

21 *Early Lincoln Wills,* p. 79.

Me Deus in the Peterhouse library catalogue, was probably inspired by John Newton, a close friend and colleague of Richard Scrope from at least 1376, and an executor of Richard's brother Sir John Scrope in 1405.[22] It was probably through his friendship with this family that Newton had access to the autographed manuscripts that he used when studying Rolle's works. In his library there was a volume of the hermit of Hampole's works and a glossed psalter which may have been Rolle's Latin commentary on the psalms.[23] This Peterhouse circle read Rolle with discernment, and they were among the first to recognize the close affinity between Rolle's mystical writings and Suso's emotive and autobiographical *Horologium Sapientiae*, which arrived in England around 1380.[24] One half of the surviving English manuscripts of the *Horologium* also contain the works of Rolle; and William Noion, Thomas Arundel and Thomas of Barnard Castle were among the earliest readers. Noion, who, like Thorpe, was a member of Arundel's household in 1380, left Archbishop Arundel a small book called the *Horologium* 'in which I have had much pleasure in my life'; and he bequeathed another copy to Thomas of Barnard Castle.[25] Robert Alne, who was a fellow of Peterhouse during Barnard Castle's long mastership, obtained from his friend Thomas Hebbenden, who was ordained by Bowet in 1421 and whose early career was spent in York, a copy of Rolle's *Melos Amoris*, which was in the same volume as the *Horologium*; he left instructions to Hebbenden, who was his executor, to give the work to Cambridge University library; and he owned another copy of the *Horologium* which he bequeathed to his brother John Alne, a Carthusian of London.[26]

The arrival of Arundel and Newton at York in 1390, followed by that of Noion, Dalby and Scarborough, would have encouraged clergy in the diocese, especially at York Minster, to study Rolle and other contemplative writers. Robert Wyclif, who acted with Newton as an executor to Sir John Dependen and as a co-sponsor of a student at Oxford, owned a volume that contained extracts from Rolle's *Contra Amatores*, the Commentary on Job, *Judica Me Deus*, and *Emendatio Vitae*; on the fly leaf there are documents relating to property transactions in the diocese witnessed by the owner.[27] In 1398 Edmund Daldirston, a York chantry priest, left a library consisting of 'a highly recommended' book of *The*

22 James, *Peterhouse Catalogue*, n. 218.

23 Reg. Test. I, fo. 168; TE, I, p. 364ff. Newton as vicar general would also have been associated with Henry Lord FitzHugh after Richard Scrope's death: FitzHugh was appointed keeper of the temporalities of the see of York.

24 R. Lovatt, 'The Influence of the Religious Literature of Germany and the Low Countries on English Spirituality c. 1350 – 1475', (Oxford Univ. D.Phil. thesis, 1965) p. 94ff.

25 Reg. Test. I, fo. 139.

26 TE. II, p. 78.

27 Deanesly, *The Incendium Amoris*, p. 58; Camb. Univ. Lib., MS., F.F. 1, 14, fo. 183.

Mending of Life by Richard Rolle, a psalter and books of grammar, which were to be left to his chantry for the use of his fellow cantarists.[28] Walter Bruge, a canon of York, bequeathed a glossed psalter, probably Rolle's, and a copy of *Piers Plowman* in 1395; in 1398 a York chaplain, Thomas Monkton, bequeathed a copy of the *Emendatio Vitae*, and John Kendale, a vicar choral of the minster by 1409 and a friend of John Newton, to whom he gave a psalter, owned a copy of *Piers Plowman*.[29] Such early interest in Langland's work — which may owe something to the fact that it was copied at Lichfield into the same volume as Rolle's works during Scrope's episcopate — is an indication of the spiritual awareness of the York clergy in this period.

After Arundel's departure to Canterbury the diocese was administered by Scrope, Bowet, Newton and their clerks. Under their influence the study of contemplative literature became an established tradition among the York clergy. Bowet's interest in contemplation and the eremitic life was shown by his ownership of Anselm's *Cur Deus Homo*, and he is credited in the Syon catalogue with the authorship of a guide to the religious life.[30] Stephen Scrope, the archdeacon of Richmond, owned an early fourteenth century manuscript containing saints' lives, a Meditation of Bonaventura on the Passion and a life of the Virgin.[31] Treasurer John Newton made a significant contribution towards the studying of contemplative literature at York when he bequeathed to the cathedral library a volume containing Hugh of St Victor's *De Institucione Noviciorum*, and the works of John of Hevenden, Richard Rolle and Walter Hilton; this volume may well have summarized the main achievements of the eremitic movement in the north-east.[32] The collection of eremitic writings in the minster would have been further supplemented by Robert Ragnall who had a collection of devotional works, unfortunately not itemized, in the library he offered to the canons in 1430.[33]

By the end of this year the only surviving member of Arundel's circle of former Ely servants was Mr John Gylby, the rector of Knesall in Nottinghamshire. The dominant figures in the cathedral were now the canons and vicars choral who had started their careers serving members of this circle. Unlike their patrons they spent most or all their lives in the service of the church in York; the exceptions being Hebbenden and Alne; and they devoted themselves to administration, liturgical services

28 B.I.H.R. Prob. Reg. 3, fo. 16; J. H. Moran, 'Education and Learning in the City of York', *Borthwick Paper*, 55, (1979), 30.
29 B.I.H.R. Prob. Reg. I, fo. 81; Reg. Test. I, fo. 225.
30 ibid, fo. 216.
31 Oxford, Bodl. MS. Balliol, 227.
32 Reg. Test. I, fo. 168; TE, I, p. 364ff.
33 Reg. Test. I, fo. 202.

and the study of contemplative literature. Robert Wolveden, the treasurer from 1426 to 1431, probably consulted a recluse while he was Richard Scrope's precentor at Lichfield, for he bequeathed a book of devotion which had been written by the anchorite of Lichfield; this may have been an English version of the *Ancren Riwle*, known as *The Treatise on Five Wits*, which is ascribed in one manuscript to one Lichfield.[34] Wolveden, like other York clerks, may have shown an interest in Rhineland spirituality because he also bequeathed a book that was transcribed by John Arston, a German notary from the diocese of Mainz who had a large library and lived in York; he made his will in 1432 on the same day as Wolveden and was buried in the cathedral.[35] In the same year Robert Semer, the sub-treasurer of York, who had been ordained by Richard Scrope and who had acted as one of John Newton's executors, bequeathed to Robert Helperby, a vicar choral who was buried in the cathedral aisle in 1435, an important volume containing Rolle's *Commentary on Job* and other works by the same author; Semer also owned a copy of St Bridget's *Revelations* and bequeathed a *Horologium* to Robert Skelton, a penitentiary of York Minster.[36] One of the leading vicars choral in this period was Richard Ulleskelfe, the sub-chantor of the cathedral from 1419 – 21 who received help early in his career from John Newton who granted him a dispensation in 1403 allowing him to take orders despite his illegitimacy. Ulleskelfe acted as Richard Pittes' executor and received a *Veritas Theologiae* from Robert Semer; in 1446 he left *The Meditations of St Anselm* to a John Wooley and a *Horologium* to his chaplain John Kexby, who was involved in propagating the cult of Richard Scrope.[37] These clerks had access to autographed manuscripts of Rolle's which they may have obtained from members of Arundel's circle: Thomas Beelby, a canon of York and a benefactor in the will of William Waltham, left William Duffield, a residentiary canon and benefactor in Robert Alne's will, the autographed version of Rolle's Latin psalter and a volume containing Rolle's *Commentary on Job*, which, as it was valued at 8s 4d, may also have been an autograph.[38]

The devotional interest of these clerks ensured that there was enthusiasm for Rolle's works in York Minster in the second half of the fifteenth century. Duffield, who had been Archbishop John Kempe's diocesan official in Rochester and Chichester before accompanying him to York to serve as his chaplain and as a proctor in the court of York in

34 ibid, I, fo. 235; Doyle, 'A Survey', II, p. 135.

35 TE, III, p. 91.

36 *Calendar of Reg. Scrope*, p. 48; Reg. Scrope, fo. 175; Reg. Test. I, fo. 236; F. Harrison, *Life in a Medieval College*, (London, 1952), p. 306.

37 Reg. Test. I, fos. 236, 259; Harrison, pp. 158 – 62; Reg. Scrope, fo. 129v.

38 Reg. Test. I, fo. 261.

1439, was probably especially influential.[39] So too was Archbishop Thomas Rotherham, a former chancellor of Cambridge, who professed in his will his orthodoxy and devotion to the Holy Name, and who founded Jesus College in Rotherham in 1486 in honour of the Holy Name of Jesus.[40] The influence of high ranking officials in the diocese and the cathedral was also responsible for the increasing interest shown in Rolle's works by chantry priests of the minster during the fifteenth century, perhaps because of the influence of members of Arundel's circle. During Wolveden's treasurership in 1427 an inventory of the goods of a priest of the cathedral choir, Henry Thorpthorp, revealed two books and a quire of unspecified writings by Richard the hermit.[41] Another minster priest, William Gate, William Waltham's former chaplain, bequeathed in 1431 Rolle's Commentary on Job and the *Meditations of St Anselm* to Richard Drax, a chantry priest of York.[42] In 1452 Robert Est, a chantry priest who owned a large library, brought Rolle's autographed latin psalter from the effects of William Duffield for 14s 8d, and he left it in 1467 to the nuns of Hampole, who already owned the autograph of Rolle's English psalter.[43] Est's friends included Thomas Synson, owner of St Mechthild's *Revelations*, and Thomas Howren, the rector of All Saints' Church in North Street, from whom Est obtained a copy of St Bridget's *Revelations*.[44] The participation of York chantry priests in the corporate life of study and prayer that the residentiary canons and vicars choral shared within the cathedral and its close and the bedern of the vicars choral, was facilitated in 1461 by the foundation near the east end of the cathedral of St William's college for chantry priests. By 1467 the college had its own library, and in 1479 Thomas Pynchbek, a chantry priest of York who owned a copy of Rolle's *Commentary on Job*, left the library a glossed psalter which was probably Rolle's.[45] The literacy and spirituality of these men gives an indication of how far chantry priests had progressed from the time when Thoresby tried to instil into chantry priests of the diocese a rudimentary sense of liturgical and parochial duty.

In no other cathedral during this period was there such an impressive increase in standards of scholarship, especially in the study of contemplative literature. By 1412 Exeter Cathedral had its own library of

39 TE, III, p. 132.
40 Pfaff, *Liturgical Feasts*, pp. 30, 70; TE, IV, pp. 138 – 48; Emden, BRUC, pp. 489 – 90.
41 Unpublished Borthwick Institute inventory; see G. R. Keiser, 'Lincoln Cathedral Library Manuscript 91: The Life and Milieu of the Scribe', *Studies in Bibliography*, 32 (1979), 172.
42 Reg. Test. I, fo. 233; TE, III, p. 58.
43 Reg. Test. I, fo. 331; TE, III, p. 160.
44 TE. III, p. 199; Reg. Test. I, fo. 317.
45 Dobson, 'A History of York Minster, the Later Middle Ages', p. 97; Moran, 'Education and Learning', p. 29; TE, III, p. 199.

legal and theological texts, but the intellectual interests of the cathedral clergy were narrowly professional: the canons bequeathed law texts necessary for the administration of the cathedral; they showed no interest in either the classics, twelfth century spirituality or the contemplative writers of the north-east; the vicars choral and chantry priests owned the breviaries, psalters and missals that they needed for their liturgical duties; and there is no evidence that any of them possessed the culture and spirituality of Ulleskelfe or Est.[46] This superior scholarship of the York clergy in the fifteenth century also illustrates the way the concept and performance of the pastoral office had diverged in both dioceses from the period when Thoresby and Grandisson had essentially worked in unison on the same problems. Between 1370 and 1450 the clergy of York would go far beyond the rudimentary instructions for parish priests and their flocks provided by Thoresby and Gaytrick when they attempted to adapt Rolle's teachings and provide supplementary spiritual instruction for priests and laymen. Within this more sophisticated dimension of pastoral care the York clergy were, initially at least, on their own.

Pastoral Care and the Eremitic Movement

Evidence that Arundel's clerks considered at an early stage in their careers the pastoral ramifications of the growing interest in Richard Rolle and eremitic reaching is provided by the pastoral manuals of the 1380s and 1390s. The most striking aspect of the association of *Pupilla oculi* with Cambridge graduates and northerners is that most of the owners had some interest in the writings of Rolle and the patronage of recluses: John Newton, William Duffield, Nicholas Holme, Thomas Markaunt and John Maltster were all owners of the works of Richard Rolle; Robert FitzHugh was the son of Henry the lord of Tanfield who owned an autograph manuscript of the hermit's works; Thomas Langely and Thomas Fishbourne were associated with Syon, where there was a collection of Rolle's writings and three copies of *Pupilla oculi*; and James Pagula was a rector of All Saints', a church associated with a number of recluses. An indication that Burgo himself anticipated and desired the circulation of the *Pupilla* among such a devotional elite is provided in his decision to omit from the *Oculus sacerdotis* the brief devotional passages urging strong feelings; he probably regarded them as unnecessary because the northern clergy had libraries of the new devotional literature of

[46] N. Orme, 'Education and Learning at a Medieval English Cathedral: Exeter 1380 – 1448', *J.E.H.*, 32 (1981), 265 – 83.

Yorkshire.[1] The author, or authors, of *Cibus anime* and *Speculum Christiani*, by quoting the works of Rolle, were making an even more explicit association between pastoral literature and eremitic teaching; and the later owners of *Speculum Christiani*, Robert Est and Thomas Symson, were students of Rolle. The authors of such handbooks, and their readers, were clearly making some effort to reconcile the teachings of Rolle with the performance of pastoral duty. The pastoral problems facing Thoresby and his clerks were dauntingly simple by comparison. These sophisticated men realized that despite their sometimes heavy involvement in government responsibilities, they needed to impart some of their education to the parish priests of the diocese if the laity were going to be given basic religious and moral instruction. The pastoral issues facing Arundel's clerks were more complex because they needed to provide the growing numbers of priests and laymen interested in eremitic teachings with spiritual guidance, and before doing so they needed to decide how they were going to reconcile this and other pastoral and public duties with their own growing interest in scholarship, and especially the contemplative arts. Walter Hilton's writings express the problems facing northern civil servants, lawyers and priests of the diocese of Ely and Cambridge University who had contemplative aspirations but neither the freedom nor the inclination to become recluses. In all these works the author presupposes that he is addressing a more spiritually sophisticated readership than the simple parish priests for whom Thoresby and Gaytryge wrote.

The most firmly dateable of Hilton's works is *De Utilitate et Prerogativis Religionis*, a letter in which the author encourages an exchequer clerk in his intention to enter the Carthusian order while admitting his own unworthiness to take such a step.[2] This letter reveals Hilton's preoccupation as a North Lincolnshire clerk with the spiritual problems facing many northerners destined to follow the traditional paths of government service established by Thoresby. References in the letter to the heretics who opposed private religion suggest that it was composed after Wyclif's condemnation on this point in 1382, and probably in 1384 or 1385, for the clerk concerned, Adam Horsley, joined Beauvale Charterhouse in 1386. Hilton was a solitary at the time of writing the letter, but the tone suggests that he was not far from joining a religious order himself; he probably joined the Augustinian canons around 1386, and probably abandoned his legal studies to become a hermit around 1384, fired no doubt by the example of Rolle, whose cult had recently been established at Hampole in 1382. The earliest of these Latin letters to provide an

1 Ball, 'Education of Secular Clergy', p. 234ff.

2 Hilton's *Latin Writings*, ed. J. P. Clark and Cheryl Taylor (Analecta Cartusiana, 124, Salzburg, 1987).

indication of the date of composition is *De Imagine Peccati*, a letter addressed to a friend, a high ranking ecclesiastic who, like Hilton, denounced a worldly career, honours and benefices, but had not found peace of soul. In this letter Hilton gives an unhappy account of his own conversion to the solitary life and attempts to formulate a way of life that satisfies his contemplative aspirations and sense of social duty. The lack of reference to heresy and absence of the expression of any intention to join a religious community, a prospect considered in the letter to Horlsey, indicates that this was an earlier letter written shortly after Hilton left Cambridge, around 1384.[3] In the *Epistola ad Quemdam Seculo Renunciare Volentem*, he addressed a fellow canonist, Dr John Thorpe, who had experienced a religious conversion after suffering imprisonment and sickness; Hilton discusses the tensions facing men who had legal training and contemplative aspiration.[4] While observing his friend's unsuitability for the life of a recluse, he advised him to give up legal practice and employed his own legal knowledge to give the recipient canonical advice on the question of salvation in the case of unpaid debts for which Thorpe had been imprisoned.[5] Hilton, however, was no longer practising law and alluded to his having given up a promising legal career for the service of God. This, the more confident tone of the letter, and Hilton's suggestion that the recipient was unsuitable to take vows and join a religious community, suggests that the letter was written at Thurgarton priory. Two other letters which have no indications of the date of composition are *Epistola de Leccione*, which was written for a parish priest bound to the recitation of canonical hours who had withdrawn from worldly conversation and renounced some form of doctrinal error;[6] and *Firmissime Crede*, probably an extract from a larger work on the scruples regarding absolution following a religious conversion, which was addressed to a parish priest who had been educated at university, probably Cambridge, and who was a member of a college.[7] Hilton's two surviving English works, the *Scale of Perfection* and the *Epistle on Mixed Life*, were probably both written at Thurgarton, and were in part concerned with the needs of former colleagues and secular clerks in general. The *Scale* has a practical and restrained survey of the contemplative life which was applicable to a wide range of people including solitaries, regular and secular clergy, and it appealed to anyone of sufficient education and devotion who aspired to a life of reading, meditation and activity. The 'ghostly friend' to whom book two was dedicated may therefore have been a person of

3 Hilton, *Latin Writings*, i, pp. 75 – 91.
4 ibid, ii, pp. 249 – 303.
5 ibid, ii, p. 264.
6 ibid, ii, p. 220ff.
7 ibid.

similar background and education as the author.[8] Hilton defined the life of such people as a 'medled lyf'. As a canonist he would have encountered this term in the writings of Hostiensis, and he gave some advice on how to live such a life in his *Epistle on Mixed Life,* which he partly directed at secular clergy.[9]

The internal evidence of these Latin letters and English pastoral works suggests that Hilton, like Burgo, was writing for Cambridge and Ely administrators from the north-east; and this is further corroborated by common factors in the later careers of Hilton, the recipients of the Latin letters, and members of Arundel's circle. Hilton's decision to enter the small priory of Thurgarton (where according to one manuscript tradition of the *Scale* he died in 1396) did not preclude his doing pastoral work, or his involvement in the secular world. By following John Thweng's example Hilton was making an acceptable compromise that allowed him to combine a religious life with some pastoral service: the canons were the most pastorally orientated order, and in theory they were allowed, by canon law, to exercise the cure of souls. Characteristically, however, Hilton did not impose his choice on his readers and he generally tried to help them to find a way in secular life to integrate their spiritual needs. All the recipients of these letters, like the author, had at some time a secular career which they were unable to discard easily or to integrate into a contemplative life. They included an exchequer clerk turned Carthusian; a solitary who was formerly a prosperous benefice holder; an ecclesiastical lawyer and Cambridge graduate; and two secular priests, one of whom was a university graduate, probably of Cambridge. They were therefore part of the same secular world and felt the same tensions as Hilton's fellow northerners, Cambridge graduates and Ely diocesan administrators. These tensions concerning the pulls of the contemplative and secular lives provide the background and inspiration to Hilton's writings. Only one member of the Arundel circle actually made the transition from secular to religious life. Mr Ralph Selby left York, where he was sub-dean, to become a privileged monk of Westminster.[10] Others maintained close connections with religious communities: John Waltham, the bishop of Salisbury, who appointed Selby as his executor, gave £500 to the monks of Westminster;[11] and Thomas Dalby probably had close connections with Thurgarton near the end of his life. Others in the circle had links with the Carthusians, the

[8] Russel-Smith, 'Walter Hilton', 205, 208; M. G. Sargent, 'The Transmission by the Carthusians of Some Late Medieval Spiritual Writings', *J.E.H.* 27 (1976), 237.

[9] For printed editions of the *Epistle on the Mixed Life* see *English Prose Treatises of Richard Rolle of Hampole,* ed. R. Perry (London, E.E.T.S., 1886), pp. 19 – 42; *Yorkshire Writers,* I, pp. 264 – 92.

[10] Emden, *BRUC,* p. 517.

[11] E. H. Pearce, *The Monks of Westminster,* (Cambridge, 1916), pp. 128 – 9.

order especially praised by Hilton: Mr Richard Scrope's arms are on the doorway to one of the cells of Mount Grace, and Thomas Arundel joined the Mount Grace fraternity. While most of Hilton's Cambridge and Ely associates remained in secular life many, like Richard Scrope and John Newton, managed to retain their enthusiasm for books, including contemplative literature, and they used ascetic language in their wills in the manner espoused by Walter Hilton in the *Epistle on Mixed Life*.

Given the common secular background and contemplative aspirations of Hilton and Arundel's other administrators it is possible that Hilton, who had a larger audience in mind than the original recipients of his letters, may have written his works to help his fellow Cambridge and Ely clerks who may also have introduced him to Rolle's writings. This is also suggested by the tangible connections existing between the two known recipients of the letters, Adam Horsley and John Thorpe, with this circle of northerners. Horsley was probably from Horsley in Derbyshire ten miles from Beauvale. Like many northerners he was in the king's service, which he entered while Thoresby was archbishop; and in 1369 he was rewarded with the presentation of a church within the king's gift, St John Staunford in Nottinghamshire in the diocese of York. He had a successful career in the exchequer, and in 1375 he was appointed controller of the Great Roll. His associates in the Exchequer were Yorkshiremen: in 1384 he acted as executor to William Yaule, parson of Kirklington near Ripon and the king's remembrancer.[12] As a northerner in the Treasury it is likely that he was helped by the head of the Exchequer, Richard Scrope of Bolton. Horsley, as a royal servant, found, like Thoresby and others before him, that high rank and prestige in government service increased the difficulties of leaving: an indication that he was detained in the king's service after expressing a desire to leave is provided in the unusual enforcement of a legal technicality requiring Horsley to obtain the permission of his bishop (Alexander Neville, archbishop of York) to join the Carthusian order.[13] Hilton applied his legal knowledge to the problem and pointed out in his letter to Horsley that canon law allowed clerks to enter monastic orders without the permission of their bishops. Horsley finally entered Beauvale in the diocese of York in 1386 when he secured the permission of the general chapter of the Urbanist observance of the Carthusian order. Horsley died at Beauvale in 1423/4, having lived as a Carthusian monk *laudabiliter*.[14] Hilton's other named recipient, John Thorpe, described as a king's clerk of Ely and Norwich diocese, had less contact

12 CPR, 1381–85, p. 541; CPR, 1377–81, p. 110; 1367–70, p. 281; CPR, 1370–74, p. 285; CCR, 1384, p. 605.

13 Russel-Smith, 'Walter Hilton', 12.

14 M. G. Sargent, 'James Greenhalgh as Textual Critic', *Analecta Cartusiana*, 85 (Salzburg, 1984), ii, p. 570ff. and p. 44 addendum; Hilton, *Latin Writings*, ii, p. 361.

with the diocese of York, but he was a Cambridge graduate in canon law by 1388 and would therefore have had contact with other members of Arundel's circle: in 1391 he heard a case in the court of chivalry along with other doctors of law including Mr John Barnet, a member of Arundel's household, and Richard Lord Scrope of Bolton.[15] Despite his conversion and intention to enter a vowed religious life, Thorpe, unlike Hilton, continued to practise law and to hold benefices, including a canonry in Lincoln Cathedral from 1389 until his death in 1421, and two incompatible rectories of Erpingham (1393 to 1403) and Winterton (1396 to 1406) in Norfolk.[16] Many of his interests and connections were in this region. He was possibly related to Sir Edmund Thorpe, and he was associated with the Norfolk knight Sir Miles Stapleton of Ingham and Bedale with whom he appeared in property transactions in 1397 and 1401.[17] Thorpe's association with Miles Stapleton, who was both a member of the family who were patrons of Rolle, and responsible for supporting Julian of Norwich, may explain Hilton's influence on this Norwich recluse, which is apparent in her *Revelations of Divine Love*. Thorpe may also have influenced Julian's follower Emma Stapleton, daughter of Miles Stapleton and anchoress of the Carmelite priory of Norwich: the Norwich Carmelite John Thorpe was one of Emma's counsellors in 1421; he was mentioned in Edmund Thorpe's will in 1393 along with Miles Stapleton and was probably a relative of the Cambridge lawyer.[18]

Some of the first readers of Hilton's works were naturally members of Arundel's circle. Thomas Fishlake translated the *Scale of Perfection* into Latin, possibly before Hilton's death in 1396, and probably with his consent and collaboration: several of the manuscripts of the Latin text have a summary of book two, written in the first person, and therefore presumably as a guide to the translator. Furthermore, the translation was undertaken at the instigation of another member of the Arundel circle, John Pole, the Carmelite of the Cambridge and Coventry convent.[19] The presence of Pole and Mr Richard Scrope at Coventry probably explains why the earliest surviving versions of the *Epistle on the Mixed Life* and book one of the *Scale* are found in the two closely related Simeon and Vernon manuscripts, which may have been produced in the scriptorium of Lichfield cathedral under the direction of Richard Scrope.[20] Both these manuscripts contain amalgamated versions of

15 Aston, *Thomas Arundel*.
16 Russel-Smith, 'Walter Hilton', 212ff; CPR, 1388 – 92, p. 508; Emden, *BRUC*, p. 586.
17 Russel-Smith, 210.
18 ibid. The connection between Dr J. Thorpe and the Carmelite of the same name may explain Bale's knowledge of Hilton's letter to Thorpe.
19 ibid, p. 206.
20 Simeon MS: BL MS Add. 22283; Vernon MS, Oxford, Bodl. Eng. poet. a.1. Doyle, 'A Survey', I, p. 245.

Rolle's *Form of Living* and *Ego Dormio,* which are only found in the authoritative volume of Rolle's works that was compiled at Lichfield from early Rolle manuscripts and from which the Vernon and Simeon manuscripts were descended, perhaps with the intervention of a single exemplar.[21] Other evidence which connects the Vernon and Simeon volumes to Lichfield is the presence of marginal notes referring to their use for copying parallel tests while they were still available to the scribes; in the margins to one of the works in these volumes, *Speculum Vitae,* there is a memorandum concerning a John Scryveyn, a property owner in St Paul's, a centre of the book trade, who copied three or four folios for Thomas Lord Henelay, a canon of Lichfield.[22] Scrope, while he was archbishop of York, also helped an early owner of Hilton's *Scale of Perfection,* Margery Pensax, an anchoress of Hawton, Nottinghamshire, near Thurgarton. In 1399 he made the unusual concession of allowing her to chose a new cell and a prelate to seclude her.[23] John Newton, whose collection of the works of Augustine, Bernard and the Victorines reveals the same theological influences that occur in Hilton's works, showed his interest in the mixed life by bequeathing to York minster library a copy of Maurice the prior of Kirkham's *Contra Salomita,* an abstract on the comparison of the two Marys which would be read in chapter. Newton also bequeathed a collection of Hilton's works to the canons, which were in the volumes of the works of Rolle and other northern writers; as all Newton's works were in Latin, it is possible that this volume contained the Latin epistles and Fishlake's translation of the *Scale.*[24] Thomas Dalby would also have been an early reader of Hilton's writings and probably visited Hilton at Thurgarton: four years after Hilton's death in 1400, Dalby made a bequest to the prior of Thurgarton. Dalby appears to have influenced the interest shown in the works of Hilton and his community at Thurgarton by his successor to the York prebend of Tocklington, Robert Wolveden, a clerk of Richard Scrope's along with Thomas Hilton. In 1432 Wolveden left a book of devotion written by Hilton to his executor John Langtofte, a York Minster priest and former chaplain of Thomas Walleworth; and he also made a bequest to his brother who resigned as prior of Thurgarton in 1434.[25] It is

21 Oxford, Bodl. Rawlinson Rawl. A. 389. See Doyle, 'A Survey', II, p. 162ff. for discussion of the Simeon and Vernon manuscripts.

22 ibid, II, p. 165. The name on fo.1 of Simeon is perhaps that of Arundel's sister, Joan Bohun, a widow who lived in retirement in the Ely diocese between 1377 and 1399, possibly at Denny. Doyle, 'A Survey', I, pp. 208 – 10.

23 *Reg. Scrope,* p. 73; Margery turned up in a London cell six months later and lived there for eighteen years.

24 Evidence of an interest in Hilton's works among the fellows of Peterhouse is provided in Univ. Coll. 28, a manuscript of a *Scale of Perfection* with an ownership note on fo. 137: 'Mr Thomas Ashes book of Peterhouse'.

25 Y.M.L. Reg. Test, I, fo. 235 and 152.

possible that the two Wolveden brothers encouraged an interest in Hilton and the contemplative life at this community. Alesia Deyncourt, who left a French bible to Mary Roos, was buried at Thurgarton in 1433 in a plot of her choice, and Robert Wolveden witnessed her will.[26] Just as they encouraged an interest in Rolle's works among the York Minster clergy, so Arundel's clerks established a tradition of studying Hilton at the minster. Robert Est, the chantry priest who studied Rolle's writings, also owned books by Hilton, probably books one and two of the *Scale*, which he left to his nephew. Many of the surviving fifteenth century manuscripts of the *Scale* and the *Epistle on the Mixed Life* are derived from the north-Midlands and are found in volumes containing pastoral material, which suggests ownership wy secular clergy of York.[27] The combination of such material with Hilton's works demonstrates how working priests were attempting to live mixed lives of contemplation and pastoral administration: one Latin volume from York contains chapters three and four of the *Epistle on the Mixed Life* and notes on parish administration; another, which had an obit on the fly leaf for John Marshall, a residentiary canon of York and the probable owner, contains books one and two of the *Scale* and Thoresby's *Lay Folk's Catechism*, neatly demonstrating the growing spiritual dimension to the lives of secular priests of York since Thoresby's time.[28]

Further evidence of the close connection between pastoral instruction for secular clergy and contemplative teaching is provided in the third book of *Cibus Anime*.[29] The compiler resolves the contradictions between the teachings of Rolle and Hilton by complementing their different strengths: Rolle's superior literary instincts for rhythm and images, demonstrated by the communication of strong emotional, sensory experiences; and Hilton's more cautious sense of social responsibility and perceptiveness, to produce, in a pastoral manual addressed to secular clergy, instructions close in tone to the *Epistola de Utilitate*, for a similar audience of ecclesiastical lawyers and administrators contemplating joining a religious order. The first section of the book uses quotations from Fishlake's Latin translation of the *Scale* to demonstrate, in a manner reminiscent of the *Epistle on Mixed Life*, the complexities of divorcing oneself from the world and counsels the reader against such

26 MS. Harl. 6970, fo. 29; cited Dugdale, *Monasticon*, VI, p. 190. Wolveden the prior of Thurgarton knew Henry Lord FitzHugh of Tanfield, who was interested in contemplative communities, including the Brigittine Order. In 1417 they both received a commission, along with Thomas Langley, bishop of Durham, who was also involved in the foundation of Syon, to control for four years the affairs of the priory of Torksey in Lincolnshire. *Reg. Chichele*, I, pp. 323 – 4. For Alesia Deyncourt's will see *Early Lincoln Wills*, p. 160.

27 Rawl. A355; Chetham 6690; Doyle, 'A Survey', I, p. 243ff.

28 Ashmole 751; Rawl. c. 285; Doyle, I, p. 243ff.

29 For further discussion see V. Gillespie, '*Cibus Anime*'.

extreme measures as giving away all of one's money instead of keeping sufficient to support life and avoid sin. Hilton is also used to analyse motivations behind the decision to leave the world and to provide practical advice on the discipline necessary to begin ascetic contemplation. The second half of the book deals with the contemplative life and the different stages of religious experience, and is therefore heavily dependent on Rolle's *Emendatio Vitae* and *Incendium Amoris*.[30] If the third book of *Cibus Anime* is by the author of the first two books, then it is likely that it was produced at York Minster; or it may have been an addition made by a monk of Mount Grace, which since 1398 had replaced Beauvale as the natural focus for the devotional aspirations of York Minster clergy, including Arundel and his clerks.

In the period between 1350 and 1400 there were other writers from the north-east with links with Hilton who were adjusting the hermit's calling for educated secular clergy. Although the author of *The Cloud of Unknowing* was writing primarily for recluses advanced in contemplative disciplines, he also addressed himself in this work to those living in the world who wished to know more about contemplative experience; and it is possible that the original recipient of *The Cloud* was a secular turned solitary.[31] He was described as previously being a servant of the 'special servants of God where he had learned to live more specially and ghostly in this service'; this may be a precise description of a Carthusian redditus of Beauvale, the only Carthusian monastery in the north in the fourteenth century; if so the recipient may have been Adam Horsley, the former exchequer clerk and recipient of Hilton's *Epistola aurea de origine religionis*,[32] which provides specific advice concerning the experience of the 'fire of love'. The author of the *Cloud* may have had connections with Hilton and his circle; both writers knew of one another: in *The Cloud* there is a reference to 'another place of another man's work', and there is considerable doctrinal interdependence between the works of both authors.[33] The similarity of dialect in the earliest manuscripts of *The Cloud* and *The Scale* implies, but does not prove, that both men spent much of their lives in the north-east Midlands.[34] The place where they met may have been Beauvale Charterhouse, the home of Adam Horsley. In any conversations they may have had the works of Rolle would have figured prominently. This circle may have produced another reflection

30 ibid.

31 *The Cloud of Unknowing*, p. 137.

32 Doyle, 'A Survey', I, pp. 274–77.

33 *The Cloud of Unknowing*, p. 198.

34 See Horstmann, *Yorkshire Writers*, I, pp. 175–83 for observations on the Yorkshire dialect of early manuscripts of *The Scale*. See also *The Cloud of Unknowing*, pp. ix–l for Hodgson's observations on the dialect of early manuscripts of *The Cloud of Unknowing*.

on the mixed life: the *Speculum Vitae humanae* is a compendium of the spiritual life which was compiled about 1390 and is attributed in the Syon catalogue to *Adam Cartusianus*; it was compiled in the mid-fifteenth century by John Gisburn, a residentiary canon of York.[35] Three Carthusian monks bearing this name were alive at the turn of the century, and the most likely candidate as author of the *Speculum*, considering the extensive use made of the works of Hilton in this work, is Adam Horsley of Beauvale. The *Speculum* provides, through use of quotations from the works of Rolle, St Bridget, Suso and Hilton, a summary of the spiritual options available to the devout, a debate on the conflicting claims of the active and contemplative lives and a summary of the values of the 'mixed life'. Other members of Arundel's circle besides Hilton may have articulated the spiritual needs and problems of public men. According to Bale and the Syon library catalogue, Richard Scrope was the author of a collection of letters while he was archbishop of York, and in the same catalogue Henry Bowet is credited with the authorship of a guide on the religious life.[36] John Newton compiled a table of chapter headings for Rolle's *Incendium Amoris* which summarized the hermit's teachings and provided some of his own independent insights on the inter-relationship between the active and contemplative lives.[37] In one of these headings Newton also defined the 'mixed life' — which Rolle never did — from the perspective of one who had remained active in the world. Another Carthusian writer who was probably a contemporary of Horsley's at Beauvale was the Carthusian monk whose objections to the potentially harmful aspects of Rolle's teachings were answered by the Norwich hermit Thomas Basset in *Defensorium contra Oblactractores*. The unique surviving copy of the *Defensorium* was written at Vadstena around 1400, which indicates that Rolle's critic was writing in the last two decades of the fourteenth century at the same time as Hilton and the author of the *Cloud*. Beauvale was probably at this time a centre for the study of Rolle's[38] works, which would have been introduced to the monastery by York monks such as Thomas Braystones, owner of the *Incendium Amoris*, who died at Beauvale in 1376.

Most of the religious writers of the north, from Nassington to Hilton and his circle, were at some time in their careers secular clergy, and their preoccupations were different from men who had spent their entire lives within a monastery. They were concerned with the tension between the

[35] Merton Coll. Oxf. MS. 204 fos. 4 – 180. The work also known as the *Speculum Spiritualium*. See Allen, *Rolle, Writings*, pp. 405 – 6. There was a manuscript of the *Speculum Spiritualium* at Mount Grace. See Brown, 'History of Mount Grace', 204. See also Oxford Bodl. Lib. MS. 450 (Summ. Cat. 2398).

[36] *Catalogue of Syon Library*, p. 126; Tanner, p. 658; Bale, VII, p. 36.

[37] Emmanuel Coll. Camb. MS. 35; Deanesly, *The Incendium Amoris*, pp. 60 – 62.

[38] Sargent, 'Criticism of Rolle', 160 – 87.

conflicting ties of public and private life to a greater degree, and they identified with the monk bishops Augustine and Gregory on a much more personal level. Furthermore, by writing about the secular life as well as the contemplative life, they were articulating the needs and conflicts of their fellow canonists and ecclesiastical administrators at Cambridge and York. It is possible to see in the penitential language used by many of these clerks when writing their wills, an admission of the difficulties they experienced in integrating contemplation with pastoral activity and the distractions of public life. Arundel, when he was archbishop of York, was, according to the Lollard who translated and adapted Ullerston's tract on bible translation between 1401 and 1407, ready 'on the morowe to leve up his office of chaunceler and forsake the world' after delivering a sermon at the funeral of Queen Anne about the negligence of the clergy.[39] In his will in 1414 Arundel described himself as a miserable sinner and an unworthy and lukewarm minister, and ordered a lowly funeral for his foetid, putrid cadaver; in the same year Newton, who recalled with gratitude Arundel's patronage, reflected on the uselessness of his life and the fact that all he could offer to God, in whose infinite mercy he trusted, was his perishable and worthless body.[40] In the following year Richard Pittes, describing himself as an unworthy canon of York, left his sinful soul, with as much devotion as possible, to his saviour and redeemer Jesus Christ, and his vile body to the cathedral; and in 1416 William Waltham described his corpse as a cadaver.[41] These extreme penitential statements were too rare in this period to be labelled as conventional rhetoric, and they bear some affinity with the language and sentiments of the letters Hilton wrote to those attempting to reconcile the active and contemplative lives. In the letter on the mixed life Hilton refers to the worthlessness and the pomp of this world and the dark night of fleshy corruption,[42] and in a letter (*Epistola de Leccione*) to a priest who subsequently became a solitary he pointed out his friends defects in order that he would turn in on himself to recognize his weakness, corruption and misery; and he urged the recipient of the letter to meditate on the bluntness and deformity into which he has fallen through sin and the bestial state of his soul.[43]

Two preoccupations emerge from the letters of Hilton and the wills of his fellow Cambridge canonists: a sense of failure and a hatred of the

39 Trin. Coll. Camb. MS. 333 ff. 26 – 30b, printed Deanesly, *Lollard Bible*, pp. 437 – 45. See p. 445.
40 *Sede Vacante Wills*, iii, pp. 81 – 2; Y.M.L. Reg. Test. I, fo. 168; cf. McFarlane *Lancastrian Kings*, p. 204 – 5.
41 Y.M.L. Reg. Test. I, fo. 172; fo. 139.
42 *Epistle on Mixed Life*, ed. Horstmann, pp. 265, 268.
43 Hilton, *Latin Writings*, ii, p. 238.

flesh. Behind this sense of failure lay the weight of pastoral responsibility which had increased from 1350 as northern clerks, who had grown up during the period of Thoresby's tenure of the see of York, placed greater demands on themselves and were in turn the subject of the increased expectations of an increasingly pious and knowledgeable laity. This can be seen in an incident described by Margery Kempe, who preached to the York chapter her favourite sermon about non-resident priests neglecting their pastoral office and exchanging their benefices like men of the world; Margery claimed that the chapter was moved and that the archbishop, Henry Bowet, was so smitten with remorse that he confessed to her in private begging her forgiveness.[44] The expression of hatred for the flesh represented a desire to reject the world and to participate in the eremitic life; but the feelings behind it were perhaps more complex and ambigious than those experienced by recluses of the thirteenth and early fourteenth century. Richard Rolle, when describing his first attempts to live as a hermit, drew on the hagiographic and ascetic traditions of the northern saints, and dramatically depicted his struggle to free himself from the temptations of the world in an encounter with the Devil in the form of a young woman. Behind this simple account of sexual temptation there lay an unambiguous understanding of the sacrifices and struggle necessary to become a recluse; but things were not so clear-cut for the religious writers of the late fourteenth century. Worldly temptation was something they could not hope to defeat or protect themselves from, because in attempting to reconcile contemplative aspirations with public careers, they continually compromised themselves; they therefore saw sin and temptation in a less dramatic way as something insidiously elusive unless defined as hypocrisy. When they confessed to this sin they captured their sense of unease with a world in which they could achieve success through a network of patronage and ambition, and satisfaction through the application of a comfortable conformist religion. In Hilton's Latin letters sexual anxieties are subsumed by this sense of hypocrisy, by the writer's awareness that he and other clergy faced a choice between exploiting patrons and benefices to do something socially useful, or to lead less socially useful and equally parasitical lives as hermits.

Wyclif's denunciation of patronage, church property and papal provisions amounted to a condemnation of the compromise of secular life, in which he felt he was heavily implicated. His preoccupation with the sin of hypocrisy meant that his tempting devil or antichrist took the form of holders of high office within the church and eventually the church itself. He resolved his own sense of his hypocrisy by turning against the church that had implicated him in his sin and by contrasting

44 *Book of Margery Kempe*, p. 316.

the visible church of antichrist to the invisible predestined church of the elect. The pastoral reforms within the church of York and burgeoning interest in contemplative life among secular clergy had created tensions distinctive to the late fourteenth century which would have emerged in confessions as well as the religious literature and wills. The Augustinian canons John of Bridlington and William Sleightholme, a prominent confessor in the diocese, discussed the way the compromises and complexities of the secular world blurred the issues of sin and temptation. Sleightholme asked the prior why the devil no longer appeared to men in visible form, and Thweng replied that men were once of firmer faith; but now they no longer needed the devil to help them to fall.

Enough evidence survives to indicate that there was an increasing commitment to the pastoral office, and a self-critical anxiety about the distractions and privileges of ecclesiastical office among Arundel's circle. This explains why leaders of the church like Philip Repingdon, a friend of Arundel's, could have held Wyclifite beliefs, and shows that Lollardy among court and university circles in the late fourteenth century was more of a state of mind among an educated elite aware of their superior education and privileges. There was, however, one crucial difference between the circles of Wyclif and Arundel: much of the thought of Wyclif was a socially negative outcome of his inner conflicts, and his followers, apart from translating the bible, produced little in the way of a constructive social programme. Arundel and his clergy transmitted their personal conflicts into a constructive programme of pastoral teaching, Hilton and his fellow administrators at Ely and York recognized that they were not in a position, as secular priests and lawyers, to follow eremitical counsel in an unqualified way; and in their cautious personal response to the teachings of Rolle and Suso they exerted a sober influence on their colleagues at York in the first three decades of the fifteenth century. In addition the eremitic movement presented them with an opportunity to satisfy the demands of the active and contemplative lives by asserting their control over it, a paradox that would not have escaped their attention. They were well positioned, through their friendship with Richard Scrope, to recognize that Rolle would be read and imitated outside their own circle; they would have been among the first to observe the wider implications of the eremitic movement, represented by the cult of Richard Rolle established between 1381 and 1383 and the activities of the Scrope and Stapleton families and Richmondshire anchoresses. Their pastoral reaction to Rolle's teaching would have a crucial influence on the subsequent development of contemplation in the north-east, and ultimately in the rest of the kingdom.

One of the most urgent problems that these clerks faced in the 1380s was the uncontrolled dissemination and copying of manuscripts of

Rolle's writings which produced many corrupt texts. In this period Rolle's most popular work, his English commentary on the psalms, was interpolated with Lollard doctrine, perhaps by the Leicester hermit William Smith, and copied. It is even possible that the Hussites were taking Rolle's works out of the country: one version of the *Incendium* ends with a colophon giving the approbation of the future Innocent VII, found otherwise only at Prague; this copy occurs in a paper volume containing a compilation, also unique to Prague, and many works connected with the Hussites.[45] There was therefore an urgent need for manuscript scholars who could correct faulty copies against authoritative texts, transcribe sound versions and establish an authoritative canon of Rolle's writings. Arundel's clerks developed the necessary skills at Peterhouse, Ely and York. They used tables as study aids and these could be used to compare the contents of different manuscripts. One of Arundel's chaplains compiled a table and index to Nottingham's commentary on Clement of Llanthony 'out of pity for students', and Richard Scrope provided tables for his letter collection.[46] John Newton may have encouraged the practice of compiling tables at Peterhouse and York. In 1406 John Harwood, an advocate of the court of York who referred to Newton as 'my special lord', left Newton 'a quire of paper ruled in red according to the letters of the alphabet, called a table',[47] The copies of Seneca's letters and Gregory's *Moralia* that he left to Peterhouse had tables and indexes.[48] Newton may have influenced the Peterhouse fellow Robert Alne who bequeathed a copy of Boethius's *De Consolatione* with tables to John Oteringham.[49] Members of this circle saw and developed the potential of cathedrals as centres of book production. Richard Scrope was probably responsible for the compilation of a number of manuscripts at Lichfield; John Clifford, the treasurer of York, bequeathed in 1393 an annotated missal and portifor which had been copied for him by the scribe John Grenealke; Thomas Dalby employed the chapter clerk Thomas Dautre as a scribe, and Robert Wolveden employed John Arson to copy books.[50] Some had scribal experience: John Oteringham was employed in 1396 writing documents; Thomas of Barnard Castle, who had been guilty of forging documents in his youth, was, as Arundel's registrar in Ely, responsible for the compilation of the bishop's register, parts of which he copied himself; and John Newton,

45 Vienna MS. 4483 (National Bibliothek); Allen, *Writings*, pp. 39 – 40.

46 B. Smalley, 'Which William of Nottingham', *Medieval and Renaissance Studies*, 3 (1954) 211.

47 Y.M.L. Reg. Test. I, fo. 142.

48 Y.M.L. Reg. Test. I, fo. 168; James, *Peterhouse Catalogue*, pp. 133, 164; Deanesly, p. 67. In Newton's first year as master the college compotus role has an entry 'for paper and parchment for rolls and *quaterni*'.

49 TE, II, p. 78.

50 TE, I, p. 166; Y.M.L. Reg. Test. I, fo. 124; 235; Aston, *Thomas Arundel*, p. 313; *Cal. Pap. Reg. Letters*, v, 1396 – 1404, p. 586.

as vicar general in York, wrote part of Arundel's register and copied a book of chronicles which was in the possession of John Harwood.[51]

Evidence that these clerks used their tables and scribal skills to correct faulty manuscripts and to exercise control on the production and circulation of Rolle's writings, survives in the work of John Newton. Newton would have regarded this as crucial pastoral work, not just because it could prevent lollard heresy from being confused with the teachings of a popular holy man, but also because it was a way of preventing people from taking Rolle's excessively emotional and sensational accounts of his mystical rapture — which was only one aspect of his teaching — out of context and giving it undue prominence. The nuns of Hampole had done this in their attempts to get Rolle canonized by compiling a biographical office from the rapturous passages in the *Incendium*.[52] Newton may have been involved in an attempt to ensure that this was not done with the liturgy at St Mary's Abbey in York, an important centre for Rolle's manuscripts. On 16 May 1390 Arundel conducted a visitation of the abbey and discerned some notable defects, as a result of which Newton and Thomas Walworth were appointed on 30 May to elucidate the ambiguities and variations which had been introduced into the divine service, reintroducing order by cutting out superfluities and adding 'whatever else was fitting in modern times'.[53] It is perhaps in the context of his work at St Mary's, which went on until 1398, and developments at Hampole that Newton's efforts in restoring and correcting the incomplete versions of the *Incendium Amoris* should be seen.

Although the only surviving translation of the *Incendium* dates from 1384, it is likely that there were other translations of this work at the time that Newton was treasurer of York. Margery Kempe's reference to having a priest read the *Incendium* to her long antedates Misyn's translation and suggests that this priest and others were translating and extemporizing this work. Newton witnessed the free use made of the *Incendium* not only in the Hampole nuns' biographical office, but in two separate tracts that were partially compiled from the *Incendium*. Shortly after Rolle composed the *Incendium*, a scribe compiled a treatise known as *Oleum effusum*, using Rolle's commentary on the canticles and the fervid autobiographical passages from chapters thirteen and fifteen of the *Incendium* that were later used by the Hampole nuns in compiling Richard Rolle's office. The scribe then made another separate work out of a letter of Anselm's to recluses and the non-autobiographical

51 Deanesly, *The Incendium Amoris*, pp. 68 – 72; Y.M.L. Reg. Test. fo. 142; see Ch. 5.

52 *The Ordinal and Customary of the Abbey of Saint Mary*, York, ed. L. McLachlan and J.B.L Tolhurst (Henry Bradshaw Society, lxxiii, lxxv, 1936 – 7), i, pp. 1 – 2.

53 Aston, *Thomas Arundel*, p. 287.

passages from the *Incendium*, which he probably intended for the use of a religious house. The rapid copying and circulation of Rolle's works, including both of these texts, confused later scribes who treated them as separate works of the Hampole hermit.[54] Eleven versions of the text containing the non-autobiographical passages of the *Incendium* and Anselm's letter survive, and Newton worked on one of them, restoring it to its original length by carefully inserting at relevant placed in the margins or on separate sheets the missing autobiographical passages from the *Incendium*.[55] In doing so he established that the text containing the commentary on the canticles and the autobiographical passages from chapters ten and fifteen of the *Incendium* was not a separate work of the hermit's, and alongside these autobiographical passages, which he had included in his restored version of the *Incendium*, he left the marginal direction referring his readers to the 'tract called *Oleum effusum*'.[56] Using the same methods, Newton also restored a short version of the *Judica Me Deus*, which was probably in the same manuscript. He added to the corrected manuscript a table of chapter headings summarizing the contents of the *Incendium*, which he presumably used to assist him in his corrections. The restored text of the *Incendium* was in a confused order, and Newton left the table with the corrected version to assist subsequent readers, prefacing it with the heading 'This table was added to this book by Mr John Newton'.[57] At the end of the *Incendium* Newton also supplied the following note: 'This was corrected from the book which the holy Richard of Hampole wrote in his own hand'.[58] The manuscript that Newton used to correct these corrupt versions of Rolle's works was probably the autographed volume of the *Incendium* and *Judica Me Deus* given by Henry Lord Scrope of Masham to Henry Lord FitzHugh in 1415; Newton may have had access to this volume through Richard Scrope.[59]

The manuscript that Newton actually worked on no longer survives, but it may have formed part of the volume of Rolle's works that Newton left to the cathedral, to be horned and nailed in the library in 1421.[60] It

54 Deanesly, pp. 60 – 62.

55 ibid; see Emmanuel Coll. Camb. MS. 35 fos. 76, 78, 79, 81, 84, 85b, 86, 97b, 98 and 99 for examples of the additions made by Newton to the corrupt text of the *Incendium*. These are not, as M. Deanesly thought, in the hand of Newton himself, but they are the corrections of a York minster clerk in the mid fifteenth century who was using Newton's methods on another copy of the short version of the *Incendium*. See following page.

56 Emmanuel Coll. Camb. MS. 35, fos. 16 – 19; Deanesly, p. 14.

57 ibid, fos. 59 – 61b.

58 ibid, fo. 19.

59 *Foedera*, IX, p. 276.

60 *York Fabric Rolls*, p. 45. The account roll for December 1421 contains a reference to the payment of Thomas Horner of Petergate and Ralph Lorymer of Coney Street, for horning and nailing the forty books given it the cathedral library by Newton: none of the books in Newton's 1414 bequest had therefore been lost.

was used by other cathedral clergy who studied the hermit's works. Newton's original chapter headings were used by Richard Misyn in his English translation of the *Incendium*, which he made in 1434 at the request of Margaret, a recluse of Heslington near York and a member of the York Corpus Christi Guild in 1429.[61] Misyn had many connections with York: like Newton he was a close associate of the archbishop of York, acting as a suffragan between 1458 and 1462 to Laurence Booth; and he was also a member of the Corpus Christi guild.[62] When he made his translation Misyn may well have used Newton's authoritative text, corrected from the original manuscripts. Newton's corrected manuscript would also have been used by cathedral clergy who were correcting short versions of the *Incendium*, and evidence of their work survives in an Emmanuel College manuscript written by two scribes, which contains Rolle's Latin works, the *Psalter, Melos Amoris, Super Mulierem Fortem, Contra Amatores Mundi*, and the short versions of the *Incendium* and *Judica Me Deus*. In this manuscript a third scribe has added in margins and on separate pages the missing passages of the *Incendium* and *Judica Me Deus*, together with Newton's marginal directions, presumably using Newton's corrected manuscript in the cathedral; this third scribe also left a copy of Newton's tables and headings in the Emmanuel manuscript to help subsequent readers to make sense of the restored texts.[63] The York Minster origin of the Emmanuel manuscript is suggested by the hands of all three scribes, which are all academic and suggest the professional notarial training of a cathedral. The high looped and rounded script of the three scribes suggests a date between 1450 and 1470 for the manuscript, and the script bears a close similarity to that of a copy of Rolle's *Emendatio Vitae* which was written by a public notary about 1470.[64] The hand of one of the scribes also bears a resemblance to that of John Gisburn, a precentor and residentiary canon of York in 1463,

61 *The Fire of Love and the Mending of Life, translated by Richard Misyn, 1434 – 5*, ed. R. Harvey (London, E.E.T.S., 1896); *Register of the Guild of Corpus Christi*.

62 ibid, p. 62; Emden, *B.R.U.O.*, II, p. 1286.

63 Emmanuel Coll. MS. 35, fos. 59 – 61b; see page 247.

64 Allen, *Writings*, p. 232; M. B. Parkes, *English Cursive Book Hands* (Oxford, 1969), p. 15; MS. Bodl. Lib. Oxford 456 (Sum. Cat. 2412), fo. 9. I am grateful to the late Mr Croft, librarian of King's College Cambridge, for his help in dating this manuscript. A. I. Doyle has also assigned the period 1450 – 70 for Emmanuel Coll. Camb. MS. 35 (Bull. John Rylands Lib., xxxix, (1957 310 – 11). This, and the fact that the manuscript was annotated by a Carthusian monk, James Greenhalgh, in the early sixteenth century, has led M. Sargent to assume that the Emmanuel College manuscript is of Carthusian origin and that it was corrected by an unknown Mr John Newton, who was presumably a monk of the order, between the years 1450 and 1470. There is no evidence for such a speculation, and in fact the connections of Newton and other northerners with Syon would explain why Greenhalgh, who worked in Syon library, was using the York treasurer's methods of manuscript study. M. Sargent, 'The Transmission by the English Carthusians of some Late Medieval Spiritual Writings', *J.E.H.*, 27 (1976), 234.

who compiled a volume of northern devotional works, including extracts from the works of Rolle, the *Speculum Vitae*, and the writings of Suso. Gisburn's manuscript also contains a table of chapter headings similar to those found in the Emmanuel manuscript, which summarize the contents of the *Speculum Vitae*.[65] It is therefore probable that the Emmanuel manuscript was copied and rapidly corrected from Newton's own manuscript within the York circle of John Gisburn and Robert Est, the chantry priest who owned Rolle autographs.

Other members of Newton's circle at York Minster studied and copied manuscripts using tables. William Waltham, Newton's executor, probably arranged the copying of parts of Rolle's Latin psalter when, in 1416, he left the residentiary canon Thomas Beelby, the owner of Rolle's autographed Latin Psalter, four marks and asked his executors to have interpolations from the psalter copied into his bible.[66] The Peterhouse fellow Robert Alne, who owned books with tables, may have compiled tables to aid the study of Rolle's *Melos Amoris*, which he received from Thomas Hebbenden: part of a glossary survives from an early fifteenth century manuscript of the *Melos* which was in York in the early seventeenth century and was compiled by 'different doctors'.[67] The other cathedral clergy who owned autographs and authoritative volumes, such as Robert Semer, William Gate and William Duffield, may have studied and compiled manuscripts of Rolle's writings.

By exerting such responsible control over the production of Rolle's works, the York clergy were able to give their qualified approval to the widespread dissemination of the teachings of Rolle and Suso. The remarkable congruity of thought between Walter Hilton and Julian of Norwich in terms of maturity, restraint and common sense, suggests that Hilton had a direct influence on the Norwich anchoress (he may have met her) in modifying the influence of Rolle. The circulation of Rolle's works in East Anglia in the beginning of the fifteenth century may have been encouraged by Newton and Wolveden who held benefices there.[68] Newton left his volume of Rolle's works to be horned and nailed in the cathedral of York where it was accessible for the local gentry. His friend Mr John Gylby may have left similar works among the collection of books that he left to his parish church of Knesall: the one specified work was a small psalter with devout prayers.[69] Nicholas Love

65 Merton Coll. Oxford, MS. 204, fos. 4 – 180; Gisborn, a residentiary canon 1463 – 1481, had been Archbishop William Booth's personal chaplain as early as 1451. Dobson, 'Residentiary Canons', 163.

66 Y.M.L. I, fo. 262.

67 TE, II, p. 78.

68 Emden, *B.R.U.C.*, pp. 421 – 22; Le Neve, *Fasti Ecclesiae Anglicanae*, IV, p. 27. Wolveden was appointed archdeacon of Norwich in 1406.

69 TE, II, p. 51.

probably supervised the translation of Suso's *Horologium*, which was completed at Mount Grace by 1419 while he was prior, and this work was circulated among the local gentry.[70] York clergy who were among the delegates at Constance secured formal approval for Rolle's teaching at a time when the English nation was anxious to establish the orthodoxy of Oxford and take a strong stand against heresy; one of the main topics of interest at Constance was the confirmation of St Bridget's canonization, and in pressing her claims, Geoffrey, the abbot of Byland in Cleveland, compared her revelations to those of Rolle, quoting the opening lines of the prologue to the *Incendium Amoris*. Other northern delegates may also have proclaimed the sanctity of Rolle's experiences and introduced his works to the European delegates. Thomas Spofforth, the abbot of St Mary's, a centre for the study of Rolle's works, gave his chaplain Christopher Braystones an indulgence of forty days for devout readers of the *Incendium*, which he 'so highly esteemed'.[71] However, the approval of the York clergy was guarded, especially when they considered the implications of the wide circulation of Rolle's more extreme works. They were perhaps responsible for the fact that the most popular of his writings in the fifteenth century were the more moderate commentaries on the psalms and the book of Job. They certainly recognized that the control they had exerted over the production of the manuscripts of the *Incendium* needed to be applied to the teachings themselves, and without this, it is doubtful if they would have permitted the dissemination of his writings.

The potential that Rolle's works had to inspire the enthusiasm of laymen would have been immediately apparent. In his autobiographical accounts of the first steps he made to become a hermit and his first sensational religious experiences there is an element of amateur exuberance. He also used his charismatic personality to arouse the admiration of a circle of followers among the Yorkshire gentry. By the 1380s admiration for his teaching and for the recluse as a holy man was growing and could be seen in the cult of Rolle and in the increasing incidence of patronage of recluses in the diocese. However, although he inspired popular support and even emulation, he made no real attempt to tailor his teachings for those who had neither the capacity or opportunity to lead a full contemplative life. In spite of his exuberance, Rolle used elitist language and maintained the tone of professional mystique when addressing a circle of disciples who were not amateurs; furthermore his descriptions of religious experience were vague and

70 Lovatt, 'The Influence of Rhineland Spirituality', p. 168; Zeeman, *Archiv fur das Studium der Neueren Sprachen*, p. 117–18.

71 Lovatt, 'The Influence of Rhineland Spirituality', p. 93. Spofforth was a monk of St Mary's during Newton's visitation of the abbey; Allen, *Writings*, p. 214; Deanesly, p. 52.

used primarily to assert his own prestige as an expert in the contemplative discipline. He provided little practical advice or help to those in the active life, and little in the way of cautionary advice for potential followers. This lack of guidance must have been alarming to the northerners in Arundel's circle. The libraries of these men reveal them to have been versatile scholars who were accustomed to recognize the general ethical principles governing different professions, and who attempted to give these disciplines a social and human dimension. During their years at Cambridge, Ely and York they applied these criteria to the professional teachings of the recluse and adapted them for the less educated priests and laymen outside their own refined circle. This was a pastoral programme that represented an important advance upon the educational policies of Thoresby and his clergy.

Arundel's clerks, in their capacity as professional advocates in ecclesiastical court and as archdeacons, vicars general, and later as bishops and archbishops, must have viewed with alarm the prospect of enthusiastic followers of Rolle neglecting their social and domestic responsibilities. They attempted to demonstrate that participation in the eremitic life was compatible with other public roles besides those of priest and lawyer, including those of landlord, tenant, householder and housewife. One writer from the north-east with possible links with Hilton's circle was the translator of the *Abbaye du saint Espirit*. The original, written at the turn of the fourteenth century, was one of the earliest works to provide guidance to those outside the monastery, and was addressed to sisters who would be in religious orders but for poverty, fear of families or marriage bonds.[72] The *Abbaye* attempted to show such people the possibility of living the religious life in the spirit through an allegorical description of a convent, built on the foundations of conscience in the heart of a person living an active life. The translator, who was writing in the period between 1350 and 1400, added some of Rolle's characteristic descriptions of the warmth of God's love in an attempt to demonstrate the possibility of attaining such experiences in the active life.[73] Walter Hilton similarly replaced the monastic vows with the dictates of conscience in a letter to a laywoman, an account of which precedes a copy of the English version of the *Abbey of the Holy Ghost* in one manuscript.[74] Hilton's *Epistle on Mixed Life* was partially intended to help secular clergy, but he envisaged a wider audience and originally dedicated it to a 'worldly lord', a gentry householder who was probably

[72] Pantin, *The English Church*, p. 253.
[73] For the English version see *Yorkshire Writers*, I, pp. 321 – 37; *Religious Pieces*, ed. Perry, pp. 49 – 56.
[74] Richle, *English Mystics*, p. 19; MS. Harl. 2406.

a widower.[75] Hilton gave this squire specific and pragmatic advice on how to integrate his contemplative enthusiasm with his social responsibilities so that neither his personal stability, nor his household and family were adversely affected. More exhortations of this nature were provided in another late fourteenth century English prose work called *Of Angel's Song,* which was probably by Hilton or one of his followers from the same area: the work survives in six unrelated manuscripts, four of which are in northern dialect, and the ascription to Hilton occurs in an early sixteenth century manuscript.[76] The author addressed himself in this work to those who did not have the time or the expertise to master the contemplative techniques expounded by Rolle and the author of the *Cloud;* reapplying an old doctrine of the contemplative life he warned against trying to use these techniques in an effort to have a religious experience and suggested that instead of striving too hard they should regard experiences, if and when they came, as gifts of grace.[77]

Hilton and his circle also concerned themselves with the psychological and emotional implications of Rolle's idosyncratic writings. In *The Cloud of Unknowing, The Scale of Perfection* and the treatise *Of Angel's Song,* warnings are given to the followers of Rolle about the dangers of self-deception inherent in attempting to bring about the physical experiences of *calor, dulcedo* and *canor.* By concerning themselves with religious experience, Hilton and other clerks in Arundel's circle were attempting to guide people along a path of religious sensibility which took them away from the elitist metaphysical abstractions of the author of *The Cloud* and the ecstasies that Rolle claimed could be attained through fasting, repetition of the Holy Name or at the elevation of the host; instead they directed them towards the normal emotional responses that were appropriate to married couples and their families. Christ's passion was therefore seen to be the focal point of the piety of such people: it could arouse the charitable impulses towards dependents and the less fortunate on which the stability of parish society depended. Much of the pastoral work that Arundel and his clerks did towards the end of the fourteenth century was concerned with the provision of meditations on Christ's life which would achieve this objective.

Such work was an urgent priority by the 1380s when the popularity of Rolle's English translation on the psalms was becoming evident and the

75 For printed editions of *The Epistle on the Mixed Life,* see *Prose Treatises of Rolle,* ed. Perry, pp. 19 – 42; *Yorkshire Writers,* I, pp. 264 – 79.

76 There are two printed editions of this work: *Yorkshire Writers,* I, pp. 175 – 183; *Of Angel's Song,* ed. T. Takamiya (Tokyo, 1977). The four surviving manuscripts are B. Mus. Ms. Add. 127592 (West Yorks.); C.U.L., Ms. Dd. (Westmorland) and Linc. Cath. Lib. Ai 17 (fo. 17ff.). The last three manuscripts contain *The Scale of Perfection.* See Takamiya, p. 7.

77 *Yorkshire Writers,* p. 177ff; *Of Angel's Song,* p. 13.

circle of Wyclif had translated the bible into English. Arundel and his clerks would have been concerned about the implications of the wide circulation of both of these works. The English psalter contained Rolle's idiosyncratic responses to the scriptures, and a vernacular Lollard bible in the hands of the less educated was potentially a more socially divisive threat than eremitic teaching because it could be used to criticise the church and its institutions. They therefore recognized the need for a translation that harmonized and expanded the four gospels into a narrative of Christ's life that could be used in private meditation and for communal reading in religious houses and devout households. The attitudes towards the study of the bible and its pastoral application shared by the York Minster clergy towards the end of the fourteenth century were an important factor in the provision of affective meditations on the life of Christ. In the first half of the fourteenth century pastoral theology, as seen in preaching manuals such as the *Oculus Sacerdotis* and *Speculum Vitae* with their complex schemes of vices and virtues, was still influenced by a specialized and technical allegorical understanding of scripture. But in this period commentators such as Nicholas Trevet and the Franciscan Nicholas of Lyre concentrated on the literal and historical sense of the bible, and analysed events from the perspective of psychological motivation; this was an essential precondition to an affective response to the New Testament.[78] The libraries of York ecclesiastics show that they were in sympathy with this method of studying scriptures: the commentaries of Nicholas de Lyre were owned by Robert Ragnall, Richard Holme, a canon of York, Robert Alne and John Newton, who bequeathed the commentaries of Lyra and Trivet to York Minster library.[79] Arundel's circle in particular studied the principles of writing gospel harmonies as a means of overcoming the obstacles to meditation provided by the difficulties and contradictions of the four gospel narratives. The gospel harmony and commentary of Clement of Llanthony, *Unum ex quatuor,* was still used in the fifteenth century, and his commentary, discussing the relationship between the gospels, was adapted early in the fourteenth century by William of Nottingham into a comprehensive apparatus for the study of the scriptures.[80] Thomas Arundel owned the postills of Nottingham which descended into the hands of Thomas Langley, bishop of Durham; and John Waltham, the sub-dean of York, left his old college of Balliol *unum librum concordantiorum Nottyngham Super Evangelia.* A table of contents was compiled for this manuscript by Arundel's chaplain to aid

78 B. Smalley, 'The Church's Use of the Bible in the Middle Ages', in D. E. Nineham (ed.) *The Church's Use of the Bible, Past and Present* (London, 1963), p. 64.

79 TE, III, p. 89; TE, II, pp. 96, 78; TE, I, p. 366.

80 B. Smalley, 'Which William of Nottingham', 200 – 10.

students and dedicated to the archbishop, who is depicted above the tables sitting in his pastoral chair and holding in his arms the book, which is open at the page saying *quod factum in ipso vita erat*.[81] These canon tables were designed for the purpose of aiding meditation on the four gospels; and it is significant that members of Arundel's circle such as John Newton had designed tables for reading Rolle's works. They clearly saw the creation of a gospel harmony as a pastoral responsibility and turned to the prolix and febrile meditations of the Franciscans for help.

This had of course been done earlier by Rolle in his *Meditations on the Passion*; but Rolle responded to the Fransciscan meditations with poetic intensity, developing vivid and personal images in a manner which Julian of Norwich was to emulate; Hilton, on the other hand, accompanied his Franciscan inspired meditations with spiritual advice that was characteristically practical and full of common sense. The *Stimulus Amoris*, or *Prick of Love*, attributed in two early northern manuscripts to Hilton and found in the Vernon and Simeon manuscripts, was freely expanded by Hilton from James of Milan's *Stimulus Amoris* into a book of thirty-eight chapters consisting of meditations on the Passion and a treatise on the spiritual life.[82] In this work Hilton was concerned to ensure that meditation on the Passion helped to reinforce a sense of social duty, and he reminded his readers to wash Christ's feet by attending to subjects and tenants.[83]

The most influential version of Christ's life to be produced by Arundel's circle was *The Mirror of the Blessed Lyfe of Jesu Crist*, Nicholas Love's paraphrase of the Pseudo-Bonaventuran *Meditationes Vitae Christi*. The circumstances surrounding the composition of this work, which was begun in 1408, suggest that Arundel and his clergy were consciously asserting control over the production and circulation of religious literature. In the same year Arundel published a provincial constitution entitled *Quia insuper nova via* in which he forbade the reading of any books composed since Wyclif's time in schools, hostels, halls or any other place in the province of Canterbury until they were examined by the universities. In another decree, *Periculosa res est*, he enacted that no one could translate on their own authority any holy text into English, and no such translation made since the time of Wyclif could be read until it was approved by the local bishop.[84] *The Mirror*,

81 ibid, 211; Balliol Coll. Oxford, MS. 33. A note on the fly leaf in a handbook of 1400 records Waltham's donation. For Waltham's will see Y.M.L. Reg. Test., fo. 166. For the depiction of Arundel in his pastoral robes see Pacht and Alexander, *Illuminated Manuscripts*, III, plate LXXXIII, 739 (9).

82 Doyle, 'A Survey', I, pp. 207 – 13.

83 J. A. W. Bennett, *Poetry of the Passion* (Oxford, 1982), p. 60.

84 *Concilia*, ii, p. 284 – 86.

which met with Arundel's approval as a spiritual guide and a gospel translation, was their answer to the Lollard Bible. Discussion between the two men on this subject may have occurred in 1409 when Arundel joined the Mount Grace fraternity: Love's completed work was dedicated to 'some devout soules', a description that would fit the lay fraternity of the house.[85] In 1410 Love travelled to London with his completed translation and submitted it to Arundel for his inspection, and the archbishop of Canterbury confirmed that it should be distributed to edify the faithful and to confute the heretics or Lollards.[86] There were similarities between this partnership of Arundel and the monk of Mount Grace and that of Thoresby and Gaytrick of St Mary's Abbey: Thoresby and Gaytrick provided, in the *Lay Folk's Catechism*, a guide to the moral principles and social conduct of the active life; Love and Arundel were responsible for a guide to the emotional and spiritual values appropriate to those living 'a perfighte actyf lyfe'.[87] Love, as a lay official of a monastery engaged in such external business of the house as endowments, privileges, lay servants and patrons, was in a position to appreciate the religious needs of laymen. His translation abbreviated the one hundred and sixty chapters of the Meditationes to sixty-three; he added imaginative additions of his own to aid the meditation of 'common persones and symple souls', who needed to be fed with the 'mylke of lygte doctrine not with sadde mete of grete clergie and of hige contemplacioun'.[88] Love warned his readers about the dangers of the amateur enthusiasm for the eremitic life and striving for supernatural experiences, and provided them with an alternative source of spiritual fulfilment in a realistic biography of Christ; by concentrating on tangible human relationships, he hoped to arouse objective and affective responses to the Passion.

This circle may also have been responsible for providing gentry householders with practical advice on how to structure their meditations on the Passion around their daily work. *The Holy Boke Gratia Dei* was written in prose that reflects the influence of Rolle, and the author wrote the treatise after the appearance of the English version of *The Abbey of the Holy Ghost*, from which he borrowed.[89] The surviving manuscripts suggest that the work was written at Mount Grace, where it was copied,

[85] Thompson, *The Carthusian Order in England*, p. 339.
[86] M. Deanesly, *The Lollard Bible* (Cambridge, 1920), pp. 325 – 30; M. Deanesly, 'Vernacular Books in England in the Fourteenth and Fifteenth Centuries', *M.L.R.*, xv, (1920), 353.
[87] *The Mirror of the Blessed Lyfe of Jesu Crist*, ed. Powell, pp. 8 and 165.
[88] ibid, p. 158.
[89] *The Holy Boke Gratia Dei*, ed. M. L. Arntz, in *Elizabethan and Renaissance Studies*, ed. J. Hogg, (Salzburg, 1981). For another edition see *Yorkshire Writers*, I, pp. 305 – 21.

probably during Love's years as prior between 1410 and 1417.[90] The earliest manuscript, which contains copies of the *Holy Boke* and Love's *Mirror*, was in the possession of the Ingelby family, the patrons of Mount Grace, and on one of the folios there is the name of a *conversus* of the house at the time of the dissolution.[91] The other two independent surviving manuscripts are also, on the basis of linguistic evidence, from the north-east.[92]

Arundel and his clerks were concerned that the teachings of the recluse, especially on religious experience, would degenerate, as they were disseminated to the less sophisticated, into a crude materialistic religion in which people strove for spurious physical experiences of warmth or sweetness and practised deception on themselves and others. Through their writings on the Passion, these clergy found a way of teaching gentry householders to rely on what was both inside themselves and yet fundamentaly true and consistent with external reality. However, they also needed to impart this teaching to a wider audience that had neither the education or financial means to read such works as the *Mirror*. They saw, in the cult of the Eucharist, how widespread the spiritual problems they had diagnosed among some of the followers of Rolle really were, and they realized that their opportunity to exert a control on religious sensibility at a fundamental level lay in their influencing attitudes towards the host. As lay devotion culminated in the cult of the Eucharist in the fourteenth century the host was regarded by the laity as a corporeal reality: it was worshipped behind rood screens and venerated as a relic when it was taken on processions. Rolle and John Thweng may have encouraged a more spiritual and interior contemplation of the mysteries of the mass, but among their less sophisticated followers, such as Margery Kempe, they simply aroused ostentatious displays of ecstasy or grief that were equally extroverted. The reaction of Wyclif to the cult of the Eucharist made a moderate solution an urgent priority. Regarding all this as deception and a gross material misrepresentation of a spiritual reality, he tried to demonstrate this reality in the language of optics by showing that the host's significance was spiritual in the sense that it was a reflection of Christ's heavenly body: the host remained on the altar after

90 *V.C.H., Yorks.*, III, p. 192; C.P.R., 1410 – 16; C. Zeeman, 'Nicholas Love: A Fifteenth Century Translator', *Review of English Studies* (1915), 118.

91 G. R. Keiser, 'The Holy Boke Gratia Dei', *Viator*, 12 (1981), 289 – 317; Huntington Lib. MS. 148.

92 Linc. Cath. Lib. MS. A.1.17; Arundel 507. For description of the manuscripts and a discussion of their dialects, see *The Holy Boke Gratia Dei*, ed. Arntz, pp. vi – xl; H. E. Allen, 'Some Fourteenth Century Borrowings from the Ancren Riwle', *M.L.R.*, xviii (1923), 6.

consecration as bread and wine like the surface of a reflecting mirror.[93] Arundel — whose reverence for the host was noted by the St Alban's chronicler — and the other clerks of his circle probably had an equally profound understanding of the spiritual significance of the Eucharist; but although they shared Wyclif's distaste for the material debasement of religion, they opposed his teachings on the Eucharist, not because of the metaphysical subtleties of his argument, but because of their asocial implications. He reduced the sacramental significance of the host and treated it as a stimulus to internal prayer, thereby negating the traditional social functions of the host.[94] Daily mass, which followed confession, restitution and penance, affirmed the individual's reconciliation with his community; and the annual procession of the host, accompanied by the performance of cycle plays by the competing craft guilds and culminating in the celebration of mass, demonstrated the social concord of the towns of the north in the fourteenth century. Wyclif's neglect of the social dimension to religion reflected his relative isolation within the theology schools of Oxford, but Arundel and his clergy were working churchmen; when Arundel, in an incident described by the St Alban's chronicler and Walsingham, rebuked the courtiers at Coventry for turning their backs on the host when it was being carried through the streets, he was objecting to their asocial conduct rather than their blasphemy, and he compared it to the pageantry and devotion of the great processions of the host that he had witnessed in the streets of the strongly communal Italian towns.[95] He and his clergy were confronted by two extremes of religious behaviour that coalesced around attitudes to the Eucharist: on the one hand there was a religion that was introverted, elitist and socially divisive or unhealthily private and emotional; on the other hand there was the crudely material popular worship of relics and idols. They characteristically steered a middle way and found a compromise consistent with their philosophy of the mixed life.

Nicholas Love and his fellow clergy, who were familiar with figurative and metaphysical concepts, did not answer Wyclif with dogma. Like him they saw the host as a mirror; but instead of providing a mirror image of the heavenly body of Christ within the individual mind, they saw it reflecting the earthly body of Christ that existed within a community held together by the charity that Christ showed in his

93 J. I. Catto, 'John Wyclif and the Cult of the Eucharist', in K. Walsh and D. Wood, eds. *The Bible in the Medieval World* (Oxford, 1985), pp. 273 – 75.

94 J. Bossy, 'The Mass as a Social Institution', *Past and Present*, (1983) 29 – 61; M. James, 'Ritual, Drama and Social Body in the Late Medieval English Town', *Past and Present*, xcviii (1983), pp. 3 – 29.

95 *Cronica Monasterii S Albani*, ed. H. T. Riley, (R.S., 1866), pp. 391 – 94; McFarlane, *Lancastrian Kings*, p. 221.

passion. The Guild of Corpus Christi was founded by the clergy of York in 1408 as a means of popularizing this image of the host. This popular guild was administered by the clergy of York: in the year of its foundation there were seventy-five clerical members, from whom a master and six priests were appointed to supervise the Corpus Christi celebrations.[96] Arundel may have encouraged the foundation, and he would have certainly approved. His former servants were influential figures in the guild: in 1412 John Newton, Stephen Scrope and Robert Wolveden all joined, along with Thomas Spofforth, the abbot of St Alban's.[97] The residentiary canons, whose chapter house was illuminated with scenes from Christ's life, may have influenced the composition of the guild's ordinances which claimed for the Eucharist the function of arousing compassion for Christ's life and the poor of the city: the guild was responsible for maintaining ten poor people and finding beds daily for seven paupers.[98] Love's *Mirror,* which was begun in the same year as the guild's foundation, would have helped guild members to comprehend the host in this way, and it is significant that many members owned copies including Thomas and John Dautre, Sir Robert Roos and Elizabeth Sewerby.[99] One guild member, John Malster, a priest of the chantry of St Thomas Martyr in St Saviour's church since 1402, transcribed a copy of the *Mirror* and showed his appreciation of the link made in the work between affective piety and social charity when he bequeathed it to the inmates of St Leonard's hospital.[100] The possibility that Love composed *The Mirror* for the guild is strengthened when it is considered that he appended to the *Mirror* a treatise on the Eucharist. In this work he claimed that the prime function of the Eucharist was to instill into communicants the memory of Christ's life in the world; and in both *The Mirror* and *The Treatise on the Sacrament* he identified Christ's body with the social body through charity and compassion.

In their attempts to demonstrate the figurative significance of the Corpus Christi procession as an image of Christ's charity and the social concord of the city, the York clergy could rely on the dramatic witness to both of these principles provided in the plays of Christ's Passion, staged by the different guilds on the days of the procession, or, after 1423, on the following day. By the end of the fourteenth century the Passion was

96 H. F. Westlake, *The Parish Guilds of Medieval England,* (London, 1919), p. 54.

97 For record of membership see *Register of the Guild of Corpus Christi*. For the objectives of the original founders see *Extracts from the Municipal Records of the City of York,* ed. R. Davies, pp. 227 – 29.

95 ibid, pp. 15, 30, 241, 246; Westlake, p. 54. For details of the window of York Chapter house, see J. Knowles, *Essays in the History of the York School of Glass Painting* (London, 1936).

99 TE, II, p. 59 and 96; B.I.H.R. Prob. Reg. 2, fo. 413.

100 *Calendar Reg. Scrope,* p. 33; B.I.H.R. Reg. Scrope, fo. 34v.

becoming centrally important in the cycle, and it is possible that Love's meditations were written with their dramatic potential in mind. Franciscan preachers were fond of dramatic gestures, and the dramatic and pictorial possibilities of the original Latin version of the *Meditationes* were enhanced by illustrations in manuscripts of Love's translation, which contained many dramatic incidents, passages of dialogue and even costume directions.[101] This suggests that Love was inspired by the York plays and perhaps hoped to influence their development. He certainly influenced the latest and most important reviser of the York cycle, who between 1415 and 1431 contributed a number of original plays in alliterative verse, including eight on the Passion.[102] The identity of the playwright, known as the 'York Realist', remains unknown; he was probably a clerical member of the guild like William Revetour.[103] These eight plays show a considerable realism in the depiction of a contemporary setting for the Passion, and they concentrated on the mental and emotional processes of characters, integrating human emotions and compassion with religious meditation. Their author had the same intention as Nicholas Love, to arouse affective meditations on the Passion; in the Corpus Christi cycle these would reach a climax in the *Mortificacio Christi*.[104] If they were written before 1426 these plays would have earned the approval of the Franciscan preacher William Melton who praised the religious value of the York Corpus Christi plays in a sermon delivered in York.[105] Devotional innovations also occurred in the Corpus Christi plays of the nearby town of Wakefield, which were performed in the natural amphitheatre of the disused quarry of Goodbower. This cycle may have originated from the pastoral initiative of either Archbishop Arundel or Archbishop Scrope and their circles. Towards the end of the fourteenth century the town, anxious to demonstrate its new found prosperity from the cloth industry, borrowed and adapted the York cycle using pastoral manuals of the diocese: the play of Christ's exposition of the Ten Commandments in

101 Bennett, *Poetry of the Passion*, p. 55.

102 C. Davison, 'The Realism of the York Realist and the York Passion', *Speculum* (1975), 270ff; the eight passion plays that the 'York Realist' wrote were plays XXVI, XXVIII – XXXIII inclusive, and XXXVI of the Corpus Christi cycle. This cycle survived in B.M. MS. Add. 35290, a formal copy made between 1430 and 1440 for the corporation of the city from single plays in the hands of guilds or trading companies. See Craig, *Religious Drama*, p. 234.

103 TE, II, p. 117.

104 Craig, *English Religious Drama*, pp. 205 – 10. These plays also survive in a mid-fifteenth century manuscript that is a formal register of the plays collected from individual trading companies. The plays written by the 'Wakefield Master' are Noah (number III in the cycle), Prima Pastorum (XII), Secunda Pastorum (XIII), Herod (XVI), and Colphizacio.

105 E. K. Chambers, *The Medieval Stage* (Oxford, 1903), ii, 402.

the temple was expanded using the exposition found in *Speculum Christiani*.[106] The most important devotional expansion to the original York cycle was made around 1430 by the 'Wakefield Master' who added five new, realistic plays to the Wakefield cycle that demonstrated the desirability of integrating religious piety with a full range of honest, human emotions and a sophisticated sense of humour and humanity.[107] The Corpus Christi celebrations, and especially the Passion plays, represented the culmination of the York clergy's teaching on the mixed life. They were the means by which the laity, and many priests, could be weaned from their preoccupations with supernatural and material phenomena towards an appreciation of the symbolic functions of religious ritual, which could nurture a religious sensibility that integrated the interior and the external, that is, normal healthy human impulses with the social life of the community.

Between 1380 and 1430 households of York clergy had assumed responsibility for communicating and adapting eremitic teaching for the laity through contemplative literature and such non-literary forms of religious expression as the Corpus Christi processions and the cycle plays. In doing so they elaborated considerably on the rudimentary education that Thoresby and his clergy provided for laymen in an attempt to create a more stable parish society. Nevertheless, increased lay piety and initiative, in its extreme manifestations, posed a threat to the very social stability that the pastoral bishops of the mid-fourteenth century had helped to create. This could be observed in the activities of the lay preachers during the peasant's revolt of 1381; in the sermons of the Lollard hermits, Smith and Swinderby, and in the devotional novelties of Northern Europe and Italy, represented by the Waldensians, the Flagellants and the Free Spirit heresies. Arundel and his clerks therefore had to concern themselves with what people were thinking and feeling; and, in distinguishing genuine piety from heresy and religious extremism, they were responding in a judicial and pragmatic way to problems they regarded as being social rather than exclusively abstract and theological.

Since the thirteenth century bishops and their officials were responsible for supervising recluses and ensuring that their activities could be accommodated within their local communities. This involved conducting investigations into potential recluses' suitability for an eremitical life, ensuring that they had adequate means of support and that they were not deserting dependents. The bishop or one of his officials conducted the rite of enclosure, and subsequently they supervised all of the

[106] A. C. Cawley, 'Middle English Versions of the Decalogue with Reference to the English Corpus Christi Cycles', *Leeds Studies in English* New Ser., VIII (1975) 129–40.

[107] Craig, *Religious Drama*, pp. 205–10.

anchorites, contacts with the community such as approving grants of alms, granting licences to hear confession, and granting the recluse premission to leave or change a cell.[108] Arundel and his clergy performed all these duties: as bishop of Ely, Arundel issued a forty day indulgence in 1376 to all those who would contribute to the support of William Cower, a hermit of Canterbury; he personally received the vows of chastity of Lady Isabella Countess of Suffolk in 1381 and Catherine, widow of William Bernard in 1385 (when Thomas Dalby was also present);[109] and Richard Scrope, besides his patronage of Margery Pensax while archbishop of York, enclosed Richard Peckard in 1390 at the Blackfriars in Lancaster while he was bishop of Lichfield, and licensed him to hear confessions.[110] However, these clerks were also faced with the more complex problems of evaluating the religious convictions of professional recluses, and more dauntingly still, those of pious laymen who were attempting to live like recluses without ecclesiastical supervision, direction and approval.

Their most urgent concern was to prevent the teachings of Rolle, and indeed their own instructions on the contemplative life, from being over-simplified and distorted by over-enthusiastic and irresponsible followers. Hilton, while still at Cambridge, was familiar with the excesses indulged in by some members of the Brethren of the Free Spirit in Picardy and the Rhineland and referred to them in his translation of Louis Fontibus, by condemning those who considered they had the 'freedom of spirit' to perform deeds of immorality.[111] He was clearly concerned about the possibility of distortion of some of his own characteristic assertions: in the *Scale of Perfection* he advised followers to progress beyond religious customs and not to value these more highly than 'the fredom of thin hert'.[112] The author of the *Cloud* was also concerned with the problem of distinguishing extreme piety from heresy and referred to heretics as 'the devil's contemplatives'.[113] The rest of Arundel's circle concerned themselves with such distinctions in a more practical sphere in their diocesan work. In July 1389 John Waltham, bishop of Salisbury, assisted by Cambridge clerks Robert Ragenhill, the archdeacon of Dorset, and Ralph Selby, Waltham's executor, examined the opinions of a self-appointed lay preacher, William Ramsbury, who had slept with several women while believing, in accordance with one of

108 Warren, *Anchorites*, p. 45ff.
109 E.D.W. Reg. Arundel, 1893 – 96, pp. 53, 153; 1896, p. 47.
110 *V.C.H. Lancs.*, ii, p. 103.
111 *Eight Chapters on Perfection*, ed. F. Kuriyagawa (Tokyo, 1971), ii, 196 – 212.
112 *The Chastizing of God's Children*, ed. J. Balzire and E. College (Oxford, 1957), p. 37ff; Riehle, *Middle English Mystics*, p. 25ff. R. E. Lerner, *The Heresy of the Free Spirit* (Berkeley, 1972). *Scale of Perfection*, ii, pp. 12, 21, 76, 99.
113 *Chastizing*, p. 40.

the tenets of the sect of the Free Spirit that it was not a sin carnally to know a woman.[114] The delicate and patient enquiries that they were prepared to make in order to give a cautious approval to sincere followers of Rolle who were untainted by heresy and who did not represent a threat to society, is best illustrated in their treatment of a Lynn burgher's daughter, Margery Kempe.

Norfolk, like the diocese of York, was an important source of benefices for Cambridge graduates, and Margery's activities were carefully supervised by Cambridge scholars like Alan or Lynne. She was also strongly influenced by the spiritual movements of the north-east: she visited Yorkshire in the summer of 1413 and was in York for the performance of the Corpus Christi plays; she left the city on 23 July for Bridlington where she visited the shrine of St John of Bridlington and her confessor, William Sleightholme. Margery visited York diocese again in September 1417, by which time she would have had the works of Rolle and Hilton read to her, including the *Incendium Amoris*.[115] Margery was especially influenced by Richard Rolle: in one of her revelations God says to her 'Thou art to me a singular love and therefore have a singular grace in heaven'; this term singular was used by Rolle to apply to the third and highest form of love when the soul feels the fire of Christ's love as a 'finger feels a flame burning'. Margery repeatedly claimed to have experienced this. She was also influenced by her interviews with Sleightholme and imitated St John of Bridlington to the extent of publicly demonstrating her ability to weep at the elevation of the host. However, the Lollard movement and rumours of religious excesses on the Continent helped to create a climate of public opinion in which it was advisable for recluses and religious enthusiasts to establish their orthodoxy. An anchoress of York who had loved Margery Kempe well refused to see her in 1417 because of her reputation.[116] The patient and sympathetic treatment Margery received from Arundel and his circle contrasted markedly with the hostility shown towards her by many laymen and clergy. She visited Arundel on her return from York in 1413 to secure his approval of her vow of chastity; although his household disapproved of her he gave her a long audience in his garden at Lambeth palace as she described her manner of life, her contemplative experiences and her gift of weeping. Arundel's approval was couched in the same language that was used in the *Epistle on Mixed Life* and *The Holy Boke Gratia Dei* to describe the contemplative experiences of the devout layman: he 'was ryght glad þat owyr mercyful Lord Cryst Ihesu

114 A. Hudson, 'A Lollard Mass', in A. Hudson, *Lollards and their Books* (Oxford, 1985), p. 111; M. Aston, 'Lollardy and Sedition' in M. Aston, *Lollards and Reformers* (London, 1984), pp. 17–18.

115 *The Book of Margery Kempe*, p. 154.

116 ibid, p. 119.

schewyd swech grace in owry days'; the archbishop gave her letters granting her the privilege of choosing her confessor every Sunday.[117] During her next visit to the diocese in 1417 her public sermons, delivered in defiance of Arundel's constitutions, her criticisms of the clergy and her displays of weeping, aroused the opposition of the townsfolk of Hessle, where she narrowly escaped burning, and Beverley. John Duke of Bedford, his confessor John Rikinghale, who was Bowet's suffragan, and leading friars were also hostile towards her.[118] Despite this, Margery was able to leave the diocese safely, after spending fifteen days at York Minster and visiting her confessor William Sleightholme at Bridlington, largely because of the protectors and friends she could count on among the York Minster clergy. Those she particularly mentioned with praise were: John Kendale, a friend of Newton's, and a vicar choral of the minster and priest of the chantry of either Richard Scrope or Henry Bowet;[119] and Dr John Aclomb, or Akum, another member of this Cambridge circle of northerners who were students of contemplative literature, Akum was a theology graduate (B.Th. by 1406 and a Doctor of Theology) probably of Michaelhouse. In York he held the rectory of St Margaret's, Walmgate in 1410 and a canonry in the college of the chapel of St Mary and Holy Angels in 1417. He was also in the service of Bishop Langley of Durham in 1411.[120] These men and the other cathedral clergy who were students of Rolle's works approved of Margery's piety, and they were able to do so because they had the necessary experience in adapting eremitic teaching for laymen to establish her orthodoxy and to give her protection. She was examined at York by the chapter, which included the residentiary canons William Waltham, William Cawood, Robert Wolveden and Stephen Scrope. These men were readers of Suso's *Horologium*, and one of Suso's revelations had inspired the heretical belief in free love among the Brethren on the Free Spirit in Cologne and Bohemia; Margery was therefore questioned by a great clerk and doctor (perhaps Scrope) on the text *Crescite et Multiplicamini*.[121] Archbishop Bowet and his household examined her further at the insistence of Rickinghale and Bedford.[122] Bowet was quite capable of conducting this enquiry for he had other investigations into eremitic enthusiasm: in 1410 he made an extensive visitation of Hampole and drew up ordinances concerning the accommodation and conduct of the many visitors to the priory, who had presumably come to see Rolle's shrine. The archbishop

117 ibid, pp. 35 – 6.
118 ibid, pp. 129, 130, 132, 134.
119 ibid, p. 120.
120 ibid; Emden, *BRUC*, p. 4.
121 ibid, p. 121.
122 ibid, pp. 122 – 28.

tested Margery's knowledge of the articles of faith and questioned her on her white mantle because of its resemblance to the gowns worn by the flagellants; but her main concern was to establish her innocence regarding Bedford's charge that she had advised John Beaufort's daughter, Lady Joan Greystoke, to leave her husband. Bowet seems to have been puzzled and embarrassed by Margery but many of his clerks, including 'a good sad man' and his steward John, spoke up for her, and she was given a safe escort to Bridlington and out of the diocese.[123]

Besides concerning themselves with keeping the followers of Richard Rolle free from the excesses of continental sects, Arundel's clerks also needed to disentangle genuine independent piety from the new English Lollard heresy: one Cambridge scholar, Thomas Markaunt, fellow of Corpus Christi in 1413, owned Rolle's *De amore* and a book of 'Wyclif's *Opiniones*'.[124] By the 1380s hermits and itinerant preachers were spreading Wyclif's doctrine, often simplifying and distorting it in the same way as some of the followers of Rolle misinterpreted his teachings. Cambridge University was at the forefront of the church's stand against Lollardy and the chancellor of the university, John de Burgo, probably at the instigation of the clergy in Arundel's circle such as John Newton, acted promptly to mitigate the influence of Wyclif's teaching at a parish level by answering his attacks on secular clergy, the doctrine of transubstantiation, and the concept of private religion, in the pastoral manual *Pupilla oculi*, which was addressed to all curates. An illustration of Burgo's concern to encourage the clergy to preserve orthodoxy is his provision of a clause in the *confiteor* for sinning in faith: 'I have sinned in faith, I have believed all, I have wavered, I have discovered, defended and followed heresy'.[125] The same caution can be seen in his restriction of the discussion of preaching to the basic Pecham syllabus, a precaution inspired by Lollard preachers.[126] In answer to criticisms of the clergy, Burgo unconditionally asserted the dignity and importance of all ordained secular clergy to whom obedience is due regardless of the failings of individual priests: tithes must therefore, he says, be paid to all priests.[127] The source of this respect is not the priest's parochial zeal but his role as intercessor. For this reason Burgo placed special emphasis on the sacrament of the Mass. As a theologian he answered Wyclif's denial of transubstantiation, using Richard of St Victor and Scotus, with an academic demonstration that the matter and form of the bread is converted by consecration to the matter and form of the body of Christ;

123 ibid, pp. 122 – 28; B.I.H.R., Reg. Bowet, ii, fos. 101 – 2; Palmer, 'The Career of Henry Bowet', pp. 72 – 77.
124 Emden, *BRUC*, pp. 390 – 91.
125 Ball, 'Education of Secular Clergy', p. 320.
126 ibid, p. 281ff.
127 ibid, p. 320.

with philosophical exactness Burgo exposed the philosophical position inimical towards transubstantiation, including Wyclif's,[128] and concluded: 'And so after consecration the substance of the bread does not remain, as certain new-fangled modes falsely boast, nor any substance but only the true body of Christ under species of bread'.[129] In his response to Wyclif's attacks on the theory of transubstantiation, Burgo helped to arouse a devotional reverence for this sacrament: he placed it at the beginning of his work as the most important of the sacraments, and instead of rationalizing its meaning and purpose, like Pagula, he provided technical and priest-orientated instructions to emphasize that the celebration of mass by the priestly intercessor, regardless of the human frailties of the celebrant, was the most important duty for all clergy, whether they had cure of souls or not, and all were bound to celebrate whenever they had the opportunity.[130] Burgo's elevation of the importance of the mass amounted to a ratification of its growth as a stimulus to emotional, private religious experience which had been encouraged by Richard Rolle. Owners of the *Pupilla*, when annotating the section on the Eucharist with descriptions of the mass as a sacrifice, and with prayers of praise offered to God with purity of devotion, conceived of the mass as a form of private worship rather than a congregational service.

Nicholas Love, an associate of Arundel and the Cambridge educated clergy of the diocese of York, endorsed Cambridge teaching on transubstantiation using the same language as Burgo. However, while Burgo answered Wyclif's followers as a theologian with logic, Love, in the *Mirror of the Blessed Life of Jesus Christ*, argued that transubstantiation was a miracle defying natural law and reason which could not be understood through 'bodily felygne, es in sight, taste and touchynge' or the intellect:

> 'the sacrament of the altar, made by virtue of Christ's words is truly God's body in form of bread, his true blood in the form of wine, and the form of bread and wine seem to all bodily senses of man bread and wine in the same manner as it was before, nevertheless it is not so in substance, but only God's flesh and blood in substance. So that accidents of bread and wine miraculously, against man's reason and common order of nature be there in holy sacrament without their natural subject; and true Christ's body that suffered death on the cross is there in the sacrament bodily under form and likeness of wine substantially and wholly without feigning and deceit and not only in figure as false Lollards say'.[131]

Love claimed that transubstantiation could not be empirically observed,

[128] ibid, pp. 65 – 70.
[129] ibid, p. 322.
[130] ibid, p. 262.
[131] *Mirror*, pp. 206 – 8.

and his original contribution to the controversy was to assert that it could be privately experienced at mass by the devout. Lollards, he claimed, scorned the miracle because they 'tasteth nought the swettnesse of this preciouse sacrament'; and the proof of transubstantiation therefore could only be found within the hearts of those who experienced Christ's love. They provided witness to 'a gracious worchynge in sensible felynge of this blissid sacrament; the whiche marveylous worchynge and felynge abouen commoun kynde of man scheweth and proueth souereynly the blessid bodyly presence of Jesu in that sacrament'. Their human bodies constituted the form of bread within which the substance of Christ was manifested at the elevation of the host. Nicholas Love furthermore tried to define for the confusion of 'alle false Lollards, and in comfort of 'alle sincere louers and worchippers of this holy sacrament' the actual 'felynge' which he claimed was a sensation of the blessed bodily presence of Christ within the body of one touched by grace: 'thorogh the whiche he feleth him sensibly, with unspeakable ioye, as he were ioyned body to body'. Although admitting that he had never had the experience himself, he provided a long description of it, drawn from Rolle's accounts of the sensations of the heavenly fire of love, warmth, sweetness and sound in the *Incendium Amoris*. The presence of Christ within the human body, testified by Rolle and another man of Love's acquaintance, provided proof that although no one can see the bodily presence of Jesus in the sacrament of the altar and the bread seems to remain bread, his presence can be felt: 'Oure Lorde Jesu schewynge sensibly his blessed, delectable bodily presence in the most excellent sacrament of the awter, in manere as the forsaide persone that feleth it mygte telle it so in partye'.[132] Nicholas Love's association of Rolle's accounts of his experience of the fire of love with the Eucharist helped to nullify the controversial aspects of the Hampole hermit's teaching, and demonstrated that the clergy of the north could use devotional teaching with its emphasis on personal experience, to answer Wyclif, not only in the practical, pastoral sphere, but in those areas of theology and logic where his challenge was most formidable.

Walter Hilton was another northerner (and a Cambridge academic) who responded to Wyclif's writings with an assertion of the importance of ritual and the sacraments. He may have first written *De Ymaginibus*, a disputation against heretics on the subject of images, as a respondent in the faculty of canon law when he would qualify for the chancellor's licence to incept.[133] Aware of the iconoclastic implications of Wyclif's attack on the idolatry of images of Christ and the saints in churches, he

132 ibid, pp. 208 – 9.
133 Clark, 'Walter Hilton', 16.

countered the Lollard emphasis on the written word of the bible by defending the use of images as books for the illiterate layman and aids to devotion which lead the simple to spiritual knowledge. Images, according to Hilton, were material in the sense that Christ's manhood was material; they and signs such as the host, were memorials of the human nature of Christ, tokens of the absent friend like the king's seal, in a life where there could only be desire and longing.[134] Hilton also emphasized in the *Scale of Perfection* the importance of the sacraments as a means of nourishing the less spiritually refined. Thomas Arundel shared Hilton's anxiety about the iconoclastic implications of Lollardy, and is reported to have said at the trial of William Thorpe in 1407: 'were it a fair thing to come into a church and see therein none image'.[135] Hilton also responded to Wyclif's attacks on private religion, although in a more direct manner than Burgo. While *De utilitate Prerogativis* was written to answer Horsley's private reservations about entering a religious life, the scale of the work shows that the author was meeting Wyclif's objections to the monastic life by giving a defence of the religious life that included a historical account of its origins and specific allusions to the heretical opposition of opponents of private religion. In his letter to Dr John Thorpe Hilton even used legal arguments to defend private religion.

Many of the pastoral ideals shown in the work of Burgo, Hilton and Love can also be seen in the active steps taken by the northerners and Cambridge scholars of Arundel's circle against heresy after 1380. As early as 1382 Arundel forbade anyone from preaching without a licence from the bishop of Ely in an admonitory letter sent to John Newton, his official.[136] This measure was occasioned by the part played by vagrant clergy in the peasant's revolt of 1381, in which Cambridge university suffered particularly. Arundel's action accords with the reservations that Burgo expressed about preaching in *Pupilla oculi*. Arundel and his clerks were also responsible for implementing an ecclesiastical policy between 1384 and 1411 that subjected vernacular religious literature to the careful supervision of scholars before approving it for general circulation. This policy was a response to the dissemination of Lollard criticisms of the church in the vernacular, some of which were interpolated into the popular religious treatises of Yorkshire: Rolle's *Commentary on the Psalms* and Gaytryge's version of Thoresby's *Catechism* were interpolated with Lollard doctrine, perhaps as early as 1381 to 1385 when the Lollard English bibles were being produced. An

134 Aston, 'Lollards and Images', in *Lollards and Reformers*, p. 143ff. Russel-Smith, 'Walter Hilton', 210ff.
135 Aston, 'Lollards and Images', pp. 165 – 67; *Concilia*, iii, pp. 326 – 7.
136 E.D.R. Reg. Arundel, 1395 – 6, p. 168; for text of letter see Aston, *Thomas Arundel*, pp. 402 – 3.

early attempt to exert some control on the circulation of vernacular texts was made in 1384 when the acting chancellor of Cambridge, John Burgo, and his council of doctors of both laws, subjected a manuscript containing the *Speculum Vitae* of the Yorkshireman William Nassyngton to a close five day examination.[137] Apart from Burgo, the other northerner definitely involved in the examination was John Newton, the master of Peterhouse, for the manuscript was tested in every college; Arundel himself, as bishop of Ely, would also probably be involved. The composition and dissemination of the vernacular religious writings of the north was presenting authorities with a worrying problem and it was a major issue in the 1380's, as can be seen in Sir Henry Francis' attempt to secure papal approval for his translation of the Chester cycle plays.[138] The climax to the attempts made by Arundel's Cambridge and York clerks to supervise laymen's reading of religious literature came between 1408 and 1411. In 1408 Arundel, as archbishop of Canterbury, issued constitutions forbidding the reading of books composed since the time of Wyclif until they had been examined by the universities, and preventing anyone from translating any holy text on their own authority[139]: in 1411 Nicholas Love submitted to Arundel his *Mirror* as an alternative to the Lollard gospels.

Cambridge was also at the forefront of the church's initial investigations into Lollardy. Arundel, as local diocesan, was closely involved in university affairs and visited King's Hall in July 1383 because of the negligence of the warden and general defects among the scholars[140]; this may have been an investigation to forestall heresy in the college. Cambridge clerks were certainly prominent in early heresy trials. The Dominican John Paris was present at the council convened by Courtenay at Blackfriars in London to condemn Wyclif's errors in June 1382,[141] and at the trial of Henry Crumpe at Stamford in May 1392.[142] The opinions of the hermit William Swinderby were pronounced heretical in 1391 by the Yorkshireman William Colville, the chancellor and master of Michaelhouse, and other Cambridge scholars,[143] and on the same occasion the masters of theology at Cambridge and members of the four orders of friars were involved in the trial of Walter Brut.[144] Arundel's clergy continued to regard careful and patient investigations into heresy as an important aspect of pastoral work after they left Cambridge. It is

137 Aston, pp. 322–23; Pantin, *English Church*, pp. 229–30.
138 Salter, *Drama in Chester*, p. 8.
139 Lyndwood, *Provinciale* (Oxford, 1676, repr. Farnborough, 1969), p. 284.
140 E.D.R. Reg. Arundel, 1896, p. 177.
141 *Fasc. Zizan*, (R.S., London, 1858), pp. 286, 498, 343.
142 ibid, p. 347, 357.
143 *Reg. Johannis Trefnaunt*, ed. W. W. Capes (Hereford, 1914), p. 365.
144 ibid, p. 359.

likely that Hilton was actively involved in such work when he moved to Thurgarton priory in Nottinghamshire: in 1388 a commission was granted to the prior of Thurgarton to confiscate the books of Wyclif and Hereford and to arrest people teaching heresy. The prior at the time was William Saperton, but Hilton was described as a governor of Thurgarton and may have helped or even deputized for him.[145] It is also probable that his tract in defence of images reached its final form during his time at Thurgarton, and may have been used by Arundel who imposed an oath on four Nottingham suspects in 1395 that 'From this day forward I shall worship images, with praying and offering unto them in the worship of the saints that they be made after, and also I shall never more despise pilgrimage'.[146] William Swinderby found Richard Scrope a vigilant bishop of Coventry and Lichfield when he arrived in the diocese, and he was forced to move on. Scrope's friend Walter Skirlaw, the bishop of Durham, conducted a sympathetic examination of the Lollard preacher Richard Rich in 1401, and Thomas Arundel made an exhaustive attempt in 1407 to convent the Yorkshire preacher William Thorpe, who claimed to be a follower of the Bretheren of the Free Spirit. Henry Bowet assisted Arundel in the trial of John Badby at St Paul's in London, and when archbishop of York he appointed a committee which included John Paris to deal with Lollardy in 1401.[147]

In the pastoral and religious writings of Burgo and Hilton and in the careers of the northern clerks of their circle between 1380 and 1420 it is possible to discern a coherent pastoral policy. In contrast to Wyclif's more traditional concern with public worship, charity, and the parish priests' educational responsibilities, which had much in common with Pagula's and Thoresby's conception of the pastoral office, Burgo and his readers transformed pastoral duty into the preservation of doctrinal orthodoxy and respect for the priesthood as a means of encouraging and stimulating religious experience. This was achieved by their fostering liturgical richness and devotion to Christ's humanity through the sacraments, Corpus Christi processions, images, and the cycle plays. Such cultural richness, when added to the careful control of religious teaching in the vernacular, contrasts with the austerity of Lollard assertions about the primacy of the written word of the Bible.

145 Aston, *Lollards and Reformers*, p. 143. Hilton is referred to in a fifteenth century MS (Camb. MS. Ed IV 30, fo. 4) as canon and governor of Thurgarton, although the dates of the known priors, if properly transmitted, would eliminate this possibility. See *Yorks. Writers*, i, pp. 264 – 92, and Knowles, *Mystical Tradition*, pp. 101 – 2.

146 *Concilia*, iii, p. 225; C.P.R., 1385 – 89, p. 47.

147 Emden, *BRUO*, iii, p. 1708 – 10; *Reg. Chichelle*, iii, p. 57; F. D. Mathew, 'The Trial of Ric. Rich', *E.H.R.*, v, 530ff; Aston, *Lollards and Reformers*, pp. 165 – 67; *Concilia*, iii, pp. 367 – 7; *English Wyclifite Writings*, pp. 156 – 7.

Conclusion

The uniqueness of the York clergy's contribution towards the burgeoning lay piety of the fifteenth century lay in their attempts to make the composition and translation of contemplative literature an aspect of the pastoral office. Devotional literature was written in other regions and outside this circle, but seldom with a pastoral objective in mind. Henry Duke of Lancaster probably wrote his *Livre de Seynz Medicines*, an imaginative revelation of the inner life of a soldier and courtier, for the benefit of fellow courtiers and his family: one copy went to Lancaster's brother-in-law Henry Percy, who died in 1368, and this descended to Percy's daughter Mary Roos, who left *liber gallicus de Duc Lancastrie* to Isabella Percy.[1] *Pearl* — an English poem about grief that explored attitudes to providential grace and free will — had a similarly small circulation; it was probably written for the court of Richard II between 1370 and 1400 by one of the Cheshiremen who served in the retinues of John of Gaunt.[2]

One group of clergy who resembled Arundel's circle, in the sense that they produced religious literature with the intention of reaching a wide audience, were the Oxford followers of Wyclif. The circles of Peterhouse College and Cambridge and Queen's College and Oxford can be seen as twin branches that formed from the pastoral programmes and patronage of Thoresby and Islip. Both groups of clergy possessed the same scholarly interest in ecclesiastical history and the textual study of the bible; and both believed they had a pastoral mission to apply their scholarship in the service of society. But they were diametrically opposed in their attitudes towards religious teaching: Wyclif and his Oxford followers believed that they could enlighten the laity by translating the bible, thereby unlocking the source of all religious knowledge; Arundel and his clergy gave more thought to the social consequences of the uncontrolled dissemination of the sacred texts, and religious teaching in general; their policies were consequently more sophisticated than the Lollard fundamentalism. They believed in a controlled release of religious literature that had been adapted by churchmen who were mindful of the need for religion to reinforce social bonds. They established at Cambridge a tradition of writing and adapting contemplative literature in the vernacular that was maintained

1 *Livre de Seynz Medicines*, ed. E. J. Arnould (Anglo Norman Text Soc., 1940), Arnould, 'Henry Grosmont', *B.J.R.L.*, xxi (1937) 352 – 86. TE, I, pp. 59, 202.

2 *Poems of the Pearl Manuscript*, ed. M. Andrew and R. Waldron (York Med. Texts 1978); *Pearl*, ed. E. V. Gordon (Oxford, 1953); M. J. Bennett, 'Sir Gawain and the Green Knight and the Literary Achievement of the North-west Midlands', *Journal Med. Hist.*, 5 (I) (1979) 63 – 7.

by Yorkshiremen at Cambridge until the end of the fifteenth century. John Alcok of Beverley, a doctor of canon law by 1459 and a fellow of Peterhouse, wrote and translated a number of devotional works, including *The Hyll of Perfeccion* (printed by De Worde) and *The Abbey of the Holy Ghost*;[3] and William Atkynson of York diocese, a doctor of theology and fellow of Pembroke Hall in 1478, translated the first three books of Thomas a Kempis' *Imitatio Christi* into English at the request of Margaret Countess of Richmond.[4] Arundel's clerks were also among the first to recognize that the pastoral policies of Wyclif and his circle could undermine the authority of the church and many social institutions. They used their positions of dominance in Cambridge and the church in the first two decades of the fifteenth century to ensure that their educational philosophy triumphed by keeping Cambridge free of Lollard ideas and prosecuting Wyclif's followers in Oxford. In 1383 Arundel visited King's Hall, and in 1401 he conducted an episcopal visitation of Cambridge, while Stephen Scrope was chancellor, to ascertain if any members were suspected of Lollardy or heresy.[5] In September of the same year Richard Scrope, archbishop of York, issued a commission to the abbot of Leicester and others to conduct a visitation of Queen's college, Oxford and to inform him of their findings.[6] In 1411 Arundel conducted a visitation of the university because of rumours that Oxford ministers were circulating vernacular tracts to the laity.[7] A canon of York, Richard Fleming (the bishop of Lincoln who disinterred Wyclif's bones) founded the theological college of Lincoln in Oxford with the intention of defending the mysteries of the sacred page against 'these ignorant laymen who profane with swinish snouts its most holy parts'. This Cambridge circle were ultimately the more successful in reaching the laity and influencing religious practices in the fifteenth century, because they caught the mood of public opinion when they encouraged the circulation of contemplative literature and dealt with the Lollard heresy. By doing so they gave a new dimension to the pastoral office. In the mid-fourteenth century the clergy had a missionary role as Thoresby and Grandisson took moral teaching and ecclesiastical discipline to the most isolated parishes. Arundel and his clergy extended this principle of strong church government and applied it to the inner lives of parishioners as they set about influencing and monitoring what people thought and felt.

3 Emden, *BRUC*, p. 6.
4 ibid, p. 22.
5 Cobban, *The King's Hall*, pp. 102 – 3; I. J. Churchill, *Canterbury Administration* (2 vols., 1933), II, 152.
6 *Calendar Reg. Scrope*, p. 9; B.I.H.R. Reg. Scrope, fo. 119v.
7 H. Rashdall, *The Universities of Europe in the Middle Ages*, ed. F. M. Powicke and A. B. Edmen, iii, pp. 130 – 5; *Snappe's Formulary*, ed. H. E. Salter (O.H.S., lxxx, 1924), pp. 101 – 15.

The York clergy, unlike their predecessors, formulated this policy on their own. No other circle in the period between 1380 and 1450 had the same combination of pastoral, scholarly and spiritual interests. Hallum's Salisbury chapter contained distinguished scholars and pastoral reformers such as Henry Chichele, Richard Ullerston, John Chaundler and Thomas Polton, but although they exerted influence at the councils of Constance and Pisa and formulated a pastoral programme that recognized the need for resident and locally appointed clergy in the different dioceses, they showed little interest in the pastoral potential of the contemplative literature of the north-east.[8]

There were theology graduates occupying the rectories of some of the larger London churches who studied contemplative literature, but unlike the York clergy, they were primarily scholars whose personal interest in contemplation caused them to lead increasingly reclusive lives. By the mid-fifteenth century they constituted a spiritual aristocracy whose lives centred on the eremitic communities of Syon, Sheen, London Charterhouse and Eton, and not on the pastoral duties of their churches. Thomas Lawsby, the rector of St Bartholomew the Less, Thomas Westhaugh, a Pembroke fellow and rector of All Hallows the Great, and Dr John Pynchbeck, an Oxford graduate, all eventually retired to Syon. These men owned large libraries and they studied the works of the continental mystics including Suso, St Mechthild, St Bridget and Thomas a Kempis.[9] A group of theology graduates from Oxford, including John Bower, Robert Hesyll, and Thomas Barker, studied the works of Suso, Hugh of St Victor and Duns Scotus, and left their London rectories to join the austere community of Oxford graduates established at Eton in 1443.[10] The difference between the attitudes of the theologians of this community and the canonists of Peterhouse is demonstrated in the career of one of the first fellows of Eton, John Blacman. During his years at Eton he acquired a collection of theological and exegetical works of the twelfth and thirteenth centuries which reflected his academic interests at Oxford; when he joined the Carthusians in 1463 he began to study the continental mystics, including St Bridget, St Catherine of Siena, Ruysbroeck and Thomas a Kempis,

[8] Harvey, 'English Views on Reform', pp. 20. 30. 100, 172, 203, 216.

[9] R. Lovatt, 'The Imitation of Christ in Late Medieval England', *T.R.H.S.*, 18 (1968), 113–14. John Lawsby entered Syon in 1476; for his career see Emden, *B.R.U.C.*, p. 357. Westhaugh resigned as rector of All Hallows in 1459 and joined Sheen; in 1472 he was at Syon. See Emden, *B.R.U.C.*, pp. 630–31. Pynchbek entered Syon in 1459; Emden, *B.R.U.C.*, p. 466. Lawsby left over forty volumes to Syon; see Bateson, *Syon Catalogue*, pp. xxv–xxvi. For the list of books given by Pynchbek to Syon see also Bateson, pp. xxv–xxvi. For another account of this circle see Lovatt, 'The Influence of Religious Literature of Germany on English Spirituality', pp. 190–92.

[10] Emden, *B.R.U.O.*, I, p. 234 (Bower); II, pp. 922 (Hesyll); I, p. 109 (Barker). Hesyll and Barker were among the first fellows of the college.

and he amassed a collection of forty-two volumes of spiritual works. Like his contemporaries at Oxford and Eton he started his career as a scholar and ended it as a monk.[11] There is no evidence that he made any attempt to combine contemplation with pastoral work and, apart from Rolle's *Incendium* and the *Emendatio Vitae,* he owned none of the English devotional works of the north-east, nothing pertaining to the mixed life and nothing from the pen of Walter Hilton.[12] In his biography of the founder of Eton, Henry VI, Blacman expressed the distaste that these London clergy felt towards the spiritual and intellectual compromises that practitioners of the mixed life were required to make.[13] He ignored Henry's public role as a king and concentrated on his private religious life; this was characterized by such physical manifestations of devotion as his revelations from the saints, corporeal visions of the Assumption, the visualization of the Real Presence, and the hearing of voices at the elevation of the host.[14] Hilton and his circle would not have accepted such dereliction of public duty and intemperate imitation of Rolle and Suso so uncritically.

The piety of Blacman's circle and the restricted circulation of Thomas a Kempis' *De Imitatione Christi* among these theologians have been used to suggest that the *devotio moderna* failed to establish itself in a society whose spirituality was deeply conservative and stratified.[15] The reverse is nearer the truth. There is nothing so radical about Thomas's private mysticism and his revulsion at the inherent repressiveness of human societies that is not implied in the writings of Hilton and Love.[16] The York lawyers, who were the effective leaders of the spiritual movements of the fifteenth century, were reformers and innovators. They may have been cautious, but in their attempts to preserve and strengthen social structures and inner contentment, they extended the scope of the teachings of such continental mystics as Suso and helped to create the pragmatic blend of compromises that characterize English piety.

11 Emden, *B.R.U.C.*, pp. 670 – 71.

12 For a list of Blacman's books see E. Thompson, *The Carthusian Order in England*, pp. 317 – 21.

13 R. Lovatt, 'A Collection of Apocryphal Anecdotes: John Blacman Revisited', in A. J. Pollard, ed., *Property and Politics* (Gloucester, 1984). Blacman's *Collectarium mansuetudinum et Bonorum Morum Regis Henrici VI* was written while Blacman was at Witham and completed before 1485; Lovatt, p. 182. For printed edition of Blacman's biography see *Henry the Sixth: a Reprint of John Blacman's Memoirs*, ed. and trans. M. R. James (Cambridge, 1929).

14 Blacman, pp. 5, 6, 7, 8, 9 – 11, 15 – 16, 17 – 18; Lovatt, 'A Collection of Apocryphal Anecdotes', p. 182; R. Lovatt, 'John Blacman: Biographer of Henry VI, in *The Writing of History in the Middle Ages*, ed. Davis, pp. 415 – 44.

15 R. Lovatt, 'The Imitation of Christ in Late Medieval England', 117.

16 *The Earliest English Translation of the First Three Books of De Imitatione Christi*, ed. J. K. Ingram (E.E.T.S., London, 1893), pp. 11 – 13, 18, 45, 117.

There is evidence by the mid-fifteenth century that the admiration of individualistic world weariness and holy foolishness which permitted the unstable Henry VI to reign for so long was being tempered by a growing respect for practitioners of the mixed life.[17] The intellectual mentors of Thomas Gascoigne, the Yorkshire theologian who studied in Syon library and lamented his inability to undertake his pastoral duties in the rectory of St Peter Cornhill in London, were the scholar bishops Augustine and Grossteste.[18] This shift in intellectual and spiritual priorities was neatly demonstrated by a Carthusian's admiration for a northern cleric: Stoon, a monk of London Charterhouse, composed a metrical poem in honour of Richard Fleming, a canon of York and the bishop of Lincoln, praising his achievements as a scholar and patron of learning — he studied the *Horologium* and founded Lincoln College — and as a preacher and minister of the church.[19] Towards the end of the fifteenth century the ideal of the mixed life was becoming synonymous with the concept of the 'civilized man'. The versatility of the York clergy anticipated the achievements of Sir Thomas More, whose periodic retreats at London Charterhouse were just one facet of the varied life of a public, accessible, yet fundamentally private man. A closer consideration of the practice of the mixed life in the diocese, and the content of its religious literature will, therefore, provide an insight into the culture and spirituality of the period.

17 Lovatt, 'A Collection of Apocryphal Anecdotes', p. 190.

18 *Loci e Libro Veritatum*, ed. J. E. T. Rodgers (Oxford, 1881), pp. 30 – 31, 106 – 115. Gascoigne also confessed his failure to fulfil his pastoral ideals in a note he added in the margin to one of the pages of his copy of Augustine's *City of God*. See Bodl. Lib. MS. 198.

19 *Snappe's Formulary*, pp. 138 – 44; Emden, *B.R.U.C.*, II, p. 699.

CHAPTER FIVE

The Social and Domestic Content of the Religious Literature of the Diocese

Consideration has been given to the secular world of religious writers and clergy of the diocese and the formulation among circles of like-minded administrators and scholars of a pastoral policy that adapted eremitic teachings to the secular lives of their colleagues and lay folk in general. The devotional aspect of pastoral care in the late fourteenth and early fifteenth century Yorkshire and its impact on religion and society will now be considered by paying closer attention to the content of the religious literature of the north. The northern clergy of Arundel's circle provided specific practical teaching for clergy and laymen living a secular life to enable them to reconcile their spiritual and social lives in a 'mixed life'. Besides defining a non-professional religious life in the abstract terms of a mixed life, and providing a social and domestic context to the devotional literature, religious writers from Rolle to Nicholas Love showed the nobility of the diocese how to integrate teachings on mystical experience within their daily witnessing of the celebration of the mass, their participation in the sacraments, and in their public lives. The spiritual guidance provided by the Yorkshire religious writers ranged from the provision of meditations on memory that counselled an introspective detachment suitable for an educated elite, to affective depictions of Christ's life and Passion that aroused human emotions and could be disseminated to a wider lay audience through religious drama. All this religious literature demonstrated that it was possible to live a full religious, secular life, and that human feelings were the basis of all forms of religious experience. The pastoral teaching of the York clergy in this period therefore succeeded in intimately touching people of all classes.

Definitions of the 'Mixed Life'

The concept of the mixed life probably had considerable personal significance for those York clergy who developed it. Because of their commitment to the pastoral ideals of the church of York they were unable to relinquish either the responsibilities or rewards of the active life; and in the first instance the ideal of the mixed life was something that they had abstracted from their own lives of study and pastoral administration. They would have been encouraged to do this in the theological, pastoral and legal texts found in the library at York Minster and in their own private collections. These works provided specific guidance for secular clergy on how to reconcile the conflicting claims of the active and contemplative lives.

Augustine would have provided them with a basis for discussion of their experience of this conflict. He had defined the conflicting claims of the *'vita otiosa'* and the *'vita negotiosa'* in *The City of God*, and in *Confessions* he discussed the possibility of attaining interior experience between the calls of *vita negotiosa*.[1] Gregory was the first to apply such conflicts directly to secular clergy, and he maintained that it was the duty of those entrusted with the cure of souls to find a compromise between the active and contemplative lives. He observed that the introspective pastor ran the risk of neglecting the material needs of those entrusted to his care; the pastor who immersed himself in the cares of the world was liable to become afraid during private moments of silence and would long for the worldly responsibilities that he pursued with a troubled mind; such a man, Gregory warned, became a servant of his parishioners, neglecting the inner things he was supposed to teach.[2] Gregory's innovation was to fuse both vocations into a third life of simultaneous action and introspection and to claim for followers of this life the status of holy men. The basis of this life was charity: the exercise of tangible acts of love that did not weary the perception, but provided the necessary physical and spiritual nourishment for the mind unable to sustain itself in the contemplative heights alone. Those who combined action and contemplation had an inner calm and wisdom which was revealed to the world in their words and actions.[3] Their ability to remain unaffected by the turmoils of their worldly affairs was defined by Gregory in his *Moralia* as detachment.[4] Patristic writers of the twelfth and thirteenth centuries continued to discuss the need of clergy to combine both lives. In his sermons Bernard warned against the dangers of withholding contemplative gifts or dissipating them in the service of others; Aquinas, in *Secunda Secundae*, proclaimed the perfect mixture of

1 F. J. Steele, 'Definitions and Depictions of the Active Life in Middle English Religious Literature of the Thirteenth, Fourteenth and Fifteenth Centuries', (Oxford Univ. D.Phil. thesis, 1979), pp. 12 – 25, 215, 219; C. Butler, *Western Mysticism* (London, 1922), pp. 157 – 59.

2 Butler, *Western Mysticism*, pp. 118, 171; Gregory, *Liber Regulae Pastoralis*, PL lxxvii, 3, 19, 32.

3 Gregory, *Moralia*, X, PL lxxv, 938.

4 For a full discussion of the active and contemplative lives see Gregory, *Moralia*, PL lxxv, I, 761 – 6.

contemplation and external works found in a life of study and preaching to be the highest form of life: deeds of charity, he claimed, strengthened love of God and helped quell the internal passions that hindered contemplation.[5] Canonists of the thirteenth century, such as Isidore of Seville, also commented on the need to reconcile the claims of the two lives. The first to use the term *vita mixta* to describe a life of contemplation and activity was the canonist, Henry of Susa (*Hostiensis*): in his first book of the decretals he defined the *vita mixta* as the life taught and practised by Moses and Jesus.[6]

The York Minster clergy, who were not equipped by training or temperament for the specialized life of the recluses, would have turned to these texts for guidance. As canonists they would all have read Hostiensis, and members of Arundel's circle owned the works of Gregory and Aquinas. Thomas Arundel possessed a volume of Gregory's works; Thomas Dalby owned Gregory's *Dialogues*; John Newton owned Gregory's *Dialogues, Moralia*, the *Commentary on Ezechiel* and the *Pastoral Care*; Henry Bowet owned the *Pastoral Care* and the *Commentary on Ezechiel* and a collection of the works of Aquinas; Richard Pittes owned the *Moralia* and Robert Alne owned Gregory's *Homilies* and Aquinas' *Secunda Secundae*.[7] The influence of these works can be seen in the religious literature of the York clergy in which they discussed the problems of reconciling the claims of the active and contemplative lives from the viewpoint of secular clergy and lawyers.

Wyclif's experience of the conflict between the active and contemplative lives can perhaps be related to his Yorkshire origins and the spiritual problems of York careerists and secular clergy. He — like his relative Robert Wyclif — acted as a testamentary executor, to William Askeby, archdeacon of Nottingham, and he was possibly a member of Thoresby's circle. Although, as an Oxford theologian, he had little contact with his fellow northerners after 1370, he appears to have reflected on his failure to integrate his intellectual and spiritual interests with his pastoral responsibilities. He accused himself of selfish careerism and negligence of the pastoral office; but he never envisaged for himself a radical conversion by renouncing all secular privileges, either in an eremitic life, or in a life filled with pastoral work.[8] The self-knowledge that could resolve these tensions came from an understanding of both the active and contemplative lives and their successful combination. He claimed that for many the private religion of the recluse or monk could prove a bitter spring, and absorption in pastoral

5 Butler, *Western Mysticism*, p.
6 Steele, 'Definitions and Depictions of the Active Life', p. 219.
7 *Sed Vacante Wills*, iii, pp. 81 – 2; Y.M.L. Reg. Test. I, fos. 124, 168, 216; TE, II, p. 78.
8 Smalley, 'The Bible and Eternity', 77ff.

responsibilities could provide an excuse for pursuing a purely secular and unspiritual life. Wyclif, who refers to the decretals in his discussion of the mixed life, probably derived his use of the term *vita mixta* in one of his sermons from Hostiensis, and he applied it to a life in which all that was physical was not purely active and all that was spiritual was not purely contemplative, like the functioning of the physical body itself.[9] Following Hostiensis, he used Moses and Christ as examples of practitioners of this life: Christ followed the active life in the cities in the daytime by preaching, and at night he returned to the mountain to study and pray.[10] In *De Civili Dominio* Wyclif applied his discussion of the mixed life to the secular clergy by saying that they should first and foremost live contemplatively, and only then should they proceed from contemplation to perform the duties of active life.[11] Wyclif, in the same work, used Gregory's *Moralia* to claim that while contemplation was the highest form of life, it only started on earth and continued in heaven; for the purpose of this earthly life a combination of the contemplative and active lives was the state of life that was most profitable and useful.[12] The symbol he borrowed from Gregory's *Moralia* to convey the mixed life, two eyes within a single head, was probably intended to elaborate on the central image of William of Pagula's *Oculus Sacerdotis*, still the main pastoral manual for the clergy at the time Wyclif was writing.[13]

Walter Hilton was subjected to similar pastoral and legal influences, and he addressed spiritual letters to men who were attempting to reconcile their practical and legal accomplishments and secular privileges with a spiritual life. During his unsuccessful attempt to become a hermit, he wrote *De Imagine Peccati* for another recluse, in which he expressed a desire to find a middle way between the extremes of the active and contemplative lives. He describes the active life as a privileged existence wherein the social intercourse of courts, pride in high office and greed corrupts.[14] However, he also points out that conversion to a solitary life could be the mere adoption of another parasitical way of life, and ironically describes his friend's position as a recluse occupying a comfortable nest where he is fed without labour and sweat on his part, and he asks him what function he is performing.[15] Hilton, like Wyclif, was influenced by pastoral ideals and aware of the

[9] Wyclif, *Sermones*, ed. J. Loserth, 4 vols., WS (1887), ii, p. 147; *Tractatus de Civili Dominio*, ed. R. Lane Poole, 4 vols., WS (1885 – 1904), iii, p. 165.

[10] *De Civili Dominio*, i, pp. 670.77. The source for both these works was Gregory *Moralia*, lib. xxviii, PL lxxvi, 467; see Butler, *Western Mysticism*, p. 176.

[11] *De Civili Dominio*, i, p. 165; iii, p. 165; cf. Gregory, *Moralia*, lib. xxviii 33 and Gregory *Regulae Pastoralis*, ii, PL, lxxvii, 32.

[12] *De Civili Dominio*, i, pp. 170 – 77.

[13] ibid, i, pp. 170 – 77; cr. *Moralia*, PL, lxxv, 775.

[14] Hilton, *Latin Writings*, i, p. 75, 1143 – 53.

[15] ibid, p. 89.

responsibilities and privileges of his education. All men, he claimed, were set in this world to work for others: the laymen by working for his bread and the bread of others and by performing corporeal works of mercy; the secular clergy by performing spiritual works of mercy and by undertaking the cure of souls and celebrating for the dead.[16] His enumeration of the useful tasks of the clergy concentrates on the performance of the pastoral office by the humble parish priest and the observance of a religious rule by chantry chaplains and monks; he significantly says nothing about the services of his fellow York careerists as ecclesiastical lawyers, members of cathedral chapters, civil servants and diplomats. A profound sense of unhappiness at his inability to fulfil the demands of the pastoral or spiritual life is expressed:

> What do we do, your and our like, lazy useless men standing all day idle? We do not labour in the vineyard of the Lord, administering the holy rites of the church, nor do we willingly bear the yoke of obedience beneath the yoke of another --- In no way do we fill the place of any servant, even the least appointed in the church, but we are as it were left freely to our own feeling and our own free will as if in no order. We must be fearful lest we are cast away where there is no order but eternal confusion.[17]

Hilton's Latin letters reveal the extent of the development of conscience among the Cambridge educated Yorkshire clergy in the late fourteenth century. Hilton communicated to the canonist John Thorpe his scepticism about the intrinsic value of obedience to such ascetic and monastic disciplines as fasting, and analysed the religious life in such a way that the heroic confrontations with the temptations of the flesh taking place in the desert would come to appear simple and irrelevant to his readers. In *De Imagine*, the flesh was defined in social terms rather than physical drives: Hilton's description of the sin of pride entailed an analysis of dependence on secular ambition, prestigious benefices, the favours of the great, and the praise of kinsmen.[18] This was the secular world of the York careerists that Wyclif also evoked, and which was an important aspect of the collective identity of members of this class. However, Hilton's Latin letters also reveal that members of this Cambridge circle were attempting to attain full development of individual personality by showing sufficient individuality to think, feel, and act in ways that were sometimes contrary to the collective attitudes of this society. The sense of struggle within the individual conscience expressed by Hilton can be explained by the difficulties he and his

16 ibid, p. 90.

17 ibid, pp. 90 – 91, 11. 319 – 328. Hilton encouraged the recipient to use the wisdom he had acquired from his religious conversion in the active life.

18 ibid, p. 75.

readers felt in following Rolle's example of extreme individuality and in attempting to go in different directions to the ones dictated by their upbringing, education, patrons and families. The guilt they experienced was caused by the sense of gratitude and responsibility they felt towards members of this secular environment who had given them so much; and it is for this reason that Hilton, despite defending private religious life against the attacks of Wyclif, taught that vowed contemplatives should respect those in active life who had practical, pastoral commitments;[19] furthermore it was for this reason that he frequently said that the vowed religious life was not for all the spiritually gifted, and he advised John Thorpe that his calling was to live his religion in the world using his fulness of charity and other spiritual gifts.[20]

However, the York clergy did not just apply the concept of the mixed life to their own lives. Their original contribution to the debate was their application of the concept to laymen. Hilton, like Wyclif, probably first encountered the term *vita mixta* in Hostiensis when he was a canon law student, and he translated it into the 'medled lyf', the subject of his English epistle that provided spiritual direction for all those with spiritual aspirations who were leading active lives. Hilton's innovation was to extend the Gregorian treatment of the conflict between clergymen's spiritual yearnings and pastoral responsibilities into the sphere of lay piety. *The Epistle on Mixed Life* was originally addressed to a gentry householder who was probably a widower, and Hilton pronounced 'þis medled lyf best and most bihoueli', for all those "in care and gouernaunce of oþure as prelates and curates are, or in temporal soueryntе as wordly lordes and maistres are".[21] His advice to his readers not to lose their tempers if distracted by domestic crisis involving family servants and neighbours could be applied to the domestic and judicial responsibilities of the gentry; and the administration of the estates of magnates, gentry householders and high ecclesiastics is envisaged in the recommendation that: "þou schalt also loke and knowe wysli þat þi þinges and þi wordly godes be rigtly kept be seruantes, gouerned and trewely dispinded: þat þou migt be more plenteousli wiþ hem fulfille þe dedes of merci to þin euencristen".[22] The mixed life avoided the spiritual and social extremes that accompanied the contemplative vocation and the active life. Hilton counselled against choosing between these extremes by pointing out the recipient's duty towards both his spiritual aspirations and social responsibilities: he must neither absorb himself in his active affairs as if he had never felt the

19 ibid, p. 91; see also *Scale of Perfection*, i, p. 17.
20 *Latin Writings*, ii, p. 289, ll. 847 – 84.
21 Hilton, *Epistle on the Mixed Life*, ed. Horstmann, *Yorks. Writers*, i, p. 270.
22 ibid, p. 267.

fit of devotional experience; nor abandon his children and servants for a religious life, but 'meddle' the works of Martha and Mary.[23] For most people charitable social activity was an aid and not a hindrance to contemplation because it took the individual out of himself and prevented excessive fervour or disillusionment. Appropriately, Hilton used a homely domestic simile to illustrate this: good deeds, while appearing to lead the aspirant away from his goal, acted like sticks that appear to smother a coal fire before bringing it to flame: 'Hit may fal sum-tyme þat þe more troubled þat þou hast been wiþ actyf werkes, þe more brennyng desyr þou schalt haue to god'.[24]

Solitaries and Carthusian monks were actually involved in secular society, especially as spiritual guides, scribes and authors; and they concerned themselves with the problems of those attempting to live a mixed life. The author of the *Cloud of Unknowing*, who probably knew Hilton, did not really provide instructions that were suitable for most amateurs; but he categorized the spiritual experiences of those in the active life as intermittent and had followers of the mixed life in mind when he addressed his prologue to

> þoo men þe whiche þoug al þei stande in actyuete bi outwarde form of leuyng, neuerþeles yit bi inward sering after þe priue sperit of God . . . þei ben ful graciously disposid, not contynowely as it is propre to verrey contemplatyues, bot þan and þan to be parceners in þe hiegt point of þis contemplatiue act.[25]

The recipient of *The Cloud of Unknowing* may have been a Carthusian, like the former exchequer clerk, Adam Horsley of Beauvale, the possible author of the *Speculum Vitae Humanae*. This compendium of the spiritual life contained discussions on the active and contemplative lives, visionary mysticism, the Passions of Christ and Mary, the sacraments and preparations for death, all of which were illustrated with quotations from Augustine, Rolle, Bridget, Suso and Hilton. The account of the spiritual movement of the fourteenth century is concluded by a discussion of the mixed life: Gregory's *Moralia* and *Pastorale* are used to urge those who have attained the heights of contemplation to live a mixed life, and quotations are provided on the need of the clergy to persevere in the love of God while preaching to those in their care.[26]

23 ibid, p. 268.
24 ibid, p. 276. See also *Minor Works of Hilton*, ed. Jones, pp. 37 – 41.
25 *The Cloud of Unknowing*, ed. Hodgson, p. 3.
26 Merton Coll. Oxford, MS. 204, fos. 1 – 179. This work was also known as the *Speculum Spiritualium*; see Allen, *Writings*, pp. 405 – 6. There was a manuscript of the *Speculum Spiritualium* at Mt Grace: W. Brown, 'History of Mt Grace', 204. See also Oxford Bodl. MS. Bodley 450 (sum. cat. 2398).

Another Carthusian, Nicholas Love, defined the 'mixed life' in his *Mirror* as a 'perfigte actif lyffe', occurring after the active and contemplative lives and involving the governing and teaching of others for their spiritual welfare. He recommended Hilton's epistle for 'those who so wole be more pleynely be enformed and taugt in Englishe tounge' of this 'medled lyf: That is to saye somtyme actyfe and somtyme cpntemplatyf as it longeth to dyuerse persones that in worldly estate hauen grave of goostly loue'.[27]

John Newton, unlike these writers, remained in active life, but he was once a member of the same circle as Hilton, and in his will, written in 1414, he indicated that he felt Hilton's anxiety about finding a suitable way of life by proclaiming his despair at attaining happiness in a virtuous life that was full of labour, misery and confusion.[28] In his chapter headings to the *Incendium Amoris* Newton attempted more than a summary of the work: he applied Rolle's mystical experiences to his own definition of the mixed life. In the thirteenth chapter of the *Incendium* Rolle had included in his definition of solitaries those who lived physically among people and yet remained remote from them, never faltering in their heavenly longing; Newton's chapter heading says the life of the solitary is superior to the *vitam communem et mixtam* and leads to the fire of love and a joyful sweetness.[29] This is not an accurate summary: Rolle never used the term 'mixed life', and Newton was perhaps applying it to Rolle's description of those who were able to meditate among people. Newton's description of the last chapter of the *Incendium*, as a prayer for the continuation of genuine spiritual song which was not heard by lovers of the world, suggests that he had made a distinction between the continuous spiritual ecstasy striven for by the professional solitary, and the more intermittent elusive experiences attainable in the mixed life.

Religious Experience and the 'Mixed Life'

The religious writers of the diocese did more than theorize on the concept of the 'mixed life': they attempted to communicate precisely, in prose, the precise spiritual experiences attainable in a domestic or secular environment. Those who defined the mixed life in this period assumed that it was possible to attain religious experiences without ascetic exercise, the external discipline of a monastic rule or renunciation of the

27 *The Mirror of the Lyfe of Jesu Crist*, p. 165.
28 TE, I, p. 366; Y.M.L. Reg. Test., I, fo. 168.
29 *Incendium Amoris*, ed. Deanesly, p. 179; *The Fire of Love*, ed. Harvey, p. 47.

world. Such assumptions would have been encouraged in autobiographical accounts of intense or romantic experiences that were arbitrary and did not depend on hidden knowledge or skills. John Hoveden, in poems reminiscent of secular love poetry, described the *calor, canor* and *dulcedo* felt within the heart, and used the nightingale as a symbol of the mystic lover. The monk solitary of Farne, in a meditation to his guardian angel, related two experiences in Oxford when he narrowly escaped a falling wall and drowning in the river Cherwell; these brought him to a realization of God's grace and his own contemplative vocation. In his meditation on the Passion he revealed his fears of judgement and his reassurance through visions of Christ, who tells him: 'love and you will be saved'.[1]

Rolle was the first writer to make a significant contribution to arousing an interest in the possibilities of attaining emotional spiritual experiences within the domestic household, especially the private chapel. Rolle never mentioned the 'mixed life', and he was the most extreme of the fourteenth century writers in his defence of the superiority of the contemplative life; nevertheless the accounts of the subjective and sensory experiences that dominate his autobiographical writings would have been easily appreciated by his Richmondshire neighbours and patrons.[2] Rolle saw in these experiences a regenerative power, and he regarded them as the most important aspect of his life. The commentary on the canticles records his first formative experience of an inner warmth, sweetness and melody (*calor, canor* and *dulcedo*) which occurred after he had successfully dispelled an apparition of a beautiful woman by invoking the Holy Name of Jesus. He interpreted these sensations as a manifestation of God's love, aroused by his use of the Holy Name, which henceforth became the focus of his devotion.[3] In the *Incendium Amoris* he recorded that three years and four months after this temptation he saw the door of heaven swing open to reveal the face of Our Lord, and with his inner eye, *oculo intellectuali*, he was able to gaze on those in heaven. A year later he felt an 'unusually pleasant heat' and in another nine months he was kindled by a 'sweet warmth' and heard within himself 'sweet unheard melodies'.[4] Rolle regarded these intense moments as intimations of heavenly joy, and his originality lay in his determination to dedicate his life towards these experiences and to

1 *John Hoveden, Poems*, ed. Raby, p. xxii; Allen, *Writings*, p. 420. For a passage from the *Incendium* that is a prose paraphrase of Philomela see *Incendium Amoris*, pp. 259 – 60. Hoveden's *Philomela* is found in Oxford, Bodl. MS. Rawl. A. 389, a manuscript that contains many of Rolle's works.

2 Pantin, 'The Monk Solitary of Farne', 162 – 86.

3 Allen, *Writings*, pp. 70 – 78.

4 *Incendium Amoris*, p. 187 – 91, 97.

recapture their essence in rhythmical and repetitive prose autobiographies such as the *Incendium Amoris, Contra Amatores* and *Melos Amoris*. These writings had a wide appeal: the *Incendium* was addressed to all, including the unlearned: the prologue was directed at those with the greatest capacity for loving, who were prepared to forget their honours and learning.[5] The best description of the spiritual heat, sweetness and song occurs in the fifteenth chapter of the *Incendium*, which was given wider currency by its inclusion in the office compiled at Hampole c.1381.

> I was sitting in a certain chapel and while I was delighted greatly by the sweetness of prayer or meditation, suddenly I felt an unaccustomed, joyful warmth in me. Although at first I worried whence it was, eventually I realized that it was from the Creator, not from any creature, and I found it even more warm and joyful. This inestimably sweet warmth burned in my heart for nine months and some weeks before the infusion and perception of the celestial or spiritual sound of the song of eternal praise and the sweetness of invisible melody which none can know or hear but who receives it, who must be cleansed and separated from this earth.
>
> For when I sat in this same chapel and at night, before supper, and sang the psalm as well as I could, I heard above me as it were a ringing of singers of psalms — or rather, of songs. When in my prayer I fixed all my desire on heavenly things — I don't know how — suddenly I sensed in myself a symphony of song, and I felt the sweetest harmony of heaven remaining with me in my mind. For my thought was continuously turned into the song of the singers and my meditation was like a melody and I even spoke my prayers themselves and psalms in the same music. I burst out then in singing what I had before spoken out of the flowing abundance of inner sweetness — but secretly, before my Creator alone. It was not recognized by those who saw me, for if they had known, they would have honoured me immoderately, and I would thus have lost part of that beautiful flower and fallen in desolation. Meanwhile, I was wonder-struck that I, an exile, should be taken up into so great a joy that God would have given gifts to me that I did not even know how to ask for, nor thought could be given in this life even to the most holy. Thus I realized that it was not given to anyone for his merits, but freely to whomever Christ wishes. I believe, however, that no one will receive it, unless he especially loves the name of Jesus and honours it so highly that he never allows the memory of it to recede from his mind, except in sleep. To whomever it is given to do this, I believe that the other will follow.
>
> Thus it has been four years and approximately three months from the first change in my soul to the highest grade of the love of Christ which, God granting, I have been able to attain — in which grade I have resounded the divine praises with joyous song.

There is in this and other expositions of his mysticism an absence of any severe asceticism: salvation depended less on obedience to preordained

[5] ibid, pp. 145 – 8.

patterns of renunciation than on arbitrary visitations of a mystical experience, gifts of grace that came without any regard for moral worth, as tokens of predestined salvation.[6] The most favourable circumstances for the visitation of *calor, dulcedo* and *canor* was during a quiet interlude, when the lover of Christ was sitting comfortably, removed from the cares of worldly intercourse, the fatigue of travel and the discomforts of cold and hunger; but the experience could also be felt during the daily routine of walking, writing and eating.[7] Rolle's descriptions of these experiences employ the popular language of secular love poetry: his quest for the love of Jesus is described as a transference of a longing for what is beautiful and good into something worthy of this desire. This was the Holy Name of Jesus, and his thoughts objectively reach out towards this object of his love, assimilating him with his beloved, so that whenever he hears or speaks the name of Jesus he experiences delectable pleasure, is transported outside himself and becomes the most fortunate of men.[8] Such romantic introspection has close affinities with the autobiographical writings of Suso, also a devotee of the Holy Name, who depicted his relationship with Christ as a succession of oscillating emotions of depression, boredom, sadness and intense elation.[9]

Rolle was an egotist and his experiences were therefore private; however, he was not altogether self-centred and appears to have made an attempt to show anchoresses, and perhaps the neighbours he advised, how to attain them. In even his most individual of works, the *Incendium Amoris*, he expressed a need for disciples to whom he could communicate his experiences, and he acted as a spiritual advisor to recluses and laity in the diocese. His non-autobiographical epistles were the earliest works in English prose of spiritual and psychological counsel, and all were intended to help beginners in the contemplative life to attain his ecstatic experiences. *Ego Dormio*, written for a lady of Yedingham who was about to become a nun, and *The Commandment*, written for a nun of Hampole, provided an outline of the three attainable degrees of love, 'insuperable, inseparable and singular', and concentrated on the second stage, an inseparable love, 'when al þi thoght es and þi willes er gadered and festend haly in ihesu Criste sua þat þou may na tyme forgete hym'.[10] Meditative aids to master this second stage, including devotion to the Holy Name, were discussed: 'No thyng pays God sau mykel als verray lufe of þis nam Jhesu', and lyrics dedicated to

6 ibid, pp. 145 – 8.
7 ibid, pp. 174 – 7.
8 *The Fire of Love*, p. 215.
9 See Suso, *Horologium Sapienciae*, ed. J. Strange (Cologne, 1861).
10 Allen, *Writings*, pp. 251 – 6; *English Writings of Richard Rolle*, ed. H. E. Allen (Oxford, 1931), pp. 74 – 81.

Jesus were provided for use in private devotions.[11] The most sophisticated of these epistles, *The Form of Living,* written for Margaret Kirkby, offered advice on the attainment of the highest of the three degrees of love, the 'singular', a complete absorption in the love of Christ, and provided descriptions of the joys of warmth, sweetness and divine melody.[12]

Moreover, Rolle's most ambitious efforts to encourage others to strive for these experiences were his attempts to integrate them into the sacraments, especially the sacrament of penance. Like any parish priest, Rolle heard confessions, administered penance, celebrated mass, visited the sick and dying and administered extreme unction. In one of his earliest works, the confession manual, *Judica Me Deus,* he gave a mystical interpretation of the sacrament by claiming that the true penance pleasing to God was a genuine love of Christ. Throughout this work Rolle included characteristic descriptions of the mystical ecstasy which he claimed was the only secure sign of God's forgiveness.[13] *The Form of Living* was also written in the format of a pastoral manual. In the central sixth chapter, which deals with the purgative steps necessary for contemplation, there is an account of the sacrament of penance that includes a list of the various sins of commission and omission in heart, mouth and deed, and instructions on contrition, confession, satisfaction, restitution, alms giving, fasting and prayer. The following chapter demonstrates that obedience to this external code of behaviour does not bring the highest rewards, the sweetness of the Lord's love and the burning of the heart; and that it is the quality of a person's feelings that will bring the rewards of heaven and not the performance of penance: 'Forþi þe diversite of lufe makes þe diversite of halynes and of mede'.[14] Instructions suitable for laymen were provided on the means of attaining this love that were suitable for lay people were provided, including a meal-time prayer, 'loved be thou keyng'.[15] Rolle's commentary on the Decalogue, which is in the Thornton manuscript, similarly recommends the keeping of the Ten Commandments for the sake of the love of God, condemns the hypocritical performance of good deeds and mentions the three degrees of love.[16]

The daily mass itself was also regarded by Rolle as a suitable vehicle for speading his teachings. His mysticism was not abstract, and the daily routine of formal liturgical worship, shared by monks, secular clergy and laymen with private chapels, was an important stimulus to his

11 *English Writings of Rolle,* pp. 74 – 81.
12 Allen, *Writings,* pp. 263 – 68; *English Writings of Rolle,* pp. 104 – 7.
13 Allen, *Writings,* pp. 130 – 44.
14 *English Writings of Rolle,* pp. 102 – 3.
15 ibid, p. 104.
16 *Yorkshire Writers,* i, pp. 195 – 96.

imagination: in the fifteenth chapter of the *Incendium Amoris* he described its influence on his first intimation of *calor, ducedo* and *canor*. The basis of the liturgy was the psalter, which grouped together the psalms according to the offices celebrated during the day or week; and while Rolle was in a chapel, perhaps the private chapel of the Percies or Fitzhughs, he repeated to himself the psalms at vespers, the hour of the day when the melodies of the psalmody were richest, and became aware of a corresponding harmony within himself which was both delectable and heavenly.[17] Rolle transformed his glosses on the first five and a half verses of the Song of Songs and the Psalter into subjective accounts of his solitary life, his dedication to the Holy Name and the physical sensations which he regarded as his apprehension of Christ's love. In his prologue to the Middle English Psalter he urged the use of the liturgical singing of the psalms as a means of attaining religious ecstasy:

> Grete haboundance of gostly comfort and joy in God comes in the hertes of thaim at says or synges deuotly the psalms in louynge of ihu crist. Thai drope swetnes in mannys saule and hellis delite in thaire thoghtes and kyndlis thaire wills with Fyre of luf.[18]

In *The Form of Living* Rolle provides an individualistic interpretation of the liturgy which is similar to his views on the sacrament of penance. The experience of *canor* is identified when the singer of the psalms realizes that the musical accompaniments he hears can only be borne when they are in harmony with the melodies inside him; the attainment of the highest grade of love is described in terms of an inner liturgical accompaniment to the psalms, which is initiated by the chanting of the psalms, but soon develops its own inner rhythm, opposed to the scheme of the daily offices, which causes the worshipper to spend as long as a single day over one psalm:

> þan þe sange of lovynge and of lufe es commen, þan pi thoght turnes until sang and until melody, þan þe behoves syng þe psalms þat þou before syde, þan þou mon be lange aboute few psalmes þan þe wil thynk þ deed swettar þan hony, þar þan þou ert ful syker to se hym þat þou lufes.[19]

Rolle, who first came to the attention of the Daltons while celebrating a mass in Pickering church, realised the potential of the elevation of the Host as a stimulus to mystical experience; and it is probable that he

[17] *V.C.H.*, ii, pp. 97, 488. At the dower house of Percy at Seamer daily mass was said for Lady Eleanor; *Incendium Armoris*, pp. 187 – 91.

[18] Rolle, *English Psalter*, ed. H. R. Bramley (Oxford, 1884), pp. 3 – 5.

[19] *English Writings of Rolle*, pp. 105 – 7.

encouraged some form of liturgical commemoration of his experience at Hampole. This was certainly achieved by the nuns of Hampole, probably under the direction of William Stopes and Margaret Kirkby, who brought the nunnery Rolle's autograph English psalter. The mystical atmosphere of the nun's office in honour of Richard Rolle is established in the opening of the forty-second psalm: *ita desiderat anima mea ad te, Deus situit anima mea ad Deum fontem vivum. quando veniam et apparebo ante faciem Domini.*[20] Thirteen psalms were interspersed with nine biographical lessons of Rolle's life relating the evolution of his mystical ecstasy; these contained descriptions from the prologue of the *Incendium* of his first experience of the fire of love and a quotation from the *Oleum effusum* of his discovery of the power of the Holy Name. The climax to the office is in the final lesson, a description from the fifteenth chapter of the *Incendium* of Rolle's experience of *calor, dulcedo* and *canor,* which occurred when he listened to the psalms. The sung responses allude to these three attributes of Rolle's ecstasy and are perhaps an attempt by the nuns of Hampole to convey in musical terms the *canor* heard by Rolle. The response to *leccio secunda* is: *Melos canorus/Adorem sequitor,/Et dulcor ingens;/Deo laus redditur/*, and the responses to *leccio nona,* while referring to Rolle's miracles, also refer to his ecstasy: *Ad superna conscendit celitus, ubi fixus eius intuitus,/Mira vidit, gaudebat spiritus, fiebat hil aritas: dulces voces ad aurea intonant.*[21] The experiences related in the *Incendium* may also have been adapted to a monastic liturgy at the Benedictine abbey of St Mary's York. John Newton presided with the abbot of St Mary's over a commission on liturgical reforms in the house.[22] It is also possible that John Thweng encouraged a more fervent response to the liturgy at Bridlington. According to his biographers, a miraculous heat could be seen rising from his body at the moment of the elevation of the Host.[23] Around 1460 a polyphonic mass was composed to accompany St John of Bridlington's office, and a scribe, probably of chancery, provided a devout gloss to the cantus firmus 'long ioy bref langour'.[24]

Rolle's attendance at deathbeds may also have resulted in innovations in the administration of the last rites as he comforted the dying with his subjective and optimistic views on salvation. In *Contra Amatores Mundi* he used the book of Job to describe his feelings at the deathbed of his patron Lady Margery Neville: he felt a horror of her cadaver, like a wind brushing his face, and he saw an apparition that delivered a

[20] *Brev. Ebor.*, Col. 785.
[21] *Brev. Ebor*, lectio 2 and 9; Cols. 792, 807.
[22] *Incendium Amoris*, intro. p. 77.
[23] *Nova Legenda Angliae*, ii, pp. 67 – 8.
[24] 'A Polyphonic Mass of St John of Bridlington', *Eng. Church Music*, 22.

warning on the inevitability of death and the punishment of the guilty (Job iv 15). The fear inspired by her cadaver remained with him, and he was plagued by apparitions that made the inside of his cell seem loathsome; troubled by this horror, he resolved to find an explanation which would enable him to treat the same anxieties in others. He came to a realization that fear was preventing him from thinking about death; sustaining himself with his love of Jesus, he eventually came to the conclusion that most people were unable to overcome their fears of death because of a sense of sin and fear of God. His own experiences of divine love had enabled him to face death and God with equanimity, and he resolved to use his personal mysticism to teach others to fear only fear itself and to seek consolation of the Lord.[25]

Rolle also incorporated his subjective intimations on immortality into the celebration of the Office of the Dead. The source of this mass was reading from the Book of Job, which must have aroused the anxieties Rolle was attempting to combat. Through suffering, Job discovers the deceptions of high rank, wealth, pride and greed, and learns that all creatures may die at any moment, their brief lives, full of disquiet, are but a breath of wind; a man blossoms like a flower and then withers, his gold turning to ashes and his shroud to worms; he learns that it is the wicked and unrepentant who fear God and is finally reconciled to his fate and repents in dust and ashes when he realizes that everyone merits punishment. Commentaries on the Book of Job, such as the anonymous early fifteenth-century *Pety Job*, preserve the tone of bitter submissiveness found in the original texts, but Rolle's treatment was different. Around 1331, the time of his experience of the horror of his patron's death, he composed *Postillae super Novem Lectiones*, a commentary on the nine readings from the Book of Job which occur in the Office of the Dead. The primary purpose of this work, which begins *Exprimitur autem in his verbis humanae conditionis, quae non habet in hac miserabili valle manentem mansionem*, was to inspire penitence; after the penitent had acknowledged his helplessness in the face of sins, he was open to receive the foretaste of salvation in warmth, sweetness and song.[26] By introducing into his commentary this optimistic belief in the redemptive power of religious experience, Rolle had transformed the mood of the office readings. He clearly intended these readings to be more than a penitential exercise and saw them as a part of his mystical doctrine. He referred his readers to his other ecstatic works, some of which he had not yet written, for descriptions of the experiences of ecstasy that could consume the rust of sin, enabling participants in the service to quit the

25 Allen, *Writings*, pp. 456 – 57; *Brev. Ebor.*
26 Allen, *Writings*, pp. 130, 144.

world without fear and with a sense of amazement that such beauty could be experienced by mortal men in a decaying body.[27]

Rolle's influence, especially after his death, extended far beyond his patrons, neighbours and the religious houses, as many attempted to integrate his experience into the routines of their secular lives. Public men, owners of the autobiographical works of Rolle and Suso, like John Newton, Thomas Hebbenden, Robert Alne, Henry Lord Scrope and Henry Lord FitzHugh, may have entertained hopes of experiencing the fire of love. Such literature influenced the less educated: Margery Kempe was a housewife who claimed to feel 'þe hete brennyng in hir brest and at hir hert, es verily as a man shuld felyn þe material fyer yf he put hys hand or hys fynger þerin', and to hear 'a sound of melodye — as she had ben in Paradyse'.[28]

The influence of Rolle's mysticism manifests itself most clearly in the sacrament of the Eucharist. The devotional mass of the Hampole nuns could not be celebrated in the churches because the cult was unofficial, but its narrative structure recommended itself to a popular audience such as pilgrims at the shrine at Hampole. The same enthusiasm to share Rolle's fervour seems to have inspired the liturgical innovations within the private chapels of the Yorkshire nobility. Rolle's widely circulated psalter, owned by noblemen such as Henry Lord Scrope and Sir Thomas Cumberworth, may have encouraged within the private chapel a more personal and mystical participation in the liturgy. His devotion to the Holy Name was given a feast day in the Sarum calender, and the first expression of its liturgical aspect occurred in the mid-fourteenth century when indulgences for a votive mass of Jesus became common.[29] The Nevilles were probably early devotees: at Durham Cathedral there was a Jesus altar with a retable opening to reveal 'the whole passion of Our Lord Jesus Christ most richlye and curiously set forth in most lyveli colors all like the burninge gold, as he was tormented and as he hange on ye cross which was a most lamentable sighte to beholde'. Both Ralph and John Neville were buried before this Jesus altar in 1367 and 1388.[30] Sir William Beauchamp, the captain of Calias, was perhaps introduced to the works of Rolle by this family. He shared a command of 170 men with the "Lollard knight" Sir William Neville in the army of the Duke of Lancaster, and appeared with Sir William as an executor in 1382.[31] Besides his collection of the works of Rolle, Beauchamp owned a missal that is the first known liturgical book

27 ibid, p. 140.
28 *The Book of Margery Kempe*, p. 70.
29 R. W. Pfaff, *New Liturgical Feasts in Later Medieval England*, (Oxford, 1920), pp. 65 – 6.
30 ibid, p. 78.
31 McFarlane, *Lancastrian Kings and Lollard Knights*, pp. 161, 183.

before 1388 to contain a mass of the Holy Name.[32] Archbishop Rotherham enforced the observation of this cult in the diocese in 1486 when he founded Jesus College in Rotherham in honour of the Holy Name of Jesus.

The daily routine of prayer and the chanting of the psalms, prescribed in books of hours, was being changed in noble households by the addition of prayers showing the influence of Rolle's mysticism. Mary Bohun, Countess of Derby, introduced into the psalter of her father, the earl of Hereford, some personal prayers which aimed to 'inspire her heart with an intense sweetness.'[33] The book of hours illuminated by Hermann Scheere for a prominent northern family, perhaps the Scropes, contained a Latin prayer which invoked the mercy and sweetness of Christ and included a dedication to the Holy Name. The supplicant, addressing Christ directly, *O dulcissime Jesu*, asks him to reveal himself; the prayer reaches an ecstatic climax, reminiscent of Rolle, through a repetition of the Holy Name: *Jesu Jesu, Jesu O dulcissime Jesu*.[34] The Boltons' book of hours also contains a poem dedicated to the Holy Name, *O Bone Jesu, O dulcissime Jesu*.[35] Thomas Fishbourne owned a tract called *de virtute nominis Jhesu* and Robert Thornton copied into his manuscript an English translation of *Encomium nominis Jesu*, which included such characteristic expressions of Rolle's devotion as : 'This name es in myne ere heuenely sowne, in my mouthe honyfull swetnes. Wharfore na wandire þo/e lufe þat name, the whilke gyffes comforthe to me in all angwys'.[36] By the end of the fourteenth century there were many devotees to the Holy Name in the diocese. Richard Scrope founded a chapel in honour of the Holy Name in Lichfield in 1388; in 1399 Sir Philip Darcy dedicated himself in his will to 'Jesus, in thy holy name trusting', and recommended his soul to 'Thee, lord Jesus and to thy glorious mother'; and in 1449 Sir John Constable enjoined his son with a binding oath 'on the bowels of Christ'.[37] In the fifteenth century the popularity of this devotional cult was reflected in mottos inscribed on jewellery. Margery Kempe claimed that she was commanded by Our Lord to have a ring made which would be her 'bone maryd ryng to Jesus Crist', and to inscribe it with the motto *Ihesus est amor meus*.[38] The same inscription appears on the beads left by William of Wykeham to

32 Pfaff, *Liturgical Feasts*, pp. 65 – 6.

33 Catto, 'Religion and the Nobility', p. 49; Bodl. Lib. MS. Auct. D4; M. R. James, *The Bohun Manuscripts* (Oxford, 1936); M. Rickert, *The Reconstructed Carmelite Missal* (London, 1952), pp. 73 – 5.

34 Bodl. Lib. MS. Lt. Liturg. e17, fos. 111 – 112.

35 Y.M.L. MS. Add. 2.

36 *Yorkshire Writers*, i, pp. 186 – 91.

37 Pfaff, *Liturgical Feasts*, p. 79 n. 3; Apb. Reg. 16, fo. 134; Borth Inst. Hist. R., Prob. Reg. 2, fo. 242v.

38 *The Book of Margery Kempe*, p. 78.

Archbishop Arundel and on a belt bequeathed by Lady Margaret Vavasour.[39] Thomas Dautre gave the Carthusians of Hull a silver plate bearing the name of Jesus; Constance Mauley left Elizabeth Stapleton a gold ring inscribed 'Jesus be my love'; and Margaret Stapleton in 1465 gave her best gold ring, which he wore on her finger, to hang on the neck of an image of Jesus Christ at Newburgh.[40] These were also moving expressions of religious sentiment: John Castell, a residentiary canon of York, began his will in 1456 with a series of direct appeals to the name of Jesus: 'Trusting in the mercy and passion of Our Lord Jesus who is salvation, life and our resurrection — In my hour of death and judgement Jesus, Jesus is with me'.[41]

Rolle's influence could also be seen in innovations in traditional preparations for death and the liturgical commemoration of the deceased. There was a pessimistic attitude to death in this period, encouraged by epidemics of the Black Death in 1349, 1361 and 1369. Subsequent generations tended to see these as visitations of divine judgement: Thoresby in his sermons interpreted them as punishment for sins as Gascoigne was to do in an outbreak in 1451.[42] Penitential tracts on death included *The Book of Job* (Job was the patron saint against the plague), *The Art of Dying*, which was taken from Suso's *Horologium* and circulated as a separate treatise, and a guide on preparing to die that came from the popular northern poem *The Prick of Conscience*. Such literature emphasized the transitoriness of life and the suddenness of death, encouraging the sense of fear and sin that Rolle was concerned with combatting. In such an atmosphere there was an obsession with the physical process of decay depicted in funeral monuments and in the prologues to many wills in the diocese between 1370 and 1415. Those of sensitive piety who were readers of the contemplative literature of the north prefixed their wills with lamentations on the different aspects of death. Thomas Dalby contrasted his achievements and his predestined humble end with a comment on the mortality of all flesh and the circular condition of all men whose origin and end was ashes; Walter Skirlaw lamented that all knowledge and glory, like flowers in the field, was destined to die and concluded that all rational creatures, after the flowing of the course of their lives, come back to the sad thought of fearful death.[43] John Newton reflected that nothing in life is stable, constant or joyful; all was confusion, labour and misery from which no man, regardless of his high office, could be free; Henry Lord Scrope described himself as one crushed down by a brief life

39 Mauley, *Some New Light on Chaucer*, (New York, 1961), p. 507.
40 TE, I, pp. 149 – 52; 362; Y.M.L. Reg. Test. 4, fo. 116.
41 TE, III, p. 183.
42 Thompson, 'Pestilences in York', 102. *Loci e Libro Veritatum*, p. 12.
43 Y.M.L. Reg. Test. I, fo. 124; TE, I, pp. 261, 306.

full of many miseries, during which he had attempted to flee the shade knowing that nothing was permanent; and Thomas Hebbenden described death as *naturaliter formidatur*.[44] In such an atmosphere masses for the dead multiplied. The importance of the Office of the Dead in the noble chapel can be seen in the testaments of the Chaworth family of Nottinghamshire. Alice Chaworth in 1400 left a *Placebo et Dirige* to her son Sir Thomas Chaworth; in 1458 her grandson Sir Thomas Chaworth left one *Placebo et Dirige* to his son Thomas, and another in his old chapel mass book, which contained *obits* for his ancestors, to his son William.[45] It is significant that Rolle's most popular work after his psalter was his commentary on the Book of Job, which survives in forty-two manuscripts and was popular among the secular clergy of York Minster: owners included John Newton, Robert Semer, Robert Helperby, William Gate, Richard Drax, William Duffield and Thomas Pynchbek.[46] It is possible that services for the dead in this cathedral would have been strongly influenced by Rolle's mystical meditations on death and perhaps helped to lessen the severity of much traditional morality on the subject.

Introspection and Detachment

Rolle's most important contribution towards increasing the spiritual possibilities of a religious life outside the monastery and anchorage was indirect: his descriptions of religious ecstasy aroused heated debate among northern religious authors in the second half of the fourteenth century, including members of Arundel's circle, which was resolved by them moderating Rolle's teaching and formulating concepts of religious experience and meditation that were more suitable and attractive to those in secular life. After witnessing the interest that the Hampole hermit aroused in religious experience, they would have realized that the emphasis he placed on will-power in his repetitive writings made them more appropriate for the recluse than those in active life. The 'fire of love' was depicted as an invasion of the self that came about as a consequence of the recipient maintaining a harmonious relationship between a steadfast will-power and external circumstances; and the experience, closely associated with the liturgy, occurred at certain times of the day, in certain places, far away from social distractions. However inappropriate much of this teaching was for those

44 Y.M.L. Reg. Test. I, fo. 168; TE, I, p. 366; *Foedera* ix, p. 275; *Register of Langley*, pp. 159 – 62.
45 TE, I, p. 164.
46 Y.M.L. Reg. Test. I, fos. 168, 121, 233; TE, III, pp. 99, 199.

living in the active life, its potential popularity must have been self-evident: Rolle's dependence on empirical factors and his excessive emotional and sensory descriptions gave his experiences a miraculous quality that was not far removed from some of the miracles that were reported by pilgrims at the Hampole shrine. The clergy of the diocese were alarmed that these teachings had little moderate or restraining influences, and for this reason they criticized aspects of Rolle's doctrine. They saw the danger of the religious contemplation they advocated for the mixed life becoming submerged by a less sophisticated popular religious enthusiasm, generated by Rolle, that all too readily might degenerate into a literal-minded dependence on magic, supernatural phenomena and emotional impressionability. They counteracted this by formulating a less extroverted concept of religious experience, based on introspection and detachment, that required no special renunciatory gifts or extroverted, egocentric qualities, and avoided the pitfalls of emotional instability.

Most of the religious writers of the diocese in the late fourteenth century discussed Rolle's teachings on heavenly warmth, sweetness and song; and they all shared the same ambivalent attitudes when applying *calor, canor,* and *dulcedo* to their own lives and those of their immediate circle. They cautiously admired it as the reward enjoyed by a spiritual elite; but they expressed grave reservations about its application to enthusiastic lay followers. Hilton's Latin letters to fellow ecclesiastical administrators, Cambridge scholars, recluses and monks reveal the cautious attempts made by members of this circle to attain the experiences described by Rolle. In *De Imagine Peccati,* Hilton tells a fellow hermit about his devotion to the Holy Name of Jesus[1], and in *Epistola de Utilitate,* he describes for Adam Horsley the nourishing fire of love in the heart.[2] However, in all his letters Hilton counselled caution and pointed out the dangers of self-deception. In *De Imagine,* although he does not engage in conscious controversy as he does in the later *Scale of Perfection,* he does distinguish, as Rolle does not, between the experience of sweet taste that belongs to the bodily senses or imagination, and that which is properly supernatural or spiritual; moreover, he distinguishes between a devotion to the Holy Name that was similarly spiritual and interior and not bound up with physical feelings of warmth.[3] In three later works, *De Imagine Peccati, Epistola de Utilitate,* and *Epistola de Leccione* (which was probably addressed to a solitary) Hilton warned against the dangers of singularity and emphasizes the importance of discretion, including discretion in relation to sensations of warmth, sounds and smell, as the key monastic virtue which prevented pride and heresy.

1 Hilton, *Latin Writings,* i, p. 98.
2 ibid, i, p. 374, ll 843ff.
3 ibid, i, p. 94.

However, religious writers in the late fourteenth century also considered the application of Rolle's teaching to a wider, enthusiastic following, and when doing so they were more forthright in expressing their misgivings. John Thweng was noted for his ability to experience the 'fire of love', but like Hilton he was a member of an order noted for its moderation and pastoral interests, and despite the excessive admiration that he inspired during his lifetime, he appears to have been a pragmatic self-effacing man, with little patience for the extremes of religious behaviour shown by some of Rolle's enthusiastic followers. According to the bull of canonization he was, in spiritual matters, a careful man; he rebuked those who claimed to have visions of him, and when a Richmondshire anchoress confided her vision of an eagle bearing the Holy Name, he cut her short and left her. In his parting words he expressed his disappointment that while he had come to talk of the grace and goodness of God he saw that the empty talk of a demon who exploited human weakness had entered her mind.[4]

The most explicit criticisms about the potential dangers of Rolle's teaching were made in the vernacular literature of the diocese, which was directed towards novices in the contemplative profession and laymen. In *The Cloud of Unknowing* and *The Scale of Perfection* similar language is used to express doubts about the divine or diabolical origins of the experience of warmth, sweetness and song that it is possible that the writers had discussed the problem. The author of the *Cloud* warned his young disciple to hold suspect all comforts that came from an uncertain origin: 'for they may be either good or evil: done by a good angel if good, by an evil angel if evil. But the former gift can not be evil --it is performed immediately by the love of God.[5] Hilton was just ambivalent: 'For in virtues and knowing and loving of God can there be no deceit; but all such manner of things may be good, caused by the good angel, and deceitfully feigned by a wicked angel portraying himself as an angel of light'.[6] The Carthusian monk whose criticisms were recorded by Thomas Basset showed the same equivocation when he said he was not obliged to believe either that these feelings described by Rolle were spiritual or not.[7] All of these writers, while allowing for the possibility that *canor* could be genuine, implied that in most cases it was a physical sensation mistaken for a spiritual experience. Furthermore the author of the *Cloud* observed that clergy and men and women of different backgrounds, through inexperience, had been lead astray by false spirituality; after reading about the sorrowful and continual longing for God's love, they interpreted this in a physical sense, and in vain they strove to experience it, only to be left either with a physical and

4 *Nova Legenda Angliae*, ii, p. 167; for bull of canonization see Purvis, 'St John of Bridlington', 31 – 7.
5 *Cloud of Unknowing*, pp. 98 – 9.
6 *Scale of Perfection*, ed. Underhill, p. 19.
7 Sargent, 'Criticism of Rolle', 160 – 87.

spiritual torpor, or an unnatural glow within themselves; the latter was described as a spiritual warmth caused by bodily abuses and sham spirituality, a 'false knowing' which they imagined to be the fire of love, but which was a delusion of the fiend.[8] Hilton also warned directly against Rolle's descriptions of religious ecstasy saying that any sensation, whether 'sounding in the ear, or tasting in the mount, or smelling in the nose, or any sensible heat, such as glowing fire warming your breast — are not true contemplation'.[9] Later in the *Scale of Perfection* he cautioned that not all those who spoke of the fire of love knew what it was, and while he admitted that he had never experienced it himself, he attempted to prevent Rolle's followers from misinterpreting his teachings on *canor* in too literal a manner.

> This I can tell you, that it is neither physical nor phsically felt. A soul which is in the body may feel it in prayer or devotion, but he feels no bodily sense; for although its operation is in the soul, the body may warm, chafed as it were, by a sympathetic operation with the spirit. But the fire of love is not physical, for it is only in the spiritual desire of the soul. Men and women who truly feel devotion are aware of this, but some people are simple and believe that because it is called fire, it should be hot like a physical fire.[10]

Hilton clearly saw his lack of personal experience of *canor* as no obstacle to his fulfilling his pastoral duty of interpreting Rolle's teaching in a spiritual manner. In a chapter he later added to the *Scale of Perfection* he applied the same criterion to a too inflexible and literal devotion to the Holy Name, a cult inspired by Rolle: 'But now you say — I am troubled by what I find written in some men's books. As I understand it, they say that anyone who cannot love the blessed name of Jesus, or feel spiritual joy and delight in it, will be forever alien to the sovereign joy and spiritual sweetness of the bliss of heaven'.[11] Hilton's answer was to advise his readers that the name of Jesus meant health or salvation, and that: 'just as anyone who wishes to be healthy is devoted to health, so anyone who wishes for salvation is devoted to that which is signified by the name of Jesus'.[12] In the treatise *Of Angel's Song*, in answer to specific enquiried about the origin of heavenly sounds and *canor*, it is demonstrated that sweetness or song like sounding of the name of Jesus in the heart can be morally worthy when it is the result of concentration on something virtuous; but such sensations were emotional in origin and not supernatural. Devotees to the Holy Name were furthermore instructed to hold their feelings in check

8 *Cloud*, p. 86, and ch. 45, 65.
9 *Scale*, pp. 19 – 21.
10 *Scale*, p. 59.
11 ibid, pp. 104 – 108.
12 ibid.

with reason, and not to esteem them so highly: 'It sufficeth mee for to lyffe in trouthe principally and noght in felynge'.[13] All of these criticisms of Rolle's teachings provide proof that an important aspect of the pastoral work of the clergy of the diocese was to ensure that the fire of love and the cult of the Holy Name were not distorted to become sources of magic and power which could easily become a challenge to the authority of the church in the same way as Lollard claims for the word of scripture or the predestined elect. The Carthusian opponent of Rolle's followers intimated as much when he claimed that Rolle, who had deceived and ruined more men than he had helped, made men judges of themselves.

However, the criticisms of these clergy were not all negative: they all believed in the possibility of attaining the experiences described by Rolle, and they provided constructive advice to enable people to responsibly evaluate the integrity of their inner lives. These writers stressed that *canor* came to a privileged few, and that it could only be understood as a spiritual experience that came from within a devout soul. The author of the *Cloud* conceded that God sometimes enflames the body of his devout servants here in this life with wonderful sweetness and comforts which spring from within from an abundance of spiritual joy and devotion so that: 'such a comfort and such a sweetness cannot be held suspect: in fact I do not believe that the one who feels them can hold them suspect.[14] Hilton distinguished between false comforts and true comforts which, when given, incite the soul to even greater devotion. Like the author of the *Cloud* he does not specifically mention Rolle and points out that the true spiritual sensations of heat, sweetness and song may be given 'in earnest and, as it were a shadow of the glorification of the body, which it will have in bliss'.[15] In *Of Angel's Song*, similarly, it is suggested that in a soul reformed through grace to its original condition the mind is cleared of bodily worldly considerations, imaginings and fantasies, and illuuminated by grace to be enflamed with the burning love of the Holy Ghost; in such a state the soul can receive spiritual comforts such as angel's song, which are above the consideration of imagination and reason.[16] Another Carthusian of the diocese, Nicholas Love, associated the experience of the fire of love with an interiorized devotion to the celebration of mass. While conceding that there may be many people that he is unaware of who have experienced the fire of love, he knows only one person who is touched with such grace; and he gave an account of such an experience, perhaps derived from the account of a fellow monk of Mount Grace. The recipient, while meditating on Christ's Passion during mass:

13 *Yorkshire Writers*, i, pp. 175 – 82, esp. 182.
14 *Cloud*, pp. 98 – 9.
15 *Scale*, p. 23.
16 *Angel's Song*, p. 12.

> Sodynly feleth also filed in to the self body a ioye and likynge that passith with oute comparison the hygest likynge that eny creature may haue of fele as by way of kynde in this lyf; thrugh the whole ioye and likyng alle the membres of the body ben enflawmed of so delectable and ioyful an hete, that hym thinketh sensibly all the body as it were meltynge for ioye'.[17]

Perhaps the most constructive pastoral contribution that the Yorkshire religious writers of the late fourteenth century made for those wishing to attain such experiences, and for those clergy faced with the task of evaluating them, was to stress that the integrity of *canor* could be measured by the degree of humility and charity shown by Rolle's followers. Thomas Basset replied to the charges made by his Carthusian opponent about the sincerity of his own spiritual experiences by demonstrating that he at least possessed these two necessary virtues, admitting that there was no good inside him, that he did not deserve any good; Basset, with humility and charity, raised doubts about his opponents eligibility to receive the fire of love: 'My friend, God knows how you will take these words, for I am not so bold as to judge anyone except by manifest signs, and even then with a sympathetic heart. Forgive me, then, for writing to you, so literate and well educated a man, in so rude and unlettered a manner. But you know me to be a simple unlettered man, and Christ knows that his own charity urges me to write these things to you in this way; which if they have effect, I rejoice.'[18] In the treatise *Of Angel's Song* these experiences are described as gifts of charity, or grace, the true union on God and man's soul in perfect charity; and the author observes that unless the soul has perfect charity and humility it can easily fall into presumption, error, heresy and other kinds of frenzy.[19] Both Hilton and Nicholas Love provided practical advice on the attainment of this necessary humility and charity by counselling meditation on Christ's life and Passion. In the *Scale* Hilton described the spiritual vanity that was a consequence of beguiling feelings and illusions which diverted people from the 'mind and beholding of Jhesu Crist and from ghostly occupation as from prayer, and thinking of thyself, thy defaults, from the inward desire of virtues and ghostly knowing and feeling of God.'[20] However, it was Nicholas Love who provided in his gospel harmony a detailed illustration of Christ's humility and charity which he may have intended as an example for the disciples of Richard Rolle to follow if they wished to have any chance of attaining a genuine experience of the fire of love, and

17 *Mirror*, p. 209.
18 Sargent 'Criticism of Rolle', 180.
19 *Angel's Song*, p. 12.
20 *Scale*, p. 21.

if they wished to avoid the pitfalls of emotional instability, self-deception, and isolation.

These exhortations to meditate on Christ's Passion that accompanied such cautionary warnings about Rolle's teachings were an important aspect of the pastoral and religious literature of the diocese, and they will be discussed shortly. However, the York clergy realized that they needed to provide a firm foundation of psychological and spiritual teachings to convince their colleagues and sophisticated laymen that Rolle's emphasis on will power and individuality could result in alienation from community, family and the self, and that an alternative religious life was available to those which did not demand spiritual perfection. This encouraged the leaders of the church of York to teach pious men and women that religious sensibility could be consistent with ordinary human frailty, and that there was no need for them to segregate themselves from their neighbours and dependents in a search for excellence. In the writings of Augustine they had access to a religious philosophy that helped them to formulate a concept of religious introspection that made full allowance for human frailty therefore showed the pious how to reconcile themselves with others.

The basis of a detached acceptance of human limitations and the material world was Augustinian realist philosophy, which had dominated the Oxford theology schools under Bradwardine and FitzRalph. Wyclif was exposed to these influences as a theology student; he advised his students to read the *Confessions* if they wished to reach a greater understanding of God; and he attributed to Augustine his own convertion from terminism to realism, which enabled him to see all creation as a mirror of the eternal exemplar.[21] This allowed him to develop a religious philosophy with a profound sense of intellectual detachment towards reality. Wyclif saw the outside world in platonic terms as a series of fragments from God, a distraction which was mirrored in the empirical and sensory images within the human soul. Successive time and the particular beings and events within time were also an illusionary reflection of the amplified eternal present of God which contained all moments past and future: *extendo tempus de presenti sic quod omne fuit vel erit est pro tempore suo*.[22] Scripture was the mirror that revealed the creator of all this because it was the book of life that showed, in its particular historic events, God's timeless vision of the past and the future. Wyclif described the process of learning from this book of life as one of receiving light from God, from whom all knowledge comes, by divine illumination. Through contemplation of

21 Wyclif, *Summa de Ente*, ed. S. Harrison-Thompson (1930), p. 109.

22 Wyclif's theories on time are summarized by Robson in *Wyclif and the Oxford Schools*, p. 153.ff

the world, the self, and scripture in particular, it was therefore possible to ascend towards God because every man had within him an innate knowledge of things as they were in this natural order; his comprehensions were therefore not purely empirical and it was possible, and every man's duty, to progress through a hierarchy to stages of awareness from a knowledge of particular things beneath the transcendent to a deductive knowledge of God and, finally, to the highest stage of knowledge where an intuitive sense, an *instincta interna*, helps towards a knowledge of God as the first cause of all things.[23] This perception of God, described as an illumination and radiation of light in the soul, was similar to the contemplative experience envisaged by the mystical authors of the late fourteenth century.

Wyclif was also influenced by Augustine in his attitudes towards the human will. His conversion, like that of his mentor, was followed by disillusionment, but for different reasons. Unlike Augustine, he was unemotional and ascetic by temperament: he showed neither sexual guilt nor a fear of habitual pleasure, and he had put his early energies into study and public life; but he was aware that despite his concersion he had not changed much and the sins of a hard-bitten careerist such as pride, ambition and vindictiveness remained.[24] He probably found comfort from this sense of failure in the humane understanding of the limitations of the human will provided in the theology of Augustine, especially in the *Confessions* and *De Trinitate*. In his own version of *De Trinitate* and in *De Ente* Wyclif narrowed the freedom of choice allowed by Bradwardine and defined free will as the faculty by which an intellectual nature willingly cleaved to righteousness; he asserted that only God enjoyed such perfect freedom of will in that nothing could prevent Him from making a right choice: intelligent creatures were free to desire the appearance of righteousness but could be prevented from choosing it by the defection of their wills which had been ensnared by the habits of sin forged in the memory.[25] Faced with the impossibility of overcoming the self Wyclif also turned to the efficacy of grace, which is a recurring theme in his writings; his criticisms of church authority and the sacraments never extended to the sacrament of baptism.

Thomas Gascoigne, another Oxford theologian from York diocese, also absorbed himself in Augustine and quoted from most of his works, including the sermons, *De Enchiridon* and *Contra Donatistas* (a work in defence of the redemptive power of baptism). He left copies of *De Trinitate* and the commentary on the psalms to Balliol college and his

23 *Summa de Ente*, p. 108.
24 For Wyclif's conversion see Smalley, 'The Bible and Eternity', 74.
25 Wyclif, *De Ente Duorum*, ed. M. Dziewicki (London, 1909), pp. 137 – 41; Wyclif *Tractatus De Trinitate*, ed. A. Breck (Colorado, 1962). There are over a hundred references to Augustine in this work.

annotated volume of *The City of God* to All Souls. Sharing Wyclif's interest in the contemplative movement and criticisms of scholastic philosophy, he applied himself to the study of the church's redemptive role in preaching and administration of the sacraments, expressing a concern that every church in England did not have a resident pastor or a baptismal font.[26] John Castell, a residentary canon of York, theology graduate and Master of University college from 1411 to 1420, was also influenced by Augustinian theology: he compiled and transcribed a collection of theological extracts with the help of John Kexby, a York Minster priest who had been attacked by Arundel in 1409 for having Wycliffite sympathies; Castell's manuscript contained twenty-seven items, and most of them, apart from extracts from Aquinas, were the works of Augustine, including *Contra Pelagianos* and the *Confessions*.[27] Castell acknowledged his own sense of the fallibility of the human will and his trust in the efficacy of baptismal grace in his last will and testament: he requested that his perishable body be buried before the baptismal font in the metropolitan church where he had received the sacrament of baptism, declared his faith in this sacrament, which he had so frequently violated, and in the Passion, to bring about the resurrection of his perishable body.[28]

Interest in Augustine was widespread in this period and was not confined to theologians: the canonists of York Minster shared Augustine's interest in human personality and turned to his teachings on divine grace as a means of understanding and reconciling religious spirituality with human fraility. Some owned works dealing specifically with the problems of grace and free will: Newton owned *De Trinitate, Contra Pelagianos,* and *Exodus ad Literam*; Thomas Fishbourne, once a clerk of Bowet's, owned the *Epistola ad Julianum,* and Robert Alne left a copy of *De Trinitate* to Peterhouse.[29] The canonists of York, like the theologians, looked beyond the confines of their profession, and their ownership of the pastoral manuals of William of Pagula and John de Burgo suggests that they applied their interest in the principles of human behaviour and conscience to self-examination and the discharge of their pastoral duties. Hilton, a canonist who was absorbed in Augustine's writings, did this by writing English works of spiritual direction. Much of his *Scale of Perfection* was a paraphrase of book ten of the *Confessions*. In the second book of the *Scale,* Hilton showed the same faith as the theologians in the authority of the church as the dispenser of the sacrament of baptism, and he integrated the sacrament of baptism

26 Emden, *B.R.U.O.*, ii, p. 747.
27 Univ. Coll. OXford MS. 76, fos. 210, 277ff. See also R. W. Hunt, 'The Manuscript Collection of University College', *Bodl. Lib. Record*, III, (1950 – 51) 16.
28 TE, III, p. 183.
29 Y.M.L. Reg. Test I, fo. 168; TE, II, p. 78.

with the contemplative life: the first stage of the baptismal life was defined as a reformation in faith, in which grace worked outwardly and imperceptibly, both in the case of a newly baptized infant and in the turning of the will of an adult penitent.[30] But Hilton and his contemporaries were not fideists, and their originality lay in their treatment of the second stage of the baptismal life, defined by Hilton as a reformation in feeling, in which they applied the definitions of baptismal grace made in the schools to the emotional life of the individual, using subtle vernacular prose that was accessible to pious men and women in secular life.

All the religious writers of the second half of the fourteenth century shared Augustine's views of the inability of the human will to conquer sin and to approach God. In *Þe Holy Boke Gratia Dei* there is a pessimistic view of man's fallen nature, in which the will is shown to be free to do good only until the first sin, when 'þerfigte fre will in-till nedfulnes turnes'.[31] In *The Cloud of Unknowing* the efforts made to control emotions and to free the mind from habitual patterns of thought are shown to be invalid, hence the importance of the author's vision of grace, which is mentioned ninety times in this work, and which enabled men to forget their impulses rather than to conquer them; all human emotions, associations, memories and habitual patterns of thought were to be forgotten, including the contemplation of God's humanity in the Passion, because they could lead, through an inevitable train of association, to one's own life and the disintegration of personal thoughts.[32] The unknowable was to be approached through a paradoxical negation of knowledge of God or of feelings towards him in a cloud of unknowing.[33] The author provided meditative exercises to help his disciples attain a complete detachment from the world and the self which involved concentration on single words, like God, that had no associations. Although this concept of detachment was far removed from Rolle's sensual vision of God's love, the drills of *The Cloud of Unknowing* bore some similarity to the meditations on the Holy Name of Jesus espoused by Rolle.

The author of *Of Angel's Song*, probably Hilton or an associate, was unique in that he criticized both Rolle and the Cloud author for their lack of understanding about the limitations of the human will. He pointed out that followers of the *via negativa*, by concentrating on a single word such as God to the exclusion of all feelings and associations, and by believing that the absence of conscience achieved was a visit from Our

30 *Scale of Perfection*, p. 252.
31 *þe Holy Boke Gratia Dei*, ed. Arntz, p. 8.
32 *The Cloud of Unknowing*, pp. 116, 120.
33 ibid, pp. 97, 121–23.

Lord, were in danger of falling into the same self-deception as those who tried to experience the fire of love. All experiences desired by he who 'gedyrs his wittys by violence to seke and to behalde heuenly thyngys' are liable to be illusionary because they are wanted too much; their exclusive dependence on will-power and self-decipline destroyed joyful experience, mental and emotional: 'for wete þou wel þat a nakede ymagynacione of ihesu or of any gastely thynge, with owttene swetnes of lufe in þe affeccione or withowtene lyght of knowynge in resoune, es bot a blyndnes, and a waye to dessayte'.[34] The disappointment or remorse that accompanied sensory pleasure, 'the bitterness and bitynge of consyence', was seen as a consequence of the fall; but through grace it was possible to transmute such simple pleasures into an associative experience that would give a man the freedom and lordship within his own soul to see God in all things: 'some saule by vertue of charyte þat godde gyffes it es so clensede, þat all creaturs in all þat he heris, or sese, of felis by any of his wittes turns hyme till comforthe and gladnes, and þe sensualite recuyes newe sauour and swetnes in all creaturs'.[35] The author of *þe Holy Boke Gratia Dei* also felt mystical joy to be intermittent in contrast to the perpetual joy described by Rolle; he defined it as a passive experience, occurring when God 'sendes likyng to þi saule thurgh grace'.[36] The recipient should therefore be humble and content, and not unhappy when it departs like an eagle, 'Forþi thurgh his grace, he comes when he wile, and to whomever he will; and wher-so he will, parts also'.[37]

For the authors of *Of Angel's Song* and *þe Holy Boke Gratia Dei*, the Passion and the invocation of the Holy Name of Jesus were not a means to ecstasy or self-annihilation but self-affirmation. This was demonstrated by Walter Hilton who used Augustine's ideas on grace and free will to outline a theory of contemplation that did not involve abstraction from the experiences absorbed in the memory. Augustine's *De Trinitate* depicts the soul, a trinity of *Memoria, Intelligentia* and *Voluntas,* as the *Imago Dei,* obscured as a consequence of Adam's self-will by the *imago peccati,* so that the intuitive contemplation of God was lost. This work, and the tenth book of the *Confessions,* imparted to Hilton's *Scale of Perfection* a sense that there was a struggle within the intricate paths of habitual thought for a memory of a state of happiness in God's love before the fall. The strong autobiographical and psychological undertones of the *Confessions* are missing, but not the assumption that contemplation involves introspection and self-knowledge: 'For as St

34 *Yorkshire Writers,* i, p. 179. ibid; i, p. 182.
35 ibid, i, p. 177.
36 *þe Holy Boke Gratia Dei,* p. 74.
37 ibid, p. 74.

Austin saith; by the knowing of myself, I shall get the knowing of God'.[38] Also absorbed from the *Confessions* was a recognition of the impossibility of complete abstraction from and control of the thoughts and memories of the mind. Unlike the Cloud author and Richard Rolle, Hilton advocated no meditative techniques or mental drills; he showed psychological understanding of the powerlessness of the human will in the face of the vast intricacies of the human memory and the desires and responses it elicited: 'for it is not good to strive with such ther, for to put them out by mastery, for the more they strive with such thoughts the more they cleave to them'.[39] Using the same scriptural examples as Augustine, Hilton depicted the loss of God within the soul as a search for the forgotten image of a coin, lost underneath the countless and continually accumulating images of sin and distraction.[40]

Although many of Hilton's observations on memory are derived from Augustine, his original ideas about introspection and freedom from guilt were in part a direct response of the particular emotional and spiritual problems experienced by the canonists and administrators he was advising at Cambridge, and with whom he established a relationship similar to that which existed between the common lawyer Sir Thomas More and his confessor Dean Colet one hundred years later; in fact the anxieties that John Thorpe felt over confession and absolution anticipate the scrupulosity of More's confessions in his *Dialogue of Comfort*.[41]Hilton summarized the Cambridge lawyer's worries in *Epistola ad Quemdam Seculo Renunciare Volentem,* which included Thorpe's inability to renounce his sense of sin despite repeated confessions and absolutions; and his conviction that there were forgotten sins for which he had not been absolved; his conviction that he was more sorry for his failure to confess than for his conscious and unconscious sins. The specific problem underlying these worries was Thorpe's concern over the innumerable and impractical vows made in the fervour of his conversion which he had been unable to keep. Hilton perceptively concentrated on this, and by reassuring his penitent that he was not bound by these vows he created a very private, internal dimension to sin, repentance and absolution. As a canonist, Hilton pointed out that a vow made privately or even to one's confessor, rather than solemnly in church, was not subject to the church's judgement. Moreover he also suggested that his reader may have been troubled by the memory of sins committed before his conversion, and that he was projecting a remaining sense of guilt for these sins onto the lesser fault of failing to keep unrealistic vows.[42]

38 *The Scale of Perfection*, p. 92.
39 ibid.
40 ibid, p. 118.
41 Thomas More, *Utopia and Dialogue of Comfort* (London, 1968).
42 Hilton, *Latin Letters*, ii, pp. 278 – 88, ll 623 – 846.

Hilton seems to have realized that Thorpe's obsessive guilt was caused by repression, and he disclosed his own conviction that confessors when dealing with the devout needed to concern themselves with memories, conscious and unconscious, rather than obedience to external vows and ascetic rituals like fasting. Thorpe had probably vowed to join a religious order, and Hilton was suggesting that obedience to one's inner voices was more important than obedience to any rule imposed by a monastery. Moreover, in discussing absolution for these buried sins, Hilton emphasized the internal, psychological drama at the expense of the institutional power of the priest as dispencer of the sacrament. He encouraged Thorpe to remember his forgotten sins as a means of releasing himself from feelings of guilt, and compared the process to Christ's raising Lazarus from the dead; the church's role in assigning the penance that brought release from purgatory was of secondary importance, like the disciples loosening the bands of Lazarus.[43] The revival of the inner self from the dead weight of sin was achieved through self-examination and faith in Christ. Hilton, in the *Scale of Perfection*, used Augustine's *Confessions* to demonstrate how the mere act of memory, without either an effort of willpower or repression, could result in a conviction of one's inner worth. Following Augustine, he recognized that the human will was not able to exert complete control over mental processes, and he concluded that God could only be reached through the images of sin and distraction themselves by virtue of Christ's Passion. This image of God's love, forgiveness and humanity, interceded between man and his collective fall so that memories of sin were, like the outside world itself, permeated by God's presence.[44] The introspective search for the living presence of Christ within the soul that is described in the *Scale of Perfection* and *De Imagine Peccati* was, therefore, an exercise of memory that brought an intellectual and emotional detachment and a 'lifely felynge of grace' that was without remorse, and which could redeem the experiences of secular life.[45] Hilton depicted this in psychological terms in *De Imagine* by claiming that purity of intention, which was not always consciously present to the mind, but implied by the previous conscious willing of a particular end, was a gift of God with a dynamic force in holding us on our course towards God, despite our involuntary falling.[46] Hilton's writings, and especially his letter to Thorpe, establish that he saw the drama of Christ's Crucifixion and Resurrection as something that was reenacted within the individual soul any time a penitent journeyed

43 ibid, pp. 278 – 88.
44 *Scale*, pp. 80, 129.
45 *Scale*, p. 419ff.
46 *Latin Writings*, ii, pp. 278 – 88.

introspectively into his dead memories, or selves, in order to redeem them. It was for this reason that Hilton was able to tell Adam Horsley that the Christian baptismal life, and not just the vowed religious life, was a sharing in the death and Resurrection of Christ.[47]

These theories on religious detachment and introspection were intended to meet the requirements of those living the mixed life, and their application to a wide range of emotional experiences is illustrated in the close parallels between developments in secular romance and religious literature in this period. A series of tail-rhyme romances, written in the north-east in the mid-fourteenth century and collected by Robert Thornton into his family book, advised laymen against renouncing temporal responsibilities for the sake of private feelings. The heroes of these romances: *Octavian, Sir Degrevant, Sir Eglamor of Artois, Sir Ysumbras* and the *Erl of Tolous,* belong to the same class of small-holding gentry as Robert Thornton; the narratives show, in a setting more provincial than that of Chaucer's courtly love poetry, the dangers of self-orientated passion that causes a withdrawal from social and political responsibility; and they establish the state of marriage and the nuclear family as the appropriate means for integrating passion with the maintenance of a social order.[48] This sanctification of secular work within the domestic household is markedly similar to that achieved in Hilton's *Epistle on Mixed Life,* which Thornton also copied into his manuscript. The importance of the 'mixed life' as a practical reality was such that the distinctions between the two genres of secular romance and religious literature almost disappeared. In the early years of the fourteenth century human emotion, whether of a romantic or religious nature, was discussed in an oblique manner through the allegories of *Le Roman de la Rose,* the first romance to attempt an intimate depiction of the conflicting emotions of a woman in love, and *L'Abbaye de Saint-Esprit,* which discussed the contemplative life of a lady living outside a monastery. By the late fourteenth century religious writers such as Walter Hilton directly discussed and analysed the religious emotions of the pious, and Chaucer in his *Troilus and Criseyde* depicted in intimate detail the conflicting emotions of the human heart in love. But Hilton and his contemporaries, restrained by their pastoral duty to contain religious enthusiasm, could only create in their theories on the mixed life an impression of lukewarm compromise: for all their dissection of religious emotion they could not communicate the exact nature of pious laymen's emotional reaction to their social world or do justice to the

47 ibid, (Ep. de Utilitate), ii, p. 402.

48 For the printed editions see: *Sir Degrevant*, ed. C. R. Casson, (EETS, London, 1949); *The Erl of Tolous*, ed. G. Rudke (Berlin, 1881); *Octavian*, (Altenglische Bibliothek, i, Heilbronn, 1885); *Sir Eglamour* of Artois, ed. F. E. Richardson (EETS, London, 1965). For Ysumbras see *The Thornton Romances*, ed. J. Halliwell (London, 1884), pp. 88 – 120.

extraordinary degree to which they had absorbed contemplative values. This was most effectively achieved in secular literature written among the pious and sophisticated courtiers of Edward III and Richard II.

Henry Duke of Lancaster's *Livre de Seyntz Médecines* was probably written for a small circle of friends: Lancaster's brother-in-law, Henry Percy, owned a copy which he left to his daughter Mary. Only two manuscripts of the *Livre* survive, one of which bears the arms of Roos of Helmesley; members of this family were, like Lancaster, prominent crusaders: John Lord Roos, who died at Paphos during a crusade to the Holy Land, was married to Mary Percy, and it is likely that he and other members of this family would have recognized in Lancaster's book an accurate rendition of their own understanding of the dialogue between the active and contemplative lives. This vivid depiction of the inner life of a devout layman shows faith in an atonement that did not come from the exercise of will or renunciation of feeling, but from the memories and associations of his varied active life: Henry compared the soul most pleasing to Christ to an unshrivelled apple ripened by its experiences.[49] These experiences were essentially those of the senses, transformed in an active dialogue between the inner and outer man into a penitential allegory of spiritual progress. The imaginative power of the allegory shows that underlying the penitential exercises and bible reading of this apparently austere man there was a sensual and imaginative personality — he loved the feel of scarlet cloth and the smell of sweet perfumes — whose powers of association were capable of transforming his perceptions of reality into a religious vision in the manner espoused by the author of *Of Angel's Song*. Comparing himself to a tourneyer jousting for Christ, he likened the first stage of his spiritual journey, when he was in a state of sin, to the plight of a wounded soldier who is bandaged by the loving care of the Virgin; to his struggles with temptation he applied images of the crowded and colourful market place — first used by Augustine — banquets, dances and a besieged fortress; and he compared his confessions to the rooting out of foxes from their ground in the hunt and to the dissection of bodies in a Parisian medical school; the final search for spiritual peace was the seasick sailor's longing for the shore, and the preparation of the soul for God was the busy cleaning and preparation for the arrival of an important guest. Henry's piety would not have been unique, and echoes of his penitential allegory occur in the will of his son-in-law, John of Gaunt, who ordered a large tiered frame, with candles commemorating his sins of commission and omission, to be placed over his body.[50] A grandson of Richard Lord

[49] *Livre de Seyntz Médecines*, ed. F. J. Arnould (Anglo Norman Text Soc., 1940).
[50] TE, I, p. 199.

Scrope, Stephen Scrope, wrote a prologue to his translation of *The Boke of Knygthode,* dedicated to his step-father Sir John Fastolf, 'for his contemplacion and solas', which depicted the long military career of this sixty-year-old warrior as a penitential allegory. According to Scrope, Sir John had been preserved by God in all his chivalrous adventures for his greatest task, which would earn him the title of true knighthood; this task was a daily fight in his old age in which he defended his God by combatting the devil and performing deeds of spiritual chivalry.[51]

These sophisticated ideas about human impulses, memory and fate were expressed in literature that circulated among clergy and in magnate and gentry households. However, some of these concepts were given wider currency in the Corpus Christi plays of York, which were enlarged and adapted in the late fourteenth century. The typological symbolism that occurs throughout the York cycle illustrates in dramatic terms Wyclif's attempts to amplify God's time to comprehend the past, present and future simultaneously. In the York Realist's *Creation Play,* the speeches of the cherubim, who feed on the radiance of God's face, approach the mystical language of the late fourteenth century mystics.[52] All these pageants employ symbolism centering on Christ's atonement to express a vision of history that has been determined by God's grace.

Affective Piety

The religious introspection of Hilton and his contemporaries was only the polished tip of an iceberg of religious behaviour, about which they had no illusions. They realized that their introspective detachment would not satisfy the aspirations of many ordinary people whose religious impulses were extroverted and manifested in either the worship of images and relics or in physical and supernatural experiences. The cult of the Eucharist in the late fourteenth century was a focus for such popular religion, and the York clergy knew that the key to a wider participation in a more introspective and spiritual religion lay in changing attitudes towards the host. John Wyclif, who opposed the doctrine of transubstantiation and the *cultus hostie* because they savoured of idolatry, argued that the host was Christ's body only in a figurative sense because it was a created thing and a sign of God's love, fixing the attention of the mind on the creator.[1] Communion, for Wyclif,

51 *The Boke of Knyghthode*, pp. 1–4.
52 *The York Plays*, ed. L. Toulmin-Smith (Oxford, 1885).
1 Wyclif, *De Eucharista*, ed. J. Loserth, WS (1892), p. 318.

was a solemn religious occasion for reflecting on the working of grace within the soul, rather than on the phenomenal world of magic; and this depended on the faith of the recipient. The working of grace was not manifested in miracles or sensations of a physical nature, but in the devotion aroused in the pious by the knowledge of the hidden presence of God in the sacraments and in all created things.[2] Wyclif may have had in mind the Corpus Christi pageant in York when he complained that in modern churches the host was worshipped as if it were God and adorned with sumptuous ornaments and rites.[3] Sharing the same mistrust of physical sensations as his contemporaries in diocese, he was concerned that the host did not become a focus for the emotional and physical fervour encouraged by the followers of Rolle.

However, the York clergy who were more actively involved in pastoral work realized that it was not feasible for all communicants to engage in introspective reflection. They appreciated that all people shared the finer compassionate, emotional impulses and that the celebration of mass could arouse and foster such feelings if it encouraged the communicant to respond to Christ's life and Passion in an affective way. Nicholas Love, in his adaptation of Suso's treatise on the Eucharist, denied the 'magical' functions of the host and claimed that its purpose was to instil into the communicant the memory of Christ's life on earth and a realization of his continuing penance in the world:

> in sothfastness this is that hige and most noble memoriale that oweth worthily to be prentede euerge in oure mynde and to be besily ikept in the ynwarde affection of the herte into continuele mynde of hym that giueth us this swete memoriale and preciouse figte; for whos gifte is ofte tyme seene mynd is lykyngly prented in the herte.[4]

To aid the 'mynde' or memory, Love appended this treatise to his *Mirror of the Blessed Lyfe of Jesu*, and it is probable that he compiled both treatises for the use of the Corpus Christi Guild, which was founded in 1408 to ensure that the procession was an occasion for meditating on Christ's life, rather than an opportunity to witness miracles.[5] *The Mirror* has greater simplicity and cohesion than the Franciscan original and also more emphasis on realism at the expense of the supernatural: the subject matter taken from the Latin version was of a sympathetic and compassionate nature, and the highly wrought and histrionic was

2 ibid, p. 178.
3 ibid, p. 317.
4 *The Mirror of the Blessed Lyf of Jesu Crist*, p. 303.
5 In the foundation charter of Richard Scrope's chantry in Elland near Halifax it was decided that the founder, possessing a deep piety, established a chantry with ministers, to celebrate the sacrament in memory of Christ's Passion.

modified.[6] This was designed to prevent 'spiritual illusions' so that 'simple soules', who could only think in physical terms, 'mowe haue somwhat accordynge unto his affecioun where he may fede and stire his deuocioun'.[7] Love, accordingly, addressed his work to the less educated children who needed to be fed with 'mylke of lygte doctrine, not with sadde mete of grete clergie and of hige contemplacioun'.[8] For introspective writers the purpose of contemplation of the Passion was self-affirmation, achieved by diverting the attention away from the outer, material world. But Love realized that autobiographical confessions could not wean the citizens of York following the Corpus Christi pageants away from superstition and extremism; a biographical narrative of Christ's life was needed that engaged the creative emotions of ordinary people in active life and affirmed their social identities by offering, in the story of Christ's mission, a mirror of their own active lives of charity.

A piety that was emotionally responsible and moderate required an appreciation of Christ's humanity, the purpose of the institution of the Feast of Corpus Christi:

> At the bygnnynge thou that desirest to haue sorwefull compassion thorug feruent inward affecioun of the peynefull passioun of Jesu thou most in thy mynde depart in manere for the tyme the mygt of the godhede fro the kyndely infirmyte of the manhede — for ther beth many so blynded gostly by unreasonable ymaginacioun of the mygt of the godhede in Jesu that thei trowe not that eny thing mygt be peynefull or sorweful to hym as to another man that hath the kynde of man and therefore haue they non compassioun of the peynes that he suffrede.[9]

To aid his readers Love provided a realistic biography of a man and his family, portraying emotions familiar to ordinary men and women. In a manner reminiscent of John Waldeby's Sunday sermons, which called on a lay audience to imagine with *specialem affectum* the birth of Jesus in the manger, the author of the mirror attempted to arouse paternal and maternal feelings by evoking Mary's care for the newly born baby and the infant gazing at the adoring adults from the altar at Jerusalem.[10] The warmth of family life could be recognized in the intimate scenes that showed Mary's 'sewynge and spynnynge', Joseph 'worchynge in his craft of carpuntrie' and the five-year-old Jesus helping his mother by

6 L. Zeeman, 'Nicholas Love, a Fifteenth-Century Translator', *R.E.S.*, (1951), 118.
7 *The Mirror of the Blessed Lyf of Jesu Crist*, p. 8.
8 ibid, p. 8.
9 ibid, p. 44.
10 ibid, pp. 26, 37, 50.

'gede on hir errandes and halpe in that he mygte'.[11] The emotional life of the holy family, especially the relationship between mother and son, was presented with psychological realism reminiscent of Aelred of Rievaulx's compassionate participation in Christ's life and Passion in the *Rule for Contemplatives* (*De Institutione Inclusarum*). Nicholas Love shows Mary reacting to the disappearance of her twelve-year-old son in the temple in a complex way, accusing her husband and herself, and struggling to submerge her maternal instincts under religious faith.[12] In her attempts to comfort her crucified son, she feels in her helplessness a sense of shame: 'sothely I trowe that she mygy nougt speke a worde to hym for sorwe but sche mygt doo more to hym nor help hym', and this contrasts painfully with her earlier and successful attempts to comfort her sobbing infant after the circumcision:

> then mowe we ymagine and thynke howe that litel babe in his moder barne seynge him wepte and sche agenward ynwardly stired and hauinge compassioun of the sorwe and the wepynge of hir dere sonne with kissynge and spekynge comforted hym as sche mygte.[13]

Through pathos, the author was attempting to arouse emotions that could transform subjective and egocentric experiences into a response of 'sorweful compassioun' to the Passion, so that

> to hym that wolde serche the passioun of oure Lord with all his herte and all his ynward affecioun there schulde come meny deuote felynges and sterynges that he neuere supposed byfore of whiche he schulde fele a newe compassioun and a newe loue and haue goosly comfortes thorug the whiche he schulde perceyue hym self turnede as it were into a newe estate of soul.[14]

Love also tried to control the imaginative exuberance of the pious by encouraging an objective and even empathic response to the Passion. The present tense narrarive, punctuated by direct apostrophes to Jesus and Mary and by realistic fifteenth-century anachronisms, encouraged the reader to visualize the events of the nativity as if they were taking place before him: 'ymagyne we and sette oure mynde and oure thougt as we were present in the place where this was done at Bethlehem byholdyng how the three kings comen'.[15] When Joseph and Mary are forced to flee to Egypt the reader is asked to help Mary 'to bere that

11 ibid, p. 68.
12 ibid, pp. 74 – 8.
13 ibid, p. 237.
14 ibid, pp. 244 and 215.
15 ibid, p. 53.

blessed berthen the child Jesu in oure soule by deuocioun'.[16] Such absorption would reach a climax in the dramatic narrative of the events leading up to the crucifixion, and readers were asked to 'abide awhile' at Gethsemane to 'Byholde howe he is ladde of the vilest wrecches fro that ryue upward toward the citee of Jerusalem', and to pause on the way to Calvary, where 'thou schalt see harder. They stande stiffely agenst hym alle one'.[17] Such an imaginative response made reading itself an act of meditation especially suited to those with little time or aptitude for ascetic exercises.

Contemplation of the Passion was also regarded as a way of stimulating compassion for others who suffered, thereby strengthening communal feeling and charity. Hilton described Christ as the head of the spiritual body Christian society, and it behoved those living the 'medled lyf' to pay attention to his limbs, 'at ar thi children, thi seruantes, thi tenantes and all thyne euen cristyne'.[18] The ordinances of the Corpus Christi guild in 1408 discussed the mystery of Christ's appearing in the flesh and in the eucharist and provided illustrations on the unity of Christ's body, the brethren of the guild and the seven rules of charity on which the guild had been founded.[19] But Nicholas Love demonstrated the possibility of reaching a sense of contemplative detachment by demonstrating one's sense of social responsibility and the performing of deeds of charity. Christ's life 'of penaunce suffering, of perfighte charite and trewe compassion', integrated the lifelong penance of longing for the heavenly city with a genuine love of others and provided a mirror for the 'perfighte actyf lyf'.[20] His followers needed to 'haue compassion and be ynwardly sorye — for the wyked lyuynge of untrewe crisen man', and to become pilgrims, pausing to perform the works of Martha with detached compassion, without deviating from the route to their homeland.[21]

Nicholas Love and other religious writers, and Franciscan preachers such as William Melton, would have recognized the potential of the Corpus Christi plays for influencing the religious sensibility of the less literate members of the guild of Corpus Christi, and the participants in the Corpus Christi celebrations. Towards the end of the fourteenth century dramatizations of Christ's life, which occupied half of the entire cycle, reflected the affective piety of contemplative writers and served as extended meditations that would arouse the pity, compassion and

16 ibid, p. 60.
17 ibid, p. 224.
18 *Yorks. Writers*, i, p. 272.
19 English Guilds, pp. lxxxv ff.; *Extracts from Municipal Recoprds of York*, ed. R. Davies, (London, 1843), p. 240ff; Bodl. Lib. Dodsworth MS. Vol. cxxix art. 20.
20 *The Mirror of the Lyf of Jesu Crist*, p. 165.
21 ibid, pp. 48, 84.

penitence of audiences. The York nativity play was partly inspired by a meditative account of the birth of Christ in the *Revelations* of St Bridget. The Franciscan influences that can be seen in Love's *Mirror* affected the development of these plays. John Waldeby, in the Sunday sermons that he delivered at the church of Austin friars in York, dramatically showed his audiences that spectacle of Mary wrapping the torn, stretched and naked body of her son in a cloth and warming him in her lap; and he described her feelings as she became engulfed in a bitter sea of grief, unaware of her son's Transfiguration.[22] Such sermons influenced the staging of the *Depositio Christi*, the meditative climax to the Passion sequence: Mary sees her son on the cross and cries: 'Alas for louely þou laye/In my wombe, is worthely wight,/Alas, at is blossome so bright/ Untrewly is tugged to is tree'. Before she realizes he is dead, she tells him her heart is as heavy as lead.[23] The influence of Nicholas Love himself can be seen in the plays of the 'York Realist'.[24] This annonymous playwright used complex and realistic plots to make the Crucifixion into a contemporary event implicating the audience. Caiaphas was depicted as a fifteenth-century bishop who examines Christ as a heretic and, after boasting about his learning, he hands Christ over to the secular arm, represented by Pilate, a nobleman who is guilty of the aristocratic sin of pride and whose wife boasts of his lineage: 'Was nevir juge in þis Jurie of so jocunde generacion, nor of so joifull genologie to gentrys enioned'.[25] Pilate's sympathetic, yet fundamentally weak character was intimately revealed to demonstrate the audience's own implication in the crucifixion. The limitations of the convential lineage values held by Pilate, and most of the audience, were demonstrated when Pilate's standard bearers were unable to prevent his arms and banners from bowing to Christ.[26]

The identification of the Corpus Christi audience with Christ's Passion would have reached a climax during the performance of the *York Crucifixion Play*.[27] Three soldiers put Christ to death with professional detachment; they are eager to obey orders and please their superiors, showing pride in their work and a callous indifference to the suffering they are inflicting on their victim. This late fourteenth-century playwright used these soldiers to give a subtle analysis of evil, and he demonstrated the limitations of human nature in as profound a manner

22 Hackett, 'The Spiritual Life of the English Austin Friars', p. 468; Owst, *Preaching in Medieval England*, p. 120. For the affective sermons of William Rymyngton and others see Owst, *Preaching*, p. 277.

23 *The York Plays*, p. 363.

24 J. W. Robinson, 'The Art of the York Realist', *Mod. Phil.*, 60 (1962 – 63) 241ff.

25 *York Plays*, p. 271.

26 ibid, p. 326.

27 ibid, pp. 349

as any of the contemplative writers of the diocese in this period. He achieved this by using his dramatic skills to implicate the audience in the crucifixion drama. The soldiers, like Cain and Herod, are comic characters capable of generating laughter from an audience through their bungled attempts at carpentry and their indifference to the suffering they are causing. Laughter, however, gives way to shame as the cross is elevated and dropped into the mortice (a scene that influenced one of the visions of Margery Kempe)[28] and the audience realizes that they too have been guilty of the soldiers' indifference. Moreover, they are forced to accept that they too are the soldiers, sharing a mixed life that is allegorized by carpentry, the craft of Christ, and the guild staging the play: the audience are made to realize that in the course of their daily work they crucify Christ when they show spiritual blindness, indifference, cruelty and lack of charity. The symbolism of this play, while reminding the audience of their fallen nature and the spiritual significance of their daily secular lives, offered them the hope of salvation. The soldiers carry their victim and his cross, the tree of life, to Calvary and establish a trinity of Christ, crucifiers and audience to demonstrate that Christ died to make atonement for the sins so graphically revealed in this play. If the audience had participated unawares in the crucifixion of Christ, they could also, equally unconsciously, offer him comfort and sympathy while performing the daily work of their active lives: in the closely related *York Judgement Play* the souls of the saved are told by Christ that whenever they performed a charitable deed in their past lives they were feeding and comforting Christ.

The overall religious outlook of the York and Wakefield Corpus Christi cycles was optimistic; and they can be seen as celebrations of the mixed life at its fundamental level because they affirmed the experiences and emotions of secular life. The nativity plays used comedy far removed from the dark humour of the crucifixion plays to demonstrate to audiences that the charity and joy in their own lives was, thanks to Christ's atonement, a foretaste of heaven. In the Wakefield Master's nativity farce Mak, the sheep stealer, and his wife, attempt to pass off a stolen ram as an infant, and the three laconic Yorkshire sheperds, despite their anger, are unable to punish the couple because of the comedy of the situation.[29] The shepherds' reaction symbolized the arrival of tolerance and mercy with Christ's New Testament law; the audience's laughter was an expression of the joy that they felt at Christ's Incarnation. The fact that it could be expressed in such secular, and even burlesque terms, is an impressive testimony to the success with which

28 *Book of Margery Kempe*, p. 192.

29 *The Wakefield Pageants in the Towneley Cycle*, ed. A. C. Cawley, (Manchester, 1958).

the church of York made the mixed life ideal applicable throughout society.

Images that showed the pursuit of the mixed life as an imitation of Christ's life were also disseminated in the visual arts of the city of York; and they were influenced by the affective works of writers such as Nicholas Love and the York playwrights. In the windows of the York Minster chapter house the subject matter was nothing but the lives of Our Lord and certain saints and lights in the east window of the Lady chapel, donated by Richard Scrope, depicted the Virgin and child and the crucifixion.[30] In the east window of All Saints' church, North Street, there are lights showing intimate domestic scenes from the life of the Virgin; these windows, which show the donor, Nicholas Blackburn senior, and his wife kneeling in prayer, contain realistic portraits of the Virgin and St Anne that are characterized by an emotional depth.[31] Portraits of the Virgin and Child, donated to the south aisle of the church around 1440, have the same affective quality.[32] Windows donated to All Saints' Church by the merchant, Reginald Bautre, depicted the corporeal acts of mercy and were placed opposite the Passion window to demonstrate the link between active charity and meditation on Christ's life. Another parish window at St John's Ousebridge, now at the minster, vividly depicted the sufferings and the wounds of Christ.[33] In the books of hours of the nobility representations of the Passion were no longer restricted to the triumphant, chivalric coats that displayed the instruments of the Passion; illuminists were concentrating on the Five Wounds and the sufferings of Christ; a series of cartoons in the Bolton Hours provided visual meditations on the scenes from Christ's life described by Nicholas Love including the nativity and ascension.[34] The influence of Flemish realism on the paintings commissioned by the York merchants, Blackburn, Bautre and Bolton, can perhaps be explained by their trade contacts with the lowlands. The school of Herman Scheere, besides producing a York primer, illuminated the Neville Hours, and provided a Passion sequence that included representations of the betrayal and flagellation of Christ before Pilate, executed in the same affective and realistic style as the plays of the York realist.[35] Representations of the deposition of Christ's body, known as the Corpus Christi,

30 F. Harrison, *The Painted Glass of York*, (1927), p. 74.

31 E. A. Gee, 'The Painted Glass of All Saints' Church, North Street York', *Archeologia*, 102 (1969). This window was perhaps painted by John Chamber jr., who may have been associated with the school of Thornton. See C. Davison, 'Civic Concern and Iconography in the York Passion', *Annuale Mediaevale*, 15 (1974).

32 Davison, 'The Realism of the York Realist', 270ff.

33 ibid.

34 Y.M.L. 5, MS. Add. 2, fos. 35 – 40v.

35 Bodl. Lib. Lat. Liturg. fo. 2; G. M. Spriggs, 'The Neville Hours and the School of Hermann Scheere', *J.W.C.I.*, (1974).

were probably inspired by the York pageant *Mortificacio Christi* and are to be found only in the south aisle of the minster and in the York parish churches of Holy Trinity, Goodramgate, St Martin-le-Grand in Coney Street and St John Micklegate; alabaster carvers concentrated in the districts of Nottingham and York also depicted this deposition scene. The influence of affective piety can also be seen in such funerary monuments as the image of Christ in the Percy tomb at Beverley, the image of Christ crucified, before which Thomas Howren, friend of Robert Est, was buried, and the sculptured pietà procured by the Selby priest William Escryk for his burial.[36]

The realistic portrayal of personalities and their society found in religious literature and art did not represent a secular intrusion into religious art; it was an attempt to demonstrate in realist terms the close relationship between the soul, the outside world and God. The mirror, used as a title for many religious treatises, was a favourite image in this period, and the fifteenth-century Flemish artist, Jan van Eyck, included in his realistic portrait of the Arnolfini wedding a mirror reflecting his own face, the creator of this domestic world, and in the frame of the mirror he showed scenes from the life of Christ. The contemplation of Christ's life sanctified all the experiences of the active life.

The Practice of the 'Mixed Life'

This concept of the mixed life was not just an ideal imposed by the clergy on popular religious practices. The religious literature of the diocese reflected a way of life that was a reality for gentry householders and the townsmen of York. This can be established in a brief consideration of their libraries, and of the control that ordinary citizens exerted over religious culture in this period.

The interest that some pious dowagers showed in the more ecstatic works of mysticism suggests that they regarded widowhood as a release from some of the ties of active life, which provided them with the opportunity to pursue a more intense form of worship in the manner espoused by Margery Kempe, who was an adviser to Joan Beaufort. Eleanor Roos probably lived a life of seclusion at Mount Grace where she was buried in 1438; she owned copies of Hilton's *Scale of Perfection*, Rolle's book *On the Passion* and a copy of the *Revelations of St Maud*, which she left to Joan Courtenay; she also received an unspecified collection of English books from the rector of Dighton, William Authorpe, who was also buried at Mount Grace, where his relatives

[36] Y.M.L. Reg. Test., I, fo. 317.

had been mentioned in the foundation charter.[1] The other chaplains chosen by the Roos family for the living of Deighton were well equipped to advise Eleanor and her relatives on the mixed life: Dr Thomas Gascoigne, who was associated with Syon and a student of female visionaries like St Bridget, was presented to Deighton in 1433, and on his resignation he was replaced by Dr Thomas Eborall, the prominent preacher and opponent of Pecock. Agnes Stapleton, who never remarried after the death of her husband, Sir Brian Stapleton, left a collection of books in 1448 that included a book of prayer which she left to her son-in-law Sir William Plumpton; a copy of Rolle's psalter, which she left to another member of this Yorkshire family; *The Chastizing of God's Children*, which was also owned by Mary Ormsby, the wife of a common lawyer; and copies of *The Book of Vices and Virtues*, *The Prick of Conscience* and a Bonaventura.[2] The inventory of Elizabeth Sewerby, the widow of William Sewerby near Bridlington, shows that the gentry had libraries that would not necessarily be mentioned in wills: her collection, which included the pseudo-Bonaventuran *Meditations on the Passion* and an English life of Christ, reveals a special interest in the works of visionaries and female recluses, for she owned Rolle's *Meditations on the Passion* and probably his psalter, Bridget's *Revelations* and a book of *The life of St Katherine* in English, which may have been the English translation of the *Dialogues* of St Caterina of Siena, originally made for the nuns of Syon.[3] Collections such as these imply a single-minded, almost professional pursuit of eremitic ideals which suggests that widows and 'vowesses' were attempting to emulate the piety of Margaret Kirkby and other anchoresses in the diocese.

However, the success that the York clergy had in channelling enthusiasm for Rolle's teachings into a more restrained piety is testified to by the greater popularity of most of the works of Hilton and Nicholas Love in the fifteenth century. Hilton's *Scale of Perfection* and Love's *Mirror* survive in over forty manuscripts, and only Rolle's English *Psalter*, the least idiosyncratic of his works, was more popular. None of Rolle's works were printed in the fifteenth century, but *The Mirror* was printed in 1486 and *The Scale of Perfection* in 1494; both of these works and *The Epistle on Mixed Life* were reprinted in the early sixteenth century. The libraries of the gentry householders and common lawyers of the diocese, which contained an appropriate mixture of religious and secular texts, reveal a preference for sober instructions on the mixed life over the ecstatic revelations of mystics. Men who had more ties in the

1 Y.M.L. Reg. Test. 3, fo. 529.
2 *N.C.W.*, p. 116.
3 TE, II, p. 196. This inventory suggests that in many gentry households there were large collections of books that were not necessarily itemized, or even mentioned in wills.

active life than spinsters and widows were probably more prepared to identify themselves with the roles defined for them by Walter Hilton and other writers in the diocese. Sir Thomas Cumberworth, a sheriff and M. P. of Somerby in north-east Lincolnshire who was connected by marriage to the families of Scrope, Constable and Roos, owned a library that included Rolle's Psalter and Hilton's *Epistle on Mixed Life,* which he left to his chaplain; *Þe Holy Boke De Gracia,* which he left to his chantry chapel; Nicholas Love's *Mirror,* numerous prayers and meditations; and a copy of *The Canterbury Tales* which he left to his niece, Anne Constable.[4] Sir Thomas Chaworth of Ulverton in Nottinghamshire, whose daughter married into the Scrope family of Bolton, owned a similar collection that included *Þe Holy Boke de Gracia,* an English copy of *The Pelerinage of the Soul,* also entitled *Grace Dieu,* an English *Horologium,* an English and Latin *Polichronicon,* a book of 'Notes and Fines', a *Life of St Alban* and numerous service books, including a portifor that 'I always have by my side when riding'.[5] In 1446 a large volume was made for Chaworth which descended into the hands of the neighbouring family of Willoughby, and it contained Trevisa's translation of Bartholomaeus Anglicus' *De Proprietatibus Rerum, The Charter of the Abbey of the Holy Ghost,* and a tract entitled *The Medes of the Mass.*[6] Chaworth also owned another surviving manuscript that contained Lydgate's *Troy Book.*[7]

Moreover, some of the common lawyers in the diocese had a wide range of intellectual and spiritual interests. Thomas Dautre, a married York lawyer and a former chapter clerk at York, had connections with John Newton and Robert Semer. In his will, written in his own hand, he bequeathed to his son, John, also a lawyer, a pseudo-Bonaventuran Latin meditations, a book on the Trojan wars, a book of chronicles, a book entitled de *Arte Kalendarii,* a psalter, a book on the wars of Alexander; he also left to his chaplains a book on the Trojan wars, *The Book of Vices and Virtues* and Petrarch's *Africa.*[8] Sir Peter Arderne, the chief baron of the exchequer and justice of the assizes in Yorkshire, combined his public duties, which he fulfilled by serving on many commissions in the diocese, with study and contemplation; among his collection of legal texts there was a daily primer, a glossed psalter and a *Life of St Alban, A Salutation of Our Lady,* a book called *Lucerna Conscienciae,* an English *Legenda Sanctorum* and copies of Nicholas Love's *Mirror,* Chaucer's translation of Boethius, and Giles' *De Regimine*

4 *The Academy,* pp. 230 – 32, 280 – 85.
5 TE, II, pp. 220 – 28.
6 Plimpton MS. 263; Doyle, 'A Survey', ii, p. 306; *Speculum,* xvii, p. 45.
7 BL, Cotton Augustus MS. A.iv; Doyle, 'A Survey', ii, p. 360.
8 TE, II, p. 59.

Principum.[9] Many of the merchants of the city, such as Sir John Bolton and Richard Russel, also had spiritual and literary interests.[10]

The most persuasive evidence that gentry householders consciously practised the 'mixed life' and sought literature that articulated their own experiences is to be found in the library of Robert Thornton. Thornton, the lord of East Newton, was an active citizen of Ryedale and a moderate landowner and collector of taxes in the North Riding in 1453; but he was an ordinary, and by no means a leading, citizen in this area.[11] Between 1420 and 1450 he transcribed into a paper volume sixty-five items, including a prose life of Alexander the Great, an English version of St Edmund's *Speculum Ecclesiae, The Prick of Conscience*, lives of St John the Evangelist and St Christopher, numerous prayers and religious lyrics, works of devotion, romances and such practical tracts as a medical recipe.[12] Nearly all these works were written or translated in the north-east, and Thornton would have had access to them in nearby libraries in Mount Grace and in such magnate households as the Scropes of Masham.[13] He probably identified himself with the recipient of Hilton's *Epistle on the Mixed Life*, for he did not include in his volume the individualistic autobiographies of Rolle and Suso or the abstract and highly disciplined meditations of the author of *The Cloud of Unknowing*. However, he did copy those works that provided guidance on the principles of the active life and the mixed life, such as Gaytrick's translation of Thoresby's *Lay Folk's Catechism*, Hilton's *Epistle on the Mixed Life, The Abbey of the Holy Ghost* and *The Boke Gratia Dei*. The practitioner of the mixed life was given further assistance in the narrative biographies and fictional romances which dramatized conflicts between private desires and public responsibilities. The reader who indentified himself with the heroes of saints' lives and the romances, who were of the same modest gentry standing as Thornton himself, would have appreciated the dignity that erotic and religious passion could acquire when they were tempered with the responsibilities of the active life, which were epitomized in the state of marriage. The close relationship maintained in this book between the written word and the daily experiences of its owner is illustrated in *The Privité of the Passion*, which harnesses meditations on Christ's life to the different hours of the day.[14] Such literature reflected and affirmed the social world of the reader, while earlier romances and the mystical and

9 TE, II, p. 232.

10 B.I.H.R., Prob. Reg. 3, fo. 439.

11 G. R. Keiser, 'Lincoln Cathedral Library MS. 91; the Life and Milieu of the Scribe', *Studies in Bibliography*, 32, (1979) 160 – 65; see also K. Stern 'The London Miscellany', *Scriptorium* (1976), 204.

12 See D. Brewer and A. Owen, *The Thornton Manuscript, a Facsimile* (London, 1975).

13 Keiser, 'þe Holy Boke Gratia Dei', 310 for suggestion that the source of Thornton's copy of this work was Mount Grace.

14 *Yorkshire Writers*, i, pp. 198 – 218.

romantic works of Rolle and Suso used the written word as a means of escaping from the world outside the self. Thornton may have provided his family with everything they needed in terms of moral and spiritual instruction and entertainment, but he was aware of the possibility that he and his family would isolate themselves by turning to their book as an anchorage and refuge. Many of the secular and religious works that he copied into the volume warned the reader of the dangers of insularity and introversion and reminded him of his duties in a society beyond the family and its library. The artistry that this scribe showed in selecting and arranging these works was such that his manuscript can be regarded as a comprehensive witness to a married layman's emotional and spiritual life. The volume remained in the family throughout the fifteenth century, recording the births and deaths of Robert's descendents, rather like the obit roll of a monastery, and it would have served as a rule on the mixed life for the Thornton family and their neighbours.

If the Thornton manuscript was a product of the gentry household, the staging of the Corpus Christi plays was in the hands of municipal society. The York city council, an inter-guild body composed of aldermen elected annually by the craft guilds, played a prominent role in the annual performance of the great York cycle. Leading aldermen such as the merchants John Gisburn, Robert Harpham and Nicholas Blackburn jr, and aldermen Henry Wyman and his grandson William Gassoigne, paid considerable sums of money for the privilege of having the Corpus Christi cycle performed at stations outside their houses.[15] In 1415 the town clerk Roger Burton composed a list of these plays and a brief Latin summary of their contents in 1415; he added to this list the text of the lord mayor's proclamation, which was made on the vigil of Corpus Christi and preceded the performance of the plays. This proclamation shows a steadiness of moral outlook on the part of the town council: provisions were made to ensure high standards of performance, crowd behaviour, including that of knights and burghers, was to be regulated, and fines were to be imposed on inadequate standards of production or acting.[16] Between 1430 and 1440 a register or formal copy of these plays was made for the corporation of the city, perhaps by scriveners at the priory of Holy Trinity, from single plays in the hands of the ninety-seven craft guilds of the city.[17] These amateur productions dramatized the theories on the mixed life and the sanctification of daily work which were expressed by Hilton and the author of *Þe Holy Boke Gracia Dei*. The shipwrights, vintners and breadmakers who staged, with particular appropriateness to their

[15] Twycross, 'Pageant Stations at York'.
[16] L. T. Smith, *The York Plays*, pp. xi – xii.
[17] Craig, *English Religious Drama*, p. 201.

calling, *Noah's Flood, The Marriage at Cana,* and *The Last Supper,* were conducting a successful dialogue between the active and contemplative lives.

CHAPTER SIX

New Cults of Saints in the Diocese of York

Northern religious writers, expecially the clergy of Arundel's household, provided spiritual teaching for those who were not following an eremitic life. Some of their teaching was directed at sophisticated clerical lawyers, administrators, and gentry householders; however, the same concepts were adapted and disseminated to the less educated through religious art and drama. Now the relationship between the pastoral teachings of the clergy and the popular religious sensibilities of the less educated inhabitants of the diocese must be considered. The bridges between them were the new saint's cults that coincided with the eremitic movement and the production of contemplative literature, and facilitated the occurrence of a dialogue between the clerical pioneers of religious sensibility and their parishioners. The clerical households of Thoresby and Arundel played an important part in the evolution of religious culture in the period between 1350 and 1430: they educated the clergy and laity, restrained religious enthusiasm, and determined the forms it was to take by encouraging a moral and emotional awareness that was consistent with membership of a compassionate and civilized society. However, although these sophisticated clergy imposed the structure that dictated the shape of religious changes in this period, they showed a sympathetic understanding of the spiritual anxieties and needs of parishioners; the relationship between the religious teachings and convictions of the nobility of the diocese and the impulses of poorer and less educated inhabitants was far closer than a study of the contemplative literature and the evolution of the 'mixed life' ideal would suggest. The same clergy who were prominent in formulating pastoral policies between 1352 and 1430 also cooperated with magnates and gentry to establish the local and national prominence of Yorkshire saints (in fact the most popular of these new saints, Richard Scrope, was a member of Arundel's circle); and much of the initial enthusiasm and devotion that provided these cults with their hagiography came from the testimony of the humble and often illiterate pilgrims, whose accounts of miracles were recorded by priests at the grave and shrines of the saints. The new saints' cults express to some extent all aspects of the religious life of the diocese so far discussed, albeit in an idealized and supernatural form. They therefore reinforced the importance of the family and local community; idealized both the institutional conventions and pastoral reforms of the church (saints were honoured as patrons and pastors); and expressed many of the attitudes that have been detected in the religious literature of the north. Furthermore, many aspects of religious change that have been examined so far, such as the sharing of ambivalent attitudes towards a society alternately seen as a source of comfort or repression, and the growing interest in visionary mystical experience and human personality, had some inspiration, or were at least echoed, in the miracles reported by the worshippers of the Yorkshire saints. These cults are therefore evidence that there was a reciprocal relationship between eremiticism, contemplation and popular religion. They also offer proof that the pastoral reforms of the York clergy not only affected the nobility of the diocese and inhabitants of the city of York but reached rural parishioners. However, before examining these religious attitudes expressed in the worship of the saints, it is necessary to explore the mechanisms behind the creation of these cults to establish that they were the result of a cooperation between the Yorkshire nobility who supported recluses, the clergy who adapted eremitic teaching for the laity, and the ordinary unlettered people.

The Creation of Saints' Cults

In no other period since the conquest was there such a proliferation in the diocese of new and revived cults: the unofficial cults of Thomas, Earl of Lancaster, Richard Rolle, Richard Scrope, the canonization of John Thweng in 1401, and the revival of the cults of the Saxon and Norman bishops, St Cuthbert, and St William of York, indicates a level of hagiographical activity unequalled elsewhere in England. There was a local and unofficial cult in Norwich, centred on the vicar of St Stephen's, Richard Caister, who died in 1420; a revival of the cult of the Saxon saint Erkenwald in St Paul's London; and a revival of the cult of the Norman bishop of Salisbury, Osmund, who was officially canonized in 1351.[1] However, none of these cults aroused the same religious enthusiasm as the York cults, or achieved such national popularity.

The first of these new cults, that of Thomas Earl of Lancaster, was the result of cooperation between local people and the archbishop, John Thoresby. The earl of Lancaster, a northern magnate and an uncle of Edward II, was executed for treason on a hill in Pontefract and buried in

[1] For the cult of Richard Caister see Tanner, *The Church in Norwich*, p. 231.

the nearby Cluniac priory. These places soon became the foci for a cult; Edward II was forced to place a guard around the priory where the monks treasured relics of Lancaster; and pilgrims transferred their devotions to the place of his execution.[2] Miracles were reported at this spot, and a guild was established in Pontefract in honour of the Earl of Lancaster.[3] The cult soon achieved national prominence: the Benedictine monks of Durham venerated the Earl's memory and a devotional plaque, depicting his life and downfall, was to be found in St Paul's Cathedral in London.[4] It prospered because of the support of Archbishop Thoresby, who had been presented to his first living by Lancaster in 1321. In 1330 Thoresby went to the papal curia in an unsuccessful attempt to secure Lancaster's canonization, and in May 1354, despite Melton's mandate forbidding pilgrims from approaching the tomb, Thoresby permitted services to be held on the hill where the execution had taken place. A chapel was built on this site, and in May 1364 a chantry financed by Simon Simeon was dedicated to Thomas of Lancaster.[5]

Lancaster's cult commemorated the martyrdom of an important political figure in the north-east; but the cult of Philip of Beverley, established around the same time, was the first of a series of local cults that were inspired by the reputations that some clergy of the diocese acquired as holy confessors. Mr Philip Beverley of Ingelberd was a rector of Kayingham in the East Riding and a member of University College, Oxford between 1305 and 1311. During his years at Oxford he obtained a doctorate in Theology and he was regarded as the university's finest Aristotelian.[6] Between 1311 and his death in 1325 he was resident at Kayingham and became widely known as a pastor and patron; he augmented two university college fellowships in 1318 for clergy from Holderness and obtained a licence from the chapter of Beverley to build a chapel of Our Lady at Molescroft, Yorkshire in 1323.[7] Although little detail survives about his life, activities such as these probably helped contribute towards his popular reputation in Holderness as a saint. After his death his tomb in the nave of Kayingham church became a scene of miracles. These were noted in 1391 by the monks of the

2 H. Tait, 'Pilgrim Signs: Thomas Earl of Lancaster', *B. Mus. Quarterly*, xx (1932), 37 – 46; The Lanercost chronicler mentioned the miracles, the place of execution and the building of the chapel. See *The Lanercost Chronicle*, ed. J. Stevenson (Edinburgh, 1839), ii, 244 – 5.

3 Shaw, *Wills of All Hallows Church North Street*, pp. 83 – 98. John Streche, a citizen and dyer of York, bequeathed 6s 8d to the guild of St Thomas of Lancaster at Pontefract.

4 Tait, 'Pilgrim Signs', 37 – 46.

5 *Fasti Ebor.*, p. 407.

6 Emden, *BRUO*, i, p.

7 D. Robinson, 'Beneficed Clergy in Cleveland and the East Riding, 1306 – 40', *B.I.H.R.*, 37 (1969), 45.

Cistercian abbey of Meaux in Holderness who appropriated the cult when they acquired the church of Kayingham after a lengthy dispute.[8]

The cult of a contemporary of Philip of Beverley's in the East Riding, Richard Rolle, was also based on a reputation for a holy life of contemplation and teaching. Rolle's cult, like Lancaster's, began as a small priory cult celebrated among rural parishioners, and it too secured the influential support of the archbishop of York and leading magnates of the diocese. Rolle acquired a reputation among the nuns of Hampole and their neighbours as a holy man and healer with miraculous powers. The originator of the cult was his disciple Margaret Kirkby, the recluse who moved to Hampole to be near the body of her master sometime after 1357, probably between 1370 and 1380.[9] She remained there for ten years until her death, and after her arrival a biographical office was compiled at the priory using the memories of Margaret, and presumably those of the older sisters.[10] This office was intended for the use of the nuns in their own private devotions until Rolle's canonization was secured. The frequency with which this office mentions the burial of Rolle at Hampole suggests that the nuns had translated his remains to the priory church in an effort to initiate the cult. Their humble neighbours were involved in this process: Roger, from an unspecified town, built a shrine for the saint before the high altar of this church after he had experienced a series of visions of the hermit.[11] This shrine attracted many pilgrims, poor people without surnames, many of whom were from Hampole and nearby Doncaster. The accounts of the miracles they had experienced were included in the office between 1381 and 1383; their poverty explains why there were few legacies to the shrine; an exception was the bequest made by the prosperous York chandler John Croxton in 1393.[12]

The cult also had more influential supporters. An early indication of this may have been provided in the unusual concession that Margaret Kirkby secured from John Thoresby in 1357, in which she was allowed to leave her cell at East Layton to move to another cell at Ainderby, probably to be near to Rolle.[13] She must have secured the same

8 *Chronica monasterii de Melsa*, ed. E. Bond (R.S., iii).

9 This information is provided in Vienna Ms. 4483 (Nationalbibliothek), which contains the account of Rolle's life written in 1450. See also Whiting, 'Richard Rolle' 13 and Allen, *Writings*, p. 502.

10 The office must have been composed between the time of Margaret's arrival at Hampole, sometime after 1357, and 1381, when the miracles were added to the office. There is no reason to assume, as Whiting does, that it was composed immediately after Rolle's death.

11 *Brev. Ebor.*, lec. I.

12 TE, I, p. 184.

13 Reg. Thoresby, fo. 287; Whiting claims that the Margaret mentioned in Thoresby's register is not Margaret Kirkby; there are no grounds for this assertion because the register clearly gives her full name as Margaret Kirkby.

concession from the archbishop when she joined the community at Hampole. Thoresby's interest in this priory was revealed in 1374, about the time when Rolle's cult was being established, when he made his only bequest to a religious house, a substantial legacy to a Hampole nun.[14] The cult also had the backing of some of the leading magnates of the diocese. The Scropes of Masham and the Stapletons of Bedale were patrons of Margaret Kirkby, and probably of Rolle; the Scropes owned the autograph of the *Incendium Amoris*, which they may have made available for the nuns, who compiled the biographical office by using autobiographical passages from this work. It was through the help of such families that the cult achieved fame beyond the Hampole region: one interpolated southern manuscript of Rolle's psalter provides pilgrims with directions to Hampole, and some of the miracles recorded in the office were reported by pilgrims from as far afield as York, Durham, Leicester and Worksop.[15] Rolle was twice described as a holy man in the Lollard translation of Ullerston's treatise on bible translation, made between 1401 and 1407. The exhaustive visitation of the priory conducted by Henry Bowet from May to the autumn of 1409 was possibly connected with the popularity of Hampole as a pilgrimage centre; two clauses in the visitation documents deal with provisions for the sick, who may have included pilgrims seeking cures.[16] The hermit's shrine remained popular throughout the fifteenth century: a special chapel dedicated to Rolle was set aside in the priory, and there were bequests to his shrine in the beginning of the sixteenth century.[17] Rolle's cult also inspired among its followers an interest in the Swedish mystic St Bridget. Henry Lord Percy, whose family had been among Rolle's original patrons, made a vow to make a pilgrimage to St Bridget's shrine at Vadstena in the 1390s; Henry Lord Scrope of Masham, the owner of the autographed *Incendium*, was one of the earliest readers of the biographical office of St Bridget, which reached England at the end of the fourteenth century, and Henry Lord FitzHugh of Tanfield, who received the *Incendium* from Scrope in 1415, visited Vadstena in 1406 and established the Bridgittine order in England.[18]

The cult of St John of Bridlington began the same way as the Hampole cult, in a Yorkshire priory. John Thweng, like Rolle, acquired a reputation for sanctity in his lifetime: during his career as a cellarer and

14 TE, I, p. 90.

15 Allen, *Writings*, p. 173; Bodl. Lib. Ms. Laud. Misc. 286 (Sum. Cat. 1151).

16 Reg. Bowet, ii, fos. 101 – 102; Palmer, 'The Career of Henry Bowet', pp. 72 – 7; Deanesly, *Lollard Bible*, pp. 442 and 3.

17 In 1506 Richard Marreys of London, who was born in Kirkby, left money for a mass to be sung before an image of Rolle, and in 1508 Richard Royden of Levington left money for the repair of the chapel of St Richard. See TE, IV, p. 3.

18 Tait, 'The Brigittine Monastery of Syon', pp. 53, 82; *Foedera*, IX, 272 – 80.

the prior of the Austin house of Bridlington, he was known as a holy man and healer; his fame was such that as early as 1377 a manuscript ascribed the early fourteenth century Bridlington prophecies and John Erghome's commentary to John Thweng.[19] The details of Thweng's life are known because of the activities of the Bridlington scriptorium, and after his death in 1379 the canons preserved anecdotes on the wisdom and saintly conduct of their prior and of the miracles that he performed; these were collected together by a canon, probably of the priory, called Hugh; Canon Hugh wrote the first life of the saint soon after 1380.[20] At Thweng's tomb this, and probably other authentic books, were made available to pilgrims along with relics and images; miracles were soon reported at the tomb and elsewhere, and these, together with some of the miracles recorded by Hugh, were incorporated in a chronicle written at the nearby Cistercian house of Kirkstall.[21]

The cult acquired national prominence, and in 1401 Thweng became the first English saint to be canonized since Cantilupe; in 1404 his body was translated to a shrine in a church adjoining the priory. This happened because the cult secured the support of leading magnates and clergy of the diocese and the court. The family who did most to establish the cult and secure canonization were the Nevilles of Raby, whose family confessor was William Sleightholme, a canon of Bridlington and a disciple of the Thwengs. Alexander Neville, the archbishop of York, commissioned his vicar general Robert Dalton to examine the miracles in 1386, and they soon attracted the attention of Richard II who, out of regard for John Thweng, gave Bridlington a license to crenellate its buildings in 1388.[22] In 1391 the pope, in response to repeated petitions from prelates and nobles, ordered an enquiry into the miracles, which had been described by Walsingham in 1389 as so numerous and manifest that all England was struck with amazement.[23] Henry Bolingbroke made an offering at Bridlington in 1391 on his return from a crusade in Prussia; and in 1400, when he was king, he sent John Gisburn, a canon of Bridlington, to Rome to negotiate the canonization.[24] Once canonization was achieved, momentum for the cult was secured through the influence of the Yorkshire families prominent in the

19 P. Meyvaert, 'John Erghome and the *Vaticinium Roberti Bridlington*', *Speculum* (1966), pp. 656ff.

20 Purvis, 'St John of Bridlington', 152 – 201.

21 *The Kirkstall Chronicle, 1355 – 1400*, ed. M. V. Clarke and N. Denolm-Young (Bull. J. Rylands Lib., xx, 1931), pp. 100 – 137; see also P. Grosjean, *De S. Johanne Bridlingtoniensi Collectanea* (Analecta Bollandiana, ciii, 1935), p. 104.

22 For concessions to the priory see J. R. Purvis, 'Ripon Correspondence', *Y.A.S.*, xxix, (19), 157; C.P.R. 1385 – 89, p. 439.

23 *Historia Anglicana*, ii, p. 252; *Historical Letters and Papers from the Northern Registers* (R.S., 1873), pp. 420 – 21.

24 C.P.R., p. 439.

cult of Richard Rolle.[25] Archbishop Richard Scrope and the prior of Bridlington translated Thweng's remains to the adjoining church in 1404, where a shrine was prepared to receive them; this shrine was financed by an annual grant of 100 marks from the church of Scarborough, which was transferred to the priory in 1404.[26] Scrope's nephew, Henry Lord Scrope of Masham, left a collar of gold decorated with swans and white flowers to this shrine, and a silver crucifix and 100s to the priory.[27] His friend Henry, the Prince of Wales, made a visit of devotion to the shrine in 1407, in performance of a previous vow, and offered five marks at the shrine of his patron saint. When he became king in 1413 he granted the priory exemption from all expenses in coastal defence on account of his affection for the saint.[28] The Earl of Westmorland's son in law, Ralph Lord Mauley, was buried near the saint in the priory church in 1414, and Mauley's widow Matilda was buried here in 1438.[29]

With such support the shrine of St John of Bridlington became a pilgrimage centre of national importance. It was built behind the high altar 'in a fair chapel and high'; stone stairs were built on either side of the altar for a double row of pilgrims, and underneath the shrine there were five chapels with five altars containing tableaus and alabaster images.[30] Leading gentry and merchant families of the diocese made bequests to the shrine including Matilda, wife of the merchant John Holbreck, Sir Thomas Cumberworth, and Elizabeth Sewerby, who left the church 66s 8d.[31] Those who bequeathed their souls to St John of Bridlington included the York merchant John Brompton and Thomas Ardene esquire of Martin near Bridlington, who was buried in the priory church with his wife.[32] The saint also became prominent in liturgical celebrations within the priory and among gentry families in the diocese. In 1404 the chapter of Austin canons at Northampton decreed that the feast of the deposition of St John of Bridlington be celebrated in churches and monasteries of the order.[33] Eleven hymns to St John survive in liturgical books in England, including primers: the Bolton book of hours contains

25 For the bull of canonization see Purvis, 'St John of Bridlington', 31 – 7. St John's feast day was named on the day of his death on the 10th of October and his office was that of a confessor.
26 C.P.R., 1401 – 5, p. 248.
27 *Foedera*, ix, 272 – 80.
28 *Northern Chronicle*, in *English Historical Literature*, ed. C. L. Kingsford, (1913), p. 290; Purvis, 'St John of Bridlington', 157.
29 Prob. Reg. 3, fo. 546.
30 Purvis, 'Ripon Correspondence', p. 157ff.
31 TE, I, p. 331; The Academy, t, p. 220; TE, II, p. 196.
32 TE, II, p. 195; Prob. Reg. 2, fos. 86; 326.
33 E. Salter, 'Chapters of Augustinian Canons', *Lond. Cant. York Soc.*, 29 (1922), 80.

a special devotion to the saint and there is another in a northern book of hours composed between 1405 and 1413.[34] St John of Bridlington's importance in the Catholic church was recognized when he came to the attention of the leading hagiographer of the fifteenth century, John Capgrave, an Austin friar of Lynn. Sometime after 1425, when his literary career began, Capgrave added to John Tynemouth's collection of saint's lives, which he was editing, a life of St John of Bridlington. Capgrave must have had access to the records and testimony of the canons of Bridlington, for he added miracles not found in canon Hugh's work, including accounts of miracles performed by William Sleightholme, who lived until 1420.[35] Capgrave may have heard about St John of Bridlington and Sleightholme from his fellow townswoman, Margery Kempe, who made pilgrimages to Bridlington in 1413 and 1417, and from members of the Neville family of Raby who used Sleightholme and Margery Kempe as spiritual advisers.

The clergy of York who witnessed the impact of these local priory cults, and who formulated a pastoral policy to control enthusiasm for these saints, would have appreciated the potential influence that new cults could exert in popular religion. York Minster, which was under their direct control, became in this period the most important centre for the cult of saints in the country. In the fifteenth century the cathedral became the focus for a cult of a martyr, Richard Scrope, who was to eclipse Thomas Becket in popularity in the north of England. The mechanism behind this cult will be examined in some detail because it was the most popular cult in the diocese and probably the kingdom; it provides evidence of the cooperation between representatives of all the social classes in the diocese including: magnates, gentry, merchants and guildsmen of the city, and the rural peasantry. More than any other cult it demonstrated the necessity of popular support: the unpopularity of Simon Sudbury, the archbishop of Canterbury and chancellor of England, ensured that despite his importance and the manner of his death, there was no equivalent cult after his murder at the hands of the peasants of Kent and Essex and London artisans in 1381. The making of the Scrope cult therefore demonstrates the potential of the cult of saints as evidence of common religious attitudes. Richard Scrope, the archbishop of York, was sentenced to death on 8 June 1405 for placing himself at the head of a popular insurrection of priests, monks, townsmen of York, and gentry

[34] Grosjean, *Collectanea*, p. 100ff. For the hymns to St John of Bridlington see *Analecta Hymnica Medii Aevi*, ed. G. M. Dreves (Leizpig, 1905), XLVI, p. 269; XLIII, p. 193; XXVIII, p. 302; Bodl. Lib. Lat. Liturg. f2; Y.M.L. MS. Add. 2, fos. 207 – 207v.

[35] *Nova Legenda Angliae*, ii, ed. Horstmann, p. 67ff. John of Tynemouth, a Benedictine monk of St Alban's, completed his collection of the lives of English saints in 1361; see also A. de Meijer, 'John Capgrave', *Augustinia V* (1955), 400 – 40.

from the surrounding countryside.[36] The execution of the archbishop, like that of Lancaster, was followed by a popular cult that arose at the tomb and the site of the execution. Within six months of the execution the Dean of York, Thomas Langley, was cautiously referring to the phenomenon of alleged miracles reported by the citizens of York and the poor who made pilgrimages to the tomb with offerings.[37] The crowds had been so great that a wooden barricade was erected around the tomb; in September 1405 John Duke of Bedford had sent an order from Seamer to the sub-treasurer of York, enjoining him to have the fence removed and to pile logs and stones between the pillars to keep the crowds away.[38] Riots were reported in the church, and the king and council, with Thomas Arundel, agreed to allow pilgrims to visit the tomb unhindered, as long as the York clergy took no steps to advertise the miracles until they were investigated to ascertain if they were from God or just superstitions. A letter to this effect was sent to the York chapter on 3 December 1405, and in April 1406 further instructions were sent from the king's council forbidding the clergy to induce anyone to pray to the dead archbishop. Prayers were only allowed for the dead man's soul and votive offerings were to be diverted to the shrine of St William and appropriated for the benefit of the church.[39] With these restrictions lifted the offerings at the tomb became so plentiful that they contributed to the building of the lantern tower of the cathedral which had fallen down in 1405. In 1415 the yield was £73 8s and in 1419 it was £150; this unofficial shrine had become more popular than Becket's, where offerings had declined from £1,000 in 1220 to £35 in 1535.[40] A special custodian of the tomb was needed and in 1421 the keeper was John Stytenham.[41]

The field where Scrope was beheaded was also regarded as a holy place, and the cult was therefore fostered at the aristocratic nunnery of Clementhorpe overlooking this site, which received 25 marks from Scrope's confiscated property. Miracles were reported on Clementhorpe field immediately after the execution, and a chapel known as the Bishop Scrope Chapel was built on this spot.[42] In 1459 John Dautre left four torches burning at *capella domini Ricardi le Scrope extra muros* — which is probably a reference to a chapel near the nunnery.[43] The rector of St

36 P. McNiven, 'The Betrayal of Archbishop Scrope', *B.J.R.L.*, 54, (1971) 173 – 213; J. W McKenna, 'Canonization as Political Propaganda: the Case of Archbishop Scrope' *Speculum*, (1970); Jacob, *The Fifteenth Century*, p. 60.

37 *Historians of the Church of York*, iii, p. 291.

38 ibid, p. 292.

39 ibid, pp. 291 – 92; *Fabric Rolls of York Minster*, pp. 193, 292.

40 *Fabric Rolls*, pp. 225 – 28.

41 TE, III, p. 61.

42 For the report of the miracles at Clementhorpe see *Cronica Monasterii St. Albani*, ed. H T. Riley, (R.S., 1886), p. 410.

43 Prob. Reg. 2, fol. 413; TE, II, p. 59.

Michael's York, William Langton, whom Dautre had described as his spiritual father, left a bequest in 1464 to *Reverendi memoria Ricardi le Scrop iuxta Domum monalium Sancte Clement Ebor.* to intercede for his soul.[44] It was possible that Scrope's head had been placed in a reliquary and was housed in this chapel because in 1477 a lady, who was buried in the nunnery, left a gold ring set with a diamond at the head of Richard Scrope in the Scrope chapel; and in 1472 Isabella Bruce, widow of Robert Bruce and one of the Mowbrays of Easby, who was living in her widowhood in Clementhorpe where her sister was buried, also left a gold ring set with a diamond at the head.[45]

The national significance of the cult, which was implied by the popularity of these shrines, was also testified by the chroniclers. Between 1405 and 1413 Walsingham recorded in the St Alban's chronicle the miracles that occurred at the site of the execution, and in another section of the St Alban's chronicle a writer, who was critical of Henry IV, described the execution as a martyrdom.[46] The continuation of *Eulogium Historiarum* noted the illness of Henry IV, and the Godwin chronicle recorded the punishment of Scrope's judges.[47] Adam of Usk, writing around 1421, referred to the many holy miracles performed by the saint, and the chronicle of John Strecche, written by a canon of Kenilworth who was Lancastrian in sentiment, recorded for the benefit of posterity the miracles performed at the archbishop's grave.[48] The *Northern Chronicle* and the *Godstow Chronicle,* written in the early years of the reign of Henry VI, spoke of the many daily miracles continuing into their own times.[49]

The cult of Richard Scrope prospered in this way because it not only had the support of the leading magnate families and the higher clergy of the diocese, but also of the entire governing class of the diocese. Common lawyers were especially important in providing the cult with its hagiography; the execution raised important legal questions, and the establishment of a cult became a means for clergy and secular lawyers of York to express the illegality of the king's action and to assert their independence from the encroachment of central government. Many of the influential figures in the cult were secular lawyers attempting to preserve the autonomy of their profession; they would have been predisposed in Scrope's favour by their exclusion from the 1404

44 TE, II, p. 233.
45 Prob. Reg. 5 fo. 17.
46 *Cronica S. Albani,* p. 410.
47 *Eulogium Historiarum, continuation iii,* ed. F. R. Haydon (R.S., 1863); *Incerti scriptoris,* ed. J. A. Giles, (1848).
48 *Chronicon Adae de Usk,* ed. Maude Thompson, (1876), pp. 99 – 275; *The Chronicle of John Streche,* ed. F. Taylor, 1934.
49 *Godstow Chronicle,* p. 239; Kingsford, *English Hist. Lit.,* p. 282.

Coventry parliament. When the chief justice Sir William Gascoigne was asked to pass Richard Scrope's death sentence he refused; his reasons were set down by his nephew Thomas Gascoigne in his theological dictionary; Sir William asserted the distinction in canon law between laymen and clergy, which prevented an archbishop from being sentenced by a secular court.[50] Gascoigne had precedents in the cases of Archbishop Neville and Arundel, who were both found guilty of high treason and allowed to live. The York lawyer Thomas Dautre was an eyewitness at Scrope's execution, and he reverently preserved a small missal that the archbishop carried to the block. In his will in 1437 he left a rosary of 50 coral beads to his 'beloved most blessed St Richard Scrope to help with his canonization', with a prayer to God that it would be quickly granted; Dautre left Scrope's missal to his son John, along with Gascoigne's *Great Register*, which was probably given to Thomas by Gascoigne himself, in a probable attempt at preserving the memory of the chief justice's principled stand against the government.[51] John Dautre, who was also a lawyer, ensured that Scrope's relic remained in the hands of secular lawyers by bequeathing it in 1459 to his godfather William Langton, a clerk to Master Robert Esingwold, proctor of the court of York.[52] Another lawyer, Sir Brian Roucliffe of Cowthorpe, a baron of the exchequer, owned a relic of Thomas Mowbray Earl Marshal, who was beheaded along with Scrope for his part in the 1405 rebellion and buried in the Church of the Friars Minor.[53] Thomas Dautre was probably the Thomas who wrote a first-hand account of the uprising and execution of Richard Scrope; in this narrative Sir William's refusal to pass sentence is recorded in a heroic and idealistic speech; John Duke of Bedford is condemned as a traitor for his part in the execution of Scrope; and Fulthorpe, who sentenced Scrope after Gascoigne's refusal, is punished by God.[54] Dautre may have recorded these events between the death of Bedford in 1435 and his own death in 1437; but another eyewitness to the execution was Sir Thomas Cumberworth, who was also a friend of chief justice Sir William Gascoigne.[55] York lawyers were not the only ones to use a saint's cult to explore legal issues. Around 1386, John Massy based his *Life of S. Erkenwald* on the bishop of London's successful baptism and salvation of the corpse of a just pagan judge and used the saint's life to explore the

50 *Loci e Libro Veritatum*, p. 228.

51 TE, II, p. 59.

52 TE, II, p. 233.

53 TE, IV, p. 102. Mowbray was regarded as a martyr; in 1407 Richard Burgh requested burial at his feet and a drinking cup he received from the Earl Marshal was entailed in Burgh's family as an heirloom. TE, I, pp. 367 – 8.

54 *Historians of the Church of York*, iii, p. 288 – 90.

55 See J. H. Wylie, *A History of England under Henry V*, (London, 1884 – 98), App. T, for discussion of the authorship of this account.

relationship between the secular justice of Roman law and the Christian concept of God's incomprehensible justice, which was meditated through baptismal grace.[56] The revival of the cult of St Erkenwald in the late fourteenth century must have been of considerable interest to the lawyers who consulted with their clients in the porch of St Paul's, and one of the four bequests made to St Erkenwald's shrine in the cathedral was from a pleader in the common law.[57]

The cult was also fostered among the ecclesiastical dignitaries of York Minster and the leading families of the diocese, and naturally the most prominent supporters were members of Scrope's own household who were involved in the pastoral application of Rolle's teachings, and the families of Scrope of Masham and Bolton. From the moment of the execution there was considerable involvement on the part of York clergy with the popular enthusiasm for the martyred archbishop. Four vicars choral took the head and trunk of the archbishop from the field opposite Clementhorpe and reverently placed them in a place of honour in the north-east end of the choir of St Stephen's chapel.[58] That they published accounts of miracles is shown by the instructions sent from the king's council in April 1406 ordering the clergy to abstain from publishing miracles worked at the tomb. This command had to be repeated and the York penitentiary and canon William Kexby continued to report miracles.[59] The chapel of St Stephen's, where Scrope was buried and which was now the family mausoleum for the Scropes of Masham, became, under the care of the Minster clergy, a memorial to the archbishop's martyrdom. Lights in the chapel showed the martyrdom of St Stephen, the Passion of Christ and the arms of Richard Scrope.[60] The residentiary canon Thomas Greenwood left money to the shrine in return for the archbishop's prayers, and Thomas Hebbenden left an image of the virgin at the shrine.[61] Thomas Walleworth, another residentiary canon, and Stephen Scrope, the archdeacon of Richmond, were buried in this chapel, and Robert Wolveden, who was one of the five clerks pardoned after the 1405 uprising, left his arms, a wolf's head, in the chapel.[62] These former servants of Richard Scrope and the Scrope families of Masham and Bolton also promulgated the cult by commemorating the archbishop in the stained glass of the recently rebuilt choir

56 C. J. Peterson, 'The Pearl Poet and John Massey of Cotton, Cheshire', *R.E.S.*, 25 (1974), 257ff.
57 *Wills in the Court of Husting*, ii, pp. 108, 139, 160 and 203.
58 *Historians of the Church of York*, iii, p. 291.
59 ibid, iii, pp. 291–92; *Fabric Rolls of York*, pp. 193, 292. The clergy were ordered not to publish the miracles in sermons.
60 Harrison, *The Painted Glass of York*, pp. 74–84.
61 Y.M.L. Reg. Test., i, fo. 203; *Reg. Langley*, p. 159.
62 Y.M.L. Reg. Test., i, fos. 152, 235; Harrison, *The Painted Glass of York*, p. 87; Wylie, *Henry V*, ii, p. 245.

of York cathedral. They had the services of the Coventry glazier John Thornton, who was first employed at York by Richard Scrope, the former bishop of Coventry; during Bowet's archiepiscopate and Wolveden's treasurership, Thornton and his followers filled the choir with lights depicting local York saints, among whom Scrope occupied a prominent place.[63] Shortly after 1405, the Scropes of Bolton left as a memorial to their cousin a group of eight windows in the east arm of the clerestory of the westerm choir near the lantern tower; these windows contain the figures of saints, bishops and kings associated with the conversion of the north to Christianity, including the bishop saints Wilfrid and John of Beverley; one of them contains 38 shields, including the shield of the Scropes which occurs seven times, and there is a figure in the tracery of an angel holding the shield of Archbishop Scrope.[64] The Scropes of Masham were responsible for an east window in the eastern end of the clerestory of the south choir transept, depicting Richard Scrope with the nimbus of a saint and distinguished by a scroll, reading 'Archbishop Scrope'; below his feet the donor, Stephen Scrope, archdeacon of Richmond, is depicted kneeling with a prayer scroll saying *O Ricarde pastor bone tui famili miser Steph.*; also in the window is the motto IHSand the shield of Scrope of Masham impaling Chaworth.[65] In the opposite west window of the south choir transept is St William, holding a book similarly identified by a scroll, and below his feet kneels Robert Wolveden with a similar prayer scroll to Stephen Scrope's, containing the same formula.[66] Both windows, completed during the treasurership of Wolveden, have a row of armorials including: Scrope of Masham, Scrope of Bolton, Gascoigne, Wolveden and the arms of the dean and chapter; it is probable that these donors intended Scrope's sanctity to be recognized by placing him opposite St William, an established York saint.[67] Richard Scrope's arms also appear in an east window in the north transept, next to St Stephen's window. The lantern tower, which was built during the archiepiscopate of Bowet, was itself a memorial to Scrope because it was financed with funds collected at his tomb; some remorse on the part of Henry IV can be seen in his gesture of sending one of his masons, William Colchester, to assist in the building of this tower.[68]

Behind the support of the York clergy and the local gentry, all of whom were represented in the 1405 rebellion, there was the widely

63 Harrison, pp. 74 – 84.
64 ibid, p. 95.
65 ibid, p. 98; J. Haselock, 'The Stained and Painted Glass of York Minster', in G. Aylmer and R. Cant, eds., *The History of York Minster*, p. 374.
66 Harrison, p. 18.
67 ibid, p. 18.
68 J. H. Harvey, 'Architectural History of York Minster', p. 170.

recognized principle of ecclesiastical independence, the freedom of the local church and community from the central authority of the crown and parliament. This principle was asserted by proponents of the cult who drew on parallels with the cult of St Thomas Becket; even before the Scrope rebellion churchmen defending clerical privileges in taxation looked to Becket. In the Coventry parliament of October 1404, Archbishop Arundel was able, with the help of Richard Scrope, to oppose a parliamentary plan to confiscate the temporalities of the church for a year. He was reported to have sustained himself during these attacks on the church by reading a passage from the life of St Edmund archbishop of Canterbury, who had been similarly troubled by the royal exploitation of ecclesiastical wealth and had found courage from the martyrdom of Thomas Becket.[69] The rebellion of 1405 was a response to issues raised in this parliament. Scrope, with the support of five members of his chapter, placed himself at the head of a popular reform movement. A manifesto was written, probably by Oxford doctors of the northern nation, objecting to the anti-clerical proposals of this parliament, including the proposed confiscation of church property, and a list of grievances, including a demand for the reform of parliamentary elections and the appointment of local officials, was placed in public places in York.[70] The clergy and local gentry were quick to make use of the parallels between the execution of the leaders of this rebellion and the martyrdom of Becket: Bowet, Thomas Parker, and Robert Wolveden, who were all associated with the Scrope cult, and the rest of the minster clergy, donated a window in the north-west choir aisle of York minster which commemorated St Thomas the martyr.[71] A mid-fifteenth century office described Scrope as a martyr whose death in the cause of the peace of the church at the hands of the persecutor imitated the death of Thomas of Canterbury.[72]

The parallels between the Scrope and Becket cults were clearly drawn in the lives of the archbishop which were written by the York clergy with the help of the local gentry. The most important account of Scrope's execution was Thomas Gascoigne's. During his periodic ten-year residence at the small parish of Kirk Deighton near Wetherby between 1433 and 1443, Gascoigne used the first-hand testimony of relatives and friends to give an account of the execution and the subsequent miracles that depicted Scrope as a Becket-like martyr and not a traitor.[73] Among the witnesses that Gascoigne would have used were his friends and in-laws in the Roos family, who were early followers of the cult. William

69 *Cronica S. Albani*, p. 388.
70 McNiven, 'The Betrayal of Richard Scrope', 173 – 213; Jacob, *The 15th Century*, p. 60.
71 Haselock, p. 374.
72 *Political Songs of England*, ed. T. Wright (Camden Soc., 1839), pp. 268 – 72.
73 *Loci e libro Veritatum*, pp. 228 – 29.

Lord Roos was a friend of Sir William Gascoigne and he accompanied him in the royal council that dealt with the 1405 rebellion; in 1412 he bequeathed his soul to Thomas Becket.[74] Sir Thomas Roos, a member of the cadet branch of the family at Igmanthorpe, was a close friend of Gascoigne's father Richard Gascoigne, the marshal of the exchequer; his son and heir, Sir Robert Roos, possessed relics of Richard Scrope and married Joan Gascoigne, a niece of Sir William and the sister of Thomas Gascoigne.[75] Joan told her brother about a miracle told to her during her childhood at the Friars Minor of York, where Thomas Mowbray Earl Marshall was buried, concerning a successful defiance of royal strictures against making offerings at the martyr's tomb.[76] Gascoigne also had access during his residence at Deighton to the testimony of his friend Sir Thomas Cumberworth, an eyewitness of the execution, and Cumberworth gave him details of the martyrdom, including Scrope's dying words. Stephen Palmer, a citizen of York, and George Plumpton, the rector of Grasmere in 1431, whose father Sir William Plumpton was executed with Scrope, provided Gascoigne with details concerning the mysterious illness which affected the king after 1405; and John Kexby, a contempory at Oxford, may have given Gascoigne the details of the miracles witnessed by William Kexby, a canon of York.[77]

Another cleric to give an account of the miracles that discredited Henry IV was Clement Maidstone, who had heard rumours about the disappearance of the king's body on its way to burial at Canterbury while he was at the Trinitarian priory of Hounslow.[78] Both Gascoigne and Maidstone were at Syon where Gascoigne continued his hagiographic writing; both men may have been responsible for the belief, widely held in the monastery, that Syon was founded as a result of Henry IV's vow to atone for the murder of Scrope.[79] The most politically forceful account of the execution is that of one Thomas, who used the eyewitness testimony of John Corbridge to idealize Scrope as a Becket-like defender of the liberties of the church who led his followers at Shipton Moor in an attempt to obtain a remedy for the oppressive taxation of the church.[80] Thomas Dautre, the possible author, was a chapter clerk of York at the time of the execution and may have seen the parallels with Becket's martyrdom in a life of St Thomas in the

74 TE, I, p. 357.
75 Wylie, *Henry IV*, ii, p. 342.
76 *Loci e Liber Veritatum*, p. 229.
77 ibid, p. 229.
78 Maidstone's account is printed in *Anglia Sacra*, ed. Wharton (London, 1691), ii, pp. 362 – 88.
79 For a contradiction of this myth see Tait, 'The Brigittine Monastery of Syon'.
80 *Historians of York*, iii, p. 288.

windows of York chapter house. Dautre's son John owned a life of St Thomas Becket, which he probably received from his father and which he bequeathed to his son.[81] Sir Peter Ardene, chief baron of the exchequer, also owned a life of St Thomas of Canterbury which he left to his son.[82] It was the underlying principle of the inviolacy of canon and common law that would have secured for the cult the support of the influential classes of York.

The cult was also established among the citizens of York, and this was due to the support that was provided by the town council and the use that was made of the York Corpus Christi guild to popularize the saint. William Frost, mayor in 1406 and on six other occasions, and the town council frustrated attempts to quell the cult. In a York memorandum book there is a petition from four York sergeants who complained that they had been dismissed from their posts for carrying out the command of the king's son, John Duke of Bedford, to track down people offering at the tomb of the archbishop. The king granted their request to be restored to their offices, but this was resisted by the mayor and council, and the following year the elected sergeants were required to swear an oath that if they were dismissed from office they were to make no complaint to any but the mayor and council.[83] Clearly the town council saw in the execution of Scrope, and in the subsequent government measures, an issue of municipal independence similar to the principle of ecclesiastical independence appreciated by York clergy and secular lawyers. The mayor of York in 1407 was Henry Wyman, a wealthy goldsmith of Coney Street, whose only child Joan was married to William, the eldest son of chief justice Sir William Gascoigne. Wyman cherished as a relic a wooden drinking cup which the archbishop had blessed. During Wyman's second mayoralty in 1408 the Corpus Christi Guild was formed, with Wyman as a founding member, and his wife Agnes, who was also a member, presented Scrope's relic to the guild before her death in 1413.[84] The guild added to the relic a cupband and inscription, probably containing the names of members of the guild, and by 1465 this pardon cup was valued as one of the guild's most precious effects. In the annual Corpus Christi procession the host was carried through the city by the guild and during the rest of the year it was kept in a feretory. William Reventour, a guild member, left *fabriciae feretri corporis Christi Ebor.*, a silver goblet, and Isabella Bruce, a widow left

81 TE, II, p. 232. It is possible that Scrope's head was carried in a procession like St William's in a reliquary.

82 *Historians of York*, iii, p. 291.

83 *Fabric Rolls of York*, p. 193.

84 Wyman was lord mayor in 1407, 1408 and 1409. He died in 1419. See information taken from a brass in St Crux church in TE, III, p. 53n.

jewels to *feretro Corporis Christi*; it is possible that the pardon cup was carried with the host in this procession.[85] Many of those responsible for establishing the cult of Richard Scrope were members of the guild and they included: Joan Gascoigne, wife of Sir William the chief justice, who joined in 1412; Sir William Gascoigne's son William; Dame Elizabeth Plumpton, the wife of Sir William Plumpton, whose father Sir Robert Plumpton was executed with Scrope; Robert Wolveden, who joined in 1430; Sir Robert Roos, who joined in 1431; and Thomas and John Dautre. The Scropes of Masham, including Margery, the archbishop's sister-in-law, Stephen, the archdeacon of Richmond and Sir John Scrope, the fourth lord of Masham, were members. John Stytenham, the custodian of Scrope's shrine, was also a member.[86]

Despite these efforts of the governing class of the diocese, Scrope was not canonized, and his office never became official. However, his followers continued to worship him as a saint and to celebrate his office. In 1418 Katherine Craven of York bequeathed a girdle to St Richard Scrope; in 1447 Edmund de-la-Pole of York commended his soul to St Richard Scrope, and in 1468 William Haiton, keeper of Scrope's tomb, requested that his wife Margaret make an offering of 3s 4d at the execution block of *beati Ricardi le Scrope*, which was situated near the tomb.[87] Scrope's followers continued to hope for his translation: in 1467 a canon of Ripon left twenty gold nobles to be used for the shrine of the blessed Richard Scrope, 'when God grant that he should be translated'; in 1472 Robert, the abbot of Kirkby Knoll, left 'St Richard' a silver chain and asked his wife to place it at the site of the shrine, which was to be built after his translation.[88] Although Scrope was never commemorated in the liturgy of the church of York, offices to Richard Scrope occur in many of the northern primers of the gentry. The Bolton Hours, which were illuminated in the diocese between 1420 and 1430, contain a full-page illumination depicting the owners, John Bolton, the mayor of York, and his wife Alice, who were both members of the York Corpus Christi Guild, praying to St Richard; this accompanied by a prayer to the saint with seven penitential psalms, in which St Richard is invoked with St Bridget.[89] Offices to St Richard also occur in a northern primer which was illuminated by Herman Scheere between 1405 and 1413, possibly

85 TE, II, p. 117.
86 See *Register of the Guild of Corpus Christi*, ed. Skaife.
87 TE, II, p. 232; Y.M.L. Reg. Test., iv, fo. 209a.
88 *Ripon Chapter Acts*, p. 232.
89 Y.M.L. 5 Ms. Add. 2, fos. 1 – 3, 100v – 101. This manuscript was written and illuminated between 1420 and 1430 by a scribe called John for John Bolton, mercer and M.P. for York from 1427 – 28 and mayor in 1431. The manuscript remained in the family throughout the fifteenth century. For description see the *Friends of York Minster Annual Report* (1944).

for the Scrope family; and in the Mountenay Hours, which were owned by a gentry family of Nottinghamshire.[90]

In the same period during which the Scrope cult was initiated the cults of the Saxon and Norman saints were revived, and they were also focussed on York Cathedral. These cults had long commanded traditional loyalities among the citizens and clergy of York, and among the households of magnate families. York had two patron saints, St Wilfrid and St William; neither of these saints were widely known outside the diocese, and their offices only occur in the diocese of York; but they were of local significance. The canons of Ripon were dedicated to St Wilfrid and owned one of his relics; one of them, William Cawood, established a chantry in his honour. St William's feast was celebrated with enthusiasm in the city of York: the chamberlain's accounts for 1371 record that there was an annual festival celebrating his translation, accompanied by minstrels, plays, and a procession, carrying his head in a portable reliquary through the city.[91] Saints Cuthbert and John of Beverley were the patron saints of the two most important families in the north in the fourteenth century. St Cuthbert was the patron saint of the Nevilles of Raby, who fought under his banner at Neville's Cross in 1346. Ralph Neville, and his son, John, were buried next to St Cuthbert's shrine in 1367 and 1388. St John of Beverley was the patron saint of the Percy family. The ornate stone and marble screen that was made as an extension of the family tomb in 1369 was designed to carry the shrine of the saint. In 1378 the amount of offerings to be presented at this shrine was kept at 100 marks by Archbishop Neville, and the surplus was reserved for the residentiary canons. Both of these saints were known outside the diocese: the office of St Cuthbert was celebrated in missals of the use of York, Sarum, Hereford, and the feast of St John of Beverley was celebrated in York, Sarum and Hereford.[92]

By the beginning of the fifteenth century, however, these cults were undergoing a revitalization as they secured a wider and more enthusiastic following throughout the diocese and the rest of the kingdom, thanks to the efforts of the York clergy and leading gentry of the diocese. Signs of this renewed interest were appearing towards the end of the fourteenth century. In sermons delivered at the church of

[90] Bodl. Lib. MS. Lat. Liturg. f2, fo. 2; Y.M.L. MS. Add. 54, fo. 3. For additional information on Bodl. Lib. MS. Lat. Liturg. f2, an expensive prayer book with 18 large paintings, written and illuminated in the early years of the fifteenth century for a noble household: see *Bodl. Lib. Record*, iv (1952) and W. D. Macray's note in *Athenaeum*, Aug. (188). The Moutenay book of hours was still in the Moutenay family at the end of the fifteenth century. See *Archeol.*, iii, 46.

[91] J. Fowler, 'An Account of St William of York', *YAJ.*, viii, (1875), 257; *Fabric Rolls*, p. 127.

[92] G. Poulson, *Beverlac* (London, 1829), vii, p. 594.

Austin Friars at York, Friar John Waldeby commended the York saints.[93] The treasurer of York, John Clifford, chose to be buried next to St William's tomb in 1392, and Lady Joan Hesilrig left a gold brooch at the head of the saint.[94] Archbishop Richard Scrope's interest in St Cuthbert is revealed by his borrowing a copy of Bede's prose life of St Cuthbert from the library of Durham Priory.[95] Scrope's cult in turn probably encouraged his former colleagues and servants to revive the cults of these other York saints. Their interest in them is revealed in their wills: in 1415 Richard Pittes, the subtreasurer, left a necklace of gold and pearls to the 'glorious confessor St William', with instructions that it was to be placed on the reliquary containing his holy body; and in 1423 Henry Bowet commended his soul to St John of Beverley and St Wilfrid.[96] The minster clergy made these saints more widely known by commemorating them and providing narratives of their lives in the stained glass windows of the cathedral. Bowet, Thomas Parker, a residentiary canon, and Robert Wolveden, donated windows commemorating St Paul, St John of Beverley, St William, St Thomas and St Chad, whose relics were at Lichfield where Wolveden was formerly dean.[97] Between 1410 and 1430 in the clerestory windows of the north-west choir lights were inserted, commemorating bishops connected with the conversion of the north including representations of John of Beverley and Wilfrid.[98] The close connection between the cults of Richard Scrope and William is shown in the donation of lights depicting the two saints, who face one another on opposite sides of the south transept, by the same donors, Scrope of Masham, Scrope, Wolveden and the Dean and chapter.[99] The important position in the lancets beneath the rose window and above the south transept doors was used to proclaim the importance of William and Wilfrid, who are commemorated alongside Saints Peter and Paul.[100] The most impressive memorial to William was a 75ft high window in the north end of the north choir transept, donated by the Roos family of Helmesley in 1422 in memory of the 6th Lord Roos, who was named after the saint, and who died in 1414. Near the base of the window there are kneeling images of William Lord Roos' eldest son John, the 7th baron of Hamelake, his wife Margaret Despenser, and his sons Thomas, William, Sir Richard and Sir

93 Roth, *Eng. Austin Friars*, p. 401ff.
94 TE, I, pp. 166, 265.
95 Dobson, *Durham Priory*, p. 31 n. 2.
96 Y.M.L. Reg. Test. i, fos. 172, 216.
97 Harrison, *The Painted Glass of York*, pp. 88 – 9. Parker received some of R. Scrope's confiscated property and founded a chantry in his honour.
98 ibid, pp. 88 – 9.
99 ibid, p. 98.
100 ibid, p. 98.

Robert, all kneeling before the image of Our Lady.[101] The panels of this window depict episodes from the life and miracles of William, obtained from the accounts of the twelth century chronicles and York service books, which were intended for the edification and encouragement of pilgrims to his shrine.[102] Opposite this window in the south choir transept, an equally large window showing the life and miracles of Cuthbert was built between 1426 and 1437 by the bishop of Durham, Thomas Langley, who had been dean of York minster. The sources for the narrative panels of this window were two manuscripts written in Durham between 1080 and 1150 that contained illustrated versions of Bede's prose life.[103] Langley also caused a life of Cuthbert to be set up is glass in Durham Cathedral, with the help of Walter Skirlaw, and he commended his soul to Cuthbert in his will.[104]

It is difficult to say with certainty when any particular individual's interest in these Saxon and Norman saints represented anything more than a continuation of traditional local loyalties; but there does seem to have been an intensification of interest on the part of local citizens of York, and certainly a renewed national interest, which must owe something to the efforts of the York clergy and the stained glass lives in the minster. The York merchant Nicholas Blackburn, himself a donor of many windows, established a chantry in the chapel of St William at Ousebridge, and in the primer of John Bolton there are prayers to John of Beverley, William, Wilfrid and St Hilda of Whitby.[105] William and John of Beverley attracted the attention of East Anglian mystics. Julian of Norwich was devoted to John of Beverley and Margery Kempe made pilgrimages to William's tomb in 1413 and 1417. The prince of Wales made his first pilgrimage to the shrine of John of Beverley in 1408; he visited it again after his coronation and also in 1420 when he was accompanied by Queen Katherine in a visit arranged by his chamberlain Henry Lord FitzHugh, who advised the governors of the borough of Beverley on the reception of the king.[106]

The saint's cults of the diocese of York showed some things in common with the traditional and revived cults of other religions. They were controlled by regular and secular clergy, who were concerned with

[101] ibid, p. 87; Fowler, 'St William of York', 212ff.
[102] Fowler, 'St William of York', 212ff. Forty-three miracles of St William were copied onto a table in the clerestory of the cathedral of York, where they were probably used for reference.
[103] J. Fowler, 'The St Cuthbert Window of York', *Y.A.J.*, iv, (1875-6) 225; Oxford Univ. Coll. MS. 165.
[104] Fowler, 228.
[105] TE, II, p. 18.
[106] *Northern Chronicle* (Kingsford, Historical lit.), p. 290; *Chronicle of John Streche*, p. 278; Wylie, *Henry V*, iii, p. 271.

the local prestige of priories and the building projects of the minster and its central importance in the diocese. The new cult of Richard Scrope and the revived cults of John of Beverley, William and Cuthbert, commemorated in the stained glass of York Minster, were used by the canons of York to assert the historical traditions and prestige of their cathedral city. The canons of St Paul's were interested in St Erkenwald for the same reason, and the *Life of St Erkenwald* illustrated the history of the cathedral.[107] The bishop of Salisbury, Robert Hallum, and his canons, attempted to do the same thing for their cathedral between 1412 and 1416, when they tried to secure the canonization of Osmund, a former bishop of Salisbury, after recording thirty-three miracles testified by forty-six witnesses.[108]

The saints' cults of York and other cathedrals, such as Salisbury, were also responsible for an almost baroque elaboration of the religious environment, especially in York Minster. The addition of stained glass saints' lives and saints' offices in this cathedral would have created opportunities for the writing of new music, and would have enabled such musical innovations to take place as the polyphonic mass and the enlargement of the cathedral's choir, both of which occurred in the fifteenth century.[109] In this period the liturgy was being transformed as the sanctorale — the commemoration of the saint's life — occupied a more important place in the canonical hours of office. Ownership of Latin versions of the *Legenda Aurea* by Thomas Roos, Elizabeth Redman, Henry Lord Scrope and Peter Ardene; and ownership of English versions of this work by William Revetour, a chantry priest, and the merchants, Richard Russel and William Haryngton, testifies to the increasing importance of saints' lives in the liturgy. Worshippers in the cathedral of York, or in the chapels of the nobility, no longer needed to follow the daily services by the liturgical chanting of the psalter. Primers, such as the Bolton Hours, provided hymns to be sung for favourite local saints, and their offices could be celebrated in an environment of carved images and illuminated legends. The Salisbury chapter was interested in the canonization of St Osmund as a means of furthering the liturgical importance of Salisbury cathedral. Ullerston outlined his case for the canonization in a sermon delivered in 1416 when he claimed, in error, that Osmund had prescribed Salisbury's Sarum ritual, and that the canonization was therefore desired to secure

[107] T. McAlindon, 'Hagiography into Art: a Study of St Erkenwald', *Studies in Philology*, 67, (1970), 42 – 94.

[108] A. R. Malden, *The Canonization of St Osmund*, (Wilts. Rec. Soc., 1901), pp. xi – xiii, 56 – 58.

[109] P. Aston, 'Music since the Reformation', in *History of York Minster*, pp. 395 – 99, P. Aston, *The Music of York Minster* (York, 1972).

for the Use of Salisbury preeminence among any other uses in the church.[110]

However, although some of the features of these York cults can be observed in cults in other regions, there was also something distinctive about the cults of the Yorkshire saints. In no other period was there such a proliferation of cults involving so many ordinary people. The cult of St Erkenwald, of which there is little evidence apart from a sophisticated saint's life, was probably the creation of an educated minority and never really aroused popular enthusiasm: only four bequests to St Erkenwald's shrine have been recorded for the fourteenth and fifteenth centuries.[111] Pilgrims testified to the performance of miracles at Osmund's shrine; but this was only for a limited period around 1411, and the initiative, and even some of the reports, came from the Salisbury chapter.[112] This cult never really aroused the popular support that the Scrope cult inspired. All the York cults owed as much to popular initiative as to clerical direction; throughout the diocese ordinary unlettered people visited shrines, reported miracles, and followed the lives of the saints in stained glass legends, sermons, and plays. These popular cults allowed the expression of important religious feelings about local parish society, the parish church, authority and holiness, which were shared by people of all levels of wealth and sophistication. By examining these feelings more closely we can begin to understand the astonishing popularity of the saints in the diocese in this period, and the relationship between the contemplative movement initiated by the clergy and popular religious impulses.

The Social Functions of the Cult of Saints in the Diocese of York

All relics were to some degree subjected to divisive forces: the body of the martyr was decapitated; the bones of the confessor decayed; even the host, which would be regarded by some in this period as having the characteristics of a relic, was divided and consumed during the Mass. But all these relics were used to bind communities together. The procession of Christ's body through the streets of York on the Feast of Corpus Christi allowed the ninety competing craft guilds to assert their independence in cycle plays, while participating in a ritual celebrated

[110] E. F. Jacob, 'Conciliar Activity', in Jacob, *Essays in the Conciliar Epoch*, (Manchester, 1953), p. 78 – 83.
[111] *Wills in the Court of Husting*, ii, pp. 108, 139, 160 and 203.
[112] Malden, *The Canonization of St Osmund*, pp. xi – xii, 56 – 82.

the wholeness and unity of the municipal society.[1] One of the panels of the great St William window in York shows the cathedral clergy handling the scattered bones of the saint during his translation, while another depicts the procession of townsmen behind the reliquary of the patron saint.[2] These processions were regularly carried out in York, and minster expenses connected with the procession are recorded in 1340, 1390 and 1430. Guilds were established at Pontefract in honour of Thomas of Lancaster, and around Scrope's mutilated body there was established a cult that brought together minster clergy, craftsmen, city aldermen, merchants, knights and magnates of the surrounding countryside, many of whom were members of the Corpus Christi guild.[3] *The Canterbury Tales* provides an insight into the power of shrines to unify people of different backgrounds into a society of pilgrims.

A social ideology underlay this process. The offices of martyrs were celebrated as a sacrifice for a divided community. Prayers in Lancaster's office declare that the earl, when he saw that his flock was dispersed and the whole commons falling into wreck, did not shrink from dying because God had willed that the blessed Thomas, martyr and earl, should fall by the sword of the persecutor for the peace of England.[4] An office of Richard Scrope in a northern primer, which contains a full-page illumination of the decapitation, celebrates the execution as a sacrifice for the community: the archbishop, who was free from all fault, glowed like a rose for his spouse the church of York. Resemblances to the sacrifice of Christ were stressed: this office is illustrated with a devout, affecting picture of the martyr whose face is grey with suffering. William Packington's account of Lancaster's martyrdom shows the earl being stoned by the people and led to his execution on a hill at Pontefract, where he cries in despair to his God. A fourteenth century office goes further and describes his betrayal by Robert de Hagland, his arrest, and his execution on the third day of his imprisonment.[5] The accounts of Scrope's martyrdom given by Thomas Dautre and Gascoigne likewise describe the archbishop's betrayal by Bedford.[6] Gascoigne and Maidstone related the progress of the archbishop, clad in scarlet and mounted on a sorry nag, as he was taken towards York; and they described his final passion: Scrope asked his executioner to give him five wounds in memory of Christ's Passion, kissed him three times and

1 M. E. James, 'Ritual, Drama and the Social Body in the Late Medieval Town', *Past and Present*, 98 (1983), 1 – 29.
2 Fowler, 'St William', 212ff.
3 Bequests to the guild of Thomas of Lancaster were made by William Norfolk of Pontefract and John Streche of York. See TE, I, p. 281.
4 Wright, *Political Songs*, p. 270.
5 Tait, 'Pilgrim Signs', 37 – 46; *Political Songs*, pp. 268 – 74.
6 *Historians of York*, ii, pp. 306 – 11; *Loci e Libro Veritatum*, pp. 228 – 29.

forgave him; he then bent his head to receive the strokes, saying the words, *In manus tuus, Domine, commendo spiritum meum*; Scrope's biographers even noted his resurrection which was witnessed by Sibsun.[7]

Masses, whether they were celebrated in memory of Christ or the saints, also attempted to heal social divisions. The increasingly reverent attitudes towards the eucharist in this period meant that offices of saints were subordinate to the Mass, or that the Mass itself, in that it commemorated the life of Christ and venerated his relic, resembled a saint's feast in the sanctorale. Both celebrated the atonement that Christ and the saints made for the sins of the community, which in pastoral manuals of the diocese were defined as thoughts and deeds hostile to society. After the confession of such sins Mass was celebrated, the divided eucharist consumed by the officiating priest, and the pax-board was handed round and ritually kissed to symbolize the healing of the community that Christ's sacrifice had brought about.[8] The saint's office celebrated the same process: an office of Richard Scrope declares that the saint gave his blood by the rigours of the sword on St William's day, as atonement for men's sins.[9] Masses for the dead invoked the intercession of Christ and his saints for friends and relatives in purgatory; such intercession bridged the division between the Church Suffering and the Church Triumphant that had been caused by sin; masses celebrated for the good estate of the living purchased the heavenly intervention of Christ and his saints in the natural world: such intercession healed the division between heaven and a fallen world. But it was the prayers and masses for the saints that brought about the most potent manifestation of holiness in the affairs and misfortunes of men. The traditional miracles of the saints combatted the hostile forces threatening individuals and communities and demonstrated the value that people faced with stress place on concepts of wholeness and harmony that were expressed in social terms.

Much of the stress an individual would face came from outside society, from the untamed forces of the natural world; although they were ultimately under the control of God's providence, manifestations of natural power could assume, in the form of fate, an arbitrary and hostile dimension. Merchants, who invested capital in voyages and depended on the favours of fortune, had most to fear from such vagaries of nature as the storms at sea that were sometimes ascribed to demons; and when they struck the mercy and intervention of the saint was sought. The visions of the saint in his pastoral robes experienced by

[7] *Loci e Libro Veritatum*, p. 228; *Anglia Sacra*, ii, pp. 362 – 88; *Political Songs*, ii, p. xxvi.
[8] J. Bossy, 'The Mass as a Social Institution', *Past and Present*, 100, (1983), 47.
[9] Bodl. Lib. MS. Liturg. 2, fo. 146v.

sailors were an attempt to summon up, in the midst of natural disorder, an image of all that was benevolent and ordered in society. One of the miracles in the life of St John of Beverley, which was commemorated in his office, describes the vision of stricken sailors who see John approach their broken craft in a shining white raiment, looking like a pontiff, driving away the demons with his pastoral staff.[10] This miracle was used for one of the panels of the St William window which shows William relieving York merchants at sea.[11] He seems to have been invoked by merchants throughout this period, because seven silver ships given as votive offerings for deliverance from storms at sea were still at this shrine in 1509.[12] The same miracle of John Beverley probably influenced the vision experienced by five men from Hartlepool in the diocese of Durham who were overwhelmed in a storm at sea. Perceiving themselves to be in great danger, they called with weeping voices on St John of Bridlington, who they did not know but of whom they had heard much concerning his holy life. While they were praying, a man, dressed in the habit of a canon regular, placed his hand over the vessel and steadying the mast with his gracious hand he brought the vessel to safety; when the delivered men went to Bridlington to thank the prior they recognized him as the same man who had appeared to them.[13] The miracles of John of Beverley and John of Bridlington appear to have influenced the vow made by Roger Wandesford while he was in danger of drowning in a stormy sea between Norway and Scotland: in 1400 he asked his executors to make a pilgrimage to their shrine to complete his vow.[14] John of Bridlington was especially popular among merchants of the diocese including: the Boltons, who owned an office dedicated to him, John Brompton, a Beverley merchant, and the widow of York merchant John Holbeck.[15] His cult even spread to the seaports of the southeast coast, where altars dedicated to him were found in Dover and Sandwich.[16] Sailors and merchants in trouble also invoked the aid of Richard Scrope and performed pilgrimages to his shrine, either to give thanks for their deliverance, or to ask for his aid in future voyages. Around his tomb in 1509 there were votive offerings of over forty model ships of silver including a small fleet of seven ships.[17]

The hostility of nature was also experienced in sudden accidents and misfortunes, which could be confronted with the help of saints whose

10 *Vita S. Joan Bev.*, (Acta Sanctorum, Mai.), ii, p. 179.
11 Fowler, 'St William, p. 212ff.
12 *York Fabric Rolls*, p. 224.
13 *Vita S. Joannis de Bridlingtona*, (Acta Sanctorum, Octobris), v, pp. 137 – 44.
14 TE, I, p. 246.
15 TE, II, p. 96; TE, I, p. 331; Y.M.L. 5 MS. Add. 2, Fos. 207 – 207v.
16 Purvis, 'St John of Bridlington'.
17 *York Fabric Rolls*, pp. 225 – 28.

power was neither harsh nor arbitrary. William's most famous miracle is commemorated in his office and in two panels of the St William window which show the bridge over the River Ouse collapsing during a procession and sending many people into the river; William, by making a sign of the cross, stills the waters and they are all delivered unharmed. This miracle, according to the Benedictine monk of Pontefract, Thomas Castleford, also happened on Ferrybridge at Pontefract in the fourteenth century.[18] The miracle was also commemorated in a chapel errected to St William on Ousebridge in York.[19] When a bell-tower near York caught fire in 1413 there was nothing to be done to save the building, bystanders made a vow to St Richard Scrope; the fire abated, and the half burnt tower remained to record the efficacy of the sainted dead.[20] In a time when there was no accurate way of determining death, vows to the saint were often credited with causing the revival of victims of accidental drowning. The St William window commemorates the revival of a York girl, drowned in the Ouse, through a bystander binding a penny on her body in honour of St William; and the intercession of St John of Bridlington was credited with raising three men who had been drowned in wells.[21] The stories of the Hampole pilgrims gave to isolated rural parishioners a faith in providential order and mercy, which would have alleviated the sense of isolation and helplessness they must have felt when confronted with misfortune: if the stars were distant and indifferent, there was a network of shrines and pilgrim trails operating on other laws besides chance. When the son of Isabella, a lady of Leicester, was rescued from a walled well where he had remained five hours, God took pity on the grieving bystanders, and through his divine providence arranged that a pilgrim returning from Hampole should be passing through at that very moment; he told them of the mighty miracles performed there by God in answer to the prayers addressed to Richard Rolle; they followed his instructions by praying to St Richard, vowing to make an offering of a penny at his tomb, and at this the child revived.[22] Another pilgrim, from the village of Fishlake near York, publicized at Hampole St Richard's miraculous revival of her three-year-old child who had fallen in a well, in return for prayers and the measuring of a candle the length of the child's body for the saint's tomb.[23] A group of Hampole pilgrims affirmed that their promise to visit Richard Rolle's tomb to acknowledge his power to God had revived a ten-year-old boy who had been bitten by a snake while grazing his

18 Fowler, 'St William', p. 238.
19 TE, II, p. 18.
20 *Loci e Libro Veritatum*, p. 228.
21 Fowler, 'St William', 238.
22 *Brev. Ebor.*, App. lect. 6.
23 ibid, feria secunda, lec. 7.

father's sheep.[24] The saint's control over fortune was most evident around the church where his relics were housed. When the priests of the basilica of Beverley were celebrating the offices of their confessor, the unstable towers started to fall, as a gentle warning for all to leave; one of the lights of the St William window shows a stone falling upon the head of one of the canons who was sleeping during matins and who escaped unhurt.[25] Stones on the gate of Hampole churchyard and on the tomb of Rolle recorded the miracle witnessed by Roger while he was building the saint's tomb; he crashed his oxen and cart into this gate bringing the stones upon himself, and yet he escaped uninjured.[26] When Kayingham church was struck by lightning in 1391 a fire started in the nave and intercessions were offered at the tomb of Philip of Beverley; the safety of the men who put out the fire was attributed to the saint's intercession.

Sudden illness was another threat to the security of the individual that was posed by the natural world; and a large proportion of the saints' miracles were concerned with the cure of the sick. Nearly all of the thirty-three reported miracles at St Osmund's shrine were cures; most of the cures effected by St William, which were recorded in the York breviary and the minster window, involving the lame, blind, and dumb, occurred shortly after his translation; the last recorded cure at his shrine, which involved a paralysed clerk, occurred in 1418.[27] The same pattern was repeated in the fourteenth century: the translations, official and unofficial, of Richard Rolle, John Bridlington and Richard Scrope were accompanied by a spate of cures that were fantasies of dismemberment, disintegration and reintegration, closely allied to the pattern established in the translation of the physical remains of the saint. Many of the pilgrims to Rolle's shrine at Hampole were the sick, or their relatives, seeking a cure through prayer: Beatrice of York prayed at the shrine for seven days until cured of dumbness; or they were grateful convalescents completing their vows and offering to their saint the pennies and candles they had vowed to him in their moments of crisis. The relief that such measures had given to mothers in childbirth, the arthritic, the paralysed, the deaf and dumb, and the insane, was reported by these pilgrims and incorporated by the nuns into their office.[28] An external source of evidence for the curative function of this shrine was provided in 1391 by the York chandler John Croxton, who offered eight pounds of wax and a wax model of his afflicted leg.[29] A man wounded by a sword was cured at the shrine of Rolle on the advice of a priest who bound a

24 ibid, lec. 8.
25 *Vita S. Joan Bev.*, p. 293; Fowler, 'St William', 295.
26 *Brev. Ebor.*, lec. 1.
27 ibid, feria tertia, lec. I – IV.
28 ibid, feria tertia, lec. I – IV.
29 TE, I, p. 54.

penny to the wound; a child suffocated in hay was revived by an offering of a penny to the saint; and a man called Robert travels a long distance to be cured of his deafness at the shrine. Similar cures were recorded at the shrine of John of Bridlington: one Agnes was delivered of a fever; and a woman, who was a sister of one of the canons, was cured of the plague with the help of the prayers of her brother.[30] The usual cures of the blind, crippled and possessed also occurred at this shrine: one demoniac had come over 160 miles to be exorcized.[31] Contemporary chronicles testified to the procession of pilgrims that were cured of ailments at Scrope's tomb; and inventories of the contents of this tomb taken in 1509 illustrate its importance as a curative shrine. On the precious cloths that covered the tomb there were large collections of precious rings and girdles, accompanied by votive offerings of wax trindles, which were twisted around afflicted members, and the wax and silver images of the afflicted parts of the body made in expectation of, or in thanksgiving for, cures. Even by this late date there were still ten hearts, thirteen legs, six hands, sixteen eyes, ten teeth, four breasts, nine human images and two bovine. In one year alone, offerings at the tomb amounted to £2,000, which was higher than the amounts collected at Becket's shrine during the height of the cult.[32]

The saints' cures, in contrast to the painful and erratic cures of natural medicine, were painless and came as an answer to prayer, faith and pilgrimage. Isabella, who had been blind in one eye for twenty years, had tried many doctors, but had found that diligent use of natural medicines provided no help; at the tomb of Richard Rolle, after diligent prayer, the Lord considered her worthy of intercession.[33] In one of William's miracles, commemorated in the breviary of York, a woman suffering from dropsy, who despised living physicians, hastened to the living antidote of the dead physician.[34] The saints frequently cured painlessly while the sufferer was sleeping. At the shrine of John of Bridlington a demoniac was cured in his sleep when a voice told him to sing the *Te Deum*; and Robert, who had been blind for three years, heard a voice in his sleep telling him to go to Hampole, where at the tomb of the Blessed Richard he would receive clear vision.[35]

The saint's cult fulfilled the same social function in curing illness as it did in confronting misfortune; to the unknown forces outside society it opposed the social certainty of vows, votive offerings and pilgrimages, which were made to public shrines. The cure was a communal activity:

30 *Vita S. Joannis de Bridlingtona*, p. 144; *Nova Legenda Angliae* ii, pp. 73 – 4.
31 *Nova Legenda Angliae*, ii, pp. 73 – 4.
32 *York Fabric Rolls*, pp. 225 – 28.
33 *Brev. Ebor.*
34 Fowler, 'St William', 262; *Brev. Ebor.*, lec. 2 – 3.
35 *Brev. Ebor.*, Feria 4, lec. 1.

relatives and friends frequently made the pilgrimage and said the prayers, especially if the sufferer was incapacitated or insensible. Accounts of miraculous cures reveal that the whole community had been motivated to find a cure. In a period when towns shut their gates to pestilence and placed themselves under the protection of a patron saint, the exposure of the individual to illness was regarded as a threat to the whole community. When Thomas Bell of Morehow was lying ill in bed, all his neighbours despaired, until a voice told him to send his wife with a candle to be placed in the choir of All Saints' Church in Hampole. When John, who was insane, was led by his friends to the tomb of Richard Rolle, they prayed devoutly to the saint, and their friend was immediately restored to his senses to their great consolation.[36] In their curative role the saints' cults were an offshoot of pastoral reform: Thoresby encouraged the cults of Lancaster and Richard Scrope; Alexander Neville encouraged the cult of John of Bridlington; and Henry Bowet and the residentiary canons of York Minster fostered the cult of Richard Scrope.[37] The cult of saints opposed the uncertain powers and remedies of the rural pagan world with urban, or at least public, Christian cures that focussed on the bones of the saints that had been officially consecrated by the clergy and placed in shrines in public places. Communities had their own favourite saints, and the diocese itself had its own particular saints. In the cures recorded by the nuns of Hampole alongside the different saint's festivals, we can see the weaning of isolated rural pilgrims away from a natural, rustic existence, dominated by the stars and the seasons, towards the Christian rhythm of the saint's life.

In alleviating the suffering experienced from the operation of natural powers outside society, the saints were protecting communities; but they were also required to protect society from hostile natural powers that operated throughout human society, and were manifested in the oppressive exertion of secular authority. One of the functions of hagiographers was to demonstrate the superiority of the saint's powers to the power of tyrants. In the fifteenth century the head of the Trinitarian house of Knaresborough, who described himself as one who 'all yff simple be,/ Occupyes als president', wrote an English verse account of the life of the thirteenth century Yorkshire hermit St Robert of Knaresborough, and said of this saint, who was buried in the priory, 'Tyraunts trembled that did hym teyne/ Slyke selcouth was bath schewed and syne/'. According to the author of this life a squire, who attempted to evict this hermit, was visited by a black spirit and forced to

36 ibid, lec. 5.

37 Richard Scrope also attempted to help Richard II to bring about the canonization of Edward II when he went to Rome in 1397.

beg Robert's forgiveness: 'thus mesy that ys of myght wyth hys combe/ off a lyon maks a lambe/'.[38] King John visited the hermit and was challenged to a show of strength when Robert asked him to create ears of corn from nothing; the king recognized his superiority and the author comments: 'Sirres forsooth myn hertt in sonder me thynke bath wepes and wirks for wandir/ That he that was sway waike a thynge/ Durst spek sway saffly wyth hys kynge'.[39] An account is given in the life of John of Bridlington of a dispute the prior had with an official of the Duke of Lancaster who was threatening irreparable damage to the monastery; after patiently submitting to the attack John warned the official: 'Look to it that by your vicious zeal for your master which drives you daily to vex and seize our goods, you be not thrust down into Hell, there to pay the penalty forever'. In the morning the official returned, a changed man, vowing friendship to the monastery, and he steadfastly kept this vow.[40]

By reporting the posthumous miracles of martyrs, followers of their cults testified that the holy justice of heaven had not deserted a human society subjected to the coercive power of central government. Two months after his execution, the head of the Earl's steward, who was venerated as a martyr, was taken down and was reported to have shown no signs of decay. Gascoigne related that part of the barley field where Scrope's blood had trickled from the block was left untilled and bore, as he had promised, a prodigious crop with as many as seven heads of grain growing on each stalk.[41] Sir William Gascoigne heard from his niece, Joan Roos, how an old man called John Sibsun saw a vision of the archbishop's spirit commanding him to remove the logs and stones that had been placed around his tomb on government orders; under his supernatural guidance the old man's aged arms moved the weights that three men could not have lifted and placed them before the altar of the Virgin.[42] At his execution Scrope was reported to have prayed to God that the revenge of heaven would not fall on the king. Gascoigne described the king's progress in the north after the execution: there were wild storms, and the king rode over Hessay Moor in such blinding rain that it seemed as if someone had struck him a violent blow; that night, in Ripon, he awoke screaming from a nightmare, which was taken by northerners to signify that the voice of God was warning him that he would be struck by leprosy as a punishment for the death of the

38 *The Life of St Robert of Knaresborough*, ed. H. J. T. Drury (Roxburgh Club, London, 1824), p. 16. This was printed from a fifteenth century Newcastle manuscript, which also contains two Latin lives of St Robert. Another life of the saint is in Harley MS. 3775. See J. E. Wells, *A Manual of the Writings in Middle English*, 1st suppl. (Oxford, 1919); G. H. Gerould, *Saints' Legends* (Boston, 1916), p. 249ff.

39 *Life of St Robert*, p. 35.

40 *Nova Legenda Angliae*, ii, p. 72.

41 *Loci e Libro Veritatum*, p. 229.

42 ibid, p. 229.

archbishop. According to Gascoigne, the king fell ill for the next seven days, and Stephen Palmer and George Plumpton observed the large pustules on his head and hands.[43] Another northern chronicler also recorded the king's leprosy. Maidstone told a story, which he also gave to Gascoigne, that he had heard while at a Trinitarian priory of Hounslow. Within a month of the king's death a visitor to the priory told the friars that while the king's body was being conveyed to Canterbury for burial a storm had sprung up in the Thames, between Barking and Gravesend, and he, and four other men on board, took the body out of the coffin and threw it into the river; this produced an immediate calm which declared the glory of Archbishop Scrope and established him in their memories forever; then they filled the coffin with stones and buried it in Canterbury.[44] The obvious falsity of this story demonstrates the importance of the saint's cult as an outlet for discontent.

The holiness of the saint's power was also manifested in society, in the mercy that the saint showed to victims of the abrasive aspects of secular authority. In Lancaster's office the Earl, just before his execution, laments that the king of earth had deserted his people and invokes the mercy of the king of heaven.[45] The miraculous cures of the sick recorded at the tombs of the Earl of Lancaster, the Earl's steward, and Richard Scrope, were a witness to this mercy. The sinner, punished with sudden illness or misfortune, and the criminal, punished by rigour of natural law, could both find clemency through the saint's relics. Pilgrims could find protection from secular authorities through the jealously guarded privileges of the sanctuary of Beverley. The sanctuary register for the period 1478-1539 is extant and shows that within this period 469 self-confessed criminals sought the peace of St John.[46] In one of the miracles celebrated in the office of John of Beverely, a penitent thief, who is condemned to death, prays to the saint, in whose parish he had been imprisoned, to demonstrate his renowned power by releasing him; the chains and fetters are immediately loosened, and the prisoner goes to the church of Beverley and throws them down before the tomb of St John. This same miracle was recorded in the St William window.[47] The saints could also alleviate anxieties about the miscarriage of secular justice. One of the St William windows shows the saint as a merciful judge intervening in a trial by ordeal of burning.[48] The life of St John of Bridlington tells the story of a carpenter who has been fatally injured in a

43 ibid, p. 228.
44 *Anglia Sacra*, ii, p. 372.
45 *Political Poems and Songs*, p. 268 – 72.
46 For the privileges of the sanctuary of Beverley see Poulson, *Beverac*, vii, p. 594.
47 Fowler, 'St William', p. 310.
48 ibid, 310.

fall from a house.[49] His companions are suspected and all the bystanders, following the advice of one who has a great devotion to St John, pray over the dead man's body and abjure the man, in the name of the saint, to tell them if anyone is guilty; the dead man speaks and says no one is to blame for his death.[50]

Christ's saints, then, atoned for the sins which occasioned the destructive forces at work in the natural world, and which made individual and social well-being seem such a precarious thing. But the atonement of the saints offered more than a fleeting glimpse of stability because worshippers projected onto them an image of holiness that was expressed in terms of a unified and compassionate society. This was achieved through the precise social relationship that pilgrims had with their saints, in which they invested all that they valued in relationships of friendship and protection, to reflect in ideal terms the hard facts of patronage and power in this world, and judgement and punishment in the next. In moments of fear people turned to the saints who expressed an ideal view of the security offered by human society through the exercise of pastoral authority and the operation of patronage, both of which may not have been completely true in reality.

The cults of saints projected the more overtly Christian and compassionate aspects of the pastoral office. Philip of Beverley may have been absent from his rectory of Kayingham from 1306 to 1311 while he was regent master at Oxford, but after his return to Holderness he was widely regarded as a pastoral saint with the gift of second sight. In the offices of Richard Scrope the archbishop is not seen as an administrator, but a pastor who feeds the poor; a meek and obedient servant of God; a new Abel who sacrifices himself for his flock.[51] John of Bridlington was prior of a large monastery, an administrator and a landlord, but he too was seen in a pastoral role and identified in prayers with Christ the mediator who delivers men from him by his virtues; the saint was invoked with the words: *Inclite pastor*.[52] Richard Scrope and St William were depicted in York Minster lights in their pontifical vestments, and they and John of Bridlington appeared to people in trouble in priest's robes.[53]

If administration was seen in ideal pastoral terms, so too was that other aspect of the pastoral office, patronage. The saints were generous and powerful patrons: by their virtues they had become intimates in the

49 Y.M.L. 5, MS. Add. 2.

50 *Vita S. Joannis de Bridlingtona*, p. 144.

51 Y.M.L. 5 MS. Add. 2, fo. 100.

52 *Analecta Hymnica*, xlvi, p. 269; Bod. Lib. MS. Lat. Liturg. f. 2.

53 In the Bolton Hours there is a full page illumination of Scrope in full archiepiscopal vestments and in Bodl. Lib. Lat. Liturg. f. 2, fo. 2 there is a full page illumination of the decapitation which precedes the office.

court of heaven; and they were addressed as such in prayers and wills. Children were named after the saints in an attempt to attract their patronage. The most powerful and widely accessible intercessor or patron was the Virgin Mary, Mother of God. Nicholas Blackburn commended his soul to the Virgin Mary, St Anne and to all the saints who had their bright mansions in the kingdom of heaven; Thomas Howren, rector of All Saints', left his soul in 1467 to the 'multitude of sacred pities' of the Virgin Mother of Christ, for her intercession in the heavenly courts; and William Booth, archbishop of York, asked for the intercession of his patron the Virgin.[54] The Yorkshire saints were also well-connected courtiers of Christ. In a prayer, St Robert of Knaresborough is addressed: 'Hayle peirles patrone of this place/ I besek the send us grace'. He is called upon to deliver the supplicant 'fray sodan ded and dremes/ And fray all dishesse that es'. The author of his life says of the miracles performed at his grave: 'Thai may be glad and blyth that has slyke a patrone off thair place/ that ys off power for to pray/ for thare plyght bath nyght and day/'.[55] In the Bolton Hours the Boltons are shown kneeling before Archbishop Richard Scrope, a patron in life and death, asking for his prayers. A northern missal, written before 1445, contains a prayer to Scrope, the glory of York and martyr of Christ, with a picture of the supplicant asking for his intercession.[56] Scrope's nephew Stephen, who enjoyed the archbishop's patronage in his career in the church, is depicted in a York Minster window praying to his uncle : *O Ricarde pastor bone tui famuli miserere Stephani*.[57] William Pittes, treasurer of York, commended his soul to *gloriosus confessor Willielmus meorum*, and Robert Neville, bishop of Durham, commended his soul to St Cuthbert *patrono meo*.[58]

Besides this individual patronage the saint was a focus for a strong sense of collective salvation. Patron saints of parish churches interceded for the entire parish, which explains the concern of testators to be buried in their local churches. Families had their patron saints: the Scrope family, which so seriously defended the collective honour of its lineage in the Scrope-Grosvenor lawsuit, enlisted Richard Scrope, a member of their family, as their patron saint. Another proud northern affinity, the Percies, dedicated themselves to John of Beverley, and the Nevilles and their retinue followed St Cuthbert. The church of York had a historical sense of its place in the Christian cycle and a concern for the collective

54 TE., II, p. 18; Y.M.L. Reg. Test., i, fo. 317.
55 *Life of St Robert*, p. 3.
56 Y.M.L. 5 MS. Add. 2, fos. 100v – 101.
57 Harrison, *The Painted Glass of York*, p. 98; Haselock, 'The Stained Glass of York Minster', p. 378.
58 Y.M.L. Reg. Test. i, fo. 172.

fate of its members. Local saints John of Beverley and William were depicted in the west window, alongside apostles, to show that the church had its own intercessors. The cycle plays performed on Corpus Christi Day and administered by the Corpus Christi Guild would have emphasized the concept of history as a coherent progression towards the Last Judgement and its relevance to the church of York. The great east window of the choir, donated by Henry Bowet when he was candidate to the see of York in 1405-6 and built by Robert Thornton between 1405 and 1408, illustrates the words of God, *Alpha et Omega,* shown on the apex of the window by a series of panels depicting secnes from the Old Testament and the book of Revelations.[59] The Christ-like treatment of Scrope's cult, and the prominence given to him in other windows of the choir and in the guild of Corpus Christi, secured for the great church and its community proof of God's continuing mercy through this his most contemporary of apostles; and a reassurance that at the Last Judgement, at the collective end of time, the community would survive intact, as it had survived all the natural threats of this world. This sense of collective destiny under the auspices of a patron saint shows the cult of saints supporting the conventional values of familial and social religion; but there were new aspects to the cult of saints in the fourteenth century that show the development of a more personal relationship with the saints and changing attitudes to the function of society in religion.

Personal Aspects of the Cult of Saints, 1350 – 1450

The social operation of the saint's cult depended on the posthumous miracles of the saint, which were reported by pilgrims who drew on a convention established by earlier cults: many of the miracles performed at William's shrine were adaptations from those recorded at the shrine of John of Beverley; many pilgrims reporting the posthumous miracles of John of Bridlington and Richard Rolle, such as their intervention in cases of falling masonry and their revival of the dead, were relying on, or piously exaggerating, the miracles of John of Beverley and William.[1] But the hagiography of these fourteenth-century saints was independent of these traditions, and perhaps owes more to twelfth-century humanists like Walter Daniel, the author of the life of Aelred of

[59] Haselock, pp. 364 – 5.
[1] Fowler, 'St William', 202.

Rievaulx, who was interested in personality and emotions, because fourteenth-century saints' lives provide evidence of a more refined religious sensibility that was less dependent on the operation of magic and power.[2]

In the lives of Cuthbert, John of Beverley and William, which were the source of the offices of the use of York and of the stained glass legends in York, the saint's character is never explored: he remains a remote heroic figure, a powerful miracle worker. The life of St Cuthbert, which was illustrated in York minster, is dominated by fantastic and magical deeds: Cuthbert entertains an angel, and dolphins dry his hair with their breath. The cults of these saints were similarly distanced from any appreciation of personality: they were worshipped for the miracles they performed; and the aura of holiness surrounding them had much to do with the institutional manoeuvres accompanying translation and the remoteness of those who had been dead a long time. But Richard Rolle and John of Bridlington were only recently deceased; their personal charisma would have directly influenced those who contributed towards the writing of their lives. Rolle's biographical office, the outstanding saint's life of this period, was compiled from the personal memories of his lifelong disciple Margaret Kirkby and the nuns of Hampole. The author would also have had access to the testimonies of people who would have directly shaped the course of Rolle's life, such as his sister and the sons of his patron Squire Dalton, who were with Rolle at Oxford. Because Rolle died so young, these people may have outlived him by twenty years and so contributed first-hand observations to the office. Hugh, the author of the first life of St John of Bridlington, was an Austin canon, possibly of Bridlington; he may have had some first-hand acquaintance with the saintly prior, and he drew extensively on the anecdotes of older monks who knew him and who had come under his charismatic spell. In these lives the remote holiness of the long dead is replaced by the memories of people who, by recalling with warmth and humour anecdotes of the saint, including his actual words, are able to contribute towards biographies that, in their psychological realism, recreate in a full sense the personality of the holy man. Neither of these cults was entirely posthumous, and both Rolle and John of Bridlington were credited with miracles during their lifetimes and were regarded as holy men. Their hagiographers, with remarkable restraint and psychological subtlety, also demonstrated that their charismatic holiness

[2] See *The Life of Ailred of Rievaulx*, by Walter Daniel, ed. F. M. Powicke, (London, 1950) and Peter Brown's pioneering wrok on the personal aspects of saint's cults in late antiquity, esp. *The Cult of the Saints* (Chicago, 1981); *The Making of Late Antiquity* (Harvard, 1978), pp. 86 – 101; *Society and the Holy in Late Antiquity* (London, 1982), pp. 165 – 195.

depended on human qualities, on their ability to establish special relationships with people rather than on magical powers.

In the office of Richard Rolle there is a humorous, and therefore, human picture of the development of the vocation of a hermit and holy man. Rolle alarms his affectionate sister by returning suddenly from Oxford and obtaining from her two of her tunics, which he fashions into a hermit's tunic; and he then puzzles his father's former patron, the squire John Dalton, by arriving at his household in this disguise and remaining silent, only to be recognized by Dalton's sons who are on vacation from Oxford.[3] The youth and inexperience of the novice hermit is humorously illustrated when he is gently corrected by the squire for leaving the table before the others had finished.[4] The author then gives an intimate account of the development of Rolle's dedication to God by using his own words to describe his struggles with sexual temptation and the growth of his feelings of warmth towards God.

When the writer deals with the miracles performed by Rolle in his lifetime, he shows that it is the saint's human qualities: his compassion as healer and exorcist, that is the source of the miracles. The account given of Rolle's treatment of Margaret Kirkby, whom he has directed in the ordering of her life, delicately conveys the emotional force of the relationship between the holy man and his disciples. When the anchoress of Ainderby was afflicted with a loss of speech and acute pains that prevented her from resting, a 'good man' of Ainderby, knowing of Rolle's charitable affection for her, sent for the hermit. Rolle sat by her window and ate with her until the recluse, at the end of the meal, drooped her head at the window where the saint reclined and fell asleep on his shoulder; when she awoke, after a violent convulsion in which she seemed to be trying to break the window of her cell, her speech was restored. A short time later, while eating at the same window, she fell asleep, leaning on the saint as before, and the same convulsion returned, but with violent movements as if she were mad; when the holy Richard tried to hold her with his hands to prevent her injuring herself, she slipped, and in her fall awoke. After she had recovered, Richard told her that even if she had been the devil he thought he would have still held her. This was a delicate admission of his feelings for Margaret, an allusion to his earlier involvement with a young woman, which occurred shortly after he became a hermit, and which is described in the office: a very beautiful young woman, whom Rolle knew loved him with a considerable and honourable love, came to him one night and placing herself beside him, held him tightly; perceiving she was a devil tempting him in the form of a woman, he

3 *Brev. Ebor.*, lessons vii, viii.
4 ibid, lesson viii.

dispelled the apparition with the sign of the cross.[5] The writer also conveyed Margaret's strong emotional dependence on Richard, and the consequent conflict with her chosen vocation, by skilful use of the symbols of the anchorage window, which separates them, and the social ritual of eating. A sophisticated romantic unity is given to the story by the recurring illness. After this violent attack Rolle promises Margaret that as long as he is alive she will never again suffer this illness; and after several years, when her illness returns Margaret, fearing the worst, sends the same 'good man' to Hampole and learns that Rolle, faithful to his promise, has died in the same hour as the onset of her illness. The recluse spends the rest of her days at Hampole to be near his body and, presumably because the source of her conflict is now gone, the illness never returns.[6]

Rolle's high regard among noblewomen of the diocese is conveyed with similar sensitivity in a description of his attempts to comfort a dying patron, who in her fear saw the room full of demons. Rolle urged her to place all her hope in the superabundant mercy of God and in his overflowing grace, and he fervently prayed beside the woman, asking God to allow him to take away from her the fearful sight of the demons. The demons leave and disturb him instead in his cell; and after much prayer he puts them to flight and comforts the lady's friends by telling them that their friend has been saved and that after her death she will go to heaven. The inclusion in this lesson of a bystander's descriptions of the hoof marks burned in the rush-strewn floor of the lady's bedroom indicates that the less refined gossip of locals still played a part in these cults.[7]

Showing a similar concern for psychological verity, Canon Hugh and Capgrave emphasized the human qualities of John of Bridlington, which contributed towards his reputation as a holy man, and which he showed in his relationships with others. Their lives of the saint are essentially faithful accounts of the unspectacular life of a conscientious and serious prior of Bridlington who, in the execution of his duties provided his monks with an example of scrupulous compassion. He showed humility by sleeping with the monks in a small dormitory in rough bedding instead of in his prior's quarters and self-denial in his abstemiousness in eating and drinking. He was a generous cellarer who gave food to the poor, and when he was prior he remitted the rents of poor tenants and maintained poor scholars and paupers out of the wealth of the monastery. His patience and piety was shown in his habit of praying in church when all the monks were asleep, and in his careful observance of

5 ibid, lessons vii, vii.
6 ibid, lesson viii.
7 ibid, lesson viii.

the rule.[8] The most human of all his qualities was the wise tolerance he showed in dealing with his monks. A furious canon entered the hall and, hoping to enrage him, violently abused him, to which the prior answered not a word; when another monk asked him why he suffered these insults instead of sending the monk to his cell, the prior replied that rather than cast fuel on a burning house it was better to wait until the flame subsided before proceeding with suitable remedies.[9] Capgrave's work has an artistic unity similar to that of Rolle's office, and is completed when the prior hears that the monastery's great barn has been filled to unprecedented proportions with the autumn harvest of corn; sensing the completion of his work he says: 'Blessed is the Lord in his gifts for now I shall leave all in a better state than I found them, and truly now is a good hour for returning the body to the earth and the spirit to its creator.'[10] At his death he asks his monks to pardon his sins and utters such good and consoling words that none can refrain from tears.[11]

In their discussion of the saint's function as a holy man and miracle worker, Canon Hugh and Capgrave place the same emphasis on human relationships. As a result of the awe inspiring example that John set as a prior, the monks saw him as a living embodiment of holiness and preserved his commonsense pronouncements as if they were of divine origin. Hugh commented on his effect on the monks by noting that the monastery servants were restrained in the commission of evil acts by the thought of his example: for even when he was absent in body he seemed in a miraculous way to be present before them and to speak to them.[12] Both biographers give the miracles a human dimension: because of his reputation, many outside the monastery accredited the prior with performing miracles, and Hugh and Capgrave stress that St John denied his part in these miracles. When the sailors who were delivered from a storm by a vision of the prior come to Bridlington to thank him, the prior asserts that he has never left the monastery, seriously reproves them, admonishes them to be silent and tells them to enter the church where they are to give thanks to God and the Virgin; the prior further tells them to ascribe nothing to him and everything to God who alone performs miracles.[13] When a recluse told him of her vision of him in the form of an eagle, the prior cut her short and left, saying he had come to

[8] In the *Vita S. Joannis de Bridlingtona*, pp. 140 – 44, Canon Hugh gives a detached description of the daily, unostentatious acts of piety, penance and humility and compassion of a conscientious monk and prior. Capgrave gives more emphasis to St John's contemplative gifts. See *Nova Legenda Angliae*, ii, pp. 67 – 8.

[9] *Nova Legenda Angliae*, ii, p. 69.

[10] ibid, p. 75.

[11] *Vita S. Joannis de Bridlingtona*, p. 143.

[12] ibid, p. 143.

[13] ibid, p. 142.

speak with her of the grace and goodness of God, not to indulge in empty talk.[14] His biographers made no attempt to disguise the fact that the saint was a compassionate, sensible man, who was genuinely concerned about the adulation imposed on him, who denied his own powers and who placed his faith in the efficacy of prayer. Hugh described his revival of the sick through prayer and some of these accounts subtly combine practical measures with prayer. When a house beyond the circuit of the monastery caught fire, the prior set a ladder against the building until the others arrived to help, before he gave himself to prayer.[15] In his account of the miracle that John performed as cellarer when he turned loaves into stones, Hugh is careful to specify that the loaves 'seemed' stones in the canon's eyes.[16] There is a wise tolerance in Capgrave's account of the prior's conversation with a servant of the monastery, who complained that his daughter was so disfigured by a hunchback which hid her face that he could not look at her without horror: the saint rebuked the man for being ashamed of one cleansed of original sin by baptism, placed his fingers on the man's forehead and told him to do the same to her hunchback; the prior promised that he would ceaselessly pray to the Lord that she would be healed.[17] In the *Life of St Erkenwald* there is a similar disregard for the supernatural. The author, John Massey, who was possibly the *Pearl* poet, described how the bishop of London baptised the body of a just pagan which had miraculously resisted decay; the disintegration of this corpse immediately after baptism demonstrated the superiority of the Christian miracle: the operation of God's sacramental grace in a world of death and corruption.[18]

The saint's cult did not just define holiness on the basis of the saint's personality; it explored the relationship between such holiness and the society of the followers of the saint. The social and sacred functions of the bishop saints Cuthbert, William and John of Beverley, were interlocked by their occupation of recognized power niches in society; but the decision of Richard Rolle and John of Bridlington to enter a hermitage and a monastery meant that they did not hold authority in a secular world, and that they had resisted its blandishments. Such detachment was regarded as a sign of holiness and could be opposed to the harsh repressiveness or indifference of society.

In describing Rolle's wanderings, the author of the office refers to the example provided by the desert fathers and to the harassment that the

14 *Nova Legenda Angliae*, ii, p. 71.
15 *Vita S. Joannis de Bridlingtona*, p. 143.
16 ibid, p. 138. *qui in eorum aspectu lapides esse videbatur*.
17 *Nova Legenda Angliae*, ii, p. 75.
18 McAlindon, 'Hagiography into Art', 42–94. For Massey's possible authorship of *Pearl* see Peterson, 'The Pearl Poet and John Massey', 257ff.

society of evil men gave to the saints; the descriptions of Rolle's fasts and private mortifications reveal an ideal of holiness derived from the rejection of the social rituals of eating and conversation.[19] An incident which shows the saint's ability to remain detached while engaging in conversation is recorded as a miracle: the hermit is visited in his cell by his patron and other ladies who beg him to leave his writing and to give them words of edification; for two hours he continued with his writing, while exhorting them to renounce worldly vanities and to establish the love of God in their hearts; this, the writer concludes, was a thing of great wonder and would not have been possible unless the Holy Spirit were directing his hand and tongue.[20] Another time the saint was so absorbed in prayer that his cloak was taken from him without his feeling anything, and when, after stitching and patching, the ladies had replaced it on him, he still did not notice.[21] The author probably recorded this incident because the matrons showed the same concern for the hermit as the Hampole nuns; its inclusion as a miracle shows that ordinary people regarded such impractical self-absorption as holiness.

In the office there is a compatibility between the eremitic vocation and the ideal of holiness; and the Papal Bull of canonization describes John of Bridlington's profession as a monk at Bridlington Priory as a dedication to God and a removal from the world's evils and fleeting delights.[22] But Hugh the canon implies, in his account of two of John of Bridlington's miracles, that there was an incompatibility between this saint's holiness and his vocation as a monk. When he was cellarer John used to take pity on the poor and hungry men of a nearby alms house and took them loaves from the abundant monastery stores, hiding them under his cloak through humility. Rumours about this practice occasioned much discussion and disagreement over the question of his sanctity; some envious monks complained about the wastefulness of the cellarer to the prior who, knowing that their accusations proceeded from malice, did nothing. But the following day these monks obstructed the saint on his errand of piety and mercy, and the prior asked him what he carried under his cloak. Wishing his good works to be known to God alone John, like an innocent and humble man, replied for the benefit of these monks that they were stones to mend a road outside the monastery gate; the prior, who knew his holy secrets, asked him to show these stones, and when he opened his cloak the loaves 'seemed' in their eyes to be stones.[23] A similar miracle occurred when John was prior. Some noblemen of the province visited the monastery to see if

19 *Brev. Ebor.*, lessons iv, viii.
20 ibid, lesson viii.
21 ibid, lesson viii.
22 Purvis, 'St John of Bridlington', 31 – 7.
23 *Vita S. Joannis de Bridlingtona*, pp. 138 – 39.

what they had frequently heard about his holiness was true. They were received and dined in the appropriate manner, but although their host, the prior, drank from a silver cup, as was the custom for prelates and noblemen, it contained only water. One of the noblemen asked the prior if he could taste from his cup, even though his own cup was full of wine; John, not wishing to reveal his secret abstinence, said a prayer over his cup and the nobleman, after tasting it, declared that he had never tasted better wine.[24] Both these parodies of gospel miracles suggest that there is a difficulty in maintaining holiness in a community which shared such conventional social values as the acquisition of property and the provision of hospitality, and where charity and asceticism were unusual enough to be regarded as saintly virtues. John of Bridlington could appear to be a conventional monk and prior while pursuing his holy life just as Rolle could engage in conversation and have his clothes mended while remaining absorbed in private meditation. Both men possessed an innocence that enabled them to live in a profane world while remaining apart from it: it was their ability to do this that their biographers considered to be miraculous. Such miracles are very different from the miracles of earlier saints' lives and imply a popular appreciation of the values of the contemplative movement.

The same change in attitudes towards holiness can be seen in the posthumous development of the cults of the fourteenth-century Yorkshire saints. Their biographers created, through realism, a sense of intimate acquaintance with the holy man. This close relationship was also attempted in the veneration of their relics. The bones of saints, consecrated by translation into the public shrines of cathedrals, radiated in their miracles a centripetal power that brought together communities; but bones did not communicate the personality of the holy man, and the host, despite its unifying power, would have been for any an abstraction, hidden behind the choir screen. But by the late fourteenth-century another type of relic, of centrifugal power and resonant with associations of the personality of the dead, was being venerated by those who had some acquaintance with a holy man or who had contributed to the development of his cult. Personal possessions of the dead were a different sort of relic: their appeal was nostalgic and emotional, for they could evoke memories of a holy man who was recently alive and whose personality was accessible in lives written from the memories of those who had personally known the saint. They were not corporate relics, but personal mementoes that could become a focus for personal devotion to the saint. Sir Brian Stapleton, who was probably a patron of Margaret Kirkby, owned a ewer with an image of

[24] ibid, p. 142.

Our Lady which was once owned by the recluse of Hampole.[25] The canons of Bridlington, who continued to revere and remember their dead prior, preserved a collar of his as a relic. Hugh testified that when one of the novices whom he knew fell into a frenzied illness, one of the canons, who was greatly devoted to the Blessed John of Bridlington, took one of the birettas which the prior used when alive and reverently laid it on the infirm man's head saying: 'God help thee, and the blessed John of Bridlington'; the youth became calm and fell asleep, and when he awoke he was better.[26] The relics associated with the Scrope cult belong to this category: a little missal, carried at the archbishop's breast at the time of his execution, was reverently preserved by one of his chapter clerks, Thomas Dautre; and the archbishop's wooden drinking cup was venerated by Henry Wyman and his wife. Other forms of personal relic were objects associated with the passion of martyrs. In the minster there was a reliquary containing Scrope's image and a cloth stained with his blood. Relics of Christ's cross were owned by Thomas Cumberworth, who left his portion of the cross to his private chapel, and by Thomas Arundel and Thomas Haxey.[27]

Relics of the Virgin would have aroused a private and romantic loyalty. Her cult increased in importance dramatically in the diocese in the fourteenth-century: Archbishop Zouche gave an order that the Virgin was to be especially honoured in all churches; and Thoresby built the Lady Chapel in the north-east choir of the minster between 1361 and 1373 to provide a place where her daily mass could be celebrated.[28] A table with five images of Our Lady holding a series of symbolic objects and moralized in a late York Minster text was probably executed for the altar of the Virgin at this time.[29] There were centres of pilgrimage associated with her at Doncaster and Knaresborough, and she was venerated at Bridlington.[30] But there were no bones or flesh to give her cult a central focus, only vials of her milk, symbols of her love and mercy, which were venerated at Basedale nunnery and in Sir Thomas Cumberworth's private chapel at Someby, and her girdles, which were kept at many Yorkshire religious houses.[31] The most important focus for private devotion to the Virgin were the numerous painted and sculpted images which were privately owned in this period. The popularity of

25 Prob. Reg. 6, fo. 133; TE, I, p. 199.
26 *Nova Legenda Angliae*, ii, . 75.
27 *Fabric Rolls*, pp. 221; 225.
28 *Fasti Ebor.*, p. 486.
29 Gillespie, 'Speculum Christiani', p. 529.
30 For the cult of the Virgin at Doncaster see TE, III, p. 199. William Ecop, the rector of Heslerton in the East Riding, bequeathed money in 1447 for a palmer to visit eighteen major shrines in England including St William at York, the Virgin at Doncaster, Scarborough, Gisborough and Beverley and St John of Bridlington.
31 'Superstition in Yorkshire Religious Houses', *Trans. East Riding Antiq. Soc.*, (1883), i.

these images, none of which unfortunately survive, would have increased after 1408 when Arundel, in his constitutions, enjoined the veneration of crosses, saints and images.[32] None of these images would have been consecrated by the church, and their delineation of the holiness of a human face would have encouraged a worship of beauty, serenity and mercy rather than the power associated with the bones of the grave. Painted and sculpted representations of her image and the image of St Anne were to be found in households of clergy, magnates and artisans: Sir Brian Stapleton left his eldest son's widow, Lady Elizabeth Stapleton, a gilt and silver representation of the coronation of Our Lady; Philip Darcy owned an alabaster image of Anne; William Marshall in 1392 left an image of the Virgin in alabaster to St Helen's; Isabella Wyleby in 1414 left an image of the Virgin to Matilda Strangwys, and a picture of the Salutation of the Virgin to Peter Redlay; and in 1398 Agnes Bird, wife of William Bird, shipman, left an image of the Virgin to the church of St John of Beverley.[33] Henry Lord Scrope of Masham showed a special dedication to her image: in 1415 he left a painted representation of the Virgin to his wife Margery and his best statue of the Virgin, adorned with pearls, to Henry V; his inventory included paintings of the Salutation of the Virgin, a three foot image of the Virgin, and a book of masses of the Virgin.[34] York canons Richard Ulleskelfe, John Carleton, and William Waltham owned images of the Virgin; and silver and gilt images were also possessed by Michael de-la-Pole, Stephen Scrope, Thomas Gray and Matilda Marshall.[35] Representations of the Virgin and St Anne were commissioned for local parish churches: Nicholas Blackburn left £60 to contribute to the Feast of the Purification; his son Nicholas comissioned windows in All Saints' Church depicting Anne and the Virgin; and Joan Warde commissioned a painting of the Virgin.[36] Images of Our Lady in parish churches received bequests from Lady Mary Aske, daughter of Sir Robert Ughtred, and Alice Kelynghalc; and burials before her image were requested by Sir John Conyers in 1438 and John Rilleston esquire, who wished to be buried in the choir of the church of Rylstone: *coram imagine Beate*.[37] The power of such images as a stimulus to intense feeling is suggested in Thomas Dautre's request that he be buried before an image of St John the Baptist, 'whom in my youth I adored'.[38] In the Bolton Hours there are large illuminations of the

32 Wilkins, *Concilia*, iii, p. 316ff.
33 TE, I, pp. 198–99, 254, 381, 240.
34 *Foedera*, IX, p. 275; Kingsford, 'Two Forfeitures in the Year of Agincourt', 79.
35 TE, I, p. 107.
36 TE, II, p. 18.
37 TE, II, pp. 276, 373, 389.
38 TE, II, p. 59.

Virgin, Bridget, Richard Scrope and other favourite saints.[39] Such images became a catalyst for private piety and an important stimulus to the increasing visionary element in the worship of saints.

Many of the miracles performed by the saint at his shrine were essentially passive projections by pilgrims of what they understood as social justice. A more individual element in the worship of the saints can be seen in the increasing importance of visions of the saints by the beginning of the fifteenth-century which perpetuated the close ties that existed between the holy man and his clientèle. The dead saint continued to perform a role as a healer: individual fears and anxieties were confronted in visions that were a personal and imaginative projection of all that was merciful and beautiful in the individual's own imagination. The traditional function of the saint's shrine as a source of public healing was being supplemented by visions of the saint as a healing and comforting friend: Thomas Bell of Morehow was ill and lying alone; his friends had all gone on a pilgrimage to Hampole, when Richard appeared to him; he enquired about his health, placed his hand on his back and relieved him of all pain.[40] The romantic impetus given to the cult of Richard Rolle by Margaret Kirkby's accounts of her relationship with the hermit can be seen in laywomen's visions which are included in the office. A woman called Joan, who was vexed with demons, had lost her speech and bodily strength, but the Blessed Richard appeared to her and placed himself between Joan and the demons and made them depart; then as a token of the miracle he placed a ring on her finger and she recovered her speech and bodily health.[41] Another woman, in the village of Wrangbroke near Hampole, was suddenly struck by a paralytic illness depriving her of speech, and while she was fully awake she saw Richard who raised her up and restored her senses.[42] A woman called Julia, from the city of York, was vexed by demons and dumb for seven days; she was taken to Hampole, where she fell asleep at the saint's shrine and saw the blessed hermit who spoke comforting words to her, and afterwards her speech was restored.[43] A similar relationship existed with St Bridget in Gascoigne's more sophisticated Oxford circle. Discussing the ambiguity of dreams and visions and their potentially diabolic origin, he recommends Bridget as a protector against demons. He included in his life of the saint two instances of her intervention: between 1401 and 1403 a man, disturbed

39 Y.M.L. 5 MS. Add. 2, fo. 108v; Bodl. Lib. Oxford. MS. Lat. Liturg. f. 2 has pictures of the Virgin on fos. 2, 12v, 19, 44. There are also images of St Jerome on fo. 59v, and St Mary Magdalene on fo. 141v.

40 *Brev. Ebor.* lec. 5.

41 ibid, lec. 2.

42 ibid, lec. 4.

43 ibid, feria secunda lec. 3.

by Satan, was freed by a vision of the saint who spoke words of consolation; and an Oxford scholar, Mr Richard Trenaut, disturbed by a spirit, was freed after following Gascoigne's advice and using the forty prayers of St Bridget.[44]

The importance of dreams and visions in popular religion is shown in the transcription, by the beginning of the fifteenth-century, of ordinary people's dreams of purgatory. The growth of chantries in the fifteenth-century and the provision of masses for the dead may imply an institutional concept of purgatory; but the need for some people to communicate with dead friends and relatives shows that such emotions as feelings of bereavement and guilt could not always be relieved by the celebration of masses. These communications with the dead were perhaps an inevitable outcome of the increasing visionary element in the cult of saints. It is significant that the earliest of these recorded visions comes from a nun of Hampole whose brother, a Yorkshire squire, had been killed in the battle of Shrewsbury. Shortly after his death he appeared in her sleep with the same wounds on his body that she saw when he was buried; but his face was black and burning. In answer to her distress he assures her that her devout prayers for him have secured God's forgiveness and shows her some prayers and psalms which, if she says for twenty days, will deliver him from all pain.[45] In the Thornton manuscript, owned by the Yorkshire squire Robert Thornton, there is a description of a series of dreams reported in 1422 by one of the nuns of Syon, which were strongly influenced by Bridget's descriptions of the three circles of purgatory. In these dreams a deceased nun named Margaret is being punished and purified in three successive rings of fire; she asks the dreamer to obtain the intercession of her three confessors, including the prominent Westminster hermit and holy man, John London.[46]

Such visions may have been prompted by unresolved guilt feelings towards the departed which only the saint could release; the sense of guilt and forgiveness in such cases was purely personal, having little to do with the social definitions of sin and penance prescribed in a conventional confession to the parish priest; however, it had affinities with the preoccupation with the personal sense of sin shown by contemplative writers. In 1409, William Stranton, an armigerous knight from the parish of Stranton in Durham, made a pilgrimage to the cave of St Patrick's Purgatory in Lough Dergh, which was supervised by Augustinian canons. While he is sleeping in the cave he sees St Hilda of

44 *Loci e Libro Veritatum*, p. 139.

45 C.U.L. MS. Ll vi, 43, fos. 80–81b. This is a small book of prayers and offices in English which deals with the ten commandments and seven deadly sins.

46 *Yorkshire Writers*, i, pp. 383–93.

Whitby and John of Bridlington, clad in canon's habit, who tells William that he is repaying him for his many visits to their shrines; taking him by the right hand John escorts him to purgatory, where he sees his sister, long dead from pestilence, and the spirit of a man who had loved her well in life. Both inspire fear in William, who is comforted by his guide who tells him to keep in mind Christ's compassion; but William's sister complains to the saint that her brother had sinned by preventing her from marrying the man standing beside her, despite their love for one another. John then tells William that he has trespassed against God and his own soul and instructs him to confess and make penance to the prior of the purgatory, with which his sister and the man vanish. Pilgrimage to the saint's shrine was the only exception allowed in canon law for failure to make annual confession to the local parish priest; and, although confession to another priest was still required, it was the saint who became an alternative confessor to pilgrims like Stranton who were burdened with painful unconfessed sins.[47] The role of the Virgin was as a tolerant and merciful confessor was emphasized by the Dominican friar Thomas Waleys, who claimed that preachers who neglected to invoke her name were worthy of censure because they ran the risk of frightening parishioners away from church and confession.[48] The Virgin and Archbishop Scrope appeared as confessors to John Sibsun, who told his confessor, the public penitentiary William Kexby, of a series of visions experienced by him at Roucliffe in Boroughbridge: for fourteen days the Virgin and Archbishop Scrope appeared to him at his house hearing his confessions; the archbishop admonished him for his sin of harbouring a murderous intention for three years without making confession and told him to make atonement by offering a candle at his shrine.[49]

The cult of the holy man who regarded society with detachment attests to a growing conviction that a greater holiness than that dispensed by the ordained clergy in the sacraments of the church was to be found in the personality of certain individuals. Stanton's vision of purgatory reveals clergy and a vainglorous bishop being punished for their sons. Gascoigne's report of a conversation between Archbishop Henry Bowet and Henry IV shows that the clergy were aware of the implications of the popular understanding of holiness.[50] One of Bowet's clerks told an urbane joke at the archbishop's expense, explaining why bishops were no longer translated as saints: he explained that bishops received enough translation from benefice to benefice during their

[47] S. Leslie, *St Patrick's Purgatory* (London, 1932), pp. 28 – 33; Wylie, *Henry V*, i, pp. 76 – 81.

[48] Owst, *Preaching in England*, p. 346.

[49] *Anglia Sacra*, ii, p. 373.

[50] *Loci e Libro Veritatum*, pp. 22 – 3.

lifetime. The laughter this inspires proves that churchmen like Bowet were never really expected to live as confessors, and that this was an ideal projected onto the earlier bishop saints of the diocese. The same clerk observed that bishops used to accept office reluctantly, for the sake of the salvation of their souls, because they were appointed by God by virtue of their holy lives; and they proved the superiority of their divine power in their miracles. Now, this clerk pointed out, bishops were chosen by kings, and they, therefore, only had the same power as kings. Gascoigne himself, in his comment on this conversation, made an unfavourable comparison between bishops like St Cuthbert and St Edmund, and the bishops of his own time.[51] Bowet and his household recognized that the focus of holiness was not with those in secular authority who were administrators, but with those who entered monasteries or hermitages (like Bowet's former colleague Walter Hilton) and who inspired admiration because of this. These York clergy felt that the monk and the hermit bishops of Cuthbert's time were a remote ideal. Hermits and martyrs were now the important guardians of holiness, possessors of a special authority which was different from the authority of civil servants, lawyers and administrators. The mixed life ideal that the York clergy expounded was possibly an attempt to reintegrate secular authority and holiness.

Holiness, then, resided in the personality of holy men who detached themselves from a secular authority that could be harsh and repressive, and from the comforts of a society that was often self-indulgent and indifferent. This enabled them to show superior compassion, piety and ascetic restraint while remaining important figures of authority in society. This can be observed in the important position that holy men and hermits such as Robert of Knaresborough, Richard Rolle, St John of Bridlington and John of London occupied in the popular imagination. The inspiration and sweetness they brought and which derived from their remoteness from the prosaic world, introduced into popular religion a confidence in the private area of religious experience. In the life of St Robert there is a prayer in which the supplicant asks Robert to deliver him to paradise where he will 'here thi voce that ys so swette'.[52] The office of Richard Rolle described the sweet delights of contemplation that the hermit attained and acknowledged the edification that the ladies who were his patrons received from the little books that the hermit composed for his neighbours: according to the author of the office these books sounded like 'sweetest music in the hearts of the devout'.[53] His appearance, in hermit's clothes, in the vision of the

51 ibid, pp. 22 – 3.
52 *The Life of St Robert of Knaresborough*, p. 3.
53 *Brev. Ebor.*, lec. vi.

humble pilgrims at Hampole, are described as a heavenly inspiration. Roger, the householder who helped to establish the cult, saw Rolle on three successive nights and conversed with him about many things. Later he appeared for six nights, visiting him while he was awake, teaching him many secret things and inflaming him with the love of God and the spirit of holy devotion.[54] Joan, who was delivered of demons by the saint, saw him with the Virgin, who appeared in beautiful white garments.[55] The association of the hermit with visions of the Virgin is probably due to the location of the cult of the Virgin at nearby Doncaster. Julia of York saw Richard and the Blessed Virgin, the queen of heaven, in her sleep, and the brightness of this heavenly vision was of such intensity that it nearly blinded her.[56] John of Bridlington is described in a prayer as *fons deliciarum,* and in the Bolton Hours he is commemorated in a full page illumination in the same pastoral raiment that he wore when he appeared in the vision of sailors.[57] In a northern prayer book, owned by followers of the Scrope cult, the archbishop is invoked *O gemma lucis,* and the owners are depicted at the beginning of the volume praying to the Virgin, who appears to them as a celestial blue apparition surrounded by golden rays; on another page she is shown in a heavenly blue sky on a throne that is encircled by a bleeding heart.[58]

Such miracles were a manifestation of holiness that existed outside the power structures of society, in the dreams and visions of ordinary people. Miracles of power and concord were supplemented by personal inspiration and flashes of insight. The heavenly visions reported by such people indicate admiration for the visionary experiences of the fourteenth-century mystics, such as Julian of Norwich's vision of St John of Beverley, rather than the social projections of the traditional saints' cults. In his dream William Stranton was conducted by John of Bridlington to a tower from which there hung a long ladder; with the help of Jesus, and a cord that he had once lent to a merchant who had been robbed by thieves, he ascended the ladder and arrived at a beautiful country: the earth was as clear as crystal, and there were beautiful trees, sweet-smelling spices and birds singing sweet, delectable songs; he is welcomed by a company of monks, canons and priests clothed in white.[59] The tendency towards the private worship of a saint who was understood in human terms and the increasingly imaginative

[54] ibid, lec. i.
[55] ibid, lec. ii.
[56] ibid, feria secunda, lec. 2.
[57] There is a full page illumination of St John of Bridlington on fo. 46 of Y.M.L. 5 MS. Add. 2; *Analecta Hymnica,* XXVIII, p. 302.
[58] Bodl. Lib. Oxford. MS. Lat. Liturg. f. 2, fos. 2, 19.
[59] Leslie, *St Patrick's Purgatory,* pp. 32 – 33.

and individual understanding of holiness that was removed from social unity and ritual magic are all elements in popular religion contradicting the contention that the holy in the fifteenth-century was purely the extraordinary social peace of a feudal, revenge society, established in the minds of the community through sacramental rituals.[60]

The more sophisticated concepts to emerge from the contemplative movement of the diocese, and which were appreciated and understood by the educated classes of Yorkshire, were a refinement of the religious sentiment expressed in the saints' cults. Anchorite confessors who counselled obedience and detachment exerted a similar authority to the holy man, and the visionary element in the worship of the saints had affinities with the treasured experiences of some fourteenth-century mystics. The humanised portraits of the life of Christ provided in gospel harmonies echoed the interest in psychology and emotion shown in the cults of the holy men Richard Rolle and John of Bridlington, and in the personal dedication that many people showed towards individual saints. The ideal vision of a compassionate society that was expressed in many accounts of saints' miracles also finds expression in the pastoral policies of the York clergy, and especially in teachings on the mixed life, which integrate compassion and piety with secular authority. The close relationship between the sophisticated religious literature and pastoral policies of the diocese and popular saints' cults existed because the clergy of the diocese were in touch with what people felt, desired and feared; contemplative literature and the eremitic life aroused so much interest because they were so closely related to the religious impulses of the less sophisticated.

60 See the works of J. Bossy for the view that holiness was a social peace established through the sacramental rituals of a community, esp. 'Holiness and Society', *Past and Present*, 75, (1983) 119 – 37; and 'The Mass as a Social Institution', 47.ff

Conclusion

It has been established that the devotional changes of late medieval Yorkshire were, as far as the rest of England was concerned, unique to the region. However, it is also apparent from the importance of York patrons, pastors and visionaries as crown and church administrators, university scholars and diplomats, that the religious and secular life of the diocese cannot be considered in exclusively regional or national terms. It is therefore necessary to examine the relationship between religious developments in Yorkshire and in other areas of Europe where there were religious movements involving the laity, before a proper evaluation can be made of the originality of the York clergy's contribution to religion in the kingdom as a whole. This in turn will help to explain the religious controversies of the sixteenth century and the eventual establishment of a national Anglican church in terms of the spiritual traditions established in northern England rather than in terms of external continental influences.

England's isolation from France, a consequence of the Hundred Years War and the papal schism, resulted in the disruption of trade routes, pilgrim traffic, and links between the English church and Avignon, and isolated the older religious orders, especially the alien priories, from French monasteries. However, the war with France also helped to create closer links with those regions of Europe that offered the most potentially important source of religious and cultural inspiration: diplomatic alliances were established with Flanders and the German princes during the reigns of Edward III and Richard II, and these were accompanied by closer economic links: pilgrims and travellers were diverted along the Rhine; and trade links were established with Flanders and Rhineland cities; wool staples were created at Bruges, Antwerp, and Middelburgh; the merchant adventurers of York were to be found at Antwerp, Bruges, Bergen and Middelburgh; and another group of English merchants were at Danzig. Conversely there were Flemish and Lombard merchants in London. After 1378 there were also increased legal and diplomatic links with Rome.[1] However, there is little firm

1 Lovatt, 'English Spirituality', p. 30ff.

evidence that these diplomatic and economic ties resulted in a direct exchange of religious ideas, except in East Anglia. The influences on Margery Kempe, for instance, were not all northern: her pilgrimages through Holland, Constance, Florence, Rome and Venice were a direct result of these changing economic and diplomatic patterns, and they helped to shape her religious life; in Rome she met St Bridget of Sweden's servant, and Margery's other model, the blessed Dorothea of Prussia was a burgess' wife of Danzig, a Baltic port with close connections with Lynn which Margery visited in 1433 to see her son and German daughter-in-law. There were also German Dominicans in Lynn who were among her favourite confessors, and she first disclosed her revelations to a German.[2] Although religious writers of Yorkshire helped to formulate Julian of Norwich's spiritual outlook, the influence of the religious movements of the Rhineland and the Low Countries in East Anglia cannot be discounted. By 1427 there was a community of women, described as 'sisters living in chastity', who closely resembled the beguinages of cities in Flanders and along the Rhine in their adoption of an informal religious life outside the framework of an established religious order. By 1442 another such group of women were living in a Norwich tenement owned by a merchant of Bruges.[3] However, German, Prussian and Flemish influence in East Anglia was exceptional, and there is no evidence of equivalent religious influences in Yorkshire or the port of Hull. A more important agency than economic channels for the exchange of religious influences were the international communities of university scholars and monks to which the York clergy belonged. Oxford and Cambridge maintained close links with foreign universities such as Paris and Padua, and the numbers of foreign students at Oxford and Cambridge was greatest between the years 1350 and 1450; the councils, especially Constance from 1415 to 1418, provided a further opportunity for the meeting of scholars representing the various universities of Europe. While Benedictine and Cistercian orders were relatively independent and isolated in this period, the friars, canons regular, Carthusians and Brigittines maintained links with religious communities in Germany, Flanders, Italy, and Scandinavia (the Carthusians held a general chapter every four years). Furthermore, religious orders such as the Dominicans, Franciscans and Augustinians inherited and shared, through the universal Latin language of the church, common spiritual and intellectual heritages. Further opportunity for contact with the religious cultures of Europe was provided in the inter-dynastic alliances of the English royal family such as Richard II's marriage to Anne of Bohemia, the marriage

2 *Book of Margery Kempe*, p.
3 Tanner, 'Popular Religion in Norwich', pp. 64–6.

of John of Gaunt's daughters to the heirs of Castile and Portugal, and the marriage of Henry IV's younger sister Philippa to King Eric of Sweden and Denmark.

The mendicant orders had consistently transmitted religious influences from Italy to England since the thirteenth century. Italian Franciscans continued to study and teach at the universities, counselling the social and spiritual fulfilment of the self by imitating Christ's humility and charity: and it was perhaps Franciscan teaching and sermons at Oxford that inspired Rolle's romantic, emotive piety. The Cambridge Franciscan convent was a cosmopolitan community in this period,[4] and the Franciscan meditations of the life of Christ certainly influenced members of Arundel's circle including Nicholas Love, and Arundel himself, who visited Italy in 1397. The Augustinian friars shared the Augustinian heritage that included the doctrines of introspective detachment and self-affirmation, and Austin friars from Italy had a direct influence on the spirituality of members of the Arundel circle. William Flete was at Cambridge in the 1350s and was perhaps a contemporary of Hilton's during these years; Flete's *De Remediis contra Temptationes,* written before his departure from Cambridge in 1359, certainly influenced Hilton's later writings. Flete himself was influenced by the large numbers of Italian Austin friars who were introduced to Cambridge between 1355 and 1358, and who brought with them an interest in Augustine's writings and the eremitic revival in Italy: distinguished theologians such as Galvano of Padua, Gerard of Aymeric, Mathew of Poggiulo, John Heliud, and Raphael Zina, who lectured on the Bible with Flete,[5] would have spoken about the small groups of pious hermits of central Italy, and especially about the convent of Lecceto whose prior Nicolo Tini had a reputation for sanctity. By 1359 Flete was so strongly influenced by the Italians at Cambridge that he went to Lecceto and remained there until his death around 1390. Other Austin friars from Yorkshire to go to Italy included John Erghome, who was possible master of theology at Bologna in 1480, and certainly master regent of the studia generale at the Roman Curia in 1385; and John Waldeby, who visited Rome. The circle of the author of *The Cloud of Unknowing,* and the York clergy serving in Arundel's administration, were also influenced by the more individualistic and speculative writings of the German Dominicans, whose common intellectual and spiritual heritage was the scholastic theology of Aquinas and the way of self-negation counselled by Dionysius the Areopagite. Meister Eckhard (1260 – 1327) who taught at Cologne and Strasbourg,

4 Lovatt, 'English Spirituality', p. 38.
5 Emden, *BRUC,* PP. 439, 26, 456: Roth, *Austin Friars,* ii, p. 189, 195.

and his disciples Johannes Tauler (1290 – 1360) and Henry Suso (1295 – 1365) did not subordinate their neo-platonic speculations to the needs of the laity; nevertheless they found among Dominican convents, bequinages and other communities of lay folk, notably the Friends of God in the Rhineland cities of Strasbourg, Cologne and Basle, followers who aspired to become spiritual elites in a corrupt world and who were prepared to assert lay control of asceticism (one of the leading members of the Friends of God was the Strasbourg banker and religious author Rulman Merswin). There are parallels in the way these Dominicans and the author of the *Cloud of Unknowing* emphasized the *via negativa* as a form of contemplation and similarities between the circles of disciples they formed. It is possible that this can be explained not only by common Dominican influences but direct contacts between the Rhineland and England, especially at Cambridge. If the author of the *Cloud* was a Cambridge Dominican he would have come under the direct influence of the Dominican students who were sent regularly to Cambridge from the German provinces, especially at the time the author of the *Cloud* was writing, such as Segoni of Saxony in 1378; Culman of Frankfurt, who was ordained by Arundel in 1387; and John of Strasbourg, who was also ordained in Ely in 1388. Cambridge Dominicans also went to Germany, especially Cologne: Geoffrey Launde, reading a D.Th. in Cambridge in 1393, went to the Dominican convent in Cologne in 1396; and John Sygar (ordained in 1384) of the Cambridge convent was given leave to proceed to a doctorate in Theology at the Cologne convent in 1397.[6] The Rhineland mystics were studied outside the Dominican order and the *Horologium* reached England by 1380. The English Charterhouses maintained close connections with charterhouses along the Rhine like Mainz and Basle that involved the exchange of manuscripts, and Sheen was partly staffed by monks from the Low Countries. It is therefore likely that some of the early manuscripts of the *Horologium Sapienciae* were transmitted from German monasteries to English charterhouses such as Mount Grace, where it was translated into English, probably under the direction of Nicholas Love. Other clergy in Arundel's circle may also have been directly responsible for bringing Suso's work into the country: Arundel himself, Sir William Thorpe, William Noion and Thomas Barnard Castle were among the earliest owners. An indication of the way leading secular clergy of the diocese may have brought the work into England is provided in the York canon Richard Fleming's donation of a manuscript of the *Horologium* to his foundation of Lincoln College in 1428: Fleming led an assembly to Germany in 1422 and was present at the council of

[6] Emden, *BRUC*, pp. 682, 355, 573; Lovatt, 'English Spirituality', p. 38

Pavia as president of the English nation in 1423, and he would therefore have acquired his copy on one of these visits to Germany.[7]

If parallels to the emotive, individualistic writings of Rolle and the speculative teachings of the author of the *Cloud* existed among the Dominicans along the Rhine, there were also parallels to the more pastorally orientated spiritual counsels provided by Hilton and his circle among the Augustinian canons in Flanders and the Low Countries. Ruysbroeck (1293 – 1381) was, like Hilton, a secular priest turned canon: he joined the Augustinian canons of Groendael in 1349 after spending twenty-five years as a Brussels priest; and like Hilton he addressed himself to the problems arising from religious extremism, especially among the Brethren of the Free Spirit and other heretical sects whom he termed 'contemplatives gone wrong'. During his years at Groendael (1349 – 1381) he and his disciple Gerard Groote (1340 – 1385) attempted to help those in active life by converting precise philosophic, monastic mysticism into vernacular teachings that were conveyed in terms of experience and feelings, and accompanied with practical advice. Between 1345 and 1350, Ruysbroeck wrote in Flemish *De Sleestelcke Brulocht (The Spiritual Marriage)*, which dealt with the progress of the soul and the active life. A Latin version was made in Groendael between 1360 and 1372, and another Latin text was produced before 1382 by Groote entitled *Ornatus Spiritualis Desponsationis*.[8] These teachings were disseminated through the community of the Bretheren of the Common Life, founded by Groote at Derventer, in the schools and houses of the Brethren that spread throughout cities in Flanders, and in the house of the Augustinian canons at Windesheim, the nucleus of a group of reformed Augustinian convents that included St Agnietenburg near Zwolle, the house of Thomas a Kempis (1379 – 1471) the author of *The Imitation of Christ*. There is no evidence of a direct connection between these canons of Flanders and Hilton's house at Thurgarton, although Groote's version of Ruysbroeck's *Spiritual Marriage (Ornatus Spiritualis Desponsationis)*, completed before 1382, arrived in England before 1400 when it was used in the anonymous *Chastizing of God's Children*.[9] However, the parallels between the teachings and activities of the Flemish mystics and Hilton and his circle are close enough to remind us that Hilton and John Thweng belonged to an international order sharing a common heritage in the works of Augustine and common pastoral ideals. The parallels occurred to contemporaries, for in the fifteenth century the *Imitation* was frequently attributed to Hilton.

7 Linc. Coll. MS. 48; Emden, *BRUO*, i, p. 699; R. Weiss, *Bodleian Library Quarterly*, viii, 345, 347 – 59.
8 Lovatt, 'English Spirituality', p. 248.
9 ibid, p. 251.

The patronage of the eremitic movement by courtiers and nobility was in itself a European phenomenon, and the interest shown by northern courtiers, and the house of Lancaster in particular, in recluses and Carthusian monks can partially be explained by the diplomatic and family connections existing between the royal families of Europe. The patronage of eremitic movements in the Iberian penninsula in the second half of the fourteenth century by Castilian courtiers offers particularly close parallels with the activities of the English court. The king of Castile, Pedro I, and three courtiers, Fernando Yunez de Figueroa, Pedro Fernandez Pecha, Pedro's treasurer, and Alonso Pecha, St Bridget's confessor and the reviser of her Revelations; founded the new ascetic order of St Jerome in an attempt to reform the monastic ideal and to bring some of the many hermits of the peninsula under a rule. The first monastery, La Plana de Javea, was established in 1374, and by 1428 there were twenty-six Jeronimite houses founded and patronized by members of the Castilian court and aristocracy. The Spanish royal family were also patrons of the Carthusian order: Juan I, who succeeded Enrique of Trastamara in 1379, founded the Carthusian house of El Pauler.[10] The possibility of direct Iberian influence on religious patronage within the English court is suggested by the close links between the family of Lancaster and the courts of Castile and Portugal. In 1371 John of Gaunt married Pedro I's daughter Constance, and pledged himself to the recovery of her father's lost kingdom of Castile. During his Castilian campaign of 1385 to 1386 he married his daughter Philippa to Joao I, king of Portugal, and received an offer from Juan I, king of Castile of a marriage union between Gaunt's daughter Catherine, the heiress of Constance, and Don Juan's son and heir Enrique, that would confirm the Castilian succession on the heirs of a member of the Lancaster family. The proposal, which was eventually accepted, was first delivered to Gaunt in Galicia by Don Juan Serrano, prior of the shrine of Guadelupe, who with Juan I was responsible for converting the shrine to the Jeronimite monastery of Guadelupe in 1389, the scene of the first general chapter of the order in 1415.[11] Gaunt's two daughters would have participated in the subsequent royal interest in the Jeronimite and Carthusian orders. Phillipa of Lancaster, Queen of Portugal, was noted for her devotion to the daily duties of religion, and Katherine of Lancaster's husband Enrique III continued his father's grants to Jeronomite houses: their son Juan II had a Jeronimite

[10] J. R. L. Highfield, 'The Jeronimites in Spain, their Patrons and Success, 1373 – 1516', *J.E.H.*, 34 (1983).

[11] A. A. Sicroff, 'The Jeronimite Monastery of Guadelupe in Fourteenth and Fifteenth Century Spain', in M. P. Hornick, ed. *Collected Studies in Honour of Americo Castro* (Oxford, 1965) 397.

confessor.[12] Katherine herself lived until 1418, ruling for a time as regent, and she may have influenced the interest shown by Gaunt's grandson Henry V in the Carthusian monastery of Sheen, the Bridgettine house of Syon, and the reform of the Benedictine order in 1421. The interest shown by the court in the Brigittine Order and the eventual founding of Syon in 1415 was a consequence of another Lancaster marriage alliance conducted by two veterans of the Prussian compaigns, Henry IV and Henry Lord FitzHugh of Tanfield: it was while FitzHugh was negotiating in Denmark in 1406 with Erik King of Sweden and Denmark about the dowry of the English king's daughter Philippa, that he became impressed with what he saw of the Bridgettine rule.

The wider context of the religious changes in the diocese is further emphasized in the influence that northern writers exerted on the continent. Rolle's works circulated in an informal, spontaneous way before the end of the fourteenth century: the *Incendium Amoris* was found in Charterhouses in the Low Countries, and the *Emendatio Vitae* was owned by Carthusians in Mainz, Trier, and Basle; another group of Rolle manuscripts circulated among German Benedictines, and texts of *Melos Amoris* and *Emendatio Vitae* belonged to the Brigittines of Vadstena. His works were even found in Prague: some time before 1396 the archbishop of Prague gave his approval to the *Incendium*, and the Latin psalter reached the city by 1412, possibly with Hussite scholars. Wyclif's works by contrast were distributed in a more ordered fashion through the universities: *De Dominio Civili* was known in Paris by 1381 and Hus was reading Wyclif in Prague university in the 1390s.[13] Hilton and his Cambridge circle also exerted some influence beyond England, and this is implied in the spiritual doctrine of Catherine of Siena. Her letters and *Dialogues* bear a closer resemblance to Hilton's teachings than any other European literature of the late fourteenth century. The most restrained and practical of the continental mystics she, like Hilton, was pre-occupied with the sense of sin that worldly ambitions inspired, and she advocated an inner detachment which could be achieved without undue exercise of the will through introspection, memory and contemplation of the Passion; this would enable the contemplative to live an active life of affection and charity.[14] Such close parallels illustrate both writers' dependence on Augustinian theology, and a common influence on them was the Austin friar William Flete,[15] whose writings in Cambridge in the 1350's on temptation and the need to recognize the

12 S. Armitage-Smith, *John of Gaunt* (London, 1914), pp. 301 – 36.

13 Lovatt, 'English Spirituality', ch. 2.

14 Catherine of Siena, *The Orcherd of Syon*, a Middle English trans. of the Dialogues, ed. P. Hodgson and G. Liegey (E.E.T.S., London, 1966), pp. 7, 14, 26, 101.

15 M. B. Hackett, 'William Flete OSA and St Catherine of Siena', (Dublin D.Phil., 1955).

fallibility of human will power, provided a direct link between the spiritual ideals of Hilton's Cambridge circle and those of Catherine and her 'famiglia'. From his cell near the convent of Lecceto, Flete established a reputation as a religious authority: he corresponded with leading Italian mystics such as Giovanni Colombini and Giovanni delle Celle. Flete was probably responsible for the formulation of Catherine's thought through a correspondence maintained between 1363 and 1374, when he was the only one of her advisers with the necessary expertise in Augustinian theology to shape her spiritual doctrine; by 1374 he had become her chief counsellor.[16] Flete and Catherine involved themselves in the civic affairs of Siena and Florence, the politics of the schism, and the projected crusade; they also advised Sienese and Florentine noblemen on the spiritual life. Although Flete's letters to Catherine do not survive, her replies on the question of the calls of public life and the eremitic life, in which she talks about the necessity in time of schism of obeying God's will and identifying it with the will of one's neighbour,[17] suggests that they were approaching an ideal similar to Hilton's mixed life. A further link between Cambridge and Siena was established by another Austin friar and contemporary of Hilton's at the university, Giovanni Tantucci. In May 1368 he was assigned by his chapter to lecture for three years on the sentences at Cambridge (where he may have obtained his doctorate). Tantucci returned to Lecceto in 1374 to become a key adviser and confessor to Catherine until her death in 1380.[18] Given these direct Cambridge influences on Catherine between 1363 and 1380, it is possible that the English translation of her *Dialogues*, the *Orcherd of Syon*, may have been made for the nuns of Syon around 1420 by a member of Hilton's Cambridge circle. Hilton's own works were also circulated on the Continent by the end of the fourteenth century: Fishlake's Latin translation of the *Scale of Perfection* was transmitted to Vadstena from Syon, and collections of devotional texts, including Flete's *De Remediis* and extracts from the works of Rolle and Hilton, were taken to France by Charles of Orleans and John of Angoulême on their release from captivity in 1440 and 1445.

However, despite such tangible links with the Continent there is a distinctiveness to the religious changes of late medieval Yorkshire. This can partly be traced to the native devotional traditions of England which emphasized the importance of the individual solitary and which was expressed in such works as the *Ancren Riwle*. Rolle was part of this tradition, and unlike his German contemporaries Suso and Tauler, he

16 ibid, p. 190ff.
17 ibid, pp. 57 – 60.
18 ibid, pp. 168 – 74; Emden, *BRUC*, p. 576.

belonged to no religious order. Those who succeeded Rolle as spiritual leaders in the diocese continued to respect the importance of the solitary, and so while eremitic and mystical movements on the Continent tended to find communal forms of expression in such organisations as the Brethren of the Common Life and the Beguines, many participating in the devotional life in England did so as individual recluses or laymen whose only communal allegiance was to their family. Moreover, many of the communities of contemplatives on mainland Europe developed an ideological or political sectarianism: the Waldensians established throughout East Germany, Southern France, and Northern Italy tightly knit coordinated religious sects; and the Brethren of the Free Spirit, believing in the possibility of perfection on earth without ecclesiastical meditation, formed urban elites, especially among communities of Beghards and Beguines in Germany and the Low Countries. Even when devotional enthusiasm was expressed by orthodox communities, a sense of alienation from society was often implied: the Castilian courtiers, when founding the Jeronimite order, left the court to express their hostility to worldly corruption; and although the Jeronimites in the fifteenth century achieved a mixture of spiritual fervour with concern for their charitable duties, such religiosity (perhaps because of its association with Judaism) failed to take root among the Spanish people, with possibly far-reaching consequences for the future development of the nation including its failure to develop a national religious work ethic.[19] In England, however, there were no devotional sects, and there was a general and equally far-reaching integration of religious ideals with the ethics of public duty. This can be attributed to the careful supervision of devotional life (including the screening of the influences of continental mysticism) maintained by secular clergy who were following the pastoral traditions established in the diocese of York. Showing little interest in intellectual speculation and political change, they avoided the metaphysical and social excesses of continental mysticism. Like the English common lawyers who worked on precedents, they were not confined by allegiance to a single intellectual system, and in a practical manner they drew on their own experiences, as well as Franciscan, Dominican, and Augustinian teaching, to supervise, in their teaching on the mixed life and the life of Christ, the evolution of a humanized religious culture that affected people at the most humble social, intellectual and spiritual levels. The least educated of people could therefore participate in a religious life by worshipping the saints, witnessing the mass, performing plays and perhaps reciting English religious lyrics and carols.

[19] Sicroff, 'Guadelupe', p. 423.

This development of a national religious ethic in the fifteenth century, distinct from the religious movement on the Continent, must now be considered, partly to answer the frequently made claim that orthodox religion in fifteenth century England was conservative and provincial. The evidence used to justify such a claim is the limited circulation in England of the works of writers representing the *devotio moderna* such as Ruysbroeck and Kempis: the *Spiritual Marriage* and the *Imitation of Christ* were only owned and read by an elite circle of scholars and contemplatives associated with Carthusian monasteries and Syon.[20] Such provincial indifference to the more refined schools of spirituality did not end, it has been claimed, until the arrival of new ideas from Rome and Geneva in the sixteenth century. Opinions vary about the reception of these ideas in England between those who see them as heralding the end of a long spiritual drought: the conventional nature of religious customs in fifteenth century Hull have been used to justify this perception;[21] to those who see them as a violent importation of continental religious divisions which were ahistorically imposed on the native religious culture of the diocese and the rest of England. An attempt has been made to justify this latter theory by using the activities of Robert Parkyn and his circle as evidence of a failed attempt to preserve the regional traditions of late medieval Yorkshire during the Reformation.[22] Parkyn, who died in 1569, was the parish priest of Ardwick-le-Street, a church four miles north of Doncaster, which until the dissolution was in the gift of Hampole priory. This conservative Catholic priest complied with the Protestant innovations of the reigns of Edward VI and Elizabeth I, and yet worked hard to restore the devotional traditions established by Richard Rolle and Walter Hilton: he transcribed a volume of Rolle's writings and wrote a metrical Life of Christ and a number of shorter contemplative works which offered spiritual and practical advice in the manner of Walter Hilton.[23] This provincial parish priest has been seen as a reminder of what was still possible in the sixteenth century: a union between a less monolithic and moderate Catholicism and biblical humanism. The failure of this union has been attributed to the Protestant and Catholic extremists who lacked the historical perspective to recognize the importance of such men as Parkyn within the spiritual traditions of the north-east.[24] These theories rest on the false assumption that the devotional writings of Yorkshire in the late fourteenth and early fifteenth century were either spiritually or

20 Lovatt, 'English Spirituality', ch. 4.
21 Heath, 'Urban Piety', p. 229.
22 A. G. Dickens, 'The Last Medieval Englishman', in P. Brooks, (Ed.) *Christian Spirituality: Essays in Honour of Gordon Rupp* (London, 1975), 145ff.
23 ibid, 147, 160; Bodl. Lib. Oxford, MS. Lat. Thd. 15, fos. 1 – 105.
24 Dickens, p. 180.

intellectually provincial; and provincial in the sense that they never became fully integrated into the national life and be used to defend the late medieval church from radical religious ideas from abroad. The idea that the spiritual traditions of the diocese were spiritually conservative and ineffectually provincial, by the sixteenth century at least, can be refuted by pointing out the national significance of the writings of Hilton and his circle; the potentially controversial aspects of their writings, which have much in common with those works regarded as representing the *devotio moderna*; and finally by showing that the religious divisions of the sixteenth century and the eventual establishment of a national Anglican church can be traced to the writings and pastoral policies of Arundel's clergy and their successors.

Robert Parkyn was too provincial to represent the spiritual traditions of the north-east accurately. The Yorkshiremen who initiated the religious changes of the fourteenth and fifteenth centuries were, on the other hand, part of a dynamic and cosmopolitan society in which York Minster, the household of the archbishop of York, the universities of Oxford and Cambridge, the civil service in Westminster and the royal court were centres of religious culture and patronage. The importance of Wyclif as an agent of religious change and debate has been overemphasized: he was originally only one member of a society of northern clerks in the households of Thoresby and Arundel who were responsible for implementing pastoral reforms within the church of York that helped to produce a more educated and critical clergy and laity. The devotional piety that they encouraged and supervised was arguably as significant as Lollardy in the fifteenth century. By the second half of the century the national significance of contemplative writings can be measured by the activity of the printing presses: between 1491 and 1500, Wynkyn de Worde printed thirty devotional treatises out of a total of fifty-four printed works; and between 1468 and 1530 Julian Notary and Richard Pynson printed 341 works; 176 of them were of a religious nature, including 106 that can be classified as works of religious instruction and devotion.[25] The most popular were Nicholas Love's *Mirror*, which was printed nine times between 1486 and 1530, and Hilton's *Scale of Perfection*, which was printed five times between 1494 and 1533. By the second half of the fifteenth century there were circles of devout laymen attempting to live the mixed life throughout the kingdom, such as the minor gentry of Throckmorton, who received from their family confessor a series of Latin instructions bearing a close resemblance to those in *Þe Holy Boke de Gracia Dei*, and the circle of artisans and

[25] M. Deanesly, 'Vernacular Books in England in the Fourteenth and Fifteenth Centuries', *M.C.R.*, xv (1920), 355.

tradesmen in London, who had connections with Richard Whittington, and who owned some of the works of Hilton.[26]

Yorkshiremen in the fifteenth century were, therefore, of central importance in the development of lay piety throughout the kingdom; and it is possible to see the Reformation as something that developed in native soil as an intensification of the spirit of religious debate, change and self-criticism introduced by a York clergy who were anything but provincial. This can help to explain why so much of a dynamic and prosperous religious culture (illustrated by the popularity of chantries, parish priests, friars, recluses and the new saints' cults) which had evolved between 1350 and 1457 under a pastorally minded church, was swept away during the sixteenth century. The contemplative literature of the diocese contained ambiguous attitudes on the relationship between introspective piety and a personal sense of sin and the pressures and consolations of social religion and rituals. Annual confession was compulsory, and writers of penitential handbooks such as Thoresby, Pagula and Myrk analysed sins with a view to their social consequences; even compulsive sins such as gluttony were regarded as sins against the community. Penances were accordingly recommended that were public acts of atonement and reconciliation with the penitent's neighbours.[27] Hilton, Nicholas Love and other devotional writers of the period were writing for those with more individualistic understanding of sin and penance; those who, no matter how often they confessed and performed penances, still felt 'the biting and fretting of conscience', and who thought 'what is a man but his thoughts and his loves'.[28] These writers realized the inherent tensions that such people must have felt when confronted with the necessity of making their annual confessions, when they were judged in terms of their relationships with their parish neighbours and required to make public atonement. They tried to ensure that devout men and women did not harbour hostility and resentment towards their neighbours by showing them that public penances could be performed with detachment if they were regarded as just another tribulation during their days of exile as 'pilgrims and straungers'.[29] Hilton advised penitents to 'take the cross — and suffer the pain of this world awhile'; and Nicholas Love referred to 'this wrecched lyfe in penaunce'.[30] However, although York religious writers

26 See W. A. Pantin, 'Instructions for a devout and literate layman', in J. J. G. Alexander and M. T. Gibson (eds.), *Medieval Learning and Literature, Essays presented to Richard William Hunt* (Oxford, 1976), 398 – 422.

27 Myrk, *Instructions for Parish Priests*, ed. E. Peacock (London, EETS, 1868) II, 1221. Myrk's *Instructions* were taken from William Pagula's *Pars oculi*; see E. Boyle, 'The Oculis Sacerdotis of William of Pagula', *T.R.H.S.*, (1954).

28 *Scale of Perfection*, pp. 211, 77.

29 *The Myrror of the Lyfe of Jesu Crist*, p. 86.

30 *Scale of Perfection*, p. 156; *The Myrror*, p. 84.

instilled respect for authority and took pains to ensure that the development of religious sensibility did not have harmful social consquences, they could not guarantee that aspects of their teachings, like those of Rolle's, would not be taken out of context. Their teaching on penance, in which they counselled inner detachment, had socially divisive implications. Hilton advised 'thou wouldst be well paid for to be trodden and spurned under every man's feet as a thing which is outcast'; and he defined the first mystical yearnings as the moment when 'Thee thinketh that all creatures rise against thee and all thing which thou haddest delight in before turneth thee to pain'.[31] Christ, in *The Mirror*, says 'if the world hate yow, witeth wele that it hated me firste byfore yowe'; and Nicholas Love declares 'In my confusion, dejection, contempt and affliction inflicted upon me, either by myself or others I will rejoice'.[32] By recognizing the redemptive power of both affective memory and the mystical perception of reality as a penitential separation from Christ, these writers were calling attention to the repressive, stifling elements in communal religion. Hilton, like Thomas à Kempis, observed that the devout suffered in communities where priests judged on appearances and laymen informed on their neighbours.[33] Even the cults of Richard Rolle, John of Bridlington and Robert of Knaresborough expressed opposition to the abrasive and indifferent elements of social authority.

By the second half of the fifteenth century these teachings were being taken out of context, and the implicit division between institutional and private religion became explicitly polarized as clergy began to take more dogmatic stands on the issue. Reginald Pecock was a hard-working London priest, later a bishop, who shared Thomas Netter's strong sense of the church's traditions; his suspicions of personal religion and the detachment inherent in eremitic literature led him to deny any compatibility between the active and contemplative lives. Refusing to see the Martha and Mary story as a parable of the two lives, he took it literally as a rebuke of Martha's disrespect.[34] Religion was seen by Pecock in the purely public and institutional terms of social responsibility and obedience to authority: God, he claimed, was appeased by good deeds of cooperation between neighbours rather than prayers and contemplation.[35] He was dismissive of recluses, arguing that the contemplative life was less significant than the active life and that it could be confined to a few daily prayers.[36] Monasteries, he claimed, should not be contemplative communities like the Carthusians, but

31 *Scale*, pp. 39, 281.
32 *The Myrror*, pp. 213, 71.
33 *The Scale*, p. 36.
34 Pecock, *Reule of Crysten Religioun*, ed. W. G. Greet, (London, E.E.T.S., 1927), p. 490.
35 ibid, pp. 392 – 93, 414.
36 ibid, pp. 393, 397, 409, 416, 418, 479.

microcosms of society.[37] According to Pecock, God could not be reached through an individual's personal feelings and prayers, but through the institutions of the church, which were a product of reason.[38] Some of Pecock's opponents, such as John Pynchbeck, stressed the importance of private religious experience, and many of the monks of Syon who studied devotional literature showed little appreciation of the value of the mixed life or public religion.[39] In the writings of Pecock and in the opposition he aroused, there can be seen signs of the divisions that were to occur in the sixteenth century between the Protestants, who saw religion in terms of contemplating the written word of the Bible and engaging in private prayer, and the Marian Catholics, who wished to assert the primacy of institutional religion.

In the same way it is possible to see the eventual establishment of the Anglican church in England as something which grew out of the rich soil of the religious movements of the early fifteenth century, and not as something that was imposed from above in the sixteenth century by a government that had no regard for historical traditions.[40] The development of a national church led by the Crown, can be traced back to the activities of Henry V and his leading counsellors and confessors including: the Yorkshiremen, Henry Lord Scrope of Masham, Henry Lord FitzHugh of Tanfield, Stephen Patrington, Thomas Fishbourne and Thomas Langley, who were all students of the contemplative literature of the north-east, and some of the leading churchmen of Salisbury.[41] The catalyst for this development was the eremitic movement of the diocese of York. Henry V's clergy approved of this movement: Thomas Netter, one of the king's Carmelite confessors, supervised the activities of recluses in Norwich, and Thomas Langley had connections with Syon.[42] However, these churchmen would also have noticed the threats to social order and the Crown itself posed by widespread religious enthusiasm and contemplative piety. Recluses had traditionally engaged in vague prophecy; but by the end of the fourteenth century the prophecies of holy men were being used for political purposes, and recluses were becoming involved in political predictions. The Bridlington prophecies, mistakenly attributed to John

37 ibid, p. 416.

38 ibid, pp. 412 – 13; Pecock, *The Repressor of Over-much Blaming of the Clergy*, ed. C. Babbington, (R.S., London, 1860), i, pp. 28, 44, 76, ii, p. 540.

39 For the reaction against Pecock see E. J. Jacob, 'Reynold Pecock', *Proc. Brit. Academy*, xxxvii (1951), 136 – 49; J. R. Lander, *Conflict and Stability in Fifteenth Century England* (London, 1969), pp. 118 – 23.

40 J. J. Scrisbrick, in *The Reformation and the English People* (Oxford, 1984) describes Anglicanism as a return to the pre-reformation religion, p. 186.

41 For an analysis of Henry V's initiative in religious changes see Catto, 'Religious Change under Henry V', 97 – 115.

42 Tanner, *The Church in Norwich*, pp. 64 – 65.

Thweng, were used by members of the Lancastrian faction and by the supporters of the deposed Richard II. In 1407 two friars and a doctor of Divinity were executed at Tynemouth for using the prophecies to show that Richard II was still alive; and in 1403 a hermit, William Norham, was executed in York for predicting the end of Henry IV's reign.[43] Saints' cults, especially those of the martyred opponents of the Lancastrian dynasty, such as Richard II and Richard Scrope, served as a focus for discontent with the government. Anxiety concerning the growing novelties of religious belief would have reached a peak during the early years of Henry V's reign, because a growing number of serious disturbances appeared to have religious origins. One of the spokesmen for the Kent peasants who executed Simon Sudbury and other members of the government in 1381 was the malcontented and millenaristic preacher, John Ball. Wyclif and his followers were blamed for this peasant uprising, and alarm at the consequences of the Lollard movement would have increased by 1411 because of events in Bohemia, where Hus and his colleagues at Prague University were taking the kingdom along a path of radical and alarming religious innovation.

The York clergy of Arundel's circle were among the first churchmen to show an active interest in the problem of heresy, and Arundel responded to the events in Bohemia by visiting Oxford in 1411. His successor as archbishop of Canterbury, Henry Chichele, continued to take a strong stand against heresy. However, what was most important for the removal of the Lollard threat and the subsequent development of the English church was the initiative shown by Henry V. In January 1414 he put down the uprising that was led by his friend Oldcastle, near the Temple Bar in London. This skirmish aroused at least as much alarm as the magnate disputes that dominated the first fifteen years of Lancastrian rule, and even the Cambridge conspirator, Henry Lord Scrope, expressed his horror when he heard about the possibility of the Lollard involvement in the conspiracy to kill Henry V.[44] The possibility of religious war must have worried many of the king's counsellors in this period, and his clergy attempted to provide a theoretical basis for increasing royal initiative in the stamping out of heresy. Richard Ullerston first provided this in his *Petitiones*, which were written at the instigation of Robert Hallum, the bishop of Salisbury, in 1408, and presented on the advice of the royal confessor, Roger Coryngham, to Henry VI for implementation when the church was too weak to act.[45] Ullerston defined the prince's role as the protector of the church of England from external and internal threats, and he argued that heresy

43 *Cronica S. Albani*, p. 231.
44 Wylie, *Henry V*, i, 527; *Report of the Deputy Keeper of Public Records*, xliii, 1182, p. 590.
45 Harvey, 'English Views on the Reforms to be undertaken in General Councils', p. 66.

could only be defeated by royal initiative.[46] In 1415 Henry V caused the university of Oxford to draw up a list of reforms of the church to be presented at the council of Constance; forty-six petitions were presented, modelled on Ullerston's *Petitiones*, with a covering letter praising the king's role in defeating the heretics at the Temple Bar and proclaiming that the peace of the church depended on the peace of the state.[47] The letter also called for the cooperation of secular and ecclesiastical authorities at this reforming council.[48] Subsequent events in Bohemia, which was in a state of disorder between 1420 and 1434, must have convinced Henry V and his advisors of the wisdom of taking a firm line against heresy, and of state involvement in religion.

The anxiety that Henry V and his churchmen felt about heresy and the stability of the realm also manifested itself in an increasing anxiety about the difficulty of exerting any control over what people were thinking. It is in this context that the witchcraft scares of the period should be understood. In 1418 Queen Joan of Navarre was imprisoned on a charge of planning the king's death by necromancy — the fact that she owned a vial of *aqua vitae* lends substance to the charge — and in the following year the king asked all the bishops to pray against the black arts.[49] In 1441 Henry Chichele presided over the trial of Eleanor Cobham, the wife of Humphrey Duke of Gloucester; she was convicted of using necromancy and witchcraft to plot the death of Henry VI.[50] However, the most realistic and successful attempt to increase the church and the crown's authority over the spiritual lives of most Englishmen was made through the administration of confession. The leading churchmen of this period were faced with a new set of challenges. Thoresby and his clerks were concerned with showing people what to believe and instructing them in how to behave. The clerks of Arundel between 1373 and 1410 attempted to cater for the spiritual needs of people, and they exerted a similar guiding and teaching role in this area. They were so successful that the clergy of the reigns of Henry V and Henry VI, alarmed by the growth of heresy and lay piety, were confronted with the problem of needing to know more about the hidden inner lives of the growing numbers of literate and pious laymen and priests. Ullerston defined the problem in his *Petitiones*, when he claimed that the pastor's main function was to keep benefices faithful.[51] Orthodoxy was now a concern of the state, and under Henry V canonists were less concerned

46 ibid, pp. 34 – 38; Ullerston in *De Officio Militari* wrote on the knight's duty to rule.
476 ibid, p. 158.
48 ibid, pp. 148 – 50.
49 A. R. Myers, 'The Captivity of a Royal Witch', *B.J.R.L.*, 24 (1940) 263; see p. 267 for Joan's inventory.
50 R. Griffiths, 'The Trial of Eleanor Cobham', *B.J.R.L.*, 44 (1968) 381
51 Harvey, p. 67.

with the principles of moral and spiritual teaching, which Thoresby and his successors introduced into the administration of the pastoral office; and they increasingly saw pastoral care as an enquiry into the attitudes and beliefs of parishioners. William Lyndwood, a canon lawyer like Hilton and his circle, argued a case for the use of confession as a means of enquiring into people's lives; he was probably influenced to do so by his work as an official of the Canterbury Court from 1412 to 1431, when he was involved in the trials of the Lollards, William Claydon and William Taylor.[52] Lyndwood presented to Chichele his *Provinciale*, a summary and gloss on a selection of the statutes of the English church. Special prominence was given to canons concerned with the administration of confession, which was no longer merely a medium of basic religious instruction but a means of enquiring into the spiritual and intellectual lives of laymen. Many of these canons were diocesan statutes which had never been published in the councils of the province of Canterbury.[53] Lyndwood, by presenting them as provincial canon law was, as he pointed out, enlarged the competence of the archbishop's court, over which he presided.[54] The publication of the *Provinciale* in 1432, and its acceptance by both the convocations of Canterbury and York in 1462 as the recognized *Summa* of English canon law, represented an attempt to extend the importance of confessions as a means of controlling all aspects of social and spiritual life.[55] Lyndwood published a series of canons that defined the limits of the priest's interrogative power: priests were forbidden to enquire about the names of those implicated in a penitent's sin, and all confessors were bound by a seal of secrecy from revealing confessions to church authorities.[56] However, in his glosses Lyndwood, who was also an archdeacon, claimed that these restrictions could be lifted in cases where a confession implicated others who were guilty of heresy and who posed a threat to the community.[57] He also extended further the disciplinary and judicial element of confession by publishing diocesan laws that prescribed strict punishments for those laymen who failed to attend confession.[58] Pecock attempted, unsuccessfully, to extend the powers of the confessor even further in his *Donet*, written between 1443 and 1449, and *The Folewer to the Donet*, written between 1453 and 1454, in which he envisaged an examination on the basis of sins of omission and the seven virtues, as well as the Ten

52 F. W. Maitland, 'Canon Law in England, I, William Lyndwood', *E.H.R.*, (1896) 448 – 49.
53 Lyndwood, *Provinciale*, v, tit. xv, ch. 1 – 7.
54 C. R. Cheney, 'Textual Problems of English Provincial Canons', in Cheney, *Medieval Texts and Studies* (Oxford, 1973), pp. 131 – 33, 136, 167, 172, 174; *Provinciale*, iii, tit., 23.
55 Cheney, 178, *B.I.H.R.*, Reg. Booth, fo. 342b.
56 *Provinciale*, pp. 326 – 29.
57 ibid, p. 329.
58 ibid, p. 343.

Commandments and the Seven Deadly Sins.[59] Pecock even went so far as to imply that the personal sense of sin and repentance, which was encouraged by the authors of devotional works, was incompatible with penitential discipline.[60]

Henry V and his ministers may also have realized that the dangers inherent in private religion were best nullified by using contemplative piety and religious enthusiasm to help to build a more communal religion centred on the monarchy. Henry V evidently considered the royal foundations of Sheen and Syon, contemplative communities served by the royal confessor Patrington, and Fishbourne, to be prayer houses for the dynasty.[61] The king and his advisors also recognized the potential that saints' cults had for unifying local communities; they applied these cults to the services of national unity by invoking the saints to preserve the Lancastrian dynasty and to protect the realm against the French. The Bridlington prophecies were interpreted as predictions of the success of the Lancastrian dynasty; and rumours were circulated that St John of Beverley's body distilled precious drops of liquid for sixty-one days and nights when Henry V's father landed at Ravenspur.[62] During the period of Henry V's French campaigns St John of Beverley and St George became national saints. It was popularly believed that John's body distilled a precious liquid before the battle of Agincourt, and, according to Walsingham, the shrine emitted blood the entire day of the battle.[63] The cross of St George emblazoned Henry V's flagship, and the English soldiers at Agincourt all wore this emblem. After the victory the southern convocation decided that special honour should be paid to St George as England's protecting saint, and Chichele issued an order that his feast day (April 23) should be observed as a double feast, when all work should cease.[64] From the years of protracted struggle with a kingdom that had played host to the papacy a self-confident, assertive English church was emerging, which identified itself closely with the English nation; and these national saints were seen as its special protectors. Lyndwood described the victory at Agincourt as a victory for the English church, achieved through the

59 Pecock, *The Donet*, ed. E. V. Hitchcock (London, E.E.T.S., 1921); Pecock, *The Folewer to the Donet*, ed. E. V. Hitchcock (London, E.E.T.S., 1924); J. F. Patrouch Jr. *Reginald Pecock* (New York, 1970), pp. 124 – 26.

60 *Reule of Crysten Religioun*, pp. 392 – 93, 414 – 15. Pecock claimed that the serious sins were crimes of hostility against members of society, such as manslaughter, rather than the smaller sins against God, such as perjury; and he maintained that the social penance of good deeds was more important than prayer.

61 Tait, 'Bridgitine Monastery of Syon', p. 55.

62 *Historians of York*, iii, p. 288.

63 G. Poulson, *Beverlac*, (London, 1829), i, p. 184; Wylie, ii, p. 240; *Concilia*, iii, p. 379; *Foedera*, ix, p. 420.

64 Wylie, *Henry V*, ii, 239.

intercession of St John of Beverley, and he testified that a grateful king had requested special celebration of the feast day of his translation.[65] The ordination of this feast (17 December 1416) was commemorated in a document which extolled the sacred name of the English church beyond all the churches of all other countries. Gratitude was expressed for St John of Beverley, whose patronage and intercession preserved the public interest of the church and kingdom by maintaining its 'sweet repose' and securing the desired victory over 'all the enemies that make opposition from without'. This ordination charter also maintained 'that God had decreed to help his church and the kingdom of the English on account of the piety of the saints with which she gloriously shines'.[66] Naturally these patron saints were also seen as protectors against internal enemies of the realm, and they were invoked against heretics. According to the St Alban's chronicler, the bones of a burnt heretic worked the opposite way to those of a saint, being highly infectious, while Hoccleve called on all those who were of the livery of St George to stamp out Lollardy.[67]

Saint's cults were also instrumental in helping the clergy of Henry V to standardize the liturgy of the English church. The efforts made by Hallum and the Salisbury chapter on behalf of Osmund were connected with an attempt to increase the national significance of the Sarum rite, which gradually superseded all other local uses. In his sermon on the saint, delivered in 1416, Ullerston used Osmund's contribution to the liturgy of the church as a reason for canonization.[68] Chichele, who treated the Sarum ordinale as the standard use in his liturgical decrees, may have encouraged the adoption of the Sarum rite throughout the province of Canterbury, and Lyndwood defended the right of the bishop of Salisbury to ordain the rites of the province. Liturgical innovation in this period probably reflects the attempts made by leading churchmen to reverse the trend towards private devotion in the mass and to create a more public ritual for the church. Lyndwood stressed the public importance of communion in his *Provinciale,* and even the Holy Name, which was originally a focus for the private devotion of Rolle's followers, was becoming incorporated into the liturgy and was used in ordinary church services.

This development of a more state controlled, public religion was a pragmatic and moderate compromise between institutional and private religion; it therefore embodied the ideals of the mixed life and anticipated the more salient features of the Anglican church. For this

65 *Provinciale,* p. 104.
66 Poulson, *Beverlac.,* p. 787ff.
67 Wylie, i, p. 318.
68 For this sermon see Jacob, *Essays in the Conciliar Epoch,* p. 80; Malden, *The Canonization of St Osmund,* pp. 236 – 42.

reason Walter Hilton seems to have more in common with the leaders of the sixteenth-century Anglican church than the more conservative provincial parish priest of the Tudor period. Parkyn was clerical in his interests and had little sympathy with lay spiritual needs or the idea of clerical marriage: in his essay on the four lives, he defined the mixed life as the life of preaching and charity lived by Christ and his apostles, and he applied it to secular clergy.[69] Hilton, however, intended his *Epistle on Mixed Life* to be used by married laymen; and this work may have encouraged the acceptance of the idea of clerical marriage in the sixteenth century. It is, therefore, possible to regard the Reformation, with some detachment, as the evolution of a distinctively English religious culture that had been initiated by the religious changes within the diocese of York in the period between 1350 and 1450. One hundred and fifty years of Catholic history were not wiped out in the process. There were casualties: the Carthusian monasteries and the shrines of holy men were martyred at the hands of an increasingly powerful government; but even this conflict had, in a sense been anticipated by the hagiographers and pilgrims of the fourteenth century.

69 Dickens, 'The Last Medieval Englishman', p. 167.

Bibliography

A. MANUSCRIPT SOURCES

Cambridge
University Library
MS Ee, iv, 30.
MS Ff, vii, 14.
MS Ii, vi.
MS Ll, vi, 43.
MS Add. 3042.
Emmanuel College MS 35.

Oxford
Bodleian Library
MS Auct. D4.
MS Bodley 198.
MS Bodley 446.
MS Bodley 450.
MS Bodley 456.
MS Bodley 758.
MS Bodley 861.
MS Bodley 877.
MS Bodley 953.
MS c iv 2080.
MS Douce 114.
MS Douce 297.
MS e Mus. 35.
MS Eng. poet d 5.
MS Hatton 12.
MS Lat. Liturg. e17.
MS Lat. Liturg. f2.
MS Lat. Th. d. 15.
MS Laud Lat. 5.
MS Laud Misc. 286.
MS Laud Misc. 702.

MS Marshall 135.
MS Rawl. 72.
MS Rawl. A 389.
MS Tanner I.
Balliol College MS 33.
Balliol College MS 227.
Merton College MS 204.
University College MS 28.
University College MS 76.

York
Borthwick Institute of Historical Research
Exchequer and Prerogative Courts of York: Original Wills and Inventories.
Probate Registers Vols. 1 to 5.
Registers of the Archbishops of York; William Melton 1317 – 1340; William Zouche 1342 – 1352; John Thoresby 1352 – 1373; Alexander Neville 1374 – 1388; Thomas Arundel 1388 – 1386; Robert Waldby 1396 – 1397; Richard Scrope 1398 – 1405; Henry Bowet 1407 – 1423.
York Minster Library
Dean and Chapter Probate Records Vol. 1 1321 – 1493.
MS Add. 2.
MS Add. 54.
MS XVI, K.6.

B. PRINTED SOURCES

(1) Primary Sources

The Academy, V, (Lincoln, 1879).
Acts of the Chapter of Ripon, ed. J. T. Fowler (Surtees Society, 64, 1875).
Aluredi Beverlacensis, *Annales*, ed. T. Hearne (Oxford, 1716).
Analecta Hymnica Medii Aevi, ed. G. M. Dreves (Leipzig, 1905).
Acren Riwle, ed. E. J. Dobson (E.E.T.S., London, 1972)
Munimenta Academica, ed. Henry Anstey (Rolls Series, 50b). For the will of Dr Thomas Gascoigne.
Advocates of Reform, ed. M. Spinka (Library of Christian Classics, xiv, London, 1953). Translations of selected writings of Wyclif.
Angel's Song, ed. T. Takamiya (Tokyo, 1977).
Anglia Sacra, ed. Henry Wharton, 2 vols. (London, 1691).
Anominalle Chronicle, ed. V. H. Galbraith (Manchester, 1927).
Amundesham, Johanne, *Annales Monasterii S. Albani*, ed. H. T. Riley (Rolls Series 28/5 a, b, London, 1870).

Avesbury, Robert, *De Gestis Mirabilibus Edwardi Tertii*, ed. E. Maunde Thompson (Rolls Series, London, 1889).
Bale, John, *Scriptorum illustrium maioris Brytannie catalogue* (Basle, 1557).
Beverley Chapter Act Book, ed. A. F. Leach (Surtees Soc., 98, 1897, 203, 1903).
The Book of Vices and Virtues, ed. W. N. Francis (E.E.T.S., London, 1942).
Burgo, John, *Pupilla Oculi* (Paris, 1510).
Calendar of Close Rolls Preserved in the Public Record Office (Her Majesty's Stationery Office, London, 1893 –).
Calendar of Entries in the Papal Registers relating to Great Britain and Ireland, Papal Letters, ed. W. H. Bliss and J. A. Twemlow (Her Majesty's Stationery Office, London, 1893).
Calendar of Fine Rolls (Her Majesty's Stationery Office, London, 1934 – 1940).
Calendar of Patent Rolls Preserved in the Public Record Office (Her Majesty's Stationery Office, London, 1893 –).
Calendar of the Register of Richard Scrope, ed. R. N. Swanson, 2 vols (Borthwick Institute of Historical Research, York, 1981, 1983).
Calendar of the Register of Robert Waldeby, Archbishop of York, ed. D. M. Smith (Borthwick Institute of Historical Research, York, 1974).
Calendar of Wills Enrolled in the Court of Husting, ed. R. Sharpe, 2 vols (London, 1890).
Capgrave, John, *Nova Legenda Angliae*, 2 vols, ed. C. L. Horstmann (Oxford, 1901).
The Catalogue of the Library of Syon Monastery, ed. M. Bateson (Cambridge, 1898)
Catherine of Siena, *The Orchard of Syon, a Middle-English transl. of the Dialogues*, ed. P. Hodgson and G. Liegey (E.E.T.S., London, 1965).
The Chapel of St Mary's York, ed. A. H. Thompson (Y.A.J., xxvi, 1944 – 47).
The Chastizing of God's Children, ed. J. Bazire and E. Colledge (Oxford, 1957).
The Works of Geoffrey Chaucer, ed. F. N. Robinson (London, 1957).
Chronica monasterii de Melsa, ed. E. Bond (R.S., 111).
Chronicle of John Streche, ed. F. Taylor (Manchester, 1932).
Chronicle of Peter Langtoft (Rolls Series, 47, London, 1866).
Chronicon Henrici Knighton, ed. J. R. Lumby (Rolls Ser., 92, a, b, 1889 – 95).
Chronicon de Lanercost, ed. Stevenson (Edinburgh, 1839).
Chronicon Adae de Usk, ed. E. Maunde Thompson (2nd ed., London, 1904).
The Works of Sir John Clanvowe, ed. V. J. Scattergood (Cambridge, 1975).
The Cloud of Unknowing and the Book of Privy Counselling, ed. P. Hodgson (E.E.T.S. London, 1944).

Concilia Magnae Britanniae, ed. D. Wilkins, 3 vols (Oxford, 1738).

Daniel, Walter, *The Life of Aelred of Rievaulx*, ed. F. M. Powicke (London, 1950).

Sir Degrevant, ed. C. R. Casson (London, E.E.T.S., 1949).

A Dialogue Between Reason and Adversity, a late Middle English version of Petrarch's De Remediis, ed. F. N. Diekstra (Assen, 1968).

Dixon, W. H. *Fasti Eboracesses*, edited and enlarged J. Raine, (London, 1863.

Documents Relating to the Visitations of the Diocese and Province of York, (Surtees Soc., Miscellanea, ii, 1916).

The Earliest English Translation of the First Three Books of De Imitatione Christi, ed. J. K. Ingram (E.E.T.S., London, 1893).

Early English Guilds, ed. L. Toulmin-Smith (London, 1870).

Early Lincoln Wills, ed. A. Gibbons (Lincoln, 1888).

Early Meals and Manners, ed. E. J. Furnivall (E.E.T.S., London, 1868).

Ely Chapter Ordinances and Visitation Records, ed. S. J. A. Evans (Camden Miscellany, xvii, 3rd ser., lxiv, 1940).

Ely Diocesan Remembrancer, (Register Thomas Arundel) Cambridge, 1893 – 96.

English Historical Literature, ed. C. L. Kingsford (Oxford, 1913).

English Works of Wyclif, ed. F. D. Mathew (E.E.T.S., London, 1880).

Epistolario di Coluccio Salutati, ed. F. Novati (Rome, 1891).

The Erl of Tolous, ed. G. Rüdke (Berlin, 1881).

Eulogioum Historiarum, continuation iii, ed. F. R. Haydon (Rolls ser., 1863).

Extracts from the Municipal Records of the City of York, ed. R. Davies (London, 1843)

Fabric Rolls of York Minster, ed. James Raine (Surtees Soc., Durham xxxv, 1859).

Fasciculi Zizaniorum, ed. W. W. Shirley (R.S., London, 1858).

Fifty Earliest English Wills, ed. E. J. Furnivall (E.E.T.S., London).

Gale, *Registrum Honoris de Richmond* (1772).

Gascoigne, Thomas, *Loci e libro Veritatum*, ed. J. E. T. Rodgers (Oxford, 1981).

John of Gaunt's Register, 1371 – 75, ed. S. Armitage-Smith (Camden 3rd ser. xx, 1911) *1378 – 83*, ed. E. G. Lodge and R. Somerville (Camden 3rd ser. lvi, lvii, 1937.)

Gesta Abbatum Monasterii Sancti Albani, ed. H. T. Riley, 3 vols (Rolls Series, 28/4 a – c, 1867 – 69).

Registrum Abbatiae Johannis Whethumstede, ed. H. T. Riley, 2 vols (Rolls Series, 286/a, 1872).

Gesta Henrici Quinti, ed. F. Taylor and J. S. Roskell (Oxford, 1975).

Gregory, St, the Great, Pope, *Moralia in Iob*, ed. Jacques, P. Migne (Patrologia Latina, 75 – 76).

——— *Hom. in Ezech*. (Patrologia Latina, lxxvi).
——— *Liber Regulae Pastoralis* (Patrologia Latina, 77).
Henry the Sixth: Reprint of John Blacman's Memoirs, ed. and transl. M. R. James (Cambridge, 1929).
Hilton, Walter, *The Scale of Perfection*, ed. E. Underhill, (London, 1923).
——— *Epistle on the mixed life*, ed. C. Horstman.
——— *The Inner Temple Manuscript of Walter Hilton's Eight Chapters on Perfection*, ed. F. Kurigawa (Tokyo, 1971).
——— *Latin Writings*, ed. J. P. Clark and Cheryl Taylor (Analecta Cartusiana, 124, Salzburg, 1987).
Historiae Dunelmensis, ed. James Raine (Surtees Society, 9, 1839).
Historians of the Church of York and its Archbishops, ed. James Raine, Jr, 3 vols, (Rolls Series, 71, London, 1879 – 94).
Historical Letters and Papers from the Northern Registers, ed. James Raine, (Rolls Series, 61, 1873).
Þe Holy Boke Gratia Dei, ed. M. L. Arntz, (Elizabethan and Renaissance Studies, Salzburg, 1981).
Hoveden, John, *Philomena*, ed. C. Blume (Hymnologische Beiträge, Leipzig, iv, 1930).
John Hoveden, Poems, ed. F. Raby (Surtees Society, 154, 1939).
Incerti Scriptoris, ed. J. A. Giles (London, 1846).
Julian of Norwich, *Revelations of Divine Love*, ed. R. Hurdleston (London, 1927).
Julian of Norwich's Revelations of Divine Love, the Shorter Version, ed. (from MS B.L. Add. 37790) by F. Beer (Heidelberg, 1978).
Julian of Norwich, *A Book of the Showings of the Anchoress Julian of Norwich*, ed. S. B. Meech and J. Walsh (Toronto, 1978).
Kempe, Margery, *The Book of Margery Kempe*, ed. S. B. Meech and H. E. Allen (London, E.E.T.S., 1940).
The Kirkstall Chronicle, ed. M. V. Clarke and N. Denholme (Bulletin of John Rylands Library, 1931).
Lancaster, Henry, Duke of, *Livre de Seyntz Médicines*, ed. E. J. Arnould (Anglo Norman Text Soc., 1940).
Langland's William, *Vision of William Concerning Piers the Ploughman*, ed. W. W. Skeat (Oxford, 1886).
The Lanercost Chronicle, ed. J. Stevenson (Edinburgh, 1839).
The Lay Folk's Catechism, ed. T. P. Simmons and H. E. Nolloth (E.E.T.S., London, 1901).
Leland, John, *The Itinery of John Leland*, ed. L. Toulmin-Smith, 5 vols (London, 1906 – 8).
The Life of St Cuthbert in English Verse c. 1450, ed. J. T. Fowler (Surtees Society, 87, 1891).
The Life of St Robert of Knaresborough, ed. H. J. T. Drury (Roxburgh Club, 1824).

Lincoln Wills, ed. C. W. Foster (Lincoln, 1914).
Love, Nicholas, *The Mirror of the Blessed Lyfe of Jesu Crist*, ed.L. F. Powell (Oxford, 1911).
Lynwood, William, *Provinciale*, (Oxford, 1676, reprinted, Farnborough, 1969).
Market Harborough Records, ed. J. E. Stokes and W. B. Bragg (London, 1890).
Medieval Libraries of Great Britain, ed. Neil Ker (2nd ed., London, 1964).
Meditations on the Life and Passion of Christ, ed. C. D'Evelyn (E.E.T.S., London, 1921).
Memorials of Beverley Minster: the Chapter Act Book, ed. A. F. Leach (Surtees Society, 98, 108, 1897 and 1903).
Memoirs illustrative of the History and Antiquities of the County and City of Lincoln (Proceedings of the Archeological Institute, Lincoln, 1848).
Memorials of Ripon, ed. J. T. Fowler, 3 vols, (Surtees Society, 74, 78, 81, 1881, 1884, 1886).
Monstrelet, E. de, *Chronicles*, ed. T. Johnes (London, 1840).
The Myror of Lewed Men, ed. C. Horstmann (E.E.T.S., London, 1892).
The Miroure of Oure Lady, ed. H. J. Blunt (E.E.T.S., London, 1873).
Myrk, John, *Instructions for Parish Priests*, ed. E. Peacock (E.E.T.S., London, 1905).
Nicolas, N. H. *The Controversy between Sir Richard Scrope and Sir Robert Grosvenor in the Court of Chivalry*, 2 vols (London, 1832).
——— *Royal Wills* (London, 1780).
North Country Wills, ed. J. W. Clay (Surtees Society, 116, 1908).
The Northern Passion, ed. F. A. Foster (E.E.T.S., London, 1913, 1916).
Octavian, ed. Karl Vollmoller, (Altfranzösische Bibliothek 3, Heilbronn, 1883).
The Officium and Miracula of Richard Rolle of Hampole, ed. R. Woolley (S.P.C.K., 1919).
The Ordinal and Customary of the Abbey of Saint Mary York, ed. L. McLachlan and J.B.L. Tolhurst (Henry Bradshaw Society, 73 – 75, 1936 – 37).
Page, W., *Chantry Certificates in the County of York*, 2 vols (Surtees Society, 91, 92, 1894).
The Paston Letters, ed. James Gairdner, 3 vols (2nd edit., Gloucester, 1983).
Pearl, ed. E. V. Gordon (Oxford, 1953).
The Percy Chartulary, ed. W. T. Martin (Surtees Society, 117, 1909).
Pecok, Reginald, *The Repressor of Over-much Blaming of the Clergy*, ed. C. Babbington (Rolls Series, London, 1860).
——— *The Donet*, ed. E. V. Hitchcock (E.E.T.S., London, 1921).
——— *The Reule of Crysten Religioun*, ed. W. C. Skeat (E.E.T.S., London, 1927).

——— *The Folewer to the Donet*, ed. E. V. Hitchcock (E.E.T.S., London, 1924).
The Plumpton Correspondence, ed. T. Stapleton (Camden Society, 1834).
Poems of the Pearl Manuscript, ed. M. Andrew and R. Waldron (York Medieval Texts, 1978).
Political Poems and Songs, ed. T. Wright (Rolls Series 14a, London, 1856).
The Prick of Conscience, ed. R. Morris (Berlin, 1863).
Raby, F. J. E., 'A Middle English Paraphrase of Hoveden's Philomena', *Modern Language Review*, 30 (1935).
Records of the Northern Convocation, ed. J. Raine (Surtees Society, 113, 1906).
Records of Early English Drama, ed. A. T. Johnson and A. Rogerson (Toronto, 1979)
Register of Grandisson, Exeter, ed. F. L. Hingeston-Randolph, 3 vols (London, 1894 – 99).
Register of the Guild of Corpus Christi in the City of York, ed. R. H. Skaife (Surtees Society, 57, 1871).
The Register of Henry Chichele, Archbishop of Canterbury, 1414 – 1443, ed. E. F. Jacob, 4 vols (Oxford, 1938 – 47).
Register of John of Gaunt 1372 – 1376, ed. J. Armitage-Smith (Camden 3rd Ser. xx – xxi) 1911; **1379 – 1383** ed. E. C. Lodge and R. Somerville (Camden 3rd Ser. lvi – lvii) 1937.
Register of Thomas Langley, ed. R. L. Storey (Surtees Society, 164, 166, 169, 1949, 1951, 1954).
Registers of the Archdeaconry of Richmond, ed. A. H. Thompson (Y.A.J., xxx, 1930).
Religious Pieces, ed. G. G. Perry (London, E.E.T.S., 1914).
Report of the Deputy Keeper of Public Records, 43 (1882).
English Prose Treatises of Richard Rolle of Hampole, ed. R. Perry (E.E.T.S., London, 1886).
Robertus de Avesbury, *De Gestis Mirabilus Regis Edwardi Tertii* (Rolls Series, 93, 1889).
Rolle, Richard, *English Psalter*, ed. H. R. Bramley (Oxford, 1884).
——— *The Fire of Love and the Mending of Life*, ed. R. Harvey (E.E.T.S., London, 1896).
——— *The Incendium Amoris*, ed. M. Deanesly (Manchester, 1915).
——— *Meditations of the Life and Passion of Christ*, ed. C. V'Evelyn (E.E.T.S., London, 1921).
——— *English Writings*, ed. H. E. Allen (Oxford, 1931).
——— *Melos Amoris*, ed. E. J. F. Arnould (Oxford, 1957).
Rotuli Parliamentorum, ed. J. Strachey, 6 vols. (London, 1767 – 77).
Rymer, Thomas, *Foedera*, vol. IX (London, 1704 – 34).
The Saint Alban's Chronicle, ed. V. H. Galbraith (Oxford, 1937).
Saint Erkenwald, ed. Sir I. Gollancz (E.E.T.S., Oxford, 1922).

Scrope, Stephen, *The Boke of Knyghthode, translated from the French of Christine de Pisan*, ed. E. Warner (London, E.E.T.S., 1904).
——— *Epistle to Othea*, ed. C. F. Buhler (E.E.T.S., London, 1970).
Sede Vacante Wills, ed. C. E. Woodruffe (Kent Archeological Society, III, 1914).
Shaw, P. J., 'Wills relating to All Saints' North Street', in P. J. Shaw, *An Old York Church* (York, 1908).
Sir Eglamour of Artois, ed. F. E. Richardson (E.E.T.S., London, 1965).
Sir Gawain, ed. J. R. R. Tolkien and E. V. Gordon (Oxford, 1925).
Snappe's Formulary, ed. H. E. Salter (Oxford Historical Society, lxxx, 1924).
Somerset Medieval Wills, ed. F. W. Feaver (Somerset Record Society, 1901).
Speculum Sacerdotale, ed. E. H. Weatherly (E.E.T.S., London, 1936).
Strong, P. and Strong, F. 'The Last Will and Codicils of Henry V', *English Historical Review* (1918).
Stubbs, Thomas, *Lives of the Archbishops of York*, from *Historians of the Church of York*.
Suso, Henry, *Horologium Sapientiae*, ed. J. Strange (Cologne, 1861).
Tanner, Thomas, *Bibliotheca Britannico Hibernica* (London, 1748).
Testamenta Eboracensia, ed. James Raine, Vols 4, 1300 – 1429; 30, 1429 – 67; 45, 1467 – 85 (Surtees Society, 1836, 1855, 1864).
Testamenta Vetusta, ed. N. H. Nicolas, Vol. 1, (London, 1826).
Thompson, A. H., 'The Will of Master William Doune, archdeacon of Leicester', *Archeological Journal*, lxxii, (1915).
The Autobiography of Mrs Alice Thornton, ed. C. Jackson (Surtees Society, Durham, 62, 1873).
The Thornton Manuscript, a Facsimile, D. Brewer and A. Owen (London, 1975).
The Thornton Romances, ed. J. Haliwell (London, 1884).
Transcripts of Sussex Wills as far as they Relate to Ecclesiological and Parochial Subjects, up to the year 1560, ed. R. G. Rice and W. H. Godfrey (Sussex Record Society, 41 – 43, and 45, 1935 – 41).
The Tretys of the Seven Pountes of trewe loue and euerlastynge wisdame, ed. C. Horstmann, (Anglia, x, 1888).
Vita S. Joannis de Bridlingtona (Acta Sanctorum Oct., Collecta Digesta V, Brussels, 1786.
The Wakefield Pageants in the Towneley Cycle, ed. A. C. Cawley (Manchester, 1958).
Walsingham, Thomas, *Historia Anglicana*, ed. H. T. Riley (Rolls Series, 28/1 a-b, 1863 – 64).
Wills and Inventories of the Northern Counties, ed. James Raine, (Chiefly from the registry at Durham), 2 vols (Surtees Society, 38, 1835).
Wyclif, John, *De Officio Pastorali*, ed. G. Lechler (Leipzig, 1869).

——— *Tractataus de Civili Dominio*, ed. R. Lane-Poole, 4 vols (Wyclif Society, 1885 – 1904).
——— *De Ecclesia*, ed. Joseph Loserth (Wyclif Society, London, 1886).
——— *De Officio Regis*, ed. A. W. Pollard and Charles Sayles (Wyclif Society, 1887).
——— *Sermons*, ed. Joseph Loserth (Wyclif Society, 1897 – 90).
——— *De Ente Duorum*, ed. M. Dziewicki (London, 1909).
——— *Summa de Ente*, ed. S. Harrison Thompson (1930).
——— *De Trinitate*, ed. A. Breck (Colorado, 1962).
The York Breviary (Surtees Society, 75, 1882).
York City Records, ed. Angelo Raine, 3 vols (Y.A.S. rec. ser., 98, 103, 108, 110, Leeds, 1936).
The York Mercers and Merchant Adventurers, 1356 ed. Maud Sellers (Surtees Society, 129, 1917).
The York Plays, ed. L. Toulmin-Smith (Oxford, 1885).
Yorkshire Writers, Richard Rolle of Hampole and his Followers, ed. C. Horstmann, 2 vols (London, 1895).

(2) Secondary Sources

Allen, Hope Emily, 'The Authorship of the Prick of Conscience', *Radcliffe College Monographs*, 15 (1910).
——— 'Some Fourteenth Century Borrowings from the Ancren Riwle', *Modern Language Review*, xviii (1923).
——— Writings Ascribed to Richard Rolle (New York, 1927).
Amassian, M.G., 'The Rolle Material in Bradfer-Lawrence MS. 10' *Manuscripts*, 23 (1979).
Ariès, P., *The Hour of Our Death* (English edition, London, 1981).
Armitage-Smith, S., *John of Gaunt* (London, 1914).
Arnould, E. J. 'Richard Rolle and a Bishop: a Vindication', *Bulletin of John Rylands Library* (1937).
——— 'Richard Rolle's Patrons: a new Reading', *Medium Aevum*, 6 (1937).
——— Le Manuel Des Peches (Paris, 1940).
Ashmole, E., *The Institution, Laws and Governances of the Order of the Garter* (London, 1672).
Aston, Margaret, *Thomas Arundel* (Oxford, 1967).
——— *Lollards and Reformers* (London, 1984).
Aston, P., *The Music of York Minster* (York, 1972).
——— 'Music since the Reformation' in G. E. Aylmer and Reginald Cant, *A History of York Minster* (Oxford, 1977).
Aston, Trevor, 'Oxford's Medieval Alumni', *Past and Present*, 74 (1977).
——— 'Medieval Alumni of Cambridge', *Past and Present*, 86 (1980).
Attwater, A., *Pembroke College* (Cambridge, 1936).

Butler, C., *Western Mysticism* (London, 1922).

Butler, L. H., 'Archbishop Melton, His Neighbours and his Kinsmen, 1317 – 40', *Journal of Ecclesiastical History*, ii (1951).

Barnie, J., *War in Medieval Society* (London, 1974).

Barron, C. M., 'The Quarrel of Richard II with London 1392 – 97' in F. R. H. Du Boulay and C. M. Barron, *The Reign of Richard II* (London, 1971).

Bartlett, J. N., 'The Expansion and Decline of York in the Later Middle Ages', *Economic History Review*, xii (1959).

Bennett, J. A. W., *Poetry and the Passion* (Oxford, 1982).

Bennett, M. J., 'Sir Gawain and the Green Knight and the Literary Achievement of the North-West Midlands', *Journal of Medieval History*, 5 (I) (1979).

——— 'A County Community: Social cohesion amongst the Cheshire Gentry 1400 – 1425, *Northern History*, 8 (1973).

Blakiston, H. E. D., 'Two More Medieval Ghost Stories', *English Historical Review*, 38 (1923).

Bloomfield, M. W., *The Seven Deadly Sins* (Michigan, 1952).

Bossy, John, 'Blood and Baptism' in Derek Baker, ed. *Sanctity and Secularity* (Ecclesiastical History Society, 1973).

——— 'Social History of Confession', *Transactions of the Royal Historical Society*, (1974).

——— 'Holiness and Society' (Review), *Past and Present*, 75 (1977).

——— 'The Mass as a Social Institution', *Past and Present*, 100 (1983).

——— *Christianity and the West 1400 – 1700* (Oxford, 1985).

Brodrick, G. C. *Memorials of Merton College* (Oxford, 1885).

Brown, A. L. 'Privy Seal Clerks in the Early Fifteenth Century', in D. Bullough and R. L. Storey, *The Study of Medieval Records: Essays in honour of Kathleen Major* (Oxford, 1971).

Brown, J., *A History of the Metropolitan Church of St Peter's* (London, 1847).

Brown, Peter, *Augustine of Hippo, a biography* (London, 1967).

——— *The Making of Late Antiquity* (Harvard, 1978).

——— *The Cult of the Saints* (Chicago, 1981).

——— *Society and the Holy in Late Antiquity* (London, 1982).

Brown, W., 'Mount Grace Priory', *Y.A.J.*, xviii (1905).

Butler, C., *Western Mysticism* (London, 1927).

Butler, L. H., 'Archbishop Melton, his Neighbours and his Kinsmen, 1317 – 40' *Journal of Ecclesiastical History*, ii (1951).

Caiger-Smith, A., *English Medieval Mural Paintings* (Oxford, 1963).

Catto, Jeremy I., 'Religion and the English Nobility in the Later Fourteenth Century', in H. Lloyd-Jones, V. Pearl and B. Worden (eds) *History and Imagination, Essays in honour of H. R. Trevor-Roper* (London, 1981).

——— 'John Wylif and the Cult of the Eucharist', in K. Walsh and D. Wood (eds) *The Bible in the Medieval World* (Oxford, 1985).
——— 'Religious Change under Henry V, in G. L. Harriss (ed.) *Henry V: The Practice of Kingship* (Oxford: 1985).
Cawley, A. C., 'Middle English Versions of the Decalogue', *Leeds Studies in English*, New Ser., viii (1975).
Chambers, E. K., *The Medieval Stage* (Oxford, 1903).
Cheney, C. R., *Medieval Texts and Studies* (Oxford, 1973).
Chetwynd-Stapylton, H. E., 'The Stapletons of Yorkshire', *Y.A.J.*, viii (1883 – 84).
Churchill, I. J., *Canterbury Administration*, 2 vols (London, 1933).
Clarke, J. P. H., 'Walter Hilton in Defence of the Religious Life and the Veneration of Images', *Downside Review* (1985).
Clarke, M. V., *Fourteenth Century Studies* (Oxford, 1937).
Clay, R. M., *Medieval Hospitals of England* (London, 1909).
——— *Hermits and Anchorites of England* (London, 1914).
——— 'Further Studies on Medieval Recluses', *Journal of the British Archeological Association*, 3rd ser. 16 (1953).
——— 'Some Northern Anchorites', *Archeologia Aeliana*, 38, 4th ser. (1955).
Cobham, A. B., *The King's Hall* (Cambridge, 1969).
Cockayne, G. E., *The Complete Peerage*, ed. V. Gibbs, H. A. Doubleday, Lord Howard de Walden, G. H. White and R. S. Lea, 3 vols (London, 1910 – 53).
Colledge, Eric, *The Medieval Mystics of England* (London, 1962).
Colvin, H. C., *The White Canons in England* (Oxford, 1977).
Comper, Frances, *The Life of Richard Rolle* (New York, 1928).
Compton, J., 'Leicestershire Lollards', *Leicestershire Archeological and Historial Society*, 44 (1968 – 9).
Courcelle, *Les Confessions de St Augustine dans la tradition littéraire* (Paris, 1963).
Cox, J., *Annals of the Abbey of Meaux* (Transactions of the East Riding Antiquarian Society, 1893).
Craig, H., *English Religious Drama* (Oxford, 1955).
Cronin, H. S., 'John Wycliffe the Reformer, Canterbury Hall, Oxford', *Transactions of the Royal Historical Society*, 3rd Series, viii (1914).
Cross, M. Claire, 'Priests into Ministers: the Establishment of Protestant Practice in the City of York', in P. N. Brooks (ed.) *Reformation Principle and Practice, Essays in Honour of A. G. Dickens* (London, 1980).
Davidson, C., 'Civic Concern and Iconography in the York Passion', *Annuale Mediaevale*, 15 (1974).
——— 'The Realism of the York Realist and the York Passion', *Speculum* 50, (1975).
Davies, R. G., 'Thomas Arundel as Archbishop of Canterbury', *Journal of Ecclesiastical History*, 24 (1973).

Davis, Natalie, 'The Study of Popular Religion', in C. Trinkaus and H. Oberman (eds.) *The Pursuit of Holiness in Late Medieval and Renaissance Religion* (Leiden, 1974).
Davis, Virginia, 'The Rule of Saint Paul, the first Hermit in late Medieval England', in W. J. Sheils (ed.) *Monks, Hermits and the Ascetic Tradition Ecclesiastical History Society*, 22 (Oxford, 1985).
Deanesly, Margaret, *The Lollard Bible* (Cambridge, 1920).
——— 'Vernacular Books in England in the Fourteenth and Fifteenth Centuries', *Modern Language Review*, xv (1920).
Delaisse, L. M., 'The Importance of Books of Hours for the History of the Medieval Book', in *'Gatherings in Honour of D. M. Miner* (Baltimore, 1974).
Denholm-Young, N., *The Country Gentry in the Fourteenth Century* (Oxford, 1969).
Dickens, A. G., *The English Reformation* (London, 1922).
——— 'The Last Medieval Englishman', in P. Brooks (ed.) *Christian Spirituality: Essays in Honour of Gordon Rupp* (London, 1975).
——— *Lollards and Protestants in the Diocese of York, 1905 – 58* (Oxford, 1959).
Dictionary of National Biography, ed. Leslie Stephens and Lee Sidney, 63 vols (London, 1928 – 29).
Dobson, R. B., 'The Foundation of Perpetual Chantries by the Citizens of Medieval York', in G. J. Cuming (ed.) *Studies in Church History*, iv (Leiden, 1967).
——— *The Church, Politics and Patronage in the Fifteenth Century* (New York, 1984).
——— *Durham Priory, 1400 – 1450* (Cambridge, 1973).
——— 'A History of York Minster in the Middle Ages, 1215 – 1500', in Aymler and Cant, *A History of York Minster*.
——— 'The Residentiary Canons of York in the Fifteenth Century', *Journal of Ecclesiastical History*, 30 (1979).
Drake, Francis, *Eboracum* (York and London, 1736).
Dugdale, W., *Baronage of England* (London, 1675).
——— *Monasticon Anglicanum*, ed. J. Caley, H. Ellis and B. Bandinel (London, 1817 – 30).
Edwards, K., 'Bishops and Learning in the Reign of Edward II', *Church Quarterly Review*, 88 (1944).
——— *The English Secular Cathedrals in the Middle Ages* (Manchester, 1949).
Emden, A. B., *A Biographical Register of the University of Oxford*, 3 vols (Oxford, 1957 – 9).
——— *A Biographical Register of the University of Cambridge to 1500* (Cambridge, 1963).
——— 'Northerners and Southerners in the Organization of the University to 1509', *Oxford Studies presented to Daniel Callus* (Oxford

Historical Society, n.s. 16, 1964).
Evans, Joan, *English Art, 1307 – 1461* (Oxford, 1949).
Farmer, D. H., 'Stephen of Sawley, *The Month*, (1963).
Finacre, R. C., Miracles and Pilgrims, *Popular Beliefs in Medieval England* (London, 1977).
Fleming, P. W., 'Charity, Faith and the Gentry of Kent', in A. J. Pollard (ed.) *Property and Politics* (Gloucester, 1984).
Fowler, David, *The Bible in Early English Literature* (London, 1977).
Fowler, J., 'An Account of St William of York', *Y.A.J.*, viii (1875).
——— The St Cuthbert Window of York', *Y.A.J.*, vi, (1875 – 76).
Galpern, A. N., 'The Legacy of Late Medieval Religion in Sixteenth Century Champagne', in Trinkaus and Oberman, *The Pursuit of Holiness*.
Gardner, Helen, 'The Text of the Scale of Perfection', *Medium Aevum*, v (1936).
——— 'Walter Hilton and the Mystical Tradition in England', *Essays and Studies*, 22 (1936).
——— Gee, E. A., 'The Painted Glass of All Saints Church, North Street York', *Archeologia*, 102 (1969).
Gerould, G. H., *Saints' Legends* (Boston, 1916).
Gibson, S. J. W., *Wills and Where to Find them* (Liverpool, 1947).
Gillespie, V., 'The *Cibus Anime* book three, A Guide to Contemplatives?', *Spiritualität Heute und Gestern* (1982).
Goldthorp, L. M., 'Franciscans and Dominicans in Yorkshire', *Y.A.J.*, 32 (1934 – 36).
Gooder, Eileen A., 'The Parliamentary Representation of the County of York, 1258 – 1832', *Y.A.S.*, Record Series, xvi, (1935).
Gough, R., *Sepulchral Monuments in Great Britain* (London, 1786 – 96).
Gransden, Antonia, *Historical Writings in England* (London, 1976).
Grasssi, J. L., 'Royal Clerks from the Archdiocese of York in the Fourteenth Century', *Northern History*, 5 (1970).
Griffiths, R., 'The Trial of Eleanor Cobham', *Bulletin of John Rylands Library*, 51, (1068).
Grosjean, P., 'De Johanne Bridlingtoniensi Collectanea', *Analecta Bollandiana*, ciii (1935).
Gwynn, Aubrey, *The English Austin Friars in the Time of Wyclif* (Oxford, 1940).
Hackett, B., *The Spiritual Life of the English Austin Friars of the Fourteenth Century* (Studia Augustinas: Vitae Spiritualis Magister, II, Rome, 1959).
——— 'William Flete and the De Remediis contra Temptaciones', in *Medieval Studies Presented to Aubrey Gwynn* (Dublin, 1961).
——— 'William Flete', *The Month*, xxvi (1961).
Haines, R. M., *The Administration of the Diocese of Worcester in the First*

Half of the Fourteenth Century (London, 1965).
——— 'The Education of the English Clergy during the Later Middle Ages, *Canadian Journal History*, 4 (1969).
Harrison, F., *Life in a Medieval College* (London, 1952).
——— *The Painted Glass of York* (York, 1927).
Harvey, J. H., 'The Wilton Diptych', *Archeologia*, 98 (1961).
——— 'Richard II and York', in DuBoulay and Barron, *The Reign of Richard II*.
——— 'An Architectural History of York Minster from 1291 to 1558', in Aylmer and Cant, *A History of York Minster*.
——— Heath, Peter, *The English Parish Clergy on the Eve of The Reformation* (London and Toronto, 1969).
——— 'Urban Piety in the Later Middle Ages: the Evidence of Hull Wills', in R. B. Dobson, (ed.) *The Church, Politics and Patronage in the Fifteenth Century* (Gloucester, 1984).
Henderson, B. W. *History of Merton College* (London, 1869).
Hewitt, H. J. *The Organization of War under Edward III* (Manchester, 1966).
Highfield, J. R. L., 'The English Church Hierarchy in the Reign of Edward III', *Transactions of the Royal Historical Society*, 5th Ser. vi (1956).
——— 'The Jeronimites in Spain, their Patrons and Success, 1373 – 1516', *J.E.H.*, 34 (1983).
Hill, Rosalind M., *The Labourer in the Vineyard: The Visitations of Archbishop Melton in the Archdeaconry of Richmond* (York, 1968).
Hodgson, P., 'The Orcherd of Syon and the English Mystical Tradition', *Proceedings of the British Academy* (1964).
——— 'Walter Hilton and the *Cloud of Unknowing*, M.L.A., 50 (1955).
Holmes, G., *The Good Parliament* (Oxford, 1975).
Holzknecht, *Literary Patronage in the Middle Ages* (Philadelphia, 1923).
Hudson, Anne, 'The New Debate on Bible Translation, Oxford, 1401', *English Historical Review*, xc (1975).
——— *Lollards and their Books* (Oxford, 1985).
Huizinga, Jan., *The Waning of the Middle Ages* (London, 1924).
Hunt, R. W., 'The Manuscript Collection of University College', *Bodleian Library Record*, iii (1950 – 51).
Hunter, J., *Hallamshire: the History and Topography of the Parish of Sheffield in the County of York*, Revised and enlarged by A. Gatty (London, 1869.
Illingworth, W., 'A Copy of a Libel against Archbishop Neville', *Archeologia*, xvi (1812).
Jacob, E. F., 'The Beginnings of Medieval Chivalry', in E. Prestage (ed.) *Chivalry, its Historical Significance and Civilizing Influence* (London, 1928).
——— *Essays in the Conciliar Epoch* (Manchester, 1953).

——— 'Reynold Pecock', *Proceedings of the British Academy*, 37 (1951).
——— *The Fifteenth Century* (Oxford, 1961).
——— 'Christian Humanism', in J. Hale, R. Highfield and B. Smalley, *Europe in the Late Middle Ages* (London, 1965).
James, Mervym E., 'Two Tudor Funerals', *Cumberland and Westmorland Antiquarian and Archeological Society*, lxvi (1966).
——— 'The Concept of Order and the Northern Rising of 1569', *Past and Present*, 60 (1973).
——— *Family Lineage and Civil Society* (Oxford, 1974).
——— 'English Politics and the Concept of Honour 1485 – 1642', *Past and Present*, Supplement 3 (1978).
——— 'Ritual, Drama and the Social Body in the Late Medieval English Town', *Past and Present*, 98 (1983).
James, M. R., *A Catalogue of the Manuscripts in the Library of Peterhouse* (Cambridge, 1880).
——— 'The Catalogue of the Library of the Augustinian Friars at York', in *Fasciculus Joanni Willis Clark dictatus* (Cambridge, 1909).
——— *Catalogue of Manuscripts of Trinity College Cambridge.*
——— *The Bohun Manuscripts* (Oxford, 1936).
Kantorowicz, E. H., *The King's Two Bodies* (Princeton, 1957).
Keen, M. H., *The Laws of War in the Late Middle Ages* (London, 1965).
——— 'Chivalry, Nobility and the Man at Arms', in C. T. Allmand (ed.) *War, Literature and Politics in the Late Middle Ages* (Liverpool, 1976).
——— 'Chaucer's Knight', in V. J. Scattergood and J. W. Sherbourne (eds) *English Court Culture in the Later Middle Ages* (London, 1983).
——— *Chivalry* (London, 1984).
Keiser, G. R., 'Lincoln Cathedral Library Manuscript, 91: the Life and Milieu of the Scribe', *Studies in Bibliography*, 32 (1979).
——— 'Þe Holy Boke Gratia Dei', *Viator*, 12 (1981).
Kellog, A. L. and Talbot, E. W., 'The Wycliffite Pater Noster and the Ten Commandments', *Bulletin of John Rylands Library*, 42 (1959 – 60).
Kermode, J. I., 'The Merchants of three Northern English Towns', in C. H. Clough (ed.) *Profession, Vocation and Culture in Later Medieval England* (Liverpool, 1982).
Kingsford, C. L., 'Two Forfeitures in the Year of Agincourt', *Archeologia*, 70 (1919).
Knowles, David, *The Religious Houses of Medieval England* (London, 1940).
——— *The English Mystical Tradition* (London, 1961).
——— *The Religious Orders in England*, 2 vols (Cambridge, 4th edition, 1979).
Knowles, J., *Essays in the History of the York School of Glass Painting* (London, 1936).
Lander, J. R., *Conflict and Stability in Fifteenth Century England* (London, 1969).

Latham, R. E. *Revised Medieval Latin Word List* (London, 1965).
Lerner, R. E., *The Heresy of the Free Spirit* (Berkeley, 1972).
Leach, A. F., 'A Clerical Strike at Beverley Minster', *Archeologia*, lv (1896).
——— *Memorials of Beverley Minster* (Surtees Society, cviii, 1903).
L'Anson, W. L., 'Kilton Castle', *Y.A.J.*, xxii (1912 – 13).
Le Bas, H. V., 'The Founding of the Carthusian Order', in W. A. Brown, 'A History of Mount Grace'.
Le Neve, J., *Fasti Ecclesiae Anglicanae*, ed. T. D. Hardy (Oxford, 1854).
Leslie, S., *St Patrick's Purgatory* (London, 1932).
Lewis, N. B., 'The Anniversary Service for Blanche, Duchess of Lancaster', *Bulletin of John Rylands Library*, 21 (1937).
Lewett, *Studies in Manorial History* (Oxford, 1938).
Leyser, Henrietta, *Hermits and the New Monasticism* (London, 1984).
Little, A. G. *The Greyfriars in Oxford* (Oxford, 1892).
——— 'Franciscan Letters of Fraternity', *Bodleian Library Record*, v (1954 – 56).
Lovatt, Roger, 'The Imitation of Christ in Late Medieval England'. *Transactions of the Royal Historical Society*, 5th Ser., xviii (1968).
——— 'John Blacman; Biographer of Henry VI', in R. H. C. Davis and J. M. Wallace-Hadrill (eds) *The Writing of History in the Middle Ages: Essays presented to R. W. Southern* (Oxford, 1981).
——— 'A Collection of Apocryphal Anecdotes: John Blacman Revisited', in A. J. Pollard, (ed.) *Property and Politics* (Gloucester, 1984).
MacCracken, 'An English Friend of Charles of Orleans', *Publications of Modern Language Association*, xxvi (1911).
Maitland, F. W., 'Canon Law in England, I, William Lyndwood', *English Historical Review*, 11 (1896).
——— 'Wyclif's Preferments', *E.H.R.*, xv (1900).
Malden, A. R., *The Canonization of St Osmund* (Wiltshire Record Society, 1901).
Manning, Bernard, *The People's Faith in the Time of Wyclif* (Cambridge, 1919).
Mathew, F. D., 'The Trial of Richard Wyche', *English Historical Review*, v (1890).
Mathew, Gervase, *The Court of Richard II* (London, 1968).
Mauley, *Some New Light on Chaucer* (New York, 1961).
Mayr-Harting, H., 'Functions of a Twelfth Century Recluse', *History*, 60 (1975).
Meyvaert, P., 'John Erghome and the *Vaticinium* of Roberti Bridlington, *Speculum*, 41 (1966).
Moeller, Berndt, 'Religious Life in Germany at the Eve of the Reformation' in G. Straus (ed.) *Pre-Reformation Germany* (1972).
——— Moran, Hoeppner, J., 'Education and Learning in the City of

York, 1300 – 1560', *Borthwick Paper*, 55 (1979).
——— 'Literacy and Education in Northern England', *Northern History*, 17 (1981).
——— 'Clerical Recruitment in the Diocese of York', *Journal of Ecclesiastical History*, 34 (1983).
——— *The Growth of English Schooling, 1340 – 1548* (Princeton, 1985).
Morrin, M. J., *John Waldeby, O.S.A., c. 1315 – 71* (Studia Augustinia Historica Roma, 1975).
Morris, C., 'The Ravenser Composition', *Lincolnshire Architectural and Archeological Society Reports and Papers*, 10 (1963).
Morris, Colin, *The Discovery of the Individual* (London, 1972).
Murdoch, V., 'John Wycliffe and Richard Fleming, Bishop of Lincoln: Gleanings from German sources', *British Institute of Historical Research*, xxxvii (1964).
Myers, A. R., *The Household of Edward IV* (Manchester, 1959).
McAlindon, 'Hagiography into Art: a Study of St Erkenwald', *Studies in Philology*, 67 (1970).
McFarlane, K. B., *John Wycliffe and the Beginnings of English Nonconformity* (London, 1952).
——— *Lancastrian Kings and Lollard Knights* (Oxford, 1971).
——— *The Nobility of Later Medieval England* (Oxford, 1973).
McKenna, J. W., 'Popular Canonization as Political Propaganda in the Cult of Archbishop Scrope', *Speculum*, 45 (1970).
McKisak, May, *The Fourteenth Century*, 1307 – 99 (Oxford, 1959).
McNiven, P., 'The Betrayal of Archbishop Scrope', *Bulletin of John Rylands Library*, 54 (1971).
McNulty, J., 'William of Rymyngton, prior of Sawley', *Y.A.J.*, xxx (1931).
Nelson, V. A., 'Problems of Transcription of the *Speculum Vitae* Manuscripts', *Scriptorium*, 31 (1977).
O'Connor, D. E. and Haselock, J., 'The Stained and Painted Glass of York Minster', in Aylmer and Cant, *A History of York Minster*.
Orme, N., 'Education and Learning at a Medieval English Cathedral: Exeter 1380 – 1448', *Journal of Ecclesiastical History*, 32 (1981).
Owst, G. R. *Preaching in Medieval England* (Cambridge, 1926).
——— *Literature and Pulpit in Medieval England* (Cambridge, 1933).
Pacht, O. and Alexander J. J. G., *Illuminated Manuscripts in Bodley Library* (Oxford, 1973).
Palmer, G. F. R., 'The Friar Preachers of Black Friars of York', *Y.A.J.*, vi (1879 – 80).
Palliser, David M., *Tudor York* (Oxford, 1979).
Panofsky, E., *Early Netherlandish Painting* (Cambridge, 1953).
Pantin, W. A., 'The Monk Solitary of Farne: a Fourteenth Century English Mystic', *English Historical Review*, lxi (1944).

——— *The English Church in the Fourteenth Century* (Cambridge, 1955).
——— 'Instructions for a Devout and Literate Layman', in J. J. G. Alexander and M. J. Gibson (eds) *Medieval Learning and Literature, Essays Presented to Richard William Hunt* (Oxford, 1976).
Parkes, M. B., *English Cursive Book Hands* (Oxford, 1969).
Pearce, E. H., *The Monks of Westminster* (Cambridge, 1916).
Perrow, 'The Last Will and Testament as a Form of Literature', *Transactions of Wisconsin Academy of Sciences, Arts and Letters*, 17.
Peterson, C. J., 'The Pearl Poet and John Massey of Cotton, Cheshire', *Review of English Studies*, 25 (1974).
Pevsner, N., *The Buildings of England, Yorkshire: York and the East Riding* (London, 1972).
Pfaff, R. W., *New Liturgical Feasts in Later Medieval England* (Oxford, 1920).
Poulson, G., *Beverlac* (London, 1829).
Power, E., *English Medieval Nunneries* (Cambridge, 1922).
Purvis, J. S., 'St John of Bridlington, *Journal of Bridlington and Augustinian Society*, ii (1924).
——— 'Ripon Correspondence', *Yorkshire Archeological Society*, xxix (1927 – 9).
——— 'The Tables of the York Vicars Choral', *Y.A.J.*, 41 (1966).
Rashdall, H., *The Universities of Europe in the Middle Ages* (ed.) F. M. Powicke and A. B. Emden (Oxford, 1936).
Reeves, Marjorie, *The Influence of Prophecy in the Later Middle Ages* (Oxford, 1969).
Reeves, A. C., *Lancastrian Englishmen* (Washington, 1981).
Richmond, Colin, 'Religion and the Fifteenth Century Gentleman', in Dobson, *The Church, Politics and Patronage in the Fifteenth Century* (New York. 1984).
Rickert, M., *The Reconstructed Carmelite Missal* (London, 1952).
Riehle, W., *The Middle English Mystics* (London, 1981).
Riley, M. A., 'The Foundation of Chantries in the Counties of Nottingham and York, 1350 – 1400', *Y.A.J.*, 33 (1936 – 38).
Robinson, D., 'Beneficed Clergy in Cleveland and the East Riding, 1306 – 40', *B.I.H.R.*, 37 (1969).
Robinson, J. W., 'The Art of the York Realist', *Modern Philology*, 60 (1962 – 63).
Robertson J. W. 'The Late Medieval Cult of Jesus', *Publications of the Modern Languages Association*, 80 (1965).
Robson, J. A., *Wyclif and the Oxford Schools* (Cambridge, 1961).
Rosenthal, J. T., *The Purchase of Paradise* (London, 1972).
——— 'The Fifteenth Century Episcopate: Careers and Bequests', in D. Baker (ed.) *Sanctity and Secularity, the Church and the World* (Oxford, 1973).

——— *Nobles and the Noble Life* (London, 1976.
Rosewein, B. H. and Little, Lester K., 'Social Meaning in the Monastic and Mendicant Spiritualities', *Past and Present*, 62 (1974).
Roth, F., *English Austin Friars* (New York, 1966).
Russel-Smith, J. M., 'Walter Hilton and a Tract in Defence of the Veneration of Images', *Dominican Studies* (1953 – 54).
St John-Hope, W. H., 'The Architectural History of Mount Grace', in W. A. Brown, 'A History of Mount Grace'.
Salter, E., 'Chapters of Augustinian Canons', *London, Canterbury and York Society*, 29 (1922).
——— 'The Alliterature Revival', *Modern Philology*, 64 (1966 – 67).
Salter, F., *Medieval Drama in Chester* (Toronto, 1955).
Sargeant, Michael, G., 'The Transmission by the English Carthusians of Some Late Medieval Spiritual Writings', *Journal of Ecclesiastical History*, 27 (1976).
——— 'Contemporary Criticism of Richard Rolle', *Analecta Cartusiana*, 55, I (1981).
Saul, Nigel, 'The Religious Sympathies of the Gentry in Gloucestershire, 1200 – 1500', *Bristol and Gloucestershire Archeological Society Transactions*, 98 (1980).
——— *Scenes from Provincial Life. Knightly families in Sussex 1280 – 1600* (Oxford, 1986).
Scarisbrick, J. J., *The Reformation and the English People* (Oxford, 1984).
Scrope, George Poulett, *History of the Manor and Ancient Barony of Castle Combe* (London, 1852).
Sheehan, Michael, M., *The Will in Medieval England from the Conversion of the Anglo-Saxons to the End of the Thirteenth Century* (Toronto, 1963).
Schmidt, G., 'Two Unknown English Horae from the Fifteenth Century', *Burlington Magazine*, ciii (1961).
Sicroff, A. A., 'The Jeronymite Monastery of Guadelupe' in M. P. Hornick ed. *Collected Studies in Honour of Americo Castro* (Oxford, 1965).
Skaife, R. H., 'Civic Officials and Parliamentary Officials of York (York City Library manuscript).
Smalley, Beryl, *The Study of the Bible in the Middle Ages* (Oxford, 1952).
——— 'Which William of Nottingham', *Medieval and Renaissance Studies*, 3 (1954).
——— 'The Bible and Eternity, John Wycliffe's Dilemma', *Journal of Warburg and Courtauld Institute*, 27, (1964).
——— 'The Church's Use of the Bible in the Middle Ages', in D. E. Nineham (ed.) *The Church's Use of the Bible, Past and Present* (London, 1963).
Smith, David M., *Guide to the Bishop's Registers of England and Wales* (London, 1981).

Smedley, N., 'An Incised Stone from the Free Chapel of Ancres near Doncaster', *Y.A.T.*, 37 (1948 – 9).

Snape, M. G., 'Some Evidence of Lollard Activity in the Diocese of Durham in the Early Fifteenth Century', *Archeologia Aeliana* (1961).

Solloway, J., 'Archbishop Scrope', *York Minster Historical Tracts*, 15 (1927).

Somerville, R., *History of the Duchy of Lancaster*, I, 1265 – 1603 (London, 1953).

Spalding, M. C., *The Middle English Charters of Christ* (Pennsylvania, 1914).

Spriggs, G. M., 'The Neville Hours and the School of Herman Scheere', *Journal of Warburg and Courtauld Institute* (1974).

Stephenson, Mill, 'Monumental Brasses in the East Riding', *Y.A.J.* (1893).

——— 'Monumental Brasses in the West Riding', *Y.A.J.* (1900).

——— 'Monumental Brasses in the North Riding', *Y.A.J.* (1903).

Stern, K., 'The Thornton Miscellany. A New Description of Brit. Mus. Addit. MS 31042', *Scriptorium* (1976).

Stones, E. L. G., 'Sir Geoffrey le Scrope, Chief Justice of the King's Bench', *English Historical Review*, lxix (1954).

Storey, R. L., *Diocesan Administration in Fifteenth Century England* (York, 2nd ed., 1972).

Sumption, Jonathan, *Pilgrimage* (London, 1975).

Surtees, Robert, *History and Antiquities of the County Palatine of Durham*, 4 vols. (London, 1816 – 40).

Tait, H., 'Pilgrim Signs: Thomas, Earl of Lancaster', *British Museum Quarterly*, xx (1932).

Tanner, N. P., *The Church in Late Medieval Norwich* (Toronto, 1984).

Thomas, Keith, *Religion and the Decline of Magic* (London, 1971), Chapter I.

Thompson, A. H., 'The Registers of the Archbishops of York', *Y.A.J.*, 32 (1936).

——— 'The Pestilences of the Fourteenth Century in the Diocese of York', *Y.A.J.*,. lxxi (1914).

——— *The English Clergy and their Organization in the Later Middle Ages* (Oxford, 1947).

Thompson, E. M., *The Carthusian Order in England* (London, 1930).

Thrupp, Sylvia, *The Merchant Class of Medieval London* (Chicago, 1948).

Tour, T. F., *Chapters in the Administrative History of Medieval England*, 6 vols (Manchester, 1920 – 21).

Tristram, E. W., *English Wall Painting of the Fourteenth Century* (London, 1955).

Twycross, M., 'Places to hear the Play, Pageant Stations at York', *Records of the Early English Drama* (1978).

Tydeman, W., *The Theatre in the Middle Ages* (Cambridge, 1978).
Ullman, W., *Principles of Government and Politics in the Middle Ages* (4th edn, London, 1975).
Vale, M. G. A., 'Piety, Charity and Literacy among the Yorkshire Gentry 1370 – 1480', *Borthwick Paper*, 50) (1976).
——— *War and Chivalry* (London, 1981).
The Victoria History of the County of York, the City of York (Oxford, 1961).
The Victoria History of the East Riding, 2 vols (Oxford, 1969).
Walker, *A Biographical Register of Peterhouse Men* (Cambridge, 1927, 1929).
Walsh, K., *A Fourteenth Century Scholar and Primate: Richard FitzRalph in Oxford, Avignon and Armagh* (Oxford, 1981).
Warren, A. K., *Anchorites and their Patrons* (Berkeley, 1986).
Weis, Roberto, *Humanism in England During the Fifteenth Century* (Oxford, 1967).
Wells, J. E., *A Manual of the Writings in Middle English* (Oxford, 1919).
Westlake, H. E., *The Parish Guilds of Medieval England* (London, 1919).
Whiting, C. E., 'Richard Rolle of Hampole', *Y.A.J.* (1948 – 51).
Whitaker, T. D., *A History of the County of York*, Vol. I, Richmondshire (London, 1821).
Wickham, G., *Early English Stages* (London, 1966).
Wilkinson, B., 'A Letter of Edward III to his Chancellor and Treasurer', *English Historical Review*, xlii (1927).
——— *The Chancery under Edward III* (Manchester, 1929).
Index of Wills in York Registry, 1389 – 1514 (Y.A.S. rec. ser., 6, Leeds, 1889).
Dean and Chapter Wills, 1321 – 1636 (Y.A.S., rec. ser., xxxviii, 1907).
Wills . . . in the Registers of the Archbishops of York, 1316 – 1882 (Y.A.S., rec. ser., xciii, 1936).
Wilmart, A., *Auteurs Spirituels et Textes Dévots Du Moyen Age Latin* (Paris, 1932).
Wood, Anthony, *The History and Antiquities of the University of Oxford*, 2 vols (Oxford, 1676).
Wood-Legh, K. L., 'Some Aspects of the History of Chantries in the Later Middle Ages', *Transactions of the Royal Historical Society*, 48 (1946).
——— *Perpetual Chantries in Britain* (Cambridge, 1965).
Woolf, Rosemary, *The English Mystery Plays* (London, 1972).
Workman, H. B., *John Wyclif*, 2 vols, (Oxford, 1926).
Wormald, F., 'The Wilton Diptych', *Journal of Warburg and Courtauld Institutes*, xvii (1954).
Wylie, J. H., *A History of England under Henry IV* (London, 1884 – 98).
——— *The Reign of Henry V*, 3 vols (Cambridge, 1914).

Zeeman, E., 'Nicholas Love, a Fifteenth Century Translator', *Review of English Studies*, 118 (1915).
——— Ziegler, P., *The Black Death* (London, 1969).

UNPUBLISHED THESES AND DISSERTATIONS

Ball, R. M., 'The Education of English Secular Clergy in the later Middle Ages, with special reference to the Manuals of Instructions (Cambridge Univ. Ph.D. thesis, 1977).

Bartle, R. H., 'Private Book Collections in Medieval England' (Oxford Univ. B.Litt. thesis, 1956).

Boyle, L. E. 'A Study of the works Attributed to William of Pagula, with Special Reference to the *Oculus Sacerdotis* and the *Summa Summarum*' (Oxford Univ. D.Phil. thesis, 1956).

Daly, J. P., 'An Edition of the Judica Me Deus of Richard Rolle' (Univ. North Carolina Ph.d. thesis, 1960).

Doyle, A. I., 'A Survey of the Origins and Circulation of Theological Writings in English' (Cambridge Univ. Ph.D. thesis, 1956).

Ellis, R. M., 'An edition with Commentary of Certain Sections of B.M. MS Claudius of the fourteenth Century Brigittine Revelations' (Oxford Univ. D.Phil. thesis, 1974).

Given, Wilson, C. J., 'The Court and Hosehold of Edward III' (St Andrews Univ. D.Phil. thesis, 1975).

Gillespie, V. A., 'The Literary Form of the Middle English Pastoral Manual with Particular Reference to the *Speculum Christiani*' (Oxford Univ. D.Phil. thesis, 1981).

Grassi, J. L. 'Clerical Dynasties from Howdenshire, Nottinghamshire and Lindsey in the Royal Administration, 1280 – 1340' (Oxford Univ. D.Phil. thesis, 1960).

Hackett, M. B., 'William Flete OSA and St Catherine of Siena' (Dublin D.Phil., 1955).

Haren, M., 'A Study of the *Memoriale Presbiterorum*, a Fourteenth Century Confession Manual for Parish Priests' (Oxford Univ. D.Phil. thesis, 1975).

Harvey, M., 'English Views on the Reforms to be Undertaken in the General Councils 1400 – 1418, with special reference to the Proposals made by Richard Ullerston' (Oxford Univ. D.Phil. thesis, 1964).

Highfield, J. R. L., 'The Relations between the Church and the English Crown from the Death of Archbishop Stratford to the Opening of the Great Schism 1349 to 1378' (Oxford Univ. D.Phil. thesis, 1951).

Hodge, C. E., 'The Abbey of St Albans under John Whethampstede' (Manchester Univ. Ph.D. thesis, 1933).

Lovatt, R., 'The Influence of Religious Literature of Germany and the Low Countries on English Spirituality' (Oxford Univ. D.Phil. thesis, 1965).

Palmer, J., 'The Career of Henry Bowet, Archbishop of York' (Oxford Univ. B.Litt. thesis, 1964).
Peck, H. M., 'The Prophecy of John of Bridlington' (Chicago Univ. D.Phil. thesis, 1930).
Ross, G. R., 'The Yorkshire Baronage' (Oxford Univ. D.Phil. thesis, 1956).
Saul, Nigel, 'The Gloucestershire Gentry in the Fourteenth Century' (Oxford Univ. D. Phil. thesis, 1978).
Steele, F. J., 'Definitions of the Active Life in Middle English Literature of the Thirteenth, Fourteenth and Fifteenth Centuries' (Oxford, Univ. D.Phil. thesis, 1979).
Tait, M. B., 'The Brigittine Monastery of Syon with Special Reference to its Monastic Uses' (Oxford Univ. D.Phil. thesis, 1975).
Tanner, M. P., 'Popular Religion in Norwich with Special Reference to the Evidence of Wills, 1370 – 1532. (Oxford Univ. D.Phil. thesis, 1973).
Thompson, J. A., 'Clergy and Laity in London, 1376 to 1553' (Oxford Univ. D.Phil. thesis, 1960).

Index

Subjects

Names